Our Western Educational Heritage

Christopher J. Lucas

UNIVERSITY OF MISSOURI–COLUMBIA

The Macmillan Company, New York

Collier-Macmillan Limited, London

To my late father,
MARSHAL P. LUCAS

Preface

The writing of this history has been controlled by a definite viewpoint regarding the requirements of a professional preparatory program for educators and the function of educational history as one of its component elements. That view rejects the notion that only considerations of narrow, immediate utility should determine the content of the curriculum. The distinction between an "academic" and a "professional" program is never so rigorous as to demand that everything taught within the latter be directly applicable to specific situations. A radical separation of the two involves a muddle-headed notion of what preparing people for teaching and other types of educational endeavor entails. The trade-school mentality that asks that teachers be trained like mechanical technicians, that everything they are taught have a direct, discernible, and measurable outcome in their subsequent performance is a species of reductionism of the most pernicious type possible. Lawrence Cremin said it best: "Education is too significant and dynamic an enterprise to be left to mere technicians; and we might as well begin now the prodigious task of preparing men and women who understand not only the substance of what they are teaching but also the theories behind the particular strategies they employ to convey that substance."[1] History is an inescapable dimension in the theoretical study of educational methodology, content, and aims.

The student of Western educational history has not lacked resources in recent years. A considerable number of texts have appeared, most of them reasonably informative, and a few have been excellent. But the overwhelming majority has been of the invertebrate variety, a species virtually devoid of organizing structure or interpretive scheme. The writing of the present work represents a preliminary attempt to explore an alternative kind of historical narrative, one emphasizing certain broad themes running through the story of education in the West. It is to be hoped that the danger of forcing evidence to fit a particular thematic requirement is outweighed, from a pedagogical point of view, by the advantages such an approach affords. The verdict here is best left with the reader.

Secondly, this particular history pretends to be no more than a general

1 Lawrence A. Cremin, *The Genius of American Education* (Pittsburgh: University of Pittsburgh Press, 1965), p. 59. Quoted with permission.

iii

survey of educational developments. That kind of writing, as Henry Steele Commager acidly remarks somewhere, tends to rot the mind. It lacks rigor and substance. The survey invariably sacrifices detail for general contour, depth for breadth, and interpretation for exposition. Great ideas of the past —ideas that formerly stirred men's passions but perhaps do so no longer— tend to remain inert because they have to be treated so cursorily. It is easy to lose sight of the fact that hurriedly passed-over characters in the narrative were not the two-dimensional cut-outs they seem, but real flesh-and-blood individuals who experienced all the emotions men feel today. In a survey, the tendency is to loosen past events from their original living context and set them to marching across the printed page. In spite of these many draw-backs, the need remains to pull things together, to organize them as a coherent whole, and present the material in manageable form. An "over-view" sometimes reveals more than a piecemeal inspection of the historical terrain. Despite its inordinate length, students might be reminded also that the present work is only a summary of the main developments in Western education; far more has been left out than included.

An attempt has been made here to draw connections between historical phenomena and contemporary issues or problems, indirectly reflective of Dewey's point that all history is necessarily written from the standpoint of the present, and is, in an important sense, a statement not only of the past but of "that which is contemporaneously judged to be significant to the present." Where possible, discussion of the present-day relevance of histori-cal themes has been kept separate from the remainder of the text. If a skillful instructor can compensate for the hazards of re-creating the past for the sake of the present, this strategy can be extraordinarily fruitful. Those who find the interpretive chapter sections unduly intrusive may wish to omit them.

Some disclaimers are in order, because any history intended for use as a course textbook is a compromise with the requirements of scholarship, organization, and presentation. This work neither is designed to impress colleagues with the author's supposed erudition (a tactic sometimes cal-culated to mystify student readers), nor does it condescend to students, thereby insulting their intelligence. Although the result may not satisfy some academic purists, it is worthwhile mentioning that the writing of this volume was undertaken with the advice and counsel of undergraduate college students themselves. In large measure, both its organization and content were dictated by their suggestions. More specifically, they counseled against the pedagogical approach too often employed which reduces the historical narrative to such simplistic platitudes as "Plato was a great philosopher in ancient Greece who was also an outstanding educator. . . ." At the same time, they tried to save this author from the pedantry to which many textbook writers fall prey, evidenced by discussions that note how "Professors Dryasdust and Smellfungus disagree as to the precise beginnings of the common school. . . ." Hopefully, both hazards have been avoided with some measure of success.

The old truism about the impossibility of pleasing everyone is especially valid when it comes to organizing this sort of text. Some may be troubled by the scanty treatment accorded certain educational theorists and historical developments; it will be pointed out that entire cultures have been omitted from consideration. It is true that non-Western educational movements have been neglected; they deserve extended treatment in a separate work devoted to the subject. In the present volume not nearly enough has been said about the school system of the Spanish Moors and its intellectual contributions to Christian Europe. Byzantine civilization and its schools have been neglected altogether, as have developments on the African continent. By way of defense, it should be pointed out that an effort has been made to focus only upon those broad educational themes most directly in line with the Western cultural tradition. In the case of African culture and education, for example, black Americans are discovering that though their traditions are extremely important and warrant far more serious consideration than they have received to date, the social and cultural milieu in which the contemporary Afro-American inescapably finds himself derives almost exclusively from European antecedents.

Especially objectionable to some will be the inversion of historical chronology apparent in portions of Chapters 4 and 5. The single greatest contribution historical inquiry makes is to foster a sense of continuity between earlier and later events, to display the sequential evolution in time of the latter out of the former. For reasons of thematic coherence, nonetheless, the discussion of the sixteenth-century Reformation precedes the treatment of the Renaissance, even though the former was very much an outgrowth of the latter. For the same reason, consideration of the rise of scientific inquiry in the late-sixteenth and seventeenth centuries has been juxtaposed with the Renaissance revival of culture. In the first instance, at least some effort has been made to display important similarities between the Reformation and religious developments during the later Middle Ages; in the second, the attempt is to show how a literary revival paved the way for, and indeed led almost inevitably to, the birth of the modern scientific era.

The concluding chapter of this work devotes itself to a historical overview of educational theory and practice in the United States. Predictably, that exposition suffers from most of the limitations of the single-chapter approach, not the least of which is the artificial separation of American developments from European. It should go without saying that the interrelationships between the two have been profound and lasting. Those connections notwithstanding, it was determined that within the narrow limits of one book, a discussion of education in America should not be scattered throughout several chapters.

As one moves closer in time to the present, the mass of historical data becomes truly overwhelming. It becomes increasingly important to discriminate; and sometimes the process of selecting materials for exposition has to be almost arbitrary. In the final analysis, no one can be satisfied altogether with the particular judgments an author has rendered. This is true, of course, with respect to the earlier portions of this history as well, and when the presentation does not accord with any given individual's judgment on the matters at hand, due allowance must be made. (Undoubtedly, for instance, some readers may wish to take exception to the purely "secular" treatment given Judeo-Christian education.) All of this is by way of emphasizing once again that any work is written from the perspective of a particular point of view. Neither teachers nor students should be disturbed by this inescapable fact; in the case of students, they should discover as quickly as possible that worthwhile learning is best facilitated by placing oneself directly in the midst of conflicting viewpoints. As for instructors, if a text is viewed as a self-contained, self-sufficient resource, then teachers have precious little left to contribute. Whatever else stimulating instruction involves, it requires systematic compensation for the inadequacies of other learning sources.

Finally, to some extent this effort to produce another educational history has been predaceous upon the works of earlier writers. Its writing was prompted by dissatisfaction with existing texts and begun with the confident assurance that their defects could be easily avoided. The project was concluded in a spirit of profound respect for those who have tried to recount the history of education within the confines of a single volume. It is an insuperable task. At most, it is to be hoped that the present arrangement of materials will illustrate how yesterday's solutions to educational dilemmas have become today's problems. In all probability the answers of today will furnish tomorrow's questions, thus proving once again the truth of Will Durant's observation that education is and has always been a molting of dogmas, a progress in the art of doubt. The same holds true for theories about the proper conduct of that process.

Appreciation is expressed to Lloyd C. Chilton, Jr., and to Ronald C. Harris of The Macmillan Company for their active assistance in this project, and to publishers cited elsewhere who granted permission to quote from previously published sources. I am grateful to my associates who consented to review portions of a first draft, including Professors Lloyd P. Jorgenson, Ralph Glauert, William Harper, and especially Jan Stefanov. Their several suggestions have proved most helpful. I am indebted to Professor Joe Park of Northwestern University, who first introduced me to the challenges of the historical study of education; to Professors Robert B. Sutton and Bernard Mehl of Ohio State University, who directed my thinking along lines touched upon briefly in this work (although, for different reasons, both will probably disavow the intellectual parentage); and to my friend and colleague, Professor Henry

Lenz, for sharing his thoughts with me on a number of thorny historical problems. A great deal is owed my students in educational history courses. They have unknowingly demonstrated the truth of an old adage that one learns most from those one teaches. Special thanks are extended to Mrs. Karen Crenshaw for her patient labors in readying the manuscript. Without her invaluable assistance, its preparation might have been impossible. Lastly, I am grateful to my wife for her support and encouragement through a long, sometimes arduous, writing process.

Columbia, Missouri   C. J. L.

Contents

ix

3 Education for a Sacral Society   136

5   Education for a Worldly Society   271

6   Education for an Enlightened Society   324

7 Education for a Progressive Society 384

8 Education for a Free Society   468

Appendix   545

Index   581

Introduction

The massive fortress of Hohensalzburg lies sprawled across a lofty crag overlooking the Austrian city of Salzburg. Its rock-hewn battlements wind sinuously around the pinnacle, giving way to rough, vertical escarpments on every side. Stone towers jut proudly above the parapets, creating an imposing silhouette unique among Europe's strongholds. Below, nestled against the base of the precipice and extending along the meandering banks of the Salzach River, spreads the city, a riotous confusion of medieval spires, twisting streets, and colorful rooftops.

For some of Hohensalzburg's visitors, possibly only a few, the main interest lies not with impressive scenery but with the fortress itself. It pulsates with life and vigor, perhaps in the sense Collingwood intended when he said the past is not dead but living in the present. For those with a historical imagination, the citadel is a palpable embodiment of a human drama stretched across the centuries. Its walls still resound with the clamor of

1

workmen fortifying Archbishop Gebhard's redoubt during those uncertain times of the War of Investiture with the Pope. Von Keutschach stalks through gloomy corridors, ever fearful of the fifteenth-century city burghers plotting against him outside his sanctuary. Wary soldiers brace themselves for the first onslaught of a rebellious peasant mob boiling up the mount. Archbishop Paris Von Lodron nervously inspects his barricades during the Thirty Years' War and scans the horizon anxiously for signs of an approaching Swedish army.

Scenes mingle in the mind's eye. It is 1800, and Napoleon's haughty emissaries stroll leisurely through the courtyard. Or it is 1944, and Allied warplanes drone high overhead; their bombs whine past the castle's turrets to plummet into the city below. In short, the fortress is a veritable repository of images and sounds untainted with the passage of time. On the other hand, for those devoid of historical feeling and ignorant of Hohensalzburg's tumultuous past, only the murmur of present-day tourists disturbs the silence of the ages. The edifice is empty, its voice muted.

Macauley had a point in noting that the basic appeal of history is *imaginative*. Conversely the dislike of history may well be symptomatic of a failure of imagination, because after all the study of the past *is* about life and should have all the appeal of life itself.[1] Sad to say, the incapacity to transcend time's barriers is not uncommon. It leads to a profound distaste for historical study. The past for some people seems locked away in a labyrinth of hard-to-remember names and obscure events linked by a string of dates. With considerable sympathy, the authors of a charming little book, *1066 and All That,* reassure readers that theirs is a *"memorable* history of England comprising all the parts you can remember, including one hundred and three good kings, five bad kings, and two genuine dates."[2] Those bereft of the historical imagination, and hence indifferent to the study of history, might wish more such books were available.

What is missing is that certain enthusiasm for the rough stuff of human experience that accounts for the love of history, an excitement turning drudgery into delight when transformed by esthetic and intellectual involvement. "Our interest in history," writes Herbert Muller with unparalleled eloquence, "is more poetic than practical or scientific. It begins as a childlike interest in the obvious pageantry and exciting event; it grows as a mature interest in the variety and complexity of the drama, the splendid achievements and the terrible failures; it ends as a deep sense of the mystery of man's life—of all the dead, great and obscure, who once walked the earth, and of the wonderful and awful possibilities of being a human being."[3]

1 See A. L. Rowse, *The Use of History* (New York: Collier Books, 1965), p. 35.

2 Walter Sellar and Robert Yeatman, *1066 and All That* (New York: E. P. Dutton, 1931), title page.

3 Herbert Muller, *The Uses of the Past* (New York: Mentor Books, 1963), p. 42. Copyright by Oxford University Press and quoted with permission.

According to Pindar, Zeus begot Clio, the muse of history (one of nine patron goddesses of the ancient poets) with Mnemosyne, or memory. Poetry and memory—they tell something of her origin. Horace describes her as "the proclaimer," a teller of tales, and Hesiod describes her as an inspirer of epic poems. *Historia,* cognate with *story,* suggests the same general theme. History derives in a primitive, elemental way from the recounting of a narrative, beginning with tribal legends told round some primordial campfire and continuing in more complex forms today. Her attractions are as basic as they are enduring. In this very fundamental sense, apart from the subtle intellectual challenges posed by the study of the past, historical inquiry has intrinsic or "consummatory" value. History is important in the same way any liberal discipline, such as art, music, or poetry, is valuable: as a self-justifying subject with its own intrinsic end. It is not too much to claim that life's richness and diversity would be poorer without the experiences such disciplines supply.

Hard experience indicates, however, that an appeal stressing history's inherent worth will have scant impact except among those already pledged to its consummatory value. Antagonists invariably demand something more in the way of arguments to show that history has some use beyond itself, that it has instrumental utility. A host of complex, debatable issues is raised here, but most of the arguments reduce to the twofold allegation that since the present is the living sum total of the past, history helps men better understand their own time and, possibly, has predictive value for the future. "What man is," affirms Wilhelm Dilthey, "only his history tells. In vain men put the past behind them in order to begin anew. They cannot shake off the gods of the past because they become haunting ghosts. . . . The melody of our life is conditioned by the accompanying voices of the past." When contemporary critics argue that the only way to transcend history is to ignore it, George Santayana's famous dictum comes to mind with its warning that those who cannot remember the past are doomed to repeat it.

There has been a great deal of nonsense written purporting to show the direct value of history for educators. A favorite ploy is to argue that the inspiration of historical example will help turn teachers away from their autisms and lead them to emulate the practices of famous predecessors. It is true that an in-depth study of great educators from the past evokes admiration and humility, but there is no real evidence to show that historical awareness is a significant determinant of an individual's professional performance. Some will argue that the true basic problems of education are perennial, that they crop up afresh for each generation to solve in its own way. Because the answers handed down at one point in time differ substantially from those of another period, the total accumulation of partial solutions provides a wealth of valuable precedents that needs to be taken into account. There is probably some truth to that view, if not pressed too far, but its major weakness lies in the implicit assumption that the future will resemble the past.

In an age of absolutely unprecedented social, technological, and intellectual change, historical precedent may well become increasingly irrelevant. Whitehead has correctly observed that our sociological theories, our political philosophy, our practical maxims of business, our economic wisdom, and our doctrines of education descend in an unbroken line of tradition from the classical age of Greece down to the recent past. "The whole of this tradition," he argues, "is warped by the vicious assumption that each generation will substantially live amid the conditions governing the lives of its children. *We are living in the first period of human history for which this assumption is false.*" What we need to know today, as Max Lerner says, is not what great men of the past have done, but what ordinary men of the future may be doing.

There is ample reason for doubting the often repeated claim that the only way of predicting the future is to study the past. In the field of education especially it may no longer be possible to believe that teaching and learning processes will be conducted through the years ahead in roughly the same manner as before, that the conditions under which schools will function will be similar to those of the past, that the kind of challenges confronting teachers will not be of an entirely different order, or indeed that the whole societal context surrounding educational institutions will not undergo radical transformation. If at least some of tomorrow's fundamental educational issues turn out to be genuinely new, a knowledge of yesterday's perplexities may not prove particularly germane.

As a matter of fact, the most persuasive case for studying the historical development of education rests on other grounds. This is to say that history's main potential value is more subtle and indirect than many of its supporters seem to realize. Its fruitfulness derives from the *dialogue* that it generates within us between our own pedagogical wisdom and that of others separated by time. As H. I. Marrou suggests, we are sufficiently unlike our ancestors for their educational ideas to appear alien to us. Theirs may contain enough elements utterly opposed to our present thinking or our future aspirations to provide what he calls a "salutory shock." "Because this kind of dialogue is valuable," Marrou continues, "that does not mean that we are obliged to stop being ourselves; it is simply a means of acquiring culture, enlarging our perspective and stripping us moderns of that naive self-sufficiency which prevents us from imagining that anyone could be different from ourselves. But though it may force us to think, it will not necessarily change our course of action: historical example merely compels us to test the validity and cogency of the reasons for our choices—it makes our decisions conscious ones."[4] It is in its display of alternatives to our own values, beliefs, and modes of action that the study of history becomes vital.

---

[4] H. I. Marrou, *A History of Education in Antiquity* (New York: Mentor Books, 1964), pp. xii–xiii.

1 Education for a Closed Society

The paradox of education is precisely this—that as one begins to become conscious one begins to examine the society in which he is being educated. The purpose of education, finally, is to create in a person the ability to look at the world for himself, to make his own decisions. . . .

JAMES BALDWIN
A Talk to Teachers

In all societies—from societies that are very meagerly developed and have barely attained the dawnings of civilization, down to the most advanced and powerful societies—two classes of people appear—a class that rules and a class that is ruled. The first class enjoys the advantages that power brings, whereas the second, the more numerous class, is directed and controlled by the first. . . .

GAETANO MOSCA
The Ruling Class

EDUCATION AND HUMAN CULTURE

The anthropological study of primitive, preliterate cultures, both prehistoric and contemporary, might not appear germane to the history of education. It seems natural to pass over the story of mankind's beginnings because schools are virtually nonexistent and the work of education is discernible only as an integral part of the on-going culture. Education is highly informal and usually incidental to the daily activities of providing food, shelter, clothing, and defense. A primitive culture is innocent of schools, textbooks, classrooms and consciously organized curricula. However, a careful scrutiny of the earliest, simplest types of education can be a powerful tool for better understanding educational processes operative today. Primitive education, like the vastly more complex modern schooling, is basically a process of *enculturation*—the sum total of ways by which a raw, unformed human organism is inducted or initiated into a society, introduced to its culture, and becomes an effectively functioning member of the social order. Considered this way, *the nature and purpose of primitive education are fundamentally the same as those of contemporary education.* There are essential continuities between how a primitive society provides for the rearing of its young, trains them to take their place in the world as adults, and how a complex society accomplishes the same general ends via its many formal educative agencies. The emergence of a field of study known as educational anthropology in recent decades witnesses to the importance of examining such relationships between education in simple and complex societies.[1] Close analysis might demonstrate that the more objectionable features of primitive education are still prevalent in the educational practices of advanced civilizations.

The Beginnings of the Human Drama

Man's past is shrouded in mystery. Anthropologists still struggle with fragmentary data, taxonomic confusion, and underdeveloped research tools in the continuing search for human origins among the lower primates. Controversy and outright disagreement are rampant in the area and only the roughest outlines of the drama command consensus among scholars. Evidently man's early ancestors appeared on the evolutionary scene at least 750,000 years ago. Though their simian characteristics would have been unmistakable, they were upright, bipedal hominids, probably meat-eating hunters, and unquestionably toolmakers. It has been demonstrated convincingly that hominids of the late Pleistocene era possessed man's essential attributes—upright posture, a larger brain relative to body mass than that of any ape, an appetite for meat, and a rudimentary hunting culture sustained with unformed bone tools for hunting, butchering, and fighting. They were protomen, if not already men.

These australopithecines were supplanted by *Homo sapiens,* or modern man, almost three quarters of a million years ago. *Neanderthal* man, remains of which were first discovered near Dusseldorf, Germany, in 1857, was a prominent specialized subspecies of *Homo sapiens.* This group first appeared in Europe around forty thousand years ago and reigned until displaced (rather quickly) by a superior subspecies known as *Cro-Magnon* man, approximately twenty thousand years ago. The nomenclature of subsequent varieties of modern man becomes exceedingly complex. What is important to note is that distinctively human societies have existed for at least eighteen to twenty thousand years.

As *homo sapiens* consolidated his dominance over hominid competitors, he became a gatherer of foodstuffs (shellfish, fish, small animals) as well as

[1] See George F. Kneller, *Educational Anthropology: An Introduction* (New York: John Wiley & Sons, 1965).

a big-game hunter. Around 9000 B.C. man supplemented his hunting with intensive foraging for seeds, wild vegetables, and fish. Vegetation became a dietary staple. The start of the *Mesolithic* era marked the transition to food gathering, a step accompanied by the establishment for the first time of semipermanent settlements. The domestication of plants and animals soon followed. Well-developed farming communities developed. The *Early Neolithic* period was characterized by the expansion and refinement of agricultural techniques. In the Middle East it took place as early as 7500 B.C. The *Full Neolithic* era, beginning two thousand years later, saw the founding of towns and even cities, the expansion of agriculture, and the start of primitive technology. Excavations at Jarmo, at Catal Hüyükin in Turkey, and, most recently, along the Danube River prove that, contrary to earlier opinion, Neolithic settlements were common. By the time of the *Bronze Age* (ca. 3800 B.C.) isolated societies had blossomed into regional civilizations, writing had been discovered, and an urban revolution was in full swing. The *Iron Age,* which followed, starting around 2000 B.C., represents a fairly advanced stage in recorded history. Hence it can be said that "primitive" man's culture was a going concern at least nine thousand years ago.

The Nature of Culture

None of this development could have been possible without means for preserving human culture. It is man's capacity to create, sustain, and perpetuate culture that sets *Homo sapiens* apart from the lower primates. (The word *culture* here should not be taken to mean refinement, breeding, manners, or acquaintance with the fine arts, of course; anthropologically, it refers to the total shared way of life of a people.) Culture designates a more or less integrated system of learned behavior patterns characteristic of a society: all the nonbiologically inherited modes of thinking, feeling, and acting as embodied in and expressed by artifacts, values, behavior, and concepts. Customs, mores, and morals are a part of a culture. Philosophical systems, religious ideologies, political theories, language, and art are products of culture. Houses, tools, clothes, monuments, and all other physical artifacts depend upon culture. Occasionally the word *culture* is used interchangeably with *society,* although the former means ideas and beliefs primarily, whereas the latter refers to those who hold them. A society is an aggregate of people united in virtue of a shared culture.

Culture is both a product of human acts and a conditioning element for further action. Man creates culture but it, in turn, makes man. To be human is to possess a culture. The tranformation of the egoistic infant into an adult participant of the culture is what renders a man human. If the child is reared as an animal, his human potential goes unrealized. Enculturation—the process of absorbing the cognitive, affective, and behavioral patterns constituting a society—means learning explicitly or implicitly, directly and indirectly, how to be a human being competent to deal with the environment. (*Socialization,* on the other hand, is a less inclusive term which refers to the process of acquiring roles as a member of a society.)

Culture is learned. From the anthropologist's point of view, education basically means enculturation. The culture of a society must be internalized by each succeeding generation. Education, informal and formal, unconscious and conscious, is a means for the preservation of culture. Whether an Australian aborigine, a Neanderthal savage or a middle-class American, the individual is shaped and molded by his cultural milieu. The culture into which he is born largely determines his intellectual, emotional, and spiritual development. It defines how he perceives his environment and responds to it. Because cultures differ, human beings are different in terms of how they experience and express feelings. what language they speak, how they view the world through the symbolic system afforded by the various cultures, and even how certain physical traits are conditioned. Education is the force for perpetuating these life patterns, and in a very broad sense, at least, this basic function remains constant for any human culture.

SOCIETY: PRIMITIVE AND MODERN

A primitive society, in the classic definition of a "folk" society, is a small, usually isolated grouping of people. It is assumed from a study of prehistoric records such as caves, bones, implements, and other artifacts that early man developed speech and language for expressing thoughts, learned painfully to cultivate crops, devised ingenious means for hunting animals for food, and probably later domesticated and bred animals. Men congregated together under the auspices of rudimentary social conventions and gradually gained in adaptive techniques for survival. Social groupings were small in size, a few hundred people at most. Although modern technology and culture are obliterating the few surviving primitive communities, it is reasonable to assume that they approximate the conditions under which men lived in prehistorical times. There is an interesting debate among ethnologists whether some of the so-called savages tucked away in remote enclaves today truly represent an arrested stage of cultural development in human history or whether certain features of their culture are retrogressive and consequently fail to portray what life was like thousands of years ago. Either way, contemporary primitives exist in a cultural cul-de-sac; their cultures seem doomed under the impact of modern civilization. Nonetheless, the inspection of a primitive society and its culture, both prehistoric and contemporary, yields some data on man's origins despite gaps in current knowledge of the former and uncertainty regarding lineage of the latter.

The first notable feature of a primitive society is its relative *simplicity*. The social pattern of primitive groups, although varied and dissimilar in some respects, is quite homogeneous. Most constituents in a society are party to a shared body of knowledge, beliefs, values, and interests. The attitudes and activities of the community at large are known to virtually all participants of a simple culture. As a result, it is highly *integrated*. Behavioral patterns develop on a consensual basis, accompanied presumably by strong feelings of group solidarity.

The total accumulation of knowledge available in a primitive society is meagre compared with the range of human knowledge in a present-day technological society. This is not to say that the savage was or is ignorant; indeed, the very fact of his survival in a demanding environment proves otherwise. Anyone who has attempted to replicate a Stone Age knife, for example, can appreciate the difficulties of wresting sustenance using primitive methods. But the body of knowledge of a homogeneous society's culture is accessible to almost everyone. The division of labor is basically simple, even when sharply defined. In a more complex society, knowledge expands enormously, hence the operational roles of individuals become highly specialized. What is known, it has been rightly observed, expands at the expense of the individual. As knowledge proliferates, individual ignorance of the whole increases. One of the crucial problems in education today is locating ways to cope with the proliferation of knowledge. Because the "knowledge explosion" necessitates an ever-expanding specialization, the educator has to struggle with the basic issue of whether there is (or can be) a common cultural core of information that should be provided to all. Debate over school curricula usually focuses on how to establish priorities, how to transmit more data, and how much knowledge is required to sustain a minimal cultural cohesion. What are the "basic" or "essential" subjects that should be taught to everyone? How much mathematics or science or language arts should an individual know? Does specialization tend to fragment society? What undesirable consequences follow from the apparent split between the "scientific" subculture and the "literary–humanistic" subculture in the world today? Or is this division too simple, as some allege? Perhaps there are many centrifugal subcultures. How viable is the concept of a broad, liberal education in an industrial society that demands its members know more and more about less and less?

These are just some of the many pressing questions confronting those charged with the conduct of education in a complex culture. The price to be paid for an ascending order of cultural complexity is a fragmentation of social roles within society. On the one hand, the life of primitive man is not to be idealized, as not too long ago people tended to do. The "noble savage" led a far from idyllic existence. Because his repertoire of responses to environmental challenges was limited, he always ran the risk of failure. The penalty for failure could easily be death, from starvation, at the hands of wild animals, or as a result of natural catastrophes. A society whose culture is homogeneous in virtue of its simplicity is highly vulnerable. From an educational standpoint, however, the basic goal of passing on the culture was bound to be simpler than in an advanced society simply because there was less to pass on. Education, in the most immediate and direct sense, was a preparation for life and a process of living at the same time.

Another hazard of cultural homogeneity is that it seems to encourage *similar reactions to similar stimuli*. A third characteristic of a primitive society is that its members tend to respond in more or less fixed, repetitive, stereotyped ways to the circumstances arising in daily life. The problems of maintaining the economic base of a society are known to all. People necessarily live close to the basic economic realities of providing food, shelter, and clothing. The members of the community are educated to understand these necessities and how to cope with them. Specific techniques are implemented unthinkingly, if only because there is so little stimulus for experimentation. If a method for obtaining the basic needs of life works, there is little perceived need to improve upon it. "What has been, is best." This brand of hard-nosed pragmatism is understandable when there is so little room for error. If crops have always been planted in a certain way and success is not guaranteed by following an alternative method, assuredly new methods will not be tried except under exceptional circumstances. In an educational context this means the student in a primitive society is exposed to a limited range of influences. The functions of specialized groups within the community—food gatherers, hunters, weavers—are integrative and mutually reinforcing.

Societal groups will share the same values, attitudes, and ways of getting common tasks done, in sharp contrast with the situation in a modern technological culture. Of course the direction of the educative process is the same: preparing the student to function in the adult community by furnishing him with the requisite knowledge, attitudes, and values. Just as the savage must be taught how to survive as a member of the tribe, the youngster today is taught how to succeed in his community. The *social context* of education differs radically, though, because of the heterogeneity of a bureaucratic–industrial society.

This implies not just that people develop divergent reactions (behavioral patterns, attitudinal responses, and so on) to environmental stimuli, but that the variety of stimuli increases. The average person today is bombarded by competing influences, including parents, teachers, peers, and the mass media. Whereas a folk society's culture is *holistic*, a modern society's culture is fragmentary. The conflict of values represented by differing influences is at once a source of confusion for the individual and a formidable challenge for educators. The mass media familiarizes the child from an early age with the mores of many contrasting groups rather than the agreed-upon conventions of a single community. When the values held in the home obviously contradict those held in the world outside, the child is caught in the middle. His peers tacitly endorse one set of standards, his teachers another. Television celebrates certain virtues condemned by other groups or institutions with which the individual is thrown into contact. Hence, the burden of choosing (perhaps unconsciously) a set of norms, values, and opinions devolves upon the individual. As a matter of fact, specific choices are likely to be made from within the comparatively narrow range of standards typical of the middle class.

If the values taught in the school have to compete with others fostered elsewhere, the difficulty for educators is obvious. Nor is it simply a question of how to inculcate certain values in preference to others. The issue is also one of institutional choice: the school must adjudicate the conflicting demands made upon it and retain public support for its programs, all the while determining *which* mores, standards, values, and ideologies it can endorse. Furor over religious instruction in public schools illustrates how conflicts within contemporary society are fought out in the educational arena. People disagree over which beliefs are correct and how they ought to be fostered. The very fact that the school is a public institution makes it susceptible to many conflicting pressures. The historical evidence from recent decades in the United States suggests that schools have sought a common cultural denominator. They have enjoyed some success but rarely satisfied everyone. The reason is that, unlike a primitive culture, the central unifying set of values and popular beliefs may be poorly defined.

A primitive society has *few differentiated institutions*. There is no formal school because the culture does not require one. Daily experience is educational and almost every member of society serves as a teacher. Ordinary learning processes can be handled more directly by allowing the child to share actively in the life of the community. Indeed, because there are fewer skills to transmit, because knowledge is less specialized and the way of life of people is enacted before his own eyes, the student learns directly from firsthand experience. This facet of primitive education should serve as a reminder to modern educators that noninstitutionalized, informal learning is an important part of education in any culture. It is easy to forget that the student is subject to many forces besides those in the classroom. The continuing job of an effective teacher ought to be to seek ways of taking these influences into account and using them to advantage whenever possible.

Still another notable feature of primitive education is that *its objectives are almost self-evident* to the participants. The link between what is to be learned and how that knowledge will be used is directly apparent. Training for survival is something that connects with the level of experience the student handles naturally The child *sees* how and why it is necessary for him to acquire certain basic skills through unsheltered and intimate exposure. In today's schools, on the other hand, a student may be unable to perceive how the curriculum serves his interests and needs. A symptom of this is the tendency among teachers to think of motivation as an extra added ingredient, a corrective for pupil apathy that is somehow added into the educational situation. Faced with indifference, even outright hostility, the teacher feels the material has to be made more interesting in order to induce students to learn. A lag, psychological and temporal, between what society decides its youth should learn and the point when the student internalizes the requirement of knowing, say, algebra because now he finds it useful, is likely to be a veritable chasm in the classroom. It is a gap between what the student finds compelling and what the teacher deems necessary. This, of course, is again a function of a highly technological society. The problem of "motivating" the student to learn history or literature is compounded when the utility of such humane studies cannot be demonstrated readily. It almost goes without noting that the tendency toward a narrow utilitarianism is neither necessary nor inevitable in a developed culture, although it is fairly prevalent in Western countries. In the case of primitive education the problem of "motivation" is not so acute.

The family is always an important educative agency. In a folk culture it is usually an extended kin group comprising several generations traced together through the male line. In present-day Western society, the family is typically a smaller, nuclear group composed of parents and offspring. Whatever its structure, the family assumes a large share of responsibility for at least the initial phases of the child's education, beginning in earliest infancy and continuing through adolescence in some cases. From it the individual derives his own sense of identity, buttressed by a web of relations with others and sometimes by a territorial attachment associated with the family. In a simpler society, familial ties are apt to be very strong; the mobility and sheer numbers of people in an advanced culture weaken these connections.

Everyone needs a point of reference for his own sense of worth, identity, and importance. Some students of social behavior suggest that occupation rather than family has become the primary means through which personal identity is realized today, but even this has ceased to be a live option for some social groups. The worker may find it impossible to "identify with" his job. He becomes, some would say, an appendage to a production line or a cog in a bureaucratic machine. Unable to perceive the relation between his work and an end product, he is alienated—from his societal function and from himself. When the problem is aggravated by inability to identify with a family grouping, a major social problem arises. Work, family, and self-identity are parts of a common problem. Meaningful work in a primitive society is not hard to find, because all of life is dominated by the immediate need to secure basic creature comforts. But useful work, a job whose importance can be discerned without difficulty, is a rarer commodity in contemporary culture. The question is, "Can a modern culture create other social ties for its participants besides work or the family?"

Education serves to prepare people to fit certain roles in society, including economic ones. Unlike his primitive counterpart, modern man may resist his assimilation into the economic system operative in his culture. Signs point to widespread distrust on the part of the young directed against those who would lead them uncomplainingly into the world of work. It is to be hoped that most people will fit themselves into the economic structure underlying modern culture and find the life satisfactions they crave in whatever they do. The question asked: "Are there sufficient opportunities for self-expression and creativity, enough outlets for healthy idealism in the job market?" If not, then there exists a problem of major proportions. Educators share the responsibility of helping students make creative vocational choices, exhibiting the range of alternatives, and assisting the young in preparing for the vocational challenges they will encounter. An educational system that uncritically endorses the social status quo and perpetuates its liabilities is unlikely to gain the trust and support of a generation demanding instant reform of society's ills.

As a matter of fact, sociologists actually disagree on the extent of the disaffection of the young. Whether or not the family as an institution is dissolving is also uncertain. By way of contrast, nothing indicates the presence of a "generation gap" in present-day tribal cultures. Each succeeding generation appears to accept the standards and values of its predecessor.[2] Social change is nonexistent or exceedingly slow when contrasted with the rapid rate of change in a complex culture. Familial ties remain as strong as ever.

The situation is more ambiguous in present-day society. For example, the propriety of sex education in the schools is a major educational controversy today. Traditionally, the family was charged with the responsibility of introducing the facts of human reproduction to the young. It also safeguarded certain values associated with sexual behavior. The very fact that the schools are now being called upon to perform these tasks may indicate the family has partially abdicated this responsibility. Must the schools fulfill functions formerly discharged by other institutions? How many purposes can education satisfy successfully? The goals of primitive schooling are few in number and easily satisfied. At what point, it must be asked, does institutionalized education assume too many responsibilities, thereby hindering its most basic tasks?

It is interesting to note that *all societies withhold some information from the young.* The fact of male defecation is a secret kept for a time from the opposite sex in one primitive society. The truth that the wearers of ceremonial masks in dancing rituals are men, not gods, is kept from youth in other tribal groupings. In Western culture it is traditional to hide the

---

[2] Exceptions occur when a simple culture is convulsed through contact with a more advanced culture. The younger generation reflects the social conflict by selecting elements from the old and the new and attempts to forge a workable cultural synthesis.

mechanics of copulation from youngsters. Violence of all kinds—armed robbery, lynching, murder—is acceptable, or at least freely exposed via the mass media. Yet human sexuality, until recently, has been thought too controversial for preadolescents. Once again, the internal contradictions or conflicts of the culture surface in the schools.

The overriding consideration governing the purpose of primitive education is *security*. The tribe always struggles to maintain itself against formidable odds. Obtaining the basic necessities of life is fraught with peril. Wars, plagues, floods, and ecological upsets leading to the exhaustion of the food supply are always immediate possibilities. In consequence, life can be exceedingly brutal. The tribe's main job has had to be a breaking in of each new generation to the ways of life followed in the community. No halfway measures suffice: either the child thoroughly masters the rules for survival or he does not. Implicit obedience is the *sine qua non* for acceptance into the tribe. Outside it, he would die. The requisite for survival is conformity to the group's norms. At first it is entirely unconscious; later, behavior is sanctioned by tribal conventions. Education necessarily means rooting out variations in thought or practice while stamping group characteristics upon the youth. Through trial and error, by participation in ceremonies and rituals, by conscious imitation of one's elders, through the instruction received in the familial group, the child learns what is expected of him. He becomes an individual, as has been noted, only insofar as he subordinates himself to the group.

The child of a folk culture learns to accept traditions almost unthinkingly. A significant part of his education involves learning the rituals believed essential for propitiating unseen powers lurking behind every phenomenal reality. The animistic fears of tribal religion become powerful determinants of his values, attitudes, and day-to-day actions. Spirits are everywhere, in the animals he hunts, in the sky above, within the shadows of the night. The power that causes crops to grow demands elaborate sacrifices. Just as rigidly prescribed modes of behavior dictate how food and shelter are to be gained, primitive religion requires a fixity of belief. Hence, a tribal culture is extremely *conservative* and so too are its educational agencies.

In a primitive society, initiatory ceremonies (commonly called *rites de passage*) marking the attainment of manhood assume educative significance. The passage to adult status may be observed by rites admitting youth into secret societies and closed occupational groups, or by rituals associated with the onset of puberty. An initiation rite may be preceded by a long probationary period during which candidates are taught to endure hunger, pain, and hardships and are required to demonstrate mastery of skills necessary for adult life. It might not be too far-fetched to draw an analogy, as some writers have done, between primitive probation and the process of formal schooling in modern society. In both bases an arduous regimen of

the totalitarian regime of Nazi Germany partially realizes the closed society. Conversely, some of the features of an open society have been realized, if only fleetingly, in ancient Athens, Renaissance Italy, and some Western societies today.

The inspection of primitive culture and education should be an occasion for assessing contemporary education—its purpose and functions, the kind of society it serves. How "open" or "closed" is the society of this country? What consequences seem to follow for the American system of education? Upon what criteria should judgments about these consequences be based? These are inescapable questions for anyone genuinely interested in the contemporary significance of education in primitive culture.

Institutionalized education seems by its very nature to have natural affinities for the closed society. Even when it is less formal, as in a pre-literate society, it tends to reinforce established norms and encourages severe sanctions against the rare, extraordinary individual who fails to conform. Particularly does this seem true today, neither because of a sinister conspiracy by educators nor because modern society overtly endorses the more noxious characteristics of a tribalistic culture. When large numbers of children have to be handled in groups, there is an inevitable temptation to encourage conformity. Teachers want obedient, docile children similar to one another in behavior, temperament, and even learning ability. It makes them easier to discipline and control, easier to teach. Some teachers go so far as to confuse classroom "discipline" with acquiescence and passivity. "A quiet classroom," as one venerable slogan has it, "is the necessary condition for classroom learning." The school is an institution and all institutions want to run smoothly, without disruption.

The fundamental purpose of the school today, as always, is to fit young people into society. Through its efforts, youngsters are trained to cooperate in an industrial–bureaucratic society. It is a hard task: bringing people into line, showing them what constitutes acceptable behavior, how to serve society's needs. The school must succeed. Early schooling especially is crucial because it represents the child's first contact with institutionalized life. The individual must conform to its requirements as he will fit himself to the demands of other institutions throughout later life. As Nordstrom, Friedenberg, and Gold have correctly pointed out, aggressive institution-alizing in education works.[6] The Many can be managed, processed, controlled, and directed in specific paths with maximal efficiency. The "acceptable" student learns to do what he is supposed to do. He knows that the institution will reward him if he contributes to its purposes and will punish him if he controverts its will. The penalty for disobedience is social disapproval, suspicion, and economic ostracism. Such sanctions usually work just as effectively as the more drastic measures followed in a primitive so-

[6] Carl Nordstrom et al., *Society's Children: A Study of Ressentiment in the Secondary School* (New York: Random House, 1967), pp. 144–145.

ciety. School children are shaped, inexorably, unconsciously, for the practical world of Everybody.[7]

The paradox of a mass culture is that its complexity generates the same pressures for social conformity as does a primitive culture in virtue of its simplicity. Modern technology, in its present state of development, means a certain standardization of products and routines for the mass of men. It entails dependence upon machines to perform certain tasks and computers to design the machines. The social equivalent and complement is a people's willingness to accept standardization in appearance and behavior, uniformity in belief and values. Sometimes willingness converts to need: the need to find security within narrow cultural limits.

Hermann Hesse's novel *Steppenwolf* illustrates the situation vividly. Hesse depicts the bourgeois middle class as constantly seeking a balance, a mean between the opposites and extremes of human conduct. Its virtues are moderation and a morality of avoidance. The middle class, he claims, finds the path of least resistance most congenial to its temperate security. The bourgeoisie fears the uncommon, the extraordinary, the unusual. Consequently as Burns and Brauner note in support of Hesse's insight, "the machine culture with its standardization of things and routine, and the bourgeois sentiment with its security-minded abhorrence of extremes combine to provide a material and social environment in which the easiest thing to do is to adjust desires, expectations, behavior, and personality so as not to appear different."[8] Given the middle-class' cultural domination, it is altogether unsurprising that schools reinforce the bourgeois ideology.

In any society some order is necessary. Its participants need to share some basic assumptions and ways of doing things. It is vital to have some traditions to which people can adhere. A society is an impossibility unless its members cooperate and work together. Shared beliefs and customs are the social glue that keeps a culture from disintegrating and the society from dissolving. However—and this is crucial—when a society attains a level of mastery over its environment that makes it stable enough to tolerate mistakes, when the price for error is not outright destruction, then room must be made for innovation. Progress demands experimentation: in finding new modes of production, exploring untried avenues of thought, and disclosing overlooked ways of arranging social life. A culture has to find a balance, not the tepid mediocrity of bourgeois moderation, but a mean nonetheless between two opposing urges. One is the tendency to cling to imitative repetition, to obey blindly the ancestral burden of taboos and ancient customs. The other is the exploratory excitement of social novelty. A mature culture allows for change, individual and collective, in all things.

[7] Ibid., p. 145.

[8] Charles J. Brauner and Hobert W. Burns, *Problems in Education and Philosophy* (Englewood Cliffs, N.J.: Prentice-Hall, 1965), p. 121. The discussion borrows from this excellent analysis of social conformity and creativity.

Rigidity or rashness are the twin dangers it must avoid. An open society, in short, tolerates only that conformity of belief and action proved indispensable for its survival.[9] Conformity as such is not necessarily pernicious; in one sense it is obviously necessary. But conformity considered as the extension of order beyond necessity usually turns out to mean regimentation for the convenience of the dominant groups in a society. The rationalizations a society uses to justify conformity *not* shown to be essential ("We have always done things this way," or "Unorthodox ideas are dangerous," or "Pattern yourself after the group if you want to be accepted") represent so many obstacles to possible social improvements:

> Conformity . . . is social fat. The less fat the healthier the society. Today, there is so much fat it is almost impossible to feel the shape of the small core of necessary order. The general problems of freedom and tolerance involve a reducing diet that shrinks away the social fat of conformity so the solid core of necessary order can be clearly seen and used as the basis for defining liberty. . . . In a society where everyone grows up in such constant daily contact with conformity the basic problem lies in getting individuals to recognize what it is in them that makes conformity congenial. Thus the issue of conformity and creativity boils down to making the individual understand the potential for diversity implicit in human beings and hence in himself.[10]

Herein lies the basic lesson to be learned from the nature of education in preliterate societies. The contemporary school is probably too closely integrated with its society's interest groups to controvert them substantially. Yet if educational institutions are best to serve society's enduring needs, they must teach children to realize that received notions *have* to be questioned. The process of learning that all beliefs may not be warranted is a necessary one if people are to grow in their ability to tolerate differences in outlook and behavior. Individual growth depends on challenging established ways and on seeking new alternatives. The school's commitment to preserve uncritically established ideas as the only ones tolerable has to be minimized. At one level, this implies that educators adopt the following operational criterion for judging their behavior: Is this rule or imposition of order *essential* to my educational work? (One wonders how student dress codes, for example, might fare if this standard were universally applied.) At another level, curricula ought to free the individual from the tyranny of the group. Young people must be exposed freely to the ideas of other groups, systems, nations and epochs.[11] The individual has to be brought to an

[9] See Desmond Morris, *The Naked Ape* (New York: Dell Publishing Company, 1969), pp. 104–105.

[10] Brauner and Burns, op. cit., p. 132. Quoted by permission of Prentice-Hall, Inc., Englewood Cliffs, New Jersey.

[11] See Paul Nash, *Authority and Freedom in Education* (New York: John Wiley & Sons, 1966), pp. 158 ff.

awareness of his own individuality rather than his commonality. Moral autonomy, personal excellence, education for diversity—these have to become the paramount goals of education in a free society. Not education for "trained manpower" or for society's needs, but education for individual creativity and independence. Children can be induced into the culture, given a basis of common experience and knowledge essential for civilized life, without utterly suppressing their initiative or destroying their capacity to be productively different.

The alternative is a return to the closed society. The tragedy of conformity in modern education is that it is unnecessary. One can appreciate the limitations of primitive education because the conditions dictating its objectives are inherently repressive. This is not true in an industrial–bureaucratic society. Its members are fortunate enough to be able to experiment with a wide range of goals without fear of having their culture torn asunder. The unrealized potential of institutionalized enculturation consists in the exploration of this variety of educational values.

HISTORICAL ORIGINS IN MESOPOTAMIA

The Rise of the City-State

The rich alluvial plains of the Tigris and Euphrates Rivers (known to generations of modern schoolchildren as the "Fertile Crescent") were undoubtedly the site of the greatest of the very early civilizations of the Near East. A veritable revolution in man's cultural advancement—the achievement of an efficient food-producing technology—became possible with the successful domestication of plants and animals. Once man learned to cultivate the plants he had previously gathered and learned to control the reproduction of certain animals he had formerly hunted for sustenance, he was well on the way toward the radical reconstruction of human culture. Ever-increasing cultural differentiation led rather quickly to specialization within social communities. For the first time larger farming villages became not only possible but inevitable. Cities, extensive trade and commerce, large-scale warfare, and all the other accoutrements of a complex civilization were soon to follow.

The revolution in agriculture resulted in vastly more efficient modes of production. It encouraged the growth of permanent dwellings tied to a specific locale. Greater productivity freed a certain proportion of the population for other pursuits besides those directly connected with obtaining the basic necessities of life—freed to assume new roles in the social order. Food surplus created by the agricultural producers contributed to the development of a whole range of institutions greater in size and complexity than anything found in a primitive tribal society. The basic innovations in subsistence maintenance, in sum, opened up the possibility for new social processes and consequent alterations in men's patterns of interaction with one another.

It is known that at least semipermanent communities existed in the rivers' basin as early as 8000 B.C. Their inhabitants were familiar with the locale and exploited it efficiently. Clues gleaned from archeological sites of the so-called *Natufian* culture in the Palestine area, at the Kurdistani site of Zawi Chemi Shanidar, as well as the older excavations at Karim Shahir and M'lefaatin in Iraq indicate that ancient peoples in those areas possessed a well-developed culture. From remains at Hassuna along the Tigris River and at Jurmo, Iraq, it is known that the people manufactured flint tools and baked pottery, that they had attained a level of craftsmanship capable of producing finely shaped obsidian tools, and that they possessed sufficient social organization to share technological advances with the people in the region of the Amouq in Syro-Cilicia. The first villages boasted at least three to five hundred people, no mean accomplishment for such an early date. Some of the very earliest villages have been discovered along the inward slopes of the Zagros mountain crescent in Kurdistan. It took less than two thousand years for the farming-village way of life to spread down through the valleys toward the bottom lands. In the comparatively short space of three or four thousand years, agricultural innovations had changed man's life more drastically than in the preceding 250,000 years.

By 5500 B.C. the village community had fully matured. It was internally stabilized as an institution throughout southwest Asia during the following 1,500 years. Between five and six thousand years ago, agricultural settlements increased greatly in size in the Tigris-Euphrates basin. Their structural organization also changed decisively. The culmination of this process was the Sumerian city-state, of which there were several. The *Sumerians* must be counted among the earliest known people in the region and the first to develop a great civilization. Cities such as *Sumer* and *Ur* (the latter the legendary home of Abraham), and later, *Assur,* were major centers of commerce in ancient Mesopotamia. They numbered tens of thousands of inhabitants; provided the focus for elaborate military, political, economic, and religious establishments; functioned as elaborate trading centers; and helped to stimulate technology throughout that part of the world. Urbanization brought with it a stratification of social classes and an impressive array of cultural accomplishments.

The Sumerians

The early history of the Sumarians shows how political absolutism and priestly power were combined in the interest of a strong centralized state. Their record can be traced back to around 5000 B.C., though little is known of Sumerian origins. It is conjectured that their original home was on the high plateau land of central Asia. Through the greater part of their history in the Tigris–Euphrates basin, they lived in a loose confederation of city-states, each headed by a *patesi,* a leader combining the functions of chief priest, commander of the army and superintendent of the irrigation system. It is conventional to distinguish four major phases in the chronology of the rising Mesopotamian city-state: the *Ubaid* period (4000–3800 B.C.), the relatively brief *Warka* period; the *Protoliterate* period, which lasted for the remainder of the fourth millennium; and the *Early Dynastic* (3000–2500 B.C.). Archaeological explorations have uncovered the remains of work shops and storehouses clustered about buildings evidently used for cultic purposes. Most of these ruins do not predate the Early Dynastic period, but the rise of a priestly class in control of the city-state must have occurred even earlier. Priests were the first people to be released from direct subsistence labor to supervise the multitude of economic and ritual activities fast becoming essential to urban life. Some scholars conjecture that temple priests gained control over both the domesticated herds and irrigated farm lands, thereby ensuring their power over the agricultural economy of Mesopotamia as a whole. Irrigation agriculture made the vital difference between unproductive and fertile land. The class that controlled access to irrigated lands dominated the rest of the economy. The division of other social classes probably came about as the priests consolidated their power partially by determining who could use the land. Economic productivity necessitated a place for storage, exchange, and redistribution of goods. For these reasons the city was a logical device for congregating people together and setting the urbanization process in motion. And running the city fell to a priestly class. A class structure headed by priests, the rise of the city, and further urbanization must have been interrelated phenomena.

Records from the Baba temple in Girsu, for example, indicate the different allotments from lands owned by the priestly temple to its parishioners. Other texts describe the sales of houses, fields, slaves, textile goods, and cattle. Clearly, temples were centers of power. They were also a primary force for new thought patterns and the crystalization of new forms of social organization.

Only gradually was there a shift of leadership from the temple to the palace. Political organization did not begin to dominate until warrior heroes, formerly elected by a group, made good their hereditary claims to power. Kings first arose from the need for military leadership as the tempo of armed conflict increased. Warring royal authorities created constant unrest. By around 2500 B.C. they were installed more or less permanently at the apex of the social pyramid. They were rarely rivals to the priestly claims to power. On the contrary, the growing cities needed a powerful central authority to maintain the rigid social structure and to maintain the living conditions found within a city. Kings provided such an authority, and priests early founded close alliances with the political despots. Typically, the hereditary ruler was believed to be divinely inspired or even a deity himself. The status of divinity was extended through a privileged class of officeholders and the subordinate priests. No clear distinctions were made between political and religious spheres of influence; not uncommonly the king would be regarded as the chief priest. This marriage of politics and religion would produce an absolute theocracy, buttressed by a web of doctrines and dogmas reinforcing the established socioeconomic, political arrangement. It was an archetypal closed society.

Around 2500 B.C. the native Sumerians were invaded by a nation of Semites who had established themselves in a section of the valley called Akkad. Their leader was a king known as Shargena or *Sargon I,* whose conquest of the Sumerian city-states was only a prelude to the founding of the first great Semitic empire in western Asia. In the space of a few short years Sargon's domain included all the territories of the Elamites (a neighboring poeple) and all of northern Syria, to the shores of the Mediterranean. The merging of Sumerian culture and the more primitive Akkadian culture produced a strong empire and a high civilization. For almost four hundred years. Mesopotamia enjoyed a golden age of prosperity and political stability. Under Sargon's patronage, public libraries were founded in all the major cities and furnished with extensive collections. A royal library at *Ourouk* ("Town of Books") was begun, equipped with an impressive collection of documents including traditional priestly lore, histories, theological works, treaties on magic and divination, catalogues of minerals and animals, medicinal incantations, books on mathematics, astrological tablets, and technical manuals. Sargon's holdings represented an accumulation of some two thousand years of wisdom dating back as far as the literary age of a semilegendary leader, Shargena, in 3800 B.C.

Sumerian Schools

The priestly class sustained a well-defined school system designed to train leaders drawn from an elitist aristocracy. Evidently grammars and dictionaries were in common use. Two languages were taught: the ancient "classic" Sumerian of pre-Akkadian times and a Semitic tongue for daily use. The Sargon dynasty needed large numbers of civil servants, state officials, and priests, hence *temple schools* did a thriving business preparing the upper classes for their privileged positions. Training for the priesthood and preparing for a governmental career practically amounted to the same thing in these early schools, a sure indication of the close affinities between bureaucratic and theocratic power.

Sumerian schools were first established in the last half of the third millennium to train the scribes required to satisfy the economic and administrative demands of the regime. Most institutions were connected either with a major temple, the royal palace itself, or the dwelling of a provincial governor. In addition to the teaching of *cuneiform writing,* a system of pictographic symbols which gradually developed into an aggregate of almost four hundred syllabic and phonetic signs, the school served as a center

of learning and culture where scholars gathered to advance and share discoveries. Much later educational institutions became secular in nature and
were supported by tuition fees paid directly to the teachers. Throughout
the long Sumerian history, formal education was neither universal nor
compulsory and it was always reserved for the children of the wealthy class.[12]

The master of the school was known as the *ummia*, "expert," "professor,"
or "school father," whereas the student was called a "school son." A teaching assistant, the "big brother," served the *ummia* by writing tablets for
boys to copy, examined students' work, and heard their oral recitations.
Other members of the staff included "the man in charge of drawing," "the
man in charge of Sumerian," a monitor who supervised attendance, and
a "man in charge of the whip." Two courses of study were pursued by
prospective scribes. The first included taxonomic lists and compilations of
names, lexicons, and mathematical tables. The second was more literary in
character, including the study of epic tales and myths, hymns, lamentations,
essays, fables, and proverbs. Pupil workbooks excavated from Shuruppak,
dating back to around 2500 B.C., provide evidence of many hours of labor as
pupils copied down their lessons on clay tablets. Little is known about the
physical arrangement of Sumerian schools, but clues have been found from
diggings at Nippur, Sippar, Ur, and Mari, where rows of benches constructed from back brick were uncovered, seats capable of seating one,
two, or four students.

A document authorized by an anonymous schoolmaster who lived three
thousand years ago affords a vivid description of one day in the life of a
Sumerian schoolboy. He fears being late to school "lest his teacher cane
him." His mother prepares a lunch hurriedly. Evidently the young student
has a bad time of it. He misbehaves and is punished for standing up and
talking out of turn. He writes his tablet, gives a recitation, eats his lunch,
prepares a new tablet, writes his lesson upon it, is assigned some oral work,
and in the afternoon is given another written assignment. Catastrophe
strikes when the teacher severely reprimands the student for careless copy-
work. At home the boy suggests to his father that the *ummia* be invited to
dinner and bribed with presents. The father assents and the teacher is
brought to the home, where he is installed in a seat of honor, wined and
dined and given a new robe and a costly ring. The treatment has the desired
effect; the teacher then praises his charge and promises him he will "reach
the pinnacle of the scribal art" and if he applies himself diligently, he may
become a "man of learning," a leader among men.

Another literary vignette reveals that a "generation gap" existed between
Sumerian children and their parents. Pupils complained bitterly about
school, and parents, in turn, berated their offspring for being wayward, disobedient, and ungrateful. One father laments that his heart has been

12 Samuel Noah Kramer, *History Begins at Sumer* (Garden City, N.Y.: Anchor, 1959),
p. 2. The following description of the Sumerian school is taken from pp. 2–16.

"sated with weariness" over his son. He directs him to "go to school, stand before your school father, recite your assignment, open your schoolbag, write your tablet, let your 'big brother' write your new tablet for you." He then admonishes his son, "after you have finished your assignment and reported to your monitor, come to me, and do not wander about in the street."[13]

The Old Babylonian Era

As is so often the case when a strong leader passes from power, Sargon's death was the signal for the first of a series of Sumerian revolts. Gradually the administrative system crumbled under the pressure of nomadic invasions from without and internal revolts by the great city-states. One by one they began to break away from the central government. At first their revolts were suppressed; later it became impossible to keep the empire together. Ur was the first to declare its independence as an autonomous city-state. Others soon followed. About 2100 B.C. tribes of fierce barbarians from the north, known as the *Guti*, invaded the Mesopotamian basin and established their rule over all of Sumer and Akkad. Their most noted king was a tribal chieftain by the name of *Dungi*, who was determined to found a second empire on the ruins of the old. Again the Sumerians under the leadership of the city of Ur rebelled successfully against their new conquerors.

In the twenty-first century the remains of the Guti empire were annexed briefly by the Elamites and then they too fell before the onslaught of a new Semitic invasion launched by the *Amorites*, driving out from the fringes of the Arabian desert. The *Old Babylonians*, as they are commonly known, initiated the second major phase of the development of civilization in Mesopotamia. Sumerian dominance was now at the end. By 1800 B.C. the ancient Sumerian city of *Babylon* had gained ascendency in the Fertile Crescent as center for a fabulous empire—rich, powerful, and seemingly invincible.

The Babylonians established a vast autocratic state which lasted for almost two centuries. During the reign of their most famous king, *Hammurabi*, Babylonian dominion was extended as far north as Assyria, the old legal codes were gathered together and codified to produce the most systematic structure of law known to early historic cultures, and the old administrative system of government was revived and enlarged. The Amoritic Babylonians had no indigenous culture; they simply appropriated whatever was left of the old Akkadian-Sumerian culture. All vestiges of autonomy for the city-states were swept away, power was consolidated in a central state government, and the power of the king of Babylon was made absolute. Chief sanction for Babylonian political power was made to rest with religion more than with the system of law gathered in the famous *Hammurabi Code*. The king, whose influence pervaded almost all phases of daily life, popularly was believed to possess divine power. He himself was

---

13 Ibid., pp. 13–14.

not a divinity but he owed his position to the various gods revered by individual cities. Inequities in the social structure, so obviously apparent in the elevation of the privileged class over the toiling masses, were ordained by the city gods. As a result, the religious climate of opinion encouraged a perpetuation of the established social order, complete with unquestioned political totalitarianism and a priestly machinery to keep it functioning. Schooling could only be an instrument to serve the status quo.

Babylonian Schools

Schools flourished during the period of Babylonian rule as they had previously, and for the same purpose: to train priests, scribes, and civil servants to administer the central government. An elaborate system of royal taxation as well as a gross increase in trade and commerce necessitated an ever-increasing number of educated civil servants. Surviving records show that the Hammurabian legal system formed the basis for the curriculum in temple and palace schools. Aside from training in business and government, much of Babylonian education must have been directed toward the preparation of a growing priesthood, judging from the importance cultic observances played in daily life. Ancient Sumerian deities were neglected and new ones exalted in their stead. Marduk, originally a local town god of Babylon, was elevated to the highest position in the pantheon, accompanied by such important new deities as Ishtar and Tammuz. So much attention was paid to religious matters that whatever artistic and intellectual culture the Babylonians developed seemed to revolve around ritual ceremonies. It is reasonable to assume that formal schools were required to train priests to conduct rites, as well as to supervise the secular administrative system.

The Period of Assyrian Domination

Many kingdoms followed the eclipse of Babylonian power in the early half of the second millennium. Following Hammurabi's death and a succession of lesser leaders, the empire slowly declined, until its final destruction at the hands of the *Kassites,* around 1650 B.C. A period of retrogression set in, lasting over five hundred years. First one city-state would become dominant, then another. Conquerors exchanged territories a dozen times over. The third major phase in the evolution of Mesopotamian civilization began with the rise to power of a Semitic people known as *Assyrians,* inhabiting the plateau of Assur some five hundred miles up the Tigris River. By the tenth century the Assyrians had overthrown what was left of Kassite rule in Babylonia and had become acknowledged masters north, south, and east of Nineveh. Their empire grew rapidly in the following century, extending even to the Mediterranean. They were rightly feared as the most ferocious people of the area. Their mighty conscript army, strengthened with mounted cavalry and the new iron weaponry, rolled over entire nations, crushing whatever opposition it met. For the first time in recorded history a nation deliberately employed the tactics of mass terror to intimidate its subject peoples. The Assyrian empire reached its apex in the eighth and seventh centuries under *Sargon II* (ca. 722–705 B.C.), *Sennacherib* (ca. 705–681 B.C.), and *Assurbanipal* (ca. 688–626 B.C.). Syria, Israel, Phoenicia, and even Egypt all fell victims to Assyrian military prowess. Nothing much is known as yet about the Assyrian educational system except that it must have included schools to educate the vast numbers needed to administer the empire, coordinate the war machine, and consolidate power in newly conquered territories. It is recorded that King Assurbanipal, around 628 B.C., had bilingual copies of the old Babylonian library made and placed in Nineveh. Some twenty-two thousand tablets in all, it is estimated, must have been reproduced. This suggests the existence of a learned class and points to the existence of schools.

The Amoritic Babylonians or Chaldeans

The age of Assyrian supremacy came to an end in the seventh century, when the empire reached unmanageable size. The Assyrian genius for government eventually proved to be grossly inferior to their appetite for conquest, and the loosely jointed edifice began to collapse after it had been extended to Media in the east and to Egypt and Arabia on the south. In historical retrospect it seems that the more they conquered, the more they felt they had to conquer, in order to protect what they had already gained. Every success excited ambition and riveted the chains of militarism more firmly than ever. In the end their empire fell before the *Medes,* assisted by the *Chaldeans* or "neo-Babylonians," who mistakenly thought they were descended from the original Babylonians of Hammurabi's day.

The overthrow of Assyrian power began when a provincial governor, *Nabopolassar,* managed to unite dissident groups chafing under their Assyrian overlords and organized a revolt. In 612 B.C. the capture of the capital of Nineveh spelled the end of the old government. Nabopolassar was succeeded by his son, *Nebuchadnezzar,* who ruled until 526 B.C. When the last vestiges of Assyrian authority had been annihilated throughout the Fertile Crescent, the Chaldeans found themselves undisputed masters of a new cosmopolitan empire, the greatest the Near Orient had witnessed for centuries. A fourth phase in Mesopotamian civilization had begun.

Culturally, the Chaldean-Babylonians looked back to the days of grandeur of their supposed ancestors. They restored ancient law and literature, revived the essential features of the Old Babylonian economic and political system, and venerated the religious deities of an age long since gone. Marduk, who had been overthrown by the Assyrians, was restored to his central place at the head of the divine pantheon. Babylonian theology divested the gods of their anthropomorphic qualities and exalted them as transcendent, omnipotent beings. Marduk became Jupiter, Ishtar became

Venus, and other divinities were likewise associated with heavenly bodies. Chaldean literature became distinctly antiquarian in tone. Some notable innovations were made, nonetheless, especially in the fields of astronomy (stimulated by the astral theology being developed) and applied mechanics. Economically, Chaldean civilization remained unchanged: an agricultural economy supported by the lower class for the benefit of the aristocracy. Trade and business reached heights unknown in previous times.

Chaldean Education

Every Mesopotamian city had a public library of brick tablets consisting of historical and mythological writings, legal compositions, treatises on geography, astronomy and astrology, records of omens and magical formulas, poems, proverbs, and fables, grammatical disquisitions, and so forth. Sons of the priestly class were carefully instructed from boyhood up in the esoteric disciplines of medicine, law, civil government, theology, and astrology. A carefully graduated hierarchy of priestly scribes existed to service the requirements of Chaldean society. Schools were in existence wherever there were temples, palaces, and municipal storehouses. Nor was education confined to priests and scribes alone. The secular upper classes shared in formal training to some extent insofar as sons of the wealthy were chosen for civil service training at the royal court itself. Nebuchadnezzar's instructions regarding the instruction of some Jewish children, as recorded in the Book of Daniel of the Old Testament, was only the continuation of an ancient Babylonian custom. It is narrated,

> And the king spoke to Ashpenaz, the master of his eunuchs, and directed him to bring some of the children of Israel, and of the king's own sons and the princes' sons; children without faults, but well-reared, and intelligent, and trained in knowledge, and understanding science, and those of exceptional ability should be brought to the king's palace, and taught the learning and language of the Chaldeans. And the king shared his own supplies with them and wine which he drank; so sustaining them three years, that at the end thereof, they might serve the king.

This passage not only explicitly confirms the existence of a civil service training period; it implies that some form of earlier preparatory instruction on an organized basis was available to the children of the nobility.

The Persian Period

The fifth major phase in Mesopotamia, a period which actually transformed the region's cultural complex, began with the fall of the Chaldeo-Babylonian empire in 539–538 B.C. before the Elamites and Persians. The empire fell, as the Persian king *Cyrus the Great* boasted, "without a battle and without fighting." Under Cyrus' leadership, which lasted until 529 B.C., a new empire was built upon the kingdom of Lydia and Chaldean holdings, including Babylon. Cyrus' son, *Cambyses*, extended the frontiers further until they included the lowest regions of Egypt. When *Darius I* (ca. 521–486 B.C.) came to power he divided the empire into twenty-one subordinate provinces under an absolute monarchy, each province governed by a civil official or satrap. Historians concur that had the Persians not introduced a universal coinage system, built roads, developed laws, and established certain precedents for giving limited autonomy to the different peoples under a central rule, the empire-building process furthered subsequently by Alexander the Great and later by the Romans would not have assumed the shapes it did. In any case, the Persian empire was the last great empire indigenous to Mesopotamia. It lasted until 330 B.C., when its territories were annexed by Alexander.

Persian rule, like the despotisms before it, continued the tradition of authoritarian power wielded by a theocratic state. It retained many of the barbaric elements of the ancestral past, although it introduced a number of novel social innovations. A new religion, Zoroastrianism, was begun, original literary forms appeared, institutions underwent radical transformation, technology improved, and generally a new culture began to take shape. In terms of social organization the Persian pattern was a transitional one, linking primitive tribal ways with modes of life lying in the future, savagery with civilization. The Persians, it might be said, ushered in an age still chained to the present and overly respectful of the past, but destined to mark an advance in the evolution of Western culture.

Persian Education

There is some evidence to show that family upbringing, though partially brutalized by the exigencies of the day, was genial and kindly. "Up to the fifth year," according to Herodotus, children were "not allowed to come into the sight of their father, but [passed] their lives with the women." This was done so that if the child died young, the father would "not be afflicted with the loss."

Formal education for the sons of the upper class began at age five or seven and continued until age twenty-four. They were trained in the *central school* of the royal palace or at *departmental court schools* of provincial satraps. Instruction was of the nonacademic variety in the student's early years. The student was trained in the shooting of the bow, riding, the use of the javelin, and other military exercises. According to Xenophon's contemporary report in his *Anabasis*, "all the sons of the Persian nobles are educated at the Royal Palace, where they have an opportunity of learning many a lesson of virtuous conduct, but can see or hear nothing disgraceful. Here the boys see some honored by the king and others degraded, so that in their very childhood, they learn to govern and to obey." Plato, in his *Alcibiades*, speaks of the instruction of the sons of the Persian kings in the wisdom of Zoroaster as well as in justice, temperance, and courage.

At age fifteen, boys took an oath to follow the sacred laws of Zoroaster and became official servants of the state, solemnized in the reading of religious poems. For the academically inclined, those intending to follow a religious vocation continued their formal schooling for another ten years. The *Magi* (priests) oversaw systematic instruction in the culture's major literary texts, including the *Zend-Avesta,* or Bible of the Parsees, which consisted of a collection of laws (the *Venidad*), a litany of rituals (the *Visperad*), and a collection of hymns (the *Yasna*). Other subjects studied included law, medicine, astrology, and probably many others. Unlike the Sumerians and Babylonians, the Persians perpetuated their strong oral traditions and did not emphasize reading and writing until a very late date. Formal religious instruction could have been only a small part of the total educational effort. Persian culture, like its predecessors, depended heavily upon informal mechanisms for transmitting the heritage of the past, training soldiers, and training apprentices for lower-class vocations. Some historians allege the Persians were the first people to institute state controls over noninstitutionalized instruction, but the claim has little evidence for support.

HISTORICAL ORIGINS IN THE NILE RIVER VALLEY

Whether the first great civilizations of antiquity arose in Mesopotamia or in the Nile River valley is still a sharply debated question. In the *Timaeus* Plato reports that long before his own time the Egyptians considered the Greeks to be "mere children" without any appreciable traditions, which, considering the antiquity of Greek civilization, may indicate something about the age of Egyptian culture. A respectable body of authority supports the claims of the Tigris–Euphrates area, though the judgment of many scholars inclines toward the Egyptian region. Still other experts prefer Elam, a territory lying east of the Tigris–Euphrates basin bordering on the Persian Gulf. In the final analysis the issue is not crucial for the student of education; Egyptian civilization is sufficiently ancient to illustrate how formal education was conducted at the very dawn of recorded history. In some respects the Egyptian pattern shares characteristics typical in Mesopotamia; in others, certain interesting divergencies are apparent.

Almost twenty-five hundred years ago, after a trip to Egypt, Herodotus exclaimed over what he had seen. "There is no country," he marveled, "that has so many wonders." Although it extended for a distance of 750 miles, the valley of the Nile was not more than ten miles wide in some places, and its maximum width was thirty-one miles. The total area was less than eleven thousand square miles. Through uncounted centuries, the river had carved out a vast canyon bounded on either side by cliffs ranging in height from a few hundred to a thousand feet. The floor of the trench was covered with a rich alluvial deposit, which in places reached a depth in excess of thirty feet. The soil was of such amazing productivity that as many as three crops per year could be raised on the same land. The land truly was, as Herodotus observed, "the gift of the Nile."

The dwellers of the river valley enjoyed geographic advantages conducive to the growth of a high culture. To the east and west were trackless deserts, on the north was a harborless coast line, and on the south the rocky barriers of a series of cataracts which prevented the inroads of African invaders. Amidst such geographically insured isolation, one of the mightiest civilizations of all time was born.

Thirty Centuries of History

Egypt was settled by a Hamitic people as early as 18,000 B.C., according to some authorities. The earliest event in Egyptian history that can be pinpointed with any accuracy falls much later, around 5650 B.C., according to hieroglyphics found in a king's tomb at Abydos. Because there were no unified states in the valley until about 3400 B.C., the preceding centuries are referred to as the *predynastic* period. Economic conditions encouraged the growth of settled villages or "nomes" engaged in cooperative irrigation efforts. Communal relations promoted political unity as villages coalesced into independent city-states, cities into districts, and districts into two natural regions, Lower Egypt's Delta region and Upper Egypt's narrow corridor along the Nile's headwaters. Shortly after the beginning of the fourth millennium a fusion of the northern and southern kingdoms took place and the *First Dynasty* was begun under Narmer, familiarly known as *Menes*. During the first two dynasties (3100–2700 B.C.) the capital of the newly formed union was maintained at Thinis in Upper Egypt. The Third Dynasty, under Djoser (2700–2600 B.C.) transferred the seat of government to Memphis, on the southern edge of the Delta, in order to secure the advantage of a more central location for all administrative functions. It remained there for approximately four centuries. The period from about 2700 to 2300 B.C. is accordingly called the *Memphite period,* whereas the entire age of the first six dynasties (down to around 2100) is known as the period of the *Old Kingdom.*

The Fourth through Sixth Dynasties marked the first great age of Egypt. A complex hieroglyphic language evolved, monumental pyramids such as that of Khufu (Cheops) at Gizeh were erected, the Great Sphinx was built, trade flourished with nations as far away as Lebanon, and the power of the central government steadily increased. A strong theocratic state arose, headed by the king or Pharaoh (from the Egyptian *per-o,* meaning "great house" or "royal house"). The ruler's absolute authority was exercised not in his own behalf but in his capacity as the vicar of a god; the remote and majestic monarch was his agent. God-kings were themselves considered divine, however, according to the prevailing conception, and sons of the sun god Re, or Ra. They were worshiped and loyally served by subordinate priests pledged to the Pharaohs' service in both this life and in the hereafter. Government policy throughout most of the history of the Old Kingdom was based on principles of peace and nonaggression. There was neither a standing army nor a national militia. Protected on all sides, the Egyptians enjoyed a solid millennium of peace and relative prosperity.

Following the ninety-four-year reign of *Pepi II* of the Sixth Dynasty, the Old Kingdom came to an end. Usurpation of power by numerous nobles, the growth of a spirit of extreme individualism, and tax revolts against the Pharaoh's grandiose schemes for national development seem to have been responsible for the onset of a feudal period lasting between 2181 and the start of the Eleventh Dynasty in 2040 B.C. It was an age marked by violence, anarchy, aggrandizement of the power of the nobles, social revolutions by the masses, and periodic invasions.

The next major period of Egypt's long history is conventionally called the age of the *Middle Kingdom* (ca. 2133–1786). For some time the government was notably weaker, with nominal rule exercised by the dynasties of various Pharaohs but real authority gravitating into the hands of the lesser nobility. After 1950 B.C. an aggressive line of Theban rulers reunited the land and was able to regain a measure of their former power. It was a time when art, literature, and especially sculpture in Egypt reached forms never surpassed thereafter. The Middle Kingdom also brought a fusion of local deities dating from earlier dynasties and their consolidation into a universally revered god, later called Amon or Ammon-Re. In addition to the Egyptians' solar faith, a nature religion centered about various divinities achieved a synthesis in the person of a deity known as Osiris. The twin religions of Amon and Osiris came to dominate the Nile River culture permanently.

The Middle Kingdom came to an end suddenly in 1786 B.C. for reasons still unknown. A rapid succession of rulers plunged the state into anarchy. Between 1780 and 1567 B.C. rebellious nobles reduced the reigning Pharaohs to near impotence. Around the same time, the land was invaded by a Semitic–Asiatic people, the *Hyksos,* or "Shepherd Kings," who extended their sovereignty over the entire Delta region. Near the end of the seventeenth century B.C., the rulers of Upper Egypt launched a revolt, using weapons such as the horse and chariot (previously unemployed on a massive scale), and enslaved, killed, or drove out the hated invaders. *Ahmose I,* founder of the Eighteenth Dynasty (1650–1567 B.C.), became the hero of the war for national liberation and installed himself as absolute despot over all of Egypt. The regime he established was without question more highly consolidated than any that had hitherto existed.

Beginning with Ahmose, the *New Kingdom* or *Empire* (lasting until 1090 B.C.) came into being, during which time three important dynasties—the Eighteenth, Nineteenth, and Twentieth—held the reins of power. The militarism generated by Egypt's successful war against the Hyksos whetted an appetite for further victories. State policy was no longer pacific and isolationist; once humiliated by foreign rule, Egypt's leaders were resolved to prevent it from happening again. A spirit of aggressive imperialism came to the fore, leading to territorial raids deep into Asia. The lust for empire, instead of being sated by victories in Palestine and Syria, reached a zenith during the reign of *Thutmose III* of the Eighteenth Dynasty. Backed by one of the most formidable armies of ancient times, he speedily annihilated all opposition in a vast domain extending from the Euphrates to the highest cataracts of the Nile. Phoenicians, Canaanites, Hittites, and Assyrians all acknowledged Egyptian suzerainty or paid tribute.

Looted treasures and war captives flooding into Egypt gave rise to an opulent cosmopolitanism that destroyed old cultural traditions. It also inspired a golden age of architecture and painting at Karnak, Luxor, the Valley of the Kings, and Abu Simbel. A philosophical–religious literature developed rapidly, the most notable example being the *Royal Sun Hymn* of Ikhnaton. It was during the period of the New Kingdom that Pharaoh *Akhenaton* (later calling himself *Ikhnaton*) tried without success to introduce state monotheism in the form of a cult dedicated to the sun god Aton, to replace the ancestral veneration of the Theban god, Ammon-Re. By the time of the Nineteenth Dynasty (1320–1200 B.C.) under *Ramses II,* last of the great warrior-kings, the empire had begun to weaken. The next dynasty, under Ramses III through Ramses XI, brought its downfall. Most of the conquered provinces were permanently lost and those that remained could not be managed successfully. By the midtwelfth century B.C., Egypt had fallen prey to social decadence from within and barbarian invasions from without.

The *Post-Empire* period (1085–332 B.C.) was a time of general social and political decline. Libyans and Nubians swarmed freely across the land. Mediterranean pirates harried the northern coast while royal authority and prestige waned at home. Between 950 and 730 B.C. a dynasty of Libyan barbarians occupied the throne, followed by Nubians (Ethiopians) until 525 B.C. Royal tombs were robbed, the people were oppressed by corrupt officials and rapacious priests, and cities were plagued with famine and roving bands of terrorists. In the seventh century B.C., Assyrians raided deep into Egypt, sacking its major cities. A brief cultural renaissance ensued after the expulsion of the Assyrians, only to be followed by a longer twilight of foreign domination and cultural decadence. In 525 B.C. the land was conquered once again by the Persians. For two hundred years, except for a short interlude under the Twenty-eighth through Thirtieth Dynasties (404–341 B.C.), Egypt was condemned to be a minor province of the vast Persian empire.

The *Ptolemaic* period (332–30 B.C.) marked the final chapter in ancient Egypt's national history. When Persia collapsed before Alexander the Great in 323–322 B.C., its empire was carved up and Egypt became a center of Hellenic culture. Despite desperate attempts to avoid assimilation, the last of which was undertaken by Queen Cleopatra (51–30 B.C.) in her dealings with Caesar and Anthony, Egypt was finally annexed to the Romans' domain. A native Nile River valley civilization never revived again.

Egyptian Culture and Schools

The Greek description of the people of the Nile as "the most religious of men" is something of an exaggeration, yet there is no denying that belief in the supernatural was as important to the culture of the Egyptians as to any other, past or present. Religion left its unmistakable impress upon every aspect of everyday life. Politically, the government was firmly rooted as a theocracy, with the Pharaoh as chief priest of the official cults. The entire "civil" administration was not sharply separated from a priestly caste and their functions usually overlapped. Unbelievable amounts of economic energy and material resources were expended on a costly ecclesiastical system, including the tombs, pyramids, and monuments it demanded. From the very beginning, Egyptian arts and crafts developed in connection with the temples and with the religious rites of the populace. An almost obsessive concern with the afterlife prompted rulers to invest vast sums in the preparation of comfortable dwelling places for their spiritual "double," or *Ka,* which was thought to leave the individual at his death. Because the priests were custodians of culture as well as bulwarks of the political order, virtually all of Egyptian art was an expression of religious interest. Important examples of the religious influence upon literature would include the *Am Duat* or *Book of the Other World,* the famous *Book of the Dead,* the wisdom literature of Ptahhotep, the *Memphite Drama,* and to a lesser extent, the *Teachings of Dwauf,* and *Maxims of Ani.* Much of the stupendous painting, sculpture (obelisks, sphinxes, statues), and architecture for which the Nile valley civilization is so well known was motivated by theological considerations.

The Egyptian socioeconomic structure, though strikingly resistant to change, was distinguished by a surprising degree of fluidity. No inflexible caste system developed as it did in Mesopotamia and no man's position in society was unalterably fixed, in contrast with the stratified social regimes of the Tigris–Euphrates region. The class structure consisted of seven fairly well-defined levels. At the top was the royal family, served by priests and nobles; underneath the three-tiered elite was the middle-class aggregate of scribes, merchants, artisans, and farmers; beneath them labored the serfs; and on the bottom were slaves. Standing in an ambiguous position relative to the social hierarchy was a class of professional soldiers.

By the time of the Middle Kingdom, Egyptian society had become highly integrated. An elaborate social organization had been created to direct the construction and maintenance of flood-control devices along the

Nile, irrigation ditches, reservoirs, and canals. Though the riverlands were exceedingly fertile, no complex civilization was possible without institutions capable of harnessing the people to specialized tasks in order to exploit the valley's natural resources to fullest advantage. A large priestly bureaucracy to collect taxes and administer the government's various other functions became essential. Attached to the royal treasury were a number of public schools equipped for the training of the thousands of scribes within the priestly order whose services were necessary in the keeping of records and accounts in the government administration. Many scribes were also employed in a private capacity by the owners of the landed estates and by the leaders of the business world. Admission to these schools was open to any ambitious youth regardless of class. Apparently the instruction was provided free of charge by the government because of the vital need for trained manpower. In spite of their limitations, schools did provide for the poor but talented youth an avenue of escape from a life of hopeless drudgery. For this reason learning to read and write was viewed as the passport to a lucrative position and, possibly, a life of relative ease and privilege. One father, advising his son to become a scribe said, "I have never seen the smith as an ambassador nor the goldsmith as a messenger. But I have seen the smith at his work at the mouth of his furnace, his fingers like the crocodiles . . . and he stank more than eggs or fish."[14] The father's point was too obvious to miss.

At least three interrelated types of schools flourished after 3000 B.C. in Egypt: *temple schools* for training the clergy, *court schools* for preparing bureaucrats, and provincial *department schools* to equip boys for careers in private business or government. There may have been also separate military or courtly schools for the sons of the nobility who pursued careers in the Pharaoh's armed service. *Priest colleges* or higher temple schools situatéd at such great cities as Thebes, Memphis, and Heliopolis offered advanced instruction in a variety of disciplines at a level above that available in lower institutions. These higher schools supplied personnel for the learned professions.

There were several grades of scribes, ranging from simple secretaries or bookkeepers all the way up to well-educated judges, lawyers, and counselors to the head of state. Promising youths would be sent at age five or six to a village school conducted by the local temple or government department where they would learn the rudiments of their trade before being apprenticed to a master in a chosen field. Talented students might continue their education at a central temple school in one of the major provincial capitals, or even on to a higher scribal institution connected with the royal court or the main priestly temple. Prior to admittance to a temple or priest college at age seventeen, youths were expected to serve for three or

14 *The Cambridge Ancient History* (New York: Macmillan, 1923–1939), Vol. II, p. 222.

four years on a part-time basis in the office or department for which they
were being trained.

Learning to read and write must have been an arduous task. Besides the
pictographic system of *hieroglyphics* which had to be memorized, apprentice
scribes had to master a *hieratic cursive* script used for business and commercial purposes, as well as a simpler, more popular, *demotic* script used in
informal correspondance. Depending on the school and level of instruction,
the lower curriculum lasted from six to ten years. The subjects taught
might include wisdom literature plus religious commentaries, ballads,
poetry and didactic prose, music, astronomy, arithmetic, geometry, surveying, and engineering. Not everyone followed the same course of studies. At
an advanced level, students could specialize in architecture, medicine, engineering, and of course the theological mysteries of the priesthood.

Egyptian teaching techniques relied heavily upon memorization and
drill. Students spent endless hours learning to trace letters and then words
on clay tablets or broken pottery, only later graduating to the luxury of
papyrus paper. Because it was popularly believed that writing had been
invented by the god Thoth, who had imparted its secrets to the early
inhabitants of the valley, deviation from traditional literary forms was
proscribed. The school's task was to safeguard a divinely initiated literature.
Pupils were taught at an early age that if they hoped to become scribes
they had to attain perfection in reproducing the ancient texts provided as
writing models. Discipline was harsh and severe. For some infractions of
the rules, students could be flogged unmercifully or even bound in shackles
and sentenced to prison for months at a time. "The hawk is taught to fly
and the pigeon to nest; I shall teach you your letters, you idle villain!" is
the recorded utterance of one irate schoolmaster. There was a pedagogic
saying, "A young fellow has a back; he hears when we strike it." A scholar
writing to his master after having left school recalls that "his bones had
been broken like those of an ass" in the process of learning his lessons.[15]

The total social system serviced by ancient Egyptian schools was unquestionably rigid and tyrannical, as judged by the standards of a later
day. The social mandate handed down to those entrusted with the maintenance of institutions within society was clear: preserve the existing
cultural configuration in unchanging form. It was only natural that those
who passed through the formal school system, in virtue of the skills they
acquired, would rise to positions of prestige within the class structure.
Inevitably, certain advantages—social, economic, and political—accrued
to guardians of official orthodoxy. Education was the means for perpetuating
that orthodoxy, a way of life jealously perpetuated by scribal priests. Yet
even though the price paid for cultural stability must have been high, one
hallmark of Egyptian society and its subordinate system of schooling was

[15] Quoted in S. S. Laurie, *Historical Survey of Pre-Christian Education* (New York:
Longmans, Green, 1907), p. 47.

its remarkable success in preserving a great civilization for over three thousand years. The achievement has no equal in the Western cultural tradition.

CHARACTERISTICS OF EDUCATION
IN EARLY HISTORIC SOCIETIES

Western man sometimes needs to be reminded that his cultural tradition extends backward in time in a more or less unbroken line to obscure or unknown origins before the dawn of recorded history. With incredible naïveté, he is prone to forget that Western civilization antedates pre-Hellenic culture, that its threads are woven into the panoramic tapestry of Asia Minor, a very ancient land swarming with diverse peoples—Phrygians, Ionians, Chaldeans, Hittites, Lydians, Assyrians—all of whom properly may be considered bona fide cultural ancestors. It has been seen that the first great revolution in the life of man, namely, the discovery of agriculture which transformed him from a food gatherer–hunter into a food producer, occurred in western Asia. So too did that urban revolution of the fourth millennium which first opened the door to high civilization and rendered it possible. Key technological, economic, and cultural advances upon which subsequent Western societies built were made in that same area of the globe. The great Mother Goddess (not to mention her dying son) who is the oldest-known deity of mankind and who was to figure prominently in several of the religions of the West originated in western Asia Minor. Those who weary of the seemingly endless progression of Sumerian, Babylonian, Chaldean, Assyrian, Persian, and Egyptian civilizations should recall that literally thousands of years of vital human history are represented by their rise and fall. Classicists should be reminded that it was in Asia, not mainland Greece, that the Greeks first developed their brilliant civilization and that it was the ancient peoples to the east and south of the Aegean who both stimulated the Greeks and contributed immeasurably to their culture. Finally, it is essential to recall that the religion, the economy, the societal values and life styles generated among the societies of the Near East gave birth to a succession of formal educational systems long before continental Europe was anything more than a vast wilderness populated largely by primitive savages huddling in rude caves.

The necessarily cursory inspection of developments in the Nile River valley and in the Tigris–Euphrates basin suggests certain general conclusions about the nature of education in mankind's earliest civilizations. First, education considered as a process of enculturation proceeded without benefit of separate teaching institutions until a crucial point in the development of human culture had been reached. *Formal, differentiated schools first arose when the complexity of culture outstripped the capacity of its society to transmit it by informal means.* When trial-and-error methods no longer sufficed, when there was simply more to learn than could be handled through personal observation and firsthand experience, and when the educative potential of the family and extended kin grouping was exhausted, discrete educational agencies appeared on the scene.

Secondly, formal instruction in a body of knowledge was possible only when a society had achieved a degree of social complexity to permit *specialization of roles* within the community, coupled with a relatively secure economic base to free a class of people to assume teaching–learning functions. Formal schools arose when there was both a need and an opportunity to train a particular group of people in a defined body of knowledge, usually relating to the history and religion of the culture.

Thirdly, the *invention of writing* seems to have served as a catalyst for the founding of schools. The creation of a system of writing for literary and commercial purposes necessitated schools for teaching people to read and write. In ancient Sumeria the school was definitely an outgrowth of the invention of cuneiform writing, beginning with rudimentary pictographic notations written on clay tablets, probably dating back as far as the end of the fourth millennium. Notations preserved on fragments excavated at Nippur (approximately a hundred miles from modern Baghdad) are mostly administrative directives relating to routine record keeping. Much later, cuneiform evolved into a phonetic system of sufficient complexity to express very abstract thoughts in literature and theology. There is a vast difference, for example, between the crude pictographic tablets uncovered at the site of the Sumerian city of Erech, consisting of utilitarian memoranda, and the elaborate texts found at Shuruppak, another ancient city, dating from a full millennium later. Much the same development of an increasingly complex hieroglyphic system took place in Egyptian society. Writing began as a utilitarian tool and then developed into an instrument for other ends.

The invention of writing was truly a milestone in human history. Vicarious, secondhand experience mediated through written symbols vastly extended the range of information available to an individual. For the first time it became possible to preserve the record of the past in stable form. For uncounted millennia before any written languages had been devised, customs, literature, and folklore had to be transmitted orally. The entire accumulated cultural heritage depended upon memory for its preservation. But the written word fixed the record, made it less vulnerable to accidental losses, increased possibilities for its expansion. One penalty for literacy, from Sumerian and early Egyptian times on, was the tendency to become enslaved to the written word. The cultural legacy could be preserved with greater accuracy, but succeeding generations tended to revere its forms uncritically. Whereas an oral tradition could be easily modified without conscious intent on the part of a preliterate people, a recorded tradition was more permanent. Its transmutation necessarily involved a measure of deliberate, conscious effort. The record assumed a kind of authority in its own right; to tamper with it was a species of sacrilege. Hence, fourthly, the effect of early schools was to *stabilize* culture and *retard* social change, because formal educative institutions were custodians of the writing art. Now the weight of tradition bore down more heavily on the habits, values, and style of life of people within society.

Fifthly, *formal education was confined to a very small minority* of the total population. The literate person in an early historic society possessed a valuable commodity, a skill of high scarcity value. It was to be expected that he would ascend to a position of power commensurate with his ability to unravel the complexities of the scribal art. Although the lower classes were trained to specific positions by the family and other nonschool agencies, children were reared to engage in menial occupations learned through apprenticeship experience, and, in general, mass education was identical to that typical of any nonliterate people; an upper-class elite enjoyed all the advantages of formal schooling. Scribes were both administrators and religious leaders. In one Babylonian temple archive, the record shows twenty-five scribes administering a parish of over one thousand people. It is highly unlikely anyone else besides scribal priests were literate. Admittance to the upper echelons of political, economic, and religious life was made to depend upon a combination of family inheritance (Egypt was a partial exception) and literacy skills. Possession of reading and writing alone conferred position in the lower and intermediate levels of officialdom.

It is important to note that there was nothing conspiratorial about the scribal-priestly-noble monopoly of schools. One theory popular with some eighteenth-century rationalists had it that scheming, diabolical priests entered into a great historical conspiracy with political despots to strangle the liberties of the common people, to monopolize the fruits of the economy, and to forestall the spread of learning. The theory is untenable. The practical effects of an alliance of politics and religion may have been precisely as stated, but the social arrangement of an early society developed for far more complex reasons than simple conspiracy.

Sixthly, the increasingly bookish character of early formal instruction made education somewhat *esoteric,* something opaque to ordinary classes of men. In contrast to preliterate education with its highly informal characteristics and its natural accessibility to all, a penumbra of mystery surrounded the specialized arts of reading and writing. Religious sanctions supported the authority of the written word and made it inviolate.[16] Education became tied to books, thereby transforming the character of instruction more or less permanently.

Another generalization about early schooling is, predictably, that *the*

---

[16] The overly respectful awe of written language has not been confined to early peoples. Medieval monks frequently preserved the transcription errors of their predecessors when reproducing sacred texts, either unaware of what they were doing or constitutionally incapable of supplying corrections. Something about the written word instills more credibility than other forms of media. Even today, researchers have shown that the printed page lends more authority to ideas than other forms of transmitting information.

art of pedagogy was poorly developed. Methods employed laid great stress upon memorization and repetition to ensure learning. Scant attention was paid to exhibiting the meaning or application of materials in the curriculum. It was commonly believed that when teaching techniques failed, when the pupil did not perform to the instructor's satisfaction, the fault could be ascribed to indolence or stupidity on the part of the learner. Consequently, harsh discipline was the rule rather than the exception in classrooms.

Finally, *institutionalized education sanctioned a closed society.* It aimed to produce obedient citizens fitted to a tightly knit social organization in which individuals were bound by a network of traditions, obligations, and reciprocal duties. Security and stability, not autonomy and freedom, were paramount concerns reflected by the process and aim of schools in early historic societies.

THE QUESTION OF ELITISM

How does contemporary education fare as contrasted with early historic educational systems? Is there a latter-day equivalent of a priestly monopoly in control of the schools, dictating objectives, sanctioning certain class values? Are schools servants of the general social welfare or do they serve an elitist minority? It has become fashionable in recent years to allege that the latter is the case. The argument is heard that the Establishment (usually ambiguously defined) runs the educational system, bends it to its own purposes, and decides its policies. The more strident voices among student militants on college campuses, for example, have claimed that today's institutions of higher learning are mere tools for an industrial–military complex; that universities exist only for the fulfillment of designs contrived by a power elite; and that the lower schools are held in bondage to the controlling interests of this complex. Educators, it is alleged, are mere hirelings of business and political oligarchs, perpetuators of special interests.

Inequalities in the social structure are enduring features of all societies. Some people always command more power or possess more wealth than others. The question in modern times is whether the distribution of money, influence, and so on, has created a definable elite—a group of people sharing common attributes such as occupation, skill, property, ethnicity, or ability—who occupy a superior position within society. Such elitist theoreticians as Lasswell, Michels, Pareto, and others differ on the characteristics of an elite or who they are, but all tend to emphasize the importance of elites in explaining social phenomena, including education. Among the most popular writers on elites in the United States has been C. Wright Mills. He claims that American society is controlled by a power elite composed of individuals "in command of the major hierarchies and organizations of modern society."[17] The power elite is made up of business corporation heads, government officials, and military leaders bound together by certain social affinities. This top group is "increasingly unified, and often seems willfully co-ordinated." The middle socioeconomic groups are powerless because they represent "a drifting set of stalemated, balancing forces." At the bottom a mass society is emerging, also powerless and politically fragmented.[18]

Arnold Rose rejects the notion of society as a dichotomous entity made up of the ruled and the rulers, but he agrees that an elite is a powerful force. However, there is no single hierarchical and unified power bloc of interests; there are many elites, he alleges. The most influential is a political elite because it controls "the agencies of force and the instruments of legislation," has considerable access to the mass media, and uses this access to enlist the support of popular opinion.[19] As yet, little has been done to discover the precise relationships between an elitist Establishment and the schools, although preliminary observations suggest that relationships do exist.

In the first place, schools often function as instruments for elitist recruitment.[20] Babylonian administrators, officials in the temple priesthood, and wielders of political power were always graduates of the schools. The same held true in ancient Egypt, and indeed in most societies since. In England today government heads and civil servants alike are recruited mainly from the graduating classes of Eton and Harrow, Oxford and Cambridge. The so-called ivy-league schools of the United States have served an identical function: producers for an elitist group of prominent leaders in government and industry. Secondly, educational institutions provide supportive input for whomever manages society's political structure—by training children to accept certain political symbols, to be participants in political behavior. Citizenship training, whether direct or indirect, accounts for a substantial part of what schools do within the sociopolitical order.

Does an elite actually control the schools? Insofar as social values are reflected in education, the answer has to be no. Evidence is overwhelming that middle-class mores dominate educational values, and the middle class is not an elite.[21] In a direct political sense some control is exerted by an

---

17 C. Wright Mills, *The Power Elite* (New York: Oxford University Press, 1959), p. 4.

18 Ibid., p. 324.

19 Arnold M. Rose, *The Power Structure* (New York: Oxford University Press, 1967), pp. 489–491.

20 See Bryan G. Massialas, *Education and the Political System* (Reading, Mass.: Addison-Wesley, 1969), pp. 205–210.

21 The noted social critic Paul Goodman, for one, disagrees. "Some of the most important strengths that have historically belonged to the middle class," he alleges, "are flouted by the schools: independence, initiative, scrupulous honesty, earnestness, ability, respect for thorough scholarship." Rather than bourgeois, Goodman claims, "our schools have become petty-bourgeois, bureaucratic, time-serving, gradgrind-practical, timid and *nouveau riche* climbing. In the upper grades and colleges, they often exude a cynicism

"educational establishment" composed of such groups as teachers' college educators, their professional organizations, the National Education Association, and the American Federation of Teachers, linked to local school boards and regional accrediting agencies. Taken together, they may make up an influential complex, but they do not constitute an elite in the classic sense of the term, and their collective behavior does not evidence a willfully coordinated conspiracy. No one of these member groups is as powerful as such special interest organizations as the American Medical Association or the National Rifle Association in influencing federal legislation. Government at all levels exerts considerable influence on the schools in such matters as desegregation, financing, research, and manpower development. It is probably true that government, industry, and the military combine to shape contemporary education but not in the obvious sense of overt conspiratorial manipulation. The structure of school control from the Department of Health, Education and Welfare, down through various state and local levels is, for better or worse, too complex to permit a single interest group to have its way decisively.

Attempts have been made. In 1888 a speaker at the National Education Association convention advanced the thesis that "the true aim of education [was] to lead and guide, and, if need be, compel its youth to be law-respecting and law-abiding citizens" imbued with "the habits of obedience."[22] Schools today are also called upon to be instruments of social control. At the turn of this century, growing demands were made to break the elitist academic character of secondary education and expand public education at this level to all people. Strong opposition was aroused. As J. E. Russell of Columbia Teachers' College asked in 1905, "How can we justify our practice in schooling the masses in precisely the same manner as we do those who are to be their leaders?" The function of the elementary schools, according to Harvard President Charles W. Eliot in 1908, was "to sort the pupils, and sort them by their evident or probable destinies," meaning, as Woodrow Wilson put it more candidly the following year: "We want one class of persons to have a liberal education and we want another class of persons, a very much larger class . . . to forgo the privilege of a liberal education and fit themselves to perform specific difficult manual tasks."[23] Class education disguised as "equal opportunity" has always been typical of any aristocratic elite presuming to dictate to the schools. Even John Dewey, however noble his original intentions, may have lent inadvertent support to the psychology of the elite when he described progressive education as "essentially an effort to adapt the schools to the circumstances, needs and

---

that belongs to rotten aristocrats." Paul Goodman, *Compulsory Miseducation* (New York: Horizon Press, 1964), pp. 26–27.

[22] Quoted in "The Political Lie Called American Education," *The Public Life*, Vol. 1, No. 15 (August 8, 1969), p. 2.

[23] Ibid., pp. 2–3.

opportunities of industrial civilization." No actual elitist group, in the United States at least, has been successful in determining the ultimate objectives of schools. (The same cannot be said of some other modern nations.) Nonetheless, the tendency to see education as a tool for applying leverage against social needs is deeply ingrained in all cultures.

Despite the difference between early historic education and schools today in the matter of control, one fundamental similarity strikes home. The school, then and now, always serves social interests, rarely individual ones, unless they happen to coincide. Furthermore, despite some fatuous talk in some circles about the school as an active agent for social innovation, *institutionalized education never directly initiates social change*. The precepts, values, and customs it presents are those accepted by a dominant majority of people within the society, by the group who in the nature of things has a strong investment in the existing social value system. The school as a social institution, it has been correctly observed, never rises higher than its social source. One central implication follows: *the school inevitably treats students as means to social ends*. Just as the goal of Sumerian, Babylonian, Assyrian, Persian, or Egyptian education had to be, broadly speaking, meeting the "needs of society" as then understood, so also today talk about schooling for "trained manpower" or "social efficiency" shows how modern culture utilizes education for its own social purposes. The weight of history is against the possibility of an educational system serving only the interest of those being educated, recognizing no other. In fact, it is only with a great deal of imagination that one can envision the shape of an education geared to meeting purely individual needs rather than socially sanctioned ones. The very possibility of individual needs and values apart from those created by, reinforced through, and supportive of the social environment is alien to modern thinking.

In a totalitarian society education is more or less explicitly a tool for the ruling clique. The twentieth century has provided ample illustrations of how this works, including Nazi Germany, Communist China, Fascist Italy, and the Soviet Union. Although early despotisms required little in the way of institutional apparatus for a class-oriented educational system, modern authoritarian regimes need to provide mass-oriented schooling as well. This is as much a function of cultural and technological complexity as politics. Democratic societies also aspire to offer some formal schooling for everyone. In fact, the concept of mass schooling is a comparatively recent phenomenon. As for whether democratic societies inevitably turn education into an elitist monopoly or a class tool (despite protestations to the contrary), evidence is mixed. The situation differs from country to country. As noted above, in the United States there is nothing akin to the overt control of a scribal minority over schools in the ancient period. The question of whether in fact more subtle forces operate—class bias, the expressed needs of business and industry, and governmental influence—is likely to keep debate about contemporary education at a high pitch. Nor will people agree on what groups or social forces *should* control the schools. The only thing that can be said with any confidence is that education will be shaped by its supporting cultural context just as it has since before schools first appeared at the dawn of human history.

SUMMARY

Education, in its anthropological sense, denotes the process of enculturation. All societies devise ways of inducting the young into the mores, customs, traditions, and beliefs of a culture. The sum total of these learned thought and behavior patterns is both the creation and the creator of the characteristics defining the social aggregate known as a society. Education designates inclusively the processes by which individuals acquire a culture and thus become effectively functioning members of a society. It is man's capacity to sustain and perpetuate culture that accounts for his evolutionary development from a primordial simian hominid to the status of *Homo sapiens*. Thus, education is the pivotal force for cultural transmission and perhaps innovation.

Data gained from the study of prehistoric folk societies and from their contemporary equivalents illuminate primitive educational practices. Comparative analysis of this data suggests both contrasts and fundamental similarities between primitive and modern educational goals. Although a folk culture's structural simplicity makes transmission easier and a modern society's cultural complexity makes it difficult, both kinds of society aim for an integration or internal coherence through education, molding the individual into culturally acceptable patterns. The precarious socio-ecological balance of a primitive society necessitates repressive measures to ensure conformity of belief and behavior on the part of its members. The price for security is a closed society firmly committed to the enforcement of a social status quo.

Institutionalized education in a more complex industrial–bureaucratic society appears to function in much the same way. The ideology of the middle class, combined with the standardization of a mass culture required by modern technology, encourages excessive conformity. Schools tend to reinforce the modes of living that place a premium upon conformity—in values, attitudes, and behavior. If the commonly professed objective of educating the individual as an intrinsic end in himself were actually pursued, presumably far-reaching alterations within education would have to take place. Education for a genuinely open society is a live but so far unrealized possibility in contemporary life. Unlike a primitive society, modern civilization can afford errors in the quest for social and intellectual pluralism.

Early civilizations arose as a function of many factors, including an agri-

cultural revolution which freed certain classes of people from direct subsistence labor and the growth of cities as centers of trade and commerce.
The emerging social structure was hierarchical, strongly stratified, and tied
together by a central authoritarian government. Priestly scribes as the only
literate class in society served as administrators within early regimes. Increasing cultural complexity coupled with the invention of writing led to
the establishment of temple schools. Formal educational institutions were
controlled and directed by the priest-scribes in the interest of preparing
personnel for all echelons of power. Schooling was confined largely to the
aristocratic elite of the upper classes. Literacy had a high scarcity value and
tended to make education an esoteric enterprise conducted directly for the
benefit of a minority rather than for the masses. Informal enculturative
processes served to educate the majority of people for their appointed roles
within the class structure.

The monopolistic character of early schooling was not the conscious result of a scribal conspiracy to enlist education for the preservation of class
privilege. Rather, it was the natural outgrowth of many forces shaping
Sumerian, Babylonian, Assyrian, and Egyptian life. Because these cultures
were extremely conservative, absolutist, and sanctioned by a highly authoritarian ideology, schools also assumed such characteristics.

Elitist power forces exist in all societies. The allegation that contemporary education is an instrument for an established minority seems questionable at best, given the complexity of the power structures influencing
schools today. It is accurate, however, to view some institutions as instruments for elitist recruitment in that persons destined for positions of leadership are drawn from the ranks of their graduates. Moreover, so-called
citizenship training serves to reinforce political canons instituted by dominant groups within society.

Schools (ancient and modern) never directly initiate social change, though
they may help consolidate it. Schools are controlled by the societies that
sustain them; more specifically, they tend to be dominated by the most
powerful groups within society. In American society many groups rather
than a single elite decide how school will be kept. Power blocs almost invariably resist change because it threatens their position. Hence schools
cannot be initiators of social change and still be responsive to the society
they serve. A corollary is that socially defined needs take precedence over
individual ones in determining the character of education. Debate on these
complex issues is likely to continue so long as people appreciate the importance of what happens in schools.

QUESTIONS FOR DISCUSSION

1. All cultures, including primitive ones, change. New techniques and processes
   are discovered which fundamentally alter the culture's structure. How is change

possible in a tribal culture? What kinds of changes are welcomed or resisted in
modern culture?

2. How important are the educational functions of the family today as compared
with those in a simpler culture?

3. The extreme antithesis to a completely closed, tribal society is anarchy. How
"open" can a society become in its toleration of divergent beliefs and mores
before it dissolves into chaos?

4. To what extent can public schools tacitly reinforce values or ideas considered
dangerous and subversive by the majority of the society lending those schools
support?

5. Is it fair to claim that schools today are mechanisms for processing the young
to meet the needs of a bureaucratic, mechanized society? What, if anything, is
wrong with using education for preparing students for the world in which
they live?

6. Although it is clear why a scribal class developed to conduct schools, is it
equally clear why early teachers were also usually religious authorities?

7. Why would not even early civilizations mobilize resources to develop a system
of mass schooling roughly equivalent to those operating today, because schools
could be used not only as instruments of social control but also as a means
for advancing the culture? In other words, why was it not perceived that
formal education could raise the general standard of living for everyone by
facilitating a more efficient exchange and utilization of information?

8. What price, if any, has to be paid when formal education is made freely available to everyone?

9. Was the invention of writing absolutely essential to the development of the
school as a differentiated social institution? Why or why not?

10. Is it possible in a democratic society for an elite to dominate the educational
system? If possible, would it be desirable? If not, why not?

11. Which broad cultural forces are *most* influential in shaping a people's educational objectives? Do these differ from ancient to modern times?

2 Education for an Eloquent Society

At present opinion is divided about the subjects of education. People do not take the same view about what should be learned by the young, either with a view to human excellence or a view to the best possible life; nor is it clear whether education should be directed mainly to the intellect or to moral character. . . whether the proper studies to be pursued are those that are useful in life, or those which make for excellence, or those that advance the bounds of knowledge . . . men do not all honor the same excellence, and so naturally they differ about the proper training for it.

ARISTOTLE
Politics

THE GREEK MIRACLE

Ancient Hellas was a most unlikely site for a civilization whose people contributed more elements to Western culture than any other society of antiquity. The Greek peninsula is an insignificant outpost jutting into the Mediterranean. The land is rough, mountainous, unremarkable for its fertility. Its inhabitants rarely numbered more than a few hundred thousand all told. Yet despite these disadvantages, aided by a benign climate and proximity to the sea, the Hellenes were to build a mighty civilization whose cultural achievements still astound and amaze modern man.

It is true, as John Stuart Mill once remarked, that the Greeks began almost everything prized in the Western tradition: canons of art and architecture, the major poetic forms, the writing of history and philosophy, the

47

foundations of modern social and political theories, theatrical forms, legal structures, medicine, mechanics, mathematics, physics, oratory, logic, grammar, and rhetoric.

More fundamental than any of these triumphs was a habit of mind developed by the Greeks, a world view utterly unique which distinguished them from all the other Near East civilizations previously considered. To the east, human culture was based upon unreasoning obedience to authority, whether secular or supernatural, as the basic sociopolitical principle of life. Human thought, if it counted for anything, was devoted to the service of gods and god-monarchs. Its chief employment was to legitimize the status quo, to conserve and even sanctify it. Against this all too common pattern, somehow the Greeks managed early to recognize the power of human reason as a tool in the service of man. They steadfastly refused to deify political rulers and even enlisted their gods on behalf of a life of freedom and reason. For these reasons, it makes sense to affirm that if the civilizations of the Tigris–Euphrates basin contributed to the unfolding of Western culture, their influence was but a prelude (albeit an important one) to a larger performance; it was the experience in Hellas that must be considered the first major act of that vast historical drama.

The ancient Hellenes were the first to exemplify what became the spirit of Western man. They steadfastly refused to submit to the dictation of priests or even to humble themselves before their gods. They glorified man as the most important creature in the universe and organized their culture with man at its center. The Greek attitude, it would not be unfair to say, was essentially secular and rationalistic: it exalted the spirit of free inquiry even when men fell prey to intellectual despotisms, it prized freedom though the Greeks often lived in slavery, it respected the power of human reason even while demogogues rejected it. The errors of the Greeks were large but their triumphs were greater still.

The problems of the Greeks define many of the enduring questions facing modern man. Their philosophers asked all the basic questions, agreeing with the Socratic judgment that the unexamined life is not worth living. What is justice and how is it attained? How may a man best realize his fullest potential, develop his talents to the utmost, and live the good life? What is knowledge and how is it to be secured? Is morality a chimerical illustration foisted by the strong upon the weak, or a simple social convention, or an endowment from the gods? Does the human condition make sense in some fundamental way or is it all meaningless chaos? The Greeks, as Robert Ulich observes, possessed "a genius of observation, inquiry, and logical discrimination, combined with a genius of verbal and esthetic expression" that makes them worthy of emulation today, almost two thousand years after their civilization passed into history.[1] Modern man may not

---

[1] Robert Ulich, *Education in Western Culture* (New York: Harcourt, Brace, 1965), p. 19.

agree with the solutions they offered, but their profound questions endure and contemporary civilization is richer for their having raised them first. Every succeeding culture has had to come to terms, in differing ways, with the legacy of the Greek experience.

The Greeks were the first to consider consciously the perennial problems of education, to inquire about its nature, to ask how it ought to be conducted, and to ponder what ends it should serve. It should be emphasized that education was an integral part of their statecraft, deeply imbedded in a total way of life; to attempt to abstract it as a particular aspect of their culture as a whole leads to some distortion. But if understood in context, Greek educational thought is a key for illuminating other aspects of their culture, just as a study of their practices and ideals provides a useful contrast for assessing education within modern society. In the final analysis, educators may find perhaps a richer fund of inspiration in the Greek educational endeavor than in the efforts of any other ancient people. Most of the major issues and challenges in education today have had their genesis in a tradition tracing back over two millenia to that Hellenic culture.

HOMERIC HELLAS

Ethnic Origins and Early Migrations

Several of the most typical institutions and attitudes of the Greeks during their prime were modifications of a pattern which had survived from the earliest days. The foundations for much of the social and political development of subsequent centuries was laid in *Homeric* times (1200–800 B.C.). The probable original home of the Greeks was somewhere in the Danube Valley and on the steppes around the Black Sea. During the last six or seven centuries of the second millennium, Aryan tribes of Nordic and Alpine stock poured down into Greece in successive waves of migration, mingling with the native Mediterranean population. By the first millennium, a mixed race of Indo-European peoples had occupied most of the northern sections of the peninsula and a few scattered locations along the coast. At first they filtered down slowly, bringing their flocks and herds with them, and settled in the more sparsely populated areas. Many of these early immigrants seem to have belonged to the group later known as *Ionians*. Another division, the *Achaeans*, pushed farther south, conquered Mycenae and Troy, and ultimately gained dominion over Crete.

In the eleventh or twelfth century of the first millennium, a general cultural eclipse accompanied an invasion of peoples called *Dorians*, some of whom settled in central Greece. Most of them took to the sea, conquering the eastern sections of the Peloponnesus and the southern islands of the Aegean. About 1000 B.C. they captured Knossos, chief center of the thriving Minoan civilization on the island of Crete. Little is known about the de-

velopments of the next three or four centuries, but by the sixth century
B.C. a pattern becomes clear which shows a vigorous, dynamic people busily
engaged in the work of forging a new and distinctive culture.

Early Homeric Culture

The political, social, and economic life of the early Greeks, whether
Achaeans, Ionians, or Dorians, was comparatively primitive. Each little
cluster of farming villages functioned independent of external control. The
reigning monarch had little real power, his functions limited to the administration of customary law and supervision over sacerdotal rites. Organized
government was so unimportant that it is recorded that when Odysseus,
king of Ithaca, absented himself for a twenty-year period, no regent was
appointed in his stead and no session of the council of nobles or assembly of
warriors was convened. Agriculture and herding were the basic occupations
of the Homeric peoples. Except for a few skilled crafts, there was no specialization of labor and little class stratification. As in most primitive societies,
there were some dependent laborers who worked on the lands of the nobles
and served them faithfully as warriors. The religion of the time was
thoroughly polytheistic, with Zeus, god of the sky and wielder of thunder-
bolts; Apollo, the sun god; Athena, goddess of war and patroness of handicrafts; and the "implacable and unyielding" Hades, overlord of the nether-
world, as the most important deities. There was nothing of the Semite's
fear or the Egyptian's awe, no abasement of human personality before unseen powers, in the religious view of the Greek. His religion rested on a
primeval adoration of the forces and forms of nature embodied in Olympian
divinities. Gods were expressions of human thought regarding the powers
at work in nature and in man; they were merely human beings whose faults
and virtues were writ large in divine form. Morality had only the vaguest
connection with religion. Worship aimed to please the gods and to induce
them to grant favors. Notably lacking were the themes of reverence, humility, and purity of heart so typical in the Judeo-Christian tradition. Insofar as the Greeks ever bothered themselves with thoughts of an afterlife,
they believed that their ghosts or shades would wander about the land, or,
for those whom the gods had chosen to favor, would reside in a place called
the Elysian Plain.

The Achaeans probably had a system of writing as early as 1200 B.C., but
this was an exception. The Homeric Greeks were largely a preliterate
people during the greater part of their history, whose intellectual accomplishments extended no farther than the development of folksongs, ballads,
and short epics, sung and embellished by minstrels as they wandered from
one village to another. A large part of this literary material was woven
finally into two great epic cycles and put into written form sometime in
the ninth century B.C. They were ascribed to a legendary blind poet, Homer,
and called the *Illiad* and the *Odyssey*.

Homeric Education

From the ninth century B.C. on, the Greek mind was shaped decisively by the ideals expressed in the Homeric epics. Boys committed the tales to memory in childhood and studied them in their adolescence. In the figure of Achilles they saw an idealized warrior type who typified the martial virtues of a warlike people. Youths learned to revere experience and age as represented by Nestor, the leadership of the great Agamemnon, and the oratory of Ulysses. Above all, such larger-than-life figures as Achilles or Ulysses exemplified an *areté*, the distinctive excellence or virtue that bestows upon an individual a certain superiority, a condition of honor. *Areté* meant that which made an individual the very best of his kind. When Hector told Andromache his highest duty was "to win glory for my father and myself," he was seeking his *areté* in excelling over others. Every nobleman's son took to heart the battle cry of Glaucus facing Diomede: "Hippolochus begat me and I claim to be his son. He sent me to Troy, and often gave me this command, to strive always for the highest manly virtue." The aristocrat's son was to seek after great reknown, to accomplish heroic acts in the face of overwhelming odds. He validated his claim to a semidivine lineage traced back to primordial times by attaining his *areté*, perhaps by doing some notable deed that would be remembered in ages to come.

As an individual and social objective, this concept of honor was neither large nor generous. It betrayed the influence of a barbaric past too recent to be completely transcended. Homeric "excellence" as an educational ideal was manifested primarily through bravery on the battlefield and endurance in the arena, not a very lofty ideal of the human potential, but part of an ethic uniquely suited to a culture still developing out of primitive tribalism. Nor was it so different from the conception of knightly honor that was to hold sway a millennium later during the days of medieval feudal chivalry.

The Homeric epics contain scant reference to formal schooling. In the Ninth Book of the *Illiad*, Phoenix, addressing Achilles, recalls that his father, Peleus, when he sent him to war, committed him to his care. Phoenix reminds Achilles that he has been his mentor since the latter left his boyhood home "unskilled in military learning." His duty as a teacher, he says, is "to teach you to speak when speech is fit, and do when deeds are to be done; rather than have you sit dumbly for want of words; idle, for skill to move." This passage implies that young men of the *aristoi* (aristocrats, land-owning warriors) were to be educated by their fathers or their appointed surrogates, and that the content of instruction conjoined rhetorical and military training with little or no emphasis upon other areas of development. Military valor and rhetorical eloquence were the two ideals toward which education moved.

Up until age eighteen boys were retained in the family, after which they entered bands or troops to be trained in a demanding course of gymnastics, including archery, hunting, and military exercises. At age eighteen boys were also admitted to public meals and allowed to listen to the conversations of their elders. Although the defensive requirements of the state must have dominated and controlled the processes of education, the very qualities prized by the state were those thought to define the ideally developed individual. Aside from parental instruction in the home, boys were educated by an overseer appointed by the state who served as the head of the student troop or band. The curriculum included music, history, and poetry in their rudimentary forms (transmitted orally) as well as military arts. In a very real sense the state was the schoolmaster and an organized educational polity. From firsthand exposure, through imitation and example of the world around them, youths were expected to claim society's values as their own. Among the most predominant ideas they were to absorb, the concept of *areté,* or "personal excellence and distinction," the ideal of graceful expression (*eukosmia*), and the ideal of self-control and moderation (*sophrosyne*) figured importantly. These values were to enjoy a long and illustrious career in the educational aspirations of the Greeks throughout their later history.

Evolution of City-States

About 800 B.C. the relatively small village communities of Homeric Greece which had been founded on clan organizations began to give way to larger political units. As the need for defense increased, a citadel or acropolis would be built on a high location and the city grew up around it. Athens, Thebes, and Megara on the mainland were the most important of the early city-states; Sparta and Corinth dominated the Peloponnesus; and Miletus and Chalcis arose as leading municipal centers on the islands of the Aegean Sea. With few exceptions, Greek city-states went through a similar political evolution. They began their histories as *monarchies.* As a result of the gradual concentration of wealth from the land, nobles grew in economic power and wrested authority from the king. Later, the aristocracy abolished the kingship entirely and, during the eighth century, founded *oligarchies* to replace the monarchies. About a hundred years later on the average, as trade, commerce, and industry became leading pursuits and an urban middle class arose, dispossessed farmers joined forces with the bourgeois class to overthrow the land-holding oligarchs. In the resultant conflicts ambitious demagogues often appeared who used public unrest as a vehicle to sweep themselves into power. Leaving unfulfilled their earlier promises for land reform, dictators or "tyrants" seated themselves in positions of absolute authority in the city-states and transformed them into *dictatorships.* Finally, in the sixth and fifth centuries, widespread dissatisfaction with despotic rule led to the founding of *republican democracies* or, in some cases, "timocracies," that is, political franchise based on land ownership, but far more inclusive than those of an oligarchy or the ties of blood kinship typical of earlier times.

The one major city-state where the process of political evolution was arrested permanently at the oligarchic stage was ancient *Sparta*. The people of *Lacedaemonia,* with Sparta as its capital, remained fixed at a particular stage of development and never seemed to advance beyond it. One legend has it that when a group of political reformers proposed to make Sparta a democracy, they were advised curtly to try it in their families first. In any event, the Spartans retained much of the Homeric ethos; in fact, they stamped a peculiarly militaristic interpretation upon it. At a time when their neighbors were blossoming culturally, intellectually, and politically, the Spartans clung to a narrow, uncultured way of life, perhaps unconsciously seeking solace in the arts of warfare for their failure to transcend the rude achievements of Homeric times. They were to provide a depressingly clear example of the archetypal closed society, symbolized in the most literalistic fashion by the Spartan policy of discouraging foreigners from entering into the city-state's society and, more broadly, by an unbelievably xenophobic cultural life. Athens, on the other hand, another of the more important centers of Greek urban life, provided a dramatic contrast in the degree to which its inhabitants aspired in their better moments to sustain an open society. The difference between the two was clear in their respective educational practices.

THE ARMED CAMP OF SPARTA

A Fortress City

Spartan stagnation was a function of the city-state's geographical isolation and its peculiar history. Hemmed in by mountains on the west and northeast and lacking serviceable harbors, the Spartan people had little opportunity for contact with the world beyond. They never developed a middle class, as did other cities, and that lack made for a profound difference in their political evolution. Moreover, Spartans had struggled for centuries, since their original invasion into the eastern Peloponnesus, to subdue the Mycenaean population, over which they exercised nominal rule. By 800 B.C., when they finally consolidated power over all of *Laconia* (Lacedaemonia), the habit of living by the sword was so firmly fixed that it could not be overcome. In the late eighth or early seventh centuries B.C. they annexed the entire plain of Messenia west of the Maügetos Mountains, a military adventure that brought them nothing but trouble. When the conquered Messenians launched a revolt half a century later, the ensuing conflicts plunged Sparta into constant warfare from which she never was able to extricate herself. Through the remaining centuries of their history the Spartans lived in daily fear of insurrections. Hardly any feature of life was left untouched by the need to subdue and despoil hostile neighbors. Their self-imposed fear helps explain to a large extent Spartan provincialism, their conservatism, their stubborn resistance to change. The need to maintain the absolute supremacy of a citizen class over an enormous subject population required iron discipline and a stringent subordination of the individual to the collectivist state.

Prior to her Messenian conquests, Spartan life had been altogether different. The city-state was an acknowledged center of a culture famed for its artistic, poetic, literary, and musical accomplishments. Its inhabitants boasted such citizens as the lyric poet Tyrtaeus, the chordic poet Alcman, and the musician Terpander. Then martial upheaval led to an abrupt aboutface: the beauty of Spartan art vanished, the city stopped sending champions to the athletic contests, and Spartan social life assumed a coarse, harsh quality. The sudden cultural arrest and narrowing of interest turned the once glorious city into a military barracks, an armed camp concerned only with preparations for war. Sparta became, as one historian phrases it, a "barbarous city petrified in an attitude of morose distrust."[2] Henceforth, Sparta would raise a nation of soldiers rather than artists and athletes, a people seeking glory through the collective life of the *polis,* the city-state.

Spartan Culture

The population of Sparta, which numbered about 400,000 at its peak, was divided into three sharply divided classes. The ruling element was made of the master *spartiates,* descendants of the first Dorians who roamed the Peloponnesus as early as 1100 B.C. They made up no more than one twentieth of the total population. Next in order of rank were the *perioeci,* or "dwellers around" (freeborn workers without political rights). At the bottom were the *helots* (serfs or slaves), bound to the soil, universally despised, and systematically persecuted by the citizen rulers. The Spartan constitution, which tradition ascribed to a legendary lawgiver by the name of *Lycurgus,* provided for a dual system of kingships, a council of nobles, a citizen assembly, and an *ephorate,* or board of governors. *Ephors* virtually were the government: they presided over the council and assembly, controlled the state educational system, and exercised veto power over all legislation. To all intents and purposes the city-state of Sparta was an oligarchy. Its economy was designed almost solely for the ends of military efficiency and the supremacy of the Spartiate class. With its militarism, its secret police, its austere and esthetically poverty-stricken way of life, and its rigid minority rule, the Spartan system was an archetypal example of a closed society. Plutarch, speaking of Lycurgus, said it best in his *Lives* when he reported that Sparta's leader "bred up his citizens in such a way that they neither would nor could live by themselves; they were to make themselves one with the public good, and clustering like bees around their commander, be by their zeal and public spirit . . . devoted wholly to their country." The picture is not unfamiliar to twentieth-century man.

---

2 H. I. Marrou, *A History of Education in Antiquity* (London: Sheed and Ward, 1956), p. 15.

Education for a Warfare State

Because Sparta was in the center of a hostile environment, her leaders were compelled to give prominence to education in order to raise hardy citizens. "This is one point," says Aristotle in his *Politics*, "in which the Lacedaemonians deserve praise: they devote a great deal of attention to the educational needs of their children, and their attention takes the form of action on the part of the state."[3] Formal training was rigidly controlled in every detail by public authorities, under the fixed belief that children were born and bred to serve the collective. Although marriage was practically compulsory in Spartan society, little family life was permitted or encouraged; children were the property of the state, not of their parents.[4]

Discipline began in earliest infancy. It was customary to bathe the newborn child in water mixed with wine, in accordance with the belief that only a strong and healthy baby could survive the experience. A few days after the birth of a male child, a council of elders (*gerousia*), or possibly the *ephorate* itself, inspected the infant to decide his fate. If robust, he was allowed to live; if sickly and weak he would be exposed to the elements and left to die. Up to the boy's seventh year, he was left with the mother, who was charged with toughening the child through compulsory fasting and by training him to overcome fear by leaving him alone in the dark.

When the boy reached seven years of age his father, acting on behalf of the *ephors,* entrusted him to the care of a state training school headed by an appointed official known as the *paedonomos*. It is unclear whether parents bore the cost of education or whether it was paid from public revenues. There is no doubt, however, about the fact that statutory education was required for receiving state allotments and for citizenship status. All training was geared toward military ends, supplemented by exposure and merciless floggings to harden boys for the duties of war. At school, students were formed into small companies or "packs" (*ilai* or *agelai*) and these formed portions of larger companies, called *bouai*. Assisting the *paedonomos* in his duties were subordinate officers known as *bidioei;* older and abler youths were set over the younger boys as captains of the *ilai* and *bouai*. The duties of, respectively, the *ilarchai* and the *bouagores* were to supervise the gymnastic exercises of those in the lower school classes. "The governor," says Plutarch, "set over each of the bands, for their captains, the most temperate and boldest of those they called *eirens* (youths) who were usually twenty years old—two years [older than] the boys." These monitors and captains were responsible to the *paedonomos* alone. Also serving in a disciplinary capacity were attendants ominously called whip-bearers (*mastigophori*).

Accounts of the internal organization of the Spartan barracks school

---

[3] See Kenneth J. Freeman, *Schools of Hellas* (New York: Macmillan, 1922), p. 12.
[4] According to Plutarch, the tribal custom of bride capture was perpetuated, in which a man literally stole his bride from her family. As a result, it sometimes happened that husbands "had children by their wives before ever they saw their faces by daylight."

differ. In all probability there were three separate classes: one for boys aged seven to twelve, another for those aged twelve to fifteen, and a third class for youths between the ages of fifteen and eighteen. Upon first entering school, a boy's hair was cut short. He was provided with a bed of straw without blankets, given a skimpy garment, but no sandals. To accustom him to endure hunger in time of war, only meager amounts of food were provided. The remainder he had to forage for himself.

It was customary for the *eiren* to encourage pupils to steal so they would learn cunning. "The herbs of the pot," according to Plutarch's account, "they steal where they can find them, either getting into gardens surreptitiously, or creeping craftily to the common tables. But everyone who is caught is severely flogged for being careless or clumsy." To be apprehended was a serious offense because it indicated lack of foresight and cunning. Heavy whippings were the usual reward for the inept.[5]

Nothing was left undone to produce hardy soldiers capable of withstanding the rigors of famine, cold, and physical brutality. At the annual festivals of Artemis-Orthia, "whipping examinations" were administered regularly in connection with public ceremonies. "Nor must one be offended," says Solon to Anacharsis in a story by Lucian, "when you see their young men whipped at the altar and streaming with blood, while their fathers and mothers stand by begging them to suffer it courageously and even threatening them if they do not bear it with patience and resolution. Many have died under this discipline rather than acknowledge themselves unequal to it before their friends and relatives." There is every reason to believe that Lucian's description was not atypical of Sparta. Another practice calculated to produce good soldiers was the extension of permission once a year for older youths to try their hand at mortal combat. In effect, an "open season" was declared on slaves or helots. Members of packs bivouacked outside the city might set upon an unwary helot simply to gain the experience of killing a human being prior to actually going into battle.

Daily discipline in the barracks was repressive. "A spirit of discipline and obedience prevailed," says Xenophon, and youths "walked along the streets with their hands folded in their cloaks, proceeding in silence, looking neither to the right hand nor to the left, but with their eyes modestly fixed upon the ground." School years were devoted to systematic physical and military training. Led by the *ilarchai* and *bouagores,* the boys passed through a sequence of gymnastic exercises designed to develop qualities serviceable in war, principally running, leaping, fighting, swimming, throwing the discus, hunting, and wrestling. Aristotle's judgment was that Spartans "rendered their sons brutal by the exertions required of them." A

---

[5] A famous story relates how one young Spartan stole a fox but was apprehended before he could dispose of the animal. Rather than reveal what he had done, the lad hid it within his tunic while calmly engaging an elder in conversation. The fox bit his way into the boy's chest attempting to escape and the boy collapsed and died before admitting the theft. The historicity of this anecdote is doubtful but it illustrates a kind of virtue prized among the Spartans.

case in point was the *pancratium*, a personal fighting contest with no holds barred. It was not uncommon for the eyes of a contestant to be torn from their sockets in these encounters.

Besides gymnastics, students learned choral dancing, so-called "pyrrhic" or war dancing, poems celebrating the deeds of heroes, and patriotic songs. War songs and ballads of personal prowess were emphasized heavily. Portions of the laws of Lycurgus, set to music by Thaletas, were committed to memory and chanted. Authorities disagree on whether reading and writing were part of the Spartan educational regimen. Isocrates alleged that most youths could do neither, even as late as the fourth century. If literacy skills were taught, they were valued solely for their utilitarian value. The narrowness of educators in Sparta is revealed in the comment of one critic contrasting them with Athenian educators: the former, it was alleged, "consider it a bad thing for children to learn music and reading and writing; whereas the Ionians think it is shocking if they do not know these things." During the centuries when other city-states were developing a range of intellectual and literary interests, the Spartan armed camp stubbornly maintained its attachment to military drill and strenuous exercise. As Plutarch observed, "reading and writing they gave them, just enough to serve their turn; their chief care was to make good subjects and to teach them to endure pain and conquer in battle." It is not surprising that after the fifth century, Sparta never produced an artist, poet, philosopher, or musician worth remembering.

From the age of seventeen or eighteen to their twentieth year, young "budding youths" (*melleirenes*) were *ephebi,* principally occupied with drill and skirmishing. They left their barracks school, took an oath of allegiance to the state, and joined private, competing paramilitary groups engaged in public displays of military skill. At about the age of twenty, a young man (*eiren*) became a citizen and a full-fledged member of the military.[6]

According to Plutarch,

> the discipline of youths continued after they were full-grown men. No one was allowed to live as he pleased, but the city was a sort of camp in which every man had his share of provisions and business set out, and looked upon himself as not born to serve his own ends but the interest of his country. Therefore, if they were not otherwise commanded, they went to see the boys perform their exercises, to teach them something useful, or to learn it themselves of those who knew it better.

Army duty was followed by a lifetime of service in a military reserve unit whose members could be expected to be called to active duty at any time. At age thirty it was also the usual practice for a citizen to take a wife and

---

[6] Some scholars doubt whether full citizenship was bestowed until the thirtieth year, following a decade of military service.

rear a family. Another obligation of every male adult member of the community who was a citizen was to render financial support as a member of one of the *pheiditia* or military clubs which served as centers of Spartan social life.

Spartan Cultural Ideals

According to a fragment attributed to Tyrtaeus, Spartans were fond of holding festivals where there were public exhibitions of the exercises young boys had practiced for the occasion. On such days, a chorus of old men would sing: "We once were men full of vigor!" and the chorus of warriors would respond, "But we are so now; if you care, try us!" Whereupon, the chorus of young schoolboys repeated, "We shall one day be more vigorous still!" Women were likewise expected to be vigorous and hardy. To make young girls as fit as possible to be mothers of robust offspring—the most important duty of free-born women—a gymnastic course in separate schools was prescribed. Girls were divided into different classes according to age groups and set to hopping, running, wrestling, leaping, and even spear throwing. The organized curriculum also included choral dances, marching, and chanting.

Mature women entered fully into the on-going life of the state. If their husbands or sons fell gloriously in battle for their country, as at Leuctra in 371, the heroic women of Sparta offered thanks to the gods in the temples that the men had fallen so well. One such mother slew her son with her own hand because he had turned back like a coward from the battle; and another, the wife of Leonidas, admonished her son leaving for war to return *with* his shield or *upon* it. This feature of the female Spartan character is well illustrated in a famous poem of the woman Daemenata who lost eight sons in battle. "No tears she shed, but shouted 'Victory! Sparta, I bore them but to die for thee.' "

Taciturnity was a byword in Spartan life. The word *laconic* referring to a mode of speech derives from the people of the Laconian plains. The story is told of a blustering Persian king who dispatched a threatening message to the Spartans: "If I come to Greece I will lay your city in the dust." Undaunted, they replied with a single word: "If."[7] The anecdote serves as a symbol of a people who rightly took pride in their military prowess. The other side of the picture, one more terrifying in its seeming inhumanity, is revealed in the epitaph of the three hundred soldiers who fell defending the pass at Thermopylae:

> Go tell the Spartans, thou that passest by,
> That here obedient to their laws, we lie.

---

[7] Laconism is also immortalized in Leonidas' battle order at Thermopylae: "Breakfast here; supper below." Another story relates that when a group of warriors complained that their swords were too short, their leader replied that they were "long enough to reach the enemy."

It is a splendid tribute to heroism and bravery, heightened perhaps because it shows unquestioning obedience to state discipline, very much like the immortal saga of the Charge of the Light Brigade. But it also poses a reminder of how brutal and unproductive regimentation could become. As Aristotle noted, as long as the Spartans were the only Greeks pursuing military acts they were unquestioned masters, but when other city-states, some of them more broadly based in their cultural interests and educational systems, developed martial skills, the basic weakness of the Spartan ideal showed itself.

It is not the fact that the Spartans succeeded in educating for a warfare state that is so frightening; it is that they succeeded so well. Their system demanded the unconditioned subjection of the individual to the will of the community; the freedom of the individual had no existence as opposed to the requirements of the whole. The state produced grave, severe, brave, self-controlled, self-sacrificing, long-enduring warriors, respectful of elders and full of devotion to the state. But the price paid was high: crushing of personal initiative, ethical freedom, literary and scientific interest, and individuality. Total subservience of the person to the group, education by force rather than by persuasion, schooling exclusively for technique rather than for judgment—they are not unknown today. Teachers prone to use excessive repression as a disciplinary technique might well consider the long-range consequences that follow. Those who would employ education to resist inevitable change within society might ponder the Spartan failure to survive as social circumstances were altered. Spartan education demonstrates how powerful training can be in molding character to desired ends, but it also serves as a reminder of the importance of weighing whatever ends are sought. The Spartan goal was ultimately a sterile aspiration, devoid of grace, beauty, and esthetic appeal. If schools today sometimes appear to be educating for a regimented tomorrow where the fullest claims of the human spirit are ignored, educators should reflect upon the final futility of a Spartan world—austere, confining, and in a terribly important sense, inhuman.

THE TRIUMPH AND TRAGEDY OF ATHENS

A Classic Greek Drama

Athens' history began under conditions quite unlike those which prevailed in ancient Sparta, and as a result Athens developed differently. The Ionic penetration of *Attica*, the territory surrounding Athens, was not a military conquest but a gradual and peaceful immigration. No warrior caste was needed to impose its rule upon a vanquished people and consequently the base of citizenship was much broader than its Spartan counterpart. It was not long before the Athenian city-state was transformed from a predominantly agrarian state into an urban center of prosperous trade and commerce. Until the mid-eighth century, Athens, like other Greek cities, was a monarchy. During the century that followed, the council of nobles, or *Council of the Areopagus,* as it was called, gradually divested the king of his powers. The process of widening the Athenian franchise continued under pressure from peasants and a growing middle class alarmed at the ever-increasing concentration of wealth in the hands of a few entrenched oligarchs.

In 594 B.C. all contending parties agreed to the appointment of *Solon* as a magistrate with absolute power to effect needed reforms. Measures enacted included the abolition of slavery for debt, controls over land speculation, admittance of the lower classes to citizenship through legislation making them eligible for membership in the popular assembly, and the founding of a new Council of Four Hundred. But continuing dissatisfaction over economic conditions plus Solon's costly military adventures abroad led to chaos and further disillusionment. Unsettled circumstances paved the way in 560 B.C. for the triumph of the first of Athens' tyrants, *Peisistratus.* His successor, *Hippias,* was more ruthless and oppressive still.

In 510 B.C. Hippias was overthrown by a group of nobles with aid from Sparta. Factional conflict raged anew until the aristocratic *Cleisthenes* came to power. Upon taking office, he set about reforming the Athenian government by drafting a new constitution (502 B.C.) which altered the basis of suffrage and widened it, established a new Council of Five Hundred, and made it the chief organ of the government. Any free-born male could, in principle, be elected by his deme, or township, to its membership. For this Cleisthenes is rightly called the father of Athenian democracy.

Important social, economic, and cultural changes took place with the passage of time from the eighth to the sixth century. Despite the bitter cries of distress by free artisans and small landowners, a class of large landowners grew steadily in power, as did the merchant class engaged in trade and commerce. Athens embarked upon an active period of colonization throughout the Mediterranean area. At the same time, the common people within Athens slowly but surely gained in economic power, and with it came political leverage. As economic opportunities expanded, Athenian political democracy grew stronger.

Athens reached her height of political and military power in the fifth century B.C., during the so-called golden age of *Pericles* (461–429 B.C.). Her population was divided into three classes: the *citizens,* who numbered about 160,000 at most; the *metics* (resident aliens, non-Athenian Greeks), and a large number of slaves. There was evidently a surprising degree of social and economic equality among all the inhabitants, unlike the Spartan class structure. A system of direct democracy flourished, although it did not extend to the minority citizen class. Yet it must be noted that the disparity between the rich and the poor was not great. Citizens often worked in shops or tended farms, as did the lower classes. The Periclean economy remained comparatively simple, with commerce, manufacturing, and to a lesser extent agriculture the most important enterprises.

In the last century of her existence as an independent state, Athens was drawn into two great wars. The first was waged against the Persians as Athenians went to the aid of their Ionian kinsmen in Asia Minor in their struggle for freedom against the expanding Persian empire. The Persians retaliated by dispatching a powerful army and fleet to subdue the Greeks. Athens bore the brunt of the attack when she assumed major responsibility for repelling the invaders. The *Persian Wars* began in 493 B.C. and lasted, with brief interludes of peace, for about fourteen years. The Greek cities, with Athens heading a Greek alliance, or *Delian Confederacy*, emerged victorious, thus ending the Persian menace and forestalling the destruction of Hellenic ideals in a wave of Oriental despotism. The Delian Confederacy was gradually turned by Athens into a league of subservient states within an Athenian empire. Democracy as a political form continued to flourish at home in Athens but was not exported to her subject satellites.

The other of the great struggles, the *Peloponnesian War* (431–404), produced results of a quite different character. It was almost inevitable that democratic, imperial Athens should enter into a rivalry for power with aristocratic, xenophobic Sparta and finally come to blows. When the battles were over, Athens was so completely humbled that she never recovered. Athenian trade was ruined, her democracy destroyed, her population decimated. She became a subject vassal of the Spartan machine and fell prey to a host of internal social ills.

In the wake of the Peloponnesian debacle there came almost total anarchy as each city-state fought its neighbors. Spartan oligarchies replaced democracies wherever they had existed (except for a short restoration of democracy in Athens). In 371 B.C. Spartan dominion came to an end at the hands of the Thebans, who inaugurated their own rule for a short time. Nine years later war broke out once more, leaving all Greece in a state of exhaustion. Politically prostrate and helpless, Athens and her sister states were ripe for the picking by *King Philip of Macedon*. At the famed *Battle of Chaeronea* in 338 B.C., the Greeks were handed their final defeat and Athens became simply one of countless cities under Macedonian rule. Two years after Philip consolidated his power over most of the Greek peninsula he was murdered in a brawl and rule passed into the hands of his son, *Alexander*. In the space of twelve short years Alexander annexed the whole Near Orient and made of it a vast empire stretching from the Indus River to the Nile. When he died in 323 B.C. at the tender age of thirty-three, a series of wars ensued between the surviving fragments of his realm—Syria, Egypt, and Macedonia—until all were crushed finally under the advancing armies of Rome. In Athens matters came full circle, with the restoration of the monarchial form of government with which the city-state had begun its long career.

Hellenic Thought and Culture in Athens

Athens was always the hub of Hellenic life, drawing to herself the leading lights of a glorious intellectual and artistic culture without parallel in the history of Western man. Though the Athenians did not initiate every advance, they were profoundly influenced by the achievements made in all fields of endeavor. Beginning with the sixth-century Milesian movement in philosophy, the Greeks early displayed a genius for philosophical speculation. They broke through the mythological beliefs of their ancestors in seeking a purely rational explanation of the nature of the physical universe. *Thales* suggested that all things are made of water; *Anaximander* thought the underlying constituent of everything was an "ungendered and imperishable" substance; *Anaximines* argued that air was the germinal stuff of objects, mixed in varying proportions; and *Empedocles* wondered if all existence might be explained by four basic elements. Before the end of the sixth century, the *Pythagoreans* at Croton were saying that the essence of things is not a material substance at all but the abstract principle of number. The Atomists, chief among them *Leucippus* and *Democritus of Abdera,* advanced the thesis that the ultimate constituents of the universe are material atoms. The Eleatic philosopher *Parmenides* made a case for the argument that stability or permanence is the real nature of things, whereas *Heracleitus* took the opposite tack by saying that permanence is illusory, that change alone is real. In addition to metaphysical investigation, the philosophers of Athens turned to questions regarding the nature of man and his ultimate destiny, a development culminating in the great systems of *Plato, Aristotle, Epictetus,* and *Epicurus.*

Less notable were the Greek achievements in the field of science, although even here the studies of the Pythagoreans, of Aristotle, and later of Alcmeon and *Hippocrates* of Cos deserve mention. The true Greek genius manifested itself in art and literature: in the elegiac verses of Mimnermus and Theognis, in lyric poetry, and of course in the tragic dramas of *Aeschylus, Sophocles,* and *Euripides* and the comedies of *Aristophanes.* Two of the most widely read historians of all time—*Herodotus* and his younger contemporary, *Thucydides*—were Greeks. The sculptor *Phidias* was an Athenian, his craftsmanship preserved for posterity in the figure of Athena in the Parthenon or the statue of Zeus in the Temple of the Olympian Zeus. Athenian Greeks set canons of architecture revered to the present day, exemplified by the beautifully proportioned Temple of Athena Nike and of course the Parthenon. One of history's great mysteries is why so much talent revealed itself within so short a space of time. Virtually all of the preceding artists lived and worked between 525 and 380 B.C.

The religion of the Greeks had undergone a metamorphosis by the time of Pericles. In the early Aegean days of Greek culture, a primitive polytheism typical of most tribal cultures obtained. In late Homeric times, the *Iliad* and the *Odyssey* transformed vague clan deities into anthropomorphic personalities directly involved in human affairs. By the late seventh century, new religious forms had entered in: an ecstatic mystery cult which revolved around the myth of the death and resurrection of Dionysus; and the Eleusinian cult, whose central theme was the abduction of Persephone by Pluto and her redemption by Demeter, the Great Earth Mother. During the Periclean Age, the former had become an Orphic philosophy-religion, some of whose members preached a monotheistic theology of strict morality and ascetic ideals; the latter had become a secretive religious society whose mysteries were shared only by a small group of initiates. In the fifth century B.C., both the traditional rites and the authority of ancestral gods were under attack by a skeptical intellectual class. Still later, in the third and second centuries, religion lost its civic function and became more otherworldly and spiritualized. A kind of philosophical monotheism continued to gain favor among the educated classes, although most people clung to the separate gods of an earlier tradition.

Early Athenian Education

From the time of Homer to the sixth century, Athens and Sparta probably pursued the same educational objectives of preparing people for a life of military service, but where Sparta resorted to brutal regimentation and severe laws to accomplish her end, Athens never required the tightly knit system of control for molding her citizens to Homeric ideals. Athens sustained a more varied and cosmopolitan culture whose sense of democratic cooperation, personal freedom, and devotion to the state was deeply ingrained. Thucydides has Pericles formulate an ideal of democratic citizenship in a funeral oration which includes an obvious gibe against the Spartans:

> The freedom which we enjoy in our government extends also to our ordinary life. There, far from exercising a jealous surveillance over each other, we do not feel called upon to be angry with our neighbor for doing what he likes, or even to indulge in those injurious looks which cannot fail to be offensive, although they inflict no positive penalty. . . . We throw open our city to the world, and never by alien acts exclude foreigners from any opportunity of learning or observing, although the eyes of an enemy may occasionally profit by our liberality; trusting less in system and policy than to the native spirit of our citizens; while in education, where our rivals from their very cradles by a painful discipline seek after manliness, at Athens we live exactly as we please, and yet are just as ready to encounter every legitimate danger. . . .

Athens truly was, as Thucydides affirmed, "the school of Hellas."

It is presumed, from passages in Solon's laws, that formal schools of some sort existed in Athens at a very early date and became widespread by the time of the Persian Wars. Aristocratic poets such as Pindar and Theognis might scorn the replacement of private tutorship for the elite by collective institutionalized instruction, but evidently there arose a felt need for more systematic training than could be had under the informal educational forms of the Homeric past. By the sixth century B.C. it is almost certain that a well-developed school system was in existence, organized and controlled by the state, but conducted (at the lower levels at least) on a private basis.

As in Sparta, the practice of exposing an unfit infant to the elements was followed by most families, the difference being that the Athenian father, not the state, had sole responsibility for determining whether a child would live or die. On the tenth day after birth, the family assembled for a joyous celebration at which the father officially named the child. The infant was carried several times around the burning hearth by its nurse or mother, and hence the christening ceremony was called the *Amphidronia*, or "running around." On the fortieth day, the child was formally registered by the father as a member of the city ward. The initial care of the new-born child fell to a wetnurse (*titthe*) and then to a day nurse (*tithene*), assisted by the mother. The child's earliest years were easy and pleasant ones, filled with loving parental attention, toys, games, and nursery rhymes.

Around the age of seven the place of the nurse attendant was taken by a slave known as the *pedagogue*. His function was to act as moral guardian and valet to an aristocrat's son. Slaves suffering from weakness, physical defects, or advanced age became pedagogues because they could not otherwise be employed profitably by their masters.[8] Some undoubtedly abused the privileges of their station, but a few had a high conception of their function. It is said that when one was asked what his work was, he replied, "My duty is to make the good pleasant to boys."

In obedience to established custom (from the sixth or fifth century on), all Athenian free citizens sent their sons to three types of elementary schools: the *palaestra* or gymnastic school, under the direction of a *paedotribe* (gymnastic master); a *music* school (*didascalium*) under the *citharist*, or teacher of music; and a *writing* school, conducted by the *grammatist*, or teacher of letters. It may have been the case that public officials supervised the opening of schools, the hours they might keep, and so on, but institutional schools were always conducted by private entrepreneurs. Primary schools varied greatly in their academic standards, teaching competence, and physical accommodations. They might be held in the open air in some recess of a street or temple, in an unrented shop, or within the shadow of a public monument. Instruction began early in the morning and lasted until sunset.

In the earlier phases of Greek education, the teaching of letters and of

8 Pericles is reported to have said, when he saw a slave fall from a tree and break his leg, "Lo, he is now a pedagogue!"

music was often given by the same teacher or by two instructors in the same building. Later, literary instruction at the elementary level was given separate from musical training. Prior to the time of the Persian Wars, the music school was mainly a place where instrumental and vocal music was taught. The *citharist* taught his charges to play on the seven-stringed lyre, to sing, to chant, and to dance. Simple songs were dictated which children were required to learn by heart. The object of musical instruction was specifically educational, not merely ornamental. Aside from the value of developing the child's esthetic senses and the preparation it afforded the child in learning to participate in choral contests, religious festivals, and public recitations of poetry, music was believed by the Greeks to have a powerful influence on an individual's *moral* character. Plato, speaking in the *Protagoras,* says, "They make rhythm and harmony familiar to the souls of boys, that they may grow more gentle and graceful and harmonious, and so be of service both in words and deeds; for the whole life of man stands in need of grace and harmony." Music could produce a harmony and balance of the soul. As Plutarch observed confidently of the citharist's student, "music teaches him to abstain from everything that is indecent, both in word and deed, and to observe decorum, temperance, and regularity." From the ranks of those boys with a well-developed sense of melody and rhythm, a *choregos,* or dance master, picked future members of the chorus that performed at various religious and dramatic festivals in Athens.

The elementary curriculum in reading and writing, taught by the *grammatist,* prepared young boys to write both in a formal hand and a cursive script. According to Dionysius of Halicarnassus, pupils began by copying individual letters, then combined them into syllables, and finally memorized whole words. Writing was practiced on baked earthen tablets with a stylus, on wax-coated wooden boards, and later on sheets of papyrus. Pupils simply traced the outlines of letters prepared by the teacher until they learned to form them on their own. There were no accents or stops, no punctuation in the commonly used written form of ancient Greek. Sometimes counting was done on the fingers or with stones. (Higher arithmetic operations, involving a numerical system more difficult even than the Roman system, were rarely mastered.) Reading proceeded from the works of Homer, Hesiod's *Works and Days,* Aesop's *Fables,* the writings of Theognis, Phocylides, Solon, and generally, as Plato reports, "poems in which were contained many admonitions and illustrations of conduct, also praise and eulogy of distinguished men, that the boys might admiringly imitate them, and strive themselves also to become distinguished." In later years, drawing and the elements of geometry were incorporated into the primary school curriculum. Discipline at school was severe. A youth who had not been flogged, as Menander put it, had not been educated.

Elementary school teaching was regarded by Athenians as a servile occupation, unworthy of a free citizen. Because there were no qualifications (other than the ability to read) which teachers had to meet, the schoolroom became a refuge of the distressed, a haven for those who survived on subsistence wages paid by tuition fees for want of better employment. There was a proverbial saying applied to a man who had disappeared: "He is either dead or has become a schoolmaster." Lucian condemned tyrants sent to the nether world to be either beggars *or* schoolmasters. Demosthenes taunted his great rival Aeschines for having had to help his father clean out the school when he was a boy. He says in *De Corona,* "You were reared in abject poverty, waiting with your father on the school, grinding the ink, sponging the benches, sweeping the room, doing the duty of a menial rather than of a freeman's son."

The status of the *Paidotribe* in the *palaestra* was only slightly better. Gymnastic trainers were private teachers who kept a school while preparing for and aspiring to a position in one of the municipal *gymnasia.* Reflective of Athens' earlier preoccupation with military prowess, physical instruction played an important role in the educational system. The paidotribe's task was to develop in boys grace, harmony, and style through physical exercises. The program consisted of running, jumping, dancing, swimming, wrestling, and throwing the javelin and the discus. "Thus do we exercise our youth," explained Lucian, "hoping by these means to render them the guardians of our city and supporters of the commonweal, that they will defend our liberties, conquer our enemies, and make us feared and respected by all around us. . . . Our youth are thus prepared for peace and war." No separate building was required for the palaestra; its operations could just as easily be conducted in any public square or open field. It is not clear whether gymnastic training was given simultaneously with instruction by the citharist and grammatist or whether it was reserved until after elementary literary education had been concluded.

The nearest equivalent to a secondary-level school in Athens prior to the fifth century was a state-supported *gymnasium,* an enclosed stadium built around a race course and a large playing field. Its many activities were superintended by an appointed public official called a *gymnasiarch,* under whom was a staff of lesser gymnasts and paidotribes. The gymnasium was the place when youths aged fifteen or sixteen to eighteen perfected athletic skills learned in the palaestra. The sports of the *pentathlon*—javelin throwing, discus throwing, jumping, running, and wrestling—were heavily emphasized. Organized physical instruction was paid for entirely by tuition fees.

Formal education in the broadest sense of the term ended with a two- or three-year period of public military service known as the *ephebia.* The archaic values of military arts were fostered in a highly organized program of teaching, from which young cadets, or *ephebes,* graduated to full citizen status. They took an oath of allegiance to the state, promising not to desert their compatriots in time of war or to disgrace their sacred arms, and declared their loyalty to the gods and the civil magistrates. There followed a regular tour of duty in the armed services of the city-state.

Athenian Cultural Ideals

The guiding ideal of Athenian education down to the fifth century seems to have been a kind of *areté* stressing personal beauty as well as the athletic–military virtues of strength, courage, and competitiveness. It was basically an esthetic ideal, summed up in the concept of proportion or balance in all things: *aidos,* or "a feeling of respect for what is due to the gods, to one's fellow men, to oneself—reverence, self-control, modesty, fair fighting and fair play."[9] The model for Athenian youth was a man both beautiful and good, physically attractive and morally upright. As an educational end it was inseparable from what was admired in the culture as a whole.

In consequence, from the time of Solon to the age of Pericles, Athenians relied heavily on informal modes of instruction in addition to the schools already discussed. Daily life was not an adjunct to formal schooling; it was the core of education. Adolescents were introduced directly to the cultural and civic life of the city, attended productions at the theater of Dionysus, watched debates in the law courts, learned at first hand how the state's institutions functioned. Life itself, with all its varied rich appeal, was the educator for youth. They were exposed to the ferment of ideas in the marketplace, to the practical affairs of worldly men, to the religious life of feast days, cultic festivals, and public rituals. This highly unsystematic form of education sufficed exceedingly well until new political, economic, and social circumstances dictated far-reaching changes.

Later Athenian Education

About the middle of the fifth century B.C. an intellectual revolution began in Greece. Philosophers abandoned their earlier study of the physical universe and turned to a consideration of subjects more intimately related to man himself. The triumphs over the Persians at Marathon, Salamis, and Plataea brought Athens to a position of political prominence in Hellas, and with power came profound social alterations in the existing fabric of life. Themistocles had helped to transform Athens into a great maritime power. In place of an agriculturally based aristocracy, a new class of wealthy bourgeoisie arose, throwing its support to political democracy. The Periclean experiment in political freedom bred a crass egalitarianism and, for better or worse, a strong spirit of individualism. Growing luxury, it seemed to some, had weakened the moral fiber of the people. Skepticism was rampant, stimulated in part by cultural contacts with other nations. The new cosmopolitanism induced criticism, modification, and sometimes outright abandonment of older traditions and ideals, chief among these the

9 E. N. Gardiner, *Athletics of the Ancient World* (Oxford, England: Clarendon Press, 1930), p. 70.

ideal of service to the state. The ancient Olympian cosmogony seemed threatened—a new generation dared to question the very existence of the gods themselves. Disintegrative forces seemed at work everywhere. It was a time very much like the present.

Social change was reflected in the loosening of traditional educational forms. Aristophanes charged the schools with a breakdown in moral discipline and the introduction of unworthy elements into the curriculum. Old authors were replaced by modern ones. Gymnastics completely supplanted military drill. Above all, a new conception of *areté* was emerging, a cultural and educational ideal that was to shake Athenian life to its foundations. Now reformers were demanding a realignment of aim and content in formal instruction that would fortify traditional values through literary training. At the elementary level, the old esthetic and physical instruction was eliminated and literary training was made the foundation of schooling. At the upper level, the ideal of educating for the well-rounded development of the whole man gave way to the idea of training intellectuals in literary skills. Gymnasia lost their earlier upper-class exclusiveness and became centers where grammar and literary criticism were leading studies. The place of the gymnasiarch was taken over by the *grammaticus,* a teacher of grammar and rhetoric. Those youths between the ages of fourteen and eighteen who could afford to continue their studies now came to study Greece's literary inheritance—the writings of Callinus, Archilochus, Tyrtaeus, Sappho, Anacreon, and Pindar, as well as the works of Perianden, Chilon, Pittacus, Bias, and Cleobulus. By the Hellenistic period, Athens had five great literary centers of instruction: the Lyceum, the Academy, the Diogeneion, the Ptolemeion, and the school called Kynosarges, where students were schooled in the classics of Greece's long intellectual tradition. The old ephebic training underwent a similar transformation. After 335 B.C. the ephebia was no longer compulsory and its duration was shortened to one year. Linguistic training supplanted martial exercises, and whatever remained of the old athletic activities was taken over by the idle rich class and by professionals. All in all, the groundwork had been laid for a still greater transformation of Athenian education at an advanced level.

THE ORATORICAL AND PHILOSOPHICAL REVOLUTIONS IN GREEK EDUCATION

Teachers of Wisdom

The rise of the *Sophists* was both a response to changing intellectual needs in fifth-century Greece and a contributing factor to accelerated social and cultural change. Contemporaneous with the growth of commercialism and a cosmopolitan spirit there arose a diffuse spirit of inquiry or criticism that set for itself the task of rethinking inherited modes of life. Under the

assault of skeptics, established practices, existing institutions, and traditional habits of thought all appeared patently inadequate. Economic
fluidity tended to unleash a strong individualistic strain in Athenian life
which, translated into educational terms, showed itself in the demand for
an expanded kind of schooling for the *hoi polloi* ("the whole people"). It
was almost as though people instinctively felt that opportunities for success
in public life, now so much enlarged and exacting, could be created only
through a kind of intellectual training, on a scope never before attempted.
Athenian youths groped for a more "relevant" kind of education (to adopt
the current vernacular) to help prepare them for the duties of citizenship
and to assist them in gaining personal power. The question of the day was,
"What kind of education is needed for helping the individual secure
political advantage in public affairs?" An answer was provided by a new
class of teachers arriving on the scene, professing to supply the instruction
needed for success in life. These exponents of current intellectual trends
were known as "those who are wise," or Sophists.[10]

Their arrival, as depicted in Plato's *Protagoras,* was heralded by intense
excitement among the young men of Athens. Here were the first professional
teachers, exceptionally skilled ones at that (unlike most modern college
professors), opening schools in a city that had never known anything but
aristocrats' tutors, paramilitary drill masters, and humble, much-ridiculed
schoolmasters. The early Sophists had a flair for attracting prospective
students: they put on forensic exhibitions, gave sample lectures in the
public square, and had their virtues touted by former students imported
for the occasion. Some of these peripatetic teachers were charlatans and
frauds who "made the worse appear the better cause." Others were sincere,
devoted academics promising to impart a useful brand of wisdom, to arm
students for political strife and prepare them for a career in public life.
Their version of *areté* was personal political leadership, the ability to
persuade and manage other people. It seemed that Sophists were everywhere, hawking their intellectual wares and promising crowds of eager
youths that they could teach them everything necessary to the educated man.

Perhaps the most attractive feature of Sophistic teaching, so far as the
youth were concerned, was its iconoclastic spirit. The new arrivals ministered
admirably to the intellectual climate of doubt then in its ascendancy. As
the sanctions of the old mores that comfortably fitted the old city gave way,
it became possible to treat the gods lightly and decry metaphysical speculation of any sort. After all, even the ancients had failed to reach consensus
on such basic issues as the reliability of the senses and the trustworthiness
of reason. Perhaps there were no universal or ultimate ethical standards and

10 For sources on the Sophists, consult Freeman, op. cit., pp. 157–209; Frederick A. G.
Beck, *Greek Education: 450–350* B.C. (New York: Barnes & Noble, 1964), pp. 147–187; and
Werner W. Jaeger, *Paideia: The Ideals of Greek Culture* (New York: Oxford University
Press, 1945), Vol. I, pp. 298–321.

no certain truths. If everything is relative, some thinkers began to argue, then the only knowledge worth having is that which serves the interests of man the individual, instead of some abstract notion of truth in and of itself. Moreover, the curriculum offered by the Sophists was broader and more comprehensive than any previously available. It emphasized logic, grammar, rhetoric, oratory, eristics, and dialectics as the subjects most useful for preparing young men for public careers, but it went far beyond extensive training in the technicalities of speech. Though no two Sophists sponsored the same program, all allowed their instruction to extend over a wide range of subjects. Their students loved the way in which the new teachers were willing to tackle social issues frontally, usually within a frame of reference hostile to the established order. The response of modern students to latter-day Sophists is not dissimilar.

"Human excellence," proclaimed *Protagoras* of Abdera (481–411 B.C.), one of the first and greatest of the teachers of wisdom, "is the proper care of one's personal affairs, so as best to manage one's own household, and also of the state's affairs, so as to become a real power in the city, both as a speaker and man of action." His words made good sense to the ambitious, living in a society where the spoken word so potently molded public opinion. Because any aspirant to power had to be an effective public speaker if he were to be heard in the halls of government, Protagoras stressed the importance of an oratorical education. The detailed study of language—grammar, etymology, syntax—and its uses in rhetoric would help each student clarify his own thoughts and lead him to express them eloquently. The diligent student under proper supervision might learn to change, even circumvent, conventional laws by the sheer power of his argumentation.

Briefly, Protagoras' dictum, "Man is the measure of all things," comprehended the essence of the Sophist position. Truth, goodness, justice, or beauty are relative to the needs and interests of man himself. There are no absolute truths or eternal standards of rightness. Because sense perception alone is the source of human knowledge, there can be only particular truths valid for a given time and place. Morality likewise varies from one people to another. There are no absolute canons of right and wrong eternally decreed in the heavens to fit all cases; the private judgment of man alone determines what is proper. Laws and customs are only man-made conventions; they have no universal authority. Each individual should erect his own standard of authority through his own judgment and careful thought. So considered, the Sophist argument sounds a distinctly contemporary note in a world grown suspicious of absolute authority and transcendent laws.

If man is the measure of all things, the study of logic, literary criticism and oratory seemed the proper means for establishing that measure. Political virtue, the Sophists appeared to say, would follow of its own accord as oratorical skills were acquired. And if not, so much the worse for virtue; the main business of education is to learn what society requires for personal success.

There was much that was admirable in the teachings of such orators as Protagoras, *Gorgias of Leontini* (ca. 483; the Sicilian ambassador to Athens), *Hippias of Elias* (ca. 443), and lesser Sophists such as Antiphon, Prodicus, and Thrasymachus. In general, they condemned the custom of slavery, ridiculed the chauvinistic exclusiveness of Athenians, championed the rights of the common man, and preached against the folly of war. Philosophically, they turned away from abstruse speculations and, as Cicero later expressed it, "brought philosophy down from heaven to the dwellings of men." Their teachings incorporated a healthy ethical common sense, even though they sometimes advocated a crass brand of selfish opportunism. They opened formal schooling to a larger class of men and thoroughly democratized Athenian intellectual life. On the other side, the Sophistic tendency to encourage the popular belief that moral or social values could be gained on a discount basis, and their propensity to compress learning into neat little packages for sale undoubtedly weakened Athen's cultural life. In the final analysis, insofar as they hastened the decline of values better left intact, the advent of the Sophists was not an unmixed blessing.

It was inevitable that the relativism, skepticism, and individualism of the Sophists should have aroused strenuous opposition. In the judgment of the more conservative Greeks, when itinerant teachers questioned the authority of the gods and the cherished religious traditions associated with them, it was clear that the city itself was under attack. If there is no final truth, it was alleged, and if goodness and justice are merely relative to the whims of the individual, then religion, morality, the state, indeed society itself, cannot long be maintained. Critics pointed with horror to Protagoras' frank admission, "In regard to the gods I cannot know that they exist, nor yet that they do not exist; for many things hinder such knowledge." The verbal virtuosity of the Sophists aroused special ire. A sophistic character in Aristophanes' play *The Clouds* boasts, "I mean to say, we argue up or down—Take which you like—It comes to the same end." The reaction to the revolution of the Sophists was the growth of a new philosophic movement grounded upon the theory that Truth is not relative and that absolute standards do exist. Its three main supporters were Socrates, Plato, and Aristotle.

A Gadfly to Athens

The truth of Bertrand Russell's dictum, "Most men would rather die [or kill] than think," is illustrated in the fate that befell one of Athens' greatest philosophers, the teacher called *Socrates* (469–399). He was born in Athens of humble parentage, his father being a sculptor, his mother a midwife. In Plato's *Symposium*, Alcibiades describes Socrates as looking like a satyr, and Aristophanes said that he paddled through the streets "like a water-fowl" and ridiculed his habit of rolling his eyes. In Xenophon's account, Socrates was robust of body, wearing the same garment the year round, even on winter military campaign. He served as a hoplite in the army and was decorated for bravery at the siege of Potidaea (431) and the battle of Amphipolis (422) during the Peloponnesian Wars. He had a shrewish wife, Xanthippe, who berated him constantly for not being a good family provider and for frequenting the public market place so often with his friends. His ability to drink his companions under the table, all the while calmly engaging in passionate discussion, was universally admired.

From the days of his early youth Socrates had an intense concern in philosophical matters. It is unknown how he gained his education, but he was certainly familiar with the teachings of earlier Greek thinkers. Some say he was the recipient of strange "voices," and that he was given to prolonged fits of abstraction, one lasting an entire day and a night, and that while on a military expedition. Chaerephon, a devoted friend, once asked the Delphic Oracle if there was any man living who was wiser than Socrates, and the answer came back, "No." The god's response deeply disturbed Socrates. He finally concluded that if he was truly the wisest man it was because he acknowledged his own *ignorance*. He came to believe that he had been given a divinely appointed mission to combat the doctrines of the Sophists and to seek for a stable, certain wisdom, enlisting the help of anyone who consented to listen to him. He soon gathered around him a circle of ardent admirers.

In the fourth century, as has been noted, Athens was engaged in a fatal struggle for supremacy with Sparta. The impending Athenian defeat symbolized, in the eyes of many, what was wrong with her youth. Perhaps rugged individualism had sapped her inner strength. What was to replace the old intellectual and moral disciplines abandoned by the Sophists? Had emancipation in the intellectual sphere led only to bondage in the political sphere? Were there rational principles for the proper conduct of a city's affairs, and if so, had they been so neglected that the omission was leading to the downfall of Athenian sovereignty? Socrates must have asked such questions as he decried the cynical amoralism of the Sophists. Against their narrow anthropomorphism in the field of learning, Socrates stood for the transcendent claims of truth. Early in his career he turned away from the cosmological speculations of the Ionians toward man himself. In Plato's *Apology,* Socrates insisted, "But the simple truth is, fellow Athenians, that I have nothing to do with physical speculations." In opposition to the Sophists' erudite polymathy, Socrates said he had no set of doctrines of his own. Against the claim that man is the measure of all things, he argued that general principles or ideas which are identical for all are presupposed by every particular action. Justice, truth, goodness—they are not what an individual chooses to think about them, but transcendent concepts independent of private opinion. Every man's experience provides the warrant for these essential principles if only it is properly analyzed. "Know thyself," he was fond of saying, if you would seek virtue. Plato relates that Socrates said he wanted "to persuade every man among you that he must look to himself, and seek virtue and wisdom before he looks to his private interests." The existence of a strong city, he argued, depends upon enlightened citizens, true seekers after wisdom. If a man would be wise, he should seek it within, for virtue and knowledge lie latent in the human soul.

Aristotle ascribes to Socrates the method of "inductive arguments and universal definitions." He himself called it "midwifery," the bringing to birth of ideas in the minds of others in the form of clear definitions or universal concepts.[11] The *Socratic method* took the shape of a conversation or "dialectic." Socrates would engage a listener on a topic and request that some particular term used be defined more carefully. When a provisional definition was proposed, Socrates would profess his satisfaction except for one or two minor questions. As the conversation proceeded, perhaps on the topic of "virtue" or "justice," the student would be forced progressively to redefine his definition, moving inductively from particular examples of the idea under analysis to some universal definition. Socrates' aim was neither to irritate nor to embarrass, but to show his student the limit of his ignorance, to induce him to reflect for himself on his superficial view, his slipshod assumptions. Socrates was never a mere destructive critic. The final aim was to produce a consistent idea of universal validity, following from his conviction that the truth of a matter resides not in individual perceptions, as Hippias and others claimed, but in the element common to all perceptions, the concept or definition. Only a definition could save men from the relativism of the Sophists, Socrates held. According to ethical relativism, virtue varies from place to place; there can be no universal essence of morality. But if one could attain a definition of virtue which expressed its innermost nature and held true for all men, he claimed, then one could judge each individual's actions insofar as they accorded with or contradicted the universal concept of virtue. The generalized principle of virtue could then be shown to be binding upon all men aspiring to be virtuous. The final measure would not be private opinion, but objective truth.

Socrates' primary interest was ethical. Just as he believed in a stable and universally valid knowledge which man could possess if he would only pursue the right method, he argued in similar fashion that man could discover enduring principles of goodness and justice independent of the selfish desires of human beings, principles of conduct which would prove infallible guides to virtuous living, for he denied that anyone who truly knows the good can ever choose the evil. Knowledge is always sought as a means to ethical conduct, in the sense that virtue and knowledge are identical. The wise man who *knows* what he ought to do will inevitably *do* what is right.

11 It may have been a playful allusion to his mother's occupation. Etymologically, however, the term is significant: the noun *concept* comes from the verb *to conceive*, meaning "to become pregnant with." Hence, the use of maieutic, or midwifery, to bring concepts to birth.

Instances where a man commits an immoral act serve only to show that he did not actually understand the right course of action. It is inconceivable, said Socrates, that the properly educated man will be immoral because he will recognize the identity of morality and his own best ends. An action is right which serves man's true utility in the sense of promoting his true happiness. There is only one basic virtue—that which really conduces to the harmony and health of the soul.

Basically, Socrates was a spokesman for a traditionalist view of education. Mindful that high technical competence bereft of scruples or moral ends is dangerous, he devoted his career to unmasking what he considered fundamentally wrong in the Sophists' revolution of Athenian higher education. The business of forming a man, he alleged, hinges on the development of ethical virtue, virtue which *can* be taught because the process of reflection and careful analysis of alternatives will show clearly where a man's true interests lie. The education that ignores moral wisdom is a sham and a delusion. The Sophists were concerned almost exclusively with effective action, not moral conduct. They had reworked the concept of education to make it mean training for political advancement. In opposition, Socrates taught that every subject or discipline is not merely an instrument to increased efficiency or personal power, but an avenue to the truth that sets men free. Educational utilitarianism really means intellectual servitude. A Sophist's pupil might learn to make his way in the political arena but if he has not been taught morality he will still be slave to his own ambitions and desires.

What holds true for the individual is true for the state. A society cannot long endure, Socrates implied, if its members pursue exclusively selfish interests and obey only private values. Sophistic education will fragment the social order, tear it apart, and finally destroy everything worth preserving. The state must be founded on basic truths discoverable through reason, its affairs conducted by enlightened citizens respectful of rational canons of thought and obedient to them.

Socrates' life ended in tragedy. He was never popular in his role as gadfly, incessantly puncturing the pretensions of men and confounding the wise with doubts. Nor did his popularity go up when, as member of a committee of the Senate, he refused to agree to a government scheme to confiscate the property of some military leaders accused of negligence. Again, following the installation of a Spartan oligarchy in defeated Athens, he opposed an assassination plot directed against some political suspects. In the year 400 B.C. Socrates was brought to trial by Anytus and Meletus, two leaders under the brief restoration of democracy, for being too closely identified with an aristocratic, antidemocratic faction headed by his former students: Alcibiades (a traitor for Sparta) and Charmides and Critias (two of Athens' hated oligarchs). Socrates' accusers supposed that he would go into voluntary exile. When he refused to do so, he was brought into court and accused of "not worshipping the gods whom the state worships, but introducing new and unfamiliar religious practices; and, further, of corrupting the youth of Athens." It seems clear that the trumped-up charges were actually prompted by dissatisfaction with Socrates' expressions of criticism regarding the political order. Ironically enough, although Socrates was considered dangerous for associating with the politically and socially conservative oligarchs, he was also condemned for being a Sophist, introducing new ideas into Athenian life. Despite an eloquent courtroom defense, he was found guilty of all charges. Invited to suggest an alternative penalty besides death, Socrates proposed a "reward" for his service to the state. Such seeming defiance only angered the court more and he was sentenced to drink the hemlock. Socrates turned down all invitations to escape, arguing that on principle he must remain obedient to the law. In 399 B.C., surrounded by friends in his prison cell, he drank the poison and died. "Crito, perceiving it," as Plato relates the story in the *Phaedo,* "closed his mouth and eyes. This . . . was the end of our friend, a man, we should say, who was the best of all his time that we have known, and moreover, the most wise and just."

The Socratic Problem Today

Socrates' fate poses vital questions regarding intellectual freedom in all societies. How far can a society go in permitting the unrestricted exchange of ideas? What are the permissible limits of dissent? Should those who would subvert the social order go unchallenged and be allowed the liberty of expressing any ideas whatever? Throughout history there have been those who argue that some ideas—anarchism, atheism, communism, free love— are inherently intolerable and should be denied access to the market place of ideas. Unfortunately men never agree on *which* doctrines should be proscribed. Intellectual fashions change: what is heresy for one generation becomes the orthodoxy of the next. Socrates was put to death because his teachings were thought dangerous; history's verdict vindicates him as a constructive critic of his society. The abiding question in every age is how to deal with the protagonists of unpopular opinions, subversive ideologies, and allegedly immoral doctrines.

At the risk of oversimplification, it would seem that every society is caught in the tension between forces supporting total intellectual freedom and forces which would curtail it. In the one direction is a vague pervasive orthodoxy so amorphous as to be without party or sect. Its propensity is to reject "on principle" intrusions upon the existing order. Those who fear free competition of ideas stress the dangers of error and suppose the only alternative is not to run the risk. Against the benefits of intellectual liberty, they stress the overriding responsibility of freedom and the hazards of its abuse. In the other direction, there are the spokesmen for intellectual pluralism and diversity, expressed by Charles Péguy's ideal of the honest man whose life "must be an apostasy and a perpetual desertion." The man who wishes to remain faithful to the truth, he says somewhere in one of his inimitable essays, "must make himself continually unfaithful to all the continual, successive, indefatigable renascent errors." This second perspective stresses freedom of exploration, the liberty of the imagination to explore honest error because error sometimes leads to a larger truth. Against the champion of a fixed orthodoxy, his opponent refuses to embrace dogma because certitudes seem so hard to find.

The product of the tension of viewpoints is compromise. All societies strive for a balance or equilibrium. Few people will accept the often repeated claim that intellectual freedom is either unqualified or nonexistent. Instead, the values associated with a free market place of ideas are set somewhere alongside other values, such as social stability, the importunate demands of national unity (especially in times of crisis), and the need to accommodate to prevailing habits and beliefs. The task of setting limits is always an incomplete, unfinished affair. It is symbolized today by the controversy surrounding such issues as whether "subversives" (political, social, or moral) should be allowed to occupy teaching positions, whether constitutional safeguards of freedom in a democracy protect "nonverbal" forms of social protest and whether those who would destroy democracy should be allowed to avail themselves of the protection afforded by democratic institutions and processes. The problem represented by Athens' judgment on Socrates is still with modern man today—only the specific issues have changed.

The question of intellectual freedom is especially crucial in present-day democratic society, owing to the rise of an extremist pathology on the part of a political "New Left" as well as an "Old Right." Groups at either end of the continuum seek a "polarization" of views so that the middle road between anarchy and repression will no longer be possible. True Believers at both extremes tend to reject the liberal values of tolerance and sneeringly dismiss the tradition of respect for the rights of opponents. They evidence impatience, distrust, and even downright contempt for the methods and norms of democracy—the "cumbersomeness" or "sham" of representative elections, the "irrelevance" of undemonstrative majorities.[12] The major problem today is how to preserve political, social, and intellectual freedoms at a time when they are under unprecedented attack. Phrased differently, the classic dilemma of today, as always, is how to protect the right of a Socrates to be heard without being destroyed by a Sophist.

History's First Educational Philosopher

Socrates' greatest pupil, and the first systematic philosopher to consider most of the basic problems of education, was *Plato*. He was born in or near Athens in 428 B.C. of a distinguished family. Originally he was called Aristocles, according to Diogenes, but later nicknamed Plato on account of his stocky figure. He received all the advantages of an aristocratic upbring-

12 See Irving Howe, *Beyond the New Left* (New York: Dissent Publishing Corporation, 1970), Introduction.

ing and at an early age became a devoted member of Socrates' circle. He reports, writing in his *Seventh Letter* when he was around seventy-five, that "a long time ago, when I was a young man, I wanted, like so many others, to devote myself to politics as soon as I became my own master." His cousin Critias and his uncle Charmides, who served in the oligarchic government of 403, offered him their patronage if he wanted to embark upon a political career. After the death of Socrates and the fall from favor of his relatives (for having supported the oligarchic Tyranny of the Thirty), Plato found it expedient to absent himself from Athens. He withdrew to Megara, took shelter with Euclid, and may have traveled extensively. In 398 he was invited to the court of *Dionysius I,* Tyrant of Syracuse, where he probably hoped to implement some of his own developing political theories. During his stay he became close friends with the Archon's brother-in-law, a young man named *Dion.* He returned to his native state a few years later for reasons unknown and in 388 opened his own school, the *Academy,* to train statesmen in the discipline of philosophy. A return to Syracuse came about two decades later, when Plato responded to Dion's plea to supervise the education of *Dionysius II,* who had recently assumed power. The young monarch's jealousy of his uncle's close friendship with Plato led to a rupture and the latter's abrupt expulsion. A third trip back six years later, in 361, ended in failure. Plato continued (unsuccessfully) to attempt to guide political affairs in Sicily. Dion reportedly overthrew the younger Dionysius, was assassinated in turn, and Plato became involved for a time in a plot with Dion's associates to avenge the death. The demise of his protegé deeply disappointed Plato, who thought he had found a fit subject to educate as a philosopher-king. For the remaining years of his life, until his death in 348, Plato devoted himself to teaching in the Academy. As he said in the *Gorgias,* the true philosopher must turn "to the city he bears within himself." Disallusioned and misanthropic, Plato retreated to his academic grove in heroic solitude, confining his attention to the education of a select few aspirants to political power.

The Platonic Theory of Knowledge and the Doctrine of Ideas

Plato has been a towering, if controversial, figure in Western thought. Alfred North Whitehead, in his *Process and Reality,* alleged that the European philosophical tradition "consists of a series of footnotes to Plato," and Thomas Jefferson, writing to John Adams after having read Plato's *Republic,* wondered why "the world should have so long consented to give reputation to such nonsense." Whether profound truth or simple nonsense, Plato's views stoutly resist any brief exposition. A short discussion of his contribution can include only an account of those portions of his philosophical position essential for understanding his educational thought.[13]

[13] A cursory gloss inevitably introduces distortions. For fuller treatments consult John E. Adamson, *The Theory of Education in Plato's Republic* (New York: Macmillan, 1903);

Like his mentor, Plato aimed to refute the Sophist doctrine of skeptical relativism and to substitute for it a theory of an ordered stable universe in which there are absolute, transcendent standards for ethical conduct. He admitted, with Protagoras, that change and disordered flux characterize the world perceived through the human senses, but he refused to draw the conclusion that an individual's senses provide the measure of all things. Agreeing with Socrates, he argued that the objects of sense experience (*sensibilia*) do not constitute knowledge at all; true knowledge cannot be tied to the shifting and always-changing impressions of fallible perception. *Sensibilia* are relative, elusive, and subject to distortion. In the *Theaetetus* Plato concluded that knowledge is acquired solely through rational reflection, is necessarily infallible, and has for its objects whatever is stable and abiding. A sensible particular as such is indefinable and unknowable; it can become an object of rational judgment and knowledge only insofar as it is considered a "class-instance" of a universal concept. There are an infinite number of "beautiful" particular things in the world but they can be understood only when subsumed under the generic quality of "beauty," from which each takes its identity. The "knowledge" of any specific beautiful object is of the lowest kind (if indeed it is possible to have knowledge of it at all), whereas knowledge of a universal like "Beauty" *in and of itself* constitutes "real" knowledge in the highest sense of the word. So far Plato was in accord with Socrates in affirming that judgments about genuine knowledge attain the absolute and eternal only when they have universals for their objects. Particular instances of goodness may be relative to time, place, and circumstances, but the instances themselves are only good to the degree that they realize or recede from the constant, unchanging essence of Goodness.

Plato's celebrated doctrine of *Ideas* or *Forms* marks his fundamental departure from the position of Socrates. According to Aristotle at least, Plato was the first to make the further claim that universals are not just abstract forms devoid of objective content or reference. The mind *discovers* universals; it does not simply invent them. The common nature or quality of a multitude of sensory particulars which is grasped in a universal concept is not merely subjective; it has an *objective* referent. Philosophically, this is to say that universals have ontological status. To each true universal concept there corresponds an objective, hypostatic reality of a higher order than sense perception. The Form or Idea of a universal is completely unintelligible to ordinary sensory experience; it can be apprehended only by an

---

Rupert C. Lodge, *Plato's Theory of Education* (London: Routledge & Kegan Paul, 1947); Walter Moberly, *Plato's Conception of Education and Its Meaning Today* (New York: Oxford University Press, 1944); Bernard Bosanquet, *The Education of the Young in the Republic of Plato* (Cambridge, Mass.: Harvard University Press, 1917); and F. W. Russell, *The School of Plato* (London: Methuen, 1896). The interpretation here follows closely Frederick Copleston, *A History of Philosophy*, Vol. I, Part 1 (Garden City, N.Y.: Image Books, 1962), pp. 151–269.

act of the mind. Forms, Plato argued, are not mere abstractions, but spiritual archetypes or patterns of some particular class of objects or relation between objects in the sensory world. Thus, there are transcendent Ideas of the essence of Man, Justice, Proportion, Beauty, Color, Shape, Size, and so forth. These subsistent universals exist in a supersensible unchanging state and are the active causes of all perceived qualities. Although Plato experienced difficulty in tracing the connection between a perfect Form and a sensory particular, his final formulation seems to have been that all the objects of the world exist in virtue of, are "participations in," or imperfect "copies" of their corresponding Ideas. In some ineffable sense, Universals are both transcendent over and immanent in the realm of *sensibilia*.

Plato did not suppose that all the Forms existed in a state of chaotic disorganization. In certain of his dialogues, particularly the *Sophist*, he apparently posited a principle of unity for Ideas: all specific essences are unified under or subordinated to one supreme generic essence—the Form or Idea of the Good (*Agathon*), "the universal cause of all things right and beautiful—the source of truth and reason." Plato speaks as though the forms constitute a hierarchy or articulated complex, subordinate to the One (Truth, Beauty, and Goodness) at the apex as the highest and all-pervading Idea.[14]

Having postulated a theory of Forms with the Good, or the One, as active cause and guiding purpose of the whole universe, Plato believed he had satisfactorily shown that when the mind apprehends in thought an essence of something, for example, the ideal of Justice, the standard by which actions are judged just or unjust are neither purely private creations of the human mind nor are they derived from the fleeting realm of sense particulars. Their origin lies in a real, intelligible and supersensual order of reality which provides final warrant for all objective judgments about things and actions in the illusory world of experience.

The Platonic Analogy of the Cave

In Plato's most famous work, the *Republic*, he provided an analogy to help illustrate his theory of knowledge. He distinguished four levels or stages of knowing, ranging from private subjective opinion to true, absolute understanding. His readers are asked to imagine an underground cave in which human prisoners have been chained to the floor since childhood, facing the back wall of the cavern. Behind them burns a fire and between it and the captives is a low wall or embankment. Along this pass men carrying cut-out figures of real objects which, illuminated by the fire, cast flickering shadows on the wall. The prisoners in Plato's cave represent the majority of mankind, beholding only the distorted shadows of reality. Each man's view is marred by his own prejudices and passions and by the

14 As Aristotle puts it, "the Forms are the cause of the essence of all other things, and the One is the cause of the essence of the Forms."

fantasies of his fellows. His level of understanding is confined to "imagining" (*eikasia*), to knowledge of "images" and "shadows," caricatures of
reality.

Once loosened from their bonds, the prisoners are allowed to turn
around and gaze upon the concrete sensible objects which they had formerly
seen only as shadows. Now they have attained a second order of knowledge
(*pistis*), "grounded belief" of sensible particulars. Then the long-suffering
hostages are released from the cave and led out into the real world, to see
the observable world of intelligible things. Their level of understanding has
reached *dianoia,* once they are no longer blinded by daylight and able to
distinguish objects from their shadows. Corresponding roughly to Plato's
simile of the "divided line," appearing elsewhere in the *Republic,* this third
stage of knowledge apparently has to do with conceptual thought, as opposed to simple perception: the former prisoners are "endeavoring to behold those objects which a person can see only with the eye of thought."

Finally, if the men persevere with great effort, they will be able to look
directly at the sun, which represents the Form of the Good. They have
arrived at the final and highest level of understanding, that of "true certainty" (*noesis*)—knowledge of the archetypal Ideas. In fact, the thrust of
Plato's illustration is to deny Socrates' claim that all men possess a latent
ability to discover within themselves a knowledge of pure universal principles for guiding conduct. Plato's considered view was that ultimately only
a small class of men of superior intellect and insight could attain the kind
of understanding demanded. Furthermore, in the *Symposium* and elsewhere, Plato seemed to imply that the final apprehension of the Forms
was not purely a matter of intellectual cognition; a kind of mystical, ecstatic vision or intuition was also involved.

He softened this stand somewhat in his discussions of the nature of the
human soul, where it is suggested that *all* men to some degree have a
capacity for recognizing Forms. They can do so because the Ideas are "remembered" from a pre-existent state before birth when the soul beheld the
Forms in their pristine glory, unfiltered by the distortions of sensory experience. In connection with a series of proofs for human immortality in
the *Phaedo,* Plato avowed that men have a knowledge of absolute standards
or norms, otherwise they would find it impossible to make comparative
judgments of value. But absolutes do not exist in the sensory world and
sense perceptions cannot yield knowledge of the necessary and universal.
Therefore man must have known them in a state of pre-existence, however
dimly they are recalled during life.

The doctrine of *reminiscence* or *recollection* alluded to here is a cornerstone of Plato's educational theory. In the *Meno* a young man by the same
name asks "Socrates" (Plato's mouthpiece for the literary purpose of the
dialogue) whether virtue can be taught. Socrates refuses to offer a simple
answer, but agrees to help him explore the question. Meno wonders how

they can inquire into something neither of them knows. How would they recognize the answer even if they uncovered it? Socrates responds with a "likely myth" purporting to explain the process of learning in terms of remembering. The soul has stored memories within it of all knowledge it knew "before it was a man," and the act of inquiry is trying to recall something already known in a dim and confused way. "The latent power of the soul to remember truth it has already seen corresponds to the mind's power to discern unchanging forms in the changing world it confronts."[15] Socrates devises an experiment to demonstrate: a young slave boy who has had no mathematical training is induced by Socrates' insistent questioning to "remember" certain geometrical truths. Because the youth has apparently not been given the conclusions by his interlocutor and cannot have obtained them from sense perception, it is concluded that he apprehended them in a pre-existent state. Teaching has merely brought them to conscious awareness.

Education for Utopia

Whether or not the process of learning is basically recollection, education is essential for Plato because it represents the only salvation from a life free of error, prejudice, and sophistical blindness to absolute eternal truths. Education is especially crucial for those who will rise to positions of power within the state. As a political philosopher, Plato was inspired by a vision of an ideal state free from the turbulence and selfish avarice he thought was destroying his native Athens. The Platonic Utopia was to be a state which would do away with factional conflict, giving the ruling power to an aristocratic class of wise and just leaders—philosopher-kings. Not democracy or liberty, but efficiency and social harmony were the ends he sought to achieve.

In the *Republic* Plato outlined a plan for the perfect society and the educational system it would require. The state's population would be divided into three principal classes, corresponding to the three divisions of the human soul: the lowest class—men of "iron"—representing the desires or appetitive function, would include farmers, artisans, and merchants; the second class—men of "silver"—representing the spirit or will, would consist of the guardians, or soldiers; the highest class—men of "gold"—representing intellect or reason, would be made up of the rulers. Each of these classes would perform those tasks for which it was best fitted. The function of the lowest class would be the production of goods for the whole community; that of the guardians, defense; and the rulers, by reason of special philosophical aptitude, would enjoy the monopoly of power. "If a state is constituted on natural principles," Plato observed, "the wisdom it possesses as a whole will be due to the knowledge residing in the smallest

---

[15] Robert S. Brumbaugh and Nathaniel M. Lawrence, *Philosophers on Education; Six Essays on the Foundations of Western Thought* (Boston: Houghton Mifflin, 1963), p. 31.

part, the one which takes the lead and governs the rest. Such knowledge is the only kind that deserves the name of wisdom, and it appears to be ordained by nature that the class privileged to possess it should be the smallest of all." Because the state is only the individual "writ large" and justice within the soul derives from a harmonious balance of desire, will, and intellect, the justice and temperance of the ideal state would consist in the due subordination of the governed to the governing and the strict application of each class to its own unique function in the social order.

Plato was convinced that the division of the people in their several ranks should not be made on the basis of wealth or birth, but through a sifting process which would take into account each individual's ability to profit from education. Thus, the lower classes would be those who had shown the least intellectual capacity, whereas the philosopher-kings would be chosen from those who had shown the greatest. Because the state's very reason for existence is to make the good life possible for man, to develop happiness in accordance with the principles of justice, those who would conduct the life of the state he proposed would have to have attained true knowledge (*noesis*) of the Good. Plato's educational outline was designed primarily to show the kind of instruction required for producing a philosopher-ruler. His far-reaching theory of education unalterably opposed the oratorical view of training men to some specific occupational competence. The wise and virtuous ruler would govern not through any ability to gain victories in a forensic tournament, still less because he spoke eloquently, but because his rule would be patterned after a supersensible order of reality represented by the Idea of the Good. Only a few might aspire to become governors, and then only after long and arduous intellectual effort.

Summarized briefly, Plato hoped for a state in which the family and all private property would be abolished, at least for the two upper classes. The rulers would determine the genetic qualifications of all individuals and determine who would be allowed to have children. Men and women would be treated alike in every regard, even receiving the same basic kind of education supervised by the state. Early childhood would be a time for the enjoyment of simple pleasures, informal play, spontaneous games, and story-telling. Carefully censored literature and music, selected for its formative influence, would help mold the character of the developing child. From age six through ten, formal instruction would emphasize arithmetic in order to discipline the mind, followed by six or more years of learning literature, music, and higher mathematics. At age seventeen both sexes would enter upon a three-year *ephebia,* or period of military service. Upon its completion, formal education for the masses was to be concluded.

Upon reaching age twenty, a select few of the most promising students might be chosen for further instruction in mathematics. The course of studies would last a full decade. Prospective philosopher-kings (and possibly "queens"—Plato is unclear on the point) would then have attained "at last to the absolute Good by intellectual vision." Five more years of training in dialectic would follow, after which there would be a fifteen-year probationary period in which the elite group would be "sent down into the den and compelled to hold any military or other office which the young are qualified to hold." Ripened by practical experience, candidates would now be fifty years of age. They would have reached the time, as Plato described it,

> at which they must raise the eye of the soul to the universal light which illuminates all things, and behold the absolute Good; for that is the pattern according to which they are to order the state and lives of individuals, and the remainder of their own lives too, making philosophy their chief pursuit; but when their turn comes, toiling also at politics and ruling for the public good, not as if they were doing some laudable thing; but of necessity . . . then they will depart to the Islands of the Blessed and dwell there; and the city will give them public memorials and sacrifices and honor them . . . as blessed and divine.

Plato's utopian republic was a heavenly vision, not an empirical reality. He himself recognized that it might prove impossible to reinstate the (totalitarian) ethic of the ancient city-state already dying in his own time. In the *Republic* Plato says that his ideal state is a pattern by which earthly states might be set in order. "But whether it exists or even will exist on earth matters not, for the wise man will order his life after it, having nothing to do with any other." Historically, Plato was to have an enormous influence on the subsequent development of Western civilization. In educational terms, he was the first to formulate a comprehensive educational theory grounded on a philosophy. His central claims that education must not be narrowly vocational, that virtue must take precedence over utility, that knowing has a pre-eminent claim over doing, and that training must have for its ultimate end the making of the good citizen endured over the centuries, ideas which have always provoked both sharp criticism and fervent support. In the meantime, however, there were other theorists whose influence on Greek education was much more direct and immediate. It is frequently observed that classical culture was torn between two rival ideals, the one philosophical, whose protagonist was Plato, and the other oratorical, whose most important spokesman was *Isocrates.* Judging by the criterion of how late Greek schools were actually conducted, Isocrates' position was by far the most influential.

The Life and Works of Isocrates

Although neither so profound nor original a thinker as Plato, Isocrates (436–338 B.C.) typified in his views the major suppositions of Greek educational theory outside the philosophical tradition. He agreed wholeheartedly with his younger contemporary that proper education was essential for society's political leaders because it is they "who train the multitude in the ways of virtue and justice and great sobriety and who teach through the manner of their rule this very truth, namely, that every polity is the soul

of the state, having as much power over it as the mind has over the body."
In his *Panathenaicus* he phrased it strongly, "It is this which deliberates
on all questions, seeking to preserve what is good and to avoid what is disastrous and is the cause of all the things which transpire in states." Another
point upon which Isocrates was in agreement with Plato was his attitude
toward the Sophists. He assailed the eristic teachers of rhetoric for their
extravagant claims to be able to teach anyone, for a price, perfect virtue
and all useful knowledge in short order. "They pretend to search for truth,"
he fumed, "but straightway at the beginning of their professions attempt to
deceive us with lies." The Sophists who neglected all considerations of
morality for the sake of attracting large numbers of paying students he
censured as "professors of meddlesomeness and greed." Isocrates' guiding
theme, as expressed in his discourse called *Panegyricus,* was that a properly
educated orator would not be a manipulator of words for selfish advantage,
but a moral being schooled in, and governed by, the highest standards of
ethical conduct.[16]

He was born nine years before Plato, son of a wealthy flute manufacturer
named Theodorus, and studied for a time under Gorgias and other Sophists,
possibly also coming into contact with Socrates. His family's fortunes were
lost in the closing years of the Peloponnesian War and he was reduced to
earning a livelihood by composing forensic speeches for others. Although
he must have longed to try his own hand at public oratory, he was prevented from doing so because, as he reports, "I was born more lacking in
the two things which have the greatest power in Athens—a strong voice and
ready assurance—than, I dare say, any of my fellow citizens." After having
taught rhetoric at Chios for a brief period, he returned to his home state
in 403. For the next ten years he supported himself by writing speeches for
the law courts, despite his deep aversion to the work. In 392 he founded his
own school of oratory and rhetoric near the Lyceum, where, for the next
fifty-odd years, he grew wealthy and famous teaching students drawn from
all parts of the Hellenic world. He died at the ripe old age of ninety-eight,
only a few weeks after the disaster at Chaeronea. Legend has it that he
died of voluntary starvation and heartbreak over the collapse of Greek
political autonomy. His most famous works include the *Antidosis, Against
the Sophists, Areopagiticus, Panathenaicus,* and the *Panegyricus.*

Moral Education for Oratorical Eloquence

Basic to the Isocratic credo was a belief that the end of education is the
cultivation of the whole man so that his conduct in life as a private individual and public citizen will accord with virtue. The making of a man

---

[16] References to Isocrates' life and thought may be found in Moses Hadas, *Humanism:
The Greek Ideal and Its Survival* (New York: Harper & Row, 1960); R. C. Jebb, *The
Attic Orators,* Vol. II (New York: Russel and Russel, 1962); and Charles S. Baldwin,
Ancient Rhetoric and Poetic (New York: Macmillan, 1924).

consists of training in "two disciplines, physical training for the body, of which gymnastics is a part, and, for the mind, philosophy," or instruction in discourse. Isocrates would have had scant patience with the Platonic doctrine that only a select few might be trained in the canons of justice and truth, and then only after a lifetime of study. And by "philosophy" he never meant an arcane discipline taking the seeker of wisdom on flights of metaphysical speculation; for him philosophy should be taken in a much broader sense to mean the cultivated life, general culture, the whole content of a liberal education appropriate for a free man. It was, he affirmed, the rational expression (*logos*) of discourse.[17] Earlier Plato had kind words of praise for Isocrates in the *Phaedrus,* where he has Socrates laud him for his genius as a speechmaker. Isocrates will be led by a divine impulse to higher things, the character says, for "there is an element of philosophy inherent in his nature." Not evidently in the sense Plato intended. Isocrates denied that knowledge for its own sake alone has value. Knowledge is valuable only as it is employed in the framing of judgments about proposed courses of action. For him the truly educated man was "one who can deal with all that comes upon him day by day: who is honest and mannerly in society; who rules his desires; who is not spoiled by good fortune." If he was to be a student of philosophy, it would be of an altogether different kind than Plato had in mind.

In opposition to the claims of Sophists with their flagrantly shallow assurance that education could make of a man anything he desired, Isocrates was convinced that formal education could play only a subordinate role in human development. In order to attain excellence as an orator three things are required: natural aptitude, proper instruction, and extended exercise. Of the three, native talent is the most important. Because the educator has no control over inherent ability, Isocrates confined his discussion to the remaining two factors.

In training an orator, the teacher should choose for exemplary models of discourse "causes which are great and honorable, devoted to the welfare of man and our common good," not the petty, insignificant themes so favored in the shoddy practices of Sophists. In his own school Isocrates laid down a four-year curriculum, beginning with extensive instruction in the theory of rhetoric, only after which were pupils allowed to imitate the carefully selected discourses he presented. Intensive practice followed under the master's close supervision. In addition, students in his school were exposed to a broad range of subjects, including literature, logic, history, political science, art, poetry, music, and ethics, in order that they might have a sound basis for making decisions later in life. Isocrates saw clearly that oratorical skill could easily be perverted for ignoble ends, but he was

---

[17] Costas M. Proussis, "The Orator: Isocrates," in Paul Nash et al. (eds.), *The Educated Man: Studies in the History of Educational Thought* (New York: John Wiley & Sons, 1966), p. 62.

convinced that a true lover of honor and wisdom would approach oratory not just as a means for expressing ideas eloquently but as a vehicle for communicating truth, especially moral truth. He was persuaded that true eloquence must always be the reflection of a virtuous and wise mind. The study of the rhetorician's art would not only teach an individual to speak fluently but to *think* well. Good style and clear thought are indissolubly allied. "I hold that man to be wise," he wrote, "who is able by his powers of conjecture to arrive generally at the best course, and I hold that man to be a philosopher who occupies himself with the studies from which he will most quickly gain that kind of insight." Oratory was such a subject, in Isocrates' view.

The desired end product of education was to be men of good character, devoted to the public welfare: "good men in their relations to the state, to their friends, and to their own households." They would recognize that oratory is a powerful instrument to be used for serving society unselfishly, that its possession imposes an obligation to become good statesmen. Eloquence, he held, has for its aim the development of truth and is the chief agent in civilization. In the nature of things it is impossible to know whether Isocrates succeeded in making his responsible brand of oratory a handmaiden to truth and justice. It is a matter of record, however, that his students usually were remarkably effective and influential after leaving his school.[18] If his account in the *Antidosis* can be believed, upon graduation his pupils were most reluctant to leave, "So happy did they feel in their life with me, they would always take their departure with regrets and tears."

Throughout his long career Isocrates was obsessed with the idea of uniting the warring Greek states into a grand political union. Particularly as the Persian menace grew stronger, he pleaded for an end to strife in order that all Greeks might find strength in political unity as they have gained in that intellectual power deriving from their shared common culture, or *paideia*. Although he failed to see his political dream come true, his moral vision of orators as political poets, imparting esthetic form to public discourse in the interest of a common culture of enlightened men, proved more durable. Isocrates' role as the initiator of the tradition of literary humanism extended by Cicero, Quintilian, and carried on down to the present day is undisputed. Perhaps it is not too much to claim that no other single individual did more than Isocrates to validate the truth of the following famous passage from his *Panegyricus*:

So far has Athens distanced the rest of mankind in thought and in speech that her pupils have become the teachers of the rest of the

[18] There is a tradition that at the panegyric contest held at the death of Mausolus of Caria in 351, all of the contestants had received their education with Isocrates.

world; and she has brought it about that the name "Hellenes" suggests no longer a race but an intelligence, and that the title "Hellenes" is applied rather to those who share our culture than to those who share a common blood.

Aristotle

There is at least one striking similarity in the point of departure for the educational theory of *Aristotle* (384–322 B.C.), last of the great champions of the Socratic tradition, and the views of Plato and Isocrates. He shared with them the conviction that education cannot be viewed apart from the state, that in a very real sense the art of educating is but one phase of the larger art of statecraft (*politike*). An expression of the connection of the two appears in his *Politics:* "A city can be virtuous only when the citizens who have a share in the government are virtuous. . . . Let us then inquire how a man becomes virtuous. For even if we could suppose all the citizens to be virtuous, and not each of them, yet the latter would be better, for in the virtue of each, the virtue of all is involved." The view he developed, though it differed profoundly in many respects from Plato's, was structurally similar—as a social art education is part of the art of politics, whereas considered as an individual process it involves physical, spiritual, and intellectual growth. Even when condemned by critics, the Aristotelian philosophical perspective (within which his views on education appear as a distinctly subordinate part) has had an irresistible appeal in all ages, continuing down to the present day.

Aristotle was born in the town of Stageira in Thrace, bordering on the shores of the Aegean. His father, Nichomachus, was a famous physician who once served at the court of Amyntas II, father of Philip of Macedonia. At the age of seventeen he left for Athens, where he studied under the aging Plato for twenty years (367–347 B.C.) and later taught at the Academy upon completion of his philosophical training. When Plato died, leaving his school to a less-inspired disciple, Aristotle departed for Assos, on the Adramythian gulf, and joined the ranks of a Platonic circle established there some years before by two former pupils at the Academy. He founded a school in which he taught for approximately three years, meanwhile marrying a woman named Pythras, the adopted daughter of Hermias, ruler of Atarneus. From Assos he went to Mitylene on the island of Lesbos to further his growing interest in the natural sciences. In 342 B.C. he accepted an opportunity to move to the court of Philip of Macedonia to supervise the education of the king's son, Alexander. For the next seven years Aristotle served as royal tutor until the accession of his charge to the throne in 336. He was next found in Athens, in 334 B.C., where he began his own school, the *Lyceum,* in the northeast precinct of the city. The new school was apparently both a teaching institution and a center for scientific research, complete with libraries and large staff of subordinates. For the next thirteen years Aristotle plunged himself into writing and research until the local political situation dictated his leaving Athens. When Alexander died in 323 B.C, Antipater, under whose patronage Aristotle had worked, left Greece. Because Aristotle was identified with the Macedonian faction (owing to his long friendship with Alexander), he found it expedient to withdraw "lest the Athenians sin twice against philosophy," he is said to have explained wryly, and journeyed to his late mother's estate at Chalcis, on the island of Euboea. He died of illness the next year at the age of sixty-two.

Education for Self-realization

Formidable obstacles stand in the way of understanding Aristotle's educational theory: turgid prose, difficult terminology, a closely woven philosophic matrix, fragmentary sources, and the fact that his views must be extracted from a large number of writings, the most relevent being the *Politics* and his *Nicomachean Ethics*. Generally it may be said that Aristotle's comments on education are always incidental to his exposition of a broader philosophical doctrine.[19] The entire question of education first surfaces in his consideration of civil polity when he says that man is "born for citizenship" and the state exists for the attainment of man's highest good (his *summum bonum*). Man is inherently a "political animal" who realizes his innate nature only within a social community. It follows that education is a function of the state, because just as every productive art and practical science aims at some good, the end of politics is the highest or supreme good for man. Its aim is to realize the good but its central concern in so doing is to make men virtuous: "The supreme good [is] the end of political science, but the principal care of this science is to produce a certain disposition in the citizens, namely, to make them good and disposed to do what is noble." Politics, in other words, must make education its main interest and include the philosophy of education as one of its component parts.

Starting with his claim that the welfare of citizens and the good of the state are interdependent, their ends identical, namely, the promotion of goodness and virtue, the question then naturally arises, "What is the supreme good?" Beyond all lesser ends, the highest good for man, according to Aristotle, is that which is always sought for its own sake and never on account of something else. The only end pursued for itself alone is "happiness" (*eudaimonia*), an activity (*energeia*) or life of well-being and satisfac-

---

[19] Textbook treatments of Aristotle are as numerous as they are unenlightening. Among the better secondary sources from which his views on education may be gleaned: John Herman Randall, Jr., *Aristotle* (New York: Columbia University Press, 1960); W. D. Ross, *Aristotle* (Cleveland: Meridian Books, 1959); D. J. Allen, *The Philosophy of Aristotle* (London: Oxford University Press, 1952); and A. E. Taylor, *Aristotle* (New York: Dover Publications, 1955). The exposition here borrows wholesale from Brumbaugh and Lawrence, op. cit., pp. 49–75; and from William K. Frankena, *Three Historical Philosophies of Education* (Glenview, Ill.: Scott, Foresman, 1965), pp. 15–79.

tion in accordance with "virtue," or *areté* ("perfection" or "distinctive excellence"). The supreme goal and thus the highest good for man is an activity of living according to that which is uniquely distinctive of man. Man realizes himself in the exercise of whatever it is in his basic nature that makes him human in the completest sense of the term. Aristotle supports this with his contention that man has a purposive function and therefore should seek to realize that purpose, which is living a life of excellence or "virtue."

If man's highest good, happiness, depends upon the exercise of excellence, in what does that distinctive excellence consist? Aristotle's answer is to be found in his view of human nature. Man as a living organism is constituted by a single, unitary substance possessed of a number of capacities or "faculties." The lower or *"irrational"* aspect of man shares in common with animals a capacity for such basic life activities as nutritive assimilation and digestion, respiration, self-initiated locomotion, and reproduction. The nonrational or animal part of man operates partly under man's control, partly outside it. The higher or "sensitive" or "appetitive" aspect of man sustains such functions as sensing and desiring. Sensation is the link between man's irrational component and his *"rational"* or higher nature which he alone among all organisms possesses and directs. Upon sensation is built memory, imagination, and all the other mental capacities which distinguish the human being. It is man's potential for intellectual abstraction, for discursive thinking (the ordering of concepts into systematic form), and for intellectual "intuition" (the ability to grasp rational principles) that sets man apart. He has an innate desire to know, an inveterate curiosity, which leads him to systematize, structure, and explain the impressions of the sensory manifold presented to him. In the same way that the oak tree is latent within the acorn, reason lies within, in fact defines, man's basic nature. In this restricted sense man can be said to be a "rational animal." His rationality is an integral essence of his very being. Hence, according to Aristotle's teleological (purposive) philosophy, the final cause or end of man is happiness, or his highest well-being, consisting of activities conducive to the realization of rationality.

Man's supreme end is not a passive state of existence which is ever finally achieved. It is a *process* more than a destination, Aristotle seemed to imply. "This activity," he explained, "must occupy a complete lifetime; for one swallow does not make a spring, nor does one fine day. . . ." It appears there may be two interrelated kinds of excellence attained through living a life conducive to the realization of man's highest nature: an intellectual or "contemplative" kind of excellence exercised by the activity of the theoretical intellect, and a "moral" excellence, in the ordinary sense of virtue. The criterion for determining whether man's rational intellect is attaining its distinctive excellence is whether it is actively engaged in thinking that which is known to be true, or more precisely, when it disinterestedly seeks truth. Moral excellence, on the other hand, is secured under the guidance of the intellect when it engages in "practical" thinking about actions in relation to what is good or bad for human beings, when it attains knowledge of what is morally right.[20] Aristotle defined this second, or moral, type of excellence as "a settled disposition to choose the relative mean in action and emotion, this being determined in accordance with right principle, or as the man of practical wisdom would determine it." The "mean" Aristotle has in mind is a kind of balance between excess and defect, a middle ground between the extremes in conduct of a total repression of all desires (asceticism) and the uninhibited expression of all appetites and passions (hedonism). Moral virtue consists of a tendency toward moderation in all actions. So, for example, courage is a mean between unreasoning fear and foolhardy rashness, liberality between stinginess and prodigality, and so on. But how is the mean to be determined in any given case? What "right principle" or "practical wisdom" serves to indicate the middle road of moderation between two extremes? Aristotle's reply is that "it is held to be the mark of a man of practical wisdom to be able to deliberate well about what is good or beneficial for himself. . . . Practical wisdom [that which affords a principle for virtuous conduct] then is a rational disposition that grasps the truth about actions in relation to what is good or bad for human beings." This is to say that practical wisdom is knowledge of what conduces to the good, to happiness. So considered, the promotion of excellent intellectual activity is not only the end of all human action, it serves as the criterion of moral excellence.

How is a life of intrinsically excellent activities, both intellectual and moral, attained? "By some kind of study or training," was Aristotle's partial response. Education is always a purposive activity directed toward an end: the perfection or realization of man's potential nature. It aims *ultimately* to enable man to live the good life, one in which his potentiality is brought to its fullest fruition.[21] Its *proximate* aim is to cultivate or foster the dispositions essential for living the good life. Man's basic nature and the fortuitous chances of circumstance may play a large role in determining *what* dispositions are fostered as well as *how* they are developed, but as Aristotle observed, "the rest is up to education." It is this fact that explains his further comment that "education aims at filling up nature's deficiencies." Because men differ in their talents as well as in their social functions within society, the specific form and extent to which good dispositions will be fostered through education cannot of necessity be the same for all. However, generally speaking, Aristotle viewed education as a means for training men in theoretical thinking and wisdom (*sophia*), which has as its goal the

20 Frankena, op. cit., p. 38.
21 Brumbaugh and Lawrence, op. cit., p. 67. See also Frankena, op. cit., pp. 39–40.

development of knowledge which is necessary, absolute and eternal; and for training men in practical wisdom or thinking (*phronesis*) which, as has been seen, aims to direct man's moral conduct.[22]

Aristotle observed that men "learn some things by habit and some by instruction." Speaking of intellectual or theoretical excellence, he claimed it is "for the most part both produced and increased by instruction, and therefore requires experience and time." Moral excellence, however, "is the product of habit." In effect it looks as though Aristotle is denying Plato's claim that virtue can be taught, a denial strengthened by his flat assertion that men "become just by doing just acts, temperate by doing temperate acts, brave by doing brave acts. . . ." Thus, education can make a big difference in "whether we are trained from childhood in one set of habits or another." Man has a natural capacity for habit formation but there is no predetermined direction for the development of habits; he may form almost any set of dispositions. Hearing virtue preached does not guarantee that it will be learned. Nonetheless, Aristotle's settled view introduces an important qualification implicit in the earlier discussion of "practical" wisdom. Although moral virtues of themselves are produced by dispositions acquired through practice or habit, the activity of choosing them is also guided by the distinctive excellence of practical wisdom, by a rationally developed ability to see what one should do in choosing a golden mean between the extremes of conduct. Hence, moral education proceeds on the basis of *instruction* as well as practice. Moral character is formed not only by habitual action but by the deliberate taking of thought.

Returning to Aristotle's argument that education is an aspect of statecraft, there is a passage in the *Politics* which indicates the specific kind of system he advocated: The state, he affirmed, "comes into existence for the sake of life, and continues in existence for the sake of the good life. . . . The good life is the chief end, both for the community as a whole and for the individual." It can be said that *ethics* sets the direction for education and *politics* is the art for cultivating the end of education. Consequently, as Aristotle noted repeatedly, "it is best that there should be a public and proper concern for such matters." Education should be supported and controlled by the state. Its distinctive character will depend upon the particular constitution of the political system of which education is servant and preserver. States vary from one another; the shape of training in any given state must conform to that state's unique characteristics in order that citizens be trained in accordance with the way of life it supports. The only generalization Aristotle was willing to advance was that formal instruction should be "one and the same for all" (in apparent contradiction to his observation elsewhere that training should take individual differences into

22 To avoid unnecessary complications, a third kind of "productive" wisdom (*techne*) aiming to make or produce things is omitted from the discussion because it plays a minor role in Aristotle's educational theory.

account) that in order to guarantee uniformity of good citizenship teaching for everyone, education should be a state responsibility.[23]

Aristotle outlined five steps or stages in the educational process. From birth to age five, he advocated "light exercises," proper diet, regulated exposure to mild hardships to toughen the infant, and a careful regulation of the environmental influences allowed to play upon the child, but no formal lessons or organized study. During the second stage of development, from five to seven, he recommended that the child be allowed to remain in the home, because the family is the most important agent for fostering the correct dispositions leading to moral character. However, he would have educational officials closely inspect the home to be sure that the child's development was being guided in the proper direction. This is a crucial period when the child tends to imitate those around him. The third stage, lasting until puberty, would emphasize exercises for stimulating the growth of a healthy, well-developed body. All the while, by manipulating the student's natural impulses through pleasurable or painful experiences, parents would help form the fundamental habits or "dispositions of the will" later useful in attaining human excellence. The fourth period, extending from around age fourteen to eighteen, would be occupied by compulsory attendance at a state-supported school. There the youth would be given formal instruction in gymnastics, reading and writing, simple arithmetic, and drawing and music. The three basic objectives of transmitting knowledge (1) for its economic utility, (2) for its capacity to engender good citizenship, and (3) for its liberal impact in forming character would always be held in view. The fifth stage, up to the age of twenty-one, would be a time of hard physical training and military service.

Aristotle evidently believed that the curriculum he outlined was concerned primarily with the formation of moral dispositions and the capacities distinctive of man's lower or "irrational" nature. His treatment of the kind of instruction (as opposed to habituation) needed for forming the practical and the theoretical intellect is largely a matter of conjecture, because the treatise containing his position was either lost or never written. Presumably, judging from comments scattered in his writings, the curriculum would have included rhetoric, literature, geography, psychology, politics, ethics, physical science, and philosophy. The importance attached to the training of the "rational" part of man can be guessed at from the structure of his philosophy as a whole, and from his comment, "Contemplation is the highest form of human activity because the intellect is the highest part of our nature, and the things apprehended by it are the highest form of knowledge." In any event, the portions of his view that have survived have had a tremendous influence on Western philosophical and educational thought for over twenty-three centuries.

---

[23] On the topic of education for noncitizens—workers, slaves, and women—Aristotle says little, but, quoting from Sophocles, he notes that "a modest silence is a woman's crown."

THE TRANSITIONAL PERIOD OF HELLENISTIC EDUCATION

A New Civilization

The dispersion of classical Greek culture throughout the Mediterranean world was born of military and political defeat. The debacle at Chaeronea in 338 marked the beginning of the end for Hellenic hegemony, paved the way for Alexander's conquests, and was thus a symbolic turning point in history. The new epoch ushered in, beginning with the Macedonian conquest of the Greek city-states and lasting until the end of the second century of the Christian era, is conventionally called the *Hellenistic* period. The fusion of classical Hellenism with the cultures of the Near East as well as the intermingling of peoples resulting from Alexander's advances on the battlefield produced a new pattern of civilization.[24]

When Alexander the Great died in 323 B.C., his leading generals divided up the empire, with Seleucus taking possession of Syria, Mesopotamia, and Persia; Lysimachus assuming dominion over Thrace and most of Asia Minor; Cassander controlling Macedonia; and Ptolemy adding Palestine and Phoenicia to his holdings in Egypt. Two decades later intestine struggle had reduced the four states to three. During the same period, the Hellenic states waged a hard campaign for autonomy from Cassander. The so-called *Achaean League,* which included all the cities of the Peloponnesus except for Elis and Sparta, and the *Aetolian Federation,* comprised of all states in central Greece except for Athens, were temporary defensive alliances drawn up during the futile war for liberation. The issue was unexpectedly decided for all parties concerned between 146 and 30 B.C., when the entire territory passed into Roman control.

The Hellenistic period was a time of alternating prosperity and depression as trade, finance, and commerce expanded throughout the area of the former Alexandrian empire. Scores of major municipal centers grew up from provincial outposts to become bustling cities, including Antioch in Syria, Seleucia on the Tigris, and *Alexandria* in Egypt, founded by Alexander himself in 332. This last-named city became a brilliant center for Hellenistic cultural achievements. Its population grew to almost a million inhabitants by the first century B.C.; it had spacious paved streets laid out in regular order; and it boasted countless parks, schools, monuments, and splendid public buildings.

The resemblances between Hellenistic culture and modern Western culture are striking in many respects. It was a time of big business and ruthless competition, the expansion of trade and contact with new peoples, the rise of urban areas (complete with congested slums), popular devotion to creature comforts, and an obsession with material wealth. The Hellenis-

---

[24] Three noteworthy sources on the period are J. B. Bury, *The Hellenistic Age* (London: Cambridge University Press, 1923); Moses Hadas, *Hellenistic Culture: Fusion and Diffusion* (New York: Columbia University Press, 1959); and R. R. Bolgar, *The Classical Heritage and Its Beneficiaries* (London: Cambridge University Press, 1954).

tic age was increasingly distrustful of democratic forms of government and tended to embrace authoritarian rule. It was a period characterized by a grossly exaggerated emphasis upon science, a trend in the direction of narrowly specialized learning, dogmatic unbelief, and extreme skepticism.

A shift away from classical canons of balance and restraint toward sensationalism, even an exaggerated realism, was evident in almost all the arts. Sculpture grew voluptuous, emotional, grotesque, sometimes sordid. Simple dignified buildings and temples gave way to luxurious overwrought palaces, costly mansions, and imposing public monuments. Literary works, although produced in almost incredible profusion, showed little originality and less depth of thought, as compared with the productions of an earlier period. In philosophical thought, there was a palpable growth of skepticism—sometimes degenerating into a violent rejection of reason itself—and mysticism. The philosophy of *Epicureanism,* though its founder preached a life of quiet intellectual pleasures, degenerated into a warrant for nihilistic hedonism. *Stoicism,* founded on a belief that the truly virtuous man will live a life in accordance with universal reason, was translated into a counsel of despair seemingly encouraging men to accept their total impotence in the face of life's harsh realities. A still more radical defeatist philosophy was that propounded by the *Skeptics,* first begun by Pyrrho, a contemporary of Epicurus and the Stoic philosopher Zeno, and reaching its zenith in the early second century under the influence of Carneades. Most anti-intellectual of all were the *neo-Pythagoreans,* who went about teaching mystical and antirational doctrines.

In the area of religious belief, the Hellenistic age was a time in which the tendency of the masses to embrace emotional Oriental faiths flooding in from the East was clearly manifest. The Orphic and Eleusinian mystery cults attracted more votaries than ever before. Worship of the Egyptian goddess *Isis* and the astral deities of the Chaldeans was received with almost fanatical enthusiasm. The most powerful influences of all came from the offshoots of Zoroastrianism, especially from *Gnosticism* and *Mithraism.* All in all, only radically otherworldly religions seemed to satisfy the emotional cravings of the people.

The greatest cultural advances of the Hellenistic period were made in the field of science, most notably in the disciplines of astronomy, mathematics, medicine, geography, and physics. Among the leading pioneers of the last three centuries before the advent of Christianity were Aristarchus of Samos in astronomy, Euclid in geometry, Erothothenes of Cyrene and Strabo in geography, Herophilus of Chalcedon and Erasistratus in medicine, and Archimedes of Syracuse in physics.

Education and Culture: The Concept of *Paideia*

One of the most fundamental of all educational questions has to do with defining the educated man. The Greeks, for whom it was a new problem, faced it consciously for the first time in the fifth century during an age when social and intellectual forces were reshaping the character of the society. The answers they proposed, as has been seen, did not agree. Some longed for a return to the simpler virtues, the *areté,* of an earlier day. Homer could teach the heroic values, Hesiod would provide instruction in the homelier ideals of industry and frugality, and Theognis would teach young citizens the more general dispensations of the ancient aristocratic tradition. Solon, the "revered father of Athenian laws," had left a body of codes for proper conduct; their study, embodying the essence of good citizenship, would ensure properly disposed men fit to assume the duties of life within the city-state. Somewhat later, as the process of education was formalized and a systematic curriculum devised, new possibilities suggested themselves. Music would act as the sensitizer of the emotions, poetry would nourish the spirit, and gymnastics would fortify the physical body. The ideally educated man was to be a "well-rounded individual" in the most complete sense, before that term became a pedagogical cliché. Unlike the Spartan conception of the educated man as a warrior-drone, the Athenian concept made room for esthetic sensitivity as well as physical prowess. The ideal was an individual "both beautiful and good" rooted in the *areté* of political man, the servant of the *polis.* Even when oratorical skill and forensic proficiency became the hallmarks of the educated man, the earlier elements lost little of their potency in classical thought. The philosophical reaction to the Sophistic revolution, so radically opposed to it in many ways, carried a contrasting vision of what a properly educated person should be. Whereas the sophistic view of education was cast almost exclusively in instrumental terms, the philosophical viewpoint emphasized the theme of intellectualism, of knowledge for its own sake as an intrinsic good. As the classical tradition in education was redefined, synthesized, and adapted to the requirements of Hellenistic culture, both perspectives were combined in a form that was genuinely unique: the original purpose of oratorical training was lost but its content and methodologies retained; the guiding value of philosophical intellectualism was preserved in transmuted form, but the content of its instruction was largely discarded.

A useful term for gathering together the inherited beliefs, values, and symbols of Greece's greatest period is *paideia.* From the days of Socrates its meaning was systematically ambiguous, denoting as it did both "culture of the mind" or "civilized life" and the influences, processes, and techniques for the making of a man. In Hellenistic times, by a subtle extension of meaning, *paideia* came to refer to the *results* of educational effort rather than the *means* for achieving the end of education—the whole or complete man, an ideal toward which one might strive but never completely attain except through life-long endeavor. *Paideia* was an ideal of personal life enriched and nurtured by the values of classical culture, a precious possession imparted through education.[25] The historic mission of schools in the Hellenistic period was to preserve, perpetuate, and transmit that Greek *paideia*. Because the undergirding social context that had supported the classical way of life was now irretrievably lost, Hellenic culture had to be reshaped so as to permit its transmission to succeeding generations. The task of safeguarding *paideia* fell to the schools as the only organized agencies capable of performing such a service.

In the process of handing down the infinitely rich legacy of classical Greece, it was almost inevitable that its internal contradictions would show up as distortions. Residual characteristics of the old aristocratic education, such as gymnastics and music, gradually receded, their place taken by the study of language and literature. Oratory, now denuded of its practical applications because the political context which had given it birth no longer existed, survived—in fact flourished—and came to occupy a central place in the Hellenistic curriculum. It was Isocrates' cultural ideal that persisted, an ideal that was essentially esthetic, artistic, and literary, not philosophical or scientific.[26] In one sense this was unfortunate. Although it is true the Greeks rarely attained their goal of a harmonious synthesis of the developed mind in a superb body—a union of moral perfection, intellectual excellence, artistic harmony, and physical beauty—it was still an aim worth pursuing. Instead, Hellenistic thought overlooked esthetic, moral, and physical development in favor of intellectual or rhetorical training. The old conception of shaping character for social and ethical purposes was replaced by the view that the best-educated person is one who has trained his intellectual capacities as highly as possible.[27] One outcome was that as schools radiated "an expansive Hellenism as resistless as the Macedonian phalanx," to use Boyd's apt phrase, they became preoccupied with purely literary objectives.[28] If anything, this created a cleavage between life and learning that had never existed in the original culture of Hellenism.

A good case can be made for the proposition that the magnitude of Greek accomplishments so overwhelmed Hellenistic man that he imagined he could neither transcend nor improve upon them. The result was a relatively uncritical, undiscerning reiteration of established styles, habits, and beliefs. In time the freshness of classicism had degenerated into a life-

25 The concept is discussed at length in H. I. Marrou, *A History of Education in Antiquity* (New York: Mentor, 1964), pp. 140–144 ff. Marrou recounts an anecdote about the philosopher Stilpo (380–300 B.C.), who was offered compensation for any losses he might have suffered during the pillage of Megara. Upon being asked to draw up an estimate of damages, Stilpo replied that he had lost nothing, no one had taken away his "culture"—*paideia*—from him. He still retained his eloquence and learning. See also E. B. Castle, *Ancient Education and Today* (Baltimore: Penguin, 1961), pp. 101–104.

26 Ibid., pp. 296, 304.

27 R. Freeman Butts, *A Cultural History of Western Education*, 2nd ed. (New York: McGraw-Hill, 1955), pp. 66–67.

28 William Boyd, *The History of Western Education* (New York: Barnes & Noble, 1966), p. 44.

less, stereotyped orthodoxy. (Much the same thing was to take place a millennium and a half later in Western Europe upon the rediscovery of classicism.) On the other hand, it could be argued that distortion was the necessary price to be paid for preserving Greek learning. At any rate it was the Hellenistic version of Hellenism that triumphed in the end. Although reduced politically to the lowly estate of a Roman province, Greece remained a major intellectual stimulus for the emergence of a unifying civilization stretching from the northern reaches of Ireland to the hot sands of Africa and to the shores of the Indus River. It was not without reason that Horace remarked much later that "captive Greece took captive her rude conqueror and brought the arts to Latium."

Far greater attention was given to the theory and practice of education as an intentionally conducted enterprise than ever before. A list of writings on education in the Hellenistic period would include *On Education,* by Aristippus (ca 435–350 B.C.), *On Education* by Clearchus of Soloi, Theophrastus' (370–286 B.C.) *Of the Education of Rulers,* a treatise entitled *Rules of Pedagogy* by Aristoxenus, Cleanthes' *Of Education,* and Cleomenes' *Concerning Pedagogues.* More concern was shown for institutionalized schools as well, so that in its most advanced stage of development the formal Hellenistic educational structure included a wide range of schools and a complicated course of studies which began when the child was seven years of age and lasted until he was around twenty.

Hellenistic Schools and Curricula

During the third and second centuries B.C., considerable attention was paid to educational matters in municipal centers, judging from extant records of school laws passed in Teos, Miletus, and elsewhere. In the first half of the third century it is recorded that a certain Polythrus of Teos (in Asia Minor) gave his city a heavy endowment to organize and maintain a system of free elementary education for the children of the city. Likewise, at Meletus in 210 B.C. an individual named Eudemus endowed the city with money to be used in establishing a municipally controlled school system. About a hundred years later it is known that the king of Pergamon gave endowments to Rhodes and Delphi for educational purposes. There is every reason to believe that Hellenistic monarchs regularly drafted legislation on school affairs and that it was expected as a matter of course that every freeman living in or near a major city would send his progeny (of both sexes sometimes) to a city-supported or privately managed elementary school. The institution itself would be a simple affair, with classes held in some small room furnished with a few chairs or benches and an armchair for the schoolmaster. The functions of primary education were confined to teaching the basics of reading and writing, and perhaps some drawing and music. Moral training took place in the home and physical exercise was supervised by other agencies.

The teaching of reading and writing proceeded with extended drill, oral recitations, and the copying of short passages from classical authors or maxims from the poets. Physical punishments of the cruelest variety were commonly employed. One method used was to hoist an offender on the back of a classmate, whereupon the master would apply a bullock's tail or a hard leather strap until the culprit bled freely. Throughout antiquity, the pedagogical maxim "no progress without painful effort" was taken in its most literal sense. Severe discipline aside, the crude teaching methods in use by untrained teachers practically guaranteed that the learning process would be slow and cumbersome. It was not uncommon for a boy to have attended school for two or three years and still be incapable of writing his own name.

When minimal literacy had been attained, anyone desiring to go beyond the primary school stage who could afford the tuition charges was free to attend a secondary-level institution. Instruction centered around the study of literature and grammar, beginning with the works of Homer, then Sappho, Alcaeus, Pindar, Alcman, and continuing with more "modern" authors such as Menander, Euripedes, Demosthenes, Callimachus, and Epicharmus. In a peculiar reversal of means and end, it became customary to study a work of literature more for its stylistic features than for its content. An unbelievably complicated system of exercises grew around literary studies, apparently geared to produce skilled pedants capable of picking an author apart down to the bare bones rather than students enriched with a genuine understanding of literary substance. Grammar as a school subject, defined originally as "practical knowledge of the usage of writers of poetry and prose," was first systematized in the first century B.C. by *Dionysius Thrax* of Rhodes. He reportedly authored the first grammar text, in use in schools for several centuries thereafter. It did not take long before the main reason for the teaching of the subject was lost sight of and it was reduced to a dreary business where pupils had to learn the conjugation of verbs and the declension of nouns for purely disciplinary purposes. Some Hellenistic schools in addition offered courses of study in mathematics, geometry, drawing, music (as an adjunct of mathematics), and astronomy (or, more properly, astrology).

Wherever Hellenistic culture held sway, a city opened at least one *gymnasium* or sports stadium. Occasionally municipal authorities extended full financial support; more often *gymnasia* were privately conducted institutions in which gymnastics masters charged fees for teaching young men certain athletic skills. Such schools were to be found in over a hundred urban areas, and in places like Cyzicus, Cyrene, Pellene, Alexandria, Rhodes, and of course Athens many *gymnasia* were in operation. Although some retained traces of their original civic and military purpose, the devotion to athletics was their most characteristic emphasis. The gymnasial school enjoyed a wide popular appeal as the focus for an on-going sports program because it was rightly believed to provide an initiation into the ancestral Greek way of life. Closely associated with the athletic training center was the *ephebic* school. It is uncertain whether formal schools existed as such, but as the *ephebia* lost its reason for being and compulsory military service was transformed into an optional regimen of athletics, ephebic colleges became essentially "finishing schools" for an idle aristocracy trying to preserve an institutionalized anachronism. More time was spent exercising in a *gymnasium* than drilling on the parade ground. However archaic it may have become, it is almost certain that an organized course of activities in connection with ephebic training persisted as late as the third century A.D. It is not entirely misleading to talk about ephebic "colleges" or "schools" in Hellenistic times inasmuch as they added on lessons and lectures in cultural or literary subjects (sometimes hiring an itinerant *grammaticus* to supervise instruction) to the established physical program of the *palaestra* or *gymnasium*.

Quite often institutions of higher learning were direct outgrowths of ephebic-gymnasial schools, with no clear distinctions being drawn to separate secondary from higher education. Or they might be purely private ventures founded by a disciple of some outstanding philosopher or rhetorician to spread the master's teachings. Thus, for example, there appeared a number of *philosophical* enclaves, each offering a program of studies, in Alexandria, Delphi, Beirut, Antioch, Rhodes, and Pergamon. The Mecca for higher education was Athens, where four major philosophical schools were in existence: the Platonic Academy, Aristotle's Lyceum, Epicurus' "Garden," and the "Porch" (*Poecile*) of the Stoics. It seems undeniable that the philosophical schools in later years lost much of the originality and breadth of vision typical of their founders. Their instruction turned inward, their teachings became more esoteric, and they tended to become tight semireligious communities separated from the on-going life of society. When the Greek states lost their political power, ancestral and state-sanctioned theologies lost their persuasive force. Into the vacuum moved religious philosophies in an apparent attempt to fill the need for a new explanation of human destiny and the nature of the universe. The schools they founded, particularly the Epicurean, Stoic, and Cynic ones, became evangelical centers as much as academic institutions in that their graduates went about proselytizing, organizing rituals, and caring for adherents of the sect. Whatever their specific character, philosophical schools ministered to the needs of a relatively small intellectual class.

More broadly based in their popular appeal were the hundreds of *rhetorical* schools distributed throughout the Hellenistic world. Although there were many places where a student could study medicine (in Cnidus, Cos, Smyrna, Ephesus, and Laodicea), or the physical sciences, or some other discipline, anyone aspiring to be called an educated man had to have studied in the school of a rhetor. They were everywhere, in every self-respecting city. A course of studies could last four, five, even eight years or more. At first it seems surprising that so much prestige should have been given the art of oratory long after the social conditions that had produced it in the fifth century were gone. The development of eloquence and oratorical technique had been a function of particular circumstances in the autonomous democratic cities— institutions dead or dying in Hellenistic times. Virtually devoid of political influence, orators continued to practice their art and to attract students. It must be said, however, that the models for good speaking were drawn from such arid and antiseptic topics that a real split developed between oratorical interests and genuine life concerns. Marrou ascribes oratory's popularity to the fact that it provided a common standard, a common denominator of culture for all people, and a system of formal values at the heart of the Greek legacy. Hellenistic *paideia* was essentially a culture of eloquence, reminiscent of Isocrates' claim that learning to speak properly meant learning to think properly, and even to live properly. "In the eyes of the Ancients," Marrou notes, "eloquence had a truly human value transcending any practical applications that might develop as a result of historical circumstances; it was the one means for handing over everything that made man man, the whole cultural heritage that distinguished civilized men from barbarians."[29] This idea made such a powerful appeal that rhetoric or oratory remained at the heart of secular education and culture for over five hundred years.

A third major type of higher education was conducted in endowed "research" centers or "universities" scattered around the Mediterranean. By far the most important scholarly institution was located at Alexandria, where Ptolemy Soter and Demetrius of Paleron established a massive "Temple of the Muses"—a *Museum*—attracting the leading grammarians, physicians, historians, rhetoricians, geometers, astronomers, and philosophers of the third and second centuries. Because it was under royal patronage, the Alexandrian center could provide stipends for scholars, promenade halls for discussions, a vast dining hall, and other luxurious facilities. The scientist-scholars were outfitted with an astronomical observatory, a zoological collection, anatomical exhibits, botanical gardens, and a massive library containing thousands of references.[30] A partial listing of famous men who either worked, taught, or were educated at Alexandria includes Euclid, Apollonius, Eratosthenes, Timoarchus, Herophilus, Erasistratus, and Archimedes. Besides Alexandria, there were combined teaching–research complexes at Ephesus and Smyrna. Between 197 and 159 B.C. the benevolent monarch *Eumenes II* founded a major institution in Pergamon which enjoyed an excellent reputation for work in grammar,

29 Marrou, op. cit., p. 270.

30 "In this populous Egypt of ours," wrote Timon in his *Satirical Poems*, "there is a kind of bird-cage called the Museum where they fatten up any amount of pen-pushers and readers of musty tomes who are never tired of squabbling with each other." Quoted in Marrou, op. cit., p. 260. (Evidently matters have not changed much in higher education over the centuries.)

medicine, art, and literature. In the last century B.C., the city of Rhodes was a major rival to Alexandria and Athens as a scholarly enclave. Among those who were trained at Rhodes were Aeschines, Mark Antony, Pompey, Julius Caesar, Cicero, Brutus, Cassius, and Dionysius Thrax.

In the main, Hellenistic centers of learning were cultural custodians rather than places of intellectual innovation. Far more attention was paid to systematizing, cataloguing, and teaching classical lore than expanding upon it. To the extent that the Hellenistic period can be considered a transitional era in history, the chief mission of its educational agencies can be summarized as one of preservation. Although they succeeded to an admirable degree in linking Greek classicism with the culture of the Romans and later of Christian Europe, it appears in retrospect that the schools of the period may well have contributed to the bookish, pedantic, backward-looking direction most learning had assumed.

THE CONTEMPORARY PROBLEM OF *PAIDEIA*

In all probability it was the publication of C. P. Snow's *The Two Cultures and the Scientific Revolution* in 1960 that inaugurated the current phase of a controversy going back to the ancient Greeks. In *Two Cultures* he argued that the industrial revolution of the early nineteenth century was a sort of technological coup d'état which marked the beginning of the rise of applied science and wrought a cultural revolution. In its aftermath, according to Snow, Western culture has become increasingly polarized between proponents of the humanities, which deal with human nature, and advocates of the sciences and technology, which deal with physical nature. The antagonism between scientists and literary humanists has allegedly grown to the point where they share no common ground, where "a gulf of mutual incomprehension" encourages each party to retreat into intellectual provincialism and a contented specialization. Both sides issue calls for the kind of education best adapted to their own particular needs and interests, the one "liberal" and the other "technical–vocational."

There is ample reason to believe that such a simple dichotomy between two kinds of education is misleading, but it represents a very old distinction, dating back at least as far as Aristotle. Liberal education was that kind of education appropriate for free men of leisure, whereas vocational training was suited only to a lesser breed of men, primarily slaves. As an ideological distinction it was never especially troublesome, discounting the tension between those like Plato and Aristotle, who valued contemplative learning for its own sake, and Isocrates and the Sophists, who insisted on knowledge which could be usefully applied, because as interpreted in each age "liberal studies" *were* considered those essential for pursuing a given profession, whether it was rhetoric, medicine, law, or theology. Three factors brought the old Aristotelian distinction home to roost in modern times: first, the exponential growth of knowledge itself; second, the rise of technology and a consequent increase in the specialization of labor; and third, society's need to train people within formally organized programs of studies for a variety of specific occupations. From the mid-nineteenth century on, the lines of battle were drawn with some groups plumbing for a liberal humanistic kind of education and others arguing for a brand of instruction preparing people to perform particular tasks within society.

Cardinal Newman's *The Idea of a University,* first issued in 1852, laid out the arguments so far as higher education is concerned. He defined a liberal education there as a process of training the intellect, not to some specific trade or profession or to a particular study or science, but for its own sake, "for the perception of its own proper object, and for its own highest culture." Opposed to those demanding an education confined to some particular and narrow end issuing in some definite work which could be "weighed and measured," Newman asked that institutions of higher learning concentrate on training good members of society. The university should labor "at giving enlargement and sobriety to the ideas of the age, at facilitating the exercise of political power, and refining the intercourse of private life," he alleged. Newman stood squarely in the tradition initiated by Athenian philosophers.

Although Newman and others knew what they wanted to produce in the way of an ideally educated man—the individual of moral perception, esthetic sensitivity, and intellectual power—no one was quite sure how to define the *content* of a liberal education. Certain protagonists, among them President Gordon K. Chalmers, writing exactly a century later, claimed that there was a fixed curriculum to be kept in view, including history, mathematics, biology, language, literature, philosophy, and religion.[31] The Harvard University Committee, on the other hand, in its 1945 report *General Education in a Free Society* disagreed. "General education," they claimed (by which they meant something close to Newton's definition of "liberal education"), is distinguished not by the subject matter but in terms of method and outlook, no matter what the field. It could encompass any discipline. General education, the committee decided, indicates that part of a student's whole education which looks to his life as a responsible human being and citizen, as contrasted with "special education" which is concerned with the student's competence in some occupation. The task of modern democracy, the report concluded, is to preserve the ancient ideal of liberal education and to extend it as far as possible to all the members of the community. The aim of instruction should be to prepare people to become experts *both* in some particular vocation or art *and* in the general art of the free man and the citizen. Reminiscent of Whitehead's claim in

---

[31] Gordon Keith Chalmers, *The Republic and the Person* (Chicago: Henry Regnery Company, 1952).

The Aims of Education that "there can be no adequate technical education which is not liberal, and no liberal education which is not technical; that is, there is no education which does not impart both technique and intellectual vision," the Harvard committee ended its report with an optimistic call for education to produce wiser, saner, freer individuals.

The subtle shift from content to process, from defining liberal or general education in terms of consequences instead of substance, is reflective, it can be argued, of a deeper underlying crisis: *for the first time in history, modern man lacks any viable conception of an intellectual culture, a paideia.* Formerly, when each civilization attained a certain degree of self-consciousness and began to define itself, it embodied in a formal curriculum the facts and values regarded as essential for intellectual competence. The knowledge imparted succeeded in equipping men for self-understanding and control over the social order. What was learned was sufficient for assuming positions of leadership in society because being educated meant sharing in a common body of knowledge. By way of contrast, today there are no commonly shared conceptions and values whose possession defines the educated man. For reasons already alluded to, modern society lacks a unifying intellectual ideal. The lack constitutes a crisis because human cultures, like organisms, depend for survival on their internal integration, on a mode of organization which renders a shared body of experience intelligible to all members of society. A common culture is not an abstraction; it is a prerequisite for survival. It remains to examine briefly the causes of cultural disorganization, one symptom of which is the controversy between proponents of liberal versus vocational education.

Western society represents the first civilization to embrace the fundamental postulates of the scientific and technological credo.[32] The scientific culture men experience pervades almost every aspect of collective life. Even the humanities and social sciences scramble to emulate the canons and language of science to avoid any stigma of interiority; the results include humanities which are less humane and social sciences which are less social. Modern philosophies in particular appear infinitely more "scientific" but they scarcely seem any more philosophical for having aped the objectivity and quantifications of the sciences. Furthermore, the divorce between knowledge and values has been completed. In attempting to shape itself by scientific and technological knowledge, making these the foundation of its very existence, society has finally acknowledged its allegiance to means, rather than ends, methodologies rather than objectives. The exponents of the new scientific culture frankly admit that empirical, quantifiable knowledge yields nothing in the way of ends. Other forms of knowing whose stock in trade are "values" are lacking in the characteristics of genuine

[32] See John H. Schaar and Sheldon S. Wolin, "Education and the Technological Society," *The New York Review of Books* (October 9, 1969), p. 4. The following discussion borrows freely from their presentation.

knowledge and, consequently, are no longer shareable as knowledge. All
that is left are subjective preferences, the functional equivalents of values—
feelings and private sensations. It is the nature of technological–scientific
culture to render them so. Small wonder, then, that no cohesive set of values
command allegiance throughout society as a whole.

Secondly, the enormous mass of knowledge accumulated militates against
the establishment of a commonly shared culture.[33] Knowledge today is
empirical, secular, rational, and cumulative. It also grows at such a rate that
old habits, beliefs and institutions as manage to survive are transformed
beyond recognition. It is a truism to note that social change takes place
more quickly today than ever before in history. A concomitant of such
change is that concepts like "the past" or "tradition" are largely meaningless because what has been is not what will be. The future will resemble
the past less and less, or so it seems. Fewer people rather than more come
to understand the direction of change and its practical consequences for
the rest of mankind. As knowledge becomes increasingly refined or specialized, it becomes more esoteric, more removed from the world of ordinary
common experience, less accessible to the many.[34] But, again, if this is so it
means that the specialist dominates contemporary culture. There is no such
thing as an educated man in general.

Traditionally, the effort of a university was to "gather up" the surrounding culture in all of its complexity, to organize and systematize its learning,
and to present it in manageable shape to a group of learners. The end result was the *paideia,* or "culture," which distinguished an educated man.
The schools of Athens initiated this procedure and what they created was
at once a life and body of knowledge different from the "mass culture" of
society outside the academic cloister. The institution's job was essentially
assimilative: taking in new forms of knowledge and adding it to the old.
When universities were criticized, it was mainly for failure to take account
of certain areas of knowledge. In the sixteenth and seventeenth centuries
they had to assimilate modern languages and the new sciences; more recently, the various practical arts have had to be added to the mix. Now,
however, a reversal has taken place in the relationships of a society and a
university. It is society that is being told to adapt to the knowledge created
within the university, especially that developed in the new sciences of social
engineering. And a consequence of this reversal is that the universities are
floundering in disorder. There are no guidelines for performing the new
tasks undertaken by institutions of higher learning in a scientific culture.

One of these tasks, as always, is to promote a liberal education which
teaches values and molds character in the sense lauded by Newman and
the Harvard report. It has been suggested how difficult the undertaking has

33 See Daniel Bell, *The Reforming of General Education* (New York: Columbia
University Press, 1966).
34 Schaar and Wolin, op cit., p. 5.

become, given the complexity of new knowledge and the demotion of values to the status of subjective, private preferences. The problem today is not merely whether values *can* be taught and character molded by education (the ancient inquiry first launched by Socrates and Plato), but *which* values and *what kind* of knowledge need to be fostered. Glib pronouncements about the arts and humanities as indispensable for right-thinking, strong character and catholicity of taste have turned out to be unproved assumptions rather than demonstrable truths. Most educators concede as much while falling back on the claim that the traditional elements of a liberal education are still important for the productive use of leisure time, which may be true enough but a far cry from the older claim that the liberal arts curriculum *defined* a proper education. The point is, presuming the school still must lay the foundation for some general education, it is not known what form the highest liberal culture must assume in contemporary society. Modern man does not know what is appropriate for a society whose knowledge is fragmented, whose cherished beliefs are slipping, and whose values are in disarray.

The symptoms of confusion are evident everywhere, illustrated by the prevalence of survey or "breadth" courses occupying the undergraduate curriculum, and concentrated "specialized" courses for a "major," neither of which can be shown to accomplish that for which it was intended. Uncertainty regarding what an undergraduate education is all about leads to two tendencies: either the typical student is treated as a prospective graduate student and the specialization process is hastened, or he is treated as an intellectual itinerant and exposed to an unorganized smattering of studies, a dreary pastiche called "arts," in a dozen different disciplines. On the one hand, the student narrows his outlook, grows increasingly unable to relate his learning to other fields, and comes to measure his education in terms of mastery of a microspecialized body of knowledge. On the other hand, if left to his own devices, the student is intellectually fragmented, his understanding tends to remain superficial, and his knowledge becomes privatized. Most undergraduates instinctively know from experience that the concept of a general, liberal education is utterly bankrupt. Graduate students have long since forgotten they were ever exposed to any such thing.

Another task of the college or university is preparing competent people to serve society's needs. No Sophist in ancient Athens ever conceived this service so mundanely or offered it so promiscuously as the modern university. Although it is undeniable that the university is a knowledge factory and shapes the face of society, it also has to provide leadership for the technology, the new institutions, the novel modes of social life its influence calls into being. The need for "marketable skills" sets the pace for what is happening in halls of learning, so much so in fact that it seems fair to claim that the average university of today thinks of itself functionally as an appendage to the world of business, industry, and the various professions. Its task, as indicated by the growth of an "array of vocational schools of incredible variety and insignificance," to use Hutchins' harsh description, is to train people to some well-defined occupational role.[35] Critics, harkening back to the nineteenth-century liberal tradition, attack this vocational orientation because it seems to make an intellectual prostitute out of the university: the university purchases public support by pandering to society's desires for job-oriented education. Curricula proliferate endlessly in response to whatever demands are made for the moment. For a while it seemed this arrangement could last indefinitely: schools would create new knowledge, the new learning would rework society's needs, and then the schools would train people to service those needs. The system shows signs of breaking down at last, especially the last part of the equation. Trouble arises because the educational system is unable to keep up with the market and forecast what skills it is going to require five, ten, and twenty years from now. The ideal of education as a means of converting society's members into more efficient instruments of production turns out to be, as Hutchins puts it, a "melancholy instance of the general truth that a doctrine seldom gains acceptance until it is obsolete."[36] The reason for its obsolescence is that a rapidly changing technology means that the more specifically education is directed to jobs, the more ineffective it becomes. Needs change faster than the capacity to satisfy them. Automation, for example, is doing more to transform the concept of marketable skills than any other phenomenon in modern postindustrial society. Even if vocational education is thought of not as job training in specific skills but, as Sidney Hook suggests, as instruction in the basic *principles governing a whole class* of practical skills, the problem remains of bringing this occupational training in line with the larger objectives of a general education.[37] "A complete and generous education," John Milton once observed, "is one that fits a man to perform skillfully, justly and magnanimously, all the acts, both public and private, of peace and war." So far no integration between liberal and vocational education has begun to take place.

Possibly Francis H. Horn is correct when he deplores the "tragedy" of the bitter conflict within higher education over liberal and vocational, or technical and specialized, education as a failure to recognize that both the individual and society need both kinds of training.[38] Society needs the habits of mind, breadth of interest, and enlargement of spirit ascribed to the liberally educated person, *and* it needs the specialized expertise for

35 Robert Maynard Hutchins, *The Conflict in Education in a Democratic Society* (New York: Harper & Row, 1953), p. 98.

36 In his "Are We Educating Our Children for the Wrong Future?" Reprinted in Harold Full, ed., *Controversy in American Education* (New York: Macmillan, 1967), p. 128.

37 Sidney Hook, *Education for Modern Man, A New Perspective*, new edition (New York: Alfred A. Knopf, 1966), Chapter 9.

38 See his "Liberal Education Reexamined," *Harvard Educational Review* (Fall, 1956), pp. 303–314.

solving pressing problems that cannot be overcome in any other way. Having affirmed this need for well-rounded generalists who command a reflective knowledge of the whole range of human experience as well as those adept at applying more limited knowledge in a specific situation, one senses nevertheless that an answer has been achieved too quickly and too easily. It is all very well to say that general and specific education each have a place, but in fact there is no societal consensus on the relative balance to be struck between the two, on what should be included in each, or which is most important.

In a world whose future seems undecipherable, it is no longer possible to fall back on the Sophists' conception of the educated man. Civilization requires men fitted to the demands of practical life but it is not known with any certainty what kind of training best satisfies this need. The ideal of a man trained for nothing in particular but educated generally for everything is no alternative. The philosopher-king of Plato and the speculative intellect of Aristotle fail to yield a negotiable ideal of the educated man for a technological age. This is to say that neither of the basic approaches to higher education inaugurated in Athens can be followed today. Oratorical education, as conceived by Isocrates, was a noble concept—education for eloquence and virtue—but it was made to depend upon a very special conception of the culture of educated men. It was still possible to think of the ideally educated person in fairly simplistic terms. Philosophical education, as fostered in the tradition of Plato, Aristotle, and their successors, presumed an intellectual elite, men of leisure who could afford an education without any termination in the conduct of daily life. The fatal weakness of liberal education as an ideal has been its exclusiveness, its disdain for practicality, and its one-sided involvement in the life of the mind. The task today is to redefine liberalizing education in such a way that it speaks to a world whose humanity has been distorted by contemporary modes of organization and public purpose. The ancient Greek stress on "wholeness" is still relevant, but the wholeness of the educated person in the contemporary age has to depend on an awareness of what technological civilization has done to work, language, literature and art, politics, and man himself. Some will allege, as did the ancient Sophists, that no intellectual synthesis is possible. They may be correct. Perhaps no unifying vision can be successfully translated into a curriculum relevant to modern times. Still, the search for that intellectual touchstone may turn out to be the major issue facing educators today.

EDUCATION AMONG THE EARLY ROMANS

"Among the Greeks," Cicero once observed, "some devote themselves with their whole soul to the poets . . . and to the arts which mold the mind of youth to humanity and virtue. The children of the Romans, on the other hand, are brought up that they may one day be able to be of service to the fatherland, and one must accordingly instruct them in the customs of the state and in the institutions of their ancestors. . . . We must learn those arts whereby we may be of greatest service to the state, for that I hold to be the highest wisdom and virtue."[39] Lagging some two or three centuries behind the Greeks in their cultural development, the Romans finally accepted Hellenic values, but only when their own native ideals were crumbling in the face of the more luxuriant, sophisticated culture to which they had exposed themselves in the process of building an empire. The Roman mind was always more prosaic, practical, and severe than the Greek. It revered law and order, duty to the state, ancestral traditions, and the ideal of self-sufficing dignity. The popular ideal of the Romans was one of manly vigor, an ideal which tended to produce a proud, overbearing, and sometimes cruel and rapacious people. It was this fundamental difference of national temperament or character that explains why the indigenous Roman civilization could never accept fully the Hellenistic outlook. If the Romans ultimately embraced the culture of their subject people it was as a graft on a very homely Roman stock. The fruit of that union was something subtly different from either original Hellenic classicism or its Hellenistic variant.

From Monarchy to Republic

The earliest known inhabitants of the Italian peninsula were an Upper Paleolithic people called *Ligurians,* closely related to the Cro-Magnon tribes of southern France. In the Neolithic period, different people of Mediterranean stock entered the land from North Africa, Spain, and Gaul, followed during the Bronze Age by an invasion of Indo-European immigrants from the lake country north of the Alps. These latter people seem to have been the generic ancestors of all the later Italic groups, possibly related to the original Hellenic invaders of Greece. Between the twelfth and sixth centuries the early Greeks established a foothold on the peninsula, as did a people known as the *Etruscans.* Very little is known about their culture and its origins except that they probably migrated to Italy from somewhere in Asia Minor, they had an alphabet based on the Greek, a well-developed degree of skill in the metallurgical arts, a flourishing trade with the East, and a cruel, gloomy religion. It was the Etruscans who bequeathed to the later Romans the practice of divination, gladiatorial combats, and a knowledge of the basic mechanics underlying subsequent Roman architecture.

The founders of Rome (ca. 1,000 B.C.) were an Italic-Latin people who

---

39 "Passing from Athens to Rome is as passing from poetry to prose, from an artists' picnic to a business house; from a people seeking to make the present beautiful and to enjoy it rationally and nobly, to a people that subordinates present enjoyment to future gain; from a people that lives by reason to people that live by authority." Thomas Davidson, *A History of Education* (New York: Charles Scribner's Sons, 1900), p. 106.

established themselves on the Tiberine hills and plains of *Latium,* south of the Tiber River. By reason of their strategic location it was not long before they had extended their control as far as the holdings of the Volsci to the south, the Sabellians to the east, and the Etruscans to the north. By the sixth century their territory stretched from the shores of the Mediterranean to the slopes of the Apennines. Three hundred years later the Roman state had assumed mastery over the entire peninsula. In the process, primitive tribal life gave way to a monarchical form of government similar to that found in the Greek city-states during their formative stages. Sometime around 510 B.C. tradition relates that an Etruscan king whose family had usurped the royal office years before was overthrown by an aristocratic class seeking a monopoly of power. With the expulsion of *Tarquin the Proud,* Rome became an oligarchy.

The *Early Republic* (509–265 B.C.) was marked by constant warfare. As the Romans fought to expand and then maintain their control they were thrown into violent contact with such peoples as the Volsci and Aequi, and then the invading Gauls. As was to be expected, a militaristic state arose, similar in some respects to Sparta, with a sharply divided class structure. Holding most of the wealth and all of the power were the *patricians,* landowners and aristocrats. Under them were the small farmers, tradesmen, and craftsmen, called *plebians.* Growing polarization of the classes led to a series of plebian revolts, ending with a partial victory for the lower class and symbolized in the creation of the *Laws of the Twelve Tables* (a codification of ancestral law) as well as by passage of the famous *Hortensian Law* (named for the dictator Quintus Hortensius). Neither the Tables nor the Hortensian Law amounted to a charter of liberties for the common masses, but the effect of both was to improve the standing of plebians and to give them some measure of influence in what was otherwise still a despotic, aristocratically dominated oligarchy.

Social and Intellectual Culture

War and agriculture continued as the chief occupations for the bulk of Romans until a comparatively late date. Though they had some trade (evidenced by the existence of a maritime colony at Ostia in the fourth century) and craftsmanship, there were only limited contacts with other peoples beyond the Italian shores. For the most part the Romans were a provincial, insular people with little interest in anything not directly related to subsistence maintenance. They possessed a system of writing as early as the sixth century, but it seems to have been little used except for recording laws, copying treatises, and marking down orations and funerary inscriptions. Reflective of their general temperament, the religion of the Romans was worldly and practical. It had little spiritual or ethical content and the relations of the various gods to man were both external and mechanical, quite akin to a trading arrangement for mutual advantage.

Even as early as the days of the monarchy, Greek influences seem to have been felt on the Latin deities and as a result there is a striking parallel evident between the Greek and Roman pantheons. Jupiter Optimus Maximus, guardian of the Roman state and god of the sky, corresponded to the Greek Zeus; Minerva, patroness of craftsmanship, to Athena; Venus to Aphrodite as goddess of love; Neptune to Poseidon as god of the sea; and so on. When the Romans adopted Greek gods, they simply renamed them and took them much as they found them. Religion among the Romans required no dogmas and few sacraments. Morality was primarily a matter of patriotism, respect for authority and tradition, reverence for one's ancestors, and duty to country and to family.

During the early period the Roman king served as chief intercessor with the gods and appointed all the priests and priestesses for the various cults. Later the appointive power passed into the hands of a College of Priests who nominated a chief priest, or Pontifex Maximus. Although literally hundreds of gods later entered in, throughout their history Romans reserved special attention to three main deities: *Jupiter,* preserver of Roman civil life; *Mars,* the god of war; and *Vesta,* goddess of the family hearth and later protectress of the state. In large measure, the religion of the Roman state was simply the religion of the domestic hearth and family writ large. The father, or *paterfamilias,* served as both priest and magistrate for the family and his power (*patria potestas*) was absolute. It was his responsibility to weld the family together in its worship of the common household gods— the *penates,* or gods of the hearth, and the *lares,* or departed spirits of ancestors, who were regarded as still being concerned with the well-being of their descendants.

The Indigenous Roman Education

The family was the most significant institution in early Roman life and the chief educational agency. In a conception of education having to do mainly with the formation of moral character, schools either would be non-existent or would play a distinctly minor role as compared with the home.[40] There the child received his training in right conduct (*virtus*) and learned the social obligations (*pietas*) he was expected to discharge. General upbringing, or *educatio,* was jointly shared by parents, the severe discipline and magisterial authority of the father supplemented by the milder moral influences of the mother. On the eighth or ninth day after birth, a child

---

[40] Paul Monroe, *A Textbook in the History of Education* (New York: Macmillan, 1933), p. 185. Good references for Roman education abound. See Aubrey Gwynn, *Roman Education from Cicero to Quintilian* (New York: Oxford University Press, 1926); Jerome Carcopino, *Daily Life in Ancient Rome* (New Haven, Conn.: Yale University Press, 1941); A. S. Wilkins, *Roman Education* (New York: Cambridge University Press, 1914); Charles H. Coster, *Late Roman Studies* (Cambridge, Mass.: Harvard University Press, 1968); and E. P. Parks, *The Roman Rhetorical Schools as a Preparation for the Courts Under the Early Empire* (Baltimore: Johns Hopkins Press, 1945).

was formally inspected to see if it should be allowed to live. If it passed inspection, the family held a feast and a religious ceremonial at which the infant was given a name. The "naming day," or *dies nominum,* was a time for joyous celebration and extended festivities. The family at this time officially assumed the sacred task of caring for the child, educating for the future duties of adulthood.

For the next few years responsibility for rearing the child fell mainly to the mother or nurse. The Roman child was taught to be properly rever- ential to the ancestral deities, to obey his parents and all established laws, and to aspire to become a stalwart warrior and loyal citizen. The chief con- stituent of early education was custom and tradition as observed in the daily round of home activities. The father served as exemplar of the human qualities most closely associated in Roman thought with the *vir bonus—pie- tas* (filial duty, patriotism, respect for the gods), *virtus* (courageous conduct and morality), *honestas* (trustworthiness), *constantia* (firmness of character) *gravitas* (seriousness or earnestness), and *prudentia* (practical wisdom and moderation). "Among our ancestors," Pliny the Younger reported centuries later, "instruction was as much a matter of the eye as of the ear. By watch- ing their elders the young people learned what they would soon be doing themselves, and what they in turn would show their successors." Reliance upon direct imitation was the Roman way of fostering character and teach- ing skills.

Upon reaching his sixteenth year, the Roman boy went through a *rite de passage,* reminiscent of old tribal initiations symbolizing entrance into manhood. He exchanged his boyish garb, or *toga praetexta,* for the robe of a full-grown man (*toga virilis*) and had his name formally confirmed. The changing of dress was accompanied by a great domestic and public cere- mony, by religious rites, temple sacrifices, and a family festival. Henceforth, his instruction was turned over to a relative or family friend who agreed to teach the few practical skills essential to effective fighting and farming. Besides some instruction in gymnastics and weaponry, a boy from the privileged class learned to read and write, to study diligently the history of his people (one sure sign of the emerging sense of national identity of the Romans), and especially to learn the Laws of the Twelve Tables. Physical education, intended almost exclusively to prepare for military fitness, was conducted on the public exercise field, or Campus Martius. Either the father or the appointed guardian taught wrestling, running, hunting, horseback riding, and swimming.[41] Aside from the teaching of reading and writing, which was probably conducted in the home, literary education was confined wholly to oral religious hymns, martial chants, and national epics. When Cato the Elder sought to educate his son (at a much later date but in direct

[41] Music and dancing was frowned upon. It was said of someone dancing or singing in public that he must be drunk or mad. If either were taught informally, it was for purely private recreational purposes.

imitation of early practices), Plutarch's report that the father "fashioned his son to virtue—an excellent work" suggests the metaphor of a potter or sculptor rather than a teacher at work. The basic aim of indigenous Roman educational practices before they were influenced by outside cultural forces was moral rather than intellectual, practical rather than literary. It was an education appropriate for a society of soldiers and aristocrats.

There is some uncertainty as to when formal schools first appeared in Roman society. If they existed as early as the fourth or fifth century they were strictly supplemental to education conducted in the home. However, it is likely that *tabernae* (from *tabernis,* meaning "shed" or "booth") where slaves or freedmen taught the rudiments of reading and writing were in existence by the year 305 B.C., if the accounts of Livy and Camillus can be relied upon. If true, the existence of formal educational institutions would help explain the wide diffusion of literacy among the Romans prior to the third century B.C. In any case, their education seems to have remained basically the same as it had since prehistoric times, until a fateful turn of events convulsed Roman society, altered its culture, and decisively changed the character of Rome's educational processes.

THE HELLENIZATION OF ROME

Battle of the Titans

By the middle of the third century B.C. Rome headed a proud and confident state, mistress over all of Italy, its appetite whetted for further conquests. To the south lay *Carthage,* capital of a rich maritime empire stretching from Numidia to the Strait of Gibraltar. The city had originally been a ninth-century Phoenician colony which had grown through the years into a mighty Mediterranean power. Rome launched a war in 264 B.C. against the great rival over territorial claims in Sicily. The opening battle lasted for twenty-three years.[42] Roman victory in the *First Punic War* meant Carthage was compelled to surrender her Sicilian possessions and pay a heavy indemnity. Again, in 218 B.C., the Roman Senate chose to interpret Carthaginian expansion into Spain as a threat to its own interests and issued a declaration of war. The struggle raged on for sixteen years. Italy was ravaged by the armies of Hannibal, a famous Punic commander, but in the end, under the brilliant leadership of a Roman general named Scipio, Rome narrowly escaped defeat in the *Second Punic War* and humbled her great enemy. Carthage was forced to abandon all her possessions except for a narrow strip of surrounding African coastland and to make burdensome reparations. Roman avarice was still not satisfied so long as any vestiges of Carthaginian power remained. Accordingly, in 149 B.C., the Roman Senate

---

[42] The Punic Wars take their name from the Roman word *Poeni,* meaning Phoenician.

dispatched an ultimatum demanding that the Carthaginians abandon their city and move inland. For a nation dependent on sea trade, the demand was tantamount to a death sentence. As the Romans probably hoped, it was refused. The result was the *Third Punic War* (149–146 B.C.), a desperate and barbarous fight to the finish for the two titans. The final assault upon Carthage was carried right into the homes of citizens. The city's inhabitants were slaughtered or sold into slavery and the once magnificent metropolis was razed to the ground. Its land was organized as a Roman province and subdivided into estates for the victorious senators.

By the time of the destruction of Carthage, the Hellenization of Roman life was already well advanced. During the second of the wars, Rome sent expeditionary forces to punish the Syrians and Macedonians, who had entered into a Carthaginian alliance for the control of Egyptian territory (on the assumption that the Romans would be crushed). Instead, Rome conquered most of Asia Minor, subduing Greece in the process, and established a protectorate over Egypt. Thus, before the end of the second century, virtually the entire Mediterranean area had been forced to its knees. But the conquest of the Hellenistic East led inexorably to the Hellenization of Rome. After the fall of Tarentum in 272 B.C. hordes of slaves were brought to Rome. With them, they brought the important elements of Greek learning—philosophy, arts and sciences, rhetoric, grammar—"pouring in as a great flood," as Cicero described it. Military victories had brought on a cultural crisis of major proportions.

A Transitional Phase in Roman Culture

The basic question confronting Romans was whether their native vigor could withstand the mode of life fashioned in the cosmopolitan cities of the East. Were the old virtues of sobriety, gravity, and simplicity to be overwhelmed and replaced by newer ideals imported from abroad? What might be lost if Greek culture was to submerge the ancient Roman way of life and destroy traditional educational ideals? "Listen to me," one of Cicero's characters in the *Republic* is made to say, "as one not wholly ignorant of Greek ways and yet not inclined to prefer them to our own traditions. Thanks to my father, I got a liberal education, and from childhood I have sought eagerly to instruct myself. Nevertheless, experience and home education have done more to make me what I am than books." Therein lay the heart of the problem. The old Roman system of education lacked trained classes of teachers and well-developed schools, in unmistakable contrast with the elaborate institutions flourishing abroad, not to mention the skillful teachers prepared to service them. How could the best of the old Roman culture be preserved?

Meanwhile, the annexation of Greece, Macedonia, and other Asiatic provinces was rapidly turning Rome into a bilingual city. Greek was becoming fashionable as a second language for diplomats and other aristocrats of all ranks. Though Romans disdained their Greek subjects as political inferiors (after all the latter were a conquered people), they instinctively acknowledged Greek cultural superiority. Spurred by the influx of new ideas but determined never to betray their ancestral traditions, however much they were inspired by Greek models, Roman writers set out, belatedly, to draft a native literature. Such authors as Quintus Ennius, Pacuvius, and Naevius of Campania did yeoman's work in building up a body of works reflective of what was most noble in the Roman cultural inheritance.

The sudden growth of a Roman literature, coupled with the availability of Hellenistic resources, made literary instruction available for the first time. In 260 B.C., according to Plutarch, *Spurius Carvilius,* a freedman who had been a domestic tutor to a consul, opened a school and was the first to take fixed fees for his teaching. A former Greek slave, *Livius Andronicus,* who had been captured at Tarentum and set to teaching Greek to his Roman master's children, was emancipated and allowed to remain in Rome. His freedom secured, Livius Antronicus remained for the next sixty-five years (278–213 B.C.) serving as a teacher and writer. Around 250 he published the first Latin translation of Homer's *Odyssey,* followed by translations of various Greek dramas. They were so popular that their study largely replaced that of the Twelve Tables. "Up until that time," says Suetonius, "literature, far from being held in honor, was not even known; in fact, the city, rude and absorbed in war, did not yet give much attention to the liberal arts."

Greek slaves were accorded a hearty welcome in Rome. Wealthy aristocrats even sent envoys to the East to persuade Greek-speaking citizens to come to Rome where they might find ready employment as teachers and tutors. The few remaining Greek settlements in Sicily and elsewhere throughout the Mediterranean were ransacked for cultured men willing to serve as secretaries to the citizens of Rome. As Hellenistically trained ambassadors arrived, they were besieged with offers for permanent jobs. When two representatives from Athens, Carneades and Diogenes the Stoic, appeared on the scene in 155 B.C., people flocked to hear them discourse. Already, as Plutarch says, oratory was widely studied in the city. Polybius, writing around 167 B.C., refers to the large number of teachers residing in the city.[43]

One manifestation of Hellenistic influences was the rise of formal Roman schools. Primary schools—*tabernae* or *ludi* schools—vastly increased in num-

---

[43] In 167 B.C. it is reported that a Stoic philosopher by the name of Crates of Mallos (in Cicilia), a man of great learning, came to Rome as ambassador of King Attalus. He fell into an open sewer, broke his leg, and as a result was compelled to remain for some time. Polybius reports, "During the whole period of his embassy and convalescence, he gave frequent lectures, taking great pains to instruct his hearers, and he has left us an example worthy of imitation."

ber. In addition to learning the Laws of the Twelve Tables, third-century schoolboys learned to read and write (skills more broadly diffused than in previous generations), were introduced to heroic songs, public records, rude fables, and perhaps to expurgated versions of Rome's rough satires which had so long provided the literate with amusement. The masses of people, however, got little or nothing in the way of formal training. No clear differentiation was made between elementary and secondary schools, although some private schoolmasters may have offered some advanced instruction. As a rule, anything taught at a higher level was done within the home by a tutor. In the mid-second century, Polybius was still able to complain with justification that his fellow Romans were guilty of neglecting education as compared with the attention paid to schooling by the Greeks.

The Late Republic

The period from the end of the Punic Wars in 146 B.C. to the accession of Julius Caesar in 46 B.C. was one of the most turbulent in Rome's history. It was a time of class conflicts, assassinations, desperate struggles between rival dictators, constant wars, and repeated insurrections. Slave revolts in 104 B.C. ravaged Sicily and again in 73 B.C., when a slave leader by the name of Spartacus held the consuls at bay for over a year. The incident ended when he was slain in battle and over six thousand of his followers were captured and crucified. A revolt against aristocratic power by Tiberius and then Gaius Gracchus renewed a continuing struggle for power by the underprivileged orders. The chief significance of the Gracchan affairs was that it illustrated how desperate matters had become within Roman society. The Senate's resort to violence in subduing the revolt set an example of appeal to brute force which demagogues of later years were quick to follow. The declining years of the Republic also brought a succession of foreign wars— against Jugurtha, king of Numidia in northern Africa, followed by campaigns waged against the always troublesome Gauls and then against Mithradates of Pontus to forestall his territorial amibtions in Asia Minor.

Those who triumphed in battle often found they could make political capital out of success when it became common for a returning hero to be elected to consulship. In this way outstanding leaders like Marius and Sulla won grandiose honors for themselves. Unfortunately political faction sometimes degenerated into armed combat as rival commanders fought for power. Thus, for example, the general Pompey, who had won fame as the conqueror of Syria and Palestine, collided headlong with the ambitions of Julius Caesar, who had devoted his energies to a war against the Gauls. In 52 B.C. Pompey was elected sole consul and Caesar was branded an enemy of the state. With the famous pronouncement, "The die is cast," Caesar responded by crossing the Rubicon (49 B.C.) and began a march on Rome. Pompey hastily fled to the East, hoping to organize an army to help him regain control of Italy. The next year the two contending forces met at

Pharsalus in Thessaly. Pompey's forces were routed, and he fled to Egypt, only to meet death shortly thereafter at the hands of agents loyal to Caesar's faction.

After remaining for a season at the court of Cleopatra in Egypt, Caesar returned to Rome, where he was proclaimed dictator for life (46–45 B.C.). He might have done better to stay with his young paramour. The next year he was murdered by a group of conspirators headed by Brutus and Cassius, representing the old aristocracy grown fearful of absolute despotism.

The high tide of Hellenism reached its peak during Rome's last two centuries of republican rule. The earlier movement to create a native literature proceeded apace with the publication of comedies by Plautus and Terence, the lyric poetry of Catullus, the histories of Sallust, and the orations of Cicero. Philosophical influences new to Romans—Epicureanism, popularized primarily by Lucretius in the first century, and earlier, Stoicism, brought in around 140 B.C. by Panaetius of Rhodes—helped transform Latin intellectual life. As a matter of historical fact, that life was no longer specifically Roman at all after 140 B.C.; it was Hellenistic, influenced and colored by the Roman character. The old gods now paled in light of frenetic mystery cults gaining headway steadily, particularly Persian Mithraism, which was daily gaining converts from the ranks of the legions, and the orgiastic worship of the Phrygian Great Mother. Greek language and literature, logic, the study of grammar, rhetoric, art, music, geometry—all were regarded as indispensable for the educated man. The scheme of knowledge cited by Varro (born 116 B.C) represented a wholly Hellenistic conception, embracing grammar, logic, dialectic, rhetoric, geometry, arithmetic, astronomy, music, medicine, and architecture. Cicero (born 106 B.C.) gives evidence that at the beginning of his life the ancient education had been wholly overthrown.

The Native Reaction

All the while Hellenistic culture was making inroads into Roman society, conservatives were raising a chorus of protest. They inveighed against the pretensions of the *nouveau riche*, fattened by war profits, and lamented the decline of such old-fashioned ideals as self-discipline and service to the state. The "good old days" of an earlier period were romanticized and held up as an example of how the good society should be ordered.[44] Traditionalists like *Cato the Elder* (the Censor) assailed the influx of new ways as positively subversive: "Believe me," he fumed, "the Greeks are a good-for-

[44] One widely disseminated lament described Rome's native period as follows: "Then none were for the party; but all were for the state; and the rich man loved the poor; and the poor man loved the great. Then lands were fairly portioned, and spoils were fairly sold; For the Romans were like brothers; in the brave days of old."

nothing and unimprovable race. If they disseminate their literature among us, it will destroy everything." Cato's book *Of Liberal Education,* called the first Roman work on pedagogy by Quintilian, was intended to show what a *vir bonus* ought to be—orator, physician, husbandman, warrior, and jurist. Cato strove desperately to set an example to his countrymen in restoring the homely virtues of the past, and by raising his son in the archaic manner. Yet even he, despite his advice "Greek literature should be looked into but not thoroughly studied," had to compromise. There was something as pathetic as it was useless in his self-conscious attempt to turn back social change.

The tides of the times were seemingly irresistible; the gates had been open to foreign influence and the flood swept away most of the established mores and practices of the old Roman education. It was a time when neither governmental edicts nor reactional polemics availed to stem Hellenic innovations. As Suetonius relates, "Rhetoric, as well as grammar, was not introduced among us till a late period, and with . . . difficulty, inasmuch as we find that, at times, the practice of it was even prohibited." In 173 B.C. two Epicurean teachers were banished from Rome by a government ever distrustful of subversive doctrines. Then, in 161, the Senate passed an edict against all rhetoricians:

> It is reported to us that certain persons have instituted a new kind of discipline; that our youth resort to their schools; that they have assumed the title of Latin rhetoricians; and that young men waste their time there, whole days together. Our ancestors have ordained what instruction it is fitting their children should receive, and what schools they should attend. These novelties, contrary to the customs and instructions of our ancestors, we neither approve nor do they appear to us good. Wherefore it appears to be our duty that we should notify our judgment both to those who keep such schools and those who are in the practice of frequenting them, that they meet our disapprobation.

But as Suetonius concludes, in a classic understatement: "However, by slow degrees, rhetoric manifested itself to be a useful and honorable study, and many persons devoted themselves to it both as a means of defense and of acquiring reputation."

Seventy years later the last of a series of futile attempts was made to outlaw Greek schools. All of them failed to arrest the growth of Hellenistic culture and its institutionalized forms for education. Women freely engaged tutors to learn Greek. Wealthy Romans competed with one another to acquire manuscripts and teacher-slaves. Whole libraries were imported. The ideally educated man was one fit for political life through forensic skill; he would henceforth be trained not by precept and example, but in an institutionalized school.

LATE ROMAN EDUCATION

The Developed Roman School System

The line that Hellenistic studies took in Rome was grammatical and philological, rather than literary and esthetic; and in higher schools it was more rhetorical than philosophical. From around the middle of the second century B.C. onward there was a regular course of formal instruction, having "culture" or *humanitas* (the nearest Roman equivalent to Greek *paideia*) for its object, but always in subservience to oratory for the uses of public life. Although the more intellectually ambitious occupied themselves with philosophy, the intent seems to have been to gather subject material for oratorical purposes. The study of rhetoric, as accepted by the Romans, was pursued mainly as a weapon for offense and defense in the public forum or the Senate. They pretty much ignored purely speculative philosophies and the abstract scientific studies in favor at Athens, Alexandria, or Antioch. The curriculum was arranged, roughly, in three stages: the primary, consisting of reading and writing of Greek and Latin; the secondary, with instruction in grammar, philology, and literature; and finally a higher level, where an elaborate, technical study of rhetoric, dialectic, and philosophy was pursued. To the end, the dominant characteristic of Roman learning was prosaic and practical; "application" always took precedence over *humanitas.*

The basic school structure of the Hellenistic Greeks was imported intact and grafted onto the system already functioning at the primary level. "Grammar" schools at the second level may have existed as early as the third century B.C.; by the first century B.C. it is certain that both Latin and Greek language institutions existed side by side and were attracting increasing numbers of students. And despite the official disapproval already noted, systematic teaching of literature, logic, and oratory was common among the aristocratic classes by the middle of the second century.[45] Beside the Greek school arrangement, the practice was borrowed of handing over personal superintendence of boys among the wealthier classes to *pedagogi* (also called *comites* or *custodes*). The Roman pedagogue did not instruct his charge but acted as a guardian, attendant, and moral censor. Where possible, Greek slaves or freemen fluent in conversational Greek were selected for the job. Generally the Romans exercised far greater care in picking people of high moral character to be pedagogues than did the Greeks.[46]

---

[45] So far as is known, the first formal instruction in *Latin* oratory *by a Roman* was given around 128 B.C. by Lucius Aelius Praeconinus.

[46] The pedagogue was an important participant in the typical Roman learning situation. Libanius refers to him as the schoolmaster's helper in making the boy finish his homework: "What the boy gets from the teacher it is the pedagogue's job to preserve

Teachers provided their own school facilities. The *tabernae* were crude sheds or booths erected against a wall; if school was not held in such rude structures, it was held in the open air. Children sat on the floor if the school possessed one, or if in the street, on pavement stones. Higher schools were commonly held in more spacious quarters attached to larger buildings and provided with benches for students and a high seat (*cathedra*) for the master. Sometimes schoolrooms (*pergulae magistrales*) were located under the portico or veranda of some great mansion, open and accessible to all.

Up to the seventh year, the Roman child remained at home under the protection of nurse, mother, and pedagogue. Elementary education was then begun in the home or in a *ludus* school, presided over by a *ludimagister* or *litterator* (teacher of letters), where he learned to read and write.[47] Writing was taught by copying words set out by the teacher or by tracing letters inscribed on waxen tablets. Sometimes grooves were carved in wooden slabs and the instructor would painstakingly guide the student's hand. Simple calculations (with the Roman notation system of course) were learned by counting fingers or with small pebbles brought to school specifically for that purpose. The details of the reading curriculum are not known, although the main text was probably a Latin version of the *Odyssey* and (up until 80 B.C.) a copy of the Twelve Tables. In view of developments already cited, it can be said that the native Roman elementary school was never allowed to develop its own unique form; before it could do so it was supplanted by the Greek model. Although *ludus* schools were prevalent in Rome well before the first century, it required three hundred years longer at a minimum before they were spread throughout the Roman empire.

At the age of twelve, a student passed on to the school of the *grammaticus*. Two parallel institutions existed—one for the study of Greek language and literature, the other for the study of native Latin and its Roman literature. An educated individual would be conversant with both traditions. The former was a literal copy of late Greek schools found everywhere in the East; the latter, probably dating to the time of Andronicus' translation of Homer, represented a partial effort to safeguard Roman traditions. They may have been attended simultaneously, or, as some accounts have it, the practice was to attend the Greek grammar school first and then the Latin. The course of instruction carried its pupils until age sixteen. The purpose of the "grammar" school was twofold: to provide a modicum of general learning for everyone attending and to offer preparatory work for higher "professional" studies. Around 140 B.C. reliable information indi-

---

for him, by urging him on, shouting at him, fetching out the strap, wielding the stick, and, by forcing him to do his work, striving to drive into his memory the lesson he has heard." Quoted in Castle, op. cit., p. 132.

47 *Ludus* originally meant "place of exercise or play." It was later reserved for the lower school, whereas *schola,* from the Greek word for leisure, designated a higher school for oratory or philosophical discussion.

cates that over twenty celebrated schools of the *grammatici* were in operation in the city of Rome.

In the Greek school, teaching centered around Homer, Aesop, and other classical writings, portions of which had to be learned by heart. Further, thorough drill in grammar and more practice in writing was a feature of the daily routine. At the secondary level, writing was done with a sharp-pointed stylus on wax tablets and also on parchment or papyrus with pen and ink. In the Roman school the literature course studies emphasized Virgil and Horace, Sallust, Cicero, and Terence. Beginning with Varro's Latin translation of Dionysius' grammatical text, instruction in grammar employed works by such writers as Donatus, Servius, Priscian, and, in the first century, a Latin grammar authored by Remmius Palaemon. Latin rhetoric (adapted from the Greek) was accorded an important standing in the curriculum, with some attention paid to geography, music, elementary mathematics, geometry, and astronomy. After Cicero's time the Greek grammar school began to decline somewhat as the authentic Latin literature came to occupy more and more of the student's time. Common to both schools so long as they endured side by side was strict application to dictation and spelling, the learning of short tales and fables, exercises in composition and the paraphrasing of passages from selected authors, grammatical exercises on short sentences (*sententiae*) culled from the literature, and verse writing. Oral dissertations and lessons in dictation formed other important parts of the curriculum.

The opportunity to study at a grammar school was reserved exclusively for boys. If and when girls received instruction, the education was conducted within the privacy of the home. Judging from accounts left of daily life at school, the general picture is not altogether pleasant. School hours were long, beginning at daybreak and lasting until past sundown. Pupils spoke their lessons aloud, a convention which compelled the schoolmaster to outshout them in order to be heard. Martial has an amusing epigram in which he lambasts the "despised pedant" who has roused him from sleep by creating a disturbance. "Your direful threats and lashes stun my ear!" he complains. Ausonius too speaks of the school resounding with blows and the cries of children in pain. Evidently Martial's derisive reference to "melancholy rods, sceptres of pedagogues" was well understood by his audience. The cane (*ferula*) and the whip (*scutica*) seem to have been standard equipment in the classroom, so much so that the popular phrase "to withdraw the hand from the rod" was a term for leaving school.[48]

As in Greece, the teacher's position in society was extremely humble. Virtually every *ludimagister* lived in abject poverty and the situation of a *grammaticus* was not much better. Only the teacher of rhetoric in a higher school, corresponding to a modern college professor, received very much

[48] Castle, op. cit., pp. 130–131.

respect from society. In rare cases, and then only in imperial times, lower school teachers' salaries were standardized by government law and paid out of the public treasury. More often, teachers subsisted on voluntary payments, or *honoraria*, rather than fixed fees. In short, they had to take what they could get. One result, according to a first-century A.D. complaint from Petronius, was that some teachers gave up flogging and bawlings in hopes of winning their students' favor. Petronius was scornful of teachers, who, like common fishermen, baited their hooks with what they knew little fishes would eat.

During late Republican times, the school of the *rhetor* appeared, providing a course of instruction lasting two to five years. Commentators frequently note that the higher the Roman school, the more profoundly influenced it was in content and organization by the original Greek example. As in Hellenistic Greece, those who had won repute for themselves as skilled orators opened private academies and attracted students desiring to learn the art of rhetoric.[49] A favored few rhetoricians had comfortable buildings in which to lecture and study, had their salaries paid by the state, and some rose to high appointments within the government. The organization of studies in a rhetorical school and the teaching methods employed were direct imitations of schools in the East. In a half-hearted sort of way, some aristocratic Romans enrolled in rhetorical schools with the avowed aim of acquiring *humanitas,* of becoming cultured gentlemen. But that rationale ran directly counter to the deeply ingrained Roman concern for practicality, for narrow utilitarianism. Most students frankly admitted that they were engaged in purely professional studies and hoped to profit directly from the instruction. Theoretical lectures on the foundations of eloquence, thesis writing, speech making, disputations, and public declamations were aimed ultimately at turning out skilled orators for the market place.

At first those who wished further training beyond that given in a rhetor's school had to go abroad to one of the higher "university" centers at Athens, Alexandria, Antioch, Tarsus, Mitylene, or Rhodes. Many did so to receive philosophical training, which was not readily available in Rome. Later, under Vespasian, a library and *Athenaeum* similar to the *Museum* at Alexandria, although decidedly inferior to it, made advanced rhetorical training more accessible. By endowing chairs of rhetoric and exempting rhetoricians from important civil responsibilities, Vespasian enabled an intellectual class to get its education on "home territory." Nonetheless, for reasons of prestige the custom of studying abroad enjoyed continuing popularity well into the second and third century A.D.

In one major respect Roman education was superior to Greek despite the

---

[49] One cannot help wondering whether the teaching of journalism, public speaking, writing, and so forth today might not be better taught if supervised only by those having a claim to distinction in the field and practical experience at their trade.

narrower curriculum and more restricted conception of its function. The Romans achieved a thorough if pedantic mastery over the subject matter. A certain mechanical system of organizing instruction was devised, reflective perhaps of the typical Roman talent for system and order. The arrangement of studies was systematic and so were the exercises taught to generations of youth by the schoolmaster. Lessons in rhetoric at the secondary level, for example, were astoundingly thorough. Whatever they lacked in imagination they made up in organization. Although the Romans may have lacked the Greek characteristics of versatility and originality, they were masters of form and structure. It has been suggested that it was the Roman passion for system that enabled their model rather than the Greek model to be followed in later periods of educational development from the end of the medieval period down to the nineteenth century.[50]

Education During the Principate and Empire

The time of the *Principate,* dating from the victory of Octavian over Mark Antony and Lepidus and his accession to power in 27 B.C. to the reign of Diocletian in 284 A.D., encompasses a long and lurid chapter in the history of Rome. From a cultural standpoint it was an age that outshone all others. During the Principate Rome built her greatest monuments, including the Pantheon and the Colosseum. There was a new awakening of scientific interest, the growth of a distinctive art, and a period of unparalleled literary activity manifest in the works of great authors such as Seneca, Ovid, Livy, Petronius, Apuleius, Juvenal, and Tacitus. Philosophically, the Stoic writings of Epictetus, Seneca, and Marcus Aurelius invite comparison with the best produced in Greek after the fourth century B.C. But it was also, paradoxically, a time of slow but definite moral decay. A kind of popular passion for cruelty and crimes of violence grew rampant. Imperial orgies, bisexual and homosexual, became not only exceedingly common but even fashionable.[51]

The Principate was followed by a period conventionally labeled the *Empire* (284–476 A.D.). With the final establishment of a despotic state and the degradation of intellect by mystical and otherworldly religions, creative talent was virtually destroyed. Aside from neo-Platonism, interest in philosophy died out almost completely. The few literary works produced were characterized by an overemphasis upon form and a neglect of content. A barren and artificial rhetoric took the place of the study of the classics in the schools, whereas science went into a decline from which it failed to recover for over a millennium. An account of educational developments

50 Castle, op. cit., pp. 129 ff.

51 There were 32,000 prostitutes in the city of Rome alone during the reign of Trajan, according to some estimates. Emperor Tiberius Claudius Nero Caesar, who reigned between 54 and 68 A.D., was fond of being carried in procession through the streets in a cage. He would cover himself with skins and take the part of a lioness while a robust lover took the part of a male lion.

throughout the long epoch of Rome's decline and fall can mention only the most general trends within the schools.

As the Roman school system spread throughout the empire, imperial control increased. Teachers in private schools came to be paid from public tax funds collected by municipal authorities in the various towns, usually because the emperors found it advantageous to allocate monies in support of organized training. Antoninus Pius set the pattern for state control by obliging all cities to pay salaries to teachers in the lower schools. Emperor Hadrian helped to rejuvenate Athens as a center of higher learning by granting it official imperial recognition. Later, Marcus Aurelius endowed several chairs of rhetoric in Athens. By the end of the second century A.D., centralized support of schools at every level was virtually universal.

Alexander Severus in the third century A.D. established a new center of advanced studies in Rome. Gratian extended patronage to the schools in outlying provinces, mainly Gaul, as did Theodosius for the higher schools of Constantinople. By the fourth century, even though Roman rule was coming apart at the seams, schools continued to function everywhere. Augustine reports that the attacks of barbarians from the north and internal revolutions at home did nothing to lessen the continued operation of formal schools in existence everywhere the Roman legions had established dominion. The schools of the rhetoricians, he tells us, were "alive with the din of students throughout the whole world" and so they continued until they crumbled along with the once mighty empire itself.

The waning centuries of Roman rule have been examined too often to bear lengthy examination again. It is a melancholy story of more class conflict, political assassinations, domestic insurrections, and turbulent wars abroad. Even as early as Republican times signs of political instability were common. The violence of political intrigues at home were matched only by the ferocity of military exercises on the frontiers. The reign of Caesar Augustus in the first century A.D., although regarded as a time of peace and prosperity, was born of autocratic ruthlessness; Caesar's death only brought a return to upheaval, unrest, and social chaos. The third and fourth centuries witnessed the final overthrow of any form of republican government and every pretense of constitutional rule was cast aside in favor of undisguised autocracy. Diocletian, Julian, Constantine, Theodosius, and all who followed assumed absolute despotic powers. Even the celebrated *pax romana*, or "Roman peace," of the second century only temporarily arrested the gradual decay of Roman government and the seemingly inevitable collapse of social, political, and economic institutions everywhere. The peasant classes had been obliterated by the great landed estates. Provincial governments were becoming ever more inefficient. Barbarian mercenaries were making heavy inroads into the armed services and border disputes were common. Political fragmentation was accompanied by general dislocations in every aspect of life. Public morality declined and private vice and political corruption became almost socially acceptable. Christians were forever causing disturbances. The Visigoths, the Marcomanni, and the Teutons were pillaging frontier cities and growing bolder with every passing decade.

At the end of the fourth century the situation had grown desperate. Rome was sacked, first by the Visigoths and then by the Vandals. The Suevi were plundering Roman provinces with impunity. The barbarian king Odovacar deposed Emperor Romulus Augustalus and proclaimed himself ruler of Rome. By 493 an Ostrogothic king sat on the Roman throne. A dreary spectacle of ignorance, lawlessness, and disorder prevailed throughout the civilized world. The end of an era (a process rather than an event, as Gibbon noted) was at hand.

These shifts were reflected in the schools. Before its eventual disappearance and replacement by tutorial instruction once again, the *ludus* school turned exclusively to literary education, with none of the concern for developing a well-rounded individual so characteristic of its Greek counterpart. Greek grammar schools regained popularity over their Latin equivalents, perhaps because Latin grammar and literature never achieved the same degree of development as did the Greek, also perhaps because learning a foreign rather than a domestic literature seemed intellectually more prestigious. In the latter stage of its career, the Roman grammar school not only constricted its curriculum but hopelessly diluted its content.

The rhetorical schools fared no better. In a sense their usefulness was limited even before they began to function, because authoritarian regimes at Rome permitted scant opportunity for the exercise of political oratory to some tangible end. Forensic skill had long since ceased to play an important role in public life by the time the schools of the rhetors had become well established. Consequently there appeared the paradox of more and more schools to help preserve declining cultural values growing less relevant to the changing conditions of an empire moving toward a final collapse. The old Hellenistic ideal had been a *paideia*, or culture founded on the literature and philosophy of Greek classicism. The historical mission of the Romans was not to create an entirely new civilization but to add elements to that Hellenistic culture and to ensure its spread through the known world. Roman schools had become the instruments for the propagation of this culture; furthermore, they helped to shape learning in molds that could survive the centuries ahead. But the price paid for survival was high.

In the first place, the Hellenistic achievement was debased as important elements dropped out. The Roman translation was too much influenced by excessive practicality or utilitarianism. The Latin mind had little patience for disinterested research; Romans failed to understand its worth or appreciate its attractions. Speculative philosophy, with the exceptions of neo-Platonism in a limited form and a derivative brand of Stoicism, never gained an appreciative foothold in the West. At most, it served as replacement for decayed tradition and lost gods. Real philosophical activity flourished only in the East under the stimulating influence of Oriental thought. Very little was done with historical research aside from imperial chronologies and some biographies of notable political leaders. The Romans were unattracted to Hellenistic science except where applied technology could be utilized in the construction of public works. Their concerns extended only to the kind of knowledge that promised some immediate gain; the rest was ignored or shunted aside.

It has been observed often that the American temperament sometimes manifests the same antipathy to theory and disinterested learning typical of the Romans. There is a popular inclination to couple "theory" with empty speculation and impractical fancy. Whatever appears theoretical smacks of the ivory tower: it is greeted with indifference or even outright contempt. There is a long tradition going back to America's formative years when only practical results counted, not theories. American folk heroes were men of action rather than of intellect. They got the job done without recourse to obtuse theoretical considerations and, indeed, sometimes found "book-larnin'" a hindrance rather than a help. The "overeducated fool" is a common tragicomic stereotype in modern culture. Some historians account for the American distrust of learning for its own sake as a legacy from the time when colonists found themselves without a dependable body of theory to deal with the harsh conditions of the wilderness. The old social-class theory of work broke down because gentlemen suddenly found they had to till the fields and otherwise engage in menial labor in order to survive. Old precedents were shattered. Warfare against hostile natives had to be conducted in drastically different ways. The classless democratic ideal which repudiated the elitist, aristocratic monopoly of schooling also tended to reject all the activities of the upper classes, including theorizing. Whatever the reasons, a strong anti-intellectualist bias against theory has been part and parcel of the American ethos. It is manifest in the often repeated demand that education be narrowly "practical," that scholars engage themselves only in research that can be shown to have some short-range application, and that schooling must be measured primarily in terms of its monetary value. The paucity of Roman intellectual achievements could serve as a warning against carrying this practicality too far.

A second consequence of the Roman transmission of Hellenism was the progressive paralysis of the schools. It has been shown how the formal school system deleted more than it added to the Greek inheritance. Demands made upon the schools possibly proved to be too much. As family traditions were weakened and the aristocracy grew more unstable, the task of preserving Roman culture fell to formal education. Schools were viewed as the last remaining guardians of tradition, which helps explain why they were supported so lavishly. Old ideals were venerated as the bulwark against Christianity and barbarism alike. However, and this was the supreme irony for a people who took pride in their practical common sense, the schools ended up providing an education almost totally divorced from life. It was, Seneca complained, education "for the classroom, not for life." Mental agility, not training for what one ought to do, became the Romans' educational stock in trade. No informing ideal of moral excellence higher than the verbiage of rhetorical display (based on artificial and ornate models at that) shaped instruction. "An educational system with verbal eloquence as its highest ideal was condemned to decay and death by its remoteness from the realities of life and by its own inner barrenness."[52] Worse yet, in the final analysis Roman schools failed to achieve lesser goals. As Jerome Carcopino has pointed out in his instructive work *Daily Life in Ancient Rome,* because Roman culture depended so heavily on the language and literature of another people and its education on analytical studies like grammar, the sequence of learning was far removed from the ordinary interests of students. School life must have seemed especially remote for pupils in the lower schools. They left schools with a few pedestrian notions at best, ideas of little social significance painfully acquired through endless recitations before an unforgiving schoolmaster. In the fourth century military leaders could not even take it for granted that their army recruits (including those from the upper classes) would be literate.

On balance, however, despite the ultimate failure of Roman schools, the culture they had helped preserve for centuries continued to help shape the subsequent direction taken by Western civilization. Roman law, for example, was practiced even during the darkest days of the early Middle Ages and was ultimately made the foundation of most common law throughout Europe. Late Roman writers excelled in synthesizing and boiling down knowledge into simple outlines; their digests and textbooks preserved more of the elements of Hellenistic learning than would have otherwise been possible. Although these efforts were not particularly creative contributions to human culture, the works produced undeniably provided the vessels in which the remnants of the classical age could be carried conveniently through the chaotic centuries that lay ahead.

ROMAN IMAGES OF THE ELOQUENT MAN

The Greeks, from the earliest days of their history, prized eloquence as an important mark of the ideally educated man. From the time of Achilles, "skilled in words," through the Periclean age, which placed so much esteem on rhetoric, on down through the heyday of the Sophists, and continuing into the Hellenistic period through the legacy of Isocrates, Greek thought

---

[52] Boyd, op. cit., p. 82.

lauded the man who effectively employed the art of public address. Indeed, the ideal of verbal eloquence was fundamental to the Hellenistic concept of general culture, or *paideia*. When the Romans adapted Hellenistic culture as their own, they too exalted rhetorical skill as a distinguishing characteristic of the educated individual. The two most important spokesmen for Roman thought on culture and education were Cicero and Quintilian.

Cicero

Marcus Tullius *Cicero* (ca. 106–43 B.C.) was born the son of a Roman nobleman and received his training in law and rhetoric at Rome. He served in the army at age seventeen, took up a practice in court law during his mid-twenties, but was then forced into semiretirement for two years because of poor health. During his convalescence he traveled abroad, studying in Rhodes and Athens before returning to Rome to resume his law career. His many writings include *Partitiones Oratoriae, Hortensius, De Officiis, Brutus, De Inventione,* and his most famous work, *De Oratore (The Orator)*, published when he was approximately fifty years of age. His polished use of Latin helped to build his reputation as the city's foremost writer and orator of the time. Implicated in the plot to kill Julius Caesar, he tried to flee from the city but adverse winds forced his ship back to port. He returned to his villa resigned to his fate, saying, "Let me die in the country which I have often saved." Years later Augustus Caesar, who sanctioned his murder at the hands of Brutus' agents, could nonetheless say of Cicero that he was "a great man and a lover of his country."

Cicero was uncompromising in his allegiance to the ancient Roman ideal of patriotism and loyalty to the nation, a moral ideal tracing back to the ancient city-state and which insisted on the subordination of the individual to the country's interest as supreme standard for virtue. "And if our country has our love," he proclaimed, "as it ought to have in the highest degree— our country, I say . . . is the seat of virtue, empire, and dignity." In *De Oratore* Cicero set himself the task of laying down the principles for oratory upon which the education of a citizen should depend. The good society, he avowed, depends upon the fortification of public life by men educated to high moral character, trained intelligence, and an abiding loyalty to the service of the state. Society's leaders should be raised in such a way that they become good men, pure in mind and strong in body, filled with a clear sense of justice and public virtue. In order that they should govern properly, literary instruction (*institutio*) and personal development (*educatio*) should be supplemented by extensive practical experience. The transcendent ideal for Cicero was not merely *humanitas,* or "culture," but effective action in actual life. The program of studies he was advocating, he insisted repeatedly, aimed toward usefulness in public and private endeavors, not just for the sake of knowledge alone.

For the materials of an ideal education, Cicero drew upon what he thought was best in Hellenistic learning as well as elements from his native Roman tradition, trying to achieve a harmonious synthesis of the two. "We must turn to our fellow countrymen for virtue," he wrote, "and for our culture to the Greeks." Greek language and literature would have to be the cornerstones of instruction, at least until such time as Latin had developed further as a medium of communication and had given birth to a wider, richer literature. Society's future leaders should be schooled in a broad array of liberal disciplines, in "every branch of useful knowledge," in order to bring to bear on the conduct of public affairs a rich understanding of humanity and its achievements. Upon completing the curriculum of a *ludus* school, the prospective orator should study literature, mathematics, music, astronomy, rhetoric, logic, grammar, history, and civil law. Taken together, such subjects would constitute a firm foundation upon which higher instruction could proceed. "No man can be an orator possessed of every laudable achievement unless he knows everything important and all liberal arts." The student who had received a good secondary education would have studied the poets, learned history, had the meaning of words explained to him and become skilled in the "correct accent and delivery" of speeches. He would be ready for specifically professional training.

Cicero believed that higher oratorical education had six main elements. In addition to rhetoric, a student should be given lengthy instruction in literature (and grammar), history, law, and philosophy, followed by a period of experience writing, composing speeches, working in the courts, and generally absorbing the lessons of public life. The "cultured orator" would be well versed in the intricacies of law, familiar with classical literature, an avid student of the past. "To be ignorant of what happened before you were born," Cicero argued in a comment worth repeating, "is to live the life of a child forever. For what is man's life, unless woven into the life of our ancestors by the memory of past deeds?" Furthermore, a knowledge of history would be highly useful to the orator as a repository of allusions and references when making an address.

He took the same pragmatic attitude toward philosophy, viewing it and rhetoric as complementary rather than antagonistic disciplines. In order to secure "wisdom united with eloquence" an orator should be conversant with the great thoughts of Plato, Aristotle, the Sophists and most of their lesser successors. Knowledge without the ability to present it would be worse than useless, Cicero observed, but oratory without philosophical understanding would become shallow and ineffective. The orator's task should be "to set forth powerfully and attractively the very same topics which they [the philosophers] discuss in tame and bloodless phraseology." Because philosophers had withdrawn themselves from the duties of civil life, he alleged, the orator should bring their thoughts out into the market place and make them effective in the conduct of human affairs. Accordingly, the teaching of rhetoric should be based on important issues of public significance rather than the purely "literary" and artificial topics offered by rhetoricians for whom oratory had become an end in itself. This ideal— eloquent oratory wedded to philosophical wisdom—if pursued farther might well have effected a reconciliation in the opposing stands of Plato and Isocrates. Unfortunately no such synthesis was ever achieved.

Theory aside, Roman educational practice steadily manifested a retreat from the high ideals laid down by Cicero. A century later, by the time of the historian *Tacitus* (50–117 A.D.), it was necessary to recall how Cicero had insisted on a close association of formal schooling and social life. Looking at the apparent decline of learning in his own age, Tacitus ascribed it to "the laziness of the young, the carelessness of parents, the ignorance of the teacher, and the neglect of ancient discipline." What was taught within the schools in the name of oratory, he complained, was merely cheap mental gymnastics, more harmful than beneficial because, as he phrased it, "the subjects are remote from reality" and the topics used for declamation trivial, though they are "dwelt upon in grand language." Already the Ciceronian educational ideal was dying.

Quintilian

Tacitus' younger contemporary and Rome's most influential educational thinker was Marcus Fabius Quintilianus (35–95 A.D.), or *Quintilian,* as he is known to history. He was born in the town of Callagurris in northern Spain, son of a noted rhetorician. At age fifteen or sixteen he was drawn to Rome for his education, where he enjoyed a close association with a friend by the name of Domitius Afer, probably a tutor-guardian appointed by Quintilian's father. The boy studied oratory under Palaemon, a famous Roman rhetor, and became an ardent admirer of Cicero. Following Afer's death in 58 A.D., Quintilian returned to Spain for approximately eight years where he taught oratory and practiced law. He may have been a member of the inner circle of friends surrounding Galba, Rome's future emperor. At the age of thirty-three he returned to Rome and opened a school in which he taught for over two decades. While still a relatively young man, and only four years after his return to Rome, Vespasian founded a chair of Latin rhetoric for him and provided him with a generous stipend. Quintilian retired in 88 A.D. at the age of fifty-three but was persuaded by Domitian to supervise the education of his two grandnephews. As a reward he was given a consulship and many royal favors. Quintilian devoted the last two years of his life to the writing of his pedagogical masterpiece *Institutio Oratoria (Institutes of Oratory)*. He died at the age of sixty.

Like Cato and Cicero before him, Quintilian accepted as the highest human ideal "the good man skilled in speech," the orator.[53] In his writing

---

[53] Two sources for his views are H. E. Butler, *Quintilian* (Cambridge, Mass.: Harvard University Press, 1922); and W. M. Smail, *Quintilian on Education* (Oxford, England: Clarendon Press, 1938).

and thought, however, the Ciceronian ideal is more narrowly conceived, the tone is more prosaic, its expression less philosophical. Quintilian's greatest strength lay in his willingness to take up questions of educational methodology, to discuss problems of technique and their applications at length, unlike his predecessors who seemed to eschew considerations of method as too self-evident to warrant any serious consideration. Throughout the *Institutio Oratoria* the author is intent on showing how best to nourish the powers of eloquence by teaching oratory. "The first essential" of the perfect orator, according to Quintilian, "is that he should be a good man." The ideally educated man is one "who can truly play his part as a citizen and is capable of meeting the demands both of public and private business, the man who can guide a state by his counsels, give it a firm basis by his legislation and purge its vices by his decisions as a judge. . . ." In order to do so, he must have good moral character, must exhibit the highest kind of integrity, and nourish a sincere concern for the welfare of the state. "I am convinced," he wrote, "that no one can be an orator who is not a good man; but even if anyone could, I am unwilling that he should be."

The second qualification of the orator is mastery of all the liberal arts and sciences. He who speaks eloquently must have a firm grounding in all useful knowledge; he should be a true polymath. Thirdly, it almost goes without saying, he must be able to discourse fluently. To produce such a person, Quintilian was convinced there must be a clarification and gathering together of the best traditions of teaching and learning known to Romans. Virtually all his major work is devoted to a systematic exposition of an ideal educational scheme extending from earliest childhood to adulthood.

The initial part of the *Institutio* is given over to a discussion of preschool training. Quintilian was vitally interested in the child's formative years, when both moral training and the elements of literary education were acquired. Parents and nursemaids must pay strict attention to the child's contacts to ensure that unhealthy influences are avoided. It is never too early to begin instruction on an informal basis, for "though the knowledge absorbed in the previous years may mean but little, yet the boy will be learning something more advanced during that year, in which he would otherwise have been occupied with something more elementary."

Accepting the conventional wisdom of his day, Quintilian chose to ignore the question of formal education for girls. On the issue of whether boys should be educated by a tutor at home or in schools he decided in favor of the latter position. A "respectable school," he avowed, is to be recommended over the "solitude and obscurity of a private education." Children learn better in groups, they can form close friendships, they are able to profit by the examples of their classmates, and the competition afforded by a group situation can serve as a valuable stimulus for learning. The character of the schoolmaster is all-important. He must be free from the manifest taint of immorality," for unless his own character is unimpeachable, all his instruction will go for nothing. "Let him, the teacher, be free from vice himself and refuse to tolerate it in others. Let him be strict but not austere, genial but not too familiar: for austerity will make him unpopular, while familiarity breeds contempt." Quintilian had no use for flogging in the classroom, calling it "a disgraceful form of punishment fit only for slaves." Positive rewards, a good interplay of work and relaxation, a refusal to force studies prematurely, the attempt to make lessons enjoyable—all are vastly more effective because, as he observed, "study depends on the good will of the student, a quality that cannot be secured by compulsion."

The early stages of education should proceed along lines determined by the child's readiness to learn. "I am not so unacquainted with differences of age," he cautioned, "as to think that we should urge those of tender years severely, or exact a full complement of work from them." Then, illustrating his point with an unfortunate metaphor that generations of schoolmasters adopted, he noted, "Vessels with narrow mouths will not receive liquids if too much is poured into them at once, but are easily filled if the liquid is admitted in a gentle stream, or it may be drop by drop; similarly you must consider how much a child's mind is capable of receiving: the things that are beyond their grasp will not enter their minds which have not opened out sufficiently to take them in." Quintilian's point was well intentioned but the metaphor suggests a terribly passive, mechanical learning process.

Quintilian viewed memory and the capacity for imitation as the two most important essentials for acquiring knowledge. Motivation plays an important part also, and he was unusual in urging teachers to consider student interest as a factor in learning; they should do more than simply command a child to blindly memorize without understanding the material. From the teaching side, it is imperative to shape the curriculum in terms of individual achievement levels, needs, and interests. Both method and teaching objectives must be made to coincide with the characteristics of each child. "It is generally, and not without reason, regarded as an excellent quality in a master," he insisted, "to observe accurately differences of ability in those whom he has undertaken to instruct, and to ascertain in what direction the nature of each particularly inclines him, for there is in talent an incredible variety, and the forms of mind are not less varied than those of bodies." It is a point that has been largely overlooked throughout two thousand years of educational practice.

The structure of studies outlined by Quintilian was not very different from that obtaining in the better schools of his day. He thought that elementary education should enable the pupil to speak correctly, to read well, and to develop some skill in literary or poetical interpretation. The secondary-level course of studies was to embrace music, geometry, Greek syntax, linguistics, composition and literature, to be followed by a study of

Latin grammar and literature. A higher course under the direction of the rhetor would include astronomy, advanced geometry, arithmetic, music, logic, literature, ethics, history, and of course the theory and practice of rhetoric. Once graduated from such a system, Quintilian's orator was ready to go out into the world to serve the Roman state and by his example inspire others to seek virtue and honor.

In retrospect, though Quintilian came to enjoy a reputation as the most important Roman writer on education, it is in the *Institutio Oratoria* that the first signs of an intellectual stultification characteristic of later Roman educational theory and practice begin to show up. The formalization of curricula, a somewhat pedantic organization of studies, and the rejection of certain subjects as fit subjects for study are manifest in his work. Later authors were not nearly so careful in insisting on a close relation between life and learning, and before long the old model of the ideally educated man fit for political service had been replaced by the idea of an orator entertaining his audience with forensic pyrotechnics. An educational system which had relied upon the games, circuses, public baths, theaters, holidays and public festivals, the debates of the forum, and moral examples to be found in family life for the total education of the individual now gave way to one preoccupied exclusively with bookish learning in schools. The old vital connections with life had been lost. The ideal curriculum envisioned by Roman theorists had been condensed into compact derivations from secondary sources, usually dependent upon translations from the Greek into Latin. In sum, late Roman education lost any architectonic ideal of personal or social excellence and the loss was reflected not only in its poverty of curricular content, its rigidification of instructional technique, and the isolation of schooling from Roman culture at large, but also, after Quintilian's own time, in comparatively unimaginative educational theory.

SUMMARY

Both early Greek and Roman education relied heavily upon direct observation, imitation, and familial training. The content of instruction was pre-eminently moral and physical, with little emphasis upon literary skills. In Greek life the distinctive excellence, or *areté*, fostered was the heroic warrior whose physical prowess was tempered by certain moral virtues exemplified in the Homeric epics. The city-state of Sparta alone never advanced beyond a feudalistic, warlike culture and its educational ideals exclusively stressed obedience, discipline, and battlefield valor. The Spartan example illustrates education for a closed society; any assessment of its strengths and weaknesses invites comparisons and contrasts with the broad aims of contemporary education in present-day society. Athenian education, on the other hand, developed a more balanced or well-rounded conception of the ideally educated individual, although formal schools were attended only by the privileged few. The citizens of Athens placed great importance on informal means of educating the young for active participation in public political life.

A tension developed in later Athenian education, particularly in Athens, between a narrowly conceived vocational kind of training emphasizing oratorical skills as presented by the Sophists and a more general intellectual education as fostered by the founders of philosophical schools. Whereas Sophists like Protagoras, Gorgias, and Hippias envisioned education as an instrument for furthering an individual's social, political and economic fortunes, philosophical theorists, beginning with Socrates, Plato, and Aristotle, fought to preserve what they believed to be valuable elements in the older educational practices and ideals. Philosophically oriented educational thought was founded on a profound belief that education, at least for a leisured class, should aim not at the production of a skilled public speaker but at a disinterested scholar who pursues truth and knowledge for their own sake. Because the strength of a properly ordered state is proportional to the rationality and moral virtue of its citizenry, education is the handmaiden of statecraft and not merely political economics.

The tension of an oratorical *paideia* or "culture of the educated man," and a philosophical one in late Greek educational thought represents the genesis of a perennial conflict in higher education that has become especially abrasive in modern times. It sometimes assumes the form of a debate between those like Cardinal Newman and Robert Maynard Hutchins who view the university's role as providing a broad, general liberal education and those who stress its function in equipping people for specific vocations or professions. It is all very well to assert that society requires both kinds of education and hence institutions of higher learning must perform a dual task, yet in a pluralistic, heterogeneous society where few values are commonly shared and the complexity of knowledge means fragmentary specialization, it is very difficult to envision an educational structure which can successfully satisfy the needs of vocationalism and also realize the values traditionally associated with liberal education.

In Hellenistic times it was the general educational perspective of Isocrates, rather than Plato's or Aristotle's, that proved most influential in the centuries following the Greek classical period although his original perspective underwent considerable modification. Schools became agents for the preservation and transmission of the Greek legacy, but only at the cost of a progressive formalization of the original inheritance.

The Romans' function was to absorb and spread Hellenistic culture rather than to rework it completely into some higher cultural synthesis. Their assimilation of Greek learning proved to be highly selective: they discarded or ignored many structural elements and modified others. The formal school system of the Romans borrowed heavily from the Greek in terms of institutional structures even though what was taught did not encompass as many subjects. The Hellenization of Roman life obliterated the older education with minor exceptions. The last three or four centuries of Roman dominance brought a definite shift in educational objectives; as education became further and further separated from the on-going culture, it exalted the ideal of an orator as a clever manipulator of words instead of a broadly prepared statesman. Today, when the demand is made for greater relevance of schools to pressing personal dilemmas or crucial social issues, the failure of late Roman education is an apt object lesson in what happens when schools are divorced from life's realities. Nonetheless, "social relevance" can also become a procrustean standard for curricula. The shape of Hellenistic learning shows that what people unconsciously assume is valuable is not necessarily what they require. As societies change, so too must the requirements for schools and their objectives.

QUESTIONS FOR DISCUSSION

1. Analyze the following thesis: The characteristics of a flowering civilization are order and discipline. These are the conditions of growth. In decay, society is afflicted with irrationality and perversity. In its decline, the Roman Empire exhibited symptoms of such decay. Contemporary Western civilization is showing many of the same signs—disrespect for law, youthful rebellion, political and social radicalism, a decline in the social influence of religion, expansion and replacement by government of functions previously discharged in the private sector of society, and an apparent chasm between what happens in schools and what seems important in society. We are on the downward path traversed by the Roman civilization.

2. How would you support or refute the argument that when a culture turns *primarily* to schools for the conduct of education, that culture has entered a period of general decline?

3. What were the *most significant* educational differences between early Athens and early Rome?

4. Who today best represents the position of the early Sophists regarding the proper aims of education? Who defends the position of the Greek philosophers?

5. Is there any sure method for distinguishing the contemporary equivalent of a Socrates from less responsible critics of our social order?

6. Discuss the claim advanced that for the first time in history a society—our own—lacks any viable conception of a *paideia,* or "culture" of the educated man. Is the argument persuasive? Why or why not?

7. In the discussion of the decline of Hellenistic education, it is implied that an educational system requires some well-defined conception of the ideally educated individual. Does the alleged lack of such a conception help explain meaningfully why Hellenistic education was inferior to what had preceded it? What about educational theory today?

8. Why do we tend to think of a "liberal" education in terms of the content of

the arts and humanities? Assess the Harvard Committee's allegation that a "general" education could include studies in any disciplines.

9. It is reported that instruction in the *ludus* school became primarily "literary." What does this mean specifically? Compare what is taught in our elementary grades with Roman schooling at the same level. Are we preoccupied with the mastery of verbal and writing skills to the exclusion of other equally important objects of learning?

10. What factors explain the overwhelming importance of oratory and rhetoric as the foundations of instruction in Greco-Roman education? Why not the philosophical study of political theory, history, and government?

3 Education for a Sacral Society

Of course, the morality taught and enforced in the discipline of the common school is the Christian morality as laid down. . . according to its best public appreciation in Christian lands. . . . This implies, of course, the full recognition by the common school of the existence, sovereignty and providence of Almighty God and the duty of all men and of the nation to love, worship and obey God. . . .

A. D. MAYO
"Methods of Moral Instruction in Common Schools," *NEA Journal Addresses and Proceedings,* (1872)

Jesus' own recognition of the validity of certain separations was expressed in His words, "Render unto Caesar the things that be Caesar's." Thus the American public schools must be secular. It is my reasoned conviction that the day this secularism ceases, our cherished heritage of freedom is on its way out, no matter what names we pin on the pitiful skeleton that remains.

VIRGIL M. ROGERS
"Are the Public Schools 'Godless'?" *Educational Forum,* (May, 1958)

THE PEOPLE OF THE COVENANT

Education is an instrument employed by a society to transmit its culture from one generation to another. If the cultural configuration (the pattern of beliefs, values, attitudes, dispositions, and modes of behavior) is dominated by certain major ideas or values, they will figure importantly in the content of instruction imparted, just as they will shape the ends served by teaching–learning processes. It follows, naturally, that when schools exist as formal agencies within society, their transmissive role will be colored by the culture's dominant interests. In some complex cultures there is such diversity that no single unifying theme stands out clearly. For a variety of reasons special importance still may be attached to one among many educational functions and elevated to a position of prominence. The particular func-

136

tion will differ, depending on the society and historical period in question. Among the ancient Greeks, exploitation of education's *political* and *intellectual* potential seems to have been characteristic. In late-eighteenth- and nineteenth-century Europe, schools were used mainly as tools for *social* control. The school in contemporary America is expected to achieve a variety of ends—social, intellectual, political, moral—but chief among them apparently is the *economic* goal of preparing people for vocational competence.

The habit of viewing education primarily in economic terms is so deeply ingrained today that some find it hard to realize that for centuries the school's fundamental purpose was *religious*. The origin of the ties between religion and organized education in the West is very ancient, tracing back some three millennia to the Hebrews. The Judaic tradition deserves an important place in an account of educational history, if only because, like the Greco-Roman tradition, it has been a taproot of Western culture.

The story of the ancient Hebrews illustrates how a particular cultural line of development was controlled by a dominant concept or motive. The basic motif of Hebraic education within that tradition was first, last, and always religious, and when formal schools appeared their operation was dictated by the requirements of a religious faith. In the final analysis it is not misleading to affirm that the ultimate goal of education among those God-intoxicated people was the preservation of a truly sacred society.

One of the great anomalies of human history is the persistence of the Jews as a separate people. Long after their persecutors passed into oblivion, they retained their identity, culture, and faith. As Arnold Toynbee notes, the Jews ultimately proved so resistant to assimilation that the phalanx of Hellenism utterly failed to conquer Judaistic culture and finally came to terms with it by adopting a version of its fanatical religion, a faith later carried by Rome to Western Europe. Most historians agree that their peculiar persistence derives largely from a sustained, conscious educational effort to hold their culture together. It proceeded from a deep religious faith, from a consciousness of a historical legacy, and from a unique sense of destiny. It is worthwhile to examine those ideas before turning to Judaic educational institutions and ideals.

The Hebraic Religious Consciousness

The original Hebrews were a Semitic people who abandoned a nomadic existence somewhere on the Arabian peninsula early in the third millennium B.C. Following a protracted period of migration they took up residence in northwestern Mesopotamia and adapted themselves to a more or less fixed location for the next few centuries. Possibly because of antagonism toward the Chaldeo-Babylonian religion of the Chaldees at Ur, one of the most powerful cities of Sumeria and home of the original Abrahamic religion, they migrated westward across the Euphrates around 2300 B.C. and conquered the peoples inhabiting the land of Canaan or Palestine. There they remained for roughly six centuries, struggling to carve out a homeland for themselves in an area extending from Dan, in the north, to Beersheba, some 150 miles to the south. Although it was a mere sliver of land bordering on the vast desert, it must have seemed a land of "milk and honey" compared with the arid wastes beyond. Rains were plentiful and crops grew in abundance in irrigated fields. Only the occurrence of a major disaster can account for the abrupt displacement of the Hebrews from their fertile haven during the seventeenth century B.C. It was famine or plague, according to one tradition, that drove the Hebrews south, out of Canaan and as far as Egypt. They evidently settled in the Deltic region of the Nile, hoping to find a better life of peace and prosperity in the rich river basin. Instead the hapless immigrants were destined to be overrun by the native population, placed in bondage to the Pharaoh, and compelled to serve as menial laborers.

For almost three hundred years they slaved for the Egyptians until a missionary priest named *Moses* arose to assume leadership of the oppressed Hebrews, headed a successful revolt, and led his followers in an exodus out into the barren deserts of the Sinai peninsula. There they wandered for many years, engaging in petty wars with hostile tribes and in internecine strife among themselves. Scholars quarrel over the details of the Hebraic sojourn in Egypt and the legendary patriarchal migrations that followed. There is some evidence to indicate that the Pharaoh of the oppression was Rameses II (ca. 1301–1234 B.C.) and that the Exodus, involving only a very small number of emigrants, took place sometime in the thirteenth century B.C. The historicity of Moses himself is very much an open question, although critics are disposed to identify him as perhaps one of several charismatic leaders. For reasons of narrative convenience, it is expedient to assume that the Mosaic father figure to the wandering Hebrews was a single individual.

Something very powerful, a development extraordinarily important for understanding their subsequent history, happened during the wanderings in the desert. It involved a transformation of unorganized refugees into a single theocratic–political unit, inspired with a new vision destined to become the focus for their political and spiritual life—a profound consciousness of a divine mission ordained by their national deity, Yahweh. The name is obscure, possibly deriving from the Hebrew verb *hayah,* "to be." When Moses asks his name, the god replies, "I am who I am" or "I who am present." In primitive usage, Yahweh may be "the Blower" or "the Feller," a god associated with fire, smoke, or clouds, because the Semitic verb *hawah,* "to blow," may also figure as its source.[1] Whatever his origin

1 The term *Jehovah* is a thirteenth-century A.D. mistranslation from the Hebrew and was never used by either Hebrews or early Christians. Yahweh may possibly derive from an ancestral Canaanite thunder god called Yahu, according to some scholars. Some

Yahweh was to be a truly national god; to him alone were the people to give allegiance. As later re-created in Biblical lore, Yahweh summoned Moses to a mountain to deliver a proclamation: "You have seen what I did to the Egyptians, and how I bore you on eagles' wings and brought you to myself. Now therefore, if you will obey my voice and keep my covenant, you shall be my own possession among all peoples; for all the earth is mine, and you shall be to me a kingdom of priests and a holy nation." The old pre-Mosaic animism, with its necromancy, imitative magic, and scapegoat sacrifices, the traditional worship of the bull, sheep, serpents, and assorted denizens of the heavens, all were to give way gradually before a new Yahwist cult creating a community set against all other communities. The Hebrews felt called to separate themselves apart from other peoples and to build a disciplined nation obedient to a novel divine revelation. Yahweh had been the God of Abraham, Isaac, and Jacob; now he was to be the protector of his "chosen people." This was the dynamic impulse that Moses released into the mainstream of his people's life: an overpowering consciousness of a god who promised them a unique mission in the world. The theophanies or appearances of Yahweh, in burning bush and smoking mountain, in clouds by day and a pillar of fire at night, revealed an awesome, jealous deity making total demands upon his people. Something new had begun in their religious awareness.

First and foremost, Yahweh was the *only* god for the Hebrews. It is interesting to note that the First Commandment appears to assume the existence of other deities: "You shall have no other gods before (or besides) me!" It is doubtful whether Moses was a monotheist in the modern sense; more likely and less anachronistic, *henotheism* or *monolatry* best describes the Mosaic religion—belief in one god without denying the existence of other gods or without excluding the right of other peoples to worship other deities.[2] There were "gods many and lords many" for the nations, but for the Hebrews under Moses there had to be a single, undivided loyalty.

Secondly, the Mosaic Yahweh was a *spiritual* being, independent of all material existence, and was to be worshipped as a spirit, in spirit. Considering Moses' probable familiarity with such Egyptian deities as Isis, Osiris, Ptah, and Ammon, it is astounding how resistant Yahweh was to any anthropomorphic representation. He had no origin, no sexuality (as compared with the usual fertility gods), and no identification with any object or person. Moses' religion had no philosophically articulate way of formulat-

---

sources allege that *Shem Hammeyuhad* was the real and unutterable name of God, and consisted of the unpronounceable YHWH. "Yahweh" may never have had any oral pronunciation at all, but was simply a nonsense word formed by arbitrarily adding random vowels to YHWH.

2 See Norman K. Gottwald, *A Light to the Nations* (New York: Harper & Row, 1959), pp. 140–141 ff. for a discussion of this problem.

ing the transcendence of Yahweh over man and nature, but that germinal conviction was buttressed just as effectively by the prohibition against graven images. Yahweh was not an object among objects and could not be depicted as such. The proscription undoubtedly contributed to the relative aesthetic poverty of Hebraic culture in following centuries, though it did serve to keep Yahweh from becoming just another idol among literally thousands common to the area.

Thirdly, Yahweh was a *powerful* being, not yet omnipotent and infinite, but sufficiently superior over the god incarnate in Pharaoh and other Egyptian deities to free the Hebrews. At the heart of Moses' faith was the saga of Yahweh's triumph over the gods of their former captors: "It was shown you, that you might know that Yahweh he is God . . . and brought you out with his presence, with his great power, out of Egypt; to drive out the nations from before you . . . to give you their lands for an inheritance."

It has been rightly said that Moses taught Yahweh morals and eventually made him the moral conscience of his people. In an age when religion meant propitiation of the gods and when gods were not exactly models of moral virtue, Moses was the first to link religion with morality. The fact that the connection has seemed so inevitable in Western culture merely serves to show how pervasive has been the influence of a very ancient tradition going back to Mosaic times. The process of reconstruction must have continued long after Moses' own period, because it entailed the transformation of an arbitrary, wrathful god, seemingly interested as much in ritual and sacrifice as good conduct or purity of heart, into a god of righteousness and loving concern. The God who is supremely *ethical,* demanding obedience to moral law, was only partially prefigured in the Mosaic conception.

The Monarchy

The return of the wandering Hebrews to the land of Canaan was not, as implied in the Book of Joshua, a total or speedy occupation of territory already held by the Amorite Canaanites. It took several generations before a long struggle for possession succeeded. The Hebrews and Canaanites were closely related Semitic peoples, and the final triumph of the former over the latter was as much a matter of cultural assimilation as outright military triumph. Rather than an adroit single conquest, there appear to have been two major Hebrew invasions of the territory—the first from the east across the Jordan, culminating in the capture of Jericho by Joshua, followed by the fall of Shechem and Bethel, and the other from the south, into the territory later called Judah some two centuries later. Those tribes participating in the first invasion were at first loosely organized but later consolidated into a "northern" confederacy by Joshua at Shechem. Tradition relates that a covenant and legal code was established around which was gathered the nucleus of what subsequently came to be known as Israel.

Those who migrated from the south gradually formed their own "southern" confederacy of Judah.

For at least two centuries the Hebrews were governed by local chiefs or *judges* (from *shophet,* meaning "one who brings vindication, who sets things right"), some of whom enjoyed national, and not merely tribal, influence. When the invasion of the *Philistines,* a powerful people to the west, threatened to engulf both Canaanites and Hebrews, the people demanded strong leadership and political reorganization as a monarchy in order to better provide for defense against incessant attacks. *Samuel,* the last and greatest of the judges, was instrumental in establishing *Saul, the Benjamite,* as the first king of a united nation in the mid-eleventh century B.C.

Saul was a charismatic military figure whose sole aims were to expel the Philistines and to promote a militant brand of Yahwism. He began his brilliant career as a popular choice of the people, a king *primus inter pares,* able to weld other chieftains into a potent military–political force. He and his son *Jonathan* won several notable victories over the invaders, but neither were able to put down bloody internal wars of succession instigated by rival aspirants to the throne. Tragedy intervened, first, in a break with the still-active Samuel over politico-religious disagreements and second, as schizophrenic mental illness overcame Saul in later years. With all the inexorability of a Greek tragedy, events culminated in his suicide following a major defeat in battle.

The dashing young *David* succeeded Saul in 1010 B.C. through a clever combination of military and political maneuvering. Under David's reign of some forty years, the kingdom of the Hebrews achieved a pinnacle of political success. Her enemies remained quiescent everywhere. Unfortunately, with the passage of time David turned ruthless in his exercise of power. High taxation and conscription to support construction of elaborate public works, including a magnificent Temple at Jerusalem, led to widespread discontent and eventually to scattered revolts. David's successor, *Solomon,* proved to be far worse, a pampered son who had inherited most of his father's faults and none of his virtues. Contrary to popular legend, Solomon was a despotic ruler totally disdainful of good government. He encouraged luxury and ostentation and lavished tax monies on extravagant projects, the most ambitious of which was a gigantic palace modeled along Canaanite–Phoenician lines. Literally thousands of subjects were consigned to labor camps to satisfy Solomon's boundless ambitions. His death in 935 B.C. was the signal for open revolt.

Division and Conquest

Solomon's son, *Rehoboam,* made a fatal mistake in adopting a repressive policy toward the northern tribes who demanded an end to despotism. When the new monarch showed no sign of meeting their demands, the result was an uprising and declaration of independence. *Jeroboam,* a seditious leader from one of Solomon's labor battalions, assumed the new leadership. There followed a period of strife culminating in the breakup of the united monarchy. Two separate kingdoms were established: *Judah,* with its capital at Jerusalem, in the south and *Israel* (or Ephraim), with a capital at Samaria, in the north. Whereas the heavy-handed despotism of Rehoboam without question was the immediate cause of this split, many other forces were involved. The hilly terrain had always encouraged sectional insularity among the tribal amphictyonies and impeded total political unity. The northern tribes were urbane, sophisticated, and inclined toward religious syncretism, whereas the southerners were a pastoral folk devoted to nomadic ideals and loyal to ancestral pieties. Once Solomon's strong hand was removed, pent-up resentment exploded and tore the monarchy asunder.

The consequences of the schism were disastrous. Neither Israel nor Judah, occupied with internal problems, had the power or will to hold the old empire together; it simply went by default, almost overnight. Sporadic sectional warfare aggravated the deterioration. First the northern Israelites were attacked by the Assyrians (allies of Judah), subdued, and carried off to Media, where they were eventually assimilated to other Semitic peoples (thus the legend of the "lost ten tribes"). Then Judah fell when she proved powerless to resist the Babylonian invasion of King Nebuchadnezzar, an unforgiving warrior who captured Jerusalem, destroyed the temple, and led away the remaining survivors to Babylon.

Exile

Prior to this period and for centuries after, the ancient Hebrew faith was galvanized by a long line of prophets representing an ecstatic strain in Yahwism. From the time of the Philistine crisis and the founding of the monarchy, bands of intensely patriotic prophets criticized kingly conduct of the state in the light of Yahweh's covenant and law. By direct political action, through oracles and public pronouncements, they opposed every move toward foreign entanglements, denounced disregard for religious law, and exposed worship of foreign gods. The prophets persistently idealized the traditions of the past while criticizing the present in the light of those traditions. They represented an almost continuous reform movement whose aim was to reawaken memory of the now largely forgotten Sinaitic promise. The entire prophetic attack was rooted or grounded in the tradition of the Mosaic covenant. As Yahweh had come to his people through Moses and later through his spiritually designated judges, now he spoke in times of dire social crisis through his servants the prophets. Yahweh will judge his people for their impiety, they thundered, divine obligations cannot be discharged by busy religiosity or through the worship of false idols. Yahweh as accuser and judge would take action against his rebellious, willful subjects. One thinks of Amos assailing the economic and social inequalities of Jeroboam's reign shortly before the destruction of Israel. Speaking as

Yahweh's voice, he cried, "I despise your feast-days . . . though you offer me burnt offerings and your meal offerings, I will not accept them. . . . Take away from me the noise of your songs, for I will not hear the melody of your viols. But let judgment run down as waters, and righteousness as a mighty stream." As the covenantal conscience of an allegedly irresponsible social and religious order, Amos tirelessly attacked enervating luxury, judicial corruption, and class oppression: "You only have I known of all the families of the earth; therefore I will punish you for all your iniquities," he proclaimed, in the name of a wrathful Yahweh. The fury of prophets such as Hosea, Micah, and Isaiah knew no bounds when directed against religious faithlessness and impiety.

It is important to set prophetic polemics such as these in their proper context. Prior to the reign of David, the people of the northern confederacy had not embraced the Yahwist cult adopted by their neighbors to the south. Most likely their religious traditions centered around an Aaronitic cult of the bull god, or Baalism, at least until its temporary suppression during the monarchy. The secession of Israel under Jeroboam promptly led to the reestablishment of bull worship as the official religion of the northern tribes, relegating Yahwism to the status of a subordinate "underground" cult. The prophetic movement, beginning with Elijah and Elisha, drew its advocates from the ranks of those bitterly opposed to Baalism. The great eighth-century spokesmen, such as Amos, Hosea and Micah, and Isaiah, later followed by Jeremiah, Ezekiel, and a second (or third) Isaiah, were constantly engaged in the struggle against resurgent Baalism and attempted to restore the primacy of Yahwism.

Meanwhile, the Yahwist theology itself underwent radical alterations. The old tribal god of the nomadic tribes of Judah gradually became a universal deity requiring moral uprighteousness rather than conformity to ceremonial creeds. His defenders constantly upbraided kings and priests for their narrow chauvinism, championing the cause of social justice as Yahweh's divine will. Whereas early prophets like Amos seemingly accepted traditional monolatry, by the time of Jeremiah, Yahwists were proclaiming in no uncertain terms that heathen deities did not exist and that Yahweh alone had real existence. Uncompromising monotheism quickly led to the concept of religion as ethical rather than ritualistic in its foundations. The so-called Deuteronomic Reformation of the late seventh century B.C. was the final triumph of ethical monotheism wedded firmly to the legal tradition of the Mosaic covenant. For the first time all heathen cults were outlawed and a religious code was written into the state constitution of Judah. This adoption of a book of canonical scriptural codes came just in time, for the days of Judah were numbered. Once deprived of political autonomy, the conquered Hebrews could only cling to their sacred writings for a sense of identity and national purpose. Little else remained to them.

The Assyrian crisis leading to Israel's downfall and the Babylonian conquest of Judah a hundred years later necessitated a reinterpretation of the old Yahwist faith. As a chosen people, the Hebrews felt that their covenant guaranteed security, permanence, and a glorious national future. But political events contradicted this optimistic theology flatly. They even raised the question whether Yahweh was powerless to protect his people from intrusions and ultimate humiliation. Later prophets, especially Isaiah, explained that foreign invaders were the chastising rod of their god, tools to punish his people for their having strayed from the path of right-eousness. Only a pure remnant, a new Israel, would survive to rise from the fires of tragedy, to receive new promises, and to redeem Yahweh's mission on earth. Despite Israel's obliteration and Judah's destruction, this re-interpretation enabled the covenantal faith to survive the dark centuries that lay ahead. The prophetic revolution, it must be added, not only con-firmed the explicit monotheism of Hebraic religion and purified its ethical ideals, but also produced some of the most magnificent poetic literature ever recorded.

Nebuchadnezzar's army left Judah a shambles after the debacle of 587 B.C. Though the popular notion of a total deportation which left the land empty and void is erroneous, the catastrophe signaled a complete disruption of Jewish life in Palestine.[3] For those brought to Babylon, the Exile must have been especially tragic. They were strangers in a foreign land, neither totally enslaved nor entirely free. They had been torn from their homeland and wholesale loss of faith threatened. The temptation to lapse from the ancestral faith was acute, given the overwhelming evidence all around of undreamed-of wealth and the imposing temples of pagan gods. Was Yahweh, patron deity of a petty state now utterly ruined, really the only and supreme god after all? This was the basic question confronting the Jewish exiles between 587 and 538 B.C. For centuries the faith of Israel had been closely tied up with political life, first of tribal leagues, then of the united monarchy, and finally of the twin kingdoms. Some concluded with the abrupt cessation of Judean statehood that Yahweh had been vanquished by the Babylonian god Marduk, or, in default of his promises, had aban-doned his people. The sufferer of Lamentations cried out, "You have rejected me from peace; I have forgotten good, so I say, 'Gone is my endurance, my hope from Yahweh.' "

Religious thought turned pessimistic. Yahweh was conceived in still more transcendent terms; he was inscrutable, mysterious, and unapproachable. As religious observances became more formalized, synagogal worship was instituted, a priestly class expanded its influence, and observance of dietary laws came to be regarded as essential—all of these evidence of the sustained attempt to resist cultural assimilation and to preserve the religious identity

3 See John Bright, *A History of Israel* (Philadelphia: The Westminster Press, n.d.), pp. 324 ff. The name *Jew* is strictly applicable only to the Hebrews of Judah and their descendants.

of the exiles. A hard core hoped their captivity was merely an interim and that their lonely sojourn would end with a restoration of the faithful, as the prophets had continued to assure them. The bitter plight of the people, its suffering and anxiety, is hauntingly reflected in one of the Psalms:

By the rivers of Babylon, there we sat down, yes, we wept, when we remembered Zion.
We hanged our harps upon the willows in the midst thereof.
For there they that carried us away captive required of us a song; and they that wasted us required of us mirth, saying,
Sing us one of the songs of Zion.
How shall we sing the Lord's song in a strange land?
If I forget you, O Jerusalem, let my right hand forget her cunning.
If I do not remember you, let my tongue cleave to the roof of my mouth, if I prefer not Jerusalem above my chief joy.

In 538 B.C. the prophecies seemed fulfilled. A glorious new day seemed to be dawning. The Persian conquest under *Cyrus* of Babylon enabled the Jews, with official approval of their benevolent ruler, to return to Palestine and re-establish their cult there. At first only a few took advantage of Cyrus' edict, though successive migrations in later decades swelled the returning populace. The temple was rebuilt and government passed into the hands of a senate of scribes, priests, and elders (later known as the famous *Sanhedrin*). An organized system of legal formalism and of ecclesiastical ceremonial took shape, oppressive perhaps, but effective in unifying the people as a semiautonomous theocracy within the Persian empire. Under the direction of such leaders as *Nehemiah* and *Ezra,* both administrative and spiritual reforms helped the postexilic community survive a turbulent time of ritualistic readjustment and political upheaval.

The Threat of Hellenism

When *Alexander the Great* crossed the Hellespont to launch his conquest of Asia in 334 B.C. a new epoch began that was to involve little Judah as well. His inevitable collision with an already-weakening Persian empire resulted in the rout of Persian forces and the establishment of a far-flung empire that included the hinterlands of Palestine (and Judah and Samaria) as well as Egypt. The tide of Hellenism unleashed by Alexander's cosmopolitan enthusiasm for a pan-Hellenic culture caught the Jews unprepared. As a frontal challenge it tended to rigidify the main features of Judaism; indirectly, however, it broadened its contacts with other religious ideologies, some of which subtly and indirectly infiltrated into Jewish theology. Scholars dispute whether such themes as the coming of a Messiah, otherworldly salvation, a Last Judgment, and the resurrection of the dead— later firmly entrenched in Jewish theology—were native products or results of the exposure to Hellenistic thought. An irreconcilable split developed, at any rate, between those who compromised with Greek culture and those who steadfastly clung to old ways.

Decline and Dissolution

Alexander died a premature death in 323 B.C, leaving no single powerful successor. The small Judean community was caught in the midst of devastating, cruel struggles among his generals. *Ptolemy Lagi* of Egypt became the first to institute sovereignty over the Palestine area, followed briefly by the *Seleucids* (Syrians) after a century of Ptolemaic rule. The victory of *Antiochus III the Great* in 198 B.C. turned Palestine into a vassal state, an event bearing terrible fruit under a successor, *Antiochus IV Epiphanes,* who set out to extirpate Judaism as a menace to the cultural uniformity of his Hellenistic empire. His desecration of the temple at Jerusalem by the sacrifice of a pig on the altar seemed a final symbol of Judaism's demise. Jewish law was proscribed, the Sabbath could not be observed, and circumcision was forbidden. Antiochus' policies were to be strictly enforced by a garrison of troops stationed at Jerusalem. The pagan population of Palestine was urged to force Jews to participate in idolatrous rites. All these measures notwithstanding, if Antiochus believed his plan would succeed, events were to show he was mistaken. Many preferred outright revolt rather than capitulation (although of course some Hellenized Jews welcomed his edicts and gladly complied with them). Those who resisted were prepared to fight it out to the bitter end.

The struggle had its beginning when tormented Jews found a leader in the person of a priest named *Mattathias.* After the old patriach died, his son *Judas Maccabeus* (i.e., "the Hammer") took up the battle, transforming an uncertain resistance movement into a full-scale war for independence. This *Maccabean Revolt,* beginning in 166 B.C., turned into a veritable blood bath. It began as a fight for religious liberty, expanded as a war for political freedom, and finally escalated into an attempt to resurrect the ancient Jewish kingdom. Neither side was able to win a decisive victory. It must have seemed to the Seleucids that the Jews were an absolutely ungovernable people. The next set of conquerors who presumed to rule over the Jewish people fared no better.

For some time Rome had been taking an increasingly active interest in the eastern Mediterranean lands and was ready to intervene in affairs there with a high hand, long before the reign of Antiochus IV. By the year 63 B.C. Palestine, along with Syria and Egypt, had been swallowed up as a Roman protectorate. The details of Roman rule need not be considered at length; it is sufficient to note that clumsy administrative rule combined with fervent Jewish nationalism dating back to the abortive Maccabean Revolt kept the area in more or less continuous revolt. The new conquerors found it no easier to deal with their rebellions subjects than had their predecessors. Finally, in 70 A.D., Roman patience was exhausted: an expeditionary force was dispatched to destroy Jerusalem completely and annex the country as a Roman province. Most of the area's leading citizens were forced into submission, driven off, or simply executed. The dispersion (*diaspora*) of the Jews was begun, their political history abruptly terminated.

JEWISH EDUCATION

The Concept of Religious Law

It is the postexilic period in the development of Jewish religion (537 B.C.– 70 A.D.) that is most directly relevant to institutionalized Jewish education. The basic problem of the restored community following its return from Babylon was how to revive its national institutions and cult. The old pre-exilic Israelite nation was gone of course; now the question was how to construct some definition, some external form in which to retain Jewish identity, some equivalent for the old sacral state, with its geographical boundaries and ties to the soil. A new Israel could not be coterminous with any geographical or national designation, especially because Jewish enclaves were now scattered throughout the eastern Mediterranean world. The one element of the Israelite heritage that could serve as a rallying point was covenant law. The prophets had explained historical calamity as the penalty for breaching old codes, not only those of Moses but the requirements stipulated in Josiah's time in Deuteronomic law. The mark of a Jew now was made to depend upon stringent observance of religious rules involving ritual cleanliness, tithing, ceremonial purity, Sabbath worship, and cultic circumcision. Henceforth, "Israel" was defined not as a national identity or a people descended from the Israelite tribes, not as those inhabiting the old territory, not even as a community of worshippers, but as the remnant of Judah which had rallied around the old usages. Law did not regulate an already organized community; it *created* the community.[4] A Jew was one who accepted it and obeyed its provisions.

Jewish law gradually assumed authoritative written form and became canonical scripture. It also helped create the synagogue as an instrument of public worship and as a gathering place for scribes devoted to its study. In time responsibility for transmitting knowledge of the law to scribal apprentices was assumed by those who maintained the synagogue. Because not all Jews resided in a single location it was necessary to have such an institution wherever a Jewish community existed. The net effect of geographical dispersion and political oppression was to transform Judaism into a legalistic faith heavily dependent on the synagogue for its survival. At its worst, religion became a narrow legalism, a matter of fulfilling ritualistic requirements. At its best, however, it was a joyful triumph of faith over awesome

4 Ibid., p. 416.

obstacles. For the Jew his religion meant a profound devotional piety, a deep ethical sense, and a wondering trust in his God. Fulfillment of the law realized Israel's ideal of herself as the holy chosen people—as the faith was kept in every detail, so the new Israel would endure.

Jewish legalism was thoroughly ethical, capturing and preserving a moral note central in Israel's faith from its earliest beginnings. Jewish teachers continually exalted righteous behavior, obedience to parents, chastity, sobriety, and moderation in all things. They called the people to love God and neighbor and to forgive those who wronged them. God demands a penitent, obedient spirit, they taught, a person who keeps the commandments in a spirit of willing obedience instead of regarding them as burdens. The law put the final seal upon absolute monotheism ("The Lord God, He is one") in refusing to make any concessions whatever to idolatry and pagan gods. In a sense, it might be said that the ancient prophetic polemics against idols finally bore its fruit in the legal codes of later Judaism. God is all-powerful and just, even though his ways are unsearchable. He governs all nations according to his eternally valid, immutable codes. The fortunes of all peoples are guided within divine foreknowledge and led to consummation according to some final plan. His purpose will be realized, late Judaism affirmed, in a final victory over all satanic forces and the establishment of a divine beneficent rule. The community of law, the purified remnant of Israel, will triumph over the present evil age on a coming Day of Judgment. The appearance of a deliverer, a new Son of Man, will indicate that the final consummation of history is at hand. Sustained by this eschatology, faithful Jews knew what to do while awaiting the Judgment: keep the remnant of Israel pure and undefiled by instructing the young in the national history and by recalling Yahweh's covenantal promises to each new generation.

Institutional Forms

Early Hebraic education was similar in many respects to that of all primitive peoples. There were no formally organized schools as first. Education was a matter of instruction in oral traditions conducted in the home. The family always held a central place in Hebrew society, tellingly revealed in the comparison frequently drawn between the relationship of Yahweh to his people and that of a father to his children. Familial bonds embraced Yahweh himself as Heavenly Father, as one who demands implicit obedience from his children. Within the patriarchal family, children learned by exposure to group life and by participating in its activities. Young boys accompanied their fathers to the field or workshop for daily labors while young girls were trained at home in the various domestic arts. The home environment was explicitly educative in its reliance upon religious ceremonials connected with the observance of the sabbath, with seasonal feasts, and private worship. Family routine was punctuated by sacred occasions commemorating such significant events as the Passover. They offered each family member the opportunity to be reminded of the great national history and to renew his dedication to the ideals shaped by that past. The child was often given an active role to play in such observances. The correlative demand to the injunction, "My son, hear the instruction of your father, and forsake not the law of your mother," was the Deuteronomic call of parents to care for the moral and spiritual well-being of children:

> Hear O Israel, The Lord our God is one God: And you shall love the Lord your God with all your heart and with all your soul and with all your might. And these words which I command you this day shall be upon your heart: And you shall teach them diligently to your children, and shall talk of them when you sit in your house, when you walk along the way, and when you lie down, and when you rise up. . . .

Much like the Roman *paterfamilias,* the father acted as both teacher and priest, teaching his children the law and performing the rites of household worship. Down to the time of the Exile at least, family education meant instruction in the traditions of practical wisdom (such as those collected in the Proverbs of Solomon), the obligations of honoring elders and parents, the details of a long history, and explanations of an inherited lyric psalmody.

There is some evidence that writing was taught to children as early as the eighth century B.C., although probably formal instruction was confined to a special class of scribes and priests who were the depositaries of a growing judicial and historical literature. There must have been regular facilities for systematic formal instruction, because priests had to be thoroughly familiar with an elaborate sacrificial system and a body of legal codes as well. The advanced age at which priests entered upon their duties at the Temple, around twenty-five or thirty, points to the extended period of training they had to undergo.

Well before the time of Saul and David, certain priests (probably of the Levite tribe) were employed to make transcriptions, to act as notaries for the public, and to help adjudicate lawsuits. Indirect evidence suggests the existence of books and records before the monarchy, not to mention an advanced level of development in the art of writing. Furthermore, priestly functionaries were charged with the administration of an economic surplus which would almost certainly require trained personnel. Even though such technical instruction might have been sustained privately and by families, it certainly qualified as formal education.

Most people, however, were unable to write simply because it was still unnecessary. The word *school* is not mentioned in the Old Testament but some structured places of instruction were undoubtedly in existence as early as the sixth and seventh centuries B.C. Further expansion of school facilities may have been associated with the rise of the prophets. As religious revivalists outside the ceremonial priesthood grew in influence, the need for some specialized education to fit them for their role became apparent. According to rabbinical tradition, confraternities arose in connection with the prophetic movement as informal, voluntary teaching and learning groups. They constituted colleges numbering from fifty to four hundred students, or "sons of the prophets," gathered to learn at the feet of an instructor. Subjects taught included music, sacred poetry, theology, prayers, rituals of worship, and means of inducing a state of religious ecstasy. Samuel may have founded a school at Ramah in the eleventh century B.C., and other schools are known to have existed (though not as contemporary institutions) at Gilgal, Carmel, Bethel, Jericho, and Gibea. Out of these *"colleges of the prophets"* came national historians and poets promulgating the moral government of the nation and protesting against idolatries and public immorality. At the same time these schools were developing, there must have been many less formal educational influences because the prophets seem to have addressed themselves to literate audiences, some of whose members undoubtedly could read and write. A period of literary activity and instruction probably existed before the time of the first literary compositions ascribed to such prophets as Hosea and Amos.

During and immediately following the Babylonian Exile, there arose a class of learned men besides the priesthood who were coming more and more into prominence. Its members were called *scribes,* men who combined the functions of lawyers, interpreters, copyists, and professional teachers. The scribal class increased in number to become the most important and most learned sector of Jewish society. They were a lay order open to men of various organized literary guilds for instructing the young and preparing them for scribal duties. Their education involved intensive instruction covering several years in the written law and its interpretations. The multiplication of prescriptions, ritual observances, and legal dicta made for a formidable curriculum, but the learning also helped to keep Jewish culture together as a cohesive unity. The more eminent of the scribes became great teachers and expounders of the law, teaching mainly in the porches of the rebuilt Temple at Jerusalem and later at other places of public worship. Scribal schools effectively served as arenas for disputation where scholars could gather to clarify obscure or difficult parts of the law. By the beginning of the Christian era, scribal schools had acquired greater influence with the people than any other social structure. They came to be known as *Rabbinical schools,* the heads of which were called *Rabbins,* or "Masters." The level of instruction presumed some prior elementary instruction although, so far as is known, this must have been domestic because there is no evidence for the existence of elementary schools in the immediate postexilic period.

The single most important institution created during the Exile was the *synagogue.* It was a meeting place and house of worship where tight little groups could gather in expectation of an eventual return to Palestine. Within its walls the community shared its memory of the past, held itself together in the face of the blandishments of a potent but alien culture, and sharpened its social and religious life. Scribes devoted to the interpretation of the sacred books proclaimed the promises of Yahweh and helped assure the people their uphappy fate was only temporary. Elders of the community would conduct services (indicative of the lay, unsacerdotal character of popular religion) and assist the scribes in teaching the sayings of the prophets. Nor did the importance of synagogues diminish after the return from Babylon; if anything, it increased. They continued to serve as centers of religious and social life as well as schools, most notably during times when Jewish culture seemed in danger of being extinguished. This was especially the case, for example, during the attempt of Antiochus Epiphanes to eradicate Judaism by force, when Hellenism seemed to be making inroads into daily life. Greco-Roman thought often seemed a more formidable threat to Judaism than any political persecution, if only because its impact was more subtle, devious, and imperceptible.

Popular education in the synagogue centered around the system of law, morality, and ritual upon which the community faith was founded. Sometime in the third century, the *"House of Books,"* or elementary synagogal school, became commonplace as a library and place of general instruction. The *Pentateuch* (the first five books of the Old Testament) was generally accorded a central place, along with wisdom literature, in the curriculum. Thus, synagogue schools were a native growth, an almost inevitable development from earlier home instruction necessitated partly by the growing complexity of religious literature and partly by the threat of Hellenistic schools with their disruptive intellectual influence. The aims of the Jewish school were to instill a strong sense of communal identification, to preserve the heritage of the ancestral faith, and to resist every cultural pressure toward assimilation.

There is a tradition recording that *Simon ben Shetach,* around 75 B.C., inaugurated a set of educational reforms intended to spread elementary schooling more widely among the people and to institute compulsory education in Palestine. Despite advances in general education in the upper strata of society, most Jews still could neither read nor write in the generation preceding the birth of Christ. Ben Shetach's latter ambition was not realized until 64 A.D., when a high priest, *Josua ben Gamala,* first made elementary schools obligatory. Providing universal formal schooling took many years, but eventually schools were diffused everywhere there was a Jewish community and synagogue. Without gratuitous instruction, considering how dispersed the Jews were, national traditions and laws would have gradually disappeared under foreign influences. It was for this reason that the Jews were the first people of antiquity to insist upon some formal schooling *for all the people.*

The developed Hebrew educational structure did not appear until the Jews were a scattered, stateless people. In rough outline, it developed three well-defined institutions, beginning with the teaching of adults and slowly extending downward through six or seven centuries until popular education was offered to children. The elementary school, or *Beth-hasepher* (House of Books), was housed in the synagogue. Boys entered upon its sequence of studies at the age of six or seven and continued until thirteen. Under the tutelage of a scribe, the student would devote himself to the written *Torah*. The word literally means "instruction" and originally referred to the Pentateuch, but subsequently came to include a body of traditions and interpretations involving liturgy and social conduct. Aside from reading, writing and arithmetic, and the Torah, ancient Hebrew was studied, because Aramaic had long since superseded Hebrew as the vernacular language. In areas where Hellenic influences were especially strong, as, for example, at the Jewish community in Alexandria, Greek was the popular language of all Jews. When it is recalled that ancient Hebrew was innocent of vowel signs and word spacing, it can be seen how its study must have been a slow, painstaking process. After the third century A.D., the elementary curriculum of the House of Books also included the Psalms, occasionally the Prophets, and the Book of Proverbs, synagogal liturgy, and other ritual ceremonials. All signs point to a powerful, intensive course of study as rigorous as any offered in a Greek or Roman elementary school.

A higher, secondary-level education was provided by the *Beth-hamidrash,* or "House of Exposition," sometimes known as the "House of the *Midrash.*" Its subject of study was the Oral Law, or *Mishna,* codified at the end of the second century A.D. If a boy remained at school until age fifteen he was given a severe training in this legalistic interpretation of the written law. Few students completed its study.

After the destruction of the Temple by the Romans in 70 A.D., the teaching scribes, called Rabbins, discussed earlier, finally superseded the priesthood as expounders of the law and developers of the Mosaic tradition outside the Torah or Pentateuch. Their unwritten but ever-growing teachings (the Massorah and Kabbala, for instance) gave them great influence. Their guilds attracted many bright young men to courses of study of the *Talmud* (commentaries, homilies, and interpretations of oral law). A student at this higher level also learned to translate Hebrew scriptures into Aramaic or Greek, learned some Hellenistic philosophy and literature, and advanced his studies of written law. Jerusalem was a major center of higher education, although most of the major cities of Palestine boasted scribal schools to advance a youth's education as far as he was capable. Instruction proceeded much as it does at the doctoral level today, with emphasis upon individual instruction and independent research. Such famous teacher-scholars as *Shammai, Hillel,* and *Gamaliel* were products of scribal institutions.

Jewish learning as preserved and transmitted in the schools at all three levels seemed to have been determined by a complex intellectual interaction among contending parties within society. A tension between those who adhered uncompromisingly to the strict traditions of their fathers and those who welcomed the influx of Hellenic culture, beginning early in the second century B.C., seems reflected partially in the content and direction of Jewish education. On the one hand, there were the *Chasidim,* the "godly" or "pious" conservatives who insisted on a literalistic interpretation of the law in all its details. They were succeeded in the post-Maccabean period by the *Pharisees,* a separate class of puritanical fundamentalists dedicated to resistance against the Hellenistic invasion of Jewish thought and culture. Many of them taught in the synagogues, upholding the law and instructing both young and old in the doctrines of repentance for sins and the promise of forgiveness. No other group so stoutly insisted upon the absolute monotheism of Judaism in a world where polytheism was the rule rather than the exception. They set an example to potential backsliders, illustrating by their precepts and daily conduct what strict observation of legalistic religion entailed. Historians accord the preservation of Judaism through a difficult period mainly to the work of the Pharisees in the schools.

Opposed to the fundamentalists were the *Sadducees,* leaders of the Hellenizing faction. They were aristocratic priest-politicians for the most part, eager to preserve their control of Temple worship by collaboration with foreign governments in power. They rapidly declined in influence, naturally, with the destruction of the Temple in 70 A.D., but not before succeeding in introducing some innovations in the schools. Their most important contribution was to popularize the curricula and institutions of the Greek educational system, most notably the *gymnasium.* Sons of the Sadducees usually pursued a "graduate-level" course of studies at some Hellenistic center of learning in preference to the parochial education offered through the scribal or rabbinical schools. It is believed that the Sadducees also worked actively in the spread of Greek educational institutions throughout Palestine.

Still another group important to late Jewish learning, and probably an offshoot of the original Chasidim, were the *Essenes,* priestly scribes that withdrew from society to found monastic communities out in the wilderness. Little is known as yet regarding their ascetic beliefs and practices. They appear to have been religious conservatives, dedicated to preserving the purest ideals of the Mosaic faith, who spent their time copying ancient manuscripts and developing a body of esoteric theological lore. They may have founded schools; almost certainly they provided some regimen of studies for new initiates into Essenic communities, because their ranks were replenished by a constant flow of novices. The community at *Qumran,* where the famed "Dead Sea Scrolls" were discovered, appears to have been an Essene center.

Finally, another important group were the *Apocalyptists,* itinerant priests who went about preaching a vision of a coming Messianic kingdom when the wicked would perish and the righteous would reign supreme. They mingled profound piety and a strong sense of ethics with vivid imagery in their writings while helping to strengthen the reforms of the Pharisees. Students in scribal schools devoted much of their time to the analysis and interpretation of apocalyptic literature in the first century B.C. and through-out the next two or three hundred years.

Educational Ideals

Compared with the Greco-Roman tradition, Jewish culture suffers severe limitations. The Greeks were gifted in the recognition of the physical and aesthetic dimensions of life as the Jews were not. The Greeks caught most of the subtle nuances of visual and emotional experience in ways that eluded Hebraic culture. The latter displayed no talent in the visual arts, for reasons already pointed out, but also accomplished little in the way of speculative philosophy, natural science, or technology. There is little or nothing of the lively metaphysical concerns so characteristic of Western philosophy in Jewish thought. The genius of the Jew was his ability to express his religious consciousness and to infuse it with ethical power. In his writings the personal relations of man to God found a level of expression never attained by the Greek or Roman. Though the dramatic and scientific imagination remained undeveloped, his capacity for interpreting a faith in God as Creator, Preserver, and Father of his creatures and the joy (as well as the sorrow) bound up with that faith was unexcelled. What Hebrew culture missed in breadth of experience or content, it gained in depth of feeling, concentration of purpose, and level of moral insight. And it is Jewish education that most clearly reveals these tendencies, because it was so deeply conditioned by them.

Education among the Hebraic Jews through their long history aimed at a stringent separatism, the preservation of a Holy People. The com-munity's past, culminating in the Maccabean crisis, indicated clearly that it must be apart, be Jewish, or consent to the disappearance of Judaism as a distinctive entity. Its problem was standing clear of the world in order to protect its identity. It had seen members swept away from their religious moorings altogether and succumb to the allurement of foreign cultures. It knew what happened when Jews failed to stand together against the machinations of their foes, understood all too well how fellow Israelites could compromise with Gentile ways and depart from the law. This par-ticularism sometimes bred a most unlovely pride. It also engendered a piety and humility, a sense of responsibility as a Holy People. If Yahweh's purpose and rule were to be satisfied, his people must remain pure, un-defiled, ever obedient to his will. Education was based on a central con-viction that an omnipotent, righteous creator God had chosen the Hebrews as an instrument of fulfillment; that though the Jews were always in danger of forsaking this exceptional position through faithlessness, righteousness was the condition for the restoration or salvation of the people; and that instruction in the law was a powerful means of safeguarding the collective identity. Consequently, education was the creator of a cultural and civic consciousness, thoroughly religious in content and purpose. It was, as Castle phrases it, "exclusively a moral and religious education, nourished by a profound monotheism, conducted by precise regulation, centered in a written law, intimately bound up with the spiritual welfare and separateness of the Jewish people."[5]

Among them there was no humanistic ideal of excellence or level of perfection to be attained. The Jew, unlike the Greek, was not educated to a consciousness of his powers as an individual; there is no *paideia* in the precise sense of what an educated culture meant to a Hellene, no *areté* in Hebraic thought. The person was taught to be aware of his dependence upon his Creator and his human limitations before the divine omnipotence. God, not man, is the maker and measure of all things. The theme is developed with astonishing consistency throughout the evolution of Hebraic theology, from the days of Moses or the early prophets on down to the post-Maccabean apocalyptic zealots. Man is a frail reed in the hands of majestic Yahweh and must subject himself to his commandments. The only rough parallel between Hellenistic and Jewish thought is the injunction against excessive pride (*hubris* for the Greek) that calls down divine retribution upon the impiety inherent in such pride. For the Greek, however, human arrogance was an invitation for the Olympian deities to crush a man; to the Jew, pride was a symbol pointing beyond itself, to an estrangement between man and God, a sure indication of violated trust and neglect of moral duty.

Nonetheless, there were ideals, clearly articulated goals, for education. First, the aim of producing a man competent to serve *economic* needs was paramount. Unlike some strains in Greco-Roman practice, Jewish education stressed the importance of vocationalism and the dignity of labor. Every man was to be trained to a craft or trade and every woman in domestic duties. "He who does not teach his son a trade," one Talmudic judgment has it, "teaches him to be a thief." Significantly, every great Jewish preacher, scholar, or prophet was engaged in a profession of some sort. Manual labor was honored, not as a mere economic necessity, but as an enobling fulfillment of human character. Perhaps no other people throughout history has been so emphatic on this point.

Secondly, the concept of *holiness* was fundamental to the Jewish conception of the ideally educated individual. The true Jew sought a state of being traced by Yahweh himself: "You shall be holy, for I the Lord your God am holy." One cannot usurp the character of divinity but one must

---

[5] E. B. Castle, *Ancient Education and Today* (Baltimore: Penguin, 1965), p. 184.

emulate the aspect of holiness manifest in Yahweh. The striking cohesion and tenacity of the Israelite remnant was always focused around the idea of personal righteousness. It was to be achieved by moral discipline, personal and collective, by contemplation, prayer, and attention to daily conduct. Accordingly, a third, closely related mark of the Jewish educational ideal was its attention to *morality*. Both informal education and institutionalized schooling were bent to producing the ethical person. In the final analysis, what counts is what a person *is*, not what he can do or how much knowledge he possesses.

However, right conduct—one sign of the condition of holiness—depends upon knowledge. If a man exhibited a capacity to learn but did not do so, he might suffer ostracism from the community and, possibly, even civil disfranchisement. When one is ignorant of the law one cannot very well conform to it. Education among the Jews represented a great *intellectual* effort to defend themselves against spiritual conquest just as knowledge of the religious law became a source of consolation amid oppressions. Even, as has been shown, when the Jews were a dispossessed, dispersed people, they could maintain an existence, an identity, their habits and manners, through knowledge of their faith. It is fair to say, therefore, that Jewish education was thoroughly *intellectual,* in the positive sense of respect for ideas and a high tolerance for knowledge as an intrinsic value. Jewish thought has traditionally exalted the life of the mind and esteemed those devoted to scholarship.

It is tempting to conclude that education as initiated in the Hebraic tradition was primarily a matter of religious instruction. This is true insofar as its content and goals were directed toward concerns modern man would call sacred, as opposed to secular. On the other hand, no such distinction existed in Jewish culture. There were no divisions between the sacred and the secular, the religious and the profane. Life was viewed as a unitary whole and if, in retrospect, the ultimate aim of Jewish education is viewed as an effort to establish a "sacral" society consecrated by God's laws, it is only because modern man is heir to a set of distinctions introduced subsequently into Western culture. For the Jew, all of human existence was infused with the religious consciousness, a kind of global awareness that set the terms of his education: "Yahweh, he is God, there is none else. . . . And you shall keep his statutes, and his commandments . . . that it may go well with you, and with your children after you, and that you may prolong your days upon the land which Yahweh your God gives you, forever." This was the supreme directive that explains the reason for being of an education conducted down through the centuries and continuing in the present. However provincial it might seem, Jewish education has had the practical effect of preserving a cultural identity and the religious life of a people despite (and perhaps because of) horrendous persecutions in all ages. Furthermore, and aside from its own historic importance, Jewish education laid the basis for education developed in the Christian tradition.

THE PEOPLE OF THE MESSIAH

The Birth and Spread of Christianity

"I am entering upon the history of a period," Tacitus wrote of the first half of the first century, "rich in disasters, gloomy with wars, rent with seditions, nay, savage in its very hours of peace." He wrote of Rome wasted by fire, of the defilement of sacred rites, of adulteries in high places, of "seas crowded with exiles; island rocks drenched with murder. Yet wilder was the frenzy in Rome," he reported, "nobility, wealth, the refusal of office, its acceptance—everything was a crime, and virtue the surest ruin." The high hopes raised when Augustus had ascended the throne and Virgil's dream of a new Golden Age had been reduced within the short span of half a century, to the melancholy reality of an empire apparently politically and morally bankrupt. The great masses of men sought solace from a brutal age in heavenly presentiments—in the consolations of Isis, Mithra, Serapis, or Apollo. Everywhere it was predicted that Apollo or Dionysus would intervene soon in the affairs of men, that some divine vice regent would inaugurate worldwide changes to alleviate the restlessness and apprehension racking the population. Perhaps some great catastrophe was at hand, to be followed by a reign of universal harmony. Virgil himself, it was recalled, had written that there would be born a child who would "rule with his father's virtues the world at peace."

Among the Jews, such predictions were commonplace. Old Testament prophets had long ago spoken of the coming Kingdom of Yahweh, of a Day of the Lord when all earthly governments would be reduced to dust and Yahweh would appear in person to reign supreme over all the earth. Jeremiah's ancient promise that Israel would be restored under the dynasty of David was reworked by the Maccabean author of the Book of Daniel to make it appear that the restoration was close at hand. In turn, the pseudo-Daniel's description of an angelic messenger "like unto a son of man" who would herald the coming of the Kingdom of the Lord was converted in the apocalyptic Book of Enoch (ca. 95–64 B.C.) into "*the* Son of Man," savior to all faithful Jews. Thus it was not surprising that a schismatic sect of Judaism appeared on the scene which made the Messiah its central spiritual figure and the foundation for its doctrines. Its originality lay neither in the declaration that a terrible holocaust presaging the end of the temporal world was expected, a Day of Judgment ushering in the Kingdom of God, nor in the fact that its sectaries preached the advent of a Savior; its novelty was manifest in the startling practice of proselytizing Gentiles as well as Jews. The ultimate fruit of these labors was to convulse the world of antiquity and leave it forever transformed.

Very little is known about the founder of Christianity. There are no early secular sources other than two brief references in the *Antiquities* of the Jewish writer Josephus, both probably spurious. The main sources of information are the Gospels of Matthew, Mark, and Luke, authored no earlier than 66–68 A.D., and possibly much later. Behind them stands an earlier literature now lost to history, in turn resting upon an oral tradition. Because the evangelical writers adhered to the then common conception of history as a vehicle for moral edification rather than for literal transcription, the first books of the New Testament are generally distrusted by modern critics. Numerous contradictions, legends of dubious authenticity, pious interpolations designed to buttress a later doctrine or ritual, evidence of deletions, and passages describing incidents contrived to demonstrate the fulfillment of Old Testament prophecies abound. Several suspicious resemblances to the tales told of pagan gods are evident in the recounting of details from the life of Jesus Christ. At best, the over-all picture is fragmentary.

This much can be credited: around the year 5 B.C. a Jewish carpenter named Joseph and his wife Mary had a son named *Yeshu'a* (Joshua, meaning "the help of Yahweh"; in Greek, *Iesous;* in Latin, *Iesus*) who grew up in the Galilean village of Nazareth, where it is probable he was born. Yeshu'a had several sisters and four brothers. As a young man he was baptised by an Esseniclike preacher named Yohannan bar Zachariah, known to history as John the Baptist. When the latter was imprisoned and his voice silenced, the Galilean embarked upon a preaching career of his own, basing his precepts on John's doctrine of the impending Kingdom of God. His ethical code was tied to his belief in the final Apocalypse, and though it was unoriginal in virtually every respect, it was presented in a lucid and forceful manner calculated to win wide support. Jesus was quickly credited with the power to work miracles and raise the dead. Following a relatively short career, he came into conflict with Jewish or Roman law, was arrested, tried, and crucified around the year 30 A.D. His followers taught that he was the long-awaited Messiah and had been resurrected from the grave.

The thrust of his ethical teachings was to prepare his Jewish listeners for the coming of God's reign by urging repentance and baptism, thereby rendering them worthy of salvation. He considered himself an orthodox Jew and advised his disciples to shun Gentiles, from which it can be gathered that his message was directed exclusively to the Jewish community. Ethically, he exalted humility, gentleness, peace, and poverty; he remained indifferent to economic provision, government, and property; he preferred celibacy to marriage and commanded his followers to abandon their family ties.

As portrayed in the Gospels, Jesus was both a powerful, charismatic figure and unquestionably a masterful teacher. He taught with the simplicity required by his audiences, employing vivid imagery, directness of speech, and as occasion demanded, sharp sarcasm. His aphorisms were models of clarity and brevity. Rather than insinuating his lessons with reasoned argument, he relied upon similes, metaphors, and pungent aphorisms to carry the message. Clever analogies and parables are scattered throughout his recorded sayings. It is worth noting that later Christian teachers relied heavily on these pedagogical devices, so much so in fact that they became characteristic of Christian preaching.

At first the cult of the *Christiani* (from *Christos* or *Christus,* meaning "the anointed") grew slowly. It remained a minority dissenting sect within Judaism and its members continued to worship in the Temple and to observe ritual law. For almost a century its recruits were mainly Jews or converts to Judaism; later, according to the account of Justin Martyr, believers were "of all races, barbarians and Greeks, nomads and those who live in tents, whatever they may be called." Therein lay a major dilemma. So long as Christian communities included only Jews, their chief problem was contending with the orthodox Sadducees and Pharisees who denounced the cult as another instance of "whoring after new gods," of "backsliding," and who consequently rejected their teachings. But there soon arose the question of accepting pagan converts to the new faith. The result was a split between Judeo-Christians who chose to observe traditional Judaistic strictures and Hellenistic Christians who moved to disengage themselves from the parent religion. With the fall of Jerusalem and the destruction of the Temple in 70 A.D., the latter party gained the ascendancy and by the midsecond century had extricated themselves entirely from Judaic Christianity.

The foremost exponent of the Hellenizing faction and chief theologian for the messianic movement was a first-century Syrian Jew from Tarsus named *Paul,* who had been converted to the cause. Along with other apostles, he led a vigorous missionary effort through the eastern Mediterranean world which proved singularly successful. By accommodating Christian tenets to Hellenistic forms of thought he was able to communicate his message to listeners reared outside the Judaic tradition and so gain proselytes from their ranks. The Messiah figure who had proved to be "unto Jews a stumbling block and unto the Greeks foolishness" was daily gathering adherents.

Several factors militated against the spread of the new gospel. Though the heterogeneity of the imperial population made tolerant polytheism politically expedient, most outsiders regarded the "Nazarenes," as they were called, as merely another fanatical Jewish sect afflicted (in the words of Tacitus) with a "deadly superstition" originating in a frontier province. The uncompromising monotheism of Jews, as well as their persistent refusal to join in the worship of the *Divus*—the divine emperor—rendered them all exceedingly unpopular. In this respect the early Christians were regarded as equally troublesome. They too refused to support the official cults or to even recognize the validity of other faiths. The fact that the *Christiani* held meetings secretly aroused popular suspicion and antagonized almost everyone. Public officials were encouraged to spread lurid stories ascribing terrible orgiastic rites to their worship, tales quickly seized upon by the general populace. Worst of all, Christianity welcomed converts from the very dregs of society, including slaves, paupers, freedmen—all the underprivileged disdained by other sects. The pagan philosopher Celsus, about 180 A.D. poked fun at this radical egalitarianism, saying, "It is only the simpletons, the ignoble, the senseless, slaves and womenfolk and children whom they wish to persuade or *can* persuade."

And yet these apparent drawbacks were also its source of strength. Christianity had a powerful appeal for all the downtrodden who had long since abandoned any hope of bettering their lot in this world and who were drawn irresistibly to the promise of a happier life yet to come. Christians allowed women to embrace the faith, in direct opposition to the practice of excluding them from competing mystery sects. Furthermore, in an age characterized by nostalgic longing for a by-gone golden age, Christianity looked confidently to the future, expecting the return of the *Christos* and the founding of a heavenly kingdom on earth.

There were other advantages possessed by Pauline Christianity. Its devotees offered a definite historical individual of well-defined character who supplied the long-sought-after link between humanity and divinity instead of a grotesque figure drawn from some ahistorical legend. Even Jewish monotheism was made more palatable by introducing the quasipolytheistic doctrine of the Trinity and by serving Greco-Roman man worship in the deification of Jesus. Early Christians were thoroughly syncretic, drawing upon a fund of practices and doctrines already familiar to prospective initiates. Again, adherents of the Christian faith had a growing, tightly knit organizational structure which gave them a telling advantage over those mystery religions that had never achieved more than local organization. Finally, the fervor with which early Christians endured persecution and ridicule, their certain hope in salvation, could not help but impress even their most jaded opponents. For all of these reasons, the new movement rather quickly became a force with which the rest of the world had to reckon.

In the beginning Christians had no schools of their own. The phrase *Christian education* first appears around 96 A.D. in the writings of Clement of Rome, but it does not indicate any well-developed institutional apparatus for the schooling of converts to Christianity. No separate educational system was worked out among the first few generations of believers because their energies were directed first and foremost to the more immediate task of founding a system of canonical discipline, liturgy, and ethics. Education meant moral training and learning dogmas necessary for salvation, matters best handled through communal worship within communities of believers and, of course, by the family. The apostolic message had admonished parents to inculcate religious instruction in the home; it was a natural continuation of the Jewish tradition emphasizing the development of religious consciousness within the context of the family. Furthermore, because early Christians anticipated the end of the world in their own time it is hardly surprising they failed to establish schools. Schooling is a long-range endeavor and it hardly made sense to invest in it if the Second Coming of Christ was eminent. If anything, Christian education had a sacred, transcendent meaning on a level that was certainly supraschool: it was an education that could not be offered through an institution like any other profane institution, least of all a formal school. Education, in the minds of most believers, suggested training in the use of language, instruction in rhetoric, grammar, logic, and dialectic—important enough for the secular life, perhaps, but scarcely relevant to the more vital concern of attaining salvation and eternal life. Besides, a more pressing task presented itself: simple survival. There was a battle to be waged on three fronts—political, doctrinal, and cultural—and little time was left for other pursuits.

Jerusalem Versus Rome: The Political Struggle

Christian communities, like their Jewish forebears, lived apart, worshipped apart, considered themselves sojourners and strangers in a dying world, and established standards of conduct antithetical to those normally accepted by the public at large. As has been mentioned, Roman authorities first tended to regard Christians as just another extremist Jewish sect to be dealt with as circumstances demanded. Emperor *Trajan* (98–117 A.D.), in response to a request from *Pliny the Younger,* Governor of Pontus and Bithynia in Asia Minor, for a policy interpretation on an edict demanding harsh discipline for Christians made a remarkable concession. The Christians were not to be hunted out, Trajan decided, and if accused and convicted, they were not to be punished if they agreed to worship the Roman gods. Of course that was precisely what Christians refused to do and hence the source of so much hostility from the public. The authorities were inclined initially to protect the Christians from their critics, in accordance with a long-standing policy of accommodation toward all sects prevailing in areas under Roman control. Carrying out the policy in dealings with Christians was an entirely different matter, however. *Marcus Aurelius* (161–180 A.D.), for example, had to sanction persecutions in Gaul and in North Africa against the Christians when riots broke out against their separatist ways. Had he refused to bow to public pressure, open revolution could easily have ensued. The wisest course of action, it seemed, was to conclude incidents by making scapegoats of the Christians and by throwing blame on them for instigating the troubles in the first place.

The antagonism of the pagans was not altogether unreasonable, from their point of view. Why, the philosopher Celsus asked, did Christians refuse to participate in public life? If everyone were so uncooperative, it would mean the destruction of everything and every brand of religion, including Christianity, he alleged. The Christians even lacked the Jewish justification for their exclusiveness in a national sect and tradition. Could there be any possible justification, sensible men wondered, for not demanding that authorities put an end to their heresy before they completely disrupted the social order?

The first universal persecution of the Christians on a coordinated, empire-wide basis was instigated during the reign of *Septimius Severus* (193–211 A.D.). It was prompted in part by scurrilous reports that adherents of the Christian sect practiced obscene rites, including cannibalism (possibly a misinterpretation of the Eucharist) and sexual licentiousness. Prostitutes were hauled into court and promised their freedom in exchange for affidavits acknowledging their participation in Christian orgies. Public opinion demanded drastic measures. Severe penalties were levied against all converts to Christianity (and to Judaism as well). When they had no appreciable effect, mass arrests and sadistic executions followed. Wave upon wave of mass hysteria erupted until the public wearied of the blood bath.

During the period of tolerance that followed, Christians busied themselves, as insurance against further upheavals, with building an organizational structure to preserve the scattered, isolated Christian enclaves. A system of government by bishops was instituted, provision made for the financial support of clerics from a central bank, and mutual assistance programs modeled after Jewish charities or Greco-Roman welfare projects were expanded. Such activity only served to arouse more antagonism. The development of a group of people, similar to a state, within the eastern division of the empire, particularly when its members promised a classless salvation for all (even slaves), seemed dangerously subversive, a deliberate provocation against Rome's majesty. Again public pressure mounted for official action.

Finally, the apparent Christian threat was responded to by the Emperor *Decius* in 250–251. He launched a persecution during a period of political turmoil, a difficult time when he desperately required someone to blame for the over-all deterioration that had set in. Christians seemed likely candidates. The emperor's strategy was clever: no one was asked to abandon his religious faith, merely to perform a single pagan observance at a state shrine, whereupon a local Sacrificial Commission would issue a "Certificate of Sacrifice" as proof of compliance with the emperor's edict. Authorities would not tolerate any refusal to join in corporate performances upon pain of death. Either way, Christians were placed in an impossible situation. Anyone who obeyed the rule naturally lost his standing among his Christian fellows for having worshipped a false idol. Yet if he were found without a sacrificial certificate he could be executed.[6] In the end the imperial strategy failed because the resulting martyrdoms elicited public sympathy rather than satisfied any sense of popular outrage against Christians. Hordes of the faithful gladly laid down their lives in the belief that a martyr's death ensured salvation and reconcili-

---

[6] Some entrepreneurs did a thriving black market business in forged sacrificial certificates.

ation with Christ. Aside from arousing respect for the tenacity of a Christian's faith, when the victim willingly submitted to his fate, it greatly spoiled the spectacle's entertainment value.

Six years after the end of Decius' persecution, *Valerian* inaugurated a new anti-Christian pogrom. Economic considerations were involved more than religious motivations, because he was really after church properties, which had become quite extensive by the midthird century. While it lasted, money from the sale of appropriated lands rolled into the imperial coffers. Dispossessed Christians could do little but hide until the storm had passed. It was soon clear that persecution had failed to suppress the Christian menace. Valerian's son, trying a new tack, reversed his father's policy and called a halt to all official action. It may have been a mistake, from the Roman point of view. The respite allowed Christians to establish themselves more securely during the forty-year period of toleration that followed. New converts were recruited from the lower and middle classes, the number of bishops doubled, and the ecclesiastical structure of a growing church was greatly strengthened. It has been estimated that the total number of Christians tripled or even quadrupled throughout this time of relative political security.

Despite this growth, few converts were drawn from the better-educated segments of society, mainly because Christianity still seemed to offer little to people with a vested interest in preserving the existing social order. Nor did a crude, unsophisticated faith like Christianity appeal to intellectuals steeped in an older philosophical tradition. Theoretical attacks by such people as the neo-Platonist philosopher *Porphyry* and his colleague *Hierocles* probably helped create a climate of intellectual opposition to the new faith as well. It was Hierocles who became chief instigator of a Great Persecution aiming at the total and final annihilation of Christianity, thereby concluding the crucial period of noninterference that the church had used to such good advantage.

The showdown of paganism against Christianity began in 303 A.D. Emperor *Diocletian*, assisted by the lesser Caesar, Galerius, launched a death struggle designed to provide the "Final Solution" for the troublesome followers of an obscure but now notorious provincial criminal. Diocletian and Galerius were strict religious conservatives who knew this was perhaps the last opportunity to destroy the Christians and rid the empire of them forever. Christians were forbidden to gather for worship services, their sacred scrolls and churches were burned, known adherents were fired from the army and civil service, the clergy were arrested and compelled to make sacrifices to state gods. The next decade brought bloody defiance, mass tortures, and public executions.[7] Literally thousands perished. Even

---

[7] Roman tortures were fiendishly ingenious. During this and other persecutions, a wide array of techniques for inflicting pain was devised. Christians were tied to stakes and shot full of arrows. St. Catherine was tied to a revolving wheel, thus giving her name

after the abdication of Diocletian in 305, the persecution continued for a short while longer under Galerius, Diocletian's successor in the eastern provinces, until he too was resigned to abandoning the fight. Issued from his deathbed was an edict granting freedom of worship to all members of the Christian faith. Because persecution had only made them more obstinate, he lamented, henceforth they would be given clemency and allowed to live as long as they did not disturb the public order. Galerius' edict marked the first occasion when Christianity was given some measure of legal recognition. Confiscated property was restored in the western half of the empire by *Maxentius* (306–312) and Christians breathed a little easier.

For those in the East, the situation did not substantially improve. Galerius's successor, *Maximinus Daia,* fought a last-ditch struggle against Christianity's advances. The edict of Galerius was thrown out and persecutions resumed on the pretext of requests from municipal authorities at Tyre and Nicomedia that the local Christians be expelled. Daia was a bit more sophisticated in his approach to the problem of extirpating Christians. First he sought public support by circulating false confessions implicating Christians in all sorts of horrendous crimes. Next the spurious anti-Christian *Acts of Pilate* were inserted in secular school curricula. In addition to tortures and executions, Daia relied on a rival pagan organization he created to outdo its efficient Christian counterpart. An elaborate ecclesiastical system with its own priestly hierarchy was instituted in hopes of overshadowing the Church and attracting converts from her ranks. The effort came far too late. Few supported the new organization and organized Christian communities continued to flourish.

In the meantime, political events in the western empire were moving toward a climax that would bear powerful repercusions for the Christian cause. The western emperor, Maxentius, was defeated in battle in 312 at the Milvian Bridge (just outside Rome) by a rival claimant to power. The victor was a young man later known as *Constantine the Great.* Success in battle brought Constantine sole mastery of the West. It remained to be seen whether he could now extend his dominion in the East, where two co-rulers held sway. One was Maximinus Daia and the other was his rival,

---

to the popular firework. St. Apolloma had her teeth pulled out and became the patron saint of dentistry. Disembowelment with a sharpened stick inserted through the victim's posterior was common. Genital suspension, roasting on a gridiron, cooking in cauldrons and frying pans, hanging, flaying, strangulation, scourging, and goring by wild animals were common means of execution. Rape by animals was favored in public arenas. Another unusual means of execution was known as *cyphonismus,* whereby the victim was coated with honey and tortured to death by the insects that covered him. The Romans invented almost endless variations in the techniques of crucifixion. Another unique method consisted of sewing a victim inside an animal's skin and allowing it to shrink and rot in the sun. Details are chillingly described in Daniel P. Mannix's unusual work, *The History of Torture* (New York: Dell, 1964), pp. 30–42.

Licinius, who ruled the Danubian provinces. Constantine entered into a political agreement with the latter, married Licinius's half-sister, and consecrated the union in the *Edict of Milan,* which introduced complete religious tolerance for all subjects, pagans and Christians. Understandably, Daia was unhappy with the obvious political implications of the arrangement and rightly considered it a threat to his own power. It took eleven years before the situation was stabilized, ending with Licinius crushing Maximinus Daia and temporarily ruling as emperor of the East as Constantine's associate. In 324 Licinius, already weakened through indolent and cruel rule, declared war on Constantine. His armies met defeat, first at Chrysopolis, secondly at Adrianople. Licinius himself was captured at Thessalonica, where he was interned, tried, and summarily executed for treason. With his chief rival disposed of, Constantine was left as undisputed ruler of both eastern and western halves of the empire. From the outset he seems to have been determined to remove the seat of power from Rome to the east, possibly because it was politically safer there. Accordingly, in 326 the capital of Constantinople was founded at Byzantium. For over two decades, Constantine ruled from his new capital. He continued to tolerate paganism, although, as events were to show, his sympathies had been won to the Christian cause.

The Christian writers *Lactantius* and *Eusebius* report that Constantine believed he had been warned in a dream just before his fateful battle against Maxentius to inscribe the monogram XP (*Christos*) upon his soldiers' shields if he hoped to emerge victorious. Prior to his conquests in Italy Constantine also recalled a vision of a cross hanging across the sun with the injunction to "conquer with this sign" inscribed across the heavens. Of such incidents the stuff of history is made. When he came to power he initiated a series of reforms explicitly favoring the Christians. Clergy were exempted from certain municipal obligations. Provincial churches at Carthage and in other major cities were subsidized from the office of the imperial exchequer. The bishop at Rome was endowed with imposing new churches and a royal palace. Christian episcopal courts were allowed civil jurisdiction and the Church given status as a civic corporation.

Despite the vigorous impulsion to make Christianity a state religion and Constantine's own involvement in matters of Church doctrine and politics at the Councils of Arles and Nicaea, he did not officially become a Christian immediately. It can be assumed that Constantine saw in Christianity a potential agent to unify a disintegrating social culture and to quell political conflict. He personally accepted a theology of sun worship that only gradually was identified with "the lawful and most holy Christian religion." Then too he could hardly afford actually to join the Church, thereby alienating the great pagan majority of his subjects. Although he stopped short of that, he proscribed ritual prostitution, closed down some important pagan temples, passed laws against divination, confiscated temple treasuries, and finally banned all pagan sacrifices. Clearly the tide had turned in the Christians' favor even though paganism was not yet outlawed. In 337, while preparing to lead his forces into battle against Persia, Constantine fell ill. Just before he died (when he could sin no more) he consented to receiving Christian baptism at the hands of his beloved bishop and biographer Eusebius. "The miracle of miracles, greater than dried-up seas and cloven rocks, greater than the dead rising again to life, was when the Augustus on his throne, Pontiff of the gods of Rome, himself a god to the subjects of Rome, bent himself to become the worshipper of a crucified provincial of his Empire."[8]

The Ecclesiastical Church

By the beginning of the fifth century the Church was firmly established as an ecclesiastical institution. At first simple congregations had met wherever possible, with few distinctions between laity and clergy. Each independent church evolved its own structure of priests, elders, and bishops. By the second century every urban Christian community had a bishop to supervise and preside over the local clergy, his jurisdictional sphere corresponding to the *civitas*, the smallest administrative unit of the Roman state. Persecutions and the influence of pagan mystery cults drove worshippers to a hierarchical organization and a professional priesthood as guardian of some uniformity of belief. When more converts were won, distinctions of rank among bishops were instituted; those in larger cities came to be called *metropolitans*. The Roman governmental system served admirably as a model. The bishop or metropolitan corresponded to the secular municipal authority, the archbishop to a provincial governor, and a patriarch to the ruler of a division of the empire. By 400 A.D. there were patriarchs at Alexandria, Antioch, Constantinople, and Rome. The culmination of this evolution of a state within a state was a strong governmental and ecclesiastical organization capable of eventually supplanting its secular counterpart. It attained this status not as a monolithic entity, as is sometimes supposed, but as a schismatic, fragmented structure.

Even before Constantine's time, the bishop at Rome enjoyed pre-eminence over other patriarchs, partly because the city was venerated as the alleged scene of missionary activity by the Apostles Paul and Peter, partly because of the theological doctrine of Petrine Succession, mainly because Rome was also the political capital of the empire until its transfer to Constantinople. As early as the second century *Irenaeus* had advanced Rome's claim to superiority on grounds of a direct chain of authority extending from Peter down to the bishops of his own time. The eastern churches acknowledged Rome's pre-eminence but they were reluctant to admit its right to legislate for them. A dispute over the timing of the celebration of Easter led the

---

[8] Edward A. Freeman, *The Chief Periods of European History* (London: Macmillan, 1886), p. 67.

Roman bishop, *Victor,* to break with the churches of Asia Minor. Later demands that all churches be subordinated to Rome were stoutly resisted. Cultural and theological differences were only accentuated by the elevation of the patriarch at Constantinople, corresponding to Constantine's raising of that city to a place of importance. The absence of imperial government from Rome also gave the head of the Roman church greater opportunities to exercise independent civil authority. Even when Emperor *Valentinian III* issued a decree in 455 commanding all western bishops to submit to the jurisdiction of the Roman *"pater,"* or pope, many refused. They were joined by the patriarchal see at Constantinople, eventuating in a major breach between what became Orthodoxy and Catholicism.

Despite the schism of the Church, Christianity as a cultural force was well on its way to a final victory over paganism, exemplified in 391 by an edict of Emperor *Theodosius* forbidding all pagan worship. The institutional Church was steadily gaining temporal power and winning important privileges, exemptions, and endowments for itself. By 476, when the last western emperor, *Romulus Augustulus,* was deposed and a barbarian chieftain assumed the title "King of Rome," the Church was prepared to assume the work of the old Roman state. Emperor *Justinian's* closing of all pagan schools in 529, most notably at Athens, was symbolic of the Church's undisputed power by the early sixth century.

Jerusalem Against Itself: The Doctrinal Struggle

The battle for a doctrinal orthodoxy (like the struggle for political legitimacy) was not won for several centuries; in a sense it was never completed. It began in the dispute alluded to previously between those, like Paul, who argued the Christian message was intended for Gentiles as well as Jews, and those, probably James among them, who insisted that Christ's deliverance was intended only for adherents of the ancient Judaic tradition. As Christianity spread throughout the Roman world in the first, second, and third centuries, *there was no established body of doctrine defining orthodoxy,* only competing factions hurling accusations of heresy at one another. By Constantine's time, intractable schismatics of all persuasions were a far greater threat to Church unity than paganism. While the emperor was laboring to turn Christianity into a cohesive political instrument, the churches were hopelessly split by dissent. No one agreed on such weighty matters as the nature and status of Christ, the number or significance of sacraments, the legitimacy of creeds, the sources of religious truth, and similar vital questions. The philosophically oriented Alexandrians, headed by the priest *Arius,* were intent on preserving a neo-Platonic version of the Gospels. Another group, headed by Bishop *Athanasius,* bitterly contested the Arian interpretation. Dissenting puritans such as the *Nestorians* opposed all movements to organize a priestly administrative structure and supported the burgeoning monastic movement now in its first stage of development. Out of the penitential, apocalyptic villages of Asia Minor arose the cult of *Montanism*, firmly entrenched against the Hellenization of Christianity's Jewish heritage. At the same time Constantine instituted an official Christian Church, rustic, austere sects such as the *Melitians* in Egypt and the *Donatists* in North Africa were vigorously protesting the acceptance of temporary renegades back into the fold (the churches' accommodation to those who had lapsed from the faith during earlier persecutions). Extreme ascetics and mystics, such as the *Gnostics* and *Manicheans* who fought the increasing worldliness of the Church, complicated matters still further, though their own claims to represent Christianity were ephemeral at best. One of the fateful paradoxes of history was that successive attempts to convene Church councils to hammer out a doctrinal unity only seemed to aggravate tensions and create lasting disunities.

The "final" orthodoxy as it emerged in later centuries was a composite of many forces or influences bearing unmistakable traces of the Greco-Roman culture in which Christianity began. Perhaps the astounding success of the religion can best be explained by its assimilative capacity, its ability to incorporate elements from a diversity of sources. From Judaism, Christian doctrine and practice took the name of its deity, its history and world view, many of its ethical precepts, much of its literature. From the Eastern mystery religions, such as *Mithraism*, pagan *Gnosticism*, *Zoroastrianism*, and the cults of *Cybele* and *Isis*, Christianity borrowed some forms of ritual, its otherworldliness, its schedule of sacred holidays, and the concept of a primal God-Man incarnate in human form.[9] Certain strains in Christian thought almost certainly reflect tenets of Stoicism and other late Hellenistic philosophies. Christian theology drew from a variegated fund of traditions, all the while retaining its own distinctive character, which also helps explain its universal attractiveness. In the end the cosmopolitan flavor of its practices combined with its flexibility of doctrinal interpretations to transform what had once been a minor sect into a major religion.

Athens and Jerusalem: Three Points of View

The first two great challenges for Christianity were laying down a firm base of doctrines and building an institution for the propagation of the faith. The third front in the battle for survival involved the question how to come to terms with Greco-Roman culture. Could Christianity oppose the pervading Hellenism and still hope to make its message intelligible

[9] Philostratus described Apollonius of Tyana as one who taught ideals of unselfish love and the unity of deity. He performed miracles, raised the dead, and cast out demons. After his death he reappeared and ascended bodily into heaven. He was believed to be the mediating son of a god or the god in fleshly guise. The parallel with the life of Jesus is obvious. Mithraism was Christianity's chief rival, favored by many emperors, especially Diocletian, and was particularly strong as the popular religion of the army. Had the course of history been altered only slightly, it is entirely possible that some form of Mithraism might have survived to become the dominant religion in the West.

in a world wholly dominated by Hellenistic culture? Could (or should) the new faith assimilate its surrounding cultural milieu, accept its patterns of thought or intellectual structures, and still not thereby be engulfed?[10] No single answer to those queries was forthcoming, though taken together, the various positions that were advanced profoundly influenced the over-all character of early Christian education.

Basically, Christians of the first centuries elected to compromise. On the one hand, they upbraided the pagan world for its errors and adamantly tried to break with it. On the other, because the very permeability of Hellenistic culture made it difficult to resist, they tried to fuse Christian faith with pagan wisdom. The dilemma was recognized at a fairly early date: Christianity could not get along without classical learning and it could not seem to get along with it.[11] In the first hundred years, most of Christianity's followers had been poor and illiterate. As time went on, by way of contrast, there were many attracted to the new faith from the better-educated classes, people unwilling to disengage themselves from conventional learning and "the wisdom of the world." Still less were they willing to allow their children to be brought up in ignorance of Hellenistic culture. They sent them to pagan schools along with their non-Christian classmates to get a secular education. This was the practice that threw the basic issue into bold relief. The schools *were* pagan. There the child made his first acquaintance with the Olympian deities. His textbooks were filled with the old mythology he had been taught to detest at home. The feasts of Minerva, patroness of pupils and masters, were regularly celebrated, not to mention all the observances of the official state religion. He would see his place of learning lavishly decorated in honor of Flora at the appointed season. There was nothing surprising in the fact that the Christian child ran the hazard of absorbing ideas directly opposed to those of his faith. He was torn between two rival cultures, and the result, predictably, was a certain weakening or loss of religious conviction. The strategy of grafting a specifically religious kind of training onto the classical teaching received in established schools simply did not work. It failed to secure the benefits of a regular education without also endangering, even subverting Christian training in the process.

Tertullian (born circa 160), one of the Church fathers in the West, tried to take an uncompromising stand. "What has Athens to do," he exclaimed,

10 It is noteworthy that Christianity faces a similar problem today. Some adherents argue that the basic tenets of its faith need to be recast in terms that make more sense to secular man; others argue the dangers of losing essential truths in the attempt to cast off historically conditioned cultural dross. The accompanying clamor over what directions religious education should take in order to render it more relevant to the Space Age recapitulate, in generous measure, discussions about Christian education during its historical infancy.

11 Edward J. Power, *Main Currents in the History of Education* (New York: McGraw-Hill, 1962), p. 154.

"with Jerusalem? What concord is there between the Academy and the Church? What between heretics and Christians?" Secular literature should be recognized as "folly with God," he believed. Greek learning, especially philosophy, was nothing but a network of contradictions. The Christian needed only his faith: "With our faith, we desire no further belief. For this is our central faith, that there is nothing which we ought to believe besides." But even he had to grant concessions. Clearly a Christian could not be a teacher, because he would be compelled to speak of false gods and to instruct children in beliefs antithetical to religious truth. Yet Tertullian backed away from the obvious conclusion that Christian children should be forbidden to attend schools, in spite of the dangers to which they would be exposed. "How else," he asked rhetorically, "could anyone acquire human wisdom, or learn to direct his thoughts and actions? Is learning not an indispensable guide for the whole business of life?" The upshot of it all was Christians uneasily accepting the existing schools, sending their children to them, even teaching in them, trying to absorb a classical education without also accepting the culture it represented.

Another strain of thought stoutly resisted the road to accommodation. Its spirit was expressed in the *Didascalia Apostolorum* ("Apostolic Constitutions"), a third-century document addressed unofficially to the laity and clergy. "Have nothing to do with heathen writings," it enjoined bluntly, "and refrain from strange discourses, laws, or false prophets." A Christian had no need to be exposed to their errors. The Bible provided all the wisdom and knowledge one required. "If you will explore history, you have the Book of Kings; or if you seek words of wisdom and eloquence, you have the Prophets, Job, and the Book of Proverbs, wherein you will find a more perfect knowledge. . . ." If one wanted poetry, there was the Book of Psalms. He who sought a cosmology was counseled to find it in Genesis. "Wherefore," the document advised, "abstain scrupulously from all strange and devilish books." An extensive literature arose, condemning the old culture for representing an ideal hostile to the Christian revelation and urging the clergy to avoid reading the pagan authors. As *Jerome* (331–420) put it later, in censuring priests who neglected Biblical lore for profane authors, "It is a crime for them to do voluntarily what children are obliged to do for the sake of their education." Like Tertullian, he advised children to behave as though they were being given poison—the poison of non-Christian learning—and seek an antidote in religious training outside the school arranged around the teachings of the Church and in parental instruction.

Jerome's indecision in the matter is especially instructive as an example of how the early Church struggled with the question of reconciling faith and culture. As a young man, he received a thoroughly Hellenistic schooling in Rome. At the age of forty he decided to retire to the Syrian desert and cut himself off from the world. He found he could not easily repudiate his classical heritage. In his *Epistles* he recorded the anguish he suffered:

"Wretched man that I was! I fasted and I read Cicero. After passing sleep-less nights and shedding bitter tears at the thought of my sins, I took up Plautus. If at times I came back to myself and tried to read the Prophets, the simple careless style in which they were written repelled me at once." He dreamed he had died and passed before the seat of divine judgment. When he defended himself as a devout Christian, the voice of God thun-dered back, "It is false. You are a Ciceronian. Where your treasure is, there also is your heart!" Thereafter Jerome renounced pagan authors and urged others to do likewise, all the while lapsing back into quotations from classi-cal writings when lamenting his former devotion to them! In later life Jerome founded a monastery in Bethlehem where the course of instruction included many classical authors. To teach students the classics, and advise men to forget them, as he did, involved a blatant contradiction too obvious for his precepts and practice to have any substantial influence.[12] The same contradiction appeared in the writings of *Gregory the Great,* pope of the western Church from 590 to 604, who had been trained in Roman schools. He turned bitterly against pagan learning but, with Jerome, found it impossible to divorce himself from it. "I am strongly of the opinion," he wrote, "that it is an indignity that the words of the oracle of Heaven should be restrained by the rules of Donatus . . . the praise of Christ cannot lie in one mouth with the praise of Jupiter. Consider yourself what a crime it is for bishops to recite what would be improper for religiously minded laymen." His polemic only served to reflect a common phenomenon— Christians denouncing classical pagan literature in a classic style derived from their own study of it. Likewise, Church councils expressly forbade clergy to pursue pagan learning yet promulgated doctrinal creeds forged in categories of thought derived from Greek philosophy.

Only a small minority of Christians after the fourth century continued to advocate neglect of the old learning completely. One prominent spokesman for their viewpoint was *Paulinus,* a nobleman of great learning, who none-theless turned his back on the past and argued that Christianity could not afford the luxury of cultural accommodation:

Why bid the Muses whom I have disowned return to claim my devo-tion? Hearts vowed to Christ have no welcome for the goddesses of song; they are barred to Apollo. Time was when, not with equal force but with equal ardour, I could join with you in summoning the deaf Phoebus from his cave at Delphi. Now another force, a mightier God, subdues my soul. He forbids me give up my time to the vanities of leisure or business, and the literature of fable, that I may obey his laws and see his light, which is darkened by the cunning skill of the sophist, and the figments of the poet who fills the soul with vanity and false-hood and only trains the tongue.

12 William Boyd, *The History of Western Education,* 8th ed. (New York: Barnes & Noble, 1966), p. 89.

There were some, like *Basil*, who sought a middle road between accept-ance and rejection of pagan learning. In his well-known essay *On the Read-ing of the Profane Authors,* he expressly denied that a Christian curriculum could expurgate the classics entirely. What it could do, he avowed, was structure learning so that pagan authors could be interpreted according to the Gospels; the Bible was the corrective and exegetical standard for these authors. On the practical question of what to do about pagan schools, *Hippolytus* of Rome offered popular advice. "If anyone is occupied in teaching children the sciences of this world," he wrote in his *Apostolic Tradition,* "he would be well advised to give it up, but if he has no other means of livelihood, he may be excused." Hippolytus' attitude came to be widely shared in the centuries that followed. Intellectually, most Christians regarded religious training as a superimposition upon classical education rather than a substitute for it. Institutionally speaking, they compromised by permitting their members to teach in classical schools. By the fourth century, Christians were employed at all levels of instruction, from the low-est elementary grades to the highest "university-level" chairs of grammar. Even bishops of the Church commonly found employment at some point in their careers in pagan schools. Reflective of the Church's tolerant proviso on this point, many of the great apologists for Christianity, like *Justin Martyr,* called themselves philosophers, wore the traditional garb, opened schools of advanced learning, and received the back-handed compliment by their pagan colleagues of being treated as academics even as they were attacked for their Christian teachings.

A third perspective stressed the necessity of translating Christian thought into terms a classically educated pagan could understand and accept. The earliest Christians had no systematic theology, no philosophical undergird-ing comprehensible to people nurtured with Hellenistic thought. It was *Galen* who complained that the followers of Moses and Christ ordered their converts to accept everything on faith. He was substantially correct; the Christians had beliefs, not doctrines, a faith, not a set of propositions. Still, if Christianity was to win new adherents it had to be defended against criticism such as that leveled by a character from *Minucius Felix's* delight-ful dialogue, *Octavius.* The critic exclaims that people "ignorant of learn-ing, unlettered and unacquainted even with the meanest arts pronounce definitely upon the universe and the supreme power, which, after all these ages, still forms the subject of the deliberations of the philosophers." The Christians, he continues, have gathered together from the lowest dregs of the populace "ignorant men and credulous women." Who could take Chris-tianity seriously when its proponents shunned learning, thereby remaining untutored and culturally illiterate?

In the third and fourth centuries, powerful forces absolutely hostile to the spread of Christianity were still operating. The schools, in particular, were guardians of long-standing traditions that retained considerable influence among the educated classes. The opposition encountered by Constantine's reforms shows how resistant paganism was to the encroachments of the new Christian faith. Then again, there was the growth out of Alexandria of an eclectic philosophy that combined Platonic and Aristotelian tenets with Oriental mysticism, a philosophy with strong appeal as Christianity's intellectual alternative. *Neo-Platonism* was viewed by some, especially the rhetoricians and pagan philosophers, as a vindication of the old doctrines and a possible rallying ground for defense against Christianity. Its chief exponent was *Plotinus*. As developed by scholars like *Porphyry* and *Iamblichus* and their disciples, it became a formidable opponent attracting many men of letters to its defense.

Christians, now accustomed to the inevitability of their eventual triumph, cultural and religious, over paganism were given further cause for alarm when Emperor *Julian* came to power in 361, filled with determination to re-establish the pagan order. The very next year he forbade Christians to teach in the schools, the first of a series of acts designed to crush their hated faith. His anti-Christian virulence revealed itself for all to see in his proclamations on the unity of classicism and paganism, a bond which, if it had been accepted, would have isolated Christians by encouraging pagans to see them as (in Julian's phrase) "Galilean barbarians." In a letter circulated to explain the restoration of the old deities, the emperor asked, "Did not Homer, and Hesiod, and Demosthenes, and Herodotus, and Thucydides, and Isocrates, and Lysias look on the gods as the guides for all instruction?" It was impossible for Christians to teach Homer and Hesiod, he claimed, because they did not believe in their gods. The "Galileans" were dishonest in teaching what they did not themselves accept. They should either apostatize or give up their positions as teachers. The decree was later rescinded in the face of heavy opposition and Christians returned to the schools. Julian's point must have struck home, however; soon thereafter Christians began to build an extensive school system geared directly to a religious mission, schools whose curricula were derived almost exclusively from Christian sources.[13]

Three protagonists for Christianity—*Clement, Origen,* and *Augustine*—loomed large in the work to create a Christian culture and to defend it against its pagan counterpart. Or, more accurately, they sought a synthesis that could preserve the former and retain the best elements of the latter. For *Clement* (ca. 160–215) there was no real antagonism between Christianity and Hellenism. Indeed, he seems to have accepted the popular fiction that Plato was "Moses Atticized," that Christianity's basic tenets were implicit in the Greek philosophers, that they were Christians before there was a Christianity, and that a fundamental harmony existed between the Gospels and Greek learning. "There is one river of truth," he taught, "but

13 Geraldine Hodgson, *Primitive Christian Education* (Edinburgh: T. & T. Clark, 1906), p. 222.

many streams fall into it on this side and on that." Christianity is but the convergence of two streams, Judaism and Hellenism. Before Christ, "philosophy" (by which he meant learning in general) was necessary to the Hellenes to bring them closer to truth, just as Mosaic law was essential for the Hebrews. The true Christian, according to Clement, would find a rich fund of instruction in pagan learning; he would even discover that it confirmed, strengthened, and helped explain the basic doctrines of the true faith when both were viewed correctly. Thus, Clement set the tone for an emerging Christian theology congenial to Greco-Roman thought. Alexandria, where he conducted his school, had long been an outstanding center for Greek and, later, Jewish thought. In the second century an institution for the instruction of catechumens preparing for Christian baptism had been developed. Under *Pantaenus,* a Stoic convert, and then his successor, Clement, it evidently became a school of both secular and advanced religious learning. The Alexandrian school continued to function as the Christian equivalent of an institution of higher studies, offering both pagan and religious training until 415, when a Christian mob opposed to Hellenic learning attacked the school and burned its libraries. It disappeared altogether in the Arab invasion of 640.

For some fifteen years (215–230) the most brilliant spokesman for the integration of Christian and Hellenic thought was *Origen* (ca. 185–254). In his *Homilies on the Psalms,* he laid down his basic position:

> Watch this only, brethern, that no one of you be found not only not speaking or meditating wisdom, but even hating and opposing those who pursue the study of wisdom. The ignorant . . . have this worst fault of all, that of regarding those who have devoted themselves to the word and teaching as vain and useless; they prefer their own ignorance to the study and toil of the learned, and by changing titles they call the exercises of the teachers verbiage, but their own unteachableness or ignorance, simplicity.

The Church historian Eusebius reports that Origen's plan of studies was divided into two parts. The first provided a thorough grounding in mathematics, literature, and the liberal arts, especially philosophy. The second, covering a period of four years, began with grammar and logic, followed by comparative philosophy, Christian ethics, and scriptural interpretation. Clearly Origen saw no contradiction in comingling classical and religious studies; he saw them as mutually reinforcing. Although his school aroused suspicion among those pious Christians who regarded "heresy" and "school" as synonymous, it was to have an enormous influence in the East for several centuries. Origen himself was forced to leave Alexandria because of doctrinal differences with his bishop, but in Caesarea, where he resettled, he continued to teach the unity of Christian faith and classical scholarship for over twenty years until his martyrdom during Decius' persecution.

Augustine (354–430), Bishop of Hippo and foremost theologian of the Western Church, was probably most influential in working out the Christian stance toward classical culture which eventually gained widest acceptance. He reports in his *Confessions* that he had prayed God would forgive him for having enjoyed Virgil. He warned against venturing "heedlessly upon the pursuit of the branches of learning that are in vogue beyond the pale of the Church of Christ, as if these could secure . . . happiness" and advised the maxim "Not too much of anything." The classics could be used, he acknowledged, as instruments toward religious understanding, but their value was limited. At times he apparently equivocated on just how worthwhile secular knowledge could be; other times he conceded it was a question of the *uses* to which such learning was put. In his *Christian Doctrine* the point is made as follows:

> The art of rhetoric, being available for the enforcing either of truth or falsehood, who will dare to say that truth in the person of its defenders is to take its stand unarmed against falsehood? For example, that those who are trying to persuade men of what is false are to know how to introduce their subject, so as to put their hearer into a friendly or attentive or teachable frame of mind, while the defenders of the truth are to be ignorant of that art? Who is such a fool as to think this wise?

In other words, there were special hazards in an uncritical acceptance of secular learning as expressed in the classics. Christian truth was sufficient unto itself and needed no support (as Clement and Origen implied) from Hellenistic sources. On the other side, the dangers were outweighed by the hazard of *ignoring* pagan learning completely. The apologist for Christianity must come to terms with it and use it when necessary in the service of religious truth. As Augustine phrased it, "Far be it from us to suppose that God abhors in us that by virtue of which he has made us superior to other animals." Human reason, as applied to the data of secular scholarship, was not to be despised, but was to be utilized in support of religious faith. Similarly, much later, Rhabanus Maurus was to make much the same point. "When philosophers have perchance uttered some truth which agrees with our faith," he counseled, "we should not handle it timidly but rather take it from its unlawful possessors and apply it to our own use." Nonetheless, the implicit tension between faith and reason, between acceptance and criticism, would return time and time again to bedevil Christian theologians. It might even be argued that insofar as thinkers found themselves impaled upon the horns of the Augustinian dilemma, the Christian contribution to the decline of secular scholarship was accentuated. In any case, uncertain compromise seems to have been the viewpoint that won general application by succeeding generations.

The developing Christian theory of education recommended that the *content* of instruction should draw mainly from the scriptures and other

Christian writings. The classics were to be included but used sparingly. The *form* of instruction would follow the grammatical and rhetorical patterns of pagan schools. Textbook writers prepared materials suitable for Christian use along lines suggested by Augustine. Juvencus' *Historia Evangelica,* Prudentius' *Psychomachia, The Battle of the Soul,* and Martianus Capella's *De Nuptiis Philologiae et Mercurii* ("Wedding of Philology and Mercury") all represented, with varying degrees of success, the attempt to create a Christian literature based on classical models. Despite their aridity (their capacity to bore a reader is unexcelled), they enjoyed widespread popularity as texts in late Christian schools, continuing well into the medieval period.

In sum, then, the third front in Christianity's battle for survival—the confrontation with pagan culture—was won by cautiously accepting its literary traditions and pedagogical forms while grafting to them religious doctrines as these were worked out in the first few centuries of Christianity's existence. It was. not possible, in one sense, for there to be a developed system of Christian schooling until the conflict of faith and culture was well on the way toward resolution.

CHRISTIAN SCHOOLING

Institutional Forms

Aside from whatever instruction was given in the home, the first Christians made no provision for formal schooling. In the absence of any systematic beliefs, that is not surprising. If one acknowledged the fatherhood of God, repented past sins, desired to lead a godly life, and accepted in some (usually poorly defined) sense the belief that Jesus the Christ offered salvation, this was sufficient for acceptance into a Christian community. Then as Gentiles began to be accepted into the fold and the old Judaic Law was abandoned, the need for a process of instruction in the rudiments of the faith became apparent. Probably the influence of Oriental mystery cults was responsible for the stipulation of a probationary period for novitiates, a guarantee that aspirants to the faith were sincere in their intentions. The sacrament of baptism marked the entrance of a convert to Christianity; it would not do to administer the sacred rite to just anyone requesting it. One might say that preparatory instruction before baptism was intended to do for pagan converts what instruction within the Christian family did for children; that is, it indoctrinated them with the basic precepts, introduced them into a special moral climate, and habituated them to the Christian mode of thinking. Evidence is mixed on the precise character and duration of this *catechumenal* (rudimentary) instruction. It is presumed that catechumenal schools were conducted in the beginning by clerics, usually priests or bishops, or, less frequently, by laymen known for their exceptional piety. By 180 in Rome instruction was supervised by bishops, and a probationary period lasting three to five years was required before baptism could be administered. There is a literature extant that implies a carefully graded course of instruction was worked out designed to teach the essentials of church practice and religious belief as these were locally interpreted. Presumably the shape of catechumenal schooling varied from community to community for some time, because the early churches were not bound together by any formal bonds of unity and felt no need for such. The catechumenal school required no physical facilities; its curriculum could be taught wherever necessary and under a variety of circumstances. Initiatory training, usually conducted by the question-and-answer method still used by some churches today, was particularly important in the first and second centuries and may have been retained as a prerequisite for Christian standing until the ninth century, when infant baptism became a common practice. It is known that by then the probationary period had been greatly shortened, if not dispensed with entirely.

The first well-defined institution for Christian education was the *cate-chetical* school. One tradition, probably spurious, ascribes the founding of such a school to Mark, a dubious allegation because over a hundred years passed before the necessity of training people to combat their pagan opponents became acute. By then it could be seen that sincerity, piety, and missionary zeal were not nearly enough; too often an apologist for Christianity was made to look downright silly when confronted by an intellectually brilliant spokesman for some pagan cult or philosophical school. As has been observed, when Christians tried to hide behind the doctrine that childlike ignorance was the only path to salvation their stance seemed ludicrous. It impressed no one, according to critics, besides the depressed and illiterate masses who seized upon the doctrine as excuse for their lack of learning. If Christianity was to make headway among urbane, sophisticated scholars and gain their intellectual support, it had to offer "apologetic" education for its defenders. The first catechetical institution was founded in 179 by *Pantaenus* at Alexandria. Others that followed, like the school at Antioch founded by *Melchion*, a famous teacher of rhetoric, were structured closely on the Alexandrian model. Typically they were conducted by laymen only loosely supervised by ecclesiastical authorities. Their chief function was to prepare defenders of the faith. This necessarily involved a secular curriculum in addition to religious instruction. Permanent schools helped satisfy a growing demand for secular knowledge on the part of Christians, especially those converts who wanted to continue schooling beyond baptism. Schools at Nisibis and Edessa also served as preparatory centers for those desiring clerical training.

Few catechetical schools survived unchanged for very long. In the first place, responsibility for advanced religious instruction was assumed by the Church as it grew stronger. Secondly, experience showed that established pagan schools could do a better job of providing a secular instruction. With the exception of Alexandria, insofar as catechetical schools served non-religious ends, they temporarily lost their reason for being and were supplanted by other types of schools. Thirdly, the preparation of the clergy began to be regularized and so the need for schools combining sacral and secular training disappeared.

In the beginning the gathering together of Christians for communal observances had been a loosely organized, informal affair. With the growth of the hierarchical Church, however, various functionaries evolved to supervise the expanding needs of congregations. Lesser clerical officers were placed under the authority of bishops and the Church buildings erected where the latter were stationed came to be called cathedrals. Each central church or cathedral was the center for many activities, some of them educational. Bishops accepted young men willing to master the liturgy and learn Church doctrine for an apprenticeship training as future clergymen. A bishop would assume responsibility for teaching youths attached to him, and because the instruction was done in or near the cathedral, the label *cathedral school* came into common usage. As pagan schools died out, the bishop found it necessary to accept students at younger and younger ages until, finally, he was supervising their complete education, not just adding clerical training onto some foundation provided elsewhere. The seminary education of a cathedral school now had to be expanded to include an elementary curriculum as well. To meet the increased responsibility, bishops appointed other clerics to share the burden of preparing large numbers of priests and administrative officials. By the sixth century, one can speak of the *cathedral school* as a distinct institutional type offering advanced instruction for those who would accept holy orders and the *episcopal school* as a lower-level institutional type, preparatory to the cathedral school. Whereas virtually every student in the cathedral school was destined to be a cleric, this was not necessarily the case among students in the episcopal school. In its developed form, the episcopal school existed primarily to teach young children the fundamentals of religion and some elements of secular learning. The more advanced, separate cathedral school was kept busy preparing young clergymen to assist the bishop or to staff smaller churches in the outlying areas of the bishopric, the sphere of jurisdiction under the bishop.

Still other schools developed. One was the *parish school* where priests in the lesser collegiate churches located in rural areas gathered promising young boys together for a rudimentary, elementary course of studies. By assuming responsibility for the elements of minimal literacy, parish schools relieved the urban episcopal schools of some of their basic obligations when these same students came to continue their studies. These rural institutions, known as *presbyterial schools,* were essentially extensions of the episcopal school into provinces where formal schooling was a novelty. By the fifth century it is assumed parish or presbyterial schools were flourishing almost everywhere there was a church. It had become every parish cleric's duty to supervise the educational as well as the ritual activities of his congregation. Their efforts collectively laid the basis for the village school system of later ages.

When the Roman sociopolitical system collapsed, it took the classical school with it. By Merovingian times, for example, the episcopal school had become absolutely essential to provide a minimal education in the secular knowledge prerequisite to priestly training. It was the decay of pagan secular schools that undoubtedly led the *Council of Constantinople*, meeting in 381, to order the establishment of gratuitous schools for children in every major population center. In 529 the *Second Council of Vaison*, under the leadership of *Caesarius*, stipulated that "all parish priests shall gather some boys around them as lectors, so that they may give them a Christian upbringing, teach them the Psalms and the lessons of Scripture and the whole law of the Lord and so prepare worthy successors to themselves." This action was significant not only because it indicates how the close urban organization of the Church had expanded to include rural parishes, but because the Council's decision helped stimulate the further spread of presbyterial schools. By the seventh century it is known parish schools were functioning in Italy, Visigothic Spain, Gaul, Egypt, and probably many other locations.

The reasons for the disintegration of public grammar and rhetoric schools throughout the empire are too problematic to be considered in a discussion of Christian education. The *fact* of their disappearance is most important, however, because it resulted in a marked educational declension so far as general learning was concerned. Christian schools neither could nor would preserve the old literary education and its culture. Secular schools still flourished in the fourth century, but under the onslaughts of barbarian invasions, political fragmentation, and the extension of Christian schools, they were virtually nonexistent two centuries later. The decline can be traced with some accuracy in Gaul. In the fourth century, men like *Ausonius* (309–394), a distinguished rhetorician, found ready employment in the municipal schools. One hundred years later, according to the correspondence of *Sidonius Appolinaris* (430–484), schools of higher learning had gone out of business; advanced studies seem to have been pursued exclusively on a tutorial basis. In the next century even private schooling was unavailable. The case of Bishop *Gregory of Tours* (538–594) is instructive. His education at the hands of his uncle Nicetius, Bishop of Lyons, was exclusively religious. His later training under the priest Avitus was woefully meager. Gregory's deficiencies were unexceptional. In his *History of the Franks* he reported, "The cultivation of humane studies is declining, or rather dying out. . . . It was impossible to find a single person instructed in dialectic or in grammar who was capable of recounting these facts in prose or verse. Most of them lamented it and said, 'Woe to our age, for the study of letters has expired among us.' "

What then was being taught in Church schools during these centuries?

For the most part instruction was confined to religious matters. Clues are provided by an order of the *Council of Leodicea* in 367 ordering that choir boys be trained to sing at worship services, and the edict of Gregory in 595 that clergymen were not to participate in the musical portions of worship. As congregational singing died out, boys' choirs were essential for worship services. They had to be prepared to sing properly as members of choirs. Thus, in addition to his other duties, the master of the episcopal school (or the presbyterial school) had to offer religious instruction. Whether the *song* or *chantry* schools, as they were called, were initially a separate kind of institution, an emphasis within the curriculum of the episcopal schools, or something else again is rather unclear.

It remains to consider one other Christian institutional type that was to dominate whatever formal schooling existed in medieval times—the *monastic* school. There was ample precedent for the Christian asceticism that came to the fore in the third and fourth centuries. The Jewish Essenic communities, already noted, set an example of monastic piety long before the advent of Christianity. The Pythagoreans of Greece were only one among many early Greek religions with a strong ascetic bent. The Therapeutae in Egypt, the Cynics, and the neo-Platonists likewise all incorporated asceticism in their ritual observances. Among Christians two factors encouraged bodily punishments, fasting, self-flagellation, and other practices in the quest for perfect spirituality. First, Christians facing persecutions recognized they needed to learn how to endure tortures bravely for the sake of the faith. So-called *schools of martyrdom* were launched with a regimen of preparation for facing pain and even death. Church members were taught how to bear pain unflinchingly, how to prepare the body for torture, and how to avoid showing fear before the magistrates. The aim of this schooling was to create stalwart believers who could evoke admiration even as persecutors sent them to be executed. Such training was a form of asceticism in that it involved self-denial, abstention from pleasures, and a turning away from the world and the comforts of this life.

Secondly, many pious Christians grew disgusted with a degenerate society and even the churches themselves in their growing worldliness. They fled the temptations of the community to seek some purer existence in the Syrian or Egyptian deserts, living lives of absolute austerity. Hermits came to be regarded with awe for their sanctity, although their fanatical excesses of self-mutilation and grotesque tortures discredited them in the eyes of many. The spectacle of a Simeon Stylites, who reportedly perched himself atop a sixty-foot pillar for some thirty years, hardly seemed to exemplify the essence of Christian piety. Such pathological hysteria typified the early *hermitic* or *anchorite movement*. When it was discovered that the isolation of the desert easily led to insanity, the life of solitary withdrawal was condemned by Church authorities as an inappropriate form of religious devotion.

By the fourth century the hermit gave way to communal colonies of religious men dedicated to an ascetic life. *St. Anthony* (circa 250–320) is recorded to have founded a loosely organized monastery in the Nile Valley, where his followers gathered periodically for worship and instruction. But it was *Pachomius* (292–346) who laid down the pattern for *cenobitic* or communal monasticism, established the first monasteries and nunneries, and drew up a rule for their governance. Within fifty years monasticism had attracted thousands of people and had become a vital institution within Christianity.

Contrary to general opinion, early monasteries gave little attention to education. That ascetic spirit which was to dominate monasticism throughout the centuries was not calculated to encourage the spread of learning or the founding of schools. Those who had sought escape from a godless, materialistic world exhibited scant interest in promoting learning either for themselves or for others. Of course there were some, like *Cassiodorus* (ca. 480–575), who not only established monasteries but created courses of study for the benefit of their inhabitants. Cassiodorus' sevenfold grouping of secular learning (following a treatise of Cappella and the scriptural text "Wisdom has built her house, she has hewn out her seven pillars") became a popular, if unoriginal, compendium of knowledge commonly used henceforth as a medieval textbook. Nonetheless the usual character of monasticism in its early development was antipathetic to learning. Most recluses were anxious to forget anything learned earlier in schools before their conversion to an ascetic existence. When *Benedict* founded his famous monastic community at *Monte Cassino,* south of Rome, his *Rule* (ca. 523) drawn up for the monastery included no provision for study. To be sure, monks were to include reading in their daily routine and this presumes an ability to read, but Benedict himself was openly contemptuous of most learning. Despite the reputation for scholarship later enjoyed by certain Benedictine monasteries, the general picture of monastic settlements as centers where the light of learning illuminated an otherwise ignorant world needs serious qualification.

In the East monasteries found it unnecessary to engage in educational work because other schools were fairly well distributed to prepare monastic novitiates beforehand in the elements of minimal literacy. *Basil's* influential *Rule* makes no mention of education other than insisting that young boys admitted to the monastery be taught to read. Rules for women in convents reflected the same demand that nuns be able to read. If they could not, they were to be taught to do so, even though most ascetic communities, monastic or conventual, were not specifically designed for engaging in such educational labors. Centuries later there must have been reasonably extensive courses of study offered within monastery walls, especially in the West, where pagan schools died out first, for the *interni* or *oblati* (those destined eventually to become members of the community). Instruction in the rudiments of writing, reading, arithmetic, and religion culminated in initiation into the order. It is not known whether there were many schools outside the cloister for day pupils who lived at home and came only for instruction rather than preparation for monastic life. Schools for *externi* (those not permitted within the monastery) did exist in Ireland and Gaul, but they were exceptions to the general practice of confining education to those who would take religious vows. Monasteries were mainly spiritual hermitages, not educational institutions.

Educational Ideals

Christianity was a revealed religion, not an abstract theoretical system to be added to the other systems or schools of antiquity. Its founders believed their mission was to preach and proclaim, not to occupy professor's chairs. Conversion of the world, not conversion to a philosophy, was their divinely appointed mission.[14] Very soon, however, it became apparent that Christian apologists would have to borrow weapons from their adversaries. There was, as has been indicated, a divergence of attitudes regarding secular culture, depending on whether one saw it as a rival and foe of Christian faith, a useful arsenal for its defense, or even a providential preparation for the new truths. In the end it was the reconciliatory attitude that triumphed, especially as exemplified in the thought of Augustine. It is to his writings that one looks for a comprehensive view of the Christian educational ideal.

Augustine, it seems necessary to emphasize once again, endorsed the reading of pagan literature even though he had serious misgivings about it. In his tract *Christian Instruction* he acknowledged that it could be read with profit for it contained besides superstitions and false ideas "liberal instructions . . . adapted to the service of truth" and some "useful principles about morals." The student should be reminded, however, that all secular knowledge, useful though it may be, is inferior to knowledge gained from Christian Scriptures. Moreover, Augustine affirmed, the true believer should recall the observation of Corinthians that "Knowledge puffs up, but charity edifies." One was amply justified in utilizing whatever pagan arts and sciences could offer *if* these were supplemented by moral guidance. Like Cassiodorus, Augustine believed it would be safer to avoid the classical authors, but because they could be instrumental in the study of religious doctrine they should not be neglected completely. Perhaps, unlike Cassiodorus, Augustine was unwilling to go so far as to claim that all liberal culture and profane scientific thought was contained implicitly in Scripture or could be derived from it. Just as *Boethius* later taught that Hellenic thought provided forms and terminology within which Christian intellectual foundations could be framed, Augustine did attempt to build a bridge between the high culture of classicism and the spirituality of Christian thought. Classical education had posited an ideal type, a model of the educated man.

---

[14] Frederick Copleston, *A History of Philosophy*, Vol. 2, Part I (Garden City, N.Y.: Image Books, 1962), p. 27.

To it Christian thinkers like Augustine grafted a supernatural vision of man made in the image of God: "A man educated according to classical standards could become an orator or a philosopher, whichever he liked," Marrou notes. "He could choose the life of action or the life of contemplation. He was now offered a further choice, with the announcement of Good Tidings: besides these things he could now lay himself open to grace, to faith, could receive sacrament of baptism, could become a Christian."[15] Education, in the Christian mold, meant instruction in a doctrine of being, of an inner life, of a spiritual direction. It was the Christian equivalent of what antiquity had carefully reserved as a *paideia* or culture of the mind for an intellectual elite. If it makes sense to speak of a "culture of the spirit," Christianity offered it freely to the humblest of the faithful masses.

This is one side of the Christian educational ideal: the making of a faithful adherent to orthodox doctrine, not entirely ignorant of secular learning, more thoroughly schooled in the precepts of his religious faith. The other side of the ideal is social, rather than individual, public and external, not private and internal. Again, it is best expressed in the thought of Augustine. When he was converted, he accepted not only Christianity but also the Catholic Church as a historical mediator between God and the individual. Personal faith, unaided by some authoritative interpretation, was inadequate. The Christian, for Augustine, required an "ark of salvation"—the Church—to interpret God's will for man and mediate his saving grace. Love of God was best expressed in submission to it and through acceptance of its divinely commissioned authority. Without the institution, man is morally and intellectually impotent. This did not mean, naturally, that any Church member belonged automatically to the City of God any more than one outside it, governed in his conduct by love of God, justice and charity, could not belong morally and spiritually to the City of God. Undeniably Augustine believed that the historical manifestation of a heavenly city was the Church; likewise he thought the earthly city (the City of Man, "of Babylon") was to be found in the pagan empire of Rome. Yet, like the Jews, he conceived of the heavenly and earthly cities as spiritual symbols, not exactly coterminous with any actual community or organization.

This opposition of symbols leads straight to the Augustinian political perspective, also important to a Christian view of education. A properly ordered earthly state had to be founded on a bond of "faith and of firm concord, when the highest and truest good, namely God, is loved by all and men love each other in him without dissimulation because they love one another for his sake." The state, in other words, was to be informed by the higher principles of Christianity. The Church's mission was to act as a leaven of the earth, permeating the state by its precepts. Because the

---

15 H. I. Marrou, *A History of Education in Antiquity* (New York: Mentor Books, 1964), p. 426.

Church is the only perfect society (a communion of believers) and is superior to the secular state, the Church must stand above it. In maintaining this
view, Augustine helped form the medieval Church–state theory which predominated for hundreds of years (although it was never fully achieved in
actual practice). The educational corollary in its wider dimension which
followed was that Christian education must have a kind of eschatological
vision for itself, namely, the reconstruction of the social order as a heavenly
City of God. Because a society is to be defined as a "multitude of rational
creatures associated in a common agreement as to the things which it loves,"
a good society must be taught to love God, to order itself according to the
dictates of the Church. It must, finally, more fully embody the Christian
ideal by transcending its own secular nature; it must become a sacral society consecrated to God. The fate of this lofty but patently unworkable
ideal is part and parcel of succeeding developments in the history of religious thought and education.

RELIGION, EDUCATION, AND THE CONTEMPORARY SCENE

The Historic Alliance of Religion and Education

The connection between religion and education in the Western cultural
tradition has been long and intimate. For the ancient Hebrews and early
Christians alike, educational agencies were enlisted in the struggle for survival amidst a hostile cultural environment. In both cases schools became
indispensable for the preservation, transmission, and progressive enrich-
ment of a religious world view. The godly life, in the minds of the pious,
required an attitude of exclusiveness, of separation from a sinful world,
and it could not be sustained without a conscious educational effort to school
the young in its ideals. The religious "faith" taught in schools never meant
something so simple as adherence to a set of formal propositions; religion
suggested less an acceptance of dogmas and more a total orientation toward
human existence in the world, an inclusive way of looking at life. Although
schools were used to promote secular ends, these were subordinated to the
paramount aim of preserving a religious faith, in an unbroken line down
through the generations. In a world of many competing creeds, educational
institutions were intended mainly to foster commitment to a particular
religious tradition.

Christianity ultimately won out over paganism in its battle for cultural
supremacy in the late Greco-Roman period. It was only natural in succeeding centuries that schools should serve the interests of a society founded
on the principles of that religion (however great the disparity between
theory and actual practice). The culture transmitted through schools was
dominated by the precepts, values, and habits of thought of medieval Christianity. The Church for centuries was the primary custodian of culture as
well as the dominant social authority. Hence, the schools of Christendom

were its direct arm. As long as formal educational institutions were not required for socializing the young; people could be fitted to their economic functions within the social order without benefit of organized instruction; literary skills were the possession of a favored few; and so long as ordinary enculturative processes could be handled reasonably well outside the schools, educational institutions were freed to concentrate on religious concerns.

To anticipate somewhat, the advent of an anthropocentric humanism toward the end of the medieval period did not alter the situation appreciably. Nothing in Renaissance pedagogy indicates religion was de-emphasized in the schools, possibly because the brand of humanism taught within their walls was wedded firmly to traditional religious piety. Merely the form or expression of religious involvement changed. During the sixteenth century confessional revolts that divided monolithic Christianity, the pervasive use of education to advance religious objectives was only accentuated. All protagonists in the fray, both Catholic and Protestant, seized upon the school as a means of safeguarding their respective orthodoxies.

Only within comparatively recent times have educational theory and practice been divorced from theological considerations. The gradual secularization of Western society, the rise of the independent nation state, and the expansion of formal schooling for more people were undoubtedly important developments affecting the process. This is not to say that schools have become wholly secular, however, even while they are called upon to discharge an increasing number of worldly duties. In the first place, modern nation states have been unable or unwilling to assume complete responsibility for formal education. As a result, private religious agencies have stepped in to fill the gap and have continued to offer religious training as an integral part of their instruction. Secondly, schools have been presumed to play an important role in fostering both public and private morality. Conventional wisdom has long assumed that religion provides warrant and sanction for ethical behavior. Therefore, and entirely aside from its cultural importance, the teaching of religion has been deemed essential.

Seen in historical perspective, then, early Jewish and Christian educational developments represent only a preliminary chapter in the story of how religion and the schools have been tied together. A partial exception, a pattern giving rise to several vexing problems today, is found in the evolution of American schools. Before resuming the account of education since antiquity it is instructive to examine briefly some of the major issues of religion in a society which has tried to keep church and state apart.[16]

The American Transition to Church–State Separatism

The separation of church and state was virtually unknown in pre-revolutionary America. The first step toward separation came with recognition of the right to worship freely for dissenting sects. Although the majority of a

16 See pp. 499–500, 520–522.

community determined which denomination would be the established church (and thus the recipient of tax monies for the schools it maintained), in time minority religious bodies won the freedom to establish their own churches, found their own schools, and offer the kind of religious training they thought best. In effect this amounted to a multiple establishment of religion. It was not until passage of the First Amendment (1791) to the Constitution that the principle of complete disestablishment (separation of church and state) finally assumed the force of law. The Amendment held that "Congress shall make no law respecting an establishment of religion, or prohibiting the free exercise thereof." There should be an unbreachable wall of separation, in Jefferson's words, between church and state, in order to avoid all the factiousness of government intrusion into the domain of religion. The founding fathers had no personal animosity toward religion, only a fervent desire to avoid the dangers of a state-supported religion and the factionalism that had bled Europe for centuries.[17] They remembered all too well how religious controversy could tear at the body politic, how sectarian divisiveness could destroy organized social life. By denying every sect the advantage of the secular sword and by preventing the state from creating policies to further sectarian ends, they hoped to keep religious controversy out of public life.

Historically, those who framed the Constitution's Bill of Rights probably did not intend to make society secular so much as they sought to guarantee the right of states to regulate religious affairs independent of federal control and to safeguard the religious liberties of minority groups. Moreover, contrary to the polemic of some politicians and clerics today, America not only officially endorsed the ideal of religious pluralism, it specifically disavowed the concept of a "Christian" government for itself. The explicit disclaimer first appeared in a 1796 treaty with Tripoli which affirmed that "the Government of the United States of America is not in any sense founded on the Christian religion." In principle at least, the new country was completely neutral in religious matters.

America's public schools were not nearly so consistent in applying the principle of complete church–state separation. A careful examination of curricula and textbooks in early nineteenth-century schools reveals that religion *was* taught as an important part of the educational program. Initially no objections were lodged. Later, clerical intolerance over conflicting views about which religious doctrines should be taught in classrooms made public school instruction in religion virtually impossible.[18] Practical experi-

---

[17] Less than fifty years before the American Revolution, Europe was still embroiled in bitter religious dissent. In 1732, for example, the Archbishop of Salzburg took it upon himself to expel some twenty-two thousand Protestants from his Catholic realm.

[18] See Paul A. Freund and Robert Ulich, *Religion and the Public Schools* (Cambridge, Mass.: Harvard University Press, 1965); and Robert Ulich, "The Schools and Religion: The Historical Present," *Harvard Graduate School of Education Association Bulletin* (Summer, 1965), pp. 2–6.

ence showed that religious pluralism was incompatible with religious training under public auspices.

Two hundred years of legislation and litigation have confirmed the neutrality of government in matters of religion. As Chief Justice Clark of the Supreme Court observed in connection with a controversial ruling over religious observances in the public school, "We have come to recognize through bitter experience that it is not within the power of government to invade that citadel, whether its purpose or effect be to aid or oppose, to advance or retard. In the relationship between man and religion, the State is firmly committed to a position of neutrality." In the same vein, the later evolution of an American public school system was guided by the concept of religious neutrality. Considering that public schools are systematically supported by tax funds, controlled by public officials responsible to the taxpayers, and directed toward the public welfare as a whole, it has been decided they must be "nonmalevolently neutral" in all questions relative to religion. Unfortunately, the ideas of cooperative pluralism in society and public responsibility for education of all people have proved easier to formulate in theory than to implement in practice. Even with provision made for religious groups to establish and maintain their own parallel school systems, difficult problems persist.

One of the major difficulties has been a religious claim of primary responsibility for all education, both secular and religious, based on the argument that a total separation of secular and religious aspects of life is neither possible nor desirable. For a variety of reasons, Protestants have not been as militant as Catholics in advancing the claim (mainly because public schools have reflected in their practices a certain bias congenial to Protestantism). The classic statement on the question is to be found in Pope Pius XI's 1930 Encyclical *Divini Illius Magistri* ("On the Christian Education of Youth"):

> And first of all, education belongs pre-eminently to the Church by reason of a double title in the supernatural order, conferred exclusively upon her by God Himself; absolutely superior, therefore, to any other title in the natural order. . . . By necessary consequence the Church is independent of any sort of earthly power in the origin as in the exercise of her mission as educator. . . .
>
> Hence, every form of pedagogic naturalism, which in any way excludes or overlooks supernatural Christian formation in the teaching of youth, is false. . . . From this it follows that the so-called "neutral" or "lay" school, from which religion is excluded, is contrary to the fundamental principles of education. . . .

Papal pronouncements notwithstanding, expediency won out over principle in the end. When it became clear that the nation was firmly committed to religious neutrality in the schools, sectarian groups moved to fill an alleged religious and moral vacuum at the center of public education.

They have either founded their own schools or worked out a compromise through various "shared time" programs, under which a student attends a public school for instruction in certain "secular" subjects and then goes to a parochial institution for religious training. A whole complex of problems —financial, education, legal, and philosophical—is created by such an arrangement and usually no one concerned is satisfied with the results. The controversies surrounding private religious schools have been no less difficult to resolve. The perplexing dilemma of federal aid (direct and indirect) to parochial education has stimulated some casuistic distinctions that would shame a medieval scholastic. For the most part, the distinctions have only served to aggravate public discontent rather than to solve the problem.

Public and Private Education

The root idea of a strict separation of public and private school systems has come in for vigorous attack in recent years. Part of the contest over national policy centers on the question of the constitutionality of federal legislation authorizing tax support to sectarian schools. Proponents of public assistance for parochial schools have met with some success in securing textbooks, bus transportation, lunches, and other "auxiliary services" for private school pupils. Courts have held that such publicly supported services directly benefit the individual student and do not represent tacit state support for any religion. Strict separationists, in opposition, argue that piecemeal exceptions to the basic idea of keeping government out of private school financing under the "child-benefit" theory are merely devices for assisting parochial institutions by the back door while evading the constitutional prohibition of benefits by the front door.[19]

It was not until 1971 that the U.S. Supreme Court called a partial halt to increasing state support for parochial school education. In a controversial ruling (*Lemon* v. *Kurtzman*), it was held that state laws providing direct aid for the teaching of such "secular" subjects as science, mathematics, languages, and physical education in nonpublic schools, and laws allowing state-financed contributions to parochial school teachers' salaries involved "excessive government entanglement with religion" and hence were unconstitutional. Whereas bus transportation, public health services, school lunches, or textbooks made available by the state to nonpublic schools could be justified as protecting the welfare of the child, the court reasoned, the use of public funds to pay teacher salaries or other costs in sectarian schools violates the principle of church–state separation. "We cannot blink the fact," observed Justice William J. Brennan, Jr., "that the separate education those schools [i.e. church-related institutions] provide goes hand in hand with the religious mission which is the only reason for the schools' existence."

Following hard upon the court's decision were angry denunciations as well

19 See Milton Himmelfarb, "Church and State: How High a Wall?" *Commentary* (July, 1966), p. 23.

as enthusiastic expressions of agreement. Parochial-aid supporters quickly issued gloomy predictions that the demise of parochial school education was at hand. Others vowed to carry on the fight, their determination evidenced by renewed demands for direct subsidies or tax credits for parents who elect to send their children to a private school. The argument is that the state's basic reason for supporting public schools in the first place is to assist parents in providing education for children. If they elect to send their offspring to a nonpublic institution, that should not affect the state's duty to supply financial assistance. In so doing, the state acts for the family; it does not thereby endorse any particular religious beliefs. The state's refusal to extend help, it is alleged, denies parents the public assistance for education to which they are entitled as tax-paying citizens. Furthermore, when the state withholds funds, parents of parochial school pupils are in effect being taxed twice: once for the public school, and again for the private school. The standard rejoinder of opponents is to point out that the exercise of freedom of choice between public and private schools does not carry with it an option on the public treasury.[20] The added financial burden of sending children to a private school is strictly a voluntary undertaking.

Even among those with a vested interest in sectarian schools there are opponents of state support. They reason that once the government starts to finance a church-related system of education, the next step is a controlled system. Even if the "double-taxation" or the "benefit-to-students-not-religion" arguments are valid, public monies for private schools would be undesirable because it is unreasonable to think that the state would be willing to provide funds without also levying control over how they were spent—sooner or later, in lesser or greater degree.

Another argument levied against the public school is that its supportive machinery is unresponsive to changing social needs. Critics from both left and right claim that the existing public school structure should be dismantled. To pour more funds into a system in a state of advanced arteriosclerosis would produce only negligible improvements at best.[21] The basis for complaints against the public schools here is not religious in nature, but it has implications for the question of church–state separation. It is argued that only privately controlled institutions can meet the special requirements of minority ethnic or religious interests. Public schools are too often victims of a stultifying middle-class orthodoxy, critics claim; what

[20] See C. Stanley Lowell, "Shall the State Subsidize Church Schools?" *Liberty* (October, 1960), pp. 11–15.

[21] Consult Donald A. Erickson, "Public Funds for Private Schools," *Saturday Review* (September 21, 1968), pp. 66–68, 78–79. See also John Hardin Best, "Public and Private Education," *Educational Leadership* (December, 1968), pp. 250–253. For discussions of one proposed type of support, consult Christopher Jencks, "Giving Parents Money for Schooling: Education Vouchers," *Phi Delta Kappan* (September, 1970), pp. 49–52; Robert J. Havighurst, "The Unknown Good: Education Vouchers," ibid., pp. 52–53; and A. Stafford Clayton, "Vital Questions, Minimal Responses: Education Vouchers," ibid., pp. 53–54.

is needed is a diversity of institutions, each competing for pupils and public support. In order to allow for freedom of experimentation, perhaps there should be an "open market" of schools with varying arrangements of support and control. Obviously with such a system the religious question would surface if a sectarian group founded a school and appealed for public financial assistance for its maintenance. Presumably the same difficulty would exist under the "voucher" plan, whereby stipends from public tax funds would be given directly to parents to use as they saw fit in educating their children, or divided up on a per capita basis to all schools, public and parochial.

An objection to "voucher" arrangements holds that the principle of direct subsidy could be used to justify parents' school choices on any grounds whatsoever, including economic, political, social, religious, or even racial grounds. This would lead not only to a splintering of educational institutions, but to a diverse society organized along narrow sectarian, ethnic, or racial lines. The Netherlands is appealed to as a case in point. When Holland adopted a system of direct educational support for all schools, enrollment in public institutions plummeted to less than a third of the total student population. Not only did public schools suffer, but the whole of Dutch society became polarized according to sectarian affiliations. In response, those who defend the basic idea of subsidies to private schools question whether the method of financing education in Holland was a *cause* or a *symptom* of divisions within society. They point out that several other countries permitting state support for private schools have not experienced the same consequences. Against the argument that a "voucher" system of educational support would only increase the disparity between schools for the rich and the poor, that stipends would worsen existing inequalities, proponents are confident that mechanisms could be devised which would avoid any potential hazard.

Acrimony over the various issues outlined here is likely to continue. The farther arguments are extended, the more involved they seemingly become. Simplistic answers to complex questions will only continue to obscure the American dilemma over religion and education. The single conclusion that can be drawn presently with any confidence is that the traditional separation of public and private education is being scrutinized more closely than it has been for over a century.

Religious Neutrality in Public Schools

The problem of determining the practical implications of public school neutrality in religion has proved just as hard to resolve as the question of private school support. A controversy over two 1962–1963 Supreme Court rulings declaring Bible reading, recitation of the Lord's Prayer, and a "nonsectarian" prayer unconstitutional aroused a storm of protest that showed no signs of abating a full decade later. The controversy evoked an emotional backlash of frustration and anger, polarized public opinion, led to wide-spread defiance of the law, and deeply troubled people of all persuasions. Some influential figures assailed the court for establishing a religion of secularism by judicial fiat. Two Court justices admitted their own mis-givings when they observed that "untutored devotion to the concept of neutrality can lead to a pervasive devotion to the secular and to a passive or even active hostility to the religious. Such results are not only not com-pelled by the Constitution but are prohibited by it."[22] The heart of the issue is whether genuine neutrality is possible within the schools.

Many people are concerned that if religion is banned in the public schools, something of tremendous *cultural* and historical significance will be lost. As Associate Justice Tom C. Clark wrote, "It might well be said that one's education is not complete without a study of comparative re-ligion or the history of religion and its relationship to the advancement of civilization. It certainly may be said that the Bible is worthy of study for its literary and historic qualities."[23] He went on to argue that the Court's judgments did not preclude the study of religion "when presented ob-jectively as part of a secular program of education." Phrased differently, public schools can and should teach *about* religion even though they can-not seek to inculcate any particular religious beliefs.[24]

For a time it seemed as though the distinction between the teaching *of* religion and teaching *about* religion carried an easy solution to the prob-lem. The American Council on Education had long held to the position that religion could be studied in the same way as the economic and politi-cal principles and institutions of the country should be studied.[25] True neutrality respecting religious doctrines was taken to mean that public schools were debarred from teaching any of them specifically. Nor could schools either provide any "firsthand" experience of religious values through worship services or teach any doctrines antithetical to religious beliefs. Neutrality meant schools should not seek to inculcate or propagate *any* particular kind of ultimate creed, religious or antireligious.[26]

For those who view religion primarily in terms of personal involvement and moral commitment, instruction *about* religion seems hopelessly in-adequate. The "mere" objective presentation of articles of faith, some fear,

22 Quoted in Clarence W. Hall, "Is Religion Banned from Our Schools?" *Reader's Digest* (February, 1965), and reprinted in Harold Full, *Controversy in American Educa-tion, An Anthology of Crucial Issues* (New York: Macmillan, 1967), p. 321.

23 Ibid., pp. 322–323.

24 In this connection the legitimacy of religious observances—Christmas pageants, observance of Yom Kippur, or Easter observances—has remained notoriously ambiguous.

25 American Council on Education, *The Function of the Public Schools in Dealing with Religion* (Washington, D.C.: National Education Association, 1953), p. 7. See also John L. Childs, "The Future of the Common School," *Educational Forum* (January, 1957), 133–141.

26 A persuasive argument for the position appears in William K. Frankena, "Public Education and the Good Life," *Harvard Educational Review* (Fall, 1966), pp. 413–426.

may actually hinder students' ability to come to terms with their own ultimate religious affirmations. To teach *about* religion is to discourage commitment *to* religion. At this point neutralists return by saying that the school's purpose is to impart knowledge, not to instill faith. Yet if the argument that *objectivity* about religious matters is not the same as religious *neutrality,* if in fact the former tends to weaken the latter by encouraging a passive, "spectator" relationship to religion, then the schools will still not be truly neutral. Furthermore, whatever objectivity in teaching means, it cannot mean the total absence of values and a point of view. The very act of teaching about something entails standards of relevance and importance. Nothing taught in classrooms is devoid of certain value presuppositions.

Noting that education does not proceed in a moral vacuum, some disputants have suggested that the schools might teach a common faith to which everyone can assent. The secular public school is founded upon certain basic values and assumptions that arise from the effort of men working cooperatively together in a democratic society. Ingenious attempts have been made to formulate "a faith more comprehensive and profound than the warring dogmas of most existing faiths, including scientific naturalism" suitable for propagation in the schools.[27] Defenders of this position have tried to show that the teaching of a secular unifying faith is not merely a strategem of expediency but a positive opportunity to infuse teaching with values such as freedom, friendship, cooperation, creativity, and the pursuit of knowledge, to which traditional religion is not indispensable, logically or psychologically.[28] A nonsupernatural faith could still be basically religious. "A religious education," according to Whitehead, "is an education which inculcates duty and reverence. Duty arises from our potential control over the course of events. Where attainable knowledge could have changed the issue, ignorance has the guilt of vice. And the foundation of reverence," he continues, "is this perception, that the present holds within itself the complete sum of existence, backwards and forwards, that whole amplitude of time which is eternity."[29]

It is precisely the adoption of such a faith that opponents of public school neutrality fear the most. Their claim is that, protestations to the contrary, a socially based common faith is nothing less than secularized religion. If public education is denuded of all emphasis on supernaturally based values, so, it is argued, *ipso facto* it becomes immoral or at least amoral. The fundamental issue raised by this claim, the alleged dependence of morality upon religion, is a question as old as philosophy itself, not

---

27 Philip H. Phenix, "Religion in American Public Education," *Teachers College Record* (October, 1955), pp. 26–31.

28 A good discussion is provided in John Martin Rich, *Education and Human Values* (Reading, Mass.: Addison-Wesley, 1968).

29 Alfred North Whitehead, *The Aims of Education and Other Essays* (New York: Macmillan, 1929), p. 23.

to mention the further question of whether morality can be taught. Secularists argue that neither the meaning nor validity of moral values rests on religious foundations in any conventional sense. No convincing evidence exists that belief in the existence of the supernatural is an essential condition for public order or private morality.[30] This allegation, of course, runs directly counter to the religionist's belief that religious training is a necessary condition for the prevention of immorality. And it is because of this abiding disagreement on the nature and status of ethical values that the issue of religious neutrality in public schools stubbornly refuses to admit of any simple solution.

Secularism and Neutrality

The issue of religious values is only one aspect of the larger problem of teaching values generally within the schools. It is often remarked that contemporary education at all levels separates the life of personal conviction from the life of academic intelligence. Michael Novak has advanced the thesis that the seeming irrelevance of much that is taught in schools derives from attitudes fostered by a culture whose inarticulate major premise is naturalistic secularism.[31] Since the Middle Ages Western civilization has been increasingly dominated by the objectivity of scientific method and the impersonality of technology. Profound social and economic changes have molded modern man's habitual beliefs, without his being aware of it. The mass of men cling to the conventions and forms of religious faith even while an intellectual avant garde tries to indicate the emptiness of that tradition. In a line beginning with Voltaire and Hume, and extending down through Comte, Shaw, and Russell, voices are raised to show how irreligious postmedieval culture has become. "God is dead," said Nietzsche, adding, "What are these churches if they are not the tombs and sepulchers of God?" Religion has become a social amenity, not an organizing cohesive force in modern life.

A major consequence of secularism, according to Novak, is the pervasive attention to the public and the formal. The habit of thought is evidenced in education by concentration on information and technique, by instruction confined to subjects lending themselves to precise formulation. The standing assumption made is that ultimate questions, questions formerly considered religious in nature, are in principle unanswerable and hence not worth asking seriously. They are "nonintellectual, personal, and if matters of supreme importance and self-commitment, nevertheless not matters for passionate academic dispute."[32] As a result, the process of

---

[30] For example, see Sidney Hook, *Education for Modern Man, A New Perspective* (New York: Alfred A. Knopf, 1966), p. 157.

[31] Michael Novak, "God in the Colleges," *Harper's Magazine* (October, 1961), pp. 173–178.

[32] Ibid., p. 174.

acquiring knowledge, Novak argues, leaves the inner life of the student untouched. "If we cannot control the great uncertain questions in the universe, nevertheless we can make a universe of little certainties we can control."[33] Education means intellectual detachment, not self-confrontation and personal examination.

Sometimes it is argued that religious and social pluralism, rather than any lack of religious belief, accounts for the failure of schools to address value questions. Confronted by a variety of competing values in society, schools elect or are forced to play it safe by pretending that conflict does not exist. The separation of church and state controversy delivers most educators to the position of ignoring discussions of values and moral choices, in hopes that the problems involved will disappear if people do not think about them.[34] Because the social community is locked in debate over whose beliefs or values should be admitted for classroom analysis and whose should be barred, schools seek to avoid as much controversy as possible. It is far easier to assume a defensive posture, antagonize no one, and restrict learning to what can be objectified, classified—and mummified.

Neutrality, it might be said, however, does *not* require the school to encourage nonreflective attitudes. Teachers can encourage pupils to grapple with big questions even while passing on the "substantive" subjects of the regular curriculum. Course offerings on a factual, objective level can be paralleled by a subjective value dialogue sustained through the instructor's incidental comments. As Gordon Allport has rightly observed, there is a hard core of subject matter to be imparted, but it has a penumbra of moral significance that needs to be brought out explicitly.[35] The teacher's self-disclosure on value questions can lead students to self-discovery in the process of examining various alternatives. The school as a public institution need not align itself with any one set of beliefs, but this does not excuse its teachers from responsibility for raising vital issues. Failure to scrutinize competing positions has the effect of fragmenting the content of instruction and rendering it ethically bland.

Too often schools opt *ex post facto* for the safe course of rationalizing whatever value consensus has already been achieved, a course of action exciting and challenging no one, least of all students. Insofar as instruction intrudes on genuine moral concerns or controversial value questions, it typically confines itself to pious homilies, easy platitudes, and acceptable clichés. Because the least hazardous course is to teach aggregations of fact, the curriculum never gets integrated in the minds of students; subjects

[33] Ibid., p. 175.

[34] William L. Griffin, "A Needed Dialogue: Schools and Values," *The Clearing House,* Fairleigh Dickinson University (October, 1964), pp. 67–71. Several points raised here follow Griffin's discussion.

[35] Gordon Allport, "Values and Our Youth," *Teachers College Record* (December, 1961), pp. 211–219.

learned are, in Ulich's phrase, isolated islands on the *globus intellectualis*. The learner is denied the opportunity to see how what is learned is relevant, meaningful, and applicable to his conscious life; and the curriculum becomes a sort of intellectual smorgasbord leading to indigestion instead of nourishment. Worse yet, schools tend to discourage the habit of thought that allows students to understand what has gone wrong: that learning counts for very little until it has been personally synthesized, until it relates to self-understanding or wider appreciation of the individual's environment in terms of critically examined values. One of the major predicaments of education in contemporary society, indirectly related to the broader issue of moral and religious pluralism, is how to avoid the type of education that leads to ethical paralysis.

SUMMARY

Ancient Hebraic or Jewish education was profoundly colored by a religious faith, an attitude toward the national history, and a sense of a divinely appointed mission. The original faith of Abraham was transformed by Moses, following the Exodus, into the basis for a political confederacy of tribes. Following their reconquest of the ancestral homeland in Palestine, the Hebrews organized themselves as a loose theocracy governed by judges. The last of these, Samuel, helped install Saul as the first king of a united monarchy. He was succeeded, first, by David, and, secondly, by Solomon. With the abortive reign of Solomon's son, Rehoboam, the monarchy collapsed. Sectional differences resulted in the establishment of two separate nations, Israel in the north and Judah in the south. The Israelites were soon devoured by the Assyrians; Judah met destruction shortly thereafter at the hands of the Babylonians. During their fifty-year exile in Babylon, the Jewish captives fought desperately against cultural assimilation by clinging to their religious ideals. The synagogue was developed for communal worship and instruction—instruments for the preservation of Jewish identity throughout the difficult periods that followed. Political oppression under the Syrian Seleucids and cultural inroads made by Hellenism during the Alexandrian period together made the continuing struggle for survival especially difficult. When the Maccabean Revolt failed and Roman rule was firmly established, any hopes for a political restoration of the ancient monarchy disappeared. The end of the ancient Jewish political history was marked by the destruction of the Temple at Jerusalem and by the dispersion of the people during the first and second centuries A.D.

Jewish schools first appeared in the postexilic period. The developed institutional structure included the elementary school or "House of Books" (*Beth-hasepher*), the secondary-level "House of Exposition" (*Beth-hamidrash*), and the scribal or *Rabbinical* school. Broadly considered, the aim of

Jewish education was to foster a sense of religious identity as this was tied to a rich historical legacy. Its content was represented by the diverse ideals that Judaism produced in a long development from primitive monolatry to ethical monotheism. Its wisdom literature, the sayings of the prophets, the Deuteronomic Code, and Mosaic precepts provided inspiration and enlightenment for a unique people.

Neither an explicit theory of Christian education nor the apparatus for institutionalized schooling could proceed during the first few centuries of Christianity until the battle for survival in a hostile, pagan world was successful. This effort was waged on three fronts—political, doctrinal, and cultural. Politically, Christianity advanced from an oppressed Jewish sect to the status of official faith of the Roman world. It was not until the reign of Constantine that persecutions such as those of Septimius Severus, Decius, Diocletian, Marcus Aurelius, Galerius, and Maximinus Daia were halted. Although Constantine threw imperial support toward the Church, his efforts to achieve a doctrinal consensus among contending factions only aggravated dissent. It is probable that Constantine also hoped to use Christianity as a unifying force against disintegrative influences already at work in Roman society.

The Christian effort to establish a doctrinal orthodoxy has never been fully realized. Conflicts among the various parties—Athanasians, Arians, Nestorians, Donatists, Miletians, Montanists—prevented the emergence of an authoritative, universally accepted body of beliefs and practices during the first few centuries of Christianity's existence. In the end it was the assimilative capacity of the faith, its ability to borrow and adapt from many sources, that helps explain its explosive growth and eventual triumph over pagan competitors. Naturally many other factors were also involved.

The many attempts to delineate a proper relationship between religious belief and secular knowledge represented the third front in Christianity's fight to survive. There were some, like Tertullian, Jerome, and Gregory the Great, who tried with limited success to separate the two completely. Christian leaders such as Hippolytus and Basil explicitly urged compromise with pagan learning, institutions, and culture. Those who urged the road of accommodation argued that faith and secular learning could be reconciled. The stance of Clement of Alexandria, Justin Martyr, and Origen as modified in Augustine's thought finally prevailed as the most widely accepted view. On the other hand, it might be argued that when the Church was finally willing to make a cautious peace with Hellenic culture, precious little of it remained.

Aside from education in the home, the first structured religious training developed by early Christianity was catechumenal instruction for new converts to the faith. Catechetical education to train the clergy and to prepare apologists to defend Christianity against intellectual attack was the next significant move toward a system of parochial education. Cathedral schools for preparing clergymen to serve in rural parishes represented the first Church-sponsored type of formal schooling. With the decline of secular schools, it became necessary to offer a more elementary course of studies in episcopal schools. This rudimentary instruction was more widely dispersed when Church Councils ordered the establishment of presbyterial schools in outlying parishes of each bishopric. Monastic and conventual schools were outgrowths of the same need to raise the educational level of the populace, more particularly for those who would follow a religious vocation.

It would be erroneous to presume there was any single educational ideal in early Christian thought. Yet if Augustine's views are representative, they reveal a fairly distinct picture of the ideally educated Christian as one who both realizes and transcends the highest values of Greco-Roman culture. To them is added the supernatural power of divine grace as mediated by the Church. Education means pre-eminently the bringing to consciousness of God's will for men. The social extrapolation from this is education aiming ultimately at the realization of a sacral society, the fulfillment of the Heavenly City of God on earth.

QUESTIONS FOR DISCUSSION

1. Assume you are a public school teacher presenting a unit on the history of religion. Is there any important difference in saying in front of a class, "Moses received the Ten Commandments from the Lord on Mount Sinai" and "The Jews *believed* Moses received the Ten Commandments from the Lord on Mount Sinai"? If there is an important distinction, would it be as crucial for a unit on Greek mythology? Why or why not?

2. How should an elementary school teacher respond to the following query from a student: "Did God *really* make everything, the whole world, and everybody in it?"

3. Would there by any contradiction involved in agnostic or atheist parents desiring religious instruction, even parochial schooling, for their children?

4. It has been claimed that Jewish education is based on a historical consciousness. Is this any less true for Christian education—today or during its first few centuries of existence?

5. Would it have been possible for either Jews or Christians to have developed a different response besides outright refusal to the Roman demand that all religious groups show their loyalty to the state through religious observances?

6. How is the original ambivalence of primitive Christianity toward pagan culture and Hellenic learning recapitulated in contemporary religious thought? For example, do denominational differences depend partly on how various sects view the relationship between faith and secular knowledge?

7. Is it actually the case, in your opinion, that our culture has a "naturalistic secularism" for its "inarticulate major premise"? If so, how does this state of affairs affect public and private education today?

8. What groups within modern Judaism advocate, respectively, ideas similar to those of the Pharisees and Sadducees?

9. A majority of the community endorses a Christmas pageant and carol sing in a school assembly program. The parents of one school child lodge a strenuous protest against a religious observance under public school auspices. What should the principal, superintendent, or board of education do in this situation?

10. Contrast and compare Greco-Roman educational ideals with Judeo-Christian educational ideals. Which seem to be most influential in modern society? What specific themes in current educational thought appear to derive from these traditions?

4 Education for a Theocentric Society

Children, ye shall not seek after great science. Simply enter into your own inward principle and learn to know what you yourselves are, spiritually and naturally, and do not dive into the secret things of God. . . . As Saint Augustine says, "He is a miserable man who knows all things, and does not know God; and he is happy who knows God, even though he know nothing else. But he who knows God and all else beside, he is not made more blessed thereby; for he is blessed through God alone."

JOHANN TAULER
Sermons

Let us use our reason, that God may observe in us gratitude for his mercies, and that other lands may see that we are human beings, capable both of learning and of teaching, in order that through us, also, the world may be made better.

MARTIN LUTHER
Letter to the Mayors and Aldermen

THE EARLY MEDIEVAL AGE

Historians have had trouble coming to terms with that enormous portion of Western history beginning sometime around the fifth century and extending to the end of the thirteenth. Renaissance man, anxious to assert his own intellectual superiority, looked back and with pardonable arrogance designated the interlude between the eclipse of Greco-Roman civilization and the emergence of a dynamic humanistic culture in his own time as merely a "dark" interim of unrelieved barbarism and cultural stagnation. Ever since, the term *medieval* has been a patronizing synonym for "unprogressive" or "reactionary." In fact this long stretch of time was neither a single cultural unit marked solely by ignorance, superstition, and unrelieved chaos nor was it the period (as is sometimes alleged from some

199

quarters) when Western man achieved his highest cultural pinnacle. A balanced judgment will not ignore the extent to which society fell into disrepair when Rome's power faded, but neither will it depreciate how far late medieval civilization had advanced toward the flowering of Italian literary and intellectual genius known as the Renaissance, several centuries before that rebirth "officially" began.

The Middle Ages, it must be said, was a study in contrasts, in which chaos coexisted with order, ignorance with erudition, corruption with saintliness, beauty with ugliness. It was an era beknighted, yet a time evidencing considerable creativity and social ferment. If it is true that hunger, disease, and war stalked the masses of men, it is equally true that they constructed a culture boasting such triumphs as the soaring Gothic spires at Rheims, Chartres, and Paris, a rich literature, and the finely honed philosophical subtleties of scholasticism. Against the picture of political disunity must be placed the vision of a *Republica Christiana,* a spiritual commonwealth of the Christian faith united under the suzerainty of the Roman pope, holding before it a vision of a God-centered society. Any fair assessment of this vast historical time span must take both its achievements and its liabilities into account.

The historic task of medieval man was to rebuild—painfully, laboriously—upon the whitening bones of a dead civilization a new Christian civilization under the domination of the Church. The work began during a monumental night filled with the war cries of marauding barbarians, the heavy tramp of advancing invaders. Gloomy fortress-carapaces offered scant protection and less comfort in a darkened world. For some four hundred years war was the natural state of affairs, peace an abnormal pause in the beat of martial drums.

The drama opened with the great *Völkerwanderung,* or wanderings of barbarian tribes across the European continent, sometime late in the second century. Saxons, Angles, Jutes, Burgundians, Lombards, Huns, Vandals, Visigoths, Ostrogoths, Franks, Alemanni—all were involved in mass migrations prompted by wars, famines, plagues, and probably a host of other ills. They came at first in small numbers, Teutonic peoples moving across the Rhine–Danube frontier to settle along Rome's imperial outposts. Some were assimilated and taken in as *foederati,* allies of the Roman legions. Then, by the fourth century, as their homelands behind them were occupied by Asiatic tribes, their numbers swelled and they began to pile up against the Roman borders, demanding access to the territories within. They came in desperate hordes, flinging themselves across lands formerly inviolate. Visigoths and Vandals set out plundering and ravaging the imperial countryside, followed in the next century by looting, burning Ostrogoths. By the end of the fifth century Roman hegemony in the West had been vanquished, to be replaced by Ostrogothic governance in Italy, by Vandals in northern Africa, by the Anglo-Saxons in Britain, and by the

Visigoths in southwestern Gaul. Europe relapsed into stagnation. Cities shrank to towns, towns to villages, and hamlets to desolate fields. Paved roads became impassable trails swallowed up by the wilderness. The shadows of a cultural eclipse had set in.

In the long run it was the permanent conquest of Gaul by a confederation of Frankish tribes between the late fifth and early sixth centuries that was most important to the later development of Western European history. The unique contribution of the Franks was that their holdings, which came to include almost all of Christian Western Europe, served as the site for the rekindling of a new civilization and culture, represented by a gradual synthesis of Roman and Germanic elements. Beginning with the first of the Merovingian leaders in the early 400's to the start of the Carolingian dynasty in the late seventh century, there occurred the first stirrings of a new indigenous society to replace the faded glory of Rome.

EARLY MEDIEVAL EDUCATION

When the assimilative capacity of the western Roman Empire was exhausted and its territories finally overrun completely by Germanic tribes, widespread destruction obliterated much of the old culture. Cities decayed with the collapse of the Roman municipal government. Plunder and disorder brought an almost total disruption of formal education; and within two or three generations Europe had sunk to a very low intellectual level. Even the clergy were ignorant of general learning. Though some of the old Roman institutional forms were preserved, the educational system of antiquity was not among them. People viewed literary–rhetorical education with profound distrust because it was a symbol of the culture the pagan schools had served so long. It would be several centuries before the Church, as inheritor of the old legacy, felt sufficiently secure to incorporate very much secular learning into the schools it had to create to fill the educational vacuum. To the extent that the Church found itself compelled to establish a system of schools in order to illuminate faith with learning, the content of its education was directed mainly toward otherworldly concerns. That is, the growing ecclesiastical monopoly of schooling led to a restriction of learning within the limits defined by Church doctrines and institutional needs. Schooling became largely a matter of clerical training for performing religious duties, not preparation for secular affairs. Classical learning found little place in the new scheme of studies except as it could be used to support articles of religious faith.

A Celtic Cultural Outpost

Ireland was the only place in Europe where the old learning continued to flourish. Because of their relative inaccessibility, the Celts provided a haven for classical culture long after it had been obscured elsewhere. Formal education had flourished in Ireland even before Caesar's time. Celtic scholars known as *bards* or *druids* evidently had conducted schools for young nobles, imparting an extensive literary legacy through the native written language (the *ogam* or *ogham* script) centuries before Christian missionaries appeared on the scene. When monastic missionaries from St. Victor and Lerins introduced Christian learning early in the fourth century, they found a fully developed system of lower and upper schools functioning. Most of the monastics who founded churches and monasteries did not share the antipathy to pagan learning of their Italian brethren; some, as a matter of fact, had been educated in the few surviving Roman schools on the Continent. During the next two centuries the Irish were cut off from the western Church during the Teutonic invasions of Gaul and England, thus providing them with a unique opportunity to preserve the classical inheritance. The dual school system that grew up—native Irish and Christian monastic—conjoined the two traditions to the mutual advantage of both types of schools. Monks maintained interest in the native literature and language as well as in late Hellenistic learning transmitted in the study of Greek and Latin. The older Celtic schools assumed responsibility for instruction in military drill, literature, and law. Monastic schools, developing as true educational centers in their own right rather than as mere adjuncts to monasteries, provided instruction at a lower level. They may have been preparatory schools for the bardic or lay schools until the seventh century when druidic institutions died out. Monastic schools had by then opened "external" schools for the benefit of everyone, including those not intended for a clerical vocation. Unlike their continental equivalents, Irish monastic schools retained a high interest in the study of classics. As late as the ninth century if anyone knew Greek it was automatically assumed he was a product of an Irish school. Before and during the Danish invasions of the late 700's, it was Irish missionaries who were called upon to help rebuild schools and to preserve learning on the Continent. The Vikings, or Norsemen as they were more commonly called, wiped out almost every trace of Irish classical culture, but not before many learned scholars escaped to build schools in northern Frankland, Gaul, and in parts of England. In the twelfth century traces of these migrations were still evident in monasteries as far away as Bulgaria, Poland, and southern Europe.

Irish missionaries probably did a great deal to stimulate early efforts involving education in Britain, beginning in the sixth century. The first of these, *St. Columba,* founded a monastery in Iona in southwestern Scotland. He was soon followed by monks dispatched by Pope Gregory the Great to re-establish the Christian culture abruptly terminated a hundred and fifty years earlier by Saxon invasions. An ecclesiastical council held in 664 over competing claims of Celtic and Roman branches of the Church produced a decision favoring the Roman group. It resulted in a quick growth of the

Latin Church in Britain. Along with its clerics, the Church imported teachers and scholars such as the *Abbot Hadrian* and *Theodore of Tarsus* to rebuild monasteries and church schools. The most illustrious of the early English scholars was the Venerable *Bede* (673–735), who worked hard to raise standards of learning at the monasteries of Wearmouth and Yarrow. A significant number of monasteries, endowed with books from Vienna and Rome, eventually became important transmitters of classical studies. The cathedral school at York, under the directorship of the learned *Albert,* was known throughout the region for its extensive library holdings. Significantly, these included most of the important textbooks and Latin authors then known. If Bede's *Ecclesiastical History of the English Nation* is to be believed, a fairly widespread educational renaissance took place during the seventh and eighth centuries throughout Britain. During this same general period similar developments were taking place on the Continent.

The Carolingian Renaissance

Some—though precious few—of the barbarian kings in the seventh and eighth centuries who fell heir to the remains of the Roman Empire followed the old imperial precedent of supporting schools. The Ostrogothic king *Theodoric* was one who encouraged the growth of public schools in Italy during his reign, as did the Merovingian ruler *Chilperic* in Gaul. The famed *Charles Martel* and *Pepin the Short,* founders of the Carolingian dynasty in Frankland, also encouraged the settlement of scholars and missionaries in their territory. Carolus Magnus ("Charles the Great"), otherwise known as *Charlemagne,* was perhaps the foremost royal patron of learning in late eighth- and early ninth-century Europe. At his accession to the throne in 768 the general state of learning in his domain was at an abysmally low level. Monastic schools and cathedral schools were virtually nonexistent. Needless to add, the clergy were grossly illiterate. Charlemagne aimed to promote learning systematically throughout the kingdom, to force the higher clergy to reopen schools, to encourage the nobility to broaden their own education, and to attract intellectual leadership from abroad for the reforms he hoped to effect. The initial task was training clergy as teachers for the general populace. With the assistance of two Italians, *Peter of Pisa* and *Paulus Diaconus,* the former a grammarian under whom Charlemagne himself had studied and the latter a Benedictine scholar, he revitalized the royal court or palace school, sponsored the creation of an educational literature for the churches, and issued edicts for the founding of educational institutions throughout the kingdom. In a letter demanding improvement in literary standards, Charlemagne remarked, "Desirous as we are of improving the condition of the churches, we impose on ourselves the task of reviving with the utmost zeal the study of letters, almost extinguished through the neglect of our ancestors." All subjects were to cultivate the liberal arts, help create opportunities for the education of children, and support a system of schools. Though burdened with countless responsibilities, the king tried to set an example by industriously pursuing (unsuccessfully) the study of Latin and Greek, not to mention other literary disciplines.

Charlemagne's chief advisor and minister of education from 782 to 796 was a brilliant educator named *Alcuin* (735–804). He had been persuaded to resign his post as head of the cathedral school at York, where he had earlier acquired a reputation as a distinguished teacher, and to come to Charlemagne's court to direct the new reforms. Along with three advisors brought from York, Alcuin's first job was to create a model institution out of the palace school. It had been in operation for many years, thanks to Paulus Diaconus, although it had been little more than an elementary school. Under Alcuin's direction it became a center of instruction not only for members of the royal household but also for clergymen and nobles attracted from outlying districts of Charlemagne's kingdom. Other scholars joined the staff, men set to work writing hymns, poetry, capitularies to the clergy, sermons, and textbooks. To catechetical-type instruction in Church doctrine, mathematics, and writing was added a higher course of studies in astronomy, poetry, theology, and history. Before long Charlemagne's palace school was a celebrated educational institution.

Alcuin's work included the drafting of proclamations on education for other instructional centers. Before he left Charlemagne's court to become head of the abbey of St. Martin of Tours in 796, Alcuin had helped the king upgrade education among the bishops and monastery heads in the realm, organized abbey or monastic elementary schools everywhere, advanced learning for freemen of the court and children of the administrative classes, and in general had substantially improved the state of formal learning. His successor at the court, Bishop *Theodulf,* continued the revival movement. If anything, Theodulf broadened Alcuin's interest in clerical training to include universal education for all people. One order stipulated that all priests should reinstitute presbyterial-type schools in every rural community so that even children of the lower classes could receive a free rudimentary schooling. Another, issued in 802, proclaimed that everyone should send their sons to grammar schools. Further edicts stopped short at the idea of compulsory schooling but at least the opportunity to attend some school was opened to more people than ever before. Libraries grew in populated centers and at municipal cathedrals, a revision of the Vulgate translation of the Bible was undertaken, and a new interest in classical studies awakened. Over-all, an important impetus to the study of letters was provided, which led to a widespread revival of educational activity in monasteries and cathedral schools.

Alcuin's influence was considerable, taking into account those political and economic circumstances which tended to discourage the spread of learning. *Rabanus Maurus,* one of Alcuin's students and later archbishop at Mainz, helped carry on the work initiated by his mentor, earning the title First Teacher of Germany for his teaching and writing. Maurus' popular work *On the Instruction of the Clergy* was heavily influenced by Alcuin's educational treatises. Although quarrels over sovereign powers led quickly to the breakup of the Frankish empire, Charlemagne's son *Louis the Pious* swung his influence behind a Church request that grammar schools be founded in every bishopric. Louis' son, *Charles the Bald,* labored unceasingly on behalf of schools; in many respects he equalled if not surpassed the work of his grandfather.

Though few of these efforts were destined to have lasting effect, they are notable insofar as they illustrate attempts to keep the lamp of learning lit during an era of almost unrelieved darkness. It was a difficult time for educational work. The Danes were plundering and burning cities along the English coast. Nordic hordes preyed upon the northern coasts of Frankland. Scores of scholars from the battle zones flocked to Charles' court for protection, for the king's patronage had become well known. The great Irish scholar *John Scotus Erigena* (810–877), who might be called the founder of the scholastic movement, was among the great numbers of learned men finding places at the Frankish court. John Scotus, in fact, was remembered as an outstanding teacher at the palace school, perhaps excelling Alcuin himself.

Alfred's Reforms

The barbaric invasions left northern Frankland in shambles. The situation in England was no better. The general decay in learning since Alcuin's work at York was evident everywhere when *Alfred the Great,* King of Wessex, came to power in 871. His problem was identical to the one Charlemagne had faced and he responded in much the same manner. Surveying the dreary scene of libraries in disuse, monasteries reduced to rubble, and clergymen unable to translate Latin into Anglo-Saxon, Alfred determined to establish a palace school, import scholars, and revive learning within the Church. According to contemporary accounts. Alfred supported translations of such important works as Gregory's *Pastoral Care,* Bede's *Ecclesiastical History,* and Boethius' *Consolations of Philosophy.* Monasteries were rebuilt, court schools were supported from the royal treasury, and letters circulated enjoining bishops to support education among the people. Above all, Alfred tried to stimulate the development of the native Anglo-Saxon language and literature. Unfortunately, the brief renaissance of learning was obscured by Norman conquests a century later. Just as the Carolingian revival was cut off by a deluge of barbarism, so its offshoot in England was doomed by new waves of plundering raiders. Nonetheless, in the face of formidable obstacles and setbacks, these enlightened rulers, more than anyone else, helped to keep learning alive during an age of destruction, upheaval, and constant warfare. Had circumstances been more favorable it is entirely possible that the next renaissance of the twelfth and thirteenth centuries could have been hastened by at least a hundred years.

THE LATER MIDDLE AGES

The Rise and Decline of a Chessboard Society

With the collapse of Carolingian rule and its attendant lawlessness, an individual's sole hope of protection rested with some local warrior sufficiently powerful to fend off foes and fill the vacuum left by the absence of centralized government. In return for a measure of security, peasants everywhere hastened to place themselves under some overlord and to render him service. The resulting socioeconomic system of the Middle Ages was known as *feudalism,* a form of societal organization which pervaded and gave shape to all aspects of life and every institution. It arose also in response to the requirements of an agricultural economy conducted by barter and the exchange of services. As trade and external commerce were cut off, land became the main source of wealth. Regional governments found themselves unable to collect taxes and hence had to pay for services with grants of real estate or by delegating authority to landholders who could exert power over people residing on the land. Such practices became common during Carolingian times, when a monarch's retainers, known as royal *vassals,* were endowed with benefices, or estates, in exchange for military and civil assistance. This remuneration paid a vassal was known as a "feudum"—a *fief*—either title to land or the right to govern it, to exact labor from its inhabitants, and to use its revenues to meet the expenses involved in maintaining an armed force to protect it.

Royal vassals, in turn, assumed certain rights and privileges befitting their station as members of a landed aristocracy, including the authority to delegate power to subvassals. Great landowners were quick to take advantage of the lack of strong civil control to force everyone, freemen included, into becoming tenants of the land. Compulsory military service at private expense plunged the lesser ranks into debt, forcing them to yield up their own holdings to an overlord who could protest them while they worked as dependent tenants. They might serve as soldiers or as farmers, usually both. Similarly, the lower peasants sank into servitude and were fitted into the feudal system, because security had become far more valuable than freedom. Like pieces on a chessboard, everyone had his place in the social order, his moves fixed in a concerted pattern ideally suited for furthering the main activities of the age—farming and fighting. The touchstones of the feudal structure were service and loyalty (the commodities of the many) in exchange for protection and land (the commodities of the few).

Even the Church became feudalized because it also had become a great landholder, owing to the generosity of pious monarchs and lords. But this was possible on a large scale only by associating vassalage with fief-holding. A regular hierarchy of abbots, bishops, and parish clergy emerged, some of whose members might acquire fiefs, render or receive services, and even arm themselves with the secular sword. The total class structure was composed of an aristocratic elite of ecclesiastics and nobility arranged along varying grades of feudal tenure, supported by the lesser nobility and subordinate landowners pledged to their service, they in turn dependent on the toiling masses of serfs. Even the peasantry was ordered by ranks, extending downward from *villeins* (from *villa*, "farm") to lowly cotters. All classes were locked into a common mosaic. It was not without reason that a medieval rhyme went, "God hath shapen lives three; boor and knight and priest they be."

The elaborate network of connections binding emperors, kings, dukes, counts, barons, knights, and serfs together was tightly regulated by contractual relations. A formal *oath of fealty* sealed the act of homage in which a vassal pledged himself to his superior, promising to render faithful service for life and assist in the common defense. On his part, the overlord furnished land, dispensed justice, and pledged his assurance of protection over his subordinates. As these feudal contracts became hereditary, the over-all organization of medieval society was buttressed by its economic correlative, the so-called *manorial system*. The countryside was divided up into estates or manors over which the lord (*seigneur*) reigned. Around his manorial house or fortified castle would cluster the peasants' settlements and all the surrounding cultivated fields. In a very real sense everyone was bound to the soil, for except in some "free" towns owing no allegiance to an overlord, a settled existence beyond manorial borders was impossible. That state of affairs was to persist throughout Europe for centuries.

When the closed system of feudalism finally began to disintegrate, momentous political, economic, and social forces were unleased whose practical effect was to set Europe in an entirely new direction. Aided by the fragmentation of political authority, warring kings gradually succeeded in consolidating the various duchies under a semblance of centralized government once again, a process begun in England under Alfred and his successors, and accelerated after the Norman conquest. Starting with William, Duke of Normandy, and extending through a long succession of monarchs (Henry I, Henry II, John I, Henry III, Edward I), Britain moved steadily toward the political reality of the modern nation state, complete with written laws and a quasirepublican form of government. Similarly, rulership in tenth-century France (a remnant of the western Frankish kingdom) originated with the dynasty of the Capetians competing with the duchies of Toulouse, Gascony, and Aquitaine. Monarchical power expanded under the reigns of Philip I, Louis VI, Louis VII, and Philip II, and territorial consolidation continued apace under the leadership of Louis IX and Philip IV, among others. Centralized monarchies were much slower to develop elsewhere on the continent, however, even after the sequestered world of feudalism was long past. From the tenth century onward, for example, German and Italian rulers were more or less constantly engaged in a battle for supremacy with warrior-popes, their efforts at consolidation hindered by grandiose schemes of territorial conquest. Neither Frederick Barbarossa (reigned 1152–1190) nor Frederick II in the thirteenth century, two of the leading figures in the struggle for monarchial unification, succeeded in defying the temporal aspirations of the papacy. Thanks to the power enjoyed by Gregory IX, Innocent III, Innocent IV, and Boniface VIII, the dreams of a united German empire and a unified Italy were never realized. Even as late as the fourteenth century kings, emperors, and popes were locked in a battle for ultimate authority, and the question of how society was to be governed remained undecided.

Despite political anarchy, all signs pointed to a definite cultural revival across Europe even before 1000. In the succeeding three centuries, a new and vibrant civilization arose, evolving out of the poverty, ignorance, and relative stagnation of the age preceding. The Church grew ever richer and became a leading patron of the arts. Simple wooden structures gave way to Romanesque architecture, followed by the sublime creations of Gothic art. Polyphonic music and a vernacular prose appeared on the scene, accompanied by new schools of painting and sculpture. The rapid growth of trading and manufacturing towns, expanded contacts with the East, and the improvement of technology all played a role in strengthening intellectual ferment. Scholars once again turned to the ancient texts then available and undertook to disseminate their wisdom more widely. At the Norman court, in Toledo and Montpellier, in Naples and Cremona, the intelligentsia embarked upon a crusade to spread the light of learning, a labor partially deflected away from literary exegesis in the thirteenth century by the rise of a rationalist philosophical tradition emphasizing the study of logic and theology. As was to be expected, the fortunes of institutionalized education were affected by these cultural advances of the late Middle Ages.

THE DEVELOPING INSTITUTIONAL STRUCTURE OF LATE MEDIEVAL EDUCATION

Monastic Schools

The original Basilian and Benedictine Rules for the maintenance of monastic communities in the sixth century had not paid much attention to matters of education, except that reading and study should be part of the daily discipline for every monk. The monastery school did not develop until it became impossible for a novitiate to acquire reading ability in a secular school. Only when it became clear prospective monastics would have to be taught to read by the order so as to understand the Bible was some definite provision made for their instruction. Before long, monasteries were busy conducting schools for the *oblati,* even though no one had anticipated it would become their major responsibility. Schools were begun on a voluntary basis, becoming almost obligatory with the passage of time and the urging of kings and ecclesiastical authorities. The great majority of communities tended to retain their emphasis on ascetic withdrawal from society, offering only whatever instruction was minimally necessary. Yet a few, but ever-increasing number of monasteries began to collect books for their libraries and to expand their holdings by setting their members to copying texts, and eventually they became distinguished educational centers. The influence of Alfred, Alcuin, Charlemagne, Bede, and others greatly hastened the transformation of many northern monasteries into important schools whose activities completely overshadowed their contributions in fields such as agriculture, handicrafts, and manufacturing.

It is certain that by the year 1000 the medieval monastic school had evolved a regular course of studies for its novitiates. It was organized around the seven liberal arts, classified as the *Trivium* (grammar, dialectic, and rhetoric) and *Quadrivium* (arithmetic, geometry, music, and astronomy). Grammar (mainly the study of Latin) was the staple of the typical curriculum. Depending on the time and specific place, the works of *Donatus* and *Priscian* were the most popular texts employed for teaching beginning pupils. More advanced students were taught from the treatises of *Isidore* of *Seville, Boethius, Cassiodorus, Capella,* and *St. Augustine.* Alcuin's letters and the writings of Rabanus Maurus were especially favored in Frankish lands over Boethius or Donatus. After a thorough grounding in grammar, a student might be exposed to carefully edited versions of Virgil. Porphry, and Aristotle. Possibly the rhetorical works of Quintilian and Cicero were occasionally studied. As the Church's position on formal education became more definite, the range of subjects pursued in monastic schools was broadened still further. How extensive a curriculum was offered to the *externi* in "outer" schools sponsored by monasteries is purely a matter of conjecture; it probably was neither so extensive nor rigorous as that offered to promising students committed to the monastic life.

Aside from their teaching duties within or missionary activities abroad, most monks from the more active monasteries spent much time laboriously copying manuscripts, because their communities were the only book publishers left intact in society. This work was ordinarily conducted in a separate room in the monastery expressly reserved for the purpose. Virtually all the missals, psalters, compendiums of patristic writings, and Bibles available in medieval times came out of the copying room or *scriptorium* of the monastery.

Conventual Schools

Life in a convent was the only opportunity offered to women of scholarly ambition desiring to combine religious piety and the pursuit of learning under formal auspices. The same forces that led monasteries to create schools compelled nunneries to sponsor courses of studies for novitiates, but with this difference: from a much earlier date the conventual schools opened their doors to those not expecting to don a habit. It became an accepted custom (still followed today in some countries) to dispatch girls to a convent for a religious upbringing which included instruction in reading, writing, Latin, music, weaving, spinning, and needlework. It should not be supposed, however, that education in a nunnery was exclusively "domestic." The curriculum frequently included thorough studies of the *Trivium* and parts of the *Quadrivium*. Between the sixth and twelfth centuries many of the best-educated women in Europe received their formal schooling in Europe's convents. For reasons not clearly understood, convent schools appear to have declined in importance after the middle of the thirteenth century.

Cathedral Schools

Some two centuries after the educational revivals of Charlemagne and Alfred the Great, and just before Europe's great renaissance of learning, Church canon law recognized the validity of widespread popular education. The Third Lateran Council, meeting in 1189, enjoined the provision of schools for the laity as well as for clergy: "Since the Church of God, like a good and tender mother, is obliged to provide for the spiritual and bodily needs of the poor in order that they may not be deprived of the opportunity of reading . . . in every cathedral church, schools shall be opened. . . . In other churches or monasteries, also, free schools shall be re-opened."[1] Except for a long interlude between the fifth and ninth centuries, urban cathedral churches had always organized schools of some kind. By the 1100's, theology as a scholarly discipline had grown to the point where it was studied as a part of a scheme of higher studies. The cathedral school, properly speaking, had evolved from an informal *grammar school* for training clergy into an institution for highly advanced studies and was directed by the *scholasticus* or chancellor (one of four officers) of the cathedral.[2] The scholasticus probably oversaw all educational activities of a diocese while lesser clerics actually conducted the instruction. Beneath the higher school, a bewildering variety of lower educational forms developed. Among those conventionally distinguished, one may speak of *collegiate schools, chantry* or *stipendary*

---

[1] A. F. Leach, *Educational Characters and Documents* (New York: Cambridge University Press, 1911), pp. 188–189. The translation is adapted after Patrick J. McCormick and Francis P. Cassidy, *History of Education* (Washington, D.C.: Catholic Education Press, 1953), pp. 306–307.

[2] In the early medieval period there were no cathedral schools of advanced studies, only lower-level grammar schools. Alcuin and Bede, for example, describe the founding of grammar schools placed under the authority of cathedrals, and from their descriptions it is clear that the grammar schools of the eighth and ninth centuries had not yet evolved the system of studies characteristic of cathedral schools in the twelfth and thirteenth centuries.

schools, song schools, and of course, *grammar schools.* (Not all of these were in existence in any given diocese and they were not always contemporary with one another.)

Lower Church Schools

Collegiate schools were a comparatively late development, most often found from the early thirteenth to the sixteenth century. In England, where they were most typically found, they offered a combination of elementary and secondary studies, principally organized around the traditional *Trivium.* Their clientele was composed of young boys destined for secular pursuits in later life. Some graduates did enter theological studies in one or another of the cathedral schools. *Song schools* were a response to the need of churches to secure choirboys to perform during the musical portions of worship services. Instruction was roughly equivalent to that provided in the ancient presbyterial and episcopal schools of early Christian times, the only difference being that major emphasis was placed on music. The choir director, or *precentor,* assumed major responsibility for the education offered. Such schools were also created to meet identical needs in smaller parish churches. Still another kind of elementary schools which became very common was the *chantry* or *stipendary* school. A chantry (*cantaria*) was an endowment or fund established by a well-to-do parishioner or his survivors to pay for masses for the individual's soul after death. The money would be used to support an altar or special chapel in the church where the masses were offered and to pay the chantry priest assigned the task. This custom enjoyed more popularity in England than on the Continent, and it died out during the Protestant Reformation. Because saying prayers for the souls of the departed could scarcely be considered full-time employment for a priest, it became customary for him to be assigned additional duties such as the teaching of elementary school. In time, these lay-supported schools occupied the greatest portion of a cleric's time. A student usually received a very rudimentary kind of education in a chantry school, though if he were academically inclined he might advance to pursue studies in the upper cathedral school. Evidence shows that by the ninth century, a song and an elementary grammar school were attached to almost every major cathedral or collegiate church. Two hundred years later the song school had evolved beyond a chorister-training curriculum and become a true elementary school. Similarly, the grammar school was no longer merely an institution for clerical preparation because the cathedral school had assumed this function; now it had become a distinct institution for general education in its own right, roughly serving the function of an intermediate or secondary-level school today.

SECULAR EDUCATIONAL FORMS

Court Schools

The Church as an ecclesiastical institution did not enjoy an absolute monopoly in medieval schooling, owing to the existence of organized courses of study offered outside religious auspices. One kind of graduated regimen of studies was conducted in *court schools*. From Charlemagne's time onward, most of the European nobility's courts sponsored schools to help train scribes to supervise the civil administration of the realm. Not only kings but also lesser nobles appointed teachers to conduct schools for the benefit of courtesans and their offspring. Graduates found employment as clerks, tax collectors, magistrates, and so on. Nobles seeking royal favors often found it advantageous to attend a school, particularly if the ruler sought a reputation as a patron of learning to further his own political ambitions. Most often, the level of instruction was extremely primitive. Some of the more prestigious courts found it possible occasionally to expand the curricular offerings upward to include medical, scientific, and philosophical studies. King Henry II of England, for example, founded a court school in the late twelfth century whose instruction rivaled that found in many better-known cathedral schools. This type of schooling did little to contribute to the blooming medieval intellectual life of later centuries, but it was a beginning in the establishment of secular schools. So far as is known, the court schools were rarely opened to anyone besides the children of nobles and court functionaries. Royal scribes were invariably recruited from the privileged classes, which meant that court schools did little to advance the cause of popular mass education.

Feudalistic Chivalry

Indirectly, the courts were engaged in another type of education even though the school as an institutional type for the instruction involved was far less well defined. It must be remembered that the feudal noble was first and foremost a soldier. Fighting was his assigned duty and privilege. In discharging that service, he rode to battle as a member of the mounted cavalry, not as a lowly rustic foot soldier. But just as a cleric had to acquire proficiency for his chosen vocation through a long and arduous training, the feudal aristocrat with wealth and leisure enough to become a chevalier had to undergo an extended apprenticeship. The provisions which were made for preparing sons of the nobility to become knights constituted a definite kind of education, secular in content and intent, yet firmly sanctioned by the authority of the Church, because the interests of an ordered society were thought to be served by knightly ministrations. And an orderly social order was advantageous to the Church.

The term *chivalry* is employed to designate the way of life of knights—

the values, customs, responsibilities, and rights of a warrior caste. It denoted certain ideals of gallantry, honor, polite manners, and social courtesies that were supposedly exclusive to men of the knightly class, and the training required to foster chivalrous conduct is consequently called *chivalric education*. Wherever feudal institutions prevailed, the etiquette of chivalry was recognized. At its worst, chivalry simply sanctioned the homely virtues of the ancient barbarian warrior—prowess, valor, loyalty to one's plighted word, battlefield courage. At its best, however, it infused a semibarbaric outlawry with a set of higher ideals, a better sense of social obligation, and a consciousness of moral responsibility. The results included a partial check on outright social exploitation, a restraint upon pillaging and destruction by landed aristocrats, and the replacement by an ideal of regulated service in place of lawless gratification.[3]

Unless he were destined for the Church, an aristocrat's son began his training for knighthood almost as soon as he could walk. He would be set to learning horsemanship and the use of arms from the earliest age possible. When he was seven or eight, the boy would be sent to a neighboring noble's manor or perhaps to the court of a king to serve as a *page* until age fourteen. There he made himself useful in performing household chores while developing martial skills. Perhaps he might be instructed in Latin, Church creeds, some writing, music, elementary mathematics, and courtly manners by a lady of the castle. It was expected that the page would also receive training in light weaponry, wrestling, boxing, and horsemanship by soldiers and male servants. Following his apprenticeship as messenger, servant, and errand boy, the young lad graduated to the rank of *squire* ("shield-bearer") and was assigned as manservant-bodyguard to a knight. Henceforth it became his duty to accompany and assist his lord, grooming the horses, carrying weapons, following the master in tournaments or in battle. He would take charge of prisoners, help his knightly patron if he were wounded, and otherwise serve his apprenticeship. During leisure hours he learned to fence with the sword and to tilt with a lance. The diligent squire acquired skill in hunting, singing, dancing, rhyming, playing chess, and public address. The values he absorbed were those of loyalty, devotion to duty, courage, and bravery. As Chaucer phrased it, speaking of the well-rounded knight,

> He coude songes make and well endyte
> Juste and eek daunce, and wel purtreye and wryte.

Formal investiture as a knight took place around the age of twenty-one. The solemn occasion was preceded by fasting, holy confession, and a nightlong vigil spent in meditation. In the morning he knelt before his lord and

[3] Ellwood P. Cubberley, *The History of Education* (Boston: Houghton Mifflin, 1920), p. 169.

took a sacred oath "to protect the Church, to fight against treachery, to revere the priesthood, to defend the poor from injustice, to keep peace in his own province, to shed his blood for his brethren, and if necessary, to lay down his life."[4] Because the bulk of instruction received by a knight-in-training was supervised by some court, it seems fair to claim that the influence of royal patronage on secular education was twofold, as exemplified by the more formal court schools for training scribes described earlier and this less structured training for a knightly aristocrat.

Burgh or Municipal Schools

The real flowering of the Middle Ages in terms of high culture and a revival of learning took place in the twelfth and thirteenth centuries. By the 1000's, the Nordic tribes had been at least superficially Christianized and absorbed into the medieval cultural mainstream. Magyar tribes in southeastern Europe had been turned back or civilized. In England, after the invasion of William the Conqueror, there followed an unprecedented period of security, stability, and progress. Compared to what had gone before, the initial consolidation of German principalities and duchies (the legacy of Charlemagne's shattered empire), beginning with *King Otto I* in 961, ushered in a new era of prosperity under the Holy Roman Empire.[5] The re-establishment of more stable conditions promised a new moral and intellectual awakening across the continent. The Church's "Truce of God" helped to keep warring nobles in check, trade and commerce were fast developing, the Crusades were multiplying cultural contacts with established intellectual centers in the East, and scores of cathedral schools were growing into true scholarly institutions. With the Christian conquest of Toledo, in Spain, and the establishment of that city as the capital of the Kingdom of Castile, Europeans were first exposed on a large scale to the accumulated treasures of Arabic scholarship (the origins and impact of which will be considered in greater detail momentarily). Latin translations of ancient Greek, Hindu, Judaic, and Chinese classics preserved by the Moors were fast becoming available to intellectuals as far away as Scotland and Scandinavia. Returning Crusaders added to the storehouse by bringing back copies of classical literature uncovered in Syria. As with most inter-cultural contacts, the exposure to new ideas, more sources, and better texts could not help but stimulate the intellectual and social life in Christian Europe.

One culmination of this development and growth was the spread of towns and cities. Urban centers grew up near monasteries, upon the sites of ancient Roman provincial cities, or around feudal castles. The founding of

---

[4] L. F. Salzman, *English Life in the Middle Ages* (New York: Oxford University Press, 1926), p. 190.

[5] Correctly satirized by Voltaire much later as neither "holy" nor "Roman" nor an "empire."

trade routes between such centers as Bremen, Ghent, Magdeburg, London, Hamburg, Augsburg, Venice, and Genoa helped contribute to the commercial prosperity of mercantile centers. The medieval towns grew sufficiently strong by the twelfth century to revolt against their feudal overlords (or ecclesiastical supervisors) and to demand charters granting them greater autonomy. Municipal councils were formed to regulate internal civil affairs and to resist the sovereign claims of outside authorities. Merchant guilds were established for the protection and regulation of crafts. The rise of a prosperous middle class of bankers, traders, merchants, and craftsmen resulted in a demand for formal schools independent of those traditionally associated with the Church. The townspeople wanted schools similar to the cathedral grammar schools or collegiate church schools, with responsibility for their maintenance left to municipal authorities. Sometimes local clerics were permitted to accept teaching appointments from the town council; more commonly the apparent attempt by a bourgeoisie to wrest control of education from the Church was stoutly resisted.

Legally, ecclesiastical authorities had the right to proscribe the establishment of *burgh* or *municipal* schools by civil officials, but this right could be bitterly contested. In Hamburg in 1402, for instance, the city's council established four writing schools but was compelled to disband them when the local cathedral chancellor had the city's inhabitants placed under a threat of excommunication. Sixty-two years later, in Scotland, a purely municipal appointment was successfully made by secular officials in the town of Peebles. Elsewhere it took almost a century before a town provost could appoint masters to local burgh grammar schools without the approval of the cathedral chancellor. Infrequently, private elementary schools for the common townfolk were permitted, but Latin grammar (secondary) schools authorized solely by municipal administrators encountered considerable Church resistance. Perhaps the fact that Church schools did not offer instruction in the vernacular as demanded by the burgher class explains why both public and private elementary schools could do a prosperous business without ecclesiastical hindrance. This was not the case with secondary schools, however. The secular, municipal grammar schools that did appear before the fifteenth century do not seem to have differed significantly in curriculum, instructional methods, or organization from Church Latin grammar schools—from which it can be concluded that the rivalry of the two stemmed from political conflicts more than differences in educational intent. This especially appears to be the case in the German states, where the Church jealously guarded its right to license teachers as a means of controlling education. Secular schools threatened the lucrative income derived from a clerical monopoly on legal functions (record-keeping, drawing wills, preparing contracts, filing tax returns), which nonclerical graduates of a municipal school could easily perform. The Church therefore fought competition with a special ferocity. Town officers and the chancellor of a diocese might be locked in conflict for years over who was to control schools.

When compromises were worked out, they typically allowed municipalities to establish and support schools, but the right to appoint teachers was retained by the Church. In England, on the other hand, the Church monopoly of town education was broken as early as 1410 with the decision of the famous *Gloucester Grammar School Case*. The courts decided then that private and public schools could be founded and staffed without the consent or approval of the Church. In other areas, agreements to split tuition fees in municipal schools between Church and city or to make financial reparations to the clergy for lost revenue allowed total lay control of city schools. Clear precedents for total secular control of either private or public education, as a general rule, took centuries to establish. Legislation allowing parents the right to send children to *any* school, provided they could pay tuition charges, was first passed in England in the early fifteenth century. In the Frankish states, monopolistic education lasted much longer. The importance of burgh schools, aside from whoever controlled them, resided in the fact that they provided a means of entry into the upper classes for a greater proportion of a town population than ever before. Furthermore, despite a lack of curricular or instructional innovation, the burgh schools forced their churchly counterparts to serve more closely the burgeoning business and governmental interests of the bourgeois class. Civic pride played an important role in upgrading educational standards in towns, in the process attracting better teachers to whichever municipal schools received the most lavish support. Indirectly, the larger town schools may have helped galvanize a desire for more extensive instruction, a desire satisfied ultimately only with the founding of universities.

Guild Apprenticeship Training

Technical–vocational training for the medieval working class was largely a function of municipal guilds. A guild was an organization of individuals engaged in a common craft or trade banded together for the purpose of regulating business, protecting workers' interests, and setting standards of workmanship. Virtually every occupational group had its guild; taken together they completely dominated the economy of a town. Serving as combination labor unions, fraternities, and social clubs, guilds became both wealthy and politically influential. They exerted considerable power not only over municipal governments but in power centers among the higher nobility and the clergy as well. Guilds advanced education in several directions. Among their many activities burgher merchant guilds helped finance existing schools to provide a better education for members' children. When pressure was generated for the formation of a burgh school, invariably a guild or combination of guilds was behind the drive. Sometimes craft guilds organized elementary schools of their own. Beyond this kind of support, craft guilds offered another kind of training uniquely their own. Whether it was an association of leather workers, weavers, goldsmiths, masons, cloth workers, pewterers or whatever, organized plans were laid for training people in the trade concerned. Under rules drawn up by the guild as a whole, a *master* would agree to provide food, lodging, clothing, and some rudimentary instruction in reading, writing, arithmetic, and religion for a young *apprentice* during his training period. The student was expected to fulfill his side of the bargain, formalized in a contract called *articles of indenture,* by learning his master's trade and assisting him in his work.

After a stipulated period of years, the apprenticeship period was terminated and the boy was freed to leave his master's shop (provided he had learned the work to his superior's satisfaction) to seek employment in another shop as a paid workman or *journeyman.* The guild carefully regulated the amount he could earn in this manner even after he had been admitted to full membership in the association. When several more years had elapsed, the journeyman would produce a "master piece" as proof of vocational skill. If the work met high standards of craftsmanship, he would be formally approved as a master, permitted to set up his own shop, engage in a trade, accept apprentices, and hire journeymen. Here was a carefully supervised type of vocational training in which young men could learn everything essential to their trade. Without doubt many abuses of the system crept in despite the vigilance of guild inspectors. The temptation to exploit an apprentice was very real. Some masters bypassed the apprenticeship training for their sons by turning the business over to them directly. Nepotism so aggravated tensions among masters and journeymen that occasionally civil authorities intervened with regulations for the protection of all persons concerned. By and large, however, guild-sponsored training worked very well. This again was a kind of education over which the Church exerted little or no influence.

THE CONFLICT OF CRESCENT AND CROSS

It is remarkable how the Islamic contribution to the culture of Western Europe has been either underestimated or ignored. For five centuries, between 700 and 1200, a great Moslem civilization led the world in the power, order, and extent of its government, in refinement of manners, in living standards, social welfare legislation, and scholarship in such diverse fields as art, literature, medicine, jurisprudence, theology, and philosophy. Owing to contact with the culture of the Seljuq Turks during the Crusades of the eleventh through the thirteenth centuries, Christian Europe received knowledge of innumerable technological processes and artifacts, a partial list of which would include the employment of gunpowder, the use of the compass, the manufacture of paper, the pendulum clock, and a form of printing. Through exposure to Islamic civilization in Spain, Europeans were introduced to new foods and drinks, a variety of drugs, improved armaments, the game of chess, maritime codes, poetry, music, and a vastly more efficient system of numerical notation. More significantly, chief responsibility for the preservation of the treasures of antiquity, including Greek mathematics, chemistry, physics, medicine, astronomy, literature, and philosophy fell to Moslem scholars rather than to Christian savants. It is no exaggeration to say that the rise of high medieval culture in Europe previously discussed would not have assumed the form it did had it not been for the impact of this rich Islamic learning when it was transmitted to the West.

The Empire of Allah

Several factors combined to encourage territorial expansion by the followers of the prophet Mohammed (ca. 569–632)—hunger for arable land beyond the confines of the Arabian peninsula, population pressures, political turmoil, the military decline of Persia and Byzantium that made them tempting targets for conquest, and above all, a passionate religious fanaticism that welcomed death in a holy war as a sure guarantee of one's entrance into paradise. Beginning with Abu Bekr (573–624), the first Caliph of Islam following the death of Mohammed, and continuing under a long line of able leaders, the Moslems set out under the holy banner of Allah to annex an empire. In a very short time all of Syria, Persia, and Egypt fell under their control. There followed a massive wave of migration from along the shores of the Red Sea to the north, west, and east, comparable to the migration of Germanic tribes into the former holdings of the Roman empire. Before long, the conquered territories extended from the Indus River to the Atlantic Ocean, embracing parts of India, Baluchistan, Turkestan, Afghanistan, Mesopotamia, Persia, Armenia, Palestine, and Crete. Turning westward, Islamic armies advanced steadily along the north African coast, dividing the land into three provinces: Egypt, with its capital at al-Fustat; Ifrigiya, with a capital at Qairwan; and Morrocco (Maghreb), headed by the city of Fez. Later, in order to protect their northern flank on the sea, Moslem invaders embarked on a crusade to bring Corsica, Sardinia, Cyprus, Malta, and most of Sicily within their domain.

Every conquest created new frontiers which, because they were susceptible to attack, invited further expansion. Once northern Africa was subdued, it became imperative to extend the empire to the northwest. Accordingly, in 712 under the leadership of Musa ibn Nasayr, Arab governor of North Africa, a combined force of Arabs and Moors crossed the Gibraltar straits, besieged and conquered most of the cities on the Spanish peninsula, and then scaled the Pyrenees to overrun most of Gaul. For a time it appeared as though they were well nigh invincible. Not until Moslem armies had advanced over a thousand miles north of Gibraltar was the Islamic dream of making Europe a province of Damascus abruptly shattered. The decisive battle took place in 732 near the small city of Tours, where the combined forces of the Duke of Aquitaine and the Frankish King Carolus Martellus (Martel) decisively routed the invaders. Islamic forces made repeated thrusts in the years following, but eventually they were forced out of southern France altogether. Had the fortunes of war developed otherwise, Europe might easily have succumbed to Moslem culture. As it was, the new civilization that did arise was confined to the lowermost portion of Spain, behind a line running from Coimbra through Saragossa and along the Ebro River. Its cultural influence, however, could never be frustrated by a simple geographical boundary. Events would show how the presence of an alien civilization bordering upon Christendom would prove crucial to the revival of learning in the rest of Europe.

Islamic Culture and Schools

The Mohammedan faith, unlike most brands of Christianity, rarely evidenced hostility and distrust of learning. "He who leaves his home in search of knowledge," runs a maxim attributed to the founder of Islam, "walks in the path of God . . . and the ink of the scholar is holier than the blood of the martyr." From the very beginning Arabs avidly absorbed the culture of the people they conquered, in particular the surviving vestiges of Hellenistic wisdom preserved in Christian enclaves at Alexandria, Antioch, Edessa, Nisibis, Harran, and Caesarea, and throughout the major cities of Syria where Hellenicized Nestorian Christians had earlier fled the intolerance of the Eastern Church. Within a short time the urban settlements of Jund-i-Shapur, Beirut, Damascus, Cairo, Mecca, Basra, Kufa, and Baghdad had become vital centers of Arabic scholarship, where Syriac Moslems set to work translating Greek works in science and philosophy. In an age when the West had almost forgotten its classical heritage, the Arab world was busily engaged in restoring and preserving this learning and making it part of its own tradition.

As part of this momentous undertaking, the caliphs encouraged a policy of gathering neglected texts wherever they could be found, even dispatching messengers to Constantinople and other Greek cities for the purpose of procuring manuscripts. At Baghdad, around 786, it is reported that the Caliph Harounal-Raschid opened a large library, the founding of which set a precedent followed consistently by other rulers. Not many years passed before every major city had at least one public library of considerable content and generous accessibility, not to mention the various private collections housed in mosques and palaces. In 830, for example, Caliph al-Ma'mum organized at Baghdad a "House of Wisdom" (*Bayt al-Hikmah*) combining a scientific academy, observatory, treasury, and library, second only to the great *Museum* at Alexandria. The holdings at Rayy, to cite another example, were extensive enough, it is said, that ten large catalogues were needed just to list all the volumes in the library. Princes like Sahib ibn Abmas in the tenth century might personally own as many books as could then be found in all the libraries of Europe combined.

By the mid-ninth century most of the major work of translating Greek works from Syriac, Greek, Pahlav, and Sanskrit had been completed. In addition to somewhat corrupted versions of the works of Plato and Aristotle, Moslem scholars had copies of the major works of Ptolemy, Appolonius of Perga, Hero of Alexandria, Philo of Byzantium—a sizable proportion of Hellenistic philosophy, mathematics, physics, and medicine. These labors had been finished just in time, it turned out, because early in the eleventh century a wave of conservative reaction broke out at Baghdad and elsewhere, forcing large numbers of scientists, theologians, philosophers, and poets to flee the Near East and migrate westward across Africa. From there classical and Hellenistic literature was carried into the Moorish bridgehead in Spain.

Almost at once a blossoming of cultural and intellectual life occurred in the Spanish cities of Granada, Seville, Toledo, and Cordova. These Moorish centers became beehives of theologians, grammarians, rhetoricians, philologists, lexicographers, historians, anthologists, jurists, philosophers, physicians, scientists, and poets "as numerous," it was claimed, as the "sands of the ocean." The learned class, which was held in awesome repute, set about building upon and extending the lore of the past, with significant advances made in the sciences and in mathematics. At least seventy libraries were founded. Caliph Hakam II (reigned 961–967), one historian recounts, surpassed his predecessors in his patronage of learning and employed countless agents to collect books for him from the farthest reaches of the known world. It is estimated that Hakam possessed a library boasting over 600,000 volumes; four centuries later even the royal library of France had only nine hundred volumes.

Tenth-century Cordova was perhaps the leading focus of Islamic cultural achievements, although Toledo, Seville, Granada, Murcia, Almeria, Valencia, and Cadiz shared actively in the intellectual life of the period. At a time when Europe's cities were still mean overgrown towns with dirt roads and miserably crowded homes, Cordova was noteworthy for its spacious paved streets (lit at night), raised sidewalks, aqueducts, great bridges, royal palaces with innumerable minarets, and mansions equaling in beauty and luxury those of Rome in her heyday. Public baths, markets, mosques, asylums for the poor, hospitals—all unknown in Christian Europe for hundreds of years to come—were legion. Even the smaller towns were well policed, with law and order assured by governmental rule.

The Spanish outpost of Arabic culture naturally sustained a fully developed system of formal education. Basically it was an outgrowth of the pattern begun at Baghdad and Damascus well before the tenth century.

Although male children of the upper classes began their instruction under a private tutor around the age of six, young girls and children of the less privileged classes attended an elementary school, usually located in a mosque. The curriculum stressed simple reading and writing, with the *Koran* (the Islamic Scriptures) employed as a text in theology, history, law, and ethics. Tuition ordinarily was free or set very low. A classroom atmosphere of strict discipline was maintained and rote memorization was expected from every pupil. The chief instructional objective was to enable each child eventually to memorize the Koran in its entirety. Anyone who succeeded was called a *hafiz*, "holder," and was publicly honored. Secondary-level instruction for a smaller percentage of the population was provided, as well as state subsidies to the madrasas or colleges. In addition to theology and law, the curriculum encompassed the teaching of mathematics, astronomy, logic, literature, philology, rhetoric, and grammar. The proper usage of Arabic, considered the most nearly perfect language of the world, was greatly emphasized. At the first tuition fees were charged; later, private philanthropy or government aid was sufficiently generous to both pay teachers' salaries and the expenses of students.

At least seven colleges, originally founded in connection with mosques, grew large enough to qualify as universities after the old Greek models. Cordova was the greatest of these, offering advanced programs of study in chemistry, physics, mathematics, astronomy, medicine, physiology, geography, surgery, and philology. Indicative of the relatively enlightened character of these institutions is the fact that medicine was practiced in clinical laboratories, astronomy was studied in celestial observatories, and world geography was taught through the use of globes. And it was to these great centers of higher learning that European scholars like Hermann of Carinthia, Daniel Morley, Robert of Chester, Alfred of Sareshel, Plato of Tivoli, Michael Scot, and others came to sit at the feet of Moslem teaching masters and bask in the warmth of a culture then virtually extinguished everywhere else on the continent.

The Islamic Contribution

Islamic learning's influence upon Christendom proceeded along many different paths. Mention has already been made of the cultural interchange that accompanied the savage clash of East and West on the battlefields of the Holy Land. Another route was through commerce, from which Spanish-Christian armorers learned new trades and textile weavers received new inspirations. Italian bookbinders, ceramicists, metalworkers, glassblowers, and architects all found it possible to profit from the achievements of their Moorish counterparts. The practice of Spanish nobles sending their Christian sons to Islamic courts to receive a knightly education undoubtedly hastened the process of cultural assimilation. Clerics and laymen alike came to Cordova, Seville, or Toledo as students and, predictably, sometimes absorbed more than they had intended. As one pious Christian observer from northern Spain lamented, "My fellow Christians delight in the poems and romances of the Arabs; they study the works of Mohammedan theologians and philosophers, not to refute them, but to acquire a correct and elegant Arabic style. . . . Alas! The young Christians who are most conspicuous for their talent have no knowledge of any literature or language save the Arabic; they read and study with avidity Arabic books; they amass whole libraries of them at great cost; they everywhere sing the praises of Arabic lore." Finally, as has been mentioned, Moslem learning penetrated the rest of Europe as a result of outright conquest on the part of invading Christian armies.

In the final analysis, perhaps the single greatest intellectual challenge and impact of Islam was due to the threat it posed to Christian orthodoxy. Moslem scholars openly scoffed at Christianity, calling it an "astonishing superstition." Confronted by a theological system of obviously superior refinement, Christian theologians simply had no choice but to elaborate and codify their own doctrines. In this way Islamic influences provided an impetus for the development of theological scholarship in the cathedral schools of Europe. Aside from the interest shown in the medical works of Arabic physicians such as Abu Ali al-Husein ibn Sina (980–1037), known to Christians as *Avicenna,* and Abu Bekr Muhammad al-Razi (844–926), called *Rhazes,* most scholars concentrated upon those translated sources deemed useful for the advancement of theology, in particular the writings and commentaries concerning Aristotle. Especially prized were the works of the Arabic Aristotelian philosopher Abu al-Walid Muhammad ibn Rushd (1126–1198), whose name was preserved in the West as *Averroës.* Anything else in the way of secular learning, such as scientific treatises, was received with indifference or rejected as "the Devil's black arts." Nonetheless, enough had been passed on through Islamic hands and received within the cloisters of Europe to initiate a diffuse but definite intellectual awakening. Slowly but surely a long-dormant spirit of intellectual inquiry had been aroused—the end of an age was at hand. All that was required now were places in which that spirit could be nurtured.

FROM CATHEDRAL CHURCH SCHOOLS TO UNIVERSITIES

Scholasticism

The rise of the late medieval universities was closely tied to the growth of theology as a systematic, scholarly discipline. To modern men the din of theological disputation in the twelfth, thirteenth, and fourteenth centuries may seem a hopelessly arid babble, completely irrelevant to the modern era. It should be realized that for the scholastics of the medieval period the issues were live ones indeed. They were at once animated by and absorbed with questions of apparently supreme importance—questions regarding the nature of God, the relations of human reason and religious faith, the foundations of authority, and the legitimacy of certain theological doctrines. *Scholasticism* refers to a method of reasoning worked out by teachers in cathedral schools (from the word *scholasticus*), a means for employing reason in the clarification of religious truth. As an intellectual movement it began as early as the ninth century, reached its greatest heights in the twelfth and thirteenth centuries, and subsided in the fifteenth. Its influence was felt throughout the intellectual centers of Europe, and as a method of inquiry it produced almost all the intellectual achievements of the medieval period.

Early in the ninth century when *John Scotus Erigena* was master of the palace school, men were trying to reconcile the obvious contradictions in Christian doctrine inherited through the many conflicting pronouncements of popes, assemblies, bishops, and councils. Their strategy was based on an appeal to human reason and the support of philosophy to adjudicate among doctrinal inconsistencies. Erigena, for one, confidently proclaimed that true religion and true philosophy had to be in agreement; the logical analysis of the latter clarifies the former. Problems of faith, he argued, are to be solved by examining them according to logical argumentation arranged in syllogistic order. This methodology gained support several centuries later when scholars began to reflect upon the implications for religion of new floods of material being introduced. The conquests of Toledo, Sicily, and Syria made translations of Greek writers available once again. *Aristippus of Sicily* translated some of Plato's dialogues into Latin from the Arabic. James of Venice did the same for Aristotle's *Posterior Analytics*. By the beginning of the thirteenth century, scholars were wrestling with a host of problems arising from their readings of Euclid, Ptolemy, Aristotle, Plato, and other works of Hindu, Arabic, and even Chinese origin. Basically, the question was whether Christianity could be given a philosophical rationale derived from classic authors, particularly Aristotle. A beginning was made with *John of Damascus'* attempt to formulate a theology from Aristotelian metaphysics. More typical of the early response to the new learning was the position taken by *Anselm* (1033–1109), the Archbishop of Canterbury. "I do not seek to know in order that I may believe," he wrote, "but I believe in order that I may know." Or again, "The Christian ought to advance to knowledge through faith, not to come to faith through knowledge." Anselm's insistence on the precedence of faith over reason in matters of religion inevitably tended to discourage theological speculation. Nonetheless, despite his conviction that "the proper order demands that we believe the deep things of Christian faith before we presume to reason about them," he found himself embroiled in a famous philosophical dispute with *Roscellinus of Compiègne* (1050–1106) which was to have weighty consequences in the medieval intellectual arena.

For some time scholars had been familiar with Boethius' translation of a work by the neo-Platonist writer *Porphyry* (233–301) entitled *Introduction to Aristotle's Categories*. This work developed the opposing positions in the problem of universals, a highly technical issue tracing back to Plato. In the eleventh century Porphyry's oppositions became formalized in the two contending doctrines of *nominalism* and *realism*. Anselm, as realist, argued along Platonic lines that reality is reflected in our general conceptions or universal terms. Reality, insofar as it can be known at all, is apprehended indirectly by our ideas or concepts about things, not by the apprehension of the objects of concepts, whereas individual, particular things perceived by the senses are metaphysically illusory. Roscellinus, as a nominalist following Aristotle, contended that general conceptions are "mere words" without any corresponding reality. Only individual, concrete entities have existence. When the theological implications of nominalism and realism were worked out, either position could have been shown to be potentially subversive of received doctrine. Instead, the Church chose to interpret realism as a philosophical warrant for orthodoxy, whereas nominalism acquired a reputation as the philosophy of skepticism or criticism. Realism also seemed to support the traditional stance that authority in matters of faith and morals must be antecedant to rational reflection upon these matters. The more important consequence of the realist–nominalist controversy, however, was that it brought theological questions up for sustained, intensive analysis. Its impulse to new questioning came to fruition in the thought of such scholars as *William of Champeaux, Peter Abelard, Peter Lombard, Albert the Great,* and *Thomas Aquinas*.

With *Abelard,* for example, theology emerged clearly as a discrete subject for philosophical investigation. He had studied at the cathedral school of Notre Dame under William of Champeaux and later under Roscellinus but could not completely accept either of their positions. While teaching grammar and logic at Paris, Abelard published his controversial *Sic et Non,* an arrangement of authorities' opinions on such questions as whether "faith is based on reason, or no." The implication that one must reason about faith if it is to become intelligible, given the fact that authorities disagree, was spelled out explicitly, "Constant and frequent questioning is the first key to wisdom. For through doubt we are led to inquiry, and by inquiry we discern the truth." Abelard's claim that reason is prior to faith aroused immediate discussion. So too did his method of quotation from opposing authorities. It found widespread acceptance as a way of dealing with all types of questions, including nonphilosophical ones. In theology it had its greatest influence. One of Abelard's students, *Peter Lombard,* used it in his own work, the *Four Books of Sentences,* a treatise which was to systematize the teaching of theology in cathedral schools. Lombard's greatest exponent, *Albert the Great* (Albertus Magnus), extended Lombard's technique of dividing theological questions into topics from which reasoned conclusions were set down following from the analysis of each topic. He became the first scholar since John of Damascus to explicate Aristotelian philosophy within the framework of Christian doctrine. It was Albert's pioneering work toward a synthesis of religion and philosophy that influenced the greatest of the medieval scholastics, *Thomas Aquinas* (1225–1274).

Aquinas began his career studying at Monte Cassino and Naples, then continued at Paris and Cologne where he was first exposed to Albert's teachings. He served successively as a teacher of philosophy and theology at Bologna, Viterbo, Perugia, Naples, Rome, and Paris. In his monumental *Summa Theologica* Aquinas laid down the most comprehensive theological system of the medieval period, a grand attempt to harmonize Aristotle with orthodox Church doctrine. Although it would be incorrect to claim that *Thomism* became the sole philosophy of the Roman Catholic Church, it certainly has occupied a uniquely privileged position ever since. Historically, Aquinas' system is important as it illustrates how far theology had been transformed into a complex subject of scholarly study. Scholasticism began with a naive belief that Christian beliefs could be systematized as a conceptual whole, that this intellectual structure could easily be accommodated to older philosophies, and that human reason was sufficient to demonstrate the truth of the Church's authoritative dogma. With Aquinas, it became necessary to assert a distinction between dogmatic theology, which deals with matters of pure faith, and philosophy, which can only clarify certain articles of faith knowable by reason. His delimitation of these two provinces never gained universal assent but it drew attention to the enormous complexity of the theological enterprise. By the thirteenth century scholasticism had organized Church dogma to the point where theology could be a teaching subject. It was in the universities that this work was carried out.

Law and Medicine as Professional Studies

During the centuries in which theology was becoming an organized discipline, parallel movements were taking place with respect to law and medicine. These three subjects were destined to become the main specialties of early universities. Theology attracted greatest interest in northern Europe where the clerical monopoly of higher education was most complete. Law and medicine, for a variety of reasons, evolved into academic fields primarily in Italy. Possibly the fact that knowledge of ancient Roman law was never completely extinguished in the southern regions accounts for its interest among scholars in the Italian cities. Moreover, there was a longstanding tradition of lay education among the Italian nobility, especially among the Lombards, and the towns, becoming increasingly important in Italy after the tenth century, were always in need of lawyers to administer the municipal governments. Eminent law schools at Pavia, Ravenna, and Rome had been in existence for centuries before there were universities specializing in legal studies.

Basing their efforts on the work of famous scholars such as Bulgarus,

Martinus, Jacobus, and Hugo, the canonists of Bologna labored mightily at creating for the Church a comprehensive set of legal statutes for its governance. It was the Bolognese canonists, too, who were responsible from the thirteenth century onward for evolving the theory of the universal dominion of the Papacy, a doctrine which was expanded to claim political supremacy over all the peoples of the world. Another contributing factor was the need to find a legal basis from the past to support claims of independence against Teutonic rulers of the Holy Roman Empire. The so-called *investiture conflict* between 1075 and 1122 over whether king or pope had power to invest bishops with authority undoubtedly stimulated legal studies. Whatever the reasons, the first great center for the study of law was *Bologna. Inerius* of Bologna, lecturing between 1110 and 1115 on the *Code,* the *Digest,* and *Institutes* of Justinian (taken together, the *Corpus Juris Civilis*), attracted hundreds of students by the brilliance of his teaching. After his time civil jurisprudence was clearly separated from rhetoric and ranked as an important subject in its own right. Bologna's reputation throughout Europe for this kind of specialized study was further enhanced by the work of *Gratian,* a learned monk of the city, who in 1142 issued a compilation of all Church (canon) law. The *Decretum* was organized after the pattern in Abelard's *Sic et Non* except that Gratian offered positive conclusions from the evidence gathered around each topic or point of law. This work, like the Justinian compilation of civil law, organized canon law as a significant teaching subject.

The beginnings of sustained interest in medicine as a field for study occurred at *Salerno,* in Sicily. In the mid-eleventh century the study of old Greek texts by Galen and Hippocrates as well as an Islamic work authored by Avicenna began to be pursued. A Carthaginian monk, *Constantius Africanus* (Constantine of Carthage), who had fled from charges of heresy in his home city appeared at Salerno and began to lecture on medical arts. His teachings so aroused widespread interest that the city soon became famous for its medical school. The process was undoubtedly hastened by the fact that Constantius had added to Salerno's repository of Greek and Roman medical knowledge an invaluable collection of resources drawn from Arabic medical science. From an early date Salerno also maintained steady relations with the rich cultural center of Constantinople, notable in this connection for its impressive organization of hospitals and skilled physicians. *Montpellier,* in southern France, also was noted for its revival of medicine.

The Founding of Universities

According to Rashdall[6] the origins of universities are "veiled in impenetrable obscurity." Clearly, universities' growth was tied to the proliferation

---

[6] A serious student of the history of universities should consult Hastings Rashdall, *Universities of Europe in the Middle Ages* (New York: Oxford University Press, 1936). This is the classic three-volume reference for the topic.

of towns and the expanding role of the cathedral in urban life. As more and more cathedrals were built, the schools attached to them also increased in number, most notably in French lands—at Tours, Rheims, Paris, and Chartres. Swelling numbers of students drawn from the bourgeoisie were attracted to cathedral schools as the old curriculum of grammar, logic, rhetoric, geometry, arithmetic, astronomy, and music was expanded. Student enrollments were further stimulated by the advent of an era of great schoolmasters, numbering among them *Gebert,* the master of the cathedral school at Rheims in the late tenth century who later became Pope Sylvester II, and *Fulbert,* a student of Gebert's and subsequently Bishop of Chartres, not to mention Ivo, Bernard, and Thierry, all successors to Fulbert as head of the cathedral school at Chartres.

As a young monk, Gebert was dispatched by his abbot to study in Spain (a rare opportunity in itself) from where he returned enthused by his experiences at the great Moorish center of learning at Cordova. With him he brought back a restless, inquisitive spirit of intellectual inquiry. Once embarked on a teaching career at Rheims, he broke with the medieval tradition of supposing that the compilations of the Church fathers—*auctores* ("authorities")—were beyond questioning or contradiction. Henceforth, he proclaimed, his students were to study the Roman classics in the original instead of depending on extracts compiled by ecclesiastics. To accomplish this end Gebert began collecting manuscripts and built up a good-sized library for his school. Those who followed in his footsteps, most notably Abelard in Paris, infused their teachings with a critical habit of mind that students found irresistible. It was as though a door had been opened on the mind, allowing fresh currents of thought to pour in freely. Despite frequent ecclesiastical censure, a lust for learning had grown across Europe. All it needed for its fulfillment was a place where systematic instruction could be conducted on a regular basis.

The Latin word *universitas* originally meant an association or corporation of a kind common in medieval urban life, a term applicable to any guild of craftsmen, merchants, or other organized group. An academic institution was called a *studium,* or less frequently a *discipulorum,* meaning an association of persons devoted to learning and scholarly pursuits. Beginning sometime in the twelfth century a few cathedral schools began to specialize in certain higher branches of study such as law or theology. A great teacher (like Abelard at Paris) would appear, extend the scope of the school curriculum in some particular direction, and thus help the *studium* become well known for high-caliber instruction in a given field. Great numbers of students would be attracted as its reputation grew. When this happened the term *studium generale* would be used, meaning a place of study open to students from beyond the local area. The international character of their constituents was the main difference separating these *studia generalia* (later called universities) from the ordinary local *studia* out of which they evolved. Only much later was the term *universitas* restricted to a teaching–

learning community.[7] Each *studium generale* was made up of guildlike associations, called *universitates*, of scholars and teachers. There were also student *universitates* that served as protective societies for members of a common regional origin. These organizations were essential because individuals sojourning in a foreign country were otherwise defenseless. (Foreigners usually had no rights under local laws.) So, for example, all of the students from the province of Tuscany attending the *studium generale* at Bologna would band together for their mutual benefit as the Tuscan *universitate*. More commonly, student groups were known as *nations*. By the time the term *universitas* meant only an academic community rather than any kind of corporation, it referred to the total assemblage of teachers' guilds and students' nations.

Two kinds of university organization developed: the masters' university, like that of Paris, and a student or nation-dominated university, like that of Bologna. The former was controlled by teachers (masters), found commonly in German and English lands; the latter was controlled by students, most generally found in Spain, Italy, and southern France.[8] In all probability there was some rudimentary association of masters at Paris by 1150 and a similar society at Bologna not much later. At Bologna, around 1219, there were four student *universitates*—those of the Lombards, Tuscans, Ultramontanes, and Romans—reduced to two groupings a half century later— the *Citramontanes* and the *Ultramontanes*—each consisting of a number of nations. At Paris there were four nations—the Picards, the English, the Normans and the French. This fourfold division of students became something of a tradition within later universities. Each nation elected a *proctor* or *councilor* who was entrusted to protect that grouping's interests at a proctors' council. This assembly represented the student body collectively.[9] At Bologna control of the *studium's* affairs were in the hands of the student's council, whereas at Paris, and other universities modeled after its organization, the masters' guild retained power.

A Struggle for Autonomy

The fusion of *universitates* (student nations and masters' groupings) into a single *universitas* was the gradual outcome of a long struggle for independence with civil and ecclesiastical authorities. The results included many privileges not accorded other corporations, such as certain tax exemptions, immunity from military service for its constituent members, and the right to settle disputes outside the municipal courts. In 1158 at Bologna, for

[7] Dana Carleton Munro, *The Middle Ages, 395–1272* (New York: Appleton-Century-Crofts, 1922), p. 368.

[8] Friedrich Heer, *The Medieval World* (New York: Mentor, 1963), pp. 242–243.

[9] See Pearl Kibre, *The Nations in the Medieval Universities* (Boston: Medieval Academy of America, 1948) for a definitive account of these organizations.

example, the Emperor Frederick Barbarossa issued a decree bestowing special legal standing to students involved in court proceedings: their cases could be tried before the city bishop or the master's guild, rather than by civil magistrates. Also at Bologna a bitter fight was waged for the right of students to migrate and found *studia* elsewhere if they grew dissatisfied with local conditions. This was a simple enough matter because the *universitas* had no fixed facilities or permanent dwellings. Unencumbered with libraries, dormitories, and the like, the university could pick up and move elsewhere at any time. Other towns were eager to welcome an academic migration for motives easily understood. Not only was it economically profitable to host an assemblage of masters and students, but considerable political prestige was involved as well. It required the intervention of Pope Honorius III and an elaborate political compromise with city authorities before this right of secession was even unofficially recognized. A similar dispute arose in 1231 at Paris when the university (an outgrowth of the cathedral school of Notre Dame, the collegiate school of St. Genevieve, and the school of St. Victor) fought with city fathers over its right to establish board and lodging fees charged students. Again papal intervention was required. The right to suspend lectures, called *cessatio,* as a means of protest against unfair treatment or encroachments upon the university's growing sphere of jurisdiction was eventually granted by Pope Gregory IX in 1231. This turned out to be a very potent weapon in the struggle for legal autonomy. Once shut down, a university rarely reopened on the same site; it simply moved on to a more favorable locale, thereby depriving the offending city of the benefits of having a university in residence.

Ultimately universities received charters from a king or the pope formally upholding their right to strike as well as their immunity from civil jurisdiction. In 1317 the university at Bologna won complete autonomy in this respect. By 1411 criminal jurisdiction over its own members had also been granted.

Today, when student demands are heard for greater power in the operation of universities, it is interesting to note the extent of student control at Bologna and other southern universities. The student councilors ruthlessly dominated teachers' guilds. Students decided what fees would be collected, what salaries masters could receive, how classes would be conducted, and what requirements had to be met for graduation. Fines were levied on teachers for absence without leave, for digressing from the lecture material, for lecturing too fast, for failure to cover the material, for avoiding difficult explanations, even for saving important points until the end of their lectures so as to prevent students from leaving before a class was concluded! Typically, every master had to deposit a sum of money in a local banking house, from which his fines were deducted. A master could actually be expelled if he were repeatedly found guilty of such offenses. It must be remembered, however, that the students at Bologna were considerably older than today's college student. In the northern medieval universities, where most of the students were younger, masters were usually, but not always, in greater control of the institutions' administration. Where masters' guilds held sway, as in the French and English universities, the teachers carefully regulated student conduct. Pupils were forbidden to gamble or swear, they were fined for breaking curfews, and even had their table manners prescribed for them. "Cleanse not thy teeth," one regulation ordered, "with the steel that is sharpened for those that eat with thee." Even so, students constituted an influential force, as they could always desert en masse one professor's class for another's. Entering first-year students were always advised by wiser upperclassmen to sit in on several lectures before tendering a master his fee.

Three major ways of organizing and governing the university have been tried since its inception. *Student power* marked the first way. Professors had to swear absolute obedience to the student-elected student rector and obey all rules enacted. Students collected fees, paid the salaries, and laid down the rules. Teachers could not leave the university or even travel out of town, under penalty of death, without permission. As Rashdall notes, students were masters of the situation, particularly through the power of boycotting an offending professor. No professor was ever elected as university rector in the Italian universities, at least until the nineteenth century.

Even at Paris the nations exercised astounding power for several centuries. They heavily influenced the elections of rectors, which had to be conducted every month, and oversaw a variety of functions through ad hoc committees. Statutes governing internal university administration were constantly revised. Feuds over student control relating to payment of salaries, renting of school buildings, supervising lodgings, and levying fines kept Paris in such an uproar that the rector usually found it prudent to bring personal bodyguards to university meetings. Things got so boisterous that one observer during the early days at Paris reported, "Studies were in chaos . . . the rooms on one side were rented to students and on the other to whores. Under the same roof was a house of learning and whoring." Public reaction mounted over the years until early in the sixteenth century, when the French king finally overthrew the student-dominated administrative structure.

Student government did have the advantages of compelling professors to pay attention to their classes and preserving the rights of minorities at the university. And it was inexpensive. But its lack of continuity (each new generation of students felt it had a better way to overhaul the structure) and tyrannical character made it exceedingly difficult to keep the university on some even course.

The second mode of university management has been *central political control*. Rule might be exercised by king, parliament, a revolutionary government, or dictator. Autocratic rule is vastly more efficient than the anarchical. The linkage of university and state will keep the former in perfect submission to the latter. Historically, the price paid for central authority has been high, however. Universities have been dictated to, threatened, or shut down entirely; teachers have been fired for sedition, exiled for disloyalty, even executed for political heresy. Sometimes students have shared the same fates.

The third way, well developed in the American mold, has been *shared power through divided authority*. It has drawn primarily from the English collegiate model, whose beginnings will be discussed momentarily. Academic affairs are run by the professors (it is assumed they *are* the university); ideally, their actions serve the scholarly interests of teaching and research that give the university its reason for existence. The institution is maintained by professional administrators whose function is to implement faculty-initiated policy. Financing and general nonacademic policy making are reserved to a board of curators, trustees, or regents. The division of power, in theory at least, ensures that no single group can dictate decisions, only influence them. The major shortcomings of this system have been manifold. Trustees have sometimes acted autocratically, supposing everyone else, including professors, are "employees" who should be dictated to as such. Administrators, on the other hand, have often sought to apply inappropriate standards of efficiency and cost-accounting borrowed from industry which tend to thwart the academic concerns of the university. Moreover, the administrative structure easily turns into an unresponsive, rigid bureaucracy, as students well know. Thirdly, faculty members have tended to be derelict in discharging their responsibilities. Neglect of classes, obsessive preoccupation with research (the sure road to academic advancement), and rules designed to serve narrow vested interests are all signs of professional irresponsibility. Traditionally, the preceeding scheme has effectively kept students from having any say in matters that affect them within the institution. So-called student government more often than not has been confined to "sand box politics" involving matters of no real significance.

Today, when students are repudiating the *in loco parentis* function of the university (a hold-over from the days when the public required the school to be a parental surrogate) and demanding more responsibility for the management of the university, it has become increasingly clear that none of the previous models has proved itself adequate. Whereas "nonnegotiable demands" from students for increased influence over curriculum and campus rules smack of the anarchism of total student control and will be resisted, it would seem that a better balance of power among contending factions within the university will have to be achieved.

By far the most important privilege won by the early university was the right to grant teaching licenses. The battle at Paris was waged between the masters' guilds and the chancellor of Notre Dame. For centuries Church authorities enjoyed a monopoly in granting licenses to teach, the *licentia docendi.* The cathedral school chancellor not only claimed absolute power in the matter of licensing but asserted his claim to exclusive authority over all aspects of the developing *universitas.* Beginning in the early thirteenth century, masters found it necessary to appeal to the pope in resisting such claims. Papal policy tended to favor the university in these disputes. A measure of legal recognition for the masters' guild was authorized by Innocent III in 1208 and 1209. Again in 1213 he placed restrictions on the chancellor's judicial powers by forbidding him to withhold a teaching degree to anyone recommended by the masters. When ecclesiastical authorities retaliated by threatening to excummunicate the masters as a body, Innocent's successor, Honorius III, had to step in once more on the university's behalf. It required almost a century before the chancellor's privileges were reduced to the ceremonial right of conferring a license upon anyone considered qualified by the teaching masters. In the end he was obliged to accept candidates without question. In the same way, the chancellor was divested of all other powers over the university. This became the usual pattern at other universities besides Paris. Thereafter the typical university would derive its authority to grant licenses, the *jus ubique docendi,* from a papal Bull, or less frequently from an imperial charter. The university's advantage lay in the fact that its authority was more universal under such an arrangement. Once freed from purely local or sectional domination by a chancellor, an institution was able to preserve a greater measure of autonomy for itself.

Town and Gown

Questions of jurisdictional authority were critical for the evolving university, both in terms of internal control and relations with the outside community. The latter in particular was a source of controversy, owing to the riotous deportment of students in an age when men resorted quickly to physical violence. Students' unruly behavior constantly occasioned shock and horror from townspeople; it might be said the situation has not changed much since. Young scholars took to quarreling with the local burghers as readily as they fought among themselves (in the latter case sometimes pitting student nation against nation). The students raised havoc over the high cost of food and lodging, about the untended open sewers in the streets, and the quality of the fare in the taverns. There were continual lawsuits, instigated by townfolk and students alike. For its part the outside community deeply distrusted academics and jeered at the airs of both students and professors. Resentment was further aggravated when student misconduct reached intolerable proportions. In 1269, for example, an official at Paris complained that university members "by day and night atrociously wound and slay many, carry off women, ravish virgins, break into houses," and commit "over and over again robberies and many other enormities hateful to God."

On the other side, merchants of the town scarcely endeared themselves to patrons when they exploited them by charging exorbitant prices for food or rent. The resulting tensions between "town" and "gown" (so called from the academic garb then in vogue) often erupted into open warfare. Surviving annals contain accounts of bloody riots in which the opposing factions battled with pikes, cudgels, swords, bows and arrows, pails of boiling water, and even slops hurled from windows. It is recorded that on the feast day of St. Scholastica in 1214, the bell of St. Mary's at Oxford summoned the academic community to war with the townspeople. In that particular incident, the local burghers evidently carried the day, judging from one eyewitness's report: "Some twenty Inns or Halls were pillaged. Scholars were killed or wounded; their eatables and drinkables plundered; their books torn to pieces; the Halls themselves fired." Fortunately town–gown relations have improved immeasurably in the modern era, although fundamental tensions endure.

Internal Organization

A major result of the fight for the right to grant licenses was the welding together of masters' guilds into a single powerful corporation. Originally the term *faculty* meant a subject of study, but gradually it also came to designate all those teaching a given subject. The typical medieval university developed four separate divisions—arts, law, medicine, and theology. All four *faculties* were represented by *deans* who, together with the council of nations' proctors, elected a *rector* to head the university. As might be expected, in the south a university rector was usually a student, owing to the greater power of student nations. At Paris and elsewhere a rector was usually chosen from the arts faculty, because it was apt to be the largest and hence the most influential. University studies as organized around the four faculties usually required a student to finish the arts course (an expansion of the *Trivium*) before being admitted to advanced work in one of the three remaining faculties. Initially few universities possessed all four divisions, though most had a faculty of arts. Because Bologna, for example, had grown from a *studium generale* into a *universitas* owing to its prominence in legal studies, the faculty of law was created first and the other studies added later. The same pattern was repeated at Montpellier and Salerno, where medicine was established before other studies. Paris was begun as an arts school, grew as a center for theological instruction, and only much later offered courses in law and medicine. In the fourteenth century the tradition of four faculties was well established as the typical organizational pattern.

The rector of the arts faculty at Paris was officially acknowledged as university head by the pope in 1259. The institution became so well known for its instruction in theology, beginning with Abelard, that it was called the Mount Sinai of late medieval scholasticism. Credit for Bologna's fame as the acknowledged center for the study of law was owed, of course, to such scholars as Inerius and Gratian. Solerno gained its reputation in the field of medicine not simply because great teachers like Constantius had labored there but because Frederick II required all physicians in Sicily to be licensed from the masters at Salerno, beginning in 1230.

Between 1200 and 1250 nine universities were founded in Italy alone, and at least that many more were established before 1450. Some ten or twelve universities (*Salamanca* the greatest of these) were begun in Spain, their founding urged by powerful municipal interests and encouraged by royal patronage. Less successful were the half dozen or so French *studia* that attempted to become full universities. Aside from notable schools at Chartres, Angers, and Orléans, none managed to survive very long. Similarly, the university movement in England, Scotland, and Germany was delayed until late in the thirteenth century. Three hundred years later there were at least seventy-nine *studia generalia* scattered across Europe entitled to claim the title *university*.

In the north the two most important institutions were Cambridge and Oxford. A small *studium* at Oxford was evidently in existence as early as 1163, drawing students and teachers in growing numbers. It took less than a century for the school to win a royal charter, its success partially explained by an influx of people migrating from Paris who had been expelled from France during a wave of nationalistic fervor. Cambridge began with a migration of scholars from Oxford in 1209; similarly, Northampton, probably in continuous existence as a university between 1238 and 1264, was made up of migrants from both Cambridge and Oxford. Another exodus of Oxford masters to Salisbury in 1238 led to the establishment there of a *studium generale* which only lasted until 1278. As late as 1334 still another band of Oxford itinerants tried unsuccessfully to begin a new university at Stamford.

One unique feature of English and Scottish schools was the early establishment of *hospitia,* or halls, to provide students with food and lodging. The first such collegiate halls actually were begun at Paris by endowments from Count Robert of Dreux, Etienne Belot, various abbots from Clairvaux and Cluny, and the most famous benefactor of all, Robert de Sorbon, from whom the Sorbonne derived its name around 1257. The Paris colleges were essentially student domiciles under the direction of a head who was also a teacher. They rarely enjoyed any significant degree of autonomy. An altogether different situation obtained on English soil, however. Before very long, it became customary for teachers to reside with the students, to offer instruction within the living units, now called *colleges,* and to function as disciplinarians. Within a very few years colleges began to receive endowments, to assume special rights, and thus to take on a distinct character of their own. When masters began to offer lectures regularly within a college instead of a separate university lecture hall, officials dispensed with outside instruction entirely *and the colleges became the university itself.* The origins of such famous colleges as Merton and Balliol at Oxford are to be found in this practice of masters and students residing together. English colleges were autonomous corporations, headed by a principal elected by his fellows to administer the college's internal affairs. Once such institutions made an investment in fixed dwellings they of course lost their physical mobility.

It is worth noting that in the American tradition, the first institutions of postsecondary learning that made their appearance were patterned after the English collegiate model rather than the continental university structure of organization. That model included features which still persist today in many private institutions, including an instructional emphasis on nonspecialized liberal education, fixed dormitories supervised by nonacademic personnel, an atmosphere of intimate association between teachers and students, concern for moral character building, and lay control, even when ultimate authority might be vested with a private sectarian body. Traditionally, colleges and universities adhering to the collegiate pattern have viewed themselves not only as teaching institutions but as parental surrogates. In contrast, continental traditions have stressed graduate professional training, faculty autonomy, and "benevolent indifference" with respect to the private conduct of students.

Prior to the 1200's standards for qualifying as a master in a teaching guild were only loosely organized. The usual procedure was very much like the process by which an apprentice gained recognition as a master craftsman in a merchants' guild. A candidate would "hear" (attend) lectures and then present himself to a panel of masters to be examined. If the student demonstrated his proficiency in reading texts and explaining their contents to the masters' satisfaction, he was advanced to the status of assistant, equivalent to the rank of journeyman. An assistant by the fourteenth century was known as a "beginner" or *baccalaureus*. Advancement to mastership involved attending other courses for a number of years before being examined as a candidate for a teaching license. The examination, analogous to a journeyman's "masterpiece," took the form of a public disputation on a stated thesis held before a jury of masters. If judged favorably, the candidate was formally inducted into the masters' guild or faculty and awarded the title *master* if an arts teacher, *doctor* or *professor* if a teacher in one of the three higher faculties. It was a long time before separate degrees were standardized and longer still before a mastership came to signify anything more than proficiency to teach a particular subject. The early universities' purposes were largely confined to teacher preparation; professional training for practical use of a subject besides teaching it entered in long afterwards.

Curricula and Instruction

Books were exceedingly scarce in the centuries when universities were getting established. Their prohibitive cost insured student dependence on the lecture format as a means of acquiring information.[10] Such lectures could be given in wayside sheds, in the cloister of a cathedral, or, climate permitting, in an open town square. Later, teachers rented rooms where students sat on the floor, which was usually covered with straw against the dampness. Still later, physical facilities were further improved, although when good masters attracted large crowds, the antiquated rooms serving as lecture halls often failed to accommodate everyone comfortably, a phenomenon not unfamiliar to today's college students. Quite often the professor was compelled to dictate from the text so that students could keep complete notes. He would read (in Latin) from the work at hand, explain its difficult passages at great length, present glosses or commentaries on the text by other authors, lay out all the arguments and points involved, and finally, defend whatever conclusions he had reached himself. This procedure became highly formalized and was rigidly adhered to until books were more widely disseminated. Although instruction was unnecessarily drawn out, as judged by the standards of what preceded the medieval lecture for some half dozen centuries, it represented a distinct advance in methodology. A second method widely used in addition to this *ordinary* lecture was the *extraordinary* lecture conducted by a student as a training exercise for his licensing examination. The usual practice was for a candidate to hire classmates to attend and criticize his effort. A third instructional technique much in use was the debate or *public disputation* where students or masters took sides on a question and exhaustively explored all its legal or theological ramifications.

The content of university instruction varied, depending on the particular specialty of an institution. The "inferior" or lower curriculum in the arts was organized around the first three subjects of the traditional seven liberal arts, with heavy dosages from the works of Aristotle. Four to seven years were required to complete the arts course. In the faculty of law, Gratian's *Decretum* and the *Corpus Juris Civilis* of Justinian were the usual texts studied. If a student pursued medical studies, he could expect to hear lectures from translations of Avicenna, Galen, and Hippocrates. Outside of Salerno and Montpellier, interestingly, no provision was made for actual clinical experience; only book instruction was given. The consequences of this peculiar omission in terms of medical practice can easily be imagined. In a theological faculty great attention was paid to the writings of Porphyry and Aristotle, the *Sentences* of Lombard, and Aquinas' *Summa*. A student's dialectical training was organized after Boethius and sometimes Donatus.

In terms of comfort and convenience, a student's life in a medieval university certainly left much to be desired. He entered it around the age of

---

[10] It is astounding how contemporary higher education relies so heavily on the lecture as a means of transmitting information at a time when books are readily available, not to mention a multitude of other information sources.

fourteen or sixteen with no advance assurance of how many years his training might consume. It was not unusual in some cases for an individual to
associate with a university for up to twelve years and more before passing
his final examination! Some students were wretchedly poor; the majority
had their way paid by someone else, a wealthy relative or patron. Extant
documents reveal that students were pretty much like students in every
age. There are letters by young scholars written to their parents pleading for
more money to meet unanticipated expenses (carefully unitemized), just as
there are copies of correspondence from benefactors complaining about the
indolence of their irresponsible charges, or laments over the frittering away
of hard-earned money on luxuries.

The typical student arose at four or five o'clock in the morning (earlier
in the summertime), heard Mass for the next hour, and went to lectures
beginning at six. Instruction lasted about three hours, after which he
paused for a meager meal. Classes extended until late afternoon, when he
sat down to supper. Evening hours would be taken up by studying his lecture notes (or brawling in a nearby tavern). At the end of the day, according to one account at Cambridge, "half an hour was devoted to walking or
running about, that [the student] might not go to bed with cold feet."
Unless he were exceptionally fortunate, he inhabited miserable lodgings,
poorly heated and ill lit. If he ventured outside after dark, he literally took
his life in his hands. Despite all official prohibitions, many a student found
it expedient to carry a knife under his tattered gown, and he would be
ready to use it on the slightest provocation. When he wearied of his studies,
which was often, there was always ample opportunity for engaging in the
dissipations of the brothel, or for brawls with fellow students and the
townsfolk. His lot was a riotous one, when assassinations and street fighting
were a way of life.

The Universities' Influence

The importance of the universities in medieval culture can hardly be
exaggerated. As Rashdall notes, "their organization and their tradition,
their studies and their exercises affected the progress and intellectual development of Europe more powerfully or (perhaps it should be said) more
exclusively, than any schools in all likelihood will ever do again."[11] It was
in the universities that knowledge was organized, preserved, and transmitted. They became the real centers of intellectual activity where learning
was advanced, stimulated, and encouraged to a greater extent than in any
other institution. This function of the university as an oasis of intellectual
freedom in an age deeply suspicious of the slightest taint of heresy was
terribly important. It was the one place where forbidden or suppressed
questions could be discussed with what hostile critics termed "brazen impu-

11 Rashdall, op. cit., Vol. 1, p. 512.

dence." There was virtually no question too thorny, no problem touching upon the most fundamental issues of life too sancrosanct to be posed and examined in the universities of the late Middle Ages. Only in the university could there exist the critical conditions defining *Lehrfreiheit* ("freedom to teach") and *Lernfreiheit* ("freedom to learn") so essential to the mission of an educational institution. It almost goes without saying that the struggle for academic freedom has never proceeded without vigorous opposition, then or now. Just as contemporary critics yearn to transform the university into an instrument for the propagation of some partisan position or to deflect its role as social gadfly, so too did the early universities come in for their share of abuse. An address in 1290 before an ecclesiastical council by Pope Boniface VIII offers an excellent example. On that occasion the prelate vigorously chided the masters of the University of Paris for their unorthodoxy and for supposing that their wisdom was valued at the Papal Curia. "At Rome," Boniface announced, "we account them more foolish than the ignorant, men who have poisoned by their teaching not only themselves but also the entire world. You masters of Paris have made all your learning and doctrine a laughing-stock. . . . It is all trivial. . . . To us your fame is mere folly and smoke. . . ." Public figures today have shown no reluctance to engage in the same kind of polemic, directed at the same targets.

Aside from their other contributions, universities performed an extremely valuable service by turning out graduates who filled a crucial need for trained teachers at all educational levels. The growth of a learned class of men boldly proclaiming their independence from civil or ecclesiastical authority probably contributed substantially to the accelerated pace of social progress in late medieval society. Once the universities were securely established they did not hesitate to intervene in public affairs, air grievances to kings and popes alike, offer advice, and pass upon a variety of important legal and religious questions. The rise of the universities meant the Church's monopoly on learning and teaching was decisively broken. Europe's intellectual center of gravity swung from the monastic community to the school, from monks to professors. From the universities came almost all the future leaders of society. Of all the differing kinds of educative agencies devised since antiquity, it was the university whose influence would endure the longest in helping to usher in the modern age.

MEDIEVAL CULTURE AND EDUCATIONAL IDEALS

When the fourteenth-century poet Guillaume de Guilleville declared, "Your life here is but a pilgrimage," he caught the essential temper of the medieval world view. The only real significance of earthly life was that its character determined the fate of a man's soul struggling on a perilous journey toward heaven, or hell. The hazards to be met were manifold: legions of darkness—incubi, succubi, undines, witches, sylphs, and other horrors—were always at hand to ensnare the unwary. Only a steadfast pilgrim could withstand the demons of envy, pride, slander, treason, and other deadly sins. Hell's denizens might even assume the alluring forms of saintly men in order better to outwit the pious. Of course the traveler could call on powerful allies. There were always celestial guardian saints hovering nearby, ever ready to intercede with Christ on one's behalf. The merciful Virgin protected deserving souls from God's stern judgment or the spirits of malediction. And when the Day of Judgment arrived, the wicked would be thrown into eternal torment but the souls of the virtuous would ascend to a realm of perpetual bliss, there to be reunited with their Creator. In the interim, the Church—God's earthly custodian of souls—stood vigilant to protect the righteous.

This was at once the hope and obsession of medieval man. He gave it visible expression in his upwardly thrusting Gothic cathedrals, illuminated it in stained glass, and intoned it in the *Alleluia,* the *Gloria,* the *Kyrie,* and the *Agnus Dei.* His creed was rationally strengthened in the intricate structures of scholasticism and poetically depicted in the works of Dante. He extended it into the rough and tumble of secular life, as embodied in the politics of feudalism and the cult of chivalry.[12] In economic terms it was enshrined in the guild system; legally, it was implemented through civil and canon law. His culture was firmly built on a double foundation—the *civitas Dei,* or City of God, as represented by the Church, and the *civitas terrena,* or Earthly City, as represented by lay society. Its basic motif (in theory at least) was the total harmony of the individual and the social, a grand hierarchy of ascending orders in which every man had his divinely appointed position, obligations, and prerogatives. Every man acted only as member of some larger estate in fulfilling his duties to the social whole, an intricate network of mutual obligations binding everyone together under the organized power of the Church as final arbiter in all things temporal as well as spiritual. Medieval theocracy, so well defended, for example, in the thirteenth century by the powerful Pope Innocent III, was founded on the belief that power was the possessor of the truth and that any attempt to seek it elsewhere, any doubt or questioning except upon its established axioms, had to be forbidden.[13] The imperatives following from that grandiose ideal of a united Christendom under a single spiritual power armed with a secular sword found ample defense in the writings of medieval political theorists, most notably in Dante's *De Monarchia.*

[12] See "Spirit of the Middle Ages," *The History of Western Culture: The Medieval World* (New York: Life Educational Reprints No. 43), p. 4.

[13] John Herman Randall, *The Making of the Modern Mind* (Cambridge Mass.: Riverside Press, 1954), pp. 78–79.

It is impossible to locate a single ideal type for medieval man because everyone had his own place within the system. Whether one was priest, peasant, knight, doctor, or monk, each could fulfill God's will in his own unique way. If within the realm of educational thought there was any common theme, it was the belief that education must aim "to equip men for their journey to heaven rather than for their exploration of the ways of this world."[14] The prevailing habit of thought was typified in a remark of Thomas à Kempis in his *Imitation of Christ:* "Learning, when considered in itself, or knowledge upon any subject, is not to be disparaged; for it is good, and ordained of God. . . . But he is really great who is great in charity; he is really great who is little in his own eyes, and cares not for the honor of high position; he is really wise who counts all earthly things as dung that he may win Christ; he is really learned who does the Will of God, and forsakes his own will." Given such an otherworldly attitude, it is not surprising that comparatively little attention was given to the theory and practice of education.

Aside from the secular institutions for schooling previously noted, most education was intended for clerics; pedagogical theory confined itself to discussions of clerical training. One looks in vain to medieval educational treatises—for example, Maurus' *On the Instruction of the Clergy* or Conrad of Hirschau's *Dialogue on Authors* or the *Didascalicon* of Hugh of St. Victor or John of Salisbury's *Metalogicon*—for advice on the proper ends and methods of secular schools. Nowhere in the works of such diverse scholars as Cassiodorus, Isidore, or Thierry of Chartres is there any indication of a modification in the clerical frame of reference. The articulation of more secular educational ideals had to await an age that would take men's temporal aspirations into account by seeking, through education, human well-being in *this* world.

Of course if one looks back across the entire expanse of centuries when medievalism held sway, the outlines of progress can be discerned. The era began with cloistered monastics fanatically subservient to established authority. It culminated, despite lingering superstition and widespread ignorance, in the growth of educational institutions helping to bring learning back into the mainstream of society. The total impact of this blossoming cultural revival was to be greater than anyone then could have imagined.

THE CONFESSIONAL REVOLT

"Whoever examines the principles upon which that religion Christianity is founded," wrote Machiavelli in 1513, "and sees how widely different from those principles its present practice and application are, will judge that her

---

[14] Edward J. Power, *Main Currents in the History of Education* (New York: McGraw-Hill, 1962), p. 250.

ruin or chastisement is near at hand." The judgment was strangely prophetic: four years later Luther posted his Ninety-five Theses at Wittenberg,
and within a single generation half of Europe abandoned Roman Catholicism for Protestantism.

Reformational Medievalism

The Reformation was not, as it is sometimes represented, a decisive break
with medievalism. In nature and intent it was more a modification or sim-
plification of the medieval world view than an outright repudiation of it.
The reformers firmly accepted all the general features of the supernatural-
istic Christian epic, took for granted the larger outlines of its traditional
interpretation, and left its fundamental assumptions untouched. Beneath
the vitriolic anathematizations of the various sixteenth-century Protestant
creeds, the Anglican Thirty-nine Articles, the Calvinist Confession, the
Lutheran Augsburg Confession, there lay a common core of belief belonging to the same genus of thought found in medieval Catholicism's professions at the Council of Trent. Protestants exalted faith over reason, rigidly
opposed religious toleration, opposed free inquiry and the rise of science.
Roland Bainton's observation that Luther was "so much a gothic figure
that his faith may be called the last great flowering of the religion of the
Middle Ages" is an apt one.[15] Protestantism was, in the judgment of another historian, "a last medieval, a last great purely Christian, effort to
justify in action God's way to man."[16] The essential continuity of the Reformation with the Middle Ages warrants their being considered together,
despite significant historical differences.[17]

Ernst Troeltsch, in his classic *Protestantism and Progress,* makes a useful
distinction between the reformers' intentions and the consequences of their
work. They sincerely believed theirs was an *imitatio Christi,* an imitation
of Christ. Their movement was a primitivist one, which preached a return
to the simple standards of the Bible and the early Christian community.
Luther, Calvin, Zwingli, and the others did not believe they were changing
but restoring, and they would have been astonished and puzzled to be told
they were either medieval traditionalists *or* agents of progress. The irony,
as one interpreter phrases it, was that they "contributed to individualism,
although none of them were individualists in the modern sense; to nationalism, although they hoped to restore Christian unity; to democracy, al-

15 Roland Bainton, *Here I Stand* (New York: Abingdon-Cokesbury, 1950), p. 25.
16 Crane Brinton, *The Shaping of Modern Thought* (Englewood Cliffs, N.J.: Prentice-
Hall, 1963), p. 62.
17 There is no denying that the Reformation was also a product of the preceding
humanistic Renaissance. Those unfamiliar with conventional historiographical periodization may find it helpful to read the first half of Chapter 5 before returning to this discussion of Reformational developments. In chronological sequence, the rise of scientific inquiry (discussed in the latter half of the next chapter) was coincident with, and an aftermath of, intellectual developments of the sixteenth century.

though hardly any of them were democrats; to the 'capitalistic spirit,' although they were extremely suspicious of capitalists; indeed, to the secularization of society, although their aim was exactly the reverse."[18]

Luther's appeal for every man to be his own priest, because papist priests had become obstacles between man and God, clearly placed the burden of salvation upon the individual rather than upon an institution. When he declared that church councils and popes might err, he invited men to question the infallibility of all institutions. The Lutheran doctrine that the sacraments' efficacy depended upon the recipient's faith, undoubtedly provided an impulse toward individualism. The character Christian in John Bunyan's *Pilgrim's Progress* is a typical individualist pursuing his way toward the Celestial City without benefit of priests and other institutional ministrations. Nonetheless the dropping away of the sacramental system of the medieval Church and its attendant hierarchy of priests did not mean the individual was to enjoy an immediate relation with God. Protestant rebels against authority quickly supplied another intermediary in the authority of the Protestant Church with its own dogmas, laws, and clergy. Calvin's theocracy at Geneva showed unequivocally that emancipation *from* the Romish yoke meant freedom for religious belief *as decreed by Protestants.*

Politically, the Reformation was an appeal to nationalist sentiment. Reformers used the vernacular, and their translations of the Bible became the foundation of national literatures. In all Protestant lands a national church was established under the control of the local ruler. Only secular princes could provide the necessary power to help reformers make good their claims to independence. Without an appeal to nationalism against the papal claim of *Ultramontanism* (i.e., the reaffirmation of the popes' supremacy over individual governments), it is doubtful whether much headway could have been made. Taking as their text Romans 13, "the powers that be are ordained of God," Protestants were more than willing to submit to royal authority in preference to Rome's domination. They stood, in Troeltsch's phrase, for a "Church civilization" in which an infallible, historic Church claimed the right to govern society according to God's will. The claim to save souls led logically to the claim by the Church to discipline men in their worldly activities, whether in politics, business, or education. In this there was no real break from the corporate world of the Middle Ages.

The practical results, however, were altogether different. The logic of Protestant theology also led to democracy and the secularization of the state. It sought to convert the masses and to provide some rudimentary schooling for all men. Calvinism endorsed lay participation in Church gov-

18 Franklin Le Van Baumer, "The Confessional Age," in *Main Currents of Western Thought* (New York: Alfred A. Knopf, 1952), p. 169. The discussion here is dependent upon Le Van Baumer's treatment, pp. 168–174.

ernment, universal education for all classes, and popular election of ministers through the institution of the elderships. Congregational meetings helped accustom people to democratic ways. Theories of individual rights for the common man and the notion of contractual government were integral to sixteenth-century Protestant political theory. The entire theme of spiritual sovereignty residing in Church members instead of with popes, kings, or bishops (the doctrine of a priesthood of all believers) strengthened a secularized democratic movement—the last thing intended by Protestant reformers because it boldly destroyed the one great obstacle to the secular state, namely, priestly sacramental power. Once a distinction between laity and clergy was gone, and with it the sacerdotal authority of exemption from civil jurisdiction, the state was free to order social life on the basis of secular rather than sacral interests.

The Reformation had the further effect of supporting the rise of capitalism. As Weber, Tawney, and Troeltsch have pointed out, Protestantism —especially Calvinism—encouraged the competitive businessman's ethic of diligence, frugality, and thrift. It condemned sloth as sinful and endorsed work as a positive virtue. Puritan insistence on unremitting toil and diligence and on the sin of wasteful consumption combined to enjoin the amassing of wealth as a sacred duty. This Protestant ethic became the ideology of capitalism, nicely illustrated in the English cleric Richard Baxter's *Christian Directory,* a veritable handbook of middle-class Puritan moral theology. Consider the following injunction: "You may labor in that manner as tendeth most to your success and lawful gain, for you are bound to improve all your talents. . . . If God show you a way in which you may lawfully get more than in another way, if you refuse this and choose the less gainful way, you cross one of the ends of your calling, and you refuse to be God's steward." Countless other illustrations can be adduced to show how theology strengthened a capitalistic ethic. There is something grotesque in assuming, as Marxists tend to do, that economic factors were *solely* responsible for the Protestant Reformation, although of course they contributed greatly to it. More importantly, the *effect* of Protestant ethical teaching was to help expand the capitalistic spirit. Parenthetically, it is worth noting that modern educational thought has relied heavily on the Protestant ethic for legitimacy. One aspect of the crisis in education today is tied to the apparent decline of this moral and economic ideology.

Finally, neither Protestant nor Catholic reformers intended to initiate rationalist tendencies in European intellectual thought. Both groups resisted the beginning spirit of scientific inquiry. Protestants ceased to believe in saints, but they continued to believe in witches, demons, and other worshippers at the court of darkness. Luther's struggle with the Devil at Wartburg, where he threw his inkpot at the intruder, was very real for him. He thundered against reason, calling her "that silly little fool, that Devil's bride, Dame Reason," God's worst enemy; and cried, "We know that rea-

son is the Devil's harlot." His polemic was matched by the Catholic catechism devised at the Council of Trent: "Faith . . . excludes not only all
doubt, but even the desire of subjecting its truth to demonstration." To
claim, as some have done, that Protestantism was the leading edge of a
wedge prying men loose from medieval superstitions is simply erroneous.
But considered together—Calvinists, Lutherans, Socinians, Anabaptists,
Quakers—Protestant theorists did let loose, in appealing by human reason
to their respective interpretations of Christianity, a swelling tide of rationalism deepened by the popular education they required to support their positions. A certain tendency to denigrate metaphysical speculation, to fix upon
the practical and concrete, to discredit in a literalistic way most intellectual
theorizing probably helped forge a link to the scientific empiricism of later
centuries. A real breach in the closed little universe of medieval belief had
begun.

The Causes of the Reformation

The absolute authority of the Catholic Church had been under assault
for centuries before Luther's time. Fourteenth- and fifteenth-century mystics like *Johann Tauler* and *Meister Eckhart* relegated institutional apparatus to the background in their doctrine of personal salvation through
meditation and prayer alone, the practical effect of which was to weaken
the importance of sacraments, priests, and papal authority. Thirteenth-century schismatics, the *Waldensians* and *Albigensians,* crusaded in a spirit of
piety against the Church's increasing worldliness. Reforms instigated as
early as the twelfth century by *Pope Gregory VII* against ecclesiastical compromises with the political and social structure, exemplified by the founding of such new orders as the Benedictine *Cluniacs* and the *Cistercians,*
seemed to have had little effect as the Church evolved into a political, prop-
ertied power. Her moral authority suffered extensively when a secular
French king could literally kidnap the pope and transfer his court to Avignon for almost three quarters of a century. Nor was it edifying to behold
the spectacle of two rival popes at Rome and Avignon, between 1378 and
1417, each bitterly hurling accusations of heresy at one another.

On the eve of the Reformation, things had gone from bad to worse. The
secularization of parish clergy had gone so far that feudal "prince bishops,"
holding vast possessions, could arrogantly ignore the rule of clerical celibacy. Such Renaissance popes as Sixtus IV, Alexander VI, and Leo X had
become temporal sovereigns, seemingly interested only in consolidating
political power and maintaining the finances of the Curia. In faith and
deportment, they differed little from their secular counterparts. The
Church was deeply enmeshed in European political life, dramatically illustrated by the shattered ruling dynasty of the Holy Roman Empire. The
House of Hohenstaufen was merely one of several victims of papal manipulation. Various popes, beginning with *John XXII,* exploited every con-

ceivable device for extracting money for the papal coffers, to the point where holding the supreme office suggested profit, not duty. The *annate,* a fee paid to the pope in exchange for a lucrative appointment as bishop, and the *reservation,* the withholding of a bishop's first yearly income from tithes, kept a steady stream of gold flowing toward Rome. Similar fees abounded and special offices were devised. Absentee bishops, sometimes holding many appointments simultaneously, grew rich on churchly taxes. Concubinage and nepotism were rampant.

The most blatant expedient in this regard was the *indulgence.* Its underlying theory, the doctrine of a *"Treasury of Merit,"* was that Christ and the saints had accumulated more merits than needed for their own salvation. Left-over credits, so the argument went, were stored in a treasury placed by God at the disposal of the popes and capable of transfer to those whose sins were in arrears.[19] The pope could not only remit whatever penalties he had imposed but also those of purgatory. Departed souls' terms could be reduced, even canceled at papal discretion for a fee. "When the coin in the coffer rings," went the cry of indulgence collectors, "the soul from purgatory springs." A scandal involving an archbishopric at Mainz in 1517 was the immediate cause of Luther's conflict with the Church. The pope permitted the proclamation of indulgences for sale in Saxony, half of the proceeds to go to *Albert of Hohenzollern* so he could illegally buy the Church office, the other half to help pay construction costs for a new basilica of St. Peter's. The first stage of the Lutheran revolt is to be traced to protests against this indulgence sale. In the end, the Church got St. Peter's but lost Germany.

Some years before Luther's protest, other attempts at reform had been made. In England a popular Oxford preacher named *John Wycliffe* had formented criticism against the Church. He denounced the pope as the Antichrist, untiringly exposed clerical laxity, and appealed to the Bible as ultimate authority in all doctrinal matters. One hundred and fifty years before Luther, Wycliffe anticipated virtually all of the Lutheran arguments. The English reform movement spread quickly. In Bohemia, revolt broke open under the leadership of *John Huss,* a powerful preacher and university theologian at Prague. It was suppressed finally only after brutal massacres and Huss' execution at the stake for heresy. Harsh measures no longer sufficed after 1500. The rising demands for moral reform, eloquently expressed by such Catholic humanists as *Lefèvre d'Etaples* and *Erasmus of Rotterdam,* could not be set aside much longer.

Historians point to a coincidence of other factors that made the Reformation almost inevitable. Renaissance *humanism* (to be considered in Chapter 5) engendered widespread revulsion against the ascetic ideals of medieval orthodoxy. The humanistic shift of interest from heaven to earth, supported

---

[19] Roland H. Bainton, *The Reformation of the Sixteenth Century* (Boston: Beacon Press, 1956), pp. 13–14.

by new geographical explorations and the rise of commercialism, most likely helped. Extreme *nominalism,* the product of a decaying scholasticism, tended to undercut the philosophical supports of conservative Catholic theology. Above all, *German nationalism* played a part. There was tremendous ill will among Germans against the Italian papal court because it was believed, with some justification, to be sucking people dry financially to support the Italian Church. Thus, when Luther was led step by step from forensic protest to open rebellion, culminating in his excommunication in 1521, large portions of northern and western Germany were ready to support his crusade against the Church. The outbreak soon spread to Denmark, where the same grievances against Italian rule had long smoldered, to Sweden, and elsewhere. Independent reform movements quickly began in Switzerland, Scotland, and England.

Pre-Reformational Learning and Education

There is no question that the displacement of Catholic Church government by Protestant rule was partly an outcome of Renaissance humanism's spread into northern Europe. The groundwork for this latter movement had been laid in the late fourteenth century with an indigenous revival of learning centered in prosperous burgher municipalities. New universities at Prague, Heidelberg, Cologne, Vienna, Leipzig, Rostock, and Erfurt, founded between 1348 and 1409, eventually became havens for northern humanism when it gained its ascendancy beyond the Italian borders. Most of the later universities, including those at Mainz, Wittenberg, Frankfurt, Freiburg, and Basel, patronized by the burgher class and well-to-do princes, responded enthusiastically to the teaching of scholars busily importing humanism from across the Alps. Within some university communities, though, there was sharp antagonism between scholars of scholastic persuasions and those, attracted to humanism, who sought to reorient scholarship around more secular, naturalistic interests. Those receptive to reviving ancient literature, as one might expect, were more inclined to support reform movements of the Church. It only required a catalytic agent like Luther to transform a sober desire for reform into an actual rebellion activity supported by those universities where humanism held sway. "As the Renaissance spirit moved north in the fifteenth and sixteenth century," one scholar comments, "it inspired man to declare his independence of a Church that had shaped his life for centuries, create new and more vigorous institutions for his well-being, and educate for the practical world of commerce and industry, elevate the masses from abject poverty and ignorance to a position of dignity and self-respect in society, and tap the artistic veins of human imagination and sensitivity beyond anything known since the Greeks."[20] Despite profound differences, the Protestant movement and

20 S. E. Frost, *Historical and Philosophical Foundations of Western Education* (Columbus: Charles E. Merrill Company, 1966), p. 174. Quoted with permission.

northern humanism tended to be mutually reinforcing influences bringing about momentous changes in sixteenth-century education.

The advance of more secular studies in universities was accompanied simultaneously by changes in the character of lower-level education. The diffusion of schools sponsored by the *Brethren of the Common Life* did more for a general improvement of education than any other single movement. The Brethren were a unique group of ascetic, pious monastics who combined a doctrine of mystical simplicity with a strong interest in learning. Their founder, a learned Carthusian missionary preacher by the name of *Gerhard Groot* (1340–1384), very early in his career turned to education to further his teachings. Although branded a heretic by some for his denunciations of the secular clergy and denied a preaching position by his superior, Groot's ideals found concrete expression in the work of the Brethren. The brotherhood was composed of both clerics and laymen devoted to charitable works and to scholarship. From out of the *scriptoria* of their houses came a profusion of devotional tracts, textbooks, and Bibles. The Brethren staffed church and private municipal schools where they found them, and established schools where none had existed before. Their institutions became models for other schools. *John Cele's* town school at Zwolle, for example, was an outstanding institution whose innovations were widely copied by the Calvinists at Geneva, by John Sturm in his school at Strassburg, and even by the Jesuits. Its emphasis on a broad curriculum including humanistic studies as well as religion attracted admiration throughout Europe. Famous schools of the Brethren appeared at Liège, Cassel, Ghent, and Utrecht. The great humanist reformer Erasmus was once a pupil in the Brethren's school at Deventer. That by 1400 opportunities to attend some form of grammar school were common was owed partly to the Brethren's zeal for schooling.

Two outstanding educators in the early sixteenth century were *Jacob Wimpheling* (1450–1528) and *Juan Luis Vives* (1492–1540). Wimpheling graduated from a Brethren school in Alsace, and later attended universities at Erfurt, Heidelberg, and Basel. An outspoken advocate of classical studies, he did not neglect schooling for practical life. His manual for teachers, *Isodoneus Germanicus,* and the more general educational treatise, *Adolescentia,* promoted a sane balance of the old and new in pedagogical thought. Had circumstances been different, his impact on German schooling might have been more extensive than it was. Vives was as much an educational practitioner as theoretician. During his stay at Oxford, he supervised Princess Mary's personal education and that of other nobles at King Henry VIII's court. The experience prompted his writing of *Two Letters on a Plan of Studies for Youth.* With the completion of his major work, *Concerning the Teaching of the Arts,* Vives offered a broad conception of the educational process. Foster Watson calls this treatise the "most thoroughgoing educational book of the Renaissance."[21] Proper education, Vives argued, should involve the study of mathematics and the natural sciences as well as classical languages and the vernacular. Religious piety counts for little unless it is disciplined by systematic exposure to many fields of learning. Schooling is best conducted by enlightened masters willing to tailor instruction to the peculiar needs and abilities of each child. Like Wimpheling, he advocated state and municipal support of schools as a kind of social investment. Private tutorial instruction for the privileged few is hopelessly inadequate to an age of change and reform. If educational opportunities are given the masses, Vives wrote, a giant step will be made toward solving the root causes of society's ills. In this he was speaking the modern idiom.

EDUCATIONAL MOVEMENTS
IN THE PROTESTANT REFORMATION

The fragmentation of medieval Christendom had mixed effects on all forms of education. On the positive side, the Reformation contributed to the spread of schools as efforts were made in Protestant lands to instruct the masses in Bible reading, an indispensable condition for salvation. Not only was literacy disseminated more widely than ever before, but the language of instruction switched to the vernacular tongues spoken by common-folk. Prompted in part by Luther's translation of the Scriptures into German, education became "popular" in the truest sense of the term as a thousand-year-old tradition of offering formal training only in Church Latin began to fall apart. Henceforth, learning and scholarship were less isolated from the ordinary man of affairs; he too was provided access to the resources pored over formerly only within the academic cloister.

Luther was forthright in his support for popular education. Calvinists likewise zealously founded schools in Geneva, Scotland, and other lands. In Switzerland, after political turmoil had subsided, several new universities were founded. English reformers did much to help create an excellent system of popular education. It must be said that ultimately more people were given the chance to receive at least some formal instruction than ever before.

On the negative side, the Reformation added nothing to the content of education; it even narrowed it. Intense religious fervor tended to obscure educational considerations: first, because schools were seized upon as instruments for the advancement of sectarian interests, and, second, because spiritual knowledge through faith was opposed against secular, worldly wisdom through learning. The more anti-intellectualist reformers, like the

21 Foster Watson, *Louis Vives* (Oxford: Oxford University Press, 1922), p. 100.

Anabaptists, condemned secular culture as an unfit subject for study.[22] Acerbic controversy among contending sects tended to denigrate general learning; theological rectitude, not scholarship, was what counted. Antagonism against the Catholic Church generalized into opposition against any institutions of education under its jurisdiction. Inevitably Catholics shared the same prejudices against Protestant-dominated schools. Each party sought to confiscate the endowments of the other's schools, the result being that many institutions were closed permanently. Religious warfare left Europe in ruins, her schools impaired, whole populations (including teachers and students) obliterated. Bitter intolerance left little room for a very generous conception of the nature and purpose of education. This too was part of the legacy of the greatest social revolution Europe had known for centuries.

Lutheranism

Martin Luther (1483–1546) began his stormy career as a monk of the Augustinian Eremites at Erfurt. For years he quaked at the thought of death and struggled desperately for deliverance from an overwhelming sense of sinfulness. He wore himself out in strict observance of the monastic discipline, but to no avail. Suddenly, in the winter of 1512–1513 while serving as professor of Biblical literature at the University of Wittenberg, he found release in the scriptural passage, "The just shall live by his faith."

---

[22] Anabaptists were dissenters from the Reformed churches, as well as the Catholic, who "rebaptized" one another as a sign, their only sacrament, of rebirth into a community of the elect. Their opposition to a sinful world assumed militant forms: defiance of laws, total disregard for social customs, and contempt for all things secular. They affected Biblical garb, gathered occasionally in primitive communist communities, eschewed all titles and distinctions of rank, and practiced an ecstatically inspired religion. They were ferociously persecuted as anarchists, pacifists, heretics, and sexual libertines. In 1533 a New Jerusalem commune was formed at Münster in Westphalia. Jan Bockelson of Leyden, their leader, proclaimed himself the chosen savior of the people, anointed himself king, and formed a lavish court. Polygamy was introduced, and he collected a harem. Early in 1535 the deposed bishops' troops laid seige and finally destroyed the Münster community. Anabaptists soon embraced nonviolent ways and came to terms with civil society.

Michael Kraus draws startling parallels between the Anabaptists and today's student rebels. In a similar vein, Arnold Toynbee has compared contemporary dropouts and hippies to the early Christians that the Anabaptists tried to imitate. "In each instance," Kraus observes, "one finds the same total disillusionment with society—the system—and the same rejection of it in the name of a new, religiously inspired vision of the world; the same emphasis upon the elect community as the yeast in the mass and the same prophecies of impending doom should the world reject the salvation offered; and the same delight in ignorance and in non-rational experience." However, there are important differences. Today's protesting dissenters are fragmented; they lack the discipline and social cohesion within the community characteristic of Anabaptists or early Christians. Leaders of striking charisma are lacking. The appeal of those who do appear is temporary. Modern dropouts and hippies take material affluence for granted. Society today, "except for random efforts to control marijuana, the usual source of hippie ecstasy (efforts we may compare to those made by the Roman imperial authorities and the church to sequester the Bible, the source of earlier revelations), has so far been surprisingly indulgent of its dropouts." Michael Krause, "Anabaptism Reborn," *Antioch Notes*, Vol. 47, No. 1 (September, 1969), pp. 1–7.

He concluded that salvation is not to be attained according to the Catholic "way of self-help" by virtuous living and good works. Man, wretched sinner that he is, is saved through faith alone, which is a freely given gift of a merciful God. "Thereupon," he reported, "I felt myself to be reborn and to have gone through open doors into paradise." It was the turning point in his career, and for the next four years, he worked through the implications of this central theme. Finally, he felt compelled to attack the principal ecclesiastical abuses of the Church in light of his developing theology. Events moved quickly. He sent a copy of his Ninety-five Theses (intended, according to the custom of the day, as proposals for a disputation) to his archbishop along with a bluntly worded protest against the sale of indulgences. His challenge to debate was accepted by *John Maier of Eck,* a famous ecclesiastical rhetorician. Pope Leo X was furnished with copies of the arguments. The dispute escalated when it became clear that Luther repudiated the authority of the papacy. Further intransigence prompted a Papal Bull of Condemnation, which Luther scornfully burned. In January of 1521 he was officially excommunicated; three months later at the *Diet of Worms,* the German Church was finally severed from Rome. Luther went into hiding at Wartburg and did not resume his public life at Wittenberg until the following year. A flood of treatises, sermons, letters, a translation of the Bible into German, and polemic papers flowed from his pens to explain the break with Catholicism. Wittenberg assumed the lead in the reform movement. Before his death two decades later, Luther had lived to see his church become firmly established throughout northern Europe and his principal doctrines widely accepted. The heretic had found vindication at last.

Luther's first statement on education appeared in *A Letter to the Mayors and Aldermen of All Cities of Germany in Behalf of Christian Schools.* He reminded officials that spiritually the new order could not endure unless children were enabled to understand the Bible through instruction. "What would it avail," he asked rhetorically, "if we possessed and performed all else, and became perfect saints, if we neglect that for which we chiefly live, namely, to care for the young? In my judgment, there is no other outward offense that in the sight of God so heavily burdens the world, and deserves such heavy reproach, as the neglect to educate children." He once wrote that if he were not a priest, he would be a teacher. The new reformed church must take up the educational work of the old. Satan's designs are threatened by the study of languages because through it people learn God's truth: "We cannot deny that, although the Gospel has come and daily comes through the Holy Spirit, it has come by means of the languages, and through them must increase and be preserved." Here Luther was endorsing Latin schools rather than vernacular ones, a stance somewhat contrary to his aspiration to put a German translation of the Bible into the hands of everyone. More generally, his appeal to authorities was to promote schools of *all* types to fill the vacuum left by the closing of monastic, cathedral, and other Catholic Church schools.

Luther also recognized that education was essential for civil government as well as for spiritual enlightenment. Even if there were neither heaven nor hell, he affirmed, and only secular interests had to be considered, schools would be needed to train people to govern wisely and to organize social life. His *Sermon on the Duty of Sending Children to School* amplifies the point. A city's prosperity depends directly on well-educated citizens who know how to manage their possessions. Luther thought parents alone could not be entrusted with this vital service. Some lacked sufficient piety to undertake the task. Others were unqualified. "Even if parents were qualified and willing to do it themselves," he wrote to the aldermen, "yet on account of the other employments and household duties, they have no time for it, so that necessity requires us to have teachers for public schools." Luther concluded his appeal by asking officials to establish free schools as the sure guarantee of the public welfare. "For since the happiness, honor, and life of the city are commited to their hands, they would be held recreant before God and the world, if they did not day and night, with all their power, seek its welfare and improvement." Municipalities should not only maintain schools at public expense; they should make attendance compulsory if necessary, he argued. "If the magistrates may compel their able-bodied subjects to carry pike and musket and do military service, there is much more reason for them compelling their subjects to send their children to school. For there is a far worse war to be waged with the Devil, who employs himself secretly in harming towns and states through the neglect of education."

In his *Address to the Christian Nobility* Luther spelled out his ideas on education more specifically. There should be elementary schools for the teaching of languages, history, singing, mathematics, instrumental music, and religion. Higher Latin grammar schools for more advanced instruction in Greek, Latin, Hebrew, music, history, and theology would be reserved for able students destined to become teachers, clerics, or civil officials. The distinction between universal elementary education and higher language schools was never clearly spelled out in his own writings, but it became important in the organization of schools patterned after his recommendations. Luther's educational contributions were not confined to writing about education. He actively aided in the founding of schools and took a lively interest in their work. His influence on school ordinances issued for governing German Protestant churches lasted for over a century. The main burden of organizing and administering schools, however, fell to Luther's disciples.

The three educators to whose efforts Lutheran Germany owed the actual creation of schools were *Johannes Bugenhagen* (1485–1558), *Philip Melanchthon* (1497–1560), and *Johann Sturm* (1507–1589). The earliest popular schools of Protestantism were established by Bugenhagen in the towns of northern Germany. He was a Wittenberg professor who left the academic cloister to draw up school system plans in Hamburg, Lubeck, Bremen, Brunswick, and the royal realms of Denmark. At his insistence burgh schools formerly under Church control were handed over to municipal authorities who assumed responsibility for appointing teachers, establishing tuition fees, and revising curricula. Separate schools for each sex were included in the plans Bugenhagen drew up. A year after his death, his schools received official recognition in the School Ordinances of Würtemberg, and the precedent was followed by Saxony and other principalities soon thereafter. A typical organizational plan made provision for reading and writing schools, Latin schools, libraries, instruction for adults, and informal schools for religious training.

Melanchthon's work encompassed an extraordinary variety of undertakings. He was an intimate colleague of Luther at Wittenberg who, rather than Luther, did the most to transform the university into a center of Protestant studies. His work as educational counselor to civil authorities and princes went on while he was engaged in writing schools codes and helping to organize school surveys. His book *Visitation* laid the basis for a complete reorganization of schools in Saxony. The famed *Saxon Code,* with its insistence that civil authorities found schools, set the terms for education in over fifty-six cities. It prohibited the teaching of the vernacular in lower schools, stipulated what instructional strategies should be followed in the teaching of Latin (to which Melanchthon was especially devoted), and spelled out in great detail how advanced education should be conducted. His textbooks were so popular that some were still in use three hundred years later. Melanchthon found time in the midst of his other labors to draw up a constitution and plan of studies for the first Protestant higher schools at Nuremberg and Eisleben. When he died at the age of sixty-three, his methods had been so widely diffused through the teachers who had studied under him that his system was in universal use in the cities of Germany. Hardly any major educator had been uninfluenced by his teachings. Perhaps his most important contribution as reflected in the German secondary school system was his synthesis of humanistic learning and Protestant faith. It was primarily due to him, as *Praeceptor Germaniae,* that the Protestant half of Germany won ascendency over Catholicism in the realms of culture and education. The concept of classical learning as a means to *pietas literata* ("lettered piety") became the cornerstone of his educational views. As he phrased it in his inaugural address at Nuremberg in 1526, "The truths of religion and moral duty cannot be rightly perceived except by minds soundly prepared by a training based on the practice of past ages." The stature of Melanchthon in the history of this period is measured by the fact that Latin grammar and literature became the central interest of most postelementary schools for over three hundred years.[23]

[23] See Friedrich Paulsen, *German Universities and University Study* (New York: Charles Scribner's Sons, 1906), pp. 33 ff.

Melanchthon tended to seek a compromise between scriptural, catechetical studies, and classical learning, whereas Luther had distinctly emphasized the former over the latter. With the work of Johann Sturm, this order was inverted and classics placed in a position of supremacy in German secondary education. Sturm was educated under the Brethren of the Common Life and at the humanistic University of Louvain, taught briefly at the University of Paris, and accepted a post in 1537 as rector of a secondary-level *gymnasium* at Strassburg. Under his directorship of the next forty-odd years, the school was easily counted the most important classical institution on the Continent. It was organized into ten classes, with a teacher in charge of each. Pupils were accepted at the age of five or six. After graduation ten years later, they would continue schooling at a university. The purpose of education, as he stated it in his *Plan of Organization,* was piety (*pietas*), knowledge (*sapientia*), and eloquence (*eloquentia*). "Every effort of teachers and students" should be directed toward acquiring these three qualities, summed up in a "worthy piety" based on right knowledge and power of expression. An educated man must be master of pure diction, be able to use Latin skillfully, and be religious. As actually worked out in the specifics of his curriculum, Sturm's elevation of the ancient Ciceronian ideal meant *pietas* and *sapientia* were sometimes sacrificed to *eloquentia*. Rhetorical skill sometimes seemed more important than religious studies or nonclassical learning. After two or three years devoted to Latin composition and grammar, the remaining years were devoted to Latin and Greek authors, above all, the orations of Cicero. Later the curriculum was expanded to include Greek, rhetoric, and religious texts. Sturm's success is attributed to his thoroughly defined aims, systematic organization, carefully graded instruction, and broad scholarship. His school fixed the type and name of the German classical secondary school until comparatively recent times. Literally thousands of educators came under Sturm's influence. He, along with Melanchthon, helped infuse Protestant education with humanism. Herein lay a fatal flaw in Sturm's work: it was the very thoroughness of his work that encouraged less gifted imitators to transform his plan of studies into a stereotyped, rigid dogma. The insertion of classical studies into Protestant schools, it can be argued, was achieved at the cost of hastening the degeneration of precisely those humanistic studies. Latin came to be studied not as a means of intellectual stimulation, but as a purely formal end by itself. The same could be said for most of the other subjects in the curriculum.

Calvinism

Other educational reformers in the Protestant tradition took up the work initiated by Luther, Melanchthon, Bugenhagen, and Sturm. Standing behind these leaders were many lesser-known figures who accepted the fundamental Reformational doctrines and at the same time saw the need to revise the existing system of schools in order that it might better serve the ends of religious reform. More practical teaching methods, improved vernacular schools (despite the indifference of Luther and Melanchthon to them), and improved Latin schools should be included among the results of their labors. Meanwhile, independent revolts from Rome were taking place. As they succeeded in turn, the need to work out educational revisions peculiar to local conditions became apparent. The fiery *Ulrich Zwingli* (1484–1531), who led a break with the Catholic Church in the Swiss cantons, clearly saw the need for improving schools. His short treatise *The Christian Education of Youth*, published in 1523, was the first formal Protestant work on education. In it Zwingli laid out a curriculum including the study of the Bible, arithmetic, music, gymnastics, Greek, Latin, and Hebrew. His valuable work does not deserve the neglect it has suffered among historians; in all probability if Zwingli had not died an untimely death in battle, he might have used it as the basis for a fuller statement on Protestant educational thought. As it turned out, the task was left for a greater scholar-statesman than either Zwingli or Luther—*John Calvin* (1509–1569).

Calvin received his education at Paris under Mathurin Cordier, where he distinguished himself as a precocious humanist scholar. At his father's directive he pursued legal studies at Bruges and Orléans before returning to Paris when the elder Calvin died. John had intended to become a priest, but during his second stay at Paris he underwent a sudden conversion to the Protestant cause. Because it was hazardous to profess the new teachings in Paris, Calvin left hurriedly for a period of travel. In 1536 he settled in Geneva as city pastor. The next year he presented a statement of twenty-one articles of Protestant faith to the magistrates, insisting that all citizens take an oath of allegiance to them. Geneva was already persuaded to the Protestant movement in any case, although political motives as much as religious convictions were involved. Calvin and his followers saw in the confusion a unique opportunity to reorder the community under the sole control of the church. Education, he recognized, would play an important role in spreading the faith and assuring civic obedience on the part of all citizens. In a prospectus for the elementary schools, he acknowledged the dual function of schooling: "Although we accord the first place to the Word of God, we do not reject good training. The Word of God is indeed the foundation of all learning, but the liberal arts are aids to the full knowledge of the Word and not to be despised." Education, Calvin continued, is indispensable to guarantee "public administration, to sustain the Church unharmed, and to maintain humanity among men." One year later, his schemes to rebuild Geneva were shattered. Riots broke out in protest against Calvin's heavy-handed rule and he was forced to flee the city.

The next three years were spent gaining practical teaching experience under Sturm's direction at Strassburg. Those were important years for his development of an educational philosophy and a plan of school organization. Finally, in 1541, he was recalled to restore order at Geneva, a city in more or less constant upheaval since his banishment. Popular sentiment demanded his return to help restore peace; the people were thoroughly exhausted from religious controversy. Calvin's triumphant return marked the beginning of a twenty-three-year reign as chief minister of the Genevan Church. Under his iron rule, the city was turned into the "Rome of Protestantism." The remainder of his life was spent in writing, conducting conferences, administering the city, preaching, and supervising schools.

Calvin's early strong concern for education was evident in a continuing effort to build up a model school system organized mainly around the precepts absorbed at Strassburg. A Latin preparatory school replaced the earlier municipal grammar schools, with most of the basic features of the Strassburg institution incorporated in its organization. The course of study, divided by seven classes, began with elementary reading and writing as taught from Calvin's catechism. Both Latin and French were used as the languages for instruction. Greek was added in the fourth class and used for the study of the New Testament. In higher classes the subjects included elocution, rhetoric, logic, and music. All in all, it was a thoroughly humanistic type of education. A separate academy contained the advanced grades of Calvin's system. Under the capable leadership of its first rector, *Theodore de Beza,* the school was an immediate success, as measured by the fact that students from all over Europe clamored to be admitted. By the time of Calvin's death, it had become the training ground for young men interested in spreading Calvinism to other countries. Universities in England, Holland, and Scotland were virtual replicas of the original Geneva model.

Calvin's teachings were carried everywhere as a result. The *Huguenots* in France, the *Walloons* of the Belgian and Dutch Netherlands, the *Puritans* of England, the *Presbyterians* in Scotland were all Calvinist adherents. Each worked actively to reproduce the school policies of Geneva in its own region. French Huguenots founded no fewer than eight universities and thirty-two *collèges,* not to mention elementary schools. The Puritan version of Calvinism came to dominate Elizabethan Oxford and Cambridge in England. Such noted universities as Leyden, Amsterdam, Utrecht, and Groningen were infused with the Swiss reformer's teachings. Elementary schools at The Hague, in Utrecht, and in Drenthe were opened under public auspices for children of all classes. In Scotland, Genevan ideals found the widest realization. The leader of the Scottish Reformation, *John Knox* (1505–1572), was deeply impressed with Calvin's educational orders, owing to a visit of some years in Geneva. An essential part of the *First Book of Discipline for the Scottish Church,* drafted by Knox in 1560, was devoted to proposals for a comprehensive system of church-controlled schools. "Of necessity we judge it that every several church have a schoolmaster appointed, such a one as is able, at least, to teach grammar and the Latin tongue, if the town be of any reputation . . . then must either the reader or the minister there appointed, take care over the children and youth of the parish, to instruct them in their first rudiments and especially in the catechism." What was new in Knox's proposals was the prescription of universal, compulsory education within a unified national school system. The plan, unfortunately, was opposed as too expensive, and only a few of its provisions were ever carried out. Nevertheless those schools that were opened represented a real educational advance over what had earlier prevailed.

Anglicanism

The English reform movement proceeded from political, not religious motives. Northern humanism had made less of an intellectual impression; Lutheranism had gained little headway save among isolated groups at Cambridge and Oxford; and the reigning monarch, *Henry VIII*, was so loyal a subject of Rome that the title "Defender of the Faith" was bestowed upon him by the pope. Still, at the same time popular sentiment was sympathetic to Catholicism, it violently opposed the exactions of the clergy. Critical satires of the immoral priests, like Erasmus' devastating *Letters of Obscure Men*, found audiences everywhere. In 1530 King Henry petitioned the papacy for permission to divorce *Catherine of Aragon* and marry *Anne Boleyn* in order that he might have a legitimate male heir to the throne. The pope's politically motivated delay outraged the king to the point that all ties with the Roman Church were cut off in 1534 by Parliament's *Act of Supremacy*, making the king titular head of a new Church of England. The *Treasons Act* enacted shortly thereafter gave Henry a free hand against all opponents of "the papacy without the pope." The English Church assumed the functions formerly exercised by the Catholic; in many cases the same priests were retained in parish churches. Changes in Church doctrine and practice were minimal.

Educationally, more drastic alterations were effected. Between 1536 and 1539 Parliament closed every monastery in England, confiscated their properties, and converted most of the monastic houses into collegiate churches, with schools attached. University colleges were endowed to some extent from the proceeds of Catholic property. A cathedral church school at Canterbury was reformed in 1541 as a humanistic secondary school, as was a lower song school. A year before his death in 1547 Henry had another act of Parliament passed transferring power over all chantry schools to the Crown so that they might be "altered, changed, and amended to convert them to good and godly uses as in the erecting of grammar schools." Unfortunately the state found it necessary to use monies from their sale for other purposes and the intended endowments never materialized.

Henry's successor, *Edward VI*, perpetuated the new order. The *Act of Uniformity* of 1552 required everyone, including teachers and clergy, to accept the national church and tailor their beliefs to its official doctrines. Succeeding years witnessed a religious narrowing of all instruction to ensure universal orthodoxy among the populace. Teachers had to be licensed by the church, to swear an oath of allegiance, and to guarantee their instruction conformed in every particular to Anglican faith. A brief, violent restoration of Catholicism under *Mary I* ("Bloody Mary") which brought repressive legislation, terrorism, and mass executions only succeeded in alienating the people. *Queen Elizabeth I,* upon her ascension to the throne in 1558, immediately reconstituted Protestant dominion, political and educational. By this time it was commonly accepted that schooling was the concern of the church, not that of the secular authorities. The attitude hung on until well into the 1800's and unmistakably retarded the development of a state educational system. Some one hundred and thirty grammar schools were in operation during Elizabeth's reign but they were far less numerous than those formerly operated, in one form or another, under Catholic rule. Elizabethan England turned most of its energies toward the spread of charity schools, writing schools, apprenticeship institutions, and private dame schools to replace the old song, chantry, and hospital schools that had disappeared during Henry's rule.

The grammar schools that did appear were modeled after the instruction first given at St. Paul's School in London, where the humanist scholar *John Colet* had been active early in the century. A basic type for English secondary school instruction then established endured for several centuries. It has been estimated from surviving records that about one hundred and fifty humanistic grammar schools had been opened by the middle of the seventeenth century. The character of post-Reformation education in England is revealed in legislative actions relating to schools. Educational institutions became, in the phrase of the day, "nurseries of the faith," their chief mission inculcation of religious doctrine. Church officials were urged to root out all heterodox schoolmasters. Even in the universities an inquisitorial policy prevailed. In the same way, all elementary instruction was intensely religious, confined to training in sectarian literature. Any teacher suspected of departing from the formal, disciplinary regimen faced heavy fines and even imprisonment. On the other hand, English education went farther than was usual in other lands to create educational opportunities for the lower classes, exemplified in the *Poor Law* of 1601, which ordered compulsory property taxation to support apprenticeship training programs in workhouses. An added requirement that children of the poor be given formal instruction in religion became a fixed arrangement in every church parish.

English educational theory in the sixteenth century had a limited impact at best on the conduct of schools. It helped popularize humanistic learning, offered some intriguing suggestions for school curricula and discipline, and advanced the cause of English as a language of scholarship, but otherwise failed to address itself to the vital pedagogical issues of the day. *Sir Thomas Elyot* (1490–1546) and *Roger Ascham* (1515–1568) are generally regarded as the two most widely read authors on educational matters. The former's *The Boke Named the Governour* (1531) was the first educational treatise to appear in English and was a best-seller. The latter's *The Schoolmaster* (1570) also enjoyed some popularity, although there was little new in either document. The most that can be said for them is that they aided in setting the aristocratic, gentlemanly tone for English secondary education so typical during the seventeenth and eighteenth centuries. More democratic in orientation were the writings of *Richard Mulcaster* (1530–1611). His two major works, *Positions* (1581) and *Elementarie* (1582), reflected their author's keen eye for observation, his concern for quality teacher education, and his interest in state support for universal schooling. Even Mulcaster, nonetheless, endorsed the common view that too much education was socially dangerous if extended to those unfit by character or background for the life of a gentleman.

EDUCATIONAL MOVEMENTS
IN THE CATHOLIC COUNTER-REFORMATION

There were many devout people who recoiled in horror at the Protestants' exodus from the Catholic fold but who recognized an urgent need for internal reforms within the Church. The 1545–1563 *Council of Trent* was only one of several responses to popular agitation for action. Several potentially vital programs came out of that convocation. Every diocese was enjoined to establish a seminary for improving the professional preparation of priests. Stricter measures were laid down to correct abuses of clerical authority. Immorality and licentouness within the ecclesiastical hierarchy were strongly condemned, and the appeal made for churchmen to institute needed reforms in the areas of doctrine, morals, and institutional administration. Bishops were admonished to extend greater support to parish schools. The idea of free schools for the poor was endorsed as part of a larger plan for the over-all revival of Catholic education. Some reactionary prelates helped to frustrate the more forward-looking reforms of the council, however, and not nearly enough was done to satisfy liberal sentiment.

Meanwhile, the Church was engaged in other ways in the struggle to regain territories lost to Protestants, to repel their advances in countries beginning to waver, and to counter their missionary efforts among subjects remaining loyal to Rome. A two-pronged attack of force and intellectual persuasion was mounted. Where pulpit forensics unavailed, military might was employed. The Duke of Alva, under the sponsorship of Philip II, conducted a brutal campaign against Protestants in the Netherlands in an attempt to restore Church dominance. The war ended in a split between Protestant Holland and Catholic Belgium, with hundreds left dead under the smoking ruins of cities on both sides. Outbreaks elsewhere, as in

Moravia, were stamped out temporarily when Catholic sovereigns poured armies into dissident areas. In Spain, the fires of the *auto-da-fé*, or Holy Inquisition, were stoked up to burn out all heretical doctrines, dispatching their adherents in the process. Subversive texts were continually added to the *Index Expurgatorius* to prevent the spread of heresy. The war for men's minds was conducted on an educational front as well. Recently formed religious orders, such as the *Ursulines*, the *Theatines*, and the *Capuchins*, turned to the labor of educational reform, founded schools, improved instructional practices, and reorganized decayed curricula. The most outstanding of these religious associations by far was the order founded by *Ignatius of Loyola* (1491–1556).

The Jesuits

Inigo Lopez was born in Guipuzcoa, Spain, the son of a noble family. He received a somewhat meager education as page at the court of Isabella and Ferdinand but compensated for it by winning a reputation as a dauntless soldier on the battlefield under the banner of the Duke of Najera. In 1521 he was seriously wounded at the French attack on Pampeluna, the capital of Navarre. His recuperation took several months, during which time he renounced his secular vocation and consecrated himself to a life of religious service. Two years later he journeyed toward Jerusalem in hopes of helping restore the Holy Land to Christendom. The realization dawned on Ignatius that his educational background had not prepared him for any such undertaking. He resolved to return to Spain to pursue studies, first at the grammar school at Barcelona, then at the University of Alcala, and finally at Paris. The young scholar soon gathered around him a small group of devoted disciples who shared his desire to advance Catholicism against its foes. In 1534 they assembled at the church of St. Mary on Montmartre and banded together formally as a paramilitary religious order called The Regiment of Jesus, with Ignatius as its first "general." Six turbulent years followed before Ignatius and his followers were formally recognized by Pope Paul III as the *Society of Jesus*. Its founder was installed as chief officer of the Jesuit Order, a post Ignatius retained until his death sixteen years later. The central mission was to move out as a papal task force to combat Protestantism through education and missionarylike preaching wherever they were needed. The Jesuits, events showed, proved to be a powerful instrument of reform within late-sixteenth-century Catholicism.

Educational improvement was given a place of primary importance in their endeavors. *Claudius Aquaviva*, the fourth Jesuit General, appointed a committee to draw up a report for a new educational system reflecting the considered views of the whole society. It was implemented on an experimental basis, revised, and given final form in 1599 as the *Ratio Studiorum*, or Plan of Studies—the authoritative canon regulating all subjects studied within Jesuit schools. It prescribed in detail the precise methods of instruction to be followed, how schools were to be organized, how discipline should be maintained, how educational officers' responsibilities should be discharged, and the exact aims to be pursued.

The Jesuit school structure was divided into two courses: the lower preparatory sequence beginning for boys aged ten, which took them through a six-year course of grammar, humanities, and rhetoric; and a higher three-year plan of studies involving sciences, mathematics, and philosophy. Institutions for the first course were known as *studia inferiora* and the second course was conducted in *studia superiora*. Taken together, the schools were called colleges. Each college was governed by two officials—a *rector* appointed by the pope responsible to the *provincial* of the regional area and a *prefect of studies*. Beneath these were the *corrector* or official disciplinarian, student supervisors, and the students themselves. Discipline in these schools was firm but not repressive. Every effort was made to make learning interesting. Students were expected to memorize lessons delivered orally, although detailed explanations, drill, and frequent repetitions were instituted to help each pupil with his work. Also offered were such incentives as prizes, student ranks, and public disputations to facilitate the learning process. Carefully regulated hours of study punctuated with physical exercise set the daily pattern. This in brief was the shape of the most carefully organized, closely supervised, and rigidly maintained education ever known to western Europe.

Teachers in schools run by the Society of Jesus received the most thorough preparatory training available. "It would be most profitable for the schools," reported Aquaviva's original drafting committee, "if those who are to be preceptors were privately taken in hand by some one of great skill, and for two months or more were trained by him in the method of reading, teaching, writing, correcting, and managing a class. If teachers have not learned these things beforehand," it was added, "they are forced to learn them afterwards at the expense of their scholars; and then they will acquire proficiency only when they have already lost in reputation; and perhaps they will never unlearn a bad habit." (Contemporary critics of professional teacher education would do well to ponder the point.) The actual system of teacher preparation worked out was much more elaborate. Candidates wishing to teach were accepted only after they completed the lower course of studies. A two-year period of spiritual discipline followed before admittance into the three-year upper course sequence where prospective teachers majored in the subject they would teach. At that time young men were allowed to observe master teachers while teaching as a "scholastic" in the lower classes. This probationary period, or *juniorate*, led to an additional three or four years of university studies in philosophy, mathematics, and sciences. A preliminary teaching experience lasting three or four more years was required before final ordination as a master teacher.

The rigor of this training helps account for the spectacular success of

Jesuit schools. It is also true that besides preparing first-rate teachers, the Jesuits had the advantage of a regularized plan of study, a plan progressively refined and improved as it was tested by successive generations of dedicated teachers. Even opponents had to acknowledge their superiority in the field of education. The Protestant Lord Bacon, speaking in the early seventeenth century, remarked, "As for the pedagogical part, the shortest rule would be, consult the schools of the Jesuits; for nothing better has been put into practice." (He is said to have added ruefully, "They are so good that I wish they were on our side.") Furthermore, the Jesuits were careful to found schools only when and where there were sufficient endowments to enable them to offer instruction on a gratuitous basis. Students might have been charged fees for lodging and food when necessary, but there were never any tuition costs. As might be expected, this practice won widespread acclaim and contributed to their spectacular success in educational endeavors.

The Jesuit impact on the spread of schools was unequalled. By 1600 over two hundred "colleges," universities, and training seminaries had been founded. The total number doubled in the next century alone. Northern France, Belgium, Austria, Hungary, and Poland were the chief beneficiaries of Jesuit educational work because the struggle with Protestantism was most intense in those areas.

Notable for its lack, it must be said, was Jesuit interest in lower-school education. Except in missionary situations on the North American continent, the Society of Jesus rarely opened elementary schools, and when it did, control was relinquished as soon as possible. The reasons for this neglect are unclear; in all probability the Jesuits felt that the need for renewal was greatest at higher educational levels and that their over-all contribution should be made where it would have the greatest impact. The fact that no provision was made for introducing lay teachers in their schools (following the medieval concept of a clerical monopoly in education) also set limits upon the total Jesuit effort on behalf of expanded schooling, but in all fairness neither omission should detract from the positive contributions this religious teaching order made.

Despite deserved criticism for subordinating liberal learning to doctrinal proselytizing, their resistance to further innovation, and their inflexible authoritarianism, there is no denying that the Jesuits did more to upgrade secondary-level education in Catholic countries than any other group. Their universities were citadels of humanistic scholarship. It is not too much to claim that they were the first line of defense against Protestant incursions, more effective perhaps in the long run in redirecting the attention of the Catholic Church to the need for better schools than even the Protestants themselves.

Other Catholic Orders

Of course there were many other teaching societies besides the Jesuits who developed Catholic schools. Some of these have been mentioned earlier. The *Oratory of France,* established by *Cardinal de Berulle* in 1611, worked actively for the improvement of music schools and seminaries for priests in France. The *Piarists,* a religious teaching order concerned with elementary education, founded schools modelled after the Jesuitical organizational scheme as adapted for lower schools in Italy, Spain, Moravia, and Bohemia. The *Jansenists* or Port Royalists, founded by St. Cyran and Cornelius Jansen in opposition to the Jesuits, inaugurated the famous "little schools of Port Royal" experiment in progressive education between 1646 and 1661. Their influence far exceeded their numbers, persisting even after the dispersal of the society under Jesuit pressure. Catholic charity schools for the poor were maintained by several orders. The most important of the teaching orders concerned exclusively with elementary education was the *Brothers of the Christian Schools,* founded by Father LaSalle at Rouen in 1684. His major work on education, *The Conduct of Schools* (1720), was a vigorous defense of free primary schools for religious instruction in the vernacular. Aside from the elementary schools conducted by the Brothers, at least two teacher-training normal schools were put into operation at Paris and Rheims in the late 1600's. Some fifty schools of differing types were eventually developed in the first century of the order's existence. A distinctive contribution to educational practice made by LaSalle was "ability grouping" by classes, with each class provided with an older student monitor to assist the teacher in instruction.

Generally, the Protestant Reformation compelled leaders of the Catholic Counter-Reformation to extend existing church systems of schools. At least thirteen different teaching orders, some temporary, others still in existence today, were begun between 1535 and 1684, all for the express purpose of assisting the Church to overhaul or expand schooling from the primary to the university level.

EDUCATIONAL IDEALS OF THE CONFESSIONAL AGE

The fatal weakness of sixteenth and seventeenth century religious fervor was its stubborn refusal to abandon the medieval theocratic ideal. So long as all accepted the theory that the pope was God's vicar on earth delegating authority to civil rulers, and submitted to the Church as interpreter of the will of God, society was held together. Culturally, theocracy (and more generally the whole theocentric habit of thought applied to other aspects of culture) exacted heavy penalties insofar as it retarded the growth of rational and scientific inquiry, but it served Europe well enough for over a millennium. Unhappily, Protestant reformers persisted in exalting the ideal even as their own actions rendered it impossible of realization. Events of the Reformation in German lands, especially the peasants' revolts against their princes, led Luther to exclaim, "The princes of this world are gods, the common people are Satan!" He wholeheartedly endorsed the view that civil authorities must govern and church authorities serve as their counselors. It was not far from this to the theory of the divine right of sovereignty, that the authority of the civil ruler proceeds from God himself. "It is in no wise proper," Luther insisted, "for any one who would be a Christian to set himself up against his government, whether it act justly or unjustly." Calvin retained the Catholic theory, substituting the Church of Geneva for the Church of Rome, and insisted on absolute obedience: "Out of her bosom . . . there can be no hope of remission of sins, or any salvation. . . . It is always fatally dangerous," he wrote in his *Institutes,* "to be separated from the Church." In England, church and state were united in the person of the king. *Which* church, then, ought the Christian obey? The answer of the *Peace of Augsburg* in 1555 was to let each prince choose between Catholicism and Lutheranism and to compel his subjects to follow course—*cuius regio eius religio* ("whose region, his religion"). No other doctrinal possibilities were even considered. The inevitable result of each group's refusal to extend to others the same toleraton it claimed for itself was war. And so there followed two centuries of intermittent religious conflict during which Catholics and Protestants vainly tried to re-establish their own versions of the theocratic state.

The long and tragic period between Emperor Charles V's declaration against German Lutheran princes in 1546 to the *Peace of Westphalia* in 1648 represented a century of harsh, vindictive strife when men slaughtered one another *omnia ad majorem Dei gloriam* and for the salvation of souls. The last three decades of that terrible time, the *Thirty Years' War* (1618–1648), was the culmination of pious ferocity set to plundering and pillaging. The German states were reduced to ruins, half their population destroyed, and most of their property obliterated. Widespread starvation led to cannibalism. In France the attempt to root out Huguenots killed thousands. In the massacre of St. Bartholomew's eve in 1572 alone, fifty-five thousand Protestants perished in a single night. The toleration promised by the *Edict of Nantes* in 1598 was rarely extended and the decree itself was revoked in 1682. It took far too many years before all parties were exhausted, settled for peaceful coexistence, and accepted a *pax dissidentium,* the peace of those who agree to differ. The aftermath of the religious wars was hatred, suspicion, and mutual intolerance. Each church turned inward to supervise its own house and sectarian schools became guardians of the respective orthodoxies.

Much of the earlier educational progress was swept away by religious warfare. Those elementary vernacular schools that did manage to survive or were later founded depended almost exclusively for support on the scanty finances of their denomination. Doctrinal training far overshadowed their other educational aims. The situation involving secondary schools was only slightly better. They tended to confine their attentions to Latin-based instruction for preparing leaders to direct the new social and religious order. In all, the end of a confessional age meant the process of educational rebuilding had to begin again; new and better schools were needed to service the growing demand for more universal education in a dawning secular age. The practice of using schools to promote allegiance to sectarian creeds and obedience to religiously based moral precepts would continue for several centuries more. On the other hand, genuinely new cultural forces were appearing that spelled the beginning of the end for that long, intimate association of religious interests with educational concerns that began when the Church assumed control over schools in late antiquity.

It is worth recalling in this connection how closely the Reformation was tied to the first organized educational efforts of settlers in colonial America. Though historians are prone to exaggerate the point, those who founded the Massachusetts Bay Colony and other communities to follow included many refugees from the religious warfare and intolerance raging throughout Europe. In New England especially, religious antagonism to the Established Church of England bore heavy responsibility for the public commitment to education prevalent during the seventeenth century. The founding fathers at Plymouth, as well as leaders in Connecticut, New Hampshire, and Maine, had a compelling motive to attend to the literacy of their offspring, believing as they did that a child's salvation depended in generous measure on his or her ability to read and understand the Bible. Thus it is not surprising to note a close correlation between the scope of educational ferment sustained by colonists and the degree of religious urgency they experienced. As private schools with secular aims began to supplant theologically oriented public institutions in New England in the late 1600's, the pious rightly feared that the end of a theocentric civilization was drawing near.

For several reasons religious motives did not play as important a role in the founding of schools in New York and Pennsylvania, but there is abundant evidence to show how the southern Anglican colonies moved quickly to provide catechistic instruction for apprentices and paupers, as well as Latin grammar schools geared to the requirements of the clergy. In these respects the settlers at Virginia and elsewhere were no different from their northern counterparts in emphasizing the religious importance of organized schooling. As in Europe, dissenting minority sects made heroic efforts within the limitations of their limited resources to set up educational institutions in which theological rectitude could be nurtured and sustained.

There was little new in Reformational Catholic thought on education, with the important exceptions of better attention to school organization and management and the drive to introduce humanistic studies into the curriculum. The basic aim, as always, was to instill traditional loyalty to the tenets of the Catholic faith. The ideally educated individual remained a faithful servant of Mother Church, obedient to her will, always ready to fulfill his functions, be they clerical or lay, within the divinely appointed social order. He might be highly critical of the Church, but ultimately he would remain within the fold.

The erudite Dutch cleric Erasmus (whose specific educational views will be considered later) provides a worthy illustration of how Catholic educational and intellectual ideals could be expressed with unequalled eloquence. He voiced his hopes for a saner world as follows: "Now that I see that the mightiest princes of the earth . . . have drastically cut down all warlike preparations and concluded a firm and, I hope, unbreakable treaty of peace, I feel entitled to hope with confidence that not only the moral virtues and Christian piety but also true learning, purified of corruption, and the fine disciplines will revive and blossom forth. . . ." Erasmus penned this vision just one century before the advent of those religious wars which were to decimate the population of Europe and reduce its cities to smoking ruins. Happily he did not live to see the worst excesses of religious intolerance. As for himself, he stood for a humane kind of educational system, one in which there would be achieved a high synthesis of religious devotion tempered with the wisdom of antiquity. With the possible exception of Melanchthon, no Protestant educational reformer was more devoted to the ideal of unifying faith and reason and making them the interdependent foundations of learning.

Rare among his contemporaries, he was exquisitely sensitive to the need for enlisting schools in the pursuit of larger objectives than sectarian orthodoxy. He further understood that whatever the subject matter involved, whether sacred learning or secular, educational practice remained slave to drudgery and pedantry. "Look," he demanded, "at how your hard-plodding students, by a close sedentary confinement to their books, grow mopish, pale, and meagre, as if by a continual wrack of brains, and torture of inventions, their veins were pumped dry, and their whole body squeezed sapless." Teachers fared no better in his estimation. "I knew an old sophister," he satirically related, "who after threescore years' experience in the world had spent the last twenty of them only in drudging to conquer the criticisms of grammar, and made it the chief part of his prayers that his life might be spared until he had learned how rightly to distinguish between the eight parts of speech—which no grammarian had yet accurately done."[24] Unfortunately, his fellow Catholic educators were too concerned with the idea of education as religious indoctrination to worry much about the human costs involved or even to comprehend his criticisms of school practice. Beyond this, his vision of the Christian humanist as an educational

---

[24] Few observers would care to deny that both images are still very much a part of the contemporary educational scene.

image had to await a later day to receive a hearing, in an age when passions had cooled and the fires of sectarianism had subsided.

Much the same held true for Protestant educational thought too of course, although its protagonists could with equal facility perceive the shortcomings of prevailing pedagogical norms. Luther was quick to disparage the existing grammar schools for teaching the student "only enough bad Latin to become a priest and read Mass . . . and yet remain all his life a poor ignoramus fit neither to cackle nor to lay eggs." Universities, he avowed, were dens of murderers, temples of Moloch, synagogues of curruption; "nothing more hellish . . . ever appeared on earth . . . or ever would appear"; and he was satisfied that they were "only worthy of being reduced to dust." Lamenting the fact that in the German provinces schools were everywhere being allowed to go to ruin, Luther acidly complained that "princes and lords were so busily engaged in the high and important affairs of the cellar, the kitchen, and the bedchamber that they had no time" to support education.

More positively, Protestants held before them a lofty vision of what educational endeavor, rightly conducted, might accomplish. "Christian knowledge," according to Melanchthon, was knowledge of man's freedom from domination by the papist machinery of salvation. Secular learning, as taught in schools, ought to lead to "true and substantial wisdom" which consists of knowledge of the things of this world but also the things of God. Learning, Calvin affirmed, "is not only an incitement to seek after God, but likewise a considerable assistance towards finding Him." The true Christian diligently pursues his secular calling under established civil law. Schools exist to prepare the individual to take his place in the social and economic order, to foster habits of obedience, thrift, hard work, and sobriety. On another level, schools must teach people to read the Bible with understanding because it alone is the source of truth that sets man free. It reveals that man is justified by faith alone, that good works proceed from a righteous heart; it teaches the rules of human conduct and everything else necessary to the Christian life. On this all parties agreed, however much they disputed the particulars. In the final analysis, the greatest setback to meaningful education toward these ideals was the obsessive preoccupation of educators with such theological specifics. An analysis of the contemporary educational significance of these historic events must await closer inspection of the more worldly type of education that grew up just before and after the confessional interlude had passed.

SUMMARY

Several significant attempts were made to rebuild schools after the Roman empire disintegrated. One outgrowth of the survival of classical learning in Ireland was a limited reconstruction of schools throughout Britain in the seventh and eighth centuries. The so-called Carolingian Restoration under Charlemagne, Alcuin, and others aided in the spread of educational institutions in Frankish lands between 768 and 900. King Alfred of Wessex in England in the same way sponsored a cultural revival in the late ninth century which helped expand educational interests. A fully developed system of education under Church auspices did not begin to function until at least the eleventh century. Among its institutional forms must be counted the internal and external monastic and conventual schools, collegiate schools, chantry or stipendary schools, and lower and upper cathedral church schools. The secular system of education that grew up paralleling the religious one was composed of royal court schools, institutions for the conduct of chivalric training, burgh or municipal schools, and guild schools.

The university as a distinct institutional type had its origins in upper cathedral church schools, beginning late in the eleventh century. Its growth was closely tied to the development of scholastic theology, medicine, and law as organized subjects for instruction. Organized around teaching faculties and student nations, such universities as those at Paris, Bologna, Salerno, and Salamanca offered more advanced instruction than had ever previously been offered in Europe. Their effects, culturally and socially, on education were far-reaching. Some scholars allege they helped to accelerate the pace of social progress and hastened the end of the medieval period. Educational ideals up until the thirteenth century were a function of an elaborately constructed world view dominated by religious interests. Educational theory and practice were mainly concerned with other worldly values. Schools existed above all to train priests for their ministry. The sociopolitical context of all education supported the maintenance of a theocratic state, variously interpreted or reflected by the music, art, theology, economics, and political theory of medieval culture.

The sixteenth-century Protestant Reformation spelled the demise of the grand medieval synthesis, a consequence wholly unintended by religious leaders. The confessional age they ushered in contributed greatly to the rise of individualism, democracy, nationalism, capitalism, and even rationalism, though Luther, Calvin, Zwingli, and other reformers exhibited little sympathy for such movements. They probably remained unaware of the directions in which European life began to move. The essential theme that binds medieval and reformational education together was the continuing concern to use education in the furtherance of religious ends. Protestants and Catholics alike were quick to recognize that education was a potent tool for consolidating religious reforms. With the advent of the Catholic Counter-Reformation and the work done by new teaching orders such as the Ursulines, the Jesuits, the Jansenists, and the Brothers of the Christian Schools, education became a battle ground in the struggle for religious loyalties. Schools now became means to serve narrow doctrinal interests instead of educational concerns in the broader sense. Because Protestants and Catholics alike accepted the venerable ideal of a theocratic society but disagreed on whose version should prevail, the struggle for supremacy indirectly retarded as much as it aided the growth of educational institutions.

QUESTIONS FOR DISCUSSION

1. Suppose the Latin Church had not evolved as a temporal power in European affairs. What consequences might have followed for the development of education between the sixth and sixteenth centuries?

2. On the basis of your general knowledge of the period, how accurate is it to claim that medieval society was "more religious" than our own? How affected are contemporary social institutions, including education, by religious concerns?

3. Why did the Catholic Church vigorously oppose municipal control of burgh schools and yet sanction the chivalric education for knighthood which was equally secular in character?

4. If universities today were organized according to the medieval student nation-dominated pattern at Bologna and elsewhere, what consequence, good and bad, would follow for modern higher education?

5. Why do institutions of higher education today lay claim to certain privileges functionally similar to the *jus licentia docendi* and *cessatio*? Precisely what rights do universities claim for themselves? Are these claims fully justified?

6. Contrast early Jesuit teacher education with secular teacher-preparation programs today. What are the most important similarities and differences? Evaluate the claim of Aquaviva's committee that prospective teachers need a thorough grounding in methodology before they are allowed to teach on their own.

7. More books have been written about Martin Luther than about any other Christian figure, including Jesus Christ. Every age has been able to find in him a religious hero (or villain) suited to the time. Compare Roland Bainton's biography *Here I Stand*, with playwright John Osborne's depiction in *Luther*. Why is there perennial disagreement on Luther's place in history?

8. Was religious intolerance an inevitable feature of the post-reformational period? Upon what points might Catholic and Protestant educators have agreed? (Consider the latter question in light of Sturm's school at Strassburg.)

9. Could the Protestant Reformation have been averted? Would it have been desirable to do so? What might have been the educational results if Catholicism had succeeded in suppressing Protestantism? Consider the possible results for education if there had been no proliferation of confessional denominations; that is, if the Lutheran and Catholic churches had been the only contending groups. Might not the growth and development of their respective schools have taken a different course?

10. The correlative academic freedoms of teaching and learning had their origins in the evolving medieval university. Ever since, the concept of "academic freedom" has provoked controversy and confusion. Consider the following questions carefully and attempt to formulate your own answers to them:

a. Note that originally "academic freedom" referred to the corporate autonomy of the university *as an institution* and the collective rights of its personnel. Why has this concept now been extended to refer to the *individual* within the institution?

b. *Lehrfreiheit* ("freedom to teach") is most simply defined as the right of a university scholar to communicate the content of his discipline and to share the results of his research without restrictions or censorship. *Why* should a professor enjoy this right? What is the stronger argument on behalf of teaching freedom: the constitutionally guaranteed rights of free speech for the professor as private citizen, or the need for special dispensations in virtue of the nature of his professional activity? In other words, is his academic freedom a "right" or a "privilege," or both?

c. What limitations, if any, should be placed on the "extramural" utterances of the teacher, that is, his public remarks outside the classroom, in light of the argument that he is inevitably identified in the public mind as a spokesman for his institution?

d. Academic tenure (the right to hold an academic position indefinitely except in cases where it can be shown that the teacher is guilty of gross neglect of duty, disruptive conduct, or immoral and illegal behavior) and "due process" (provision for orderly hearings and procedures governing dismissals) have traditionally been regarded as the twin safeguards of academic freedom. Evaluate the argument that an alternative to the granting of tenure must be found because it allows incompetent teachers immunity from dismissal.

e. As a student you enroll in a course only to find that the instructor in charge is guilty of any or all of the following offenses: habitual tardiness or absence from class, unpreparedness, arbitrary and unfair grading practices, repeated introduction of totally irrelevant material, persistent refusal to answer questions, and insistence upon student agreement with positions taken by the instructor in class. What recourse do you have as a student? Do these offenses represent infringements upon your *Lernfreiheit,* your freedom to learn?

f. Suppose that your college or university enacts policies forbidding peaceful demonstrations or the extension of an invitation to speak on campus to someone deemed "subversive" by administration officials. Would such policies abrogate your *Lernfreiheit?* What about policies establishing mandatory residence in institutional dormitories, curfews, or forbidding coed "visitations" in student living quarters? In these latter cases, is any question of "student academic freedom" involved?

g. Should either professors or students enjoy special immunity from civil law, as they did in the early universities? May an institution of higher learning impose special *nonacademic* requirements on its faculty or students as conditions for being admitted to, or remaining in good standing with, the formal academic community?

h. What action on the part of students, teachers, or outside groups might represent an encroachment upon the *collective* academic freedom of a college or university?

i. What special limitations, if any, on academic freedom might be appropriate to a sectarian or denominational institution of higher learning? For example, should a teacher or student in a religious school be allowed to profess openly any agnostic or atheistic views?

j. Assess the argument that academic freedom cannot be allowed to protect an "irresponsible" individual who advocates heterodox or subversive opinions.

k. It is frequently alleged that secondary school or elementary school teachers should not enjoy the same measure of academic freedom as a professor in a collegiate setting, owing to the relative immaturity and impressionability of lower-school students. It is further argued that younger students cannot be allowed the prerogatives implied by *Lernfreiheit*. Analyze these positions.

l. Why does "academic freedom" pose important issues in the first place? Why are academic freedoms so frequently attacked, even by college and university graduates, sometimes by professors themselves?

5 Education for a Worldly Society

Reflecting now as to whence it came that in ancient times the people were more devoted to liberty than in the present, I believe that it resulted from this, that men were stronger in those days, which I believe to be attributable to the difference of education. . . .

NICCOLO MACHIAVELLI
The Discourses on Titus Livy

We must not forget that true distinction is to be gained by a wide and varied range of such studies as conduce to the profitable enjoyment of life.

LIONARDO BRUNI
Concerning the Study of Literature

THE RENAISSANCE

With the passing of the Confessional Age of religious reform, the medieval world view was irrevocably shattered. Its thrust to reconstitute the old theocratic ideal prevalent during the Middle Ages crumbled under a surging tide of nationalism and a spirit of individualism, whereas the unrealized Christian vision of a society united in peace and security under hierarchical authority faded in the harsh light of contemporary reality: divided authority, endemic war, and the disintegration of long-accepted beliefs. All of these were prevalent so long before the age of Luther, Calvin, Zwingli, and Loyola that it is tempting to view the sixteenth century's obsessive preoccupation with religious matters as an historical anachronism in its own time, as a temporary interlude within a broader movement away from the

271

medieval perspective beginning as early as the twelfth and thirteenth centuries. To the extent that the Reformation and Catholic Reformation can be understood as unsuccessful attempts to renovate traditional social and intellectual norms, they were a reaction *against* the gradual shift away from a religiously dominated culture toward a worldly one. Basically, changes in the way in which men looked at themselves in relation to the universe, and, consequently, alterations in the values considered important had been developing over several centuries. An important revolution in ways of thinking and believing had begun at least two or three hundred years before the final fragmentation of medieval Catholicism. As it gained momentum the transition from otherworldly to more secular concerns involved profound differences in social, political, economic, and intellectual life, all antipathetic to the reformational leaders' intentions.

The conventional term employed to denote the rise of worldliness ushering in the modern period is the *Renaissance* ("rebirth"), that time between the beginning of the fourteenth and the close of the fifteenth century. The label is misleading if it suggests a sudden cultural revival unrelated to such earlier forces as the growth of politically emancipated towns, the rise of commerce and trade, the replacement of guilds by bankers and entrepreneurs, the spread of universities, and the decline of other medieval institutions. Traditional scholarship has tended to exaggerate the novelty of the Renaissance in relation to the age immediately preceding it. For example, Jacob Burckhardt's classic study *The Civilization of the Renaissance in Italy*, first published in 1860, represented the rebirth as a decisive break with the medieval past. As the opening chapter of the modern era, Burckhardt claimed, it was a revolt against the asceticism, collectivism, and authoritarianism of the Middle Ages. Later research has tended to blur the lines separating the medieval period from the Renaissance and to deemphasize the decisiveness of the changes that took place. Furthermore, the revival beginning in Italy was only a part of much broader changes. Perhaps the most defensible generalization that can be made is that the dawning era was a time when man was rediscovering himself and his potential for self-development in this world.

Certain distortions are introduced, again, if the aspect of this movement known as the Renaissance is viewed primarily as an antireligious influence. Although it is true that those who helped bring about a cultural revival often bitterly criticized the Church, ridiculed the scholastics, and in other ways repudiated the *ancien régime,* their iconoclasticism is understandable. Owing to the so-called "Babylonian Captivity," the Great Schism, and the rapacious territorial ambitions of the Italianate papacy mentioned previously, the Church's over-all authority had greatly suffered. It became fashionable in German lands (to cite but one symptom of general dissatisfaction) to speak of "die tote Hand"—the dead hand—of the Church on economic progress. Scholars like *Rabelais* and *Boccaccio* never tired of poking fun at licentious priests, friars, and monks, though there is nothing to indicate they abandoned the conventional piety of their forefathers. Few professed doubts (at least publicly) about Christian belief even when they assailed its alleged institutional custodian. Nor were Renaissance men latter-day rationalists, as it was once fashionable to argue. They were never totally emancipated from the medieval tendency of looking for authoritative answers in the writings of their predecessors. They shared that same deference toward tradition and the love of abstract, deductive thought typical of the medieval schoolmen they so thoroughly detested; and their intellectual frame of reference was religious-humanistic, not scientific. Nonetheless, the change in tone was unmistakable. Renaissance thought, although not scientific, contributed to the scientific revolution by its interest in ancient culture and the standards of scholarship that came into play for handling the texts of antiquity. More broadly, the accent was placed on the practical and concrete instead of the abstract, on individualism instead of communalism, on the active rather than the contemplative side of life. All these tendencies helped to foster the growth of a lay, secularized society more congenial to scientific interests.

The Nature of Humanism

The keynote of the shift to worldliness, so well exemplified in the spirit of the Renaissance, was an emphasis on man. Pico della Mirandola's *Oration on the Dignity of Man* sang praises for human life as it can be lived upon earth without reference to any destiny in the hereafter. Pico has God address humanity with a reminder that it is free to answer the call of experience, "We have set thee at the world's center that thou mayest from thence more easily observe whatever is in the world. We have made thee neither of heaven nor of earth, neither mortal nor immortal, so that with freedom of choice and with honor, as though the maker and molder of thyself, thou mayest fashion thyself in whatever shape thou shalt prefer." Man, not God, became the center of the universe. The frank enjoyment of sensuous pleasure, the exaltation of secular life, the beauties and joys of life lived to its fullest—those were the themes now dominating European culture. Renaissance *humanism* (from *humanitas,* meaning "culture") as a habit of thought was intoxicated by a sense of opening vistas, a broader social and cultural horizon, the possibilities of self-realization freed from old bonds. Roland Bainton has suggested that the humanistic spirit was a reaction of Hellenic anthropomorphism against Hebraic theocentricity, better still, an exaggeration of Greek elements in the Christian synthesis.[1]

It is true that most humanists continued to live securely within the Aristotelian-Christian universe of striving and purpose, and assumed a moral

[1] See his "Man, God, and the Church in the Age of the Renaissance," in *The Renaissance* (New York: Harper Torchbook, 1962), pp. 77–96.

order in which evil actions brought down retribution from on high.[2] But in the frenzied enthusiasm for a world where the widest range of interests was made to revolve around man the individual, early humanists at least saw a need for compromise between the old and the new. They sensed a certain incongruity between elements of the Christian tradition and the emergent naturalistic, almost pagan view of man's life and its scene. Francesco di Petracco (1304–1374), the greatest representative of Renaissance humanism, reports how agonizing the choice between traditional piety and worldliness could become.

"A stubborn and still undecided battle," he confessed in his *Secretum*, "has been long raging on the field of my thoughts for the supremacy of one of the two men within me." His two men were the spiritual, otherworldly man of Augustine's *Confessions* and the worldly man of humanism who lusts after the beauties of nature. As in Augustine before him, the theme is one of divided loyalty: he felt caught between the authority of the old and the call of the new.

Petrarch, as he is more commonly known, was the son of a Florentine notary. He was an avid learner who plunged himself into the study of the humanities at Carpentras and law at Montpellier. He took ecclesiastical orders and was supported by a rich patron, Giacomo Colonna, of the famous Italian Colonna family. Freed from the need to make a living for himself, he ardently pursued his literary interests. Almost from the beginning, he was disdainful of the chief interests of the medieval past—monastic asceticism, arid scholasticism, academic legalism—and attracted to the glories of the past. He mourned his having been born out of his time, "Among the many subjects which interested me, I dwelt especially upon antiquity, for our own age has always repelled me. . . . In order to forget my own time I have constantly striven to place myself in spirit in other ages, and consequently I delighted in history." This delight led him far and wide in the search for traces of the classical past. Devoted above all else to the stately cadences of Ciceronian Latin, he was insatiable in his search for ancient Roman manuscripts, despite the indifference or hostility of some to this work.

His first major discovery, two previously unknown orations of Cicero, was made at Liège where they had lain mouldering for centuries in a monastic collection. Another of Cicero's letters was found a dozen years later at Verona. So enthusiastic was Petrarch over these discoveries that he launched a correspondence (necessarily one-sided) with the leading lights of the Greco-Roman age to inform them that once again men were learning from their writings. Petrarch devoted the remainder of his life to recovering, copying, and editing classical manuscripts, with time some-

2 Le Van Baumer, ed., "The Renaissance," in *Main Currents of Western Thought* (New York: Alfred A. Knopf, 1952), p. 109.

how reserved for writing hundreds of letters, lyrics, sonnets, and ballads in the vernacular language for popular consumption.

Petrarch's passion for Latin classics soon infected others. Massive fortunes were spent for manuscripts by such prominent figures as Pope Nicholas V and Niccoli, Cosimo de Medici, and Lorenzo the Magnificent. Wealthy merchants, princes, and bishops vied with one another in amassing collections of the works of Cicero, Quintilian, Tacitus, and the other writers of antiquity. Castles and monasteries all over Europe were ransacked for traces of an ancient culture that had again caught the imagination of men.

Before his death Petrarch summed up an attitude toward life that reveals a careful compromise between traditional piety and secularism. "There is a certain justification for my way of life," he wrote. "It may be only glory that we seek here, but I persuade myself that, so long as we remain here, that is right. . . . So this is the natural order, that among mortals the care of things mortal should come first; to the transitory will then succeed the eternal; from the first to the second is the natural progression." Some have called Petrarch "the first modern scholar and man of letters" or "the morningstar of the Renaissance," and his career seems to offer ample warrant for such appellations. The conception of culture as essentially *Studia humanitatis ac litterarum* (the study of humanity and letters), originally acclaimed by Cicero, became Petrarch's own. His love of classicism, equaled only by a passion for poetry celebrating earthly joys, was tempered by allegiance to the spiritual strictures of Augustine, his religious mentor. In these divided loyalties Petrarch represented the merging of disparate traditions that is termed Renaissance humanism. Three viewpoints, the classical, the medieval, and something else still unshaped, came together in a radically new perspective on man and the world he inhabited. Petrarch was among the first to sense how little the future need resemble the immediate past; others soon came to share that vision.

Humanism, considered as a general social and *intellectual* tendency, accentuated developments in process long before the Italian Renaissance began. Knowledge once united under the aegis of theology had begun to break up into its several compartments even before humanists explicitly rejected the scholastic synthesis. Far from seeing theology and philosophy in the relation of mistress and handmaiden, humanists viewed them as divergent, even contradictory quests for truth. The old epistemological problem of universals over which schoolmen had shed so much blood was abandoned in favor of questions of ethics, the nature of man, and freedom of the will. The idea of man's inherent sinfulness and the doctrine of the Fall of Man were at least implicitly rejected. In their place humanists emphasized man's protean nature, his possibilities for self-improvement. This latter idea, as will be seen, significantly influenced Renaissance thought on education, in addition to whatever force it had for religious and philosophical thought.

As a *religious* and *scholarly* movement, humanism was primarily a fusion of what Erasmus called "the philosophy of Christ" with the moral wisdom of the Greco-Roman tradition. It taught the importance of ethics over theological dogma, internal piety over external churchly observances. Its dominant mood was critical, well illustrated in the work of Nicolas of Cusa and *Lorenzo Valla* in exposing a document known as the *Donation of Constantine* which had long been used by the Church in support of its claims to temporal power. Emperor Constantine, so the claim ran, had made a gift of the western half of the Roman empire to Pope Sylvester I in gratitude for being cured of leprosy. Hence, the Church argued, there was historical precedent for its authority over all lesser earthly governments. Valla and others showed unmistakably that the *Donation* was filled with anachronisms, that it was at best a pious hoax perpetrated only a few hundred years earlier. The same spirit of scholarship was applied in producing better translations of the Vulgate Bible and in developing alphabetical dictionaries for foreign languages, lexicons, glossaries, grammars, and other analytical tools of inquiry. It questioned the legitimacy of medieval pilgrimages, the veneration of relics, and similar ecclesiastical customs of the Church, thereby helping to encourage the forces of religious reform.

In northern Europe, where emigrating scholars introduced the revival of learning begun in Italy, humanism tended to be more religious in tone than in southern regions. Humanist scholars like *Johann Reuchlin, Lefèvre d'Étaples,* and *John Colet* aspired to infuse Church and state with a greater sense of piety and moderation than either seemed to manifest on the eve of the Reformation. The new studies were first introduced by a Spanish scholar, Mebrissensis, at Seville and Salamanca around 1473. Two students of Italian scholarship, *Thomas Linacre* (1460–1524) and *William Grocyn* (1446–1514), brought Greek learning to Oxford where it was warmly received. The first German to study in Italy, so far as is known, was a *Peter Luder* (1415–1474), who tried with limited success to awaken an interest in classicism at Erfurt and Leipzig. More influential were two learned Dutch scholars, *Johann Wessel* (1420–1489) and *Rodolph Agricola* (1443–1485), who made Heidelberg a famous haven for humanist studies. These *"spare"* humanists, to use Crane Brinton's descriptive label, discovered in classicism the ideals of clarity, sobriety, moderation, and decorum. The "classical spirit" interpreted through this kind of humanism was a tendency to regard the regular, the universal, the uniform as a sort of standard for life. "Spare" humanism meant a habit of simplifying, with reverence for rules and formulas. Christian humanism, so considered, was a type of religious piety much better suited to an increasingly lay society than medieval religiosity. Its cultivation of *pietas literata* ("wise and eloquent piety") as the end product of scholarship and learning serves as a kind of hallmark of the Christian–humanist synthesis.

Religious humanism was more closely allied with the Renaissance program of *social reform* than the more secular version of humanism popular in Italy. It was a self-conscious rebellion against all that seemed stale, constricting, and obsolete within the old order. Humanists were in the vanguard of those trying to renovate society from top to bottom or at least to come to terms with a rapidly changing social system, symbolized by the turbulent politics of warring princes, novel forms of commercialism, the acquisitive economics of capitalism, and the machinations of the Church.

Southern, Italian humanism was predominantly (though not exclusively) a *secular* movement. It reached its greatest heights in the fifteenth century (the Italian *Cinquecento*), though it persisted well into the next two hundred years. Perhaps it was inevitable that Renaissance humanism should originate in Italy. Its inhabitants had been among the first to reconstruct a viable social political order after the floods of early medieval barbarism subsided, and their city-states were the first to benefit in wealth and prestige from the Crusades as well as the recovery of industry and trade. Surrounded constantly by the physical artifacts of the Roman Empire, Italians believed themselves to be the most direct heirs of the classical legacy. They were the first and most vigorous protagonists in the long struggle against the overbearing dominance of the Holy Roman Emperor and the papacy. These *"exuberant"* humanists, to borrow Brinton's happy phrase once again, were dynamic, Faustian spirits openly embracing the extreme individualism of the age they did so much to help bring about. Theirs was a restless, zestful rejection of tradition and authority whenever these seemed to threaten their pursuit of pleasure. The names of the great ruling houses suggest themselves: the Medici, the Borgias, the Sforzas, and the Viscontis—lusty leaders of the Renaissance, Machiavellian in demeanor, but liberal in their sharing of the fruits of power. They became great patrons of such artists as da Vinci and Cellini, who produced the magnificent paintings, sculpture, and architecture of the period. They may have been cruel, amoral, vulgar, but no one excelled them in their frankly pagan enjoyment of the life of the appetites. Their outlook was reflected in the motto over Rabelais' utopian Abbey of Thélème: *Fay ce que vous vouldras* ("Do what you will"). Whatever was brilliant and exciting about the Renaissance was owing to those bawdy, daring free spirits who rebelled against the cosmology of their predecessors and reinstated man as center and measure of all things. Shakespeare's *Romeo and Juliet* and *The Taming of the Shrew* distill something of their spirit.

Finally, enough has been said to indicate that humanism was an aesthetic *literary* movement. The search for cultural norms to replace those overthrown led back to the examples of antiquity. Humanists possessed, or, rather, were gradually coming to possess, what their medieval predecessors did not have, a knowledge of Greek. Interest in classic literature actually went back to the establishment of the universities when John of Salisbury collected poetical writings for his own edification. Dante, who preceded

Petrarch by only one generation, filled his writings with pagan references as well as Christian symbols. Evidently *some* knowledge of Greek and Latin authors was possible as early as the fourteenth century, but the spread of this knowledge took much longer. Outside of Ireland, the ability to read and write Greek had been extinct for half a millennium except among a few scattered scholars. One would think that Byzantine scholars fleeing from the Turks after the fall of Constantinople in 1453 might have brought Greek to the West rather quickly; actually it came gradually through less direct cultural contacts with the eastern Mediterranean world. In any case a revival of Greek studies followed hard upon the interest in Latin authors instigated by Petrarch, Flavio Blondo, Ciriaco of Ancona, and Poggio Bracciolini. It began in Italy when a Greek monk visited the pope as an ambassador from Constantinople in 1339 and again in 1342, bringing his knowledge of Greek with him.

The first and most distinguished among a flood of scholars in the fourteenth and fifteenth centuries who imported Greek language and literature to Europe was a Byzantine noble, *Manuel Chrysoloras* (1355–1415). Sent as envoy to Venice from the East because of his fame as a teacher of rhetoric at Constantinople, Chrysoloras remained in Italy at the invitation of Florentine scholars, accepting a post as professor of Greek letters at the University in Florence. He taught there for four years before moving to the University of Pavia. His pupils from both institutions became dedicated propagandists in behalf of the new learning. Their translations of the classics helped promote an enthusiastic if temporary rage for the works of Xenophon, Plutarch, Plato, Aristotle, Aeschylus, and Sophocles, a contagion that moved steadily northward when it began to subside in Italy. Guarino da Verona, for one, was untiring in his efforts to popularize the lost writings of classical Greece. Aruispa and Filelfo, other students of Chrysoloras, joined the ranks of such scholars as Theodorus of Gaza and *Demetrius Chalcondyles* in making translations of old manuscripts more readily available to the literate public. Never perhaps since the advent of the Sophists in Athens had there been so much ferment in learned circles. It required the entire fifteenth century for the Italians to assimilate or intellectually digest the restored treasures of Greco-Roman culture.

In the meantime a creative outburst of vernacular writings by authors infected with the humanistic spirit began to make itself felt. The new wave of literature, thoroughly courtly and aristocratic in its origins, was led by Florence, Naples, and Ferrara. Italians, more than anyone else, provided distinguished models of good literary form for the rest of Europe, in defiance of the tradition which held the use of the vernacular unsuited for literary usage. The *novelle* (short story) form became immensely popular, as did the pastoral romance and the romantic epic. One of the earliest works in Italian prose to reflect humanistic interests was Boccaccio's *Decameron,* but his *Ameto* and the *Ninfale Fiesolano* are also worthy of admiration as examples of the literary renaissance. His poems, translations of the classics, and prose soon found an avid audience everywhere. So too did Sannazaro's *Arcadia,* another illustrious illustration of how the pastoral romance as a literary form had been developed. The cause of vernacular writing as replacement for medieval Latin was indisputably advanced with the publication of epics by Pulci, Boiardo, and Ariosto. To be sure, the literary revival was not confined to Italy. In Spain Cervantes' *Don Quixote* was a masterly obituary for the antiquated ideals of chivalry. Camoen's *Lusiads* revealed how well the Portuguese could adapt the epic form for their own uses. In England authors were busily engaged in creating a native literature for the developing English language, seen in Chaucer's *Canterbury Tales,* the best example of the vernacular turned to literary usage, and Spenser's *The Faerie Queene,* which began as a direct imitation of Ariosto's style in the *Orlando Furioso.* The tradition of northern humanism with its special emphasis on Christian ethics was manifest in the English use of satire to belittle the great and exalt the lowly. Erasmus' *In Praise of Folly* had no equal in this respect, except possibly the *Letters of Dark Men* of Ulrich von Hutten, an attack on monkish ignorance, or Sebastian Brant's famed *Ship of Fools.*

The name of the French physician and monk *François Rabelais* (1494–1553) must not be omitted from a roster of humanist literary greats. His two major works, *Gargantua* and *Pantagruel,* constituted a devastating, sometimes hilarious exposure of medieval pedagogy. Rabelais was not the first to make a case for humanistic studies and methods, but he was certainly among the most effective. A good education, he argued, reflected a balance of physical pursuits and academic learning, enriched always by firsthand observation of the world. In place of scholastic studies, a man should learn Greek, Latin, Hebrew, Chaldee, and even Arabic. Subjects such as arithmetic, philosophy, music, geometry, history, and the various sciences should also be included. Education for actual living, according to Rabelais, must become something very different in an age fraught with rich possibilities for self-improvement and intellectual stimulation.

EDUCATIONAL AND CULTURAL IDEALS OF EARLY HUMANISM

The Educated Man

The transformation of European culture accompanying the shift to a more worldly society involved far more than popular contempt for medieval schoolmen, the veneration of Ciceronian Latin as an exemplary style, and a love of ancient learning and writings. It entailed the elevation of new cultural values, among these a passion for the things of this world, a sense of the beauties of nature, and an increased hope and confidence in the individual's capacity to free creative talent. Humanist thought fervently stressed the possibilities of self-improvement through education. "Believe me," said Erasmus, "men are not born, they are made." *"Educatio superat omnia."* "Handle the wax while it is soft, mould the clay while it is moist, dye the fleece before it gathers stains." This basic optimism regarding human nature is evident in a comment of the Italian Guazzo. "Nature," he wrote, "always tends to the best: so that of good parents ought naturally to come good children, and if it turns out sometimes otherwise, the fault is not to be imputed to nature. For if one looks advisedly into the matter, he shall see that for the most part it happened not by birth, but by the bringing up." Working on this assumption, humanists flooded bookstalls with educational treatises on the proper means and ends of education. Not since the days of the Greeks and Romans had so many taken pen in hand to address the perennial problems of educators. Among the writings of the period must be mentioned Pietro Paolo Vergerio's *On Liberal Studies* (1402), a controversial plea for the inclusion of Latin literature in a liberal education, Lionardo Bruni's *Concerning the Study of Literature* (1415), which expresses the humanist mania for ancient literature as well as the attention being paid to the education of women, Leone Battista Alberti's *On the Family* (ca. 1430), Aeneas Silvius' *On the Education of Youth* (1445), Battista Guarino's *On Teaching and Learning* (1459), and Maffeo Vegio's *On the Liberal and Moral Education of Children* (1450).

The ideal type was Cicero's statesman and Quintilian's "good man skilled in speaking," a man of moral and intellectual excellence fitted for life as a good citizen. In fleshing out their portrait of the idea, it was only natural that reformers should have recourse to the examples of the highest civilization they knew, the classical. What better way, they must have asked themselves, to usher in a new golden age than to reproduce the statesmen, the orators, the rhetoricians of ancient Rome? If the world was becoming ever more "Machiavellian," all the more reason to substitute for medieval abstractions the humanistic wisdom of antiquity as guide to high-minded action.

There was little if anything of the democratic spirit in the Renaissance ideal. Even the very titles of works on education (*The Education of a Christian Prince, The Governor, The Complete Gentleman*) evidence an aristocratic bias. Yet the humanist aristocracy did not entirely exclude the "base-born"; it was to be an elite of talent and style rather than an aristocracy of birth. "Nobility Dative, being truly derived and raised for itself," observed Thomas Milles in his *Catalogue of Honor* (1610) is to be more admired than "that which is Native and descended from another." Nevertheless, the interest of the humanists was fixed mainly on the kind of education required by a ruler or prince. Baldassare Castiglione's *The Courtier* comes to mind for its picture of the *novi homines* who were displacing the feudal nobility. An individual capable of adorning a kingly court and dispensing sage advice to his ruler must be a *homo universale,* a "universal man," developed fully in all his faculties. He was to be a skilled polymath in everything. Very few people, all things considered, could attain such a stringent ideal. Henry Peacham's *The Complete Gentleman* epitomized the transformation of the medieval knight into the "complete" Renaissance man and at the same time reveals how Hellenistic the change was: "Respect and honor are to be attributed to eloquence, whereby so many have raised their esteem and fortunes, as able to draw civility out of barbarism, and sway whole kingdoms." Clearly, the status of eloquent generalist as an educational product belonged to the few, not the many.

In Castiglione's thought the ideal man should reflect the classical rule of harmony or proportion among the claims of body, heart, and head. The character of proper education, accordingly, will mirror and minister to all three claims. This theme found fuller expression among the more sober-minded "spare" humanists than it ever did among "exuberant" humanists. The much broader theme underlying Renaissance man's idealized picture of himself is summed up in the Italian word *virtù.* It derives from the Latin *vir,* man, but emphasizes "virtue" as well as "manliness." "Talent" in the widest sense comes closest in meaning. *Virtù* was an upper-class ideal (one to which at least some gifted persons of lower origins might rise) descended partly from the ideals of chivalry. It was made to emphasize a code of conduct involving striving, pushing, competing for the development of all one's potential. "Whatever a man can be, that he should become."

The common interpretation of this maxim was apt to be promiscuous, because *any* quest to excel at something would suffice in a wild scramble of the talents, including those displayed in Don Juan's 1,003 female conquests. The joyful, fearless exercise of all man's powers involved in seeking *virtù* could express humanist exuberance in an astonishing variety of forms— bestial drunkenness, benign abstinence, or a pleasant temperance. The cultivation of every natural impulse could and often did lead to excess. Certain humanists at least seemed to yearn romantically for the overpowering, the heroic, and perhaps because of this there is a sense of strain in the lusty rowdiness of a Rabelais or the frenetic activism of a Cellini. On the other hand, the exuberant expression of the Renaissance ideal with its attempt to transcend all limitations could, paradoxically, mask a special humility. "You follow infinite objects," said Cosimo de Medici, "you place your ladders in the heavens, I on earth, that I may not seek so high or fall so low." The ideal was an anthropocentric one insofar as it set up the full, complex human being as a standard for thought and conduct, but in one sense it was not nearly so ambitious as the medieval aspiration to bind all creation within the confines of an intellectual system. Medieval man sought to comprehend the divine; the natural man of the Renaissance rested content if he found himself. The flavor of the humanist ideal was also unmistakably hedonistic—"Let us enjoy the papacy," said Leo X, "now that God has given it to us"— and its morals were tolerant enough. "If we are not ourselves pious," Pope Julius II remarked, "why should we prevent other people from being so?"

The divergent stream of northern, spare humanism was more austere in tone. Castiglione's stress on balance in the art of living was carried further in the gentle, academic humanism of an Erasmus, More, or Montaigne. The counterpoint to concern for a happy, wholesome enjoyment of the goods of human life was a greater degree of reverence for the Greek ideal of moderation and a golden mean. Like their Faustian compatriots, northern humanists were persuaded of the superiority of the natural life over medieval formalism, convention, and sacerdotalism. Yet the ideal of human excellence they respected was not that of *virtù,* nor did they view the overthrow of medievalism as an invitation to abandon all guidelines for living. Their humanism was more akin to the Puritan ethic of middle-class virtues: self-discipline, seriousness, diligence, and Stoicism. Not prodigal excess but moderation was the end served by education in the well-rounded development of mind and body. In the end it was this ideal of the educated man that most directly influenced humanist educational theory, even though it did not long prevail in actual practice.

Education for Worldliness

The diffuse but insistent yearning for a fuller and larger life outside the confines of old modes of thought and practice first made its influence felt in education at the courts of wealthy patrons inclined toward the revival of learning. Florence, in particular, became one of the main centers for literary savants with the establishment under princely patronage of a humanistic university in 1348. The *Platonic Academy,* a self-conscious imitation of its Athenian predecessor, was opened during the reign of Lorenzo de Medici to further the spread of a Christian Platonism. Academies organized after the Florentine model quickly began in Padua, Venice, Naples, and Rome and served to popularize classical studies. By and large, existing Italian schools (except for the universities) appear to have responded eagerly to the renewed interest in Latin and Greek.

Most likely, the treatises of Vergerio (*On Liberal Studies* and his exposition of Quintilian's *Education of an Orator*) helped to call attention to the fundamental ideals of humanistic education. The uncompromising stand for a broadly based curriculum and an awareness of the need to vary instruction for individual students, expressed in Quintilian, became mandates for Christian liberal education in Vergerio's proposals. Most educators of the fifteenth and sixteenth centuries were familiar with his work. The course of study recommended was basically a modification of the seven arts, yet the faint beginning of interest in science is evident also in his attitude toward the subjects of the *Quadrivium.* "The knowledge of nature," Vergerio observed, "the laws and the properties of things in heaven and in earth, their causes, mutations and effects—this is a most delightful and at the same time most profitable study for youth." There is nothing yet of the enthusiasm for natural science evident in later curricular proposals, but at least a beginning had been made in widening the curriculum beyond the study of logic, language, and literature.

Vergerio's theoretical work was realized in practice a few years later by a remarkable practitioner of humanistic education, *Vittorino da Feltre* (1378–1446), who has been often lauded as "the first modern schoolmaster." (The term flatters some modern educators.) More than any other single individual of the Italian revival, Vittorino translated the essential spirit of educational reform into concrete realities. Some of his innovations compare favorably with the most progressive tendencies in public education today. He seems to have been one of those rare gifted individuals (like Froebel, Pestalozzi, and Montessori in later centuries) endowed with a natural capacity for adopting theory to practice successfully. In Vittorino one finds an excellent illustration of Renaissance education at its best.[3]

The Schoolmaster of Mantua

Vittorino had studied for some time at Padua under Giovanni de Ravenna, a pupil of Petrarch and probable custodian of Petrarch's library at the university, during the time Chrysoloras was teaching Greek at Florence. Vittorino shared in the ferment over classical studies at Padua, soon attracting attention as a Latin stylist in his own right. After receiving his arts degree and completing further work in mathematics (then an unrecognized subject in university study), he taught grammar for two decades before pursuing Greek at Venice. At the age of forty-five, probably dissatisfied with his initial attempt to found a school in that city, he was persuaded by the Marquis of Mantua, Gianfrancesco Gonzaga, to undertake the education of his five children. Gonzaga vacated a palace adjoining the royal mansion, which he called *La Gioisa* ("House of Pleasure"), to house Vittorino's new school, now renamed *La Giocosa,* designating a place of learning. From the very beginning it was clear that a model institution would be created. Around the physical plant, gardens were landscaped to provide an idyllic, pastoral setting for the new school. Nothing was spared in providing facilities for instruction. So many wealthy noble families hastened to enroll their sons that Vittorino shortly had over seventy pupils boarded under his tutelage. Almost half of the students (at Vittorino's insistence) came from poor families and were given free lodgings, meals, and tuition. *La Giocosa's* first master was determined to introduce an equalitarian note into what might

3 See William Harrison Woodward, *Vittorino da Feltre and Other Humanist Educators* (London: Cambridge University Press, 1921), and also his *Studies in Education During the Age of the Renaissance* (London: Cambridge University Press, 1906).

otherwise have been a very aristocratic boarding school. His pupils, of both sexes, ranged from six to twenty-seven years of age.

Careful, lengthy study of Latin and Greek authors, instruction in Latin declamation and composition, and reading from the histories of Plutarch and Livy formed the basis of the curriculum. To these pursuits was added the study of Biblical passages, writings of the Church fathers, and various sermons. No provision for vernacular instruction was made, however. Choral singing and dancing helped provide recreational interludes in the regimen of studies as did classes in drawing—all radical departures from established usage. Indicative of the courtly, chivalric strain in Vittorino's educational orientation, games and exercises were introduced as a regular part of the daily routine. These innovations drew scholars to Mantua from all parts of southern Europe to observe the school. Other schools were begun along similar lines, but few enjoyed Vittorino's success and none fully attained in practice the curricular breadth or comprehensiveness of aim realized in his *Giocosa*. The fact was that Vittorino's practices represented something genuinely new in his own day. Recognition of the simple truths that children learn best in pleasant surroundings, that play can be effectively conjoined to work, that good bodily health is basic to efficient learning, and that, as Woodward puts it, a school must become a community created a striking contrast between the Mantua school and others in operation elsewhere. Vittorino's concern for character building and his intent to produce scholars ennobled with a sense of social conscience were reflected in his methods. First and foremost, he understood how important it was to individualize instruction as much as possible in helping to develop the talents of each student. Secondly, Vittorino departed from the usual tendency to regard teaching as transmission of content instead of seeing it as a skill, as a set of techniques to be developed. Though he knew that "discipline" had to be learned if the student was to become a dutiful, complete citizen schooled in the classical literatures, it could be fostered in humane ways. Much attention was given to making learning as enjoyable as possible. Vittorino could scarcely have fit the popular schoolmaster's image decried in Petrarch's scathing criticism: "Let those . . . teach who like disorder, noise, and squalor; who rejoice in the screams of the victim as the rod falls gaily, who are not happy unless they can terrify, flog, and torture." The melancholy truth is that until very recent times the general horror described here has been more faithful to the actual conduct of formal schools than would be a description of Vittorino's house of learning. This is not to say that the educational program at Mantua was without fault; in many respects it was deficient. But the revival of music and physical exercise within the curriculum set a good precedent for instruction in these areas in later centuries. Vittorino's break with the tradition holding liberal studies as "merely" preprofessional training rather than as important subjects in themselves also created a precedent for other educational experiments. The idea that moral character should be a primary concern for the educator, especially when he is involved in training society's leaders, had too often been neglected before Vittorino's time. For those with discerning eyes, the result, a disintegrating religious and civic leadership within the social structure, had long been evident.

Guarino da Verona

Another humanist educator of note was an older contemporary of Vittorino, *Guarino da Verona* (1374–1460). He is remembered primarily for having studied under Chrysoloras while the latter still resided in Constantinople and for having brought back to his native Verona several translations of Greek manuscripts. During his tenure as professor of Greek at Ferrara, Guarino also drafted numerous important translations, among these the commentaries on Persius, Plutarch's *Lives,* a work by Strabo, and writings by Martial, Aristotle, Cicero, and Juvenal. His reputation as an educator depends on a short treatise authored by his youngest son, *Battista Guarino,* a description of his father's pedagogy entitled *On Teaching and Learning.*[4] It is taken from the elder Guarino's work at the court of Marquis Niccolo in Ferrara where he supervised the education of the despot's son for a number of years. Like the school of Mantua, the palace or court school at Ferrara stimulated considerable interest from scholars abroad. They came from as far away as Germany and England to absorb firsthand the humanistic learning incorporated in the curriculum. The great humanist Agricola, for example, is thought to have spent four years at Ferrara under Battista after the latter had succeeded his father as schoolmaster.

With Guarino, the beginnings of a degeneration in educational theory and practice begin to appear, a kind of declension that plagued later humanistic thought. Unlike Vittorino, there are signs in Battista's work that knowledge of the classics was coming to be regarded solely as a self-sufficient end instead of basically the means to a balanced, well-rounded personality. What might have been a salutary concern for the *forms* learning should take seemingly overshadowed concern for the *content* of education at Ferrara. "I have noted," wrote the younger Guarino, "that ability to write Latin verse is one of the essential marks of an educated person. I wish now to indicate a second which is of at least equal importance, namely, familiarity with the language and literature of Greece." Greek and Latin as formal studies might be entirely unobjectionable except that Guarino makes it clear he is more interested in teaching grammatical rules and stylistic form than literature itself. The danger of attaching an exaggerated value to proficiency in the use of language was always implicit in humanism; now it began to show itself in the ways classical learning was transmitted through the schools. Even today educators are painfully learning

---

[4] Sometimes more accurately translated as *On the Method of Teaching and of Reading the Classical Authors.*

anew that verbal skills are not the only important ones to be developed through schooling. Growing recognition that modern education has unwittingly emphasized verbal learning and skills associated with language usage is stimulating interest in other significant kinds of abilities. Diagnostic and evaluation instruments commonly used today have repeatedly been shown to favor a relatively narrow range of skills. The interest in recent years has been to broaden the development of human potential through new testing devices, curricular forms, and pedagogical techniques.

The Decline of Southern Humanism

Later Italian Renaissance educators fell prey to the same disastrous involvement with form and style coloring Guarino's perspective. Perotti's grammatical texts, for instance, greatly elaborated the forms through which language studies were conducted. Pedantic admiration for Cicero's style was carried to such absurd lengths that by the end of the fifteenth century there were Ciceronian scholars who refused to use any words or constructions not used by the master. A major controversy arose, ironically reminiscent of the schoolmen's debates in medieval universities, between those like *Politian* who refused to ape Cicero as the sole model for composition and those like *Pietro Bembo* (1470–1547), the Venetian "prince of stylists," who was an absolute purist worshipping at Cicero's shrine.[5] This loss of vision of the original purposes of scholarship and rigid formalism, sometimes referred to as *Ciceronianism,* provided endless targets for ridicule among saner humanists.

Educationally, overemphasis on language affected schooling. Succeeding generations of educators after the Guarinos lost the creative spirit stirred originally by classical literature and confined themselves to the joyless analysis of literary forms and rules. Just as in the late Hellenistic period when students were condemned to memorizing trite maxims or copybook phrases culled from the wisdom of Roman writers (the *sententiae* of the *ludus* school text and the *exempla* of the rhetorical schools), humanist schools apparently found nothing more important to teach than grammatical formulas. Textual criticism, not appreciation of content, the rules of Quintillian, not his breadth of vision, became the dominant themes. There is some truth in Randall's assessment of the consequences:

These things doomed Europe to centuries of schooling in the polished and studied but meagre literature of Rome, to a formal and barren preoccupation with the bones of language, with style engraved on mediocre thought, to the sodden horrors of imitation Horace and

[5] Bembo went so far as to advise shunning portions of the Bible because they might spoil one's appreciation of Ciceronian style. Interestingly, his personal ambitions finally won over his scholarly persuasions. When Pope Paul III offered him a cardinal's hat, Bembo renounced classical studies and assumed a position as bishop of Bergamo and Gubbio.

veneer Virgil; if they did not stifle scientific thought, they at least guaranteed that no school boy should hear of it. In countless ways the world has paid dearly for the revival of learning.[6]

Northern Humanist Education

The decay of humanist educational theory and practice in northern Europe was just as marked, but it did not occur quite so rapidly as in Italy. Humanism seemed to answer to the vague yearnings for better modes of life in most of the areas where it was introduced, despite the schools' failure to respond to the changing spirit of the times to any noticeable degree until classicism, and more generally the whole revival of learning, had long been accepted by the learned classes. It seems accurate to claim that most formal educational institutions continued well into the sixteenth century to monopolize their students' energies with the study of Church Latin and the traditional grammatical pursuits. However, enthusiasm for classical studies as well as something of the secular spirit typical in Italy did find fertile soil in many places, including the aristocratic, upper-class schools of England. These secondary-level institutions, peculiarly called *"public" schools* although they were conducted under private auspices, were begun with the founding of Winchester in 1382 by William of Wykeham. The superiority of their instruction warranted their reputation as fit preparatory centers for society's future leaders. Perhaps because they were relatively free from outside interference, they most readily embraced the new learning imported by scholars educated in Italy. Judging from the way classes were conducted and reports of the subjects taught, Scottish secondary schools in particular led the way in educational innovation. The barbarisms of medieval Latin were replaced by purer models from the classical period. Antique literature almost completely supplanted the Patristic writings as a major subject of study, that is, until the Reformation. Some of the pedagogical techniques in favor at the better Italian courtly schools were adopted with considerable success.

Humanistic studies first found favor among educators in the Netherlands. It should be recalled that in Italy, no strong centralized government developed in the face of pressures from the papacy and the incursions of French invaders. The various Italian cities grew up as autonomous states, each with its ruling family. Almost every school worth mentioning that appeared between the thirteenth and sixteenth centuries either was directly connected with a ruler's court or was founded under his paronage. The situation in the Netherlands, indeed virtually everywhere in Europe, was different. Effective political authority was established throughout broad regional areas, thereby removing the need for protection under feudal nobles while at the same time enabling cities to expand their various activities.

[6] John Herman Randall, *Making of the Modern Mind* (Cambridge, Mass.: Riverside Press, 1954), p. 121. Quoted with permission.

Guild and burgh schools as products of this urban life gradually became extremely important factors in the extension of educational opportunities to all classes throughout the late fifteenth and early sixteenth century. Most of these schools offered little more than a rudimentary, elementary-level kind of education but it was in the vernacular, which rendered it appropriate for the working classes, and it was available to anyone able to pay tuition charges. As early as 1391, for example, the English monarch Richard II denied a petition from the House of Commons that children of common parentage be barred from burgh schools even though their parents could afford the entrance fees. The same arrangement held true in the Netherlands, owing to the impressive influence of municipal schools partially supported by prosperous merchants. The cities' school systems were so well developed in fact that some institutions were beginning by the 1500's to offer the equivalent of a secondary education to constituents. The impact of the revival of learning is apparent in the fact they were called *Latin grammar schools,* because advanced instruction had been renovated to reflect interest in literary studies derived from the Greco-Roman period.[7]

The ready welcome given humanism by town schools can also be accounted for in the pioneering work of the Brethren of the Common Life—not that its members were necessarily all humanists by persuasion, but they did organize institutions thoroughly and they were open to the possibilities inherent in curricular proposals launched by humanist scholars. Above all, grammar as a subject of study had rarely subordinated the study of literature; this naturally created an atmosphere congenial to the less formal strain of classicism. As is often the case, a few important individuals, rightly placed, could exercise disproportionate influence in affecting the direction education would take. *Alexander Hegius,* for one, who served as headmaster of the Brethren's school at Deventer between 1465 and 1498, was an enthusiastic convert to humanism. "To the Greeks," he exclaimed in his treatise *On the Usefulness of Greek,* "we are indebted for everything." Because the schools of the Brethren were far superior to other schools during this period and the ablest students everywhere enrolled in them, the convictions of Hegius counted for something. No records survive that reveal how his passion for Hellenism was mirrored in the Deventer curriculum, but it is known the Brethren's school at Liège around the end of the fifteenth century was patterned closely on Hegius' model. An eight-year sequence of studies began with Latin grammar and selected prose readings, introduced the study of Greek and history in the fourth year, and continued with advanced teaching of Greek literature and composition. Between the sixth and seventh years, a student was given logic, rhetoric, Euclid, Roman law, and more Greek. The last two years were devoted to philosophy and

---

[7] The name *Latin grammar school* is not as significant in this respect as it might appear, however, because the only real curricular change was the teaching of classical instead of Church Latin.

theology. A large staff of teachers was employed at Liège, where none of the classes was allowed to exceed ten students. Older pupils were employed to assist teachers in routine assignments and to help supervise classes. There is some reason to believe this school pattern obtained widely in those Brethren schools where humanism infiltrated. Liège, with an enrollment of over two thousand, remained the largest school of its kind.

Interest in a literary revival in France began as a byproduct of invasions into Italy launched by Charles VIII and Louis XII between 1494 and 1512. Politically, the temporary occupations of cities like Florence, Naples, Rome, and Milan were an abysmal failure, but culturally they were important because the retreating armies carried back the new learning. Libraries, a royal press, and schools were set up to promote humanism when Francis I took the throne resolving to support arts and letters. Typical of the work being done was the reorganization of a town school at Bordeaux in the early 1500's. The *Collège de Guyenne*, as it was called, was known for its extensive library holdings, well-educated teachers, and a liberal curriculum rarely equaled north of the Alps. At a higher level the famed *Collège de France* at Paris opened its doors to offer instruction in Latin, Greek, and even Hebrew. Lesser municipal colleges spread throughout southern France, although not in the north where religious controversy accompanying the outbreak of the Reformation made the founding of schools almost impossible. Indicative of the favor humanism won among the noble classes was the appointment of a humanist scholar, *Guillaume Budaeus* (1467–1540), as royal librarian in 1522. His dictum that all men, even kings, should devote themselves to the liberal culture of Greek and Latin won widespread assent in courtly circles.

The humanist revival in German lands began, as was mentioned earlier, as a movement within such universities as Tübingen, Leipzig, Heidelberg, and Vienna. It was serviced by a small but growing number of scholars convinced that the future lay with the radical overhaul of traditional curricula. Despite vigorous opposition from fanatics like Johann Pfefferkorn (a Jewish convert to Christianity who argued the best way to convert Jews to Christianity was to deprive them of their literature), the learned humanist scholar *Johann Reuchlin* (1455–1522) prevailed in his celebrated struggle to make the study of Hebrew part of the German universities' curriculum.[8] Newly founded universities at Wittenberg, Königsberg, Marburg, and Jena were soon organized around classical studies and did much to insure the eventual triumph of humanism over scholasticism in German higher education. Aside from the introduction of Latin studies in German secondary schools

---

[8] Reuchlin was summoned before Emperor Maximilian to defend his contention that chairs of Hebrew be instituted at every German university. His opposition accused him of heresy and complicity in a Jewish plot aimed at subverting Christian truth. The controversy was submitted to the universities for a judgment which proved hostile to Reuchlin. In the end it required a papal decision on his behalf before Hebrew studies were allowed at Tübingen and Heidelberg.

founded by the Brethren of the Common Life, there was a strong movement to instigate classical training at commercial city schools in such diverse locations as Bremen, Hamburg, Strassburg, Ilfeld, Dantzig, and Nuremberg. Except for Sturm's *Gymnasium* at Strassburg and its imitators, humanistically oriented secondary schools met with a poor reception from the burgher classes. They correctly saw that liberal studies offered at best a circuitous preparation for a successful business career. What they demanded was vernacular instruction in commercial subjects, not formal instruction in Greek, Latin, or Hebrew literature. The outcome was an unfortunate cleavage in German education persisting for centuries: on the one hand, elementary vernacular schools, burgher writing schools, and business institutions for the commercial class and, on the other, Latin secondary schools for the intellectual aristocracy.

Humanism in England, first introduced at Oxford by Linacre, Grocyn, and Colet in the last decade of the fifteenth century, failed to make much headway except in the colleges of English universities until Henry VIII and Elizabeth I lent support to a literary revival at the royal court. Their interest in university reforms began a drive to convert Cambridge and Oxford from preparatory schools for scholastic theologians into schools where secular political leaders might obtain a professional education. John Colet's revamped *St. Paul's School* in London set the pattern for humanist secondary education in English lands. Its course of study based on William Lily's *Latin Grammar* (a famous text for generations, whose popularity surpassed that of Donatus) provided an exemplary education in classical and religious education, through which passed a succession of brilliant clerics, scholars, statesmen, and men of letters. Despite denunciations of heresy by the Bishop of London, Colet's alleged "temple of heathenism and idolatry" won so much popular favor that within a century almost every English secondary school had fallen under its influence. *Richard Mulcaster* (1531–1611), headmaster of the famous Merchant Taylor's School in London, was typical in his advocacy of physical sports, games, music, drawing, and classical Greek and Latin as the foundations of the secondary curriculum.

A multitude of factors aside from humanism help explain the gradual expansion of schooling everywhere in Europe in the fifteenth and sixteenth centuries. In Switzerland the unique form of democratic self-government practiced in the cantons encouraged public concern for universal literacy. If even commoners were to have a say in the halls of power, it was thought necessary they be given an opportunity to learn to read and write. A combination of private schools, municipal schools, and religious institutions served this end. Economic reasons undoubtedly prompted support for vernacular schools in areas where merchants' associations discovered they were essential for maintaining a supply of clerks, bookkeepers, and accountants. The invention of printing with movable type in the 1400's and better paper inevitably facilitated the exchange of information as books became both cheaper and more plentiful. It has been shown how the Protestant Reformation lent urgency to the need for literacy because reading the Bible now became a religious obligation—an activity possible only if one had received some education. When all of these civic, economic, and religious reasons are considered, it can be seen how varied were the forces shaping the character of education in a worldly society.

LATER HUMANIST EDUCATIONAL THOUGHT

Erasmus

There is ample justification for considering *Desiderius Erasmus* of Rotterdam (1466–1536) the most significant literary scholar and educational theorist of the early sixteenth century. He, more than anyone else, worked out the underlying arguments supportive of practical efforts by practitioners like Hegius and countless others whose names have not survived. Erasmus looms the largest among those endeavoring to give a Teutonic cast to humanist learning, to make it a vital force within northern schools. Just as the Englishman Mulcaster was later to remark that he loved Rome, but London better, favored Italy but England more, Erasmus perceived that if the revival of learning was to have any lasting effect in northern Europe, it would have to be given a new expression more appropriate to the changing social context. "In my youth," he reflected, "such gross barbarism prevailed in our Germany that it was counted heresy to have anything to do with Greek literature. For this reason I have tried in my own feeble way to raise the young people from the mire of ignorance to pure studies. I have not written for Italy but for Holland, Brabant and Flanders." In this, his success was unarguable.

Erasmus was born at Gouda, and began his formal education there. After an inauspicious start, he continued at the church school in Deventer where, despite his aversion to memorizing "foolish Latin verses," he came to appreciate classical learning then beginning to shape the Brethren's school. He remained for nine years as a student of Hegius and his assistant, Johannes Sinthius. At his father's request he studied for a monastic career at Hertogenbosch and was ordained a priest in 1492. His first assignment as private secretary to the Bishop of Cambrai proved fortunate because it allowed him to pursue his studies, initially at St. Gregory's at Steyn and finally at the University of Paris. The pervasive devotion to scholastic studies then typical at Paris had little attraction for the young Erasmus. However, the sojourn offered valuable opportunities to meet and talk with several important humanist reformers in attendance. In 1499 he accepted an invitation from a kindred spirit, Lord Mountjoy, to return with the latter to England. During his brief visit he met the leading lights of the humanistic movement at Oxford, an experience which fired him with an ambition to further his own classical studies. Following a six-year period in Paris and other cities, he went back to England to accept a teaching assignment with the sons of the royal physician, Baptista Boerio. The task provided him with a long-awaited chance to visit Italy, home of the revival of learning. In company with Boerio's sons, Erasmus studied at Turin and later at Bologna, earning a Doctor of Divinity degree and completing his study of Greek. He then returned to England filled with a desire to share his learning with others under the benign patronage of the new reigning monarch, Henry VIII. The next four years were spent assisting Dean Colet at St. Paul's and teaching Greek at Cambridge. A period of literary activity at Basle was followed by a brief stay in Louvain from 1517 to 1521, during which time his literary reputation was gradually spreading through all of Europe. Sectarian strife finally dictated a return to Switzerland where he remained for the last few years of his life.

There is in Erasmus that characteristic concern for a common "culture of the mind" derived from both Christianity and Greco-Roman thought so characteristic of spare humanism. No one believed more deeply than he that "a man ignorant of letters is no man at all," but he was unwilling to suppose liberal knowledge is sufficient by itself; it has definite ends to realize in the life of an educated man. "The first and most important part of education," he avowed, "is that the youthful mind may receive the seeds of piety; next that it may love and thoroughly learn the liberal studies; third, that it may be prepared for the duties of life; and fourth, that it may from the earliest days be accustomed to the rudiments of fine manners."[9] Those four qualities, piety, love of learning, fitness for public life, and personal style, distinguish the ideally educated man, as discussed throughout his many writings on education, including *The Education of a Christian Man, On the Liberal Education of Boys from the Beginning,* and *On the Right Method of Instruction.*

Erasmus would have agreed with Augustine's rueful admission that if he were faced with the choice of death or returning to primary school, he would choose death. Like others before him, he detested those masters— "school tyrants"—who "expect their little pupils to act as though they were but diminutive adults." Erasmus had little patience with schoolmasters who hammered grammatical rules into children's heads without allowing them a chance to speak Greek or Latin and see how the rules applied. The result, he fumed, was wayward teachers who caused children "to hate learning before they know why it should be loved." The only way of acquiring the power of speaking a language, he said, was not by learning rules, "but by daily intercourse with those accustomed to express themselves with exactness and refinement, and by copious reading of the best authors."

9 Consult William Harrison Woodward, *Erasmus Concerning Education* (London: Cambridge University Press, 1904), pp. 73 ff.

Furthermore, learning should be a pleasurable experience: "By the teacher's gentleness and courteous behavior . . . by his wit and subtle practice . . . he shall choose diverse pretty means to make learning pleasant to a child and pull him away from the feeling of hard labor."

In an almost Rousseaulike passage Erasmus recognized the value of natural and spontaneous involvement of the learner as an effective teaching technique. "Lead the beginner to face his unfamiliar matter with self-confidence," he urged, "to attack it slowly but with persistence. We must not underrate the capacity of youth to respond to suitable demands upon the intelligence. . . . The child," he continued, "like every other creature, excels in the precise activity which belongs to it . . . follow nature, therefore, in this, and so far as is possible take from the work of the school all that implies toilsomeness, and strive to give to learning the quality of freedom and enjoyment."

The too common practice of divorcing language studies from the world of experience, Erasmus believed, could be remedied by combining the teaching of classical literature with instruction in many other subjects, including geography, agriculture, mythology, history, astronomy, and so on. The larger end of a generous education is the growth of intelligence and an increase in knowledge about the world. Progress toward these goals is affected by three factors: an "innate capacity for being trained, partly native bent towards excellence"; training itself, or "the skilled application of instruction and guidance" involved in pedagogy; and practice to reinforce what is taught. The significance of Erasmus' careful analytic discussion of educational technique resides not in these now-pedestrian distinctions so much as in the fact that he paid attention to methodological considerations in the first place. It is almost as though most early humanist educators knew full well *what* they hoped to achieve but remained indifferent to questions about *how* they would go about it. The intense concern for effective methodology in Erasmus' thought was something of a novelty in his time.

Very much like Luther he further saw the fundamental *social* importance of education. His stress on a parental obligation to educate children ("Your children are begotten not to yourself alone but to your country: not to your country alone but to God") might have been taken from one of Luther's tracts, so closely does the rationale follow. The state's responsibility for founding educative agencies is also similar to the Lutheran position: "It is a public obligation," he declared, "in no way inferior to the ordering of the army." As for securing qualified teachers, "it ought to be public care and charge." On the latter point, it must be said, Erasmus was a tragic figure, a voice crying in the wilderness of religious warfare and hatreds aroused by the Lutheran revolt. The all-pervading confusion brought about by clashes between Protestants and Catholics guaranteed for some time that state officials would be unable to make any provision for formal schools.

Erasmus seems to have been more dedicated to the concept of liberal education than was Luther, even though the latter's own proposals endorsed humanistic learning. His refusal to follow Luther's break with Catholicism, despite their common hostility toward ecclesiastical abuses and doctrinal developments, may conceivably have reflected Erasmus' stronger belief that proper education would help reform the Church. Furthermore, though both aimed to foster piety through learning, Luther was quick to attack those humanists who rejected his religious stand—sometimes scorning their scholarship in the process. Erasmus had some justification for his lament that in areas where Lutheranism prevailed, learning was neglected. Luther "heaps hatred and contempt on the classical studies," he complained, "and that is fatal to us without being helpful to him." Phrased differently, Luther was willing to allow humanistic studies if they fostered religious truth; Erasmus took more seriously the idea that classical education, rightly directed, *would* lead to piety.

The fatal flaw in Erasmus' educational position was its aristocratic disregard of vernacular languages and apparent lack of interest in the needs of people destined to pursue careers outside the halls of academia or courtly circles. Classical language and literature could never fulfill their requirements for a worldly education. There is no denying that Erasmus' school texts and educational treatises were enormously helpful. He was brilliant when attacking an already dying medieval culture and scorning its educational canons. Nevertheless, what he failed to see was that however noble and elevated might be the classical ideal, it could not offer much to the vast majority of people who needed a broader interpretation of humanistic tenets. The new forms of knowledge then appearing which had no direct connection with Greco-Roman life needed to be brought into the mainstream of popular education, but this Erasmus neglected to do. Even *Juan Luis Vives* in the generation following Erasmus, who did so much to broaden humanism in its educational bearings, offered little that was relevant to schooling for men doing the ordinary work of society. His interest lay exclusively with an aristocracy of letters for the scholarly caste.

Vives

The latter half of the sixteenth century was marked by renewed interest in questions of educational technique. The beginnings of an incipient psychology of learning are discernible in Vives' works, the two books *On the Subjects of Study* and his *On the Teaching of the Several Subjects* in particular. Instead of dwelling on method in terms of teaching subject matter, he fastened on the correlative aspect of education as a learning process. Vives showed how memorization could be facilitated through the association of ideas and the logical ordering of facts in a coherent sequence. In his major work, *The Method of Learning*, he anticipated a great many of the later proposals to arrange learning experiences so the student progresses from individual facts to general concepts. His recognition of individual differences in learning abilities made him a pioneer in problems of educating the mentally and physically handicapped as well as a strong advocate of sense experience as the basis of learning. With Vives there is also more recognition of the place of vernacular language learning as a foundation for studying classical languages than in Erasmus, although he did not go so far as to make the former a separate subject in the curriculum.

Ramus

Peter Ramus (1515–1572), French scholar and Protestant reformer, similarly placed great importance on the role of experience in acquiring knowledge. His proposals regarding teaching, however, did not reflect the inductive approach. Instruction should begin, he claimed, with the general and move to the specific. Once discrete facts are learned, the teaching movement should reverse itself by relating specific information back to those more general concepts from which particular facts take their meaning. Ramus shared in the growing concern among forward-looking reformers for greater utility in education. Knowledge is useless unless it issues in practice; it is not something that can simply be stored away, he argued. One learns grammar, for example, in order to speak correctly and not because it has intrinsic value by itself. The same holds for all the liberal arts, in the very literal sense that they are *"arts"*—means to some further end. When taught correctly, the various subjects will be brought into direct relation with their daily applications. These arguments were developed at some length in Ramus' attacks on formalism within higher education. In addition to the working out of new methods, he aimed to expand the types of subject matter included in university curricula. Unfortunately, his reforming work was cut short in the nightmare of the St. Bartholomew's Day massacre; Ramus was among the slaughter's victims. Despite his untimely death those efforts bore fruit in years to come. Logic was dethroned from its position as most important subject of the *Trivium,* to be replaced by new forms of grammar. Literature and history evolved as separate studies, as did arithmetic, geometry, and astronomy. Algebra, trigonometry, and geography were added to the old *Quadrivium.* The teaching of music became more common and its content more varied.

Rabelais

Some glimmering of interest in the natural sciences as academic subjects of study appears in the writings of most educational theorists throughout this period. *Rabelais,* for example, has Gargantua write a letter to his son Pantagruel outlining an ideal curriculum. The usual Greek, Latin, and other language studies are advocated, but also the sciences, "As to the knowledge of the works of nature, I would have you devote yourself to the study of it." Pantagruel is to be a "very abyss of knowledge" about man and his natural environment. All the facts of daily experience should be the stuff for an encyclopedic education. This was a common strand of thought tying together curricular proposals with the wide desire for better educational methodology in the last half of the sixteenth century.

Montaigne

All the individuals considered so far drafted their reforms mainly as gestures of protest against the objectionable features of late medieval education. The next step to be taken was a critical assessment of humanistic practices gradually displacing established usages. Signs existed that the same loss of vision evident in Italian Ciceronianism was beginning to infect humanism in the North. Despite significant extensions of learning into new areas beyond antique letters and recognition that all studies should find practical application, humanism as a reform movement was losing its force. Classical studies tended to become disciplinary ends in themselves instead of liberating pursuits, and the generous conception of the well-rounded man, exemplified by Castiglione's courtier, was lost sight of entirely. In its prime, humanism had offered one answer to men's quickened impulses toward the claims of everyday life. With the passage of years it hardened into a new formalism, mute on questions about how wider knowledge of the universe could be brought within the province of the schools. Instead of restoring the Hellenic ideal of *paideia,* it erected a scholarly pedantry as stultified as anything found in scholastic thought. The time was ripe for a better expression of human aspirations based not on the past, but on a vision for the future. What kind of education would be required to realize that vision was still an undecided question.

Some indication of the direction to be taken appeared in the educational writings of a precocious young Frenchman, *Michel de Montaigne* (1533–1592). At a very early age Michel's father resolved to provide him with the best education obtainable. The young boy lived for some years with a German family where only Latin was spoken in the household. By the time Michael was admitted to the *Collège* of Guyenne at six years of age he spoke it fluently although he knew no French. His first exposure to formal schooling was evidently traumatic. Years later he recalled teachers who never stopped "bawling into our ears, as though they were pouring water into a funnel" and who saw their students' tasks as "only to repeat what has been told us."[10] Upon graduation Montaigne undertook legal studies at Toulouse and then served in a variety of administrative posts.

In the various essays he drafted concerning education, *On Pedantry, Of the Education of Children,* and *Of the Affection of Fathers to Their Children* chief among them, Montaigne never forgot the educational stupidity to which he had been exposed. "We direct all our efforts to the memory and leave the

[10] The best way to absorb the flavor of Montaigne is to consult his original writings. See *The Complete Works of Montaigne* (Stanford, Calif.: Stanford University Press, 1957).

understanding and the conscience empty," he complained in *On Pedantry*. "Like birds which go forth from time to time to seek for grain and bring it back to their young in their beaks without tasting it, our pedants go gathering knowledge from books and never take it further than their lips before disgorging it. And what is worse, their scholars and their little ones are no better nourished by it than they are themselves. It passes from one person to another and only serves to make a show or to provide entertainment."[11] Montaigne even went so far as to suggest that those *least* educated would be better people if such practices persisted. Part of the problem, he explained, was that pedagogy fastened upon knowledge without understanding. "Education has not taught us to follow and embrace virtue and prudence," he observed sarcastically in his essay *Of Presumption,* "but she has imprinted in us their derivation and etymology. We know how to decline the word virtue, even if we know not how to love it." Parents, he alleged elsewhere, "point at nothing but to furnish our heads with knowledge; but not a word of judgment and virtue." In his essay *On Pedantry,* he advanced much the same point, "To know by rote, is no knowledge, and signifies no more but only to retain what one has intrusted to our memory." Life itself, Montaigne noted, is the source of wisdom, not books. "That which a man rightly knows and understands, he is free disposer of at his own full liberty, without any regard to the author from whence he had it or fumbling over the leaves of his book. A mere bookish learning is a poor, paltry learning."

One thing teachers might do, he observed, is to let the child involve himself in the learning process. "By depriving a pupil of liberty to do things for himself we make him servile and cowardly." Secondly, pedagogical instruction should rely more on enjoyment than fear. "This method," he explained in *Of the Education of Children,* "ought to be carried on with a firm gentleness, quite contrary to the practice of our pedants, who, instead of tempting and alluring children to study, present nothing before them but rods and ferrules, horror and cruelty. Away with this violence! Away with this compulsion!" Nothing more dulls and degenerates a well-born nature, Montaigne insisted. "How much more respectable it would be to see our classrooms strewn with green boughs and flowers than with bloody birch rods. . . ." The alternative to making learning attractive, he concluded, was to "make nothing but so many asses laden with books."

A proper education naturally aims to transmit knowledge, "a great adornment and an instrument of wonderful service." No good end is served if teachers try to educate "many minds of different attainments and kinds with the same lesson and the same discipline." Individual differences among students require teachers "to direct them to the best and most profitable

---

[11] Someone once defined the university lecture as "a process whereby information is transferred from the speaker's outline to the student's notes without once passing through the head of either."

things and not to attach too much importance to those forecasts of character which we make from childish tendencies." Violence and force degrade students while destroying all desire for learning. "You may cram them full of knowledge with blows," he wrote, "but to make it of any real value you must not only get it into their minds but must espouse it to them." Knowing something by heart, accepting it merely on authority, is not knowledge. And what of the intractable child with whom no techniques seem to work and who stubbornly refuses to learn? Montaigne's facetious answer here (in his *Education of Children*) might win rueful approval from some teachers today, "Strangle him early, if there are not witnesses, or apprentice him to a pastry cook in some good town, even though he were the son of a duke."

On specific principles of instruction Montaigne had little to say, a fact he candidly admitted. He probably would have assented wholeheartedly to the rule of "learning while doing" advocated by Mulcaster in his *Elementarie*. "That rule of Aristotle must be precisely kept," Mulcaster wrote, "whereby we are taught, that the best way to learn anything well, which must afterwards be done, when it is learned, is still to be doing, while we be learning."[12] Yet Montaigne's main interest was not in formal schooling; for him the common practice of placing a child in the classroom before having a chance to mature through contact with the world of experience was a gross mistake. Only through travel and exposure to ideas on an informal basis— "no light apprenticeship," he claimed—can the individual gain the practical wisdom that makes formal instruction worthwhile. "When we have taught the boy all that is necessary to make him wiser and better, then we will explain to him about logic, physics, geometry and rhetoric, and having had his judgment trained beforehand he will soon acquire the knowledge of his choice." Instead of the "empty babble" of the classroom, learning will become at once a personal possession and an opportunity to exercise wise judgment.

In Montaigne there is a rich fund of educational advice, as worthy of admiration as anything to be found in classical writings on pedagogy. His stress on a functional concept of mind, the pragmatic utility of knowledge, the place of experience in learning, and the importance of character formation through good habits all sound a distinctly modern note. What is missing is a proper appreciation for the sciences in a formal curriculum: "at most the sciences can only teach prudence, integrity, and determination even when the best methods are employed." Lacking also is anything of the scientific approach to teaching and learning problems upon which a

---

[12] Richard Mulcaster, *Elementarie* (London: Oxford University Press, 1925), pp. 248–249. The qualification "which must afterwards be done" is an important one in the Aristotelian maxim, often neglected by those today who tout "learning by doing" as an instructional panacea. That this general principle is mistakenly attributed to John Dewey shows once again how venerable much of our contemporary educational wisdom actually is.

discipline of education might build. The ideals around which Montaigne's theories revolved were aristocratic and chivalric. For the noble gentry seeking advice on how to order tutorial instruction, Montaigne could offer much. It remained for others to incorporate his recommendations within educational systems geared for the masses of people in society at large.

All this notwithstanding, late-sixteenth-century theorists (of whom Montaigne is fairly representative) had moved some distance from the position occupied by their predecessors less than a hundred years earlier. Humanism, with all its neglect of natural science, its aristocratic cast, its overemphasis on language, was a positive influence helping to mold education through a transitional period. The broader revival of learning of which humanist education was but one manifestation might, under other circumstances, have advanced scientific inquiry, national unity, and economic progress. Instead it was irresistibly drawn to antiquity and to its cultural forms in which the ferment found expression.[13] The seventeenth century would witness an age in which men were prepared to go beyond the contributions of humanistic thought, armed with a more comprehensive understanding of the natural world and a potent tool for dealing with it—scientific method. Educational theory and practice alike would eventually benefit substantially from new social and intellectual forces in process of birth.

THE END OF AN EPOCH

Susanne Langer has advanced the hypothesis that the end of an epoch comes with the exhaustion of its motive questions.[14] The limits of thought characteristic of an age are not set from outside, by the fullness or poverty of experiences men have, as much as from within, by the powers of conception, the fruitfulness of formulative notions with which the mind interprets experiences. It is the *generative ideas* or terms in which ideas are conceived that gives a cultural period its distinctive unity. In Greek thought, philosophical questions about Being (What is the world made of? What is truth?) and, with Socrates, questions about man, set the basic forms through which philosophy, art, and literature developed. The end of Hellenism came when all the problems formulated in its terms had been exploited. What is significant about a historical period is not the answers it gives to basic questions but *how* the questions are framed and what questions are *not* raised. The next great epoch, Langer argues, was the Christian, beginning with the early Church fathers and culminating in the scholastics. Its generative ideas —sin and salvation, nature and grace, finity and infinity—provided material through which new cultural forms were worked out for over a millenium. Then these also were exhausted. Unanswerable puzzles and paradoxes

13 See Woodward, *Studies in Education*, op. cit., pp. 5–6.
14 Susanne K. Langer, *Philosophy in a New Key* (New York: Mentor, 1959), pp. 19–23 ff.

followed the completion of the scholastic synthesis. Existing economic, political, artistic, and literary ideas reached their natural limits, beyond which it was impossible to progress. There followed several centuries of sterile tradition, logic-chopping, the rehearsal of canons long since expired.

By this analysis that phrase of the revival of learning called the Renaissance was a transitional era, a bridge between the medieval world view and a new outlook born of scientific inquiry. Humanism was a mediating force which helped men bridge the gap between a theologically oriented culture and one organized around scientific interests. Humanism began in a determined resolve to break with established traditions. It ended by erecting a new dogmatism of its own, based on the cultural forms of Greece and Roman. Its generative ideas were the dignity of the individual, the intrinsic worth of the secular life, worldliness, and self-expression. When these motive concepts had been played out, men were left only with a dreary Ciceronianism, a fragmented array of competing religious ideologies, and a vague sense of discontent. The springs of philosophical thought had run dry, the limits of Europe's cultural forms completely explored. In education the great movement to infuse schools with the spirit of humanism had been accomplished. Something new was needed.

Most of the same symptoms that mark the end of an epoch are evident today. Thought is incorporated into more and more variegated "isms," be they philosophical, religious, artistic, or educational, and the clamor of their respective adherents to be heard and judged side by side increases.[15] So many millions of words have been expended to describe the various "revolutions" through which contemporary life is moving that it hardly seems necessary to describe them at length. It has become trite to speak of the "crisis" of the modern age: the dislocation of the fundamental institutions, habits, attitudes, and practices of our culture. "When a point is reached in which the major functions, the major structures, the major purposes of a culture or subculture are thrown out of joint," observes Theodore Brameld, "then its members often find themselves bewildered, lost, uprooted. They and their culture are in a state of crisis." By this definition, he continues, few thoughtful persons would care to deny that we live today at a turning point in our history.[16]

There is an ancient Chinese imprecation, "I curse you; may you live in an important age." Twentieth-century man is cursed to live in such an age; he is also challenged by its possibilities, just as Renaissance man was with the potential of his own motive concepts. The revival of learning set in motion processes of social change that have acquired momentum ever since, changes we are just now beginning to appreciate fully. The exponential growth of knowledge in the past fifty years has turned loose a technological

15 Ibid., p. 23.
16 Theodore Brameld, *Education as Power* (New York: Holt, Rinehart and Winston, 1966), pp. 10–11.

juggernaught that few profess to comprehend, much less control. The voices of reformers in the sixteenth century crying that institutions had become too unwieldy are echoed today in the charge that our present bureaucracies are unresponsive to rapid, unexpected change. The confessional theology of implacability has its analogue in the politics of our own time. Contemporary arguments that institutional behemoths are failing us and must be done away with are strikingly similar to complaints against the institutional forms of fifteenth-century Europe. Today it is argued that industrial bureaucracy arose as an adaptation from more primitive models of military and religious hierarchies and is no longer appropriate. Identical frustration was experienced by social critics three and four centuries ago as they fought against an impenetrable web of inertia and vested interests. They too felt alienated, imprisoned, and victimized by an overbearing elite, only it was ecclesiastical instead of managerial. Then, as now, men called for a radical overhaul of society's institutional structures.

The current wave of criticism directed against education, that schools do not provide moral or emotional involvement, that curricula have decayed, that universities have become stodgy and recalcitrant, is astonishingly like the charges brought against education during the age of humanistic reform. The central challenge then was to focus classical studies imaginatively on man's big needs; now it is the requirements of a technological society that demand a new kind of educational system. If Renaissance and Reformation leaders sought ways to build institutions in which people could find maximal self-realization, today's pioneers are groping for what Abraham Maslow calls "eupsychic" institutional patterns to promote the same general objective.

In the field of education indications are that theory and practice require new generative ideas. Like the American culture of which it is the ideological ally, education has been much more concerned with implementing an effective methodology than with formulating the goals for which that methodology is essential. Educators have not clearly or unequivocally focused upon the content or meaning of their social goals. The aims that do function are primarily carryovers from earlier ideals, modified in the light of a discrepancy between ambition and practice: extension of schooling to more people, equalization of educational opportunities among minorities, individualizing instruction, and so forth. Although important, because these proposals are not new, because they derive from ideas advanced at least fifty years ago, they express the ideology of a transitional culture. What is impressive about an age of revolt like the Renaissance revival of learning or the technological crisis of modern times is that men perceive more clearly what they oppose than what they support. From Petrarch to Montaigne, men struggled for release from the bondage of the past, yet few agreed on what shape their future should assume. Amidst the quest for new modes of expression in the various areas of today's culture, the same uncertainty looms large.

THE RISE OF SCIENTIFIC INQUIRY

The Scientific Revolution

The critical modern spirit of questioning that began the modern age had its beginnings in the twelfth-century revival of learning. Its first major cultural expressions, of course, were the Renaissance rejection of medievalism and the humanist interest in ancient literature. Applied to geography and commerce, worldliness led inevitably to an expansion of trade, and, with this, the discovery of better navigational routes. The Protestant Reformation and Catholic Counter-Reformation were natural outgrowths of the same relentless drive toward cultural renewal. So far as economics or politics were concerned, the modern temper burst forth with novel governmental theories, well illustrated by the French *politiques'* defense of secular sovereignty and the English development of republicanism. Thomas Hobbes' *Leviathan* (like Machiavelli's *Prince* before it) offered a dramatic break with the usual apologies for the Christian feudal state of the Middle Ages. The modern territorial state, the concept of political absolutism, and the principle of *quod principi placuit, legis habet vigorem* ("what hath pleased the prince has the force of law") spelled the end of the medieval nexus of rights and duties, counterbalanced powers, and customs. Despite lingering remnants, feudalism was dead everywhere (except in German lands) by the seventeenth century.

Above all, the 1600's were marked by the application of critical inquiry to natural phenomena—the rise of science. Herbert Butterfield, in his monumental *The Origins of Modern Science,* claims the scientific revolution was so important that it outshines everything since the rise of Christianity and reduces the Renaissance and Reformation to the status of mere episodes, minor displacements within the system of medieval Christendom. The rise of science, Butterfield alleges, was the real origin of the modern world and of the modern mentality. Beginning with Copernicus in the midsixteenth century and culminating with Newton toward the end of the next, it is so important that it makes the customary periodization of European history an encumbrance and an anachronism. Something of the change in men's attitudes toward science in a few short decades can be seen by contrasting Francis Bacon's complaint in 1605 that "matters mechanical" were esteemed "a kind of dishonour unto learning to descend to inquiry or meditation upon" with Joseph Glanvill's repudiation of ancient speculation sixty years later. "The unfruitfulness of those methods of science," Glanvill wrote in his *Plus Ultra* of 1668, "which in so many centuries never brought the world so much practical, beneficial knowledge as would help toward the cure of a cut finger, is a palpable argument." The same indication of a revolution in human thought is revealed in a letter written by John Ray (1690): "No wonder [the ancients] should outstrip us in those arts which are conversant in polishing and adorning their language, because they bestowed all their time and pains in cultivating them. . . . But those arts are by wise men censured as far inferior to the study of things, words being but the picture of things." Ray's observation here might well have served as a manifesto for seventeenth-century educational reforms.

The causes of the scientific movement were manifold. In spite of its bitter hostility to scientific learning, medieval Christianity accustomed men to the Hellenic idea of a rationally ordered creation in which orderly investigation was possible. Scholasticism encouraged the development of that conceptual precision characteristic of later scientific methodology. The Renaissance revival of antique texts and philosophies certainly whetted intellectual appetites, especially the Pythagorean and Platonic revivals in fifteenth-century Italy. Such revivals not only habituated intellectuals to think in mathematical, quantitative terms, they showed how incomplete and contradictory ancient scientific learning really was. The need for independent investigation of old problems was soon clear after the initial, uncritical enthusiasm for classicism had ebbed. Humanism also cleared the way for scientific research by removing the stigma of sin from the natural world; the favorite catch phrase was that God's word could be read in the Book of Nature as well as the Bible. Indirectly, the Reformation may have contributed to scientific progress by reducing the miraculous elements of institutional Christianity, by exalting ethics over metaphysics, and by attacking Aristotelian scientific dogma. Without question the expansion of geographical knowledge was tied to attitudinal changes favoring scientific learning. As Bacon reported, "By the distant voyages and travels which have become frequent in our times, many things in nature have been laid open and discovered which may let in new light. . . ." Finally, an economic historian of Marxist persuasions might point to the rough correspondence between the scientifically based world view of seventeenth-century philosophers and the bourgeois desire for a rational, predictable social order. A mechanical universe explainable in terms of cause and effect suggests societal stability and that is good for business.

Science as a directive force in Western civilization, displacing theology and classical letters, was more than a method of inquiry or even a body of knowledge; it was also an *attitude of mind and creator of a metaphysical world view*. Its momentous effects on culture were derived mainly from a way of looking at things more than from any specific discoveries, however important those might have been. It was the global scientific perspective that transformed philosophical theories, inspired new visions for social theorists, altered decisively men's attitudes toward fixed traditions, imposed new literary canons, and collided with orthodox theology. Above all, the scientific movement enabled the learned classes to declare their independence of the past, engendering a certain sense of condescension toward the "ancients." The future, not the past, was the Golden Age toward which society was moving on all fronts.

The Quest for Method

Surprisingly, these trends began to take shape during the confessional atmosphere of hatred, suspicion, and distrust when scientists' theories were assailed as heretical, their methods suspect as devilish art. The most famous example of how science developed comes from the field of astronomy. In 1543 a German-Polish ecclesiastic named Nicholas Kopernik (*Copernicus*) posthumously published a refutation of the old Ptolemaic theory of the universe, entitled *De Revolutionibus Orbium Celestium*. It was, as the author stated, an attempt to discover "a more rational system" for explaining irregularities in the velocity of planets in terms of a series of uniform motions. Copernicus' *heliocentric theory* with its insistence that the sun, not the earth, is the center of the solar system shook the Christian view of man's position in the universe. For advocating that heresy, an Italian Dominican monk, *Giordano Bruno* (1548–1600), was burned at the stake. A Danish investigator, *Tycho Brahe* (1546–1601), continued Copernicus' work by showing through careful observations obvious errors in the Aristotelian-Ptolemaic view. Brahe's brilliant assistant, *Johann Kepler* (1571–1630), utilized his predecessor's careful records to support the heliocentric theory's essential features. By making the novel assumption that planetary orbits describe ellipses rather than perfect circles, Kepler was able to formulate mathematically his three well-known laws of planetary motion. Experimental confirmation was furnished with the publication of the *Sidereal Messenger* in 1610, authored by a professor at Pisa, *Galileo Galilei* (1564–1642). Copernicus had shown that common sense and ordinary observation need to be supplemented with mathematical computations in the pursuit of scientific truth, Brahe and Kepler that mathematical relations in turn must be corrected by empirical observations. Now Galileo was demonstrating how these scientific methods could be used to win knowledge in fields like astronomy and physics. Galileo's advocacy of the Copernican theory more than once nearly cost him his life. In 1615 he was brought to Rome by the Inquisition and forced to recant his error as "absurd in philosophy" and "expressly contrary to Holy Scripture." Again in 1632, with the publication of his *Dialogue on the Two Chief Systems of the World*, Galileo was called before a court to abjure his heresy.[17] He escaped death by fire but remained a house prisoner of the Inquisition for the rest of his years.

Any remaining doubts over the basic validity of the Copernican hypothesis were dispelled with the publication of *Principia* (1687) by an English genius, *Isaac Newton* (1642–1727). He irrefutably showed how a mathematical method of investigation could be applied universally to problems

---

17 There is a tradition that Galileo disavowed the Copernican thesis that the earth moves around the sun before the Inquisitorial court but then muttered, "And yet it moves!" Though spurious, it seems symbolically faithful to his character. His *Dialogue* was placed on the Index and not removed until 1835. Galileo himself was not fully cleared of heresy charges until the second half of the twentieth century.

of mechanical motion. The result was an all-embracing mechanistic interpretation of the world in precise, quantitative terms. Gone was the Aristotelian–Christian universe of purposes and final causes. Not heavenly
spirits but invariable laws accounted for celestial spheres moving through
the heavens. The universe, with Newton, seemed a uniform mathematical
system, a great machine. Nature was a complex of precisely ordered properties whose connections could be expressed in mathematical terms. The
Principia laid out for all to see how the method of science worked: derivation of principles from the analysis of observed facts, deduction of the consequences following from the principles, and experimentation to validate
those deductions which thereby confirm (or invalidate) the initial hypotheses. It was not without reason that Pope's often quoted couplet applied,
"Nature and Nature's laws lay hid in night; God said, 'Let Newton be,' and
all was light." The Newtonian cosmology was to endure for two and a half
centuries until revised in light of Einstein's theories of relativity.

The first comprehensive statement of scientific method was formulated
by the English philosopher *Francis Bacon* 1561–1626). His *Advancement
of Learning* of 1605 and the more famous *Novum Organum,* published in
1620, were not planned as *countersummas* to Aristotle or the scholastics,
but they did much to discredit medieval science as "fantastic" and "delicate" and "contentious." The latter opus in particular is full of attacks on
deductive reasoning and appeals to accept the evidence of sense perception.
In showing the insufficiency of the schoolmen's deductions, Bacon went to
great lengths to demonstrate how induction lies at the heart of scientific
enterprise. A different but equally influential treatment of scientific procedure appeared in the works of a French philosopher, *René Descartes*
(1596–1650). His *Discourse upon Method* of 1637 sketched the outline of
a "universal mathematics" that would be, its author was convinced, "a
more powerful instrument of knowledge than any other that has been bequeathed to us by human agency, as being the source of all others." The
grandiose Cartesian ambition to explain all natural phenomena in purely
mechanical terms ("Give me extension and motion, and I will construct the
universe") was an important phase in the development of science through
its formative stage. Along with other prophets of the new science—Galileo,
Bruno, Newton—Bacon and Descartes produced a sweeping panoramic
view of nature unlike anything known before. All fields of thought were
stamped with the mathematical ideals of science, including education.
Bacon's views more than anyone else's fired educational theorists of the
period.

Scientific ideals captivated the imagination of the intellectual class in the
seventeenth century. Robert Boyle's *The Sceptical Chemist* (1661) and
Fontenelle's *Plurality of Worlds* (1686) were but two examples of the popular literature of the day bringing scientific thought to wider attention. New
intellectual homes for sharing scientific knowledge were founded, among

them the Lyncean Society at Rome, the Royal Society in London, the Berlin Academy, the Academy of Sciences at Paris, and the Academia del Cimento at Florence. The concept of "science" underwent a complete restriction of meaning in the seventeenth century. Up until then it had been used synonymously with the "arts"; now it came to mean exact and certain knowledge apprehended by the mind (Descartes), measured mathematically (Newton), and demonstrated by experiment (Galileo). Science meant *cumulative* knowledge, perhaps tentative and subject to revision, but ever-increasing. More broadly, the scientific distrust of unprovable hypotheses had the practical effect of placing importance on the *utility* of knowledge. "The end of knowledge," wrote Hobbes, "is power, and . . . the scope of all speculation is the performance of some action, or thing to be done." Locke reiterated the same theme, "The principal end why we are to get knowledge here," he maintained, "is to make use of it for the benefit of ourselves and others in this world."

Something must be said of the relation between science and religion in the seventeenth century. It would be too easy to conclude from theology's dethronement as a motive cultural concept that men of scientific leanings rejected religious belief. On the contrary, most of the leading researchers of the day were pious, orthodox men, and the various scientific academies more often than not included ecclesiastics on their rosters. Though it was increasingly difficult to reconcile religion and science, most scholars never embraced the militant skepticism so prevalent during the century that followed. The typical religious response was to de-emphasize supernaturalism, a tactic ably pursued in John Toland's *Christianity Not Mysterious* (1696) or John Locke's *Reasonableness of Christianity* (1695). Yet science was fostering a habit of mind potentially subversive to religious orthodoxy. The place of God in running the universe had seemingly diminished. "I perceive," says the Countess in Fontenelle's dialogue, "philosophy is now become very mechanical. I value [this universe] the more since I know it resembles a watch, and the whole order of nature the more plain and easy it is, to me it appears the more admirable." Bacon was willing to believe the word of God "though our reason be shocked at it." Locke, in opposition, refused to compartmentalize religious conviction and scientific belief. " 'I believe because it is impossible,' might," he observed, "in a good man, pass for a sally of zeal, but would prove a very ill rule for men to choose their opinions or religion by." In this lay the seeds of trouble for the years ahead.

EDUCATIONAL REALISM

The growth of scientific interests was contemporaneous with, and a formative influence upon, a diffuse educational movement termed *realism*.

Broadly speaking, realist doctrines were an outgrowth of Bacon's organizing work which gained ascendancy throughout the 1600's. Their impact on the actual conduct of schools was limited at first, although most pedagogical theoreticians served as realist spokesmen. The keynote of realism was a twofold demand: that curricula include more than humanistic–literary disciplines and that instructional practices be based on the application of scientific understanding to teaching and learning problems.

With regard to curricular matters, realism was an accommodative force seeking to replace Latin with the vernacular and at the same time to substitute new scientific or social studies for the usual linguistic pursuits. This meant an extensive broadening of school subjects at all institutional levels. Beyond this, realist reformers aimed to reorganize courses of study, to integrate the various disciplines as a coherent whole. It would not suffice, they argued, to simply tack on new courses to the old. Knowledge must be viewed holistically in all its interconnections. The aim of realist education was to unify learning in such a way that students could actually perceive internal relationships among their studies. The concept of a narrow specialist was anathema to almost all the major seventeenth-century theorists. This never meant everyone could possibly learn all there was to know, only that whatever portion of human knowledge was assimilated should be set in the broadest context possible.

Instructionally, realist pedagogy took note of rapid advances in psychological theory relating to learning. From Hobbes and Gassendi to Leibniz and Spinoza men sought improved understanding of how the human mind works. The educational correlative to this activity was a developing inductive methodology. Teachers were urged to move from the simple to the complex, from the specific to the general. A student learns best, realists affirmed, if he is presented with things before words and instances before rules. The learning process can be hastened through the use of sensory reinforcement where possible. Greater attention should be paid to drills and memory exercises. "Natural" learning can be an enjoyable experience if the teacher will take into account differences in learning ability and present only whatever is appropriate to the maturational level achieved by each student. Only then can the teacher enlist the individual's interest as a substitute for external restraints or coercion. A good teacher will always try to involve pupils in the process of inquiry rather than allowing them to remain passive spectators. It goes without saying none of this was particularly new, even in the seventeenth century; the difference was these precepts were beginning to be organized more or less systematically into a comprehensive theory of education.

So far as institutions were concerned, realists wanted more and better schools. Educational centers need not be dreary pedantic enclaves, the argument went; they can become meaningful learning centers where children will be sent to prepare themselves for everyday life in a worldly society.

Although admittedly some theorists continued to believe education should
be the exclusive possession of the special few, a growing number of educators called for the expansion of education for all people, of all classes, of
both sexes.

SCHOOL AND SOCIETY IN POST-REFORMATIONAL EUROPE

An Educational Decline

Had it not been for the Huguenot struggles, the English civil war, and
the Thirty Years' War, more educational progress along the lines sketched
above might have been made than was actually the case during the seventeenth century. Instead, the Peace of Westphalia in 1648, designed to end a
hundred years of horrible religious fratricide, was followed by yet another
century of vindictive strife, unremitting intolerance, and hatred. Europe
was depopulated, impoverished, totally unable to summon energies for any
extensive educational enterprise. Schools were either nonexistent or poorly
equipped. Insufficient endowments from the confessional churches coupled
with an absence of state aid or private generosity spelled stagnation for
schools in every area. In elementary vernacular institutions narrow sectarian religious instruction, supplemented by rudimentary teaching of reading, writing, and counting, constituted the usual curricula. Either the Bible
or a simplified primer served as the most frequently used text. The general
populace was unwilling to have public taxes levied to support primary
schools, despite Protestant injunctions for universal schooling. Naturally,
teachers were untrained and grossly underpaid. Not until society had begun
to recover from the devastations of war were the voices of educational reformers heeded in influential quarters and the yawning gap between theory
and practice narrowed. Inability to effect changes at higher school levels
proceeded from the same causes. The general indifference to education left
Latin grammar schools unaffected by the upper-class desire for vernacular,
modern language instruction. Humanistic schools, however decadent they
may have become, resisted sporadic attempts to bring in the new scientific
learning.

With the exception of English institutions of higher education, which
came under the direct influence of Bacon and Newton, European universities were not receptive to scientific interests. The seventeenth century has
been called the period of the "territorial-confessional university" dominated by a preponderance of theological interests. Where the theological
faculty prevailed over other university divisions, the institution tended to
serve narrow sectarian interests or the policies of the state. It was not until
1694 that the *University of Halle* was founded, justifiably termed the "first
modern university" for having introduced vernacular instruction, the study

of mathematics, and some sciences as regular features of the curriculum.[18] Göttingen was the only institution to follow suit, some forty-odd years later.

An Experiment at Gotha

The first educational improvement of any consequence in German territories was made in the state of Saxe-Gotha under the patronage of *Duke Ernest the Pious* (1601–1675). In 1619 he appointed the local schoolmaster, *Andreas Reyher,* to draw up a plan of reorganization for schools in part of the duchy of Weimar. Reyher's memorandum was published in 1642 under the title *Schule Methodus.* The reforms it prescribed were inspired by the most progressive theories of the time. They included a program for introducing geography, civics, and elementary science into the elementary schools, a definite system of educational control by the state, pupil examinations, compulsory attendance, and planned outlines for the teachers. As these were put into practice, several new schools were built, teachers' wages were raised, and better textbooks made available. Ernest died some thirty years after the reforms were begun, bringing the program to a close. The experiment, however short-lived, was so successful it often inspired the wry comment, "Duke Ernest's peasants are better educated than noblemen anywhere else."

Ratke's "New Method"

Less successful was the undertaking of *Wolfgang Ratke* (1571–1635), whose theories had provided inspiration for Duke Ernest and Reyher at Gotha. In 1612 he presented himself before an assembly of German princes at the Electoral Diet, held at Frankfurt-am-Mainz, with a proposal for a new educational method. It was, Ratke claimed, "fraught with momentous consequences" for teaching foreign languages more easily and quickly. His argument that a new school system built around better texts and a more efficient pedagogy would unify the people with a common language impressed his listeners, and a committee of scholars was appointed to investigate his claims further. Although Ratke was reluctant to divulge all the particulars of his scheme, the Duchess Dorothea Maria of Weimar accepted his ideas at face value and invited him to direct a court school where she and her family could learn Latin. Ratke proved successful in his initial venture, and it won him the support of Prince Ludwig von Anhalt-Köthen who opened a school at Köthen where Ratke's methods could be implemented on a larger scale. Over four hundred pupils were conscripted as subjects, facilities were turned over to this ambitious sophist, and materials prepared to help train teachers to teach foreign languages "in less time . . .

---

[18] This conservatism is not surprising. Historically, universities have been used to provide intellectual homes for new social movements, but only rarely have they *initiated* new currents of thought.

than could be done by any other method . . . and also with much less pain."
An ambitious program of studies was planned, including arithmetic, music,
religion, Greek, and Latin. The whole project failed miserably less than two
years later, the school was closed, and Ratke thrown into prison.

Poor management was the real cause of the failure. Ratke himself was
a strange, furtive individual, apparently incapable of translating what was
sound pedagogical theory into workable school practice. His major work,
published in Leipzig in 1617 as *Methodus Nova,* shows clearly the influence
of Bacon's *Advancement of Learning.* Ratke's "secret" method was nothing
more than the inductive approach to learning and teaching. Instead of
depending on rote memorization, blind acceptance of authority, and brutal
discipline, Ratke insisted the teacher must base instruction on the natural
development of the child's mind, the course of nature. Specifically, this
meant one should begin with the familiar (vernacular language), which is
learned more easily, before moving on to the unfamiliar (the study of classical or foreign languages). Instruction should fasten on one idea at a time
until it is thoroughly mastered through repetition and drill. Opportunity
should be given the student for questioning, rather than encouraging him
to learn without understanding. External constraints are vastly inferior to
student interest; brutality is a sure sign of teacher incompetence. Ratke
believed the best instructional methodology would be consistent, presenting
similar subjects in the same manner. Most important of all, the child
should have an experience upon which later explanations or elaborations
could build. In retrospect it seems strange that ordinary common sense in
classroom teaching should have been hailed as new, esoteric pedagogical
wisdom.

Educational Work Among France's Religious Orders

In France the schools' situation was only slightly better throughout the
seventeenth century. Protestant efforts to enlist royal support for a system of
vernacular primary schools which schoolchildren would be compelled to
attend were unsuccessful. The revocation of the Edict of Nantes promulgating some freedom to Huguenots led to the disappearance of all Protestant freedoms, including the right to conduct schools. After 1685, French
education was firmly under the direction of the Catholic Church. Little was
done, apart from charity schools for the poor, to meet national educational
needs until late in the century when the *Brethren of the Christian Schools*
got their start. Even Lasalle's work at Reims, Paris, and Rouen had little
real impact, despite the establishment of elementary cathedral schools
throughout France and teacher-training institutions like the College de
Saint-Yvon. Over a hundred years later, less than a thousand teachers were
actively engaged in teaching work in the Brethren's schools. Similarly, the
Order of the Oratory of Jesus, founded in 1611 for the education of priests,
opened many seminaries and colleges, but its influence was never as great as

that of the Jesuits. The Oratorians' only major innovation was to include certain modern subjects like national history, mathematics, and French language in their school curricula. More famous were those teachers organized around Jean du Vergier, Abbot of *St. Cyran,* as the *Jansenists* or Port Royalists. Their actual teaching work at Paris and then at Port Royal was cut short, thanks to Jesuit intervention at the Court, and the Port Royal schools closed less than twenty-five years after they were begun. But Jansenist reforms were destined to endure in spite of this, eventually winning enough popular approval to be incorporated into French education less than a century later. Freed from actual teaching, many of the veterans from Port Royal turned to publishing as a means to awaken interest in better education. Lancelot's *New Method,* the *Rules for Humanistic Studies* by Arnauld, and Coustel's *Rules for the Education of Children* were three of the more important publications designed to popularize Jansenist educational thought.

Three of the basic principles they enunciated have become commonplace. First, the language of instruction was French, not Latin. Experimentation in language instruction encouraged advocacy of the phonetic method of teaching reading—a procedure in frequent use today. Second, pupils were taught to write about actual things or to report on their own everyday experiences in preference to abstract grammatical exercises. Third, teaching techniques were organized strictly on the basis of what was then known about psychological functions. Children differ in their learning strategies, Coustel noted, and teachers must take account of the differences. "If a physician cannot prescribe remedies suitable for the healing of the body without knowing its various temperaments, and if a farmer ought not to set about sowing a field without knowing the quality of its soil, then beyond doubt a schoolmaster should also know the different kinds of intellect which he has to cultivate." Coustel went beyond this simple observation to discuss systematically *how* differing instructional techniques follow from the various "mental types" a teacher is likely to encounter. Reading the works of Thorndike and other leaders of the modern "child study" movement easily recalls Coustel's *Rules for the Education of Children.*

Fénelon and the Education of Women

For a time it appeared as though a positive start had been made in educating women according to new educational precepts. François de Salignac de la Mothe Fénelon (1651–1715), archbishop of Cambria, was one of many influential writers who began to raise questions about educational opportunities for the fairer sex. His *Treatise on the Education of Girls,* written in 1680, was one of the most widely read works on education of the century. Owing to his achievements as director of a proselytizing "New Catholic" Sisterhood established at Paris to win Huguenot converts, Fénelon received numerous requests for advice on how the nobility's female children should be educated. His responses do not suggest much sensitivity to women's intellectual interests nor even a very high regard for women generally, yet the very fact he thought it important to discuss their special needs indicates a more generous attitude than usual. The comment, "It is enough if one day they know how to rule their households and obey their husbands without arguing about it," from his *Treatise* typifies the general tone. This was balanced, in Fénelon's thought, by a healthy concern to give women more instruction from a wide range of subjects. Tutorial education for the privileged classes as conducted in seventeenth-century France borrowed its main practices from his recommendations.

Further Developments

Outside the home or a conventual school of some religious order like the *Ursulines,* little was available in the way of education for young girls. One exception was an unusual school endowed by the French king at *Saint Cyr,* near Versailles. Between 1686 and 1692 this liberal finishing center for upper-class girls led the way in secular education. Its founder, *Françoise d'Aubigne Maintenon* (1635–1719), had been governess to the children of the king's mistress before she herself won royal favor as courtesan. After the first few years of supervising Saint Cyr, Maintenon had a change of heart. Thereafter, the school became a sequestered cloister whose secular educational emphases disappeared entirely. What had once been a worldly curriculum encompassing history, drama, literature, and music besides the usual subjects was narrowed to the point where only domestic arts were taught.[19] Two more centuries had to elapse before anything approaching equality of educational opportunity between the sexes became possible.

Not much was done to change French higher education during this time. At Paris, Henry IV managed to force through some reforms earlier suggested by Ramus, but the effects were not long-lasting. Overall, the Jesuit plan of education dominated postsecondary institutions. In the Parisian province alone, Jesuit schools boasted an enrollment exceeding fourteen thousand; by 1700 Jesuit colleges numbered six hundred. It must be said that the Society of Jesus did offer quality education (as judged by existing standards), although its spirit and methods mirrored nothing of the growing scientific concerns. Cartesian rationalism was not strong enough yet as a cultural force to have appreciable impact, aside from the inspiration it provided Cardinal Richelieu in founding the French Academy in 1637 and such Oratorian educational theorists as Lamy, Thomassin, and Charles Rollin. Not until the eighteenth century did the scientifically influenced philosophies of a Descartes or a Bacon begin to get a hearing inside university walls.

[19] See Gabriel Compayré, *The History of Pedagogy* (Boston: D. C. Heath, 1889), pp. 220 ff.

Courtly Education

Montaigne's educational perspective of the preceding century proved exceedingly important during the 1600's. It was a characteristic expression of the nobility's attitudes toward established schools. Scorned as "citadels of pedantry," humanistic institutions seemed woefully inadequate for the practical and social interests of a cosmopolitan gentry. Renaissance classicism simply was irrelevant in an age tinctured by French language, politics, and manners; social fashions now revolved around the court of Louis XIV, not the long-gone palaces of Rome. As a result, wherever French culture held sway, the aristocratic classes often abandoned formal schools for private tutorial education. In France, Bossuet and Fénelon won reputations for themselves as tutors at the royal palace. In England, nothing less than scholars of special distinction like John Locke or Roger Ascham were good enough to educate the sons of high-ranking officials. Individual schooling was the usual pattern in other countries besides.

The upper classes did not entirely rely on private tutoring, however. There was also an *institutionalized* expression of the same dissatisfaction with narrow humanism, seen in the creation of numerous courtly *academies* at Tours, Paris, Versailles, and several other important cultural centers. Their spirit was taken from the better court schools of Guarino or Vittorino, but the curriculum and instruction were substantially different. Latin was taught perfunctorily, its place superseded by French. Modern rather than classical literature was deemed worthy of special emphasis. Some logic, rhetoric, and dialectic could be included, though always subordinated to such subjects as geography, history, politics, art, and jurisprudence. The modernization of studies was accompanied by other innovations dropped since the fourteenth century. A full regimen of games, exercises, and physical sports complemented the academic studies. The basic intent of the academies was to provide a general, liberal, and usable preparation for the public life of a gentleman. It is tempting to think that this generous kind of education might have been extended to schools for the lower classes had not the whole aristocratic regime been checked by social revolution. As it turned out, courtly education for the cultural elite did not remain in existence long enough to shape popular schooling.

The dominance of Paris and Versailles as Europe's cultural centers guaranteed the spread of courtly schools along with everything else in French fashions. At first German nobles sent their sons to one of the many academies surrounding Paris to acquire social graces unknown in their own cruder homeland. By 1649 there were twelve academies in the French capital alone, offering instruction in modern languages, mathematics, military science, and, of course, courtly arts. Through the latter half of the century, however, personal contact with the French nobility no longer was considered essential for fostering gentlemanly refinement, and native schools were built on German soil. The "knightly" academies (*Ritterakademieen*) served roughly the same ends as their French models, persisting as an important institutional type until almost the end of the eighteenth century.

English Puritanism and Education

The years 1640 to 1660 enclose an important phase in the English development of educational thought under Puritanism, a period when the reigns of James I and Charles I were marked by unusual intensity of reform interest. Discussion centered around a small but significant group of educators who, despite their differences, were united behind a drive to overhaul existing schools. *Samuel Hartlib* (ca. 1600–1670), the most influential member, was both a catalytic agent for his associates and a writer on his own. His 1650 tract entitled *London's Charity Enlarged* urged the state to found poor schools so as to spread learning among the general populace. For too long, Hartlib avowed, education had been a device for perpetuating class or rank distinctions. Schooling, he insisted, should not be reserved for the few who could afford it. His closest colleague, *John Dury* (1596–1680), took the argument further in a pamphlet called *Reformed Schools.* England desperately needs a universal, publicly financed school system for all children aged eight through fourteen, he began. The curriculum should be aimed toward occupational preparation, Dury added, and every subject should be taught in a manner leading to its natural vocational applications. *Sir William Petty* (1623–1687), another member of Hartlib's circle, echoed the appeal. In order to educate people for useful work a whole new institutional system would be needed. A common school (*Ergastulum Literarium*) open to children of all classes was the first requirement. Next there should be a workmen's college (*Gymnasium Mechanicum*), Petty urged, for common school graduates to pursue more specialized work in business and commercial subjects. Finally, an academy (*Nosocomium Academicum*) similar to the university ought to be opened, with instruction directed mainly to mechanical rather than literary interests.

Another Puritan theorist deserving attention was the cleric *Hezekiah Woodward* (1590–1675). His two most important tractates, *A Gate to Science* and *A Light to Grammar and All Other Arts and Sciences,* advocated a realist pedagogy based on sense experience. "Nothing comes into the understanding in a natural way but through the senses," he noted. Students learn best if given objects, pictures, diagrams, and other visual aids in the course of a lesson. Today when the use of visual media is standard classroom procedure, Woodward's point sounds very up-to-date. Learning does not end with a knowledge of objects, he hastened to add; there must be a natural transition from sense experience to conceptual understanding. It is as though all subjects enter the mind through "the gate of the senses" (the metaphor was not original with Woodward), are taken in, digested, and transmuted by the imagination into knowledge. The detailed strategies for accomplishing this end Woodward worked out at great length. So too did yet another of Hartlib's associates, *Charles Hoole* (1610–1667), writing in his *A New Discovery of the Old Art of Teaching School.* Unlike Woodward, Hoole's recommendations were solidly based on many years of teaching experience in Latin grammar schools.

Finally, the best known member of the group was the brilliant scholar-poet-classicist *John Milton* (1608–1674). Unlike the others he aimed to outline a "compleat and generous" education for "nobler and gentler" youth, not for commoners. His views as expressed in *Tractate on Education* are very much in the courtly aristocratic tradition. Despite this they appealed to Puritans because of Milton's insistence that private academies could vastly improve upon the sort of education ordinarily offered through Anglican-controlled Latin grammar schools. Like so many utopian idealists he utterly failed to take account of the "average" learner's inherent limitations. The enormous program of studies he proposed—encompassing mathematics, Latin grammar and literature, geometry, Greek, agriculture, philosophy, geography, physiology, poetry, modern literature, economic, politics, history, logic, rhetoric, Hebrew, and Italian—could hardly have been followed by anyone but a genius like Milton himself. Obviously no actual school implemented so ambitious a program, although some of its features were adopted in the better English academies.

Even though the Stuart restoration of 1660 thwarted Puritan educational ambitions, part of the work of Hartlib and others had a permanent effect on later English education. Two Acts for the Propagation of the Gospel enabled these dissenters (sometimes called nonconformists) to found schools throughout England and Wales. Subjects like history, trigonometry, economics, and navigation were incorporated into curricula. Realist pedagogy as practiced in these schools was so superior that its adoption was assured in more than a few of the traditional Latin institutions. Most Puritan schools were abolished when the Stuarts returned to power; a few continued to operate clandestinely; others were reconverted into grammar schools of the orthodox mold. The Act of Toleration of 1670 made it possible for dissenters to reopen schools once again and these quickly found favor when contrasted with entrenched Latin schools. In the 1700's most of England's specialized trade schools were descended from institutions governed according to precepts first popularized by men like Hartlib, Woodward, Dury, and Petty.

THE LIFE AND WORK OF JOHN AMOS COMENIUS

The Great Pansophist

The greatest single obstacle to appreciating the seventeenth-century's realist reform movement is its historic success. Most of the major theoretical tenets and many of the practical injunctions first advanced by educators during the 1600's have become firmly entrenched in modern pedagogy, so much so in fact that it is hard to see them in their original contexts. What were radical or daring ideas in the postconfessional period are now lack-luster truisms. This is very much the case when considering the greatest exponent of the realist movement, *John Amos Comenius* (1592–1670).[20]

He was born at Nivnitz in Moravia (in the kingdom of Bohemia) at a time when the tides of religious hatreds were running high. At age twelve he was enrolled at a poor village school at Straznice where, like Erasmus and Montaigne, he was appalled at the teaching methods employed. Matters were no better, he found, while attending a Moravian Latin grammar school at Prerau four years later. By the time he entered the College of Herborn in Nassau, his disgust at reigning school practices knew no bounds. Schools, he testified, were "terrors for boys and slaughter houses of the mind," "places where a hatred of literature and books is contracted, where ten or more years are spent in learning what might be acquired in one, where what ought to be poured in gently is violently forced in and beaten in. . . ." Students were stuffed with meaningless words and con-demned to memorizing unintelligible grammatical rules, without even profiting from their misery. At Herborn the young Comenius was attracted to the ideas of Ratke and Henry Alsted on how language teaching could be reformed. Although he intended to enter the Moravian Brethren min-istry, several years were required before ordination. In the interim he traveled and spent a year at Heidelberg, learning from such leading re-formers as Johann Valentin Andreä, David Pareus, and George Hartlib, the younger brother of Samuel Hartlib. Comenius returned to his native Mora-via to teach in the local Latin school, determined to put into practice some of the educational ideas he had imbibed at Heidelberg. In 1618 he assumed his clerical duties as pastor and school superintendent in Fulneck, a leading center of the Brethren.

Two years later the Thirty Years' War broke out when Comenius was only twenty-six. The next few years brought nightmarish persecutions for all Protestants in Bohemia, more terrible still for the Hussite Brethren, who were especially despised by Catholic forces. Comenius was forced to leave his expectant wife behind to lead a search for a safer haven. He finally set-tled his flock of fellow Moravians at Leszno (Lissa) in Poland. Before cir-cumstances permitted him to call for his wife and infant son, both had died of the plague in Prerov. For the next dozen years the grief-stricken father

---

[20] The literature on Comenius is enormous. Some good sources to consult include Matthew Spinka, *John Amos Comenius: That Incomparable Moravian* (Chicago: Uni-versity of Chicago Press, 1943); R. F. Young, *Comenius in England, 1641–1642* (London: Oxford University Press, 1932); F. Kozik, *The Sorrowful and Heroic Life of John Amos Comenius* (Prague: State Educational Publishing House, 1958); S. S. Laurie, *John Amos Comenius, Bishop of the Moravians: His Life and Educational Works* (Boston: Willard Small, 1885); S. S. Laurie, *John Amos Comenius* (Syracuse, N.Y.: C. W. Bardeen, 1892); N. M. Butler, *The Place of Comenius in the History of Education* (Syracuse, N.Y.: C. W. Bardeen, 1892); W. S. Monroe, *Comenius and the Beginning of Educational Reform* (New York: Charles Scribner's Sons, 1900).

plunged himself into his work as rector of a gymnasium at Leszno. This was also a period of incessant literary activity. In 1632 Comenius completed his first great educational treatise, *Didactica Magna* (*The Great Didactic*). The aim of this exposition of "the art of education and school management" was, he announced, "to seek and find a method of instruction, by which teachers may teach less, but learners may learn more." Also published was a series of graded textbooks to illustrate how his method could be applied. The first text was designed as an instructional primer to guide mothers in preschool training, entitled *The School of Infancy*. A good education, he argued there, begins at a very early age through careful supervision of the child's physical, moral, and emotional development. There followed half a dozen more books prescribing the education to be given in a vernacular school for children aged six through twelve, and an introductory Latin book called *Janua Linguarum Reserata* (*Gate of Tongues Unlocked*). Only the latter excited any attention; it quickly was translated into sixteen languages and adopted in most European countries. Its success derived from a careful arrangement of common words and idioms into sentences organized according to ascending levels of difficulty. A companion work, the *Vestibulum,* was a simpler text intended to teach each Latin word in relation to its object referent.

Comenius had by now become universally famous as an original educational theorist. In 1641 he accepted an invitation from Samuel Hartlib to come to England to help establish an academy, or universal house of learning, first proposed by Bacon and endorsed in the *Didactica Magna*. It was a most unpropitious time for the undertaking; the Irish Rebellion flared up and Parliament refused to allocate the necessary funds. The disappointed Comenius next took a commission under the chancellor of the University of Upsala in Sweden to prepare a series of textbooks for the country's schools. It was tiring work and he was happy to be released from his chores in 1648 to return to Poland as Bishop of the Moravian Church. Continuing sectarian strife brought no relief to the beleaguered Brethren; two years thereafter Comenius left his episcopal charge to found a school at Sarospatok in Hungary at the urging of Count Rakoczy. Again he confronted bitter failure. Whereas the *Sketch of a Pansophic School,* a book Comenius drew up to assist in organizing the new school, proposed a total of seven graded classes, only three were ever put into operation because of the teachers' unwillingness to follow his plan. Despite the failure, Comenius was to enjoy another kind of triumph with the publication of his *Orbis Sensualium Pictus* (*The World in Pictures*), a still more simplified version of the *Vestibulum*. It was an astounding success. The *Orbis* was basically "a word list of all the fundamental activities of life represented to the eye" —Latin words paired with their vernacular equivalents, illustrated by pictures. This simple innovation, the introduction of drawings into a textbook, awed elementary school teachers around the world.

From Hungary Comenius went back to Leszno, only to find himself caught in the midst of war between Swedes and Poles. He fled for his life, abandoning in the burning ruins of the city an invaluable collection of notes and manuscripts. The last six years of his life were spent in Amsterdam writing and tending to his pastoral duties.

Comenius' Pedagogy

Comenius' point of departure for his educational views is theological, rather than naturalistic or scientific—a point that accounts for his historical failure to effect substantial reforms within the schools during his lifetime. Few were willing to disengage his theological convictions from his pedagogy in an age when religious orthodoxy was paramount. Education for him meant a preparation for life here and for eternal life in the hereafter. We learn, he wrote, "not for the school, but for life," which is a prelude to the larger life after death. It follows that formal schooling must serve moral and religious ends first, last, and always, "Our schools, therefore, will . . . be Christian schools when they make us as like to Christ as is possible. How wretched is the teaching that does not lead to virtue and to piety." Unlike Sturm, Melanchthon, or other Protestant religious educators, Comenius never fell prey to a narrow classical humanism as the means to piety, first, because he abhorred pagan morality, and, second, despite his appreciation of ancient languages and literature, he hoped to bring the broadest possible range of subjects into the curriculum. This formative aspiration to create a system of universal knowledge as the temporal goal of learning, known as *pansophism*, has frequently been misinterpreted. Some allege Comenius believed *all* men could acquire *all* human knowledge, an idea supported in his comment that everyone is "to know all things, to do all things, and to say all things." On the face of it the claim is preposterous. In reality his call for pansophism was an appeal for a kind of basic liberal education that would connect the learner with all the fundamentals of living, but it would not of course necessarily make the learner master of those fundamentals. In modern terms Comenius was asking the question what kind of well-rounded education of mind, body, and spirit would produce the highest type of human wisdom. He believed he had uncovered clues for answering that question.

The first concomitant imperative following from the pansophic ideal is universal schooling for everyone. "The education that I propose," he wrote, "includes all that is proper for a man, and is one in which all men who are born into this world should share. All, therefore, should be educated together, that they may stimulate and urge on one another." This unalterable rejection of a dual school system, one for the classes and one for the masses (if any at all) flatly contradicted prevailing opinion in his own time. It was literally inconceivable to most people that aristocrats and peasants could be gathered together, regardless of differences in sex, religion, social position, or economic status and each individual judged on his own merits.

Some people even today refuse to accept such a notion. The second imperative, Comenius believed, was that education should begin with vernacular instruction—also a radical proposal in his day. "To attempt to teach a foreign language before the mother tongue has been learned is as irrational as to teach a boy to ride before he can walk," he exclaimed.

In the *Didactica* Comenius set forth four essential stages, each lasting six years, around which schooling should be organized: infancy, childhood, boyhood, and youth. Corresponding to these he recommended the establishment of four kinds of schools: a mother school within the home, or *Schola Materna;* a vernacular school in each town, or *Schola Vernacula;* a classical school, or *Schola Latina,* in every major city; and a university for every regional area. In the mother school the child was to be given "the rudiments of all the knowledge that we wish to give a human being for the needs of life." Essentially, this meant training the senses to connect things with words and exposing the infant to a variety of experiences. The vernacular school, the next step up the educational ladder, would provide six classes of graduated studies in reading, writing, arithmetic, history, mechanics, religion, ethics, and music. A more intensive curriculum involving four languages and all the arts and sciences would be reserved for the Latin *Gymnasium.* At this level able students would move toward the pansophic ideal of appreciating how each discrete subject relates to all other subjects, how one field of human endeavor bears upon all others. "Every branch of human knowledge" would be taught to "select intellects" capable of passing an entrance examination and entering the university. One might specialize in law, medicine, theology, or statecraft, but only after thorough exposure to other fields of study besides the area of concentration.

Schools at all levels, Comenius believed, should not "resound with shrieks and blows"; they should be places where learning is "speedy, pleasant and thorough." Discipline must be firm but never cruel: "No blows should be given for lack of readiness to learn; for if the pupil does not learn readily, this is the fault of no one but the teacher, who either does not know how to make his pupils receptive of knowledge or does not take the trouble to do so." If the teacher is unable to make an impression, beatings will have no effect. Comenius' precept here obviously exaggerates the importance of teacher effort without allowing for students' active participation in the learning process. In all probability his own unhappy school experience plus revulsion from the use of brute strength accounts for the distortion. In any case Comenius endorsed a pernicious metaphor which has plagued educational theory for millennia, "The mouth of the teacher is a spring from which streams of knowledge issue and flow over [students] and whenever they see this spring open, they should place their attention like a cistern beneath it." With this, he utterly discounted the role of self-discipline and activity on the part of learners. Fortunately this strain in Comenius' thought was counterbalanced by the injunction to make learning more meaningful by allowing students to act upon the material presented. "Artisans do not detain their apprentices with theories, but set them to do practical work at an early age," he observed, "thus they learn to forge by forging, to carve by carving, to paint by painting, and to dance by dancing. In school, therefore," Comenius insisted, "let students learn to write by writing, to talk by talking, to sing by singing, and to reason by reasoning." Here again he was directly opposed to the usual school practices of the 1600's.

What is learned must be useful for the enlargement of living, though not in any narrow utilitarian sense. "Nothing should be learned solely for its value at school, but for its use in life. . . . Whatever is taught should be . . . of practical application in everyday life and of some definite use." The *process* of learning, in order to be intelligible, must grow naturally out of the laws of human development, Comenius argued. Following Bacon, he insisted that acquaintance with facts must precede knowledge of general rules since "the mind derives the material for all its thoughts from sense," and particulars enter in through sensory experience. This suggests that human development is a sequential process in which various mental faculties mature, beginning first with the senses. "The correct order of instruction is followed," he claimed, "if boys be made to exercise, first the senses (for this is easiest), then the memory, next the understanding, and finally the judgment. For knowledge begins from sense, and passes into memory through imagination; then the understanding of universals is reached by induction from particulars; and finally comes judgment on the facts of understanding, leading to the establishment of knowledge."[21] In other words, teaching must appeal to the senses, it must allow the child to use them to manipulate his environment through pictures, models, objects, and diagrams. The root evil of much education, as Comenius saw it, was the separation of words and things. Neither makes sense without the other.

Maturational readiness is a critical variable affecting learning. "To attempt to cultivate the will before the intellect (or the intellect before the imagination, or the imagination before the faculty of sense perception), is mere waste of time," he wrote. "But this is what those do who teach boys logic, poetry, rhetoric, and ethics before they are thoroughly acquainted with the objects that surround them." This was literally the case in some schools—boys would be compelled to attend lectures on subjects in which they had absolutely no preparation whatsoever.

Comenius' passion for systematizing shows up clearly in detailed discussion of means and ends in education. He laid down sixteen fundamental rules just for the shaping of morals, and another twenty-one for instilling piety. Among the many pedagogical principles he advanced, mention of the following will have to suffice: (1) Instruction must be adapted to the age and level of maturity of each student; (2) this, in turn, implies the

21 M. W. Keatinge, *The Great Didactic of John Amos Comenius*, 2nd ed. (London: Adams and Charles Black, 1910), p. 135.

need for graduated classes conducted according to a uniform schedule with a room and teacher provided each class; 3) the relative balance of recitation, instruction, study, and recreation within each class should be determined by the physiological and psychological readiness of its members; (4) ample use should be made of training aids, laboratories, and illustrated texts; (5) learning is more efficient if the structure or form of the lesson is made clear in advance; (6) one thing should be pursued at a time, not many subjects in any given school period; (7) anything learned will be retained longer if it is related to something else learned of a similar nature —the two will mutually reinforce one another; (8) memory is a faculty which can be trained through proper exercise; (9) the precise order of instruction must be borrowed from "nature"; and because nature is consistent in its operations, a uniform instructional method must be used for teaching all subjects.

Comenius has been called one of the most comprehensive, broadest-minded, and most far-seeing educators of all times.[22] There were few problems in education he did not consider somewhere in his writings and even today his observations are worth considering at length. He may be faulted for the somewhat crude sensationalism that served as underpinning for his psychological foundations, his philosophical outlook hardly fares much better in modern eyes, and without doubt he was just plain wrong on some educational points, but the innovations now common in contemporary schooling which he advanced almost defy enumeration. If ever there lived a "man before his time" it was this realist reformer. Through no fault of his own, his influence on schools during his lifetime was minimal. It took practically two hundred years before the educational ideals of pansophic realism gained sufficient support to inaugurate lasting improvements.

SUMMARY

The cultural metamorphosis that transformed a theocentric society into an anthropocentric one after the fourteenth century was a momentous phase in the evolution of Western civilization. Renaissance humanism, its first major expression, was the dominant ideology of an increasingly worldly culture. In educational thought, to produce a *homo universale,* a "complete" man in the mold of Cicero's statesman and Quintilian's orator was the central ambition. This ideal, exemplified in the work of Vergerio, Vittorino da Feltre, or the Guarinos, proved to be a positive force for cultural renewal, at least until the breadth of vision inherent in classicism was lost sight of, to be replaced by a sterile, lifeless Ciceronianism. In northern Europe humanism represented a fusion of traditional religious piety with antique enthusiasm. Several of its proponents—Groot, Hegius, Colet, and

---

[22] Ibid. (1896 edition), p. 98.

Reuchlin—used humanism as a platform for pedagogical reforms. New schools were organized in England, France, the Netherlands, and, to a lesser extent, German lands. Curricula at almost all levels felt classical learning's influence. The old medieval pattern of studies was seriously challenged wherever humanism made headway. Its momentum was scarcely affected by the upheavals of the confessional revolts, though the same could not be said for formal institutions of learning. Very few schools remained untouched, in one way or another, by the Reformation.

During the waning years of the sixteenth century it was clear the fate Italian humanism had suffered earlier was now overtaking its institutionalized expression in the North. Schools had not really captured the Renaissance spirit; they had embalmed it. Devotion to classicism could be as confining an intellectual straitjacket as scholastic pursuits had ever been. Society was entering the throes of another revolution, the rise of science. The new challenge confronting educators was how to respond to the changing needs of a transitional culture.

The prophets of the dawning scientific age had little interest in formal schooling as such. But the appeals of Bacon, Descartes, Newton, and others to employ scientific method in many fields of human endeavor were bound to affect educators. Realism was one manifestation of general dissatisfaction with degenerate humanism. It was the force behind attempts throughout the 1600's to introduce vernacular instruction, more efficient methodologies, better schools, and broader curricula. Circumstances precluded the possibility that so radical a reformer as John Amos Comenius would be listened to in educational circles, yet indirectly his teachings affected most of the seventeenth century's leading educational theorists. Realist ideas found concrete embodiment in the labors of Reyher, Ratke, Hartlib, Woodward, and others. Limited experiments were launched by the Jansenists, the various French teaching congregations, the Puritan dissenters in England, and several members of the royalty. Moreover, in spite of universal devastation brought on by religious unrest, new kinds of schools began to appear, including courtly or knightly academies, a few institutions for women, trade and commercial schools for the lower classes, and municipal vernacular secondary schools.

QUESTIONS FOR DISCUSSION

1. What parallels can be found between the burgher resistance to humanist Latin grammar schools in the sixteenth century and criticism of university-level instruction today? Is it possible that the growing demand for community or junior colleges, trade schools, and other postsecondary vocational training centers is a function of the same forces that led to the founding of municipal vernacular schools in the 1500's or the English dissenters' schools in the seventeenth century?

2. To what extent do men share today the Renaissance belief that education's potential for social betterment is almost unlimited? And if indeed humanists were convinced that society could be improved through more and better schooling, why did they fail to urge universal, compulsory schooling for everyone?

3. Notice that during the Renaissance and again during the rise of science, older established universities did *not* take the lead in spreading the new learning. If anything, they actively resisted it. Why was this the case? Are contemporary institutions of higher learning following the same pattern?

4. Repeatedly through the writings of educational theorists there appears the claim that we learn by doing (in Aristotle, Vives, Mulcaster, Comenius, and so on). What does this really mean and what implications for teaching follow?

5. Does Langer's thesis that each historical age has its own special "motive questions" or "generative ideas" make sense to you? Why or why not? If she is correct, what have been the generative ideas characteristic of our own recent past?

6. It is commonplace to observe that we live in a scientific world. What evidence can be found for the opposing thesis, that we live in a very *un*scientific age?

7. How relevant today in a world of proliferating knowledge is Comenius' pansophic ideal? Would it be more difficult or easier to realize within today's schools? Why?

8. Despite protestations to the contrary, most teachers think of learning in terms of mastering a fixed body of knowledge. Why does this attitude hinder our alleged efforts to individualize instruction for meeting the varying needs, interests, and capabilities of students? If, as the foregoing discussion in this chapter implies, the idea of taking learning differences into account has been around for centuries, why have modern educators seemingly made so little progress toward this goal?

6 Education for an Enlightened Society

As a society becomes more enlightened it realizes that it is responsible not to transmit and conserve the whole of its existing achievements, but only such as make for a better future society. The school is its chief agency for the accomplishment of this end.

JOHN DEWEY
Democracy and Education

I may have thought the road to a world of free and happy beings shorter than it is proving to be, but I was not wrong in thinking that it is worthwhile to live with a view to bringing it nearer. . . . These things I believe, and the world, for all its horrors has left me unshaken.

BERTRAND RUSSELL
Reflections on My Eightieth Birthday

THE EIGHTEENTH CENTURY AND
THE AGE OF THE ENLIGHTENMENT

The pessimistic world view of most educated men in seventeenth-century Europe had been dominated by two almost unassailable sources of authority —Greco-Roman literature and the Scriptures. The Renaissance, with its humanist educational movement, had represented a revival of Greek and Latin learning; the Reformation had stressed the unquestionable authority of Biblical script and the writings of the Church fathers. If man needed any reminder of his vulnerability or of the omnipotence of divinity in the scheme of things, recurrent outbreaks of plague in England and the unfathomable holocaust of the Thirty Years' War in Germany afforded ample evidence of God's wrath. In the century to follow, however, the reverence with which men approached the texts that enshrined the taproots of European civilization was seriously eroded, accompanied by increasing indifference to traditional religion and the strictures of humanistic learning. The new age dawning was one of optimism, characterized by confidence in reason and natural law, by cosmopolitanism and a belief in universal progress, by a faith that humanity was at last visibly freeing itself from the superstitions, prejudices, and blind cruelty of the past. Not without justification educated men gradually came to believe that they were entering upon what they described as a *siècle de lumières*, an *Aufklärung*, or an "enlightened" era.

The *Enlightenment*, so considered, marked no cataclysmic break with the past; rather, it was a logical culmination or coming together of diverse intellectual currents set in motion by the Renaissance, the Reformation, and the rise of scientific inquiry. Any mechanical attempt to parcel out historical evolution into homogeneous and self-contained periods is foredoomed to failure; at most it can be said that the new era of the eighteenth century was a blossoming of attitudes which had already been widespread as early as the sixteenth century and even before.[1]

It would be misleading, furthermore, to suppose that man's changing way of viewing himself in relation to the world was due solely to the advances of seventeenth-century science. Although it is true that the work of Copernicus, Galileo, and Newton eroded some of mankind's pessimistic certainties about his depraved impotence to shape his material and social environment, and replaced them with new ways of looking at the universe, it is equally valid to say that the rise of science could and did buttress traditional religious piety. It did so by demonstrating new principles of order manifest in natural phenomena, suggesting to some at least the presence of a divine architect of infinite virtuosity. More significant perhaps was the way in which scientific discovery fed man's growing lust for knowledge, the *libido sciendi*, which theological dogmatism had outlawed and branded as intellectual pride.[2] Once stimulated, the desire for further discoveries in every field of human endeavor could not be denied. Now it was termed an essential component of human nature as such and restored to a place of supreme importance.

Undoubtedly, voyages of discovery beyond the sequestered shores of Europe hastened the transformation of cultural life. What the explorers did was to reveal that the better part of the globe could no longer be regarded by intellectually responsible men as merely marginally relevant to European Christian civilization. Anthropological data pouring in from

[1] Consult Norman Hampson, *The Enlightenment* (Baltimore: Penguin, 1968), pp. 15–40. Some writers compound confusion by pushing the eighteenth-century Enlightenment's beginnings all the way back to the humanistic revival of the twelfth century.

[2] This idea is expounded at length in Ernst Cassirer's monumental work, *The Philosophy of the Enlightenment* (Boston: Beacon Press, 1964), pp. 14 ff.

distant locales further impressed upon *Homo Europeensis* his insularity; he could no longer countenance the provincial assumption that the world revolved entirely around his collective person, or that the traditions of Israel, Greece, and Rome, sustained within the exclusive fraternity of the Church, encompassed everything worth knowing. A whole world, literally, awaited him without.

Clearly, it was becoming increasingly difficult to offer a rational justification for traditional beliefs, both religious and secular. Philosophically, the difficulty was compounded by an alarming tendency among some thinkers to assume that human reason was adequate to uncover truth without the supportive assistance of theology. Although Descartes, Leibniz, Spinoza, and others consistently attached conventional religious orthodoxy to their respective systems of thought, it was becoming painfully apparent that the latter were logically viable without it.[3] Pierre Bayle, for one, put it succintly when he announced, "every individual dogma . . . is false when refuted by the clear and distinct perceptions of natural reason." Similarly, Hobbes, in England, extruded religion as a source of morality and based ethical values, as well as political theory, on the human impulse toward self-preservation. Such blatant secularism inevitably contributed to a decline of the authority of the churches in European intellectual life.

Forward-thinking intellectuals were acutely aware of the need for reform in all areas of life. In art, literature, and music, an overworked form of classicism as the predominant mold held sway, tellingly revealed in the painting of Reynolds, the music of Mozart, the poetry of Pope, and the plays of Racine. In terms of economic activity, agriculture remained the most important pursuit of the laboring classes, with control of trade and commerce—mercantilism—firmly resting in the hands of privileged groups of wealthy men. Though the general decline in Europe's population during the previous century had been reversed, the general economy of the Continent had not fully recovered its lost buoyancy, partly because of the merchant guilds whose regulations perpetuated a static business complex and partly because of the landed aristocracy, which stoutly resisted any trend toward the emancipation of a formerly servile peasantry. Age-old manorial relationships governing most of society betrayed strong traces of a lingering medieval way of life.

Politically, the centralized governments of European states were growing ever more powerful and were embarking upon ambitious (and expensive) policies requiring increased taxes. Armies had grown to unprecedented size, as had the buildings demanded by royalty. Except in England, Holland, and Switzerland, power resided with absolute monarchs still claiming divine sovereignty, and even in those areas, the administration of government was controlled by a select few. In all regions the clergy constituted a privileged class alongside the nobility; and everywhere the Church was

3 Hampson, op. cit., p. 28.

successfully defending its rights as a large landowner. In Britain, to be sure, royal absolutism was tempered by a measure of civil liberty, but the situation there was a universally envied exception to the general rule. In the United Provinces, for example (a federation of several states of which Holland was the most important), there also existed a form of republican government, but it was based on a respect for feudal rights rather than on any theory of popular sovereignty and depended upon a delicate balance of power among contending patrician oligarchies. Political antiquarianism prevailed in Russia, in Italy, in Spain, and in the German principalities. The domains of the Hapsburgs and the state of Prussia were headed by paternal despots, no less authoritarian for all their relatively benign rulership. Needless to add, government in France accorded with the usual pattern of absolutist power. Complaints from the disenfranchised were rife. Injustices in the entire political, social, and economical system of Europe led to grievances, complaints unheeded led to louder protests, and finally protests generated into a concerted demand for total reform. Out of this ferment there emerged an era and a culture of the mind appreciably differen from any of its predecessors.

The Enlightenment Faith

A key to understanding eighteenth-century intellectual life, and with it many of the educational movements of the period, is provided by a congerie of beliefs about man and his society that gradually won acceptance in popular thought as the century advanced. Taken together, those affirmations represented a dynamic credo which was to prove portentous for the future, a faith strong enough to withstand determined opposition and emerge as the dominant world view of comparatively recent times. The history of mankind, it was observed, is a sad tale of oppression, tyranny, exploitation, and barbarism. The customs and institutions by which men live and to which they often fanatically cling have, through the ages, sanctioned xenophobia, corruption, organized murder, systematic cruelty, and innumerable other absurdities. The hope that all this is neither inevitable nor irremediable, that mankind is not fallen but merely a victim of itself, that man can rework his earthly lot for the better, not simply by an inward change of heart or by the enactment of some utopian scheme but by the critical employment of reason, was now becoming widely accepted as the eighteenth century wore on. As the French revolutionary St. Just phrased it, "Happiness is a new idea in Europe." For the first time in Western history, people believed they could attain a state of perfection here on earth formerly thought possible only in a state of grace and then only in an afterlife. It was a major generative idea in European culture.

The Enlightenment faith was a reaction against religious authoritarianism and political absolutism, against social inequalities and rigid class distinctions. It was a protest against all forms of lingering "medievalism" in intellectual life, unscientific habits of thought, and theories of human impotence. Underlying the rejection was a surging faith in science, in human reason, and in the common man. What grace, salvation, and predistination were to traditional Christianity, it has been said, nature, reason, and progress were to the faith of the Enlightenment. "Nature" connoted rational order, the whole Newtonian system of causes and effects governed by universal, understandable laws. It meant whatever is normatively good, orderly, and proper, as opposed to what is "unnatural"—vividly illustrated by the prevalence of vested privileges, monopolistic economic systems, and irrational modes of social organization. More precisely, "Nature" was a standard borrowed from the scientific world view and applied to the world of human affairs. "Reason" was to be the instrument for applying that standard. For the enlightened man, reason penetrated all surface divergencies, all the accretions of tradition and prejudice, to the pristine core of reality itself. It was the cast of thought that took nothing on trust, that opposed any authority, whether political or ecclesiastical, if it could not justify its claims in the light of common sense. When reason held sway, it was argued, man would discover the relations, institutions, and principles that are "natural"; when he conformed to them, he would be happy. In particular, reason revealed that inherited rights for the few, possessed at the expense of the masses, were unnatural and therefore should be revoked.

"Progress," the third keynote of the Enlightenment, served as a kind of secular eschatology for eighteenth-century intellectuals.[4] The thought of posterity, of progress, as Diderot said, could replace the idea of heaven. Once men take thought, the reasoning went, they can brush aside the failures of the past, reform their institutions, and move steadily toward a harmonious social order. The Marquis de Condorcet was convinced progress was inevitable: "Everything tells us that we are approaching the era of one of the grand revolutions of the human race . . . no bounds have been fixed to the improvement of the human faculties . . . the perfectibility of man is absolutely indefinite. . . ."[5] As soon as man learned to extend the methods of natural scientists to society, he would find Utopia just around the corner.

The French Philosophes

The revolt against the old order began in France. Nowhere else perhaps were the evils of political absolutism so apparent. During the long reigns of Louis XIV (1643–1715) and his successor, Louis XV (1715–1774), the counterpoint to courtly splendor was the general misery that made that

---

[4] See Carl Becker, *The Heavenly City of the Eighteenth Century Philosophers* (New Haven, Conn.: Yale University Press, 1963).

[5] One of the saddest ironies of history is that Condorcet wrote his optimistic treatise *The Progress of the Human Mind* (1796) while in hiding, under the death sentence from the Jacobin-controlled Revolutionary Convention of 1793–1794.

aristocratic opulence possible. The proud boast of Louis XIV that he *was* the State (*"L'État, c'est moi!"*) was perfectly true, though it could not be denied that his absolute dominion was possible only through a ruthless crushing of all independence of thought and action in political, social, and even literary spheres. The exactions of the tax collectors kept the lower classes in a state of helpless poverty. Nor was their misery relieved when the second Louis came to power. If anything, growing inefficiency within the French government continued unchecked. Efforts to alter or reform institutions were abandoned; and a corrupt administration entrenched itself still more firmly. A chaotic tax system, the erratic administration of justice, the absence of a uniform system of law, and the special privileges of the nobles and high ecclesiastics added to the woes of the masses. Louis XV continued his predecessor's inflexible rule, to the point where the rumblings of a discontented bourgeoisie may well have prompted his prophetic comment that after him would follow a general collapse—*"Après moi, le déluge!"* One might think that the genesis of reforming ideals of life would be unlikely under such conditions. And yet possibly it was *because* the French situation was so desperate that protesters found a ready audience. Other factors present included the growing self-consciousness of the middle class, popular resentment against the "iron alliance" of Church and state, and the absence of political barriers which in other lands (like Germany) robbed would-be reformers of a national public.[6]

The leaders of the Enlightenment were *philosophes,* a new intellectual class of literary men, popularizers, and propagandists, like *Montesquieu* (1689–1755), *Turgot* (1727–1781), *Diderot* (1713–1784), and *Voltaire* (1694–1778). A good case can be made for the thesis that they flourished mainly because they expressed the hopes and fears of the French bourgeois class just at a time when reform furthered the latter's interests. Without the philosophes' learned appeals to a newly awakened public opinion, an opinion increasingly hostile to the *ancien régime,* the bourgeoisie would have lacked a philosophical basis. There were, of course, other reasons why the *illuminati* (the "enlightened ones") had so much strength. Religious wars, which had immolated much of Europe in the previous century, had subsided. Trade was expanding and prosperity increasing; human life was becoming more orderly, more secure—more humane. The new scientific achievements of Galileo and Newton, the new philosophy and psychology advanced by Locke, and the vision of a world improved and shaped to men's needs and wants by the methods of scientific experiment presented by Descartes and Bacon seemed to provide the springboard for a great forward leap. Centuries-old accumulations of intellectual rubbish had been thrown

6 The Enlightenment developed in several different directions, responding to the peculiar conditions of the various countries where it penetrated. For a fuller account of these movements, in England and in German lands as well as in France, a remarkable set of references is to be found in Will and Ariel Durant's, *The Story of Civilization* (New York: Simon and Schuster, 1965), Vols. VIII, IX, and X.

out. Empiricism, unlike theological metaphysics, offered a way to certain truths which would be applied for mankind's benefit. Morality no longer seemed to need religious sanctions. In the same vein, political and economic theories had finally divested themselves of theology. "What light has burst over Europe within the last few years!" Voltaire exclaimed. "It is the light of common sense."

The major obstacle standing between men and perfectibility was the old order, symbol of unenlightenment. And so the philosophes blasted its economics, its politics, and its religion. Men like Voltaire did not foresee, nor perhaps desire, actual revolution, but their pungent criticism and countless projects for social melioration unquestionably helped to tumble the existing edifice. In particular, the Enlightenment marked the start of open warfare between science and theology in the West. Because they lacked any real historical consciousness, the reformers saw revealed religion as an imposture, fobbed off on an innocent public by rascally priests with the willing cooperation of tyrants. Voltaire's bitter advice regarding the Church —"crush the infamous thing"—seemed eminently sensible to men grown weary of trying to reform it from within. Thus, by the end of the century, a profound secularization of Western thought and culture had ensued. The Civil Constitution of the Clergy in 1790 and the systematic de-Christianizing of France during the Revolution merely represented a logical extension of anticlericalism.[7] The emergent world view of the philosophes was characterized by what Lecky calls a "declining sense of the miraculous," a world seen governed by universal law and causal order, leaving no room for religious revelation. "In all things of this kind," Voltaire remarked, "there is little need or use of revelation, God having furnished us with natural and surer means to arrive at a knowledge of them. For whatsoever truth we come to a clearer discovery of from the knowledge and contemplation of our own ideas, will always be more certain to us than those which are conveyed to us by traditional revelation."

In place of supernatural religion, the philosophes endorsed a "natural religion" consisting, in Voltaire's words, of "the principles of morality common to the human race." There certainly was a God, but his intervention on behalf of the orderly operation of the universe was probably minimal; it would be more appropriate to speak of "beneficent providence" as a principle animating man and the natural order. Few intellectuals (the expatriot Baron d'Holbach an exception) actually embraced atheism. Instead, *deism* became the typical Enlightenment stance in religious matters: a watered-down theism, an attempt to construct a religion in keeping with the scientific habit of subjecting all beliefs and practices to tests of reasonableness in this life. Its cardinal principle was *uniformitarianism,* i.e., whatever is uniform and believed everywhere by all races of men is right.

7 See Le Van Baumer, ed., "The Enlightenment," in *Main Currents of Western Thought* (New York: Alfred A. Knopf, 1952), p. 363.

Natural religion was to be a universal religion to which everyone could assent once diversive sectarian creeds were thrown overboard.

Armed with confidence in a reasoned secularism, French intellectuals set out to attack the barbarities of Western society: persecution, slavery, the brutalities of the penal codes. *Physiocrats* like Turgot and Quesnay preached the doctrine of *laissez-faire* capitalism. Montesquieu's *Spirit of the Laws* was written to show how legal standards depend upon the sovereign will of the people and hence should be modified for the benefit of the electorate they govern. History was rewritten by Gibbon and Voltaire to demonstrate the absurdity of religious strife and to mock the parochialism of providential versions of the past offered by Christian apologists. In a united phalanx, proponents of the gospel of reason set before them the work of combatting society's ills wherever they were to be found. The doctrine of rationality as against mythology, of knowledge as against dogma, of progress through education as against passive resignation of the settled order, all passed like a pollen-laden wind over Europe, upsetting every tradition, stimulating inquiry, at last fomenting revolt. To Hume, Chesterfield, Walpole, and Garrick in England; to Goethe, Eckermann, and countless others in Germany; to Franklin, Jefferson, and the other founders of the new republic in America the new ideas spread. Receptive minds everywhere were deeply stirred by the writings of the philosophes and resolved to assist in the general enlightenment of mankind. The main theme throughout was that reason teaches the necessity of mutual forbearance amidst the diversity of creeds, customs, and values of humanity. The quality of human life could be improved only if knowledge were substituted for ignorance, and reason for prejudice.[8] And of course one way to effect such a transformation was through education. The story of much eighteenth-century educational theory is an account of how men proposed to implement the Enlightenment faith.

FROM REALISM TO NATURALISM IN EDUCATIONAL THEORY

The Continuing Stagnation of Schools

The seventeenth century, in retrospect, has been viewed as essentially a time of criticism and consolidation—criticism of the prevailing social, political, religious, and economic orders; consolidation of whatever gains had been made in the fields of religious reform and scientific inquiry. In education, the critical spirit was expressed in twofold protest: (1) against a degenerate classicism that had lost its social relevance, and (2) against the schools' failure to implement progressive teaching methods. On the posi-

8 For a fuller statement of the theme, see Peter Gay, *The Science of Freedom* (New York: Alfred A. Knopf, 1969).

tive side, there were three basic changes urged by educational reformers: (1) the adoption of pedagogical techniques firmly grounded in a better understanding of psychological processes; (2) a broadening of curricula to include scientific and social studies; and (3) the expansion of educational opportunities to a wider class of people. Their urgings met with a very limited response and little headway was made toward achieving the objectives articulated by Comenius, Ratke, Hartlib, Dury, and other prominent writers. For reasons previously mentioned, the postconfessional age was far more productive of theories about education than it was prone to apply such theories in actual school practice.[9]

This contrast between the "activity of speculation and the torpor of practice," which was the distinctive feature of European education in the 1600's, became even more pronounced in the first half of the following century.[10] The great majority of people received no formal schooling at all, and those who did were victimized by atrocious school programs. The usual teaching methods followed gave primary consideration to purely verbal learning through reading, lectures, and recitations from memory. Students of every age and ability were thrown together, with chaos the predictable result. The elementary curriculum (beyond which few progressed) consisted of reading, writing, and religious indoctrination. When the teacher was unusually capable, some rudimentary arithmetic might also be included. Physical discipline was unenlightened, to say the least. Beatings, whippings, and crueler forms of physical punishment were the rule, not the exception. Teachers were woefully unprepared. Many who became schoolmasters did so because they were unfit for any other occupation ("Those who can, do; those who cannot, teach") or because they needed to supplement earnings from other full-time pursuits. At the secondary level, matters were no better. Students were taught languages through formal exercises in conjugating verbs, memorizing grammatical rules, and drilling in composition. The content of instruction was hopelessly out of touch with students' needs. Lord Chief Justice Kenyon's condemnation of English grammar schools in 1795— "empty walls without scholars and everything neglected but the receipt of salaries and endowments"—was similar to complaints against French Jesuit schools around the midpoint of the eighteenth century. The barrenness, decadence, and general deterioration of quality in higher institutions was equally universal. Perhaps the only real difference from the preceding century was more people were now aware of how bad the situation had become.

Comenius, chief prophet for the realist movement, it has been made clear, drafted his proposals for breaking this bleak pattern in the seven-

[9] The phrase is borrowed (out of context) from R. Freeman Butts, *A Cultural History of Western Education,* 2nd ed. (New York: McGraw-Hill, 1955), p. 288.

[10] William Boyd, *The History of Western Education,* 8th ed. (New York: Barnes & Noble, 1966), p. 280.

teenth century. Another important attempt to accomplish similar ends was instigated by the English scholar, philosopher, tutor, physician, and political theorist *John Locke* (1632–1704). His two major works were published in the last decade of the seventeenth century but exerted their greatest influence over a half century later. With the publication of *Some Thoughts Concerning Education* (1693) and the better-known essay *On the Conduct of the Understanding* (1690), Locke provided a philosophical base for educational realism and gave it a new cast. His insistence that all ideas come from the impingement of the external world in the form of sensations and perceptions and, accordingly, his empirical conception of the role of experience in education offered a unique warrant for realist doctrines, a justification never satisfactorily offered by earlier theoreticians."[11] For this reason Locke has been called the founder of *empirical realism* in education, to distinguish it from its parent realist movement.

Locke's Career and Pedagogical Theory

Locke was born in Wrington, England, son of a Puritan attorney. At fourteen he enrolled at Winchester School to pursue Greek and Latin studies and then attended Oxford, where he remained for almost thirty years. Between 1666 and 1675 he lived in Exeter House, the London home of the first Earl of Shaftesbury, as confidant, secretarial assistant, and resident physician. While associated with Lord Ashley, Locke tried his hand at tutoring his benefactor's son and, later, his grandson. These experiences undoubtedly helped him clarify his own educational ideas. Unfortunately, his patron fell from power in 1675 and Locke was dismissed from his position at Oxford by Charles II. There followed a period of exile in Amsterdam and Rotterdam until political circumstances permitted his return to England early in 1689. The last fifteen years of his life were spent peacefully in Essex. With his death England lost one of her foremost philosophers and men of letters.

Locke's major educational treatise is an edited compilation of letters written to a friend, Edward Clarke, consisting of recommendations for the proper rearing of a young gentleman. The primary aim of education, Locke wrote, is to foster virtue, the "first and most necessary of those endowments that belong to a man." This is secured best under a private, tutorial arrangement where the teacher's influence as a good example is likely to be greatest. In the beginning, good breeding and the formation of virtuous habits of conduct will be more important than teaching knowledge in any formal way. Prudence, soundness of judgment, a social consciousness, the proper regard of others—in the early years these are more important than bookish learning. A young man must first acquire self-discipline "that [he] is able to deny himself his own desires, cross his own inclinations, and purely follow what reason directs as best, though the appetite points the

[11] Butts, op. cit., p. 288.

other way." From the start, discipline is associated with rationality in Locke's thinking: "He that has not a mastery over his inclinations, he that knows not how to resist the importunity of present pleasure or pain for the sake of what reason tells him is fit to be done," he observed, "lacks the true principle of virtue and industry, and is in danger never to be good for anything." In order to foster self-control, the child must be gradually habituated to mild physical hardships. To discipline the mind, one begins with the body. An ascetic, spartan regimen of proper diet, personal hygiene, exercises, and sports ensures bodily vigor. When necessary, parental or tutorial constraints will be placed on the maturing student, but never when there exists an opportunity for exercising his own reason and judgment. Forming "ways of conduct as natural to a well-bred man as breathing" depends upon a delicate, always changing balance of compulsion and freedom. If punishments have to be administered, they should always be applied in such a way that the student learns from them and is encouraged to increase his own self-understanding. Nothing is worse than substituting force for reason, or depriving the learner of an appropriate measure of liberty. As Locke put it, "Children have as much a mind to show that they are free, that their own good actions come from themselves, that they are absolute and independent, as any of your proudest grown men." Self-control needs personal autonomy if it is to develop. It is not until the child has internalized the teacher's sanctions that he can acquire true virtue.

Once the basic habits leading to physical health, personal virtue, and wisdom are established, the teacher can allow for greater freedom and the fuller exercise of reason. At this point formal education commences. Locke's point of departure here was an absolute rejection of existing content and methodology in institutionalized schooling. He viewed even the better schools of his day with utter disdain; first, because they were inefficient in their techniques, and, secondly, because the classic studies they tried to teach were unfit for preparing the sons of cultivated men for their duties in a civilized life. Locke's prejudice against collective schooling reveals an aristocratic bias, but it was based on a belief that true education and school learning are inherently antithetical: "Let the master's industry and skill be never so great, it is impossible he should have fifty or a hundred scholars under his eye, any longer than they are in school together; nor can it be expected, that he should instruct them successfully in anything but their books; the forming of their minds and manners requiring a constant attention, and particular application to every single boy."

The specifics of Locke's pedagogy and ideal curriculum need not be considered at length. The program of studies advocated comprised reading and writing in the vernacular, French and Latin taught through natural conversational usage, geography, mathematics, geometry, history, more English, religion and ethics, jurisprudence, dancing, fencing, and riding. That broad curriculum was to be supplemented by games and play activity so that learning would never become drudgery. The principle to be followed was utility. Every subject studied must serve to develop virtue, wisdom, and good breeding in the individual. Narrow classical training typically relying upon memorized precepts, maxims, or rules, has no usefulness for real life. A good education, Locke maintained, will omit rhetoric, pure logic, Greek, and other specialized subjects, of interest only to academics. Probably Locke's concern to make learning directly relevant to the responsibilities of gentlemanly life accounts for this unduly utilitarian attitude, and if pressed he might not have insisted on narrow utility as the sole criterion governing what should be learned.

Until he wrote his *On the Conduct of the Understanding*, Locke offered surprisingly little in the way of specific suggestions for educational technique, other than to say that teachers should avoid allowing children to associate punishment with learning, that a diversity of methods may be necessary at different stages in the child's development, and that no single teaching approach is appropriate for all learners. He did say that learning moves best from simple ideas to more complex abstractions and therefore teaching ought to be organized in this way.

Some critics have argued Locke supported the doctrine of *formal discipline,* that is, there exist mental powers as distinct agents which can be developed through exercise. In his posthumous essay *On the Conduct of the Understanding* there is a passage to support this contention. "We are born with faculties and powers capable of almost anything," he wrote, "such at least as would carry us farther than can easily be imagined; but it is only the exercise of those powers which gives us ability and skill in anything. . . . As it is in the body, so it is in the mind; practice makes it what it is." This suggests rather plainly that education consists of training mental faculties through formal exercise in order to strengthen the mind, just as exercising muscles trains the body. As a matter of historical record, this was the common interpretation accorded Locke's views and he was appealed to in support of the practice of teaching certain subjects like rhetoric, dialectic, logic, and grammar primarily for their formal disciplinary value.[12] In his *Thoughts,* however, aside from a discussion of good habit formation, the argument rejects old-fashioned disciplinary forms of education and does not imply any transfer of training among discrete mental faculties.[13]

Throughout his writings it is evident that Locke adhered to a class-bound ideal of the gentleman as educational product, a man characterized by good breeding, fine manners, and a certain discernment of judgment. This image of man, very much in the tradition of Thomas Elyot and Montaigne,

12 A version of the doctrine of formal discipline and its related idea of transfer of training is illustrated whenever contemporary teachers defend their subjects—for example, Latin or geometry—because it helps to "train the mind" to think logically.

13 Locke even made an explicit disclaimer of a faculty theory yet the tradition that he favored it lasted for almost a century. This popular belief, not Locke himself, lent continuing credence to the theory.

depended for its realization upon proper tutelage—good education—rather than upon any accident of birth. The new bourgeois image developing in England was somewhat far removed from the old concepts of aristocratic lineage and inherited feudal prerogatives; unlike his predecessor, it was more imperative that the "new" gentleman be *trained* to assume his rank and rule in the social order. It was to this requirement primarily that Locke addressed his pedagogical thoughts. Beyond this, there is nothing to suggest any concern for the educational needs of those not destined for the upper class; indeed it probably never occurred to Locke that all children should be educated in a formal school setting. The evidence points in the opposite direction, as, for example, in his writings about a plan for the revision of the Elizabethan Poor Law dealing with pauperism. "If any boy or girl, under fourteen years of age, shall be found begging out of the parish where they dwell," he advised, ". . . they shall be sent to the next working school, there to be soundly whipped and kept at work till evening, so that they may be dismissed time enough to get to their place of abode that night." He further proposed that "working schools be set up in every parish, to which the children of all such as demand relief of the parish, above three and under fourteen years of age, whilst they live at home with their parents, and are not otherwise employed for their livelihood by the allowance of the overseers of the poor, shall be obliged to come." These schools, Locke suggested, would confine themselves to instructing young urchins in such manual skills as "spinning or knitting, or some other part of woolen manufacture." Aside from recommending that pauper children be fed with bread while in work school, supplemented "in cold weather, if it be thought needfull," with "a little warm water gruel," Locke hardly troubled himself with any consideration of the specific operation of pauper institutions.

Interestingly, there is nothing in Locke's views that logically excluded a more generous humanitarianism or the possibility of popular education. On the contrary, the larger thrust of his philosophical thought might well have impelled him in that direction. His comment, "Of all the men we meet with, nine parts of ten are what they are, good or evil, useful or not, by their education. It is that which makes the great difference in mankind," serves to illustrate the point. Or, again: "Most men come very short of what they might attain unto in their various degrees by a neglect of their understanding." Locke was convinced that there are "a great many natural defects in the understanding capable of amendment, which are overlooked and wholly neglected." Proper education, as he saw it, could lead to "enlightenment," through the release and discipline of a man's reasoning; rationality could become the governing force of the individual's judgments and of his understanding, once channeled in the right way. Like the philosophes who followed him, Locke saw education as the antidote to "enthusiasm," or the reliance on emotional conviction, as a basis of truth. In this Locke was very much an Enlightenment rationalist in his own time.

An Epistemology for Educators

Locke's philosophical position proved ultimately more important than any of his particular proposals for curriculum reform or improved teaching methods. The development of his pedagogical program, like that of most major theorists before him, proceeded not in isolation but as part of a broader theory of knowledge and a view toward human nature.[14] In his *Essay Concerning Human Understanding* Locke set as his task "to inquire into the origin, certainty and extent of human knowledge, together with the grounds and degrees of belief, opinion, and assent." His analysis and "purification of knowledge" began with a total rejection of the ancient doctrine of innate ideas, the theory propounded variously by Plato, Augustine, and Descartes that the mind has been equipped at birth with authoritative knowledge of God or the world apart from experience and mental reflection upon experience. It appeared to Locke that coming to know anything (on that view a process of "intuiting" or "remembering" true ideas) was a philosophically unsatisfactory way of providing a ground of certainty for traditional logic and theological dogmas. "Whence has [the mind] all the materials of reason and knowledge?" he asked in the first part of the *Essay*. "To this I answer in one word, from experience; in that all our knowledge is founded; and from that it ultimately derives itself."

There are no innate ideas; the only "openings" into the dark "closet of the understanding" are "external and internal sensation," Locke decided, the former being the experience of observing external sensible objects in the environment (sensation proper), the latter the experience of the mind's internal operation upon perceptions and the consciousess of its own operation, or reflection. At birth the individual is devoid of any knowledge whatever. The sole source of ideas, then, is one's sensations and his reflections upon those sensations. Phrased differently, ideas arise from the impingement of objects upon the senses and from the operations of the mind upon the sense data thus provided. The mind, he claimed in an often repeated metaphor, is a *tabula rasa,* an unblemished waxen tablet upon which experience indelibly impresses itself. This process of receiving impressions is basically passive: "These simple ideas, when offered to the mind, the understanding can no more refuse to have, nor alter, when they are imprinted, nor blot them out, and make new ones itself, than a mirror can refuse, alter or obliterate the images or ideas which the objects set before it do therein produce." After gathering in these simple perceptions, the mind combines, relates, and abstracts them to make the more complex concepts which form the substance of mental life.

Two weighty conclusions seem to follow. First, if environmental in-

[14] Peter Gay, *John Locke on Education* (New York: Bureau of Publications, Teachers College, Columbia University, 1964), pp. 5 ff. An excellent critique of educational empiricism, as derived from Locke, is supplied by Marc Belth, *The New World of Education* (Boston: Allyn and Bacon, 1970), Chapter 4.

fluences exercise a pervasive power over the mind and hence determine an individual's character, then the theological doctrine of original sin must be jettisoned. Instead of viewing education as a process of correcting faults bred in an originally depraved nature, it must be regarded as a determining factor in realizing human development for good *or* evil. The teacher's task is to furnish appropriate experiences for ensuring the right kind of growth. Education seemingly assumes an enormous potential for the development and improvement of human nature.

Secondly, inequalities in men—all the distinctions of intelligence, skill, and ability—must arise from differences in the experiences men have. All men are created equal and should therefore enjoy an equality of educational opportunity. Each growing child ought to be free to have as many beneficial experiences within his environment as possible. Nurture, not nature, is all-important. Locke softened this stand slightly by admitting there may be genetic differences in endowments. For example, in the *Conduct* he affirmed, "There is, it is visible, great varieties in men's understandings." One person's mental tablet may be different from someone else's in its receptivity to impressions. Nonetheless, Locke believed subsequent experience is the crucial variable. "I do not deny," he says, "that natural disposition may often give the first rise to [some achievement] but that never carries a man far without use or exercise. . . ."

For almost an entire century these two interrelated themes lay dormant. It was not until the Enlightenment was in full bloom that eighteenth-century educational theorists, including Condillac, Helvétius, and Rousseau, began to expand upon Locke's views (sometimes unaware of their debt) and to develop them in different directions. Gradually, however, the idea that empirical experience is the *sine qua non* of human developemnt became the cornerstone of rationalist pedagogical theory. Locke's implied suggestion that education could become a great social equalizer also had a germinal potential that social reformers were anxious to exploit. In many respects the possibilities for melioration implicit in empirical realism were probably much wider than even Locke foresaw. For these reasons his views surface repeatedly in any discussion of subsequent developments.

Enlightenment Educational Themes After Locke

Two examples will suffice to show how Locke's sensationalist psychology was applied in Enlightenment educational thought. One of the earliest treatments appeared at the century's midpoint in the writings of *Étienne Bonnot de Condillac* (1715–1780). In his first publication, *Essay on the Origin of Human Knowledge* (1746), Condillac agreed with Locke's claim that all simple ideas can be assigned an experiential or empirical origin. He more or less assumed Locke's distinction between ideas of sensation and ideas of reflection having a dual origin, respectively, in experience and mental introspection. Beyond this, in his *Treatise on Sensations* (1754) Condillac set himself the task of showing that *all* ideas, mental operations, and functions are reducible to sensations. The upshot of a long argument was that "in the natural order all knowledge arises from sensations"; even the knowledge derived from higher mental processes is "transformed sensations." The senses themselves do not appear full-blown, but are developed through use by the understanding. Educationally, this meant that the faculty of reason appears as the senses emerge and must be trained by reasoning and observation. It is wrong to assume that the child is genetically different from the adult: "Faculties of the understanding are the same in a child as in a grown-up man." "It is proved then," Condillac argued, "that the faculty of reasoning appears as soon as our senses begin to develop; and that we have the use of our senses at an early age, only because we have reasoned at an early age." Proceeding from this claim, he elaborated a proper program of studies designed to develop the faculties through which ideas are transmitted. Condillac's *Course of Instruction* (1775) began by stipulating the awakening of judgment and reasoning as the primary goal of education rather than training the senses.

Claude Adrien Helvétius (1715–1771) extended Condillac's argument that all mental phenomena are transformed sensations. In his 1758 work *On the Mind* he reduced all the powers of the human understanding to sensation or sense perception. Locke was mistaken, he claimed, in holding that man possesses faculties which transcend the level of sense. There followed a reductive analysis in which Helvétius tried to demonstrate that man is the totality of his experiences. Inequalities among men arise from the quality and quantity of experiences they undergo and are not due to differences in innate capacity. All men share a common capacity whose development is determined by chance and by education. On the basis of this sensationalist psychology he erected an interesting ethical theory. Self-love is the universal basis of human behavior, and self-love is directed to the pursuit of pleasurable satisfactions. All other loves—of power, for example —are simply transformations of the fundamental love of pleasure. All the virtues can be traced back to this. However, although self-interest is the root motive of human conduct, public interest or utility is the *norm* of morality. "The name of virtue should be given to such actions only as are useful to the public and conformable to the general interest." In order to persuade people toward benevolent conduct, according to Helvétius, a child can be taught to put himself in the place of the disadvantaged. This will cause him to have painful sensations and self-love will galvanize an impulse to relieve suffering. Through time, altruism can be conditioned by the force of association between conduct and benevolence.

Such considerations compelled him to believe that education is all-important in forming habits of conduct. Phrases like "education can do all" and "education makes us what we are" are characteristic of his writing. All of humanity's defects proceed from poor education. Society could direct its higher destinies through the type of education it imparts to its constituents if there were no obstacles standing in the way. The first order of business is to eliminate the forces of reaction. Clerical control must be broken and the schools placed out of the reach of the Church. Because no government abides by the principle of morality that "the public good is the supreme law," a new governmental system must be realized. As Helvétius put it, "Every important reformation in the moral part of education supposes one in the laws and form of government." In light of these ideas, he inveighed against political despotism, economic inequalities, the priesthood of the Church, and all else he thought detrimental to the interests of society.

Given the ambitious nature of the Enlightenment reform program, it is difficult to account for the fact that most educational writers, Condillac and Helvétius included, gave so little attention to the possibilities for social renewal latent in mass public education. Consider the comment of Duclos, in his *Thoughts on the Customs of This Century,* which was not atypical of the times: "I do not think that I have too good an idea of my century," he wrote, "but it seems to me there is a certain universal fermentation whose progress one could direct or hasten by the proper education." Yet almost all who reflected on educational questions took the existence of an unteachable majority for granted. Like Locke in the previous century, they consistently refused to follow the idea of experience as the major determinant of human behavior to its logical pedagogical conclusion. Baron d'Holbach, for one, wrote, "The people neither read nor reason. They have neither the leisure nor the capacity to do so. Books are made only for that portion of a nation which its circumstances, its education and its feelings raise above crime." Proceeding on the basis of this rather circular reasoning, the philosophes actually took pride in the fact that they wrote only for a small intellectual elite.

Voltaire's antieducational attitude was even more pronounced than most. "There is always, within a nation," he maintained, "a people that has no contact with polite society, which does not belong to the age, which is inaccessible to the progress of reason and over whom fanaticism maintains its atrocious hold." Continuing, "It is expedient that the people should be directed, not that it should be educated; it is not worthy of teaching. . . ." Clearly there was a fundamental incompatibility between two doctrines that needed to be resolved: the Lockeanlike doctrine that experience (education being an important part) molds the man, and the belief that it was impossible, or at least unlikely, that the gradual progress of educational enlightenment would eventually raise up the more intelligent of the common masses to participation in a literate society. The conflict was never fully decided in the eighteenth century; for that matter it has never been competely settled since.

A New Direction

Almost imperceptibly, as the Enlightenment era wore on, there occurred a subtle shift in emphasis in the thinking of educational theorists which paralleled a much wider reorientation of intellectual thought in eighteenth-century culture as a whole. In the first few decades of the century the primary task of social reformers was to identify and indict those institutions and ideas that were thought to be obstacles to the steady march of human progress. More broadly, the objective was to lay out a comprehensive program of societal transformation, based upon a fusion of humanist and scientific ideals inherited, respectively, from the Renaissance and the scientific revolution. The philosophes and their counterparts in English and German lands were custodians of an embattled humanitarianism deriving its strength from a multitude of sources. Not the least of these was an unflagging faith in the power of human reason to set things right once obstructions to the common welfare were confronted head on. Because man is basically rational, or so it was believed, if he behaves irrationally, that is owing to the fact that his society has corrupted his "original" nature and distorted it to perverse ends. What is needed is a total transformation of the social order, so that human nature itself can be restored to its pristine goodness.

Unfortunately, it soon became evident that matters were not nearly so simple as all that. Tyrants were not easily dislodged, nor was it clear what might replace their despotisms if they were unseated. Social institutions proved remarkably impervious to assaults and here again the question remained what new forms of social organization might be devised to discharge their functions. On a more personal level, men began to weary of argument, reason, and philosophy; they failed to satisfy or to address the impulses of the heart. There were growing doubts that man was quite the mechanical automaton some sensationalist philosophers had made him out to be, much less the creature of reason he had been portrayed. Was human "progress" as inevitable as the optimists had thought it to be, and where was it leading?

In the latter half of the eighteenth century, misgivings such as these were becoming widespread. Sentiment also came to be accepted as a source of a kind of knowledge to which intelligence could not aspire; the heart, after all, should be recognized as the legitimate consort of the head. In short, Europe was ready for a gospel that would exalt feeling above thought, or at least make them coequal. It was prepared now to entertain new inspiring visions of the world and human destiny, ideals more adequate than those which the arid intellectualism of the rationalists had been able to supply so far. Reason might erect its own tyranny of the mind, it was said; and what is needed now is a more complete image of man, one that takes into account sensation, imagination, desire, and will as well as reasoning.

These vague, amorphous tendencies of thought first came together in the person of *Jean Jacques Rousseau.* His point of departure was a sharp denial of Condillac's claim that reflection was itself a form of sensation. "Perception is feeling," Rousseau insisted, "comparison is judgment. Judgment and feeling are not the same thing." Further testimony of his opposition to the prevailing rationalism was provided in his comment, "Whatever I feel to be right is right. Whatever I feel to be wrong is wrong. . . . Reason deceives us only too often and we have acquired the right to reject it only too well, but conscience never deceives." Pure reason, as Kant was to show, led to its own antinomies, but feeling—the morally autonomous "inner voice" of man—could supply the corrective.

In many ways Rousseau was a child of the Enlightenment. He accepted its faith in "Nature" as a regulative standard for the conduct of human affairs, its optimistic faith in the innate goodness of man, and its belief in a latent providential harmony in the universe. Where he parted company was in his insistence that reform must begin within individuals' hearts, before it could reconstruct society. Possibly it is futile to try to fix precisely Rousseau's place in the intellectual developments of the eighteenth century, if only because he was such an ambivalent apostle of its internal contradictions. As this was true in his social and political philosophy, it was especially so in his educational theory. As best, one can do no better than to accept at face value Rousseau's own autobiographical judgment: "I feel my own heart and I know men. I am differently made from any of those I have seen. I dare to believe that I am different from any man who exists. If I am no better, at least I am not the same."

EDUCATION ACCORDING TO NATURE:
JEAN JACQUES ROUSSEAU

His Life and Works

"I have received, sir, your new book against the human species, and I thank you for it. . . . No one has ever been so witty as you are in trying to turn us into brutes; to read your book makes one long to go on all fours. As, however, it is now some sixty years since I gave up the practice, I feel that it is unfortunately impossible for me to resume it." So wrote Voltaire to Jean Jacques Rousseau (1712–1778) upon receiving a copy of the *Discourse on the Origin and Foundation of Inequality Among Men,* an indictment of civilization, arts, and science. Voltaire was so chagrined to see Rousseau's passion for "natural" man continued in the *Social Contract* that he wrote to a correspondent. "You see now that Jean Jacques resembles a philosopher as a monkey resembles a man." He is the "dog of Diogenes gone mad." This was the kind of reaction easily provoked by a strange, unorthodox thinker who, though influenced deeply by the intellectual currents of his day, dared to turn them in unexpected directions. As this was true in Rousseau's political thinking, so too was it characteristic of his educational views. Modern educational thought would never be the same again.

Rousseau was born in Geneva, Switzerland, the son of a watchmaker. His mother died when he was a week old, leaving him to his father's erratic care. When he was ten years old, his father became embroiled in a serious dispute and to avoid a possible prison sentence fled to Geneva, abandoning his young charge to a sister-in-law. She in turn placed Jean Jacques under the tutorship of a Reverend Labercier, the pastor at Boissy. At age thirteen his uncle apprenticed him to a notary but he showed little inclination to learn and was soon dismissed. Two years later Rousseau's uncle tried again, this time apprenticing him for five years to an engraver, but the boy ran away. In the small village of Confignon, near Geneva, Rousseau was taken in by the local cleric and introduced to a titled widow by the name of Madame de Warens. This was the beginning of a long association. It was she who persuaded the sensitive youngster to convert to Catholicism. There followed a period of wandering and vagabondage during which he served briefly as a music teacher and as a companion for a succession of wealthy women. In 1731 he rejoined Baronne de Warens and lived with her for almost thirteen years.

From 1738 to 1740 Rousseau acted as tutor to the children of the de Mably family to whom he had been introduced by de Warens in hopes he would find an independent vocation. Evidently the experience was not completely happy and he resigned in discouragement. The next few years were busy ones for Jean Jacques: he visited Paris, worked as secretary to the French ambassador in Venice for a few months, returned to Paris and formed associations with leading lights like D'Holbach, Voltaire, and Diderot. In 1743 he made the acquaintance of Thérèse de Vasseur. Rousseau was to father five children with her during the next several years only to abandon them to foundling homes.[15] A happier phase in his life began in 1749 when the Academy of Dijon offered a prize for the best essay addressed to the question, "Has the progress of science and the arts tended to the purification or the corruption of morals?" Rousseau's *Discourse on the Arts and Sciences* won the prize, making its author instantly famous. His thesis, that civilization has corrupted mankind, stirred his philosophe friends to fury. Undaunted by opposition, Rousseau drafted his second *Discourse on Inequality*, reiterating the same basic argument.

In 1754 Rousseau left Paris for Geneva and reconverted back to Protestantism to regain Genevan citizenship. Between 1756 and 1762 illness forced him into semiretirement at the Hermitage, a summer cottage provided by his patroness, Madame d'Espinay. It was a period of prolific literary activity. His major novel, *New Heloise*, came out in 1761. The next year there appeared the *Social Contract* and his book on education, *Émile*. Both works added to his personal troubles; monarchists denounced the first as sub-

15 Rousseau subsequently regretted his parental irresponsibility bitterly. Critics who point to this feature of his personal life to discredit his educational views miss an important point: an individual's private behavior should not detract from the validity of his basic ideas considered by themselves.

versive, and clergymen condemned the second as heretical. Rousseau sought refuge at Geneva, then at Yverdon, near Berne, and finally moved across the Channel to England at the invitation of David Hume. Unfortunately the hapless author developed paranoid delusions and accused his protector of plotting to destroy him. Rousseau returned to Paris for a short stay, despite the possibility of police arrest, and then spent the last two months remaining to him in seclusion at Ermenonville. He died a lonely, depressed man.

Considered as an original educational theorist, Rousseau did far more than merely attack conventional pedagogical creeds or urge the adoption of a different curriculum. Beyond his indictment of primitive teaching practices and indifferent schools, he challenged almost all the major assumptions upon which educational theory had been built up to his time. He realized more clearly than even Comenius that the child must become the starting point for any education. The educator has to study children, see them for what they are, instead of what they will become. Account should be taken of all the generic characters of mankind, including age, sex, and personality differences, and then provision must be made for an environment where each individual actualizes himself to the fullest. "Each mind has a form of its own in accordance with which it must be directed," he claimed, "and for the success of the teacher's efforts it is important that it should be directed in accordance with this form and no other." From Locke, Rousseau borrowed the idea that knowledge comes to the mind from experiences, but unlike Helvétius and Condillac, he centered attention on the active side of mental reflection in preference to the passive, sensationalist view. It is what the understanding *does* with its sensory experiences, he argued, that counts in education. The ultimate business of the educator is not to try to mold a child to a prefit pattern; aside from controlling experiences, the teacher should help the student come to terms with them in his own special way.

The best place to initiate an exploration of Rousseau's educational theory is in his social and political thought. For in his denigration of human reason, glorified by his contemporaries, and in his frontal challenge to the current notion that human progress is built upon civilized advances, he laid the groundwork for his mature reflections on the nature of education.

The Curse of Society

Rousseau began his *Discourse on the Arts and Sciences* with an apparently laudatory account of the rise of civilization: "It is a noble and beautiful spectacle to see man raising himself, so to speak, from nothing by his own exertions." Unexpectedly he then proceeded to attack civilized society as the source of all social evils. In a simpler social order human nature was no different than it is now; but men were more "open" and "sincere." Now "we no longer dare to seem what we really are, but lie under a perpetual restraint." Social conventions smother our true character and our minds "have been corrupted in proportion as the arts and sciences have improved." In the first *Discourse on Inequality* Rousseau took up the same point, in direct opposition to the usual assumption that the institutions of civilized life represent human progress. Here the task he set himself was to describe the state of nature from which man has been removed by the artificialities of his own civilization.

Primitive man was driven by two fundamental impulses: self-love, or more broadly, the instinct for self-preservation, and an innate feeling of sympathy. Self-love did not of itself involve violence or wickedness—it preceded all reflection or conscious awareness. In the *Émile*, Rousseau wrote, "The origin of our passions, the root and spring of all the rest, the only one which is born with man, which never leaves him as long as he lives, is self-love; this passion is primitive, instinctive, it precedes all the rest, which are in a sense only modifications of it." Self-preservation was primitive man's "chief and almost sole concern." This passion of self-love is not to be confused with egoism, which is a feeling which arises only in society, and which leads a man to put himself before others. Primitive man did not make the comparisons that are required for egoism to be possible. By itself self-love "is always good, always in accordance with the order of nature." Man in nature was also moved by natural compassion, "the pure emotion of nature, prior to all kinds of reflection," and it came out of self-love. What is true of mankind is true for the individual. "The child's first sentiment is self-love," Rousseau claimed in the *Émile*, "and his second, which is derived from it, is love of those about him." In a hypothetical state of nature, compassion moderated the violence of self-love in each individual, thereby contributing to the preservation of the species. It supplied the place of laws, virtues, and morals. All morality is based on these two primitive, natural feelings.

Man's vices are not natural to him, Rousseau argued; they constitute a distortion of his nature. "Our natural passions are few in number; they are the means to freedom, they tend to self-preservation. All those which enslave and destroy us have another source; nature does not bestow them on us; we seize on them in her despite." That other source is civilization. Society multiplies man's wants and needs, and this has given rise to selfishness and to the "hateful and angry passions." It was Rousseau's insistence that the moral life depends on man's fundamental passions or impulses that led him to attack those who maintained that moral education consists in eliminating them. "Our passions," he declared, "are the chief means of self-preservation; to try to destroy them is therefore as absurd as it is useless; this would be to overcome nature, to reshape God's handiwork." His exaltation of sentiment or inner feeling (*sentiment intérieur*) shows how opposed Rousseau was to the barren rationalism common in the latter half of the eighteenth century.

If morality is an extension out of basic drives and if man's corrupted state is "unnatural," how did the transition from a primitive state to organized society occur? Rousseau's first discussion of the problem appeared in the second part of the *Discourse on Inequality*. The serpent in the Edenic paradise was private property, not knowledge. "The first man who, having enclosed a piece of ground, bethought himself of saying *This is mine,* and found people simple enough to believe him, was the real founder of civil society." Property was introduced, equality disappeared, metallurgy and agriculture were begun, and human misery became a permanent feature of the human condition. "Usurpations by the rich, robbery by the poor, and the unbridled passions of both, suppressed the cries of natural compassion and the still feeble voice of justice and filled men with avarice, ambition and vice. . . . The new-born state of society thus gave rise to a horrible state of war." With private property established, government and law were necessitated to protect those who possessed nothing from those who controlled everything. "All ran headlong to their chains," Rousseau suggested, "in hope of securing their liberty; or they had just wit enough to perceive the advantage of political institutions, without sufficient experience to enable them to foresee the dangers." The results were a foregone conclusion. Government and law "bound new fetters on the poor and gave new powers to the rich; irretrievably destroyed natural liberty, fixed eternally the law of property and inequality, converted clever usurpation into unalterable right, and, for the advantage of a few ambitious individuals, subjected all mankind to perpetual labor, slavery and wretchedness."

Primitive man is naturally good and simple; civilized man in a corrupt, evil order is doomed to the tortures of self-awareness. And there is no turning back. Modern man is condemned by his reason, not saved by it, for reason gave rise to that "restless curiosity" of which civilized arts and sciences are the final products. At the conclusion of the *Discourse,* it was made clear that society cannot be abolished. There can be no "return to nature" for man. The alternative is to discover whether society can be reformed. Rousseau thus opened the way for a more positive account of political life. He phrased the problem in the *Social Contract* as follows: "Man is born free; and everywhere he is in chains. One thinks himself the master of others, and still remains a greater slave than they. How did this change come about? I do not know. What can make it legitimate? This question I think I can answer." In one way or another, the whole of the treatise is devoted to the latter question of how to justify the social order.

The Educational Program

There is a parallel question in Rousseau's thinking about education. Considering that all societal arrangements are contrary to nature, how can there be a good system of education, because it is also a part of the social fabric? He offered three distinct answers.[16] The first, as expressed in an article on political economy he wrote for Diderot's *Encyclopedia* and in a proposed constitution for Poland (*Considerations on the Government of Poland*), was that a society might be brought into conformity with nature's dictates and under such conditions a good education would be possible. Rousseau did not imply that good education was by itself enough to reform society; still less did he intend to suggest that education for proper citizenship is inevitably a "natural" education, a corrupt state necessarily demands corrupt citizens. But the potential for good in a national and public educational edifice wholly controlled by a good state he fully appreciated. The second answer, developed in his novel *The New Heloise*, posited an intermediate form between a national scheme and a purely private arrangement. Family education offers children the chance to develop their potential in a supportive environment with a minimum of restraints. A mother is the best nurse and a father is the proper teacher. His third answer, worked out in the *Émile*, was that because no ideal states exist, education according to nature would seem impossible.

At this point Rousseau was caught in the fundamental problem of educational aim—should one educate purely for the sake of the individual or must education serve society's needs?—and he agonized over it. We are "drawn this way by nature and that way by man, compelled to yield to both forces, we make a compromise and reach neither goal," he lamented. He elected not to compromise. "Natural" education, if it is to exist at all, must be conducted apart from society. The possibility of this hinges on a more careful formulation of why society's institutions repress the innately good forces of human nature. Social contrivances are not *inherently* corrupting, he seemed to say, they *become* unnatural when they begin to pervert human nature. If education faithfully allows a child's original nature to unfold according to its own internal laws, the child can be fitted to society and still retain his natural goodness. It all depends on the quality of the education he receives. "If we want to form the man of nature," Rousseau offered, "there need be no thought of making him a savage and banishing him to the woods. If he is in the whirl of social life, it is enough that he should not allow himself to be drawn into it either by his own passions or by the opinions of men; that he should see with his own eyes and feel with his own heart; and that he should be governed by no authority but that of his own reason." Paradoxically, Rousseau coupled this observation with his earlier counsel that one must remove the child to an environment safe from society's perversions in order to educate him properly. It is problematic, in the final analysis, whether he ever resolved the contradiction involved in saying one prepares the child for social life by helping him avoid it.

[16] See H. G. Good and J. D. Teller, *A History of Western Education*, 3rd ed. (New York: Macmillan, 1969), p. 207.

In any event, Rousseau's *Émile* is an outline of an ideal system of natural education which will take the unspoiled infant away from civilization, school him under the best circumstances possible, and return him to society as a mature, wholesome individual. The child is born good: "Everything is good as it comes from the hands of the Creator but degenerates once it gets into the hands of man." Degeneration can be prevented only by shielding the child from evil stimuli so that his natural goodness is preserved and his potentialities given the chance to develop. The teacher will try to foster understanding, insight, and independence of judgment as insurance against the day his charge returns to civilization. The way to begin is to make the influences impinging upon the child as consistent as possible.

Every person, Rousseau believed, has three teachers—nature, men, and things—which have to work in concert. This is practical only in a specially contrived environment manipulated by a special tutor. Education "comes to us from nature, from men, and from things," he wrote. "The inner growth of our organs and faculties is the education of nature, the use we learn to make of this growth is the education of men, what we gain by our experience of our surroundings is the education of things." The first source of education is beyond human control—organic maturational processes that proceed of their own accord. The second kind of education arises from the child's social intercourse with others. Except for the interaction between tutor and student, this phase of education is to be postponed temporarily until his habits of character and will have been strengthened and the student is prepared for the society he must eventually re-enter. The third type of education, that of things, comes from simple exposure to the physical environment. Therefore initially the educator's task is merely to adjust things to nature so that they agree. Rousseau's *Émile* indicates the procedures for accomplishing that objective.

A basic principle enunciated by Rousseau was that the child's growth from birth to adulthood is identical with the evolution of the human race —ontogeny recapitulates phylogeny. The individual's development proceeds by stages, each possessing its own special characteristics and requiring a distinctive pedagogical emphasis.

1. The period of *infancy* begins at birth and extends to five years of age. The child is an amoral, asocial creature of undifferentiated feeling. Parents should intrude as little as possible during these years. They will neither spoil nor discipline the infant, but allow experiences to form his dispositions. At most they will provide a good environment for stimulating motor activities and strengthening the senses.

2. *Childhood,* from five to twelve, is the next age, corresponding phylogenetically to the level of the primitive savage. Education appropriate to this level will be primarily negative, consisting "not in the teaching of virtue or of truth, but in the preservation of the heart from vice and the mind from error." The young boy's senses should be trained, because "the

senses are the first faculties to take form and attain perfection, and consequently should be the first to be cultivated." By this time, the student has left his home and has been placed under the direction of a dedicated tutor who will live with the boy in isolation until his education is complete. As yet the boy lacks much reasoning power, and what he learns will be dictated by his interests or needs of the moment. The tutor can stimulate self-assurance, contentment, and independence in his charge by allowing him to pursue whatever he wants. Practical experience will teach him the limits of his powers as he attempts various projects. There is no need yet for verbal learning, formal instruction, or artificially imposed constraints, Rousseau alleged.

3. The third developmental level, lasting from twelve to fifteen, is *preadolescence*. The only education appropriate now consists of teaching the student whatever he wants to know, based on his natural curiosity and love of discovery. "We should not pass too suddenly from material to intellectual objects," Rousseau warned. Through observation of phenomena in the physical environment perhaps a beginning can be made in the teaching of natural science. On the other hand, special care must be take to guard against premature learning. "It is of no use to say to the boy that he is ordered for his own good, and that, when he is grown up, he will see it." Immediate utility is the only standard to be observed. Rousseau evidently thought that spontaneous interest would arise for learning such subjects as astronomy, agriculture, geography, and the physical sciences. Somewhat inconsistently, Rousseau also recommended that the boy be taught a manual trade in a workshop specially constructed for the purpose. Later, knowing a trade would pay dividends by making the boy independent and by engendering a sense of respect for menial labor.

4. *Adolescence,* extending from fifteen to twenty years of age, marks the next level. At this stage, a more structured kind of education begins. The young man will be taught history and some religion. He will learn more about the world of men and the conditions of society. The student undergoes a rebirth as he develops such virtues as friendship, gratitude, generosity, and concern for others. His primary task is to conquer any ignoble passions he may possess and to become more patient, persevering, moderate, and self-disciplined. When he reaches his twentieth birthday he returns to society under his tutor's supervision to learn how to conduct himself in his social relations. By the time he is twenty-five his education has been completed. Now he is ready to take a marriage partner and being the life cycle anew.

Rousseau devoted part of his fifth book of the *Émile* to a discussion of education for the opposite sex. His idealized pupil finds true love in the person of the young lady Sophie. Her own upbringing, as it turns out, has been most conventional. Rousseau's few comments on the subject are strongly reminiscent of those offered by Fénelon. "Woman is made to please and to be dominated," Rousseau proclaimed, and "the whole education of women ought to be relative to men." There is nothing enlightened about Rousseau's general perspective regarding how girls are to be educated, except his observation that sex differences may require a separate kind of training.

Rousseau in Retrospect

There is no great challenge in finding fault with Rousseau's views, either his political theories or his educational ideas. His conception of nature is unclear. Anthropological and psychological data cast serious doubts on his interpretation of the genesis of society. Contradictions or inconsistencies abound in his writings. Aside from the questionable practicality of his pedagogical scheme, there are good reasons to question his formulation of developmental levels and the kinds of learning appropriate to each. All of this is to miss the point, however; literalistic criticism obscures what is enduring about his thought. Rousseau's key idea that it is the environment that provides the conditions for education is still important. The concept of learning readiness, the dangers of uncritical verbal learning, the theme of growth and discovery taking place only where there are no inhibiting constraints, the stress on freedom, the place accorded intuition, feeling, and conscience as well as rational powers are all ideas that surely strike a responsive chord with contemporary educational reformers. Rousseau's belief that man has become enslaved by artificial stimulation of his desires, that society creates a gap between the poor and the rich, that his individuality is crushed by social convention, that hypocrisy is the lubricant of social relations, are echoed in the voices of protest raised today. There is hardly a single theme in recent educational criticism that Rousseau did not touch upon somewhere.

From a historical point of view, Rousseau's influence was impressive.[17] It can be shown that educators such as Basedow, Pestalozzi, and Froebel (to mention only a few names) borrowed ideas from *Émile*. Rousseau, along with Locke, was instrumental in drawing attention to the fundamental role education must play in any lasting social reform. His educational works were translated into many languages and their ideas widely discussed by progressive-minded critics. For a time it was the fashion among German nobles to build home workshops for their sons. A new genre of literature for the young began to appear. And from Rousseau's time onward there was no longer any possibility that an educational proposal failing to consider the nature of the child could ever get a serious hearing.

[17] The student desiring further information on Rousseau will have no difficulty locating sources. Among the better offerings: William Boyd, *Emile for Today* (London: Heinemann, 1964); Boyd's *The Educational Theory of Jean Jacques Rousseau* (New York: Longmans, Green and Company, 1911); Jack H. Broome, *Rousseau: A Study of His Thought* (New York: Barnes & Noble, 1963); Thomas Davidson, *Rousseau and Education According to Nature* (New York: Charles Scribner's Sons, 1898); and G. D. H. Cole, *The Social Contract and the Discourses by Jean Jacques Rousseau* (New York: E. P. Dutton, 1950).

THE CONTRIBUTION OF JOHANN HEINRICH PESTALOZZI

Rousseau's *Émile* made a profound impression on the leading thinkers of the eighteenth century. Schiller called its author "a new Socrates" to the educational world. Kant confessed he was deeply stirred by the book. Goethe praised it as "the teacher's Gospel," and Herder proclaimed it a "divine work." Among those affected, according to his own testimony, was a sixteen-year-old Swiss boy by the name of *Johann Heinrich Pestalozzi* (1746–1827). "My visionary and highly speculative mind was enthusiastically seized by this visionary and highly speculative book," he reported. ". . . The public education of the whole world, and all ranks of society, appeared to me altogether as a crippled thing, which was to find a universal remedy for its present pitiful condition in Rousseau's lofty ideas."[18] Pestalozzi concluded, "The carriage of European education should not merely be pulled along more surely but should be turned right around and taken on to a new road."[19] That "new road" had been marked out by Rousseau; now he resolved to follow it.

It is conventional to interpret Rousseau as the original theorist and Pestalozzi as his less inspired disciple. Although it is true that the former was frequently vague on school practices whereas the latter dwelt on them at length, that Rousseau distrusted schools but Pestalozzi worked actively to promote them, and that Rousseau was content to theorize whereas his follower tried to put theory into practice, a disservice is done to Pestalozzi when his own originality is discounted. Both shared certain assumptions: man is naturally good, society corrupts his innate goodness, social reform depends partly on educational reform, education according to nature must aim to develop each child's powers in an atmosphere of freedom. Yet it was Pestalozzi, not Rousseau, who through the crucible of bitter personal defeat and failure forged a pedagogy for the modern secular elementary school. Even were this his only contribution, and it is not, his work commands a place of importance in the history of Western educational development.

His Career and Major Works

Pestalozzi was born in Zurich, Switzerland, the son of a physician. His father died when he was five, leaving young Johann's upbringing to an oversolicitous mother. The boy grew up a misanthrope, shy, maladjusted, and awkward. In spite of desperate attempts to fit in with the group, his

18 Quoted in Henry Barnard, *Pestalozzi and His Educational System* (Syracuse, N.Y.: C. W. Bardeen, 1874), p. 52.

19 Quoted in M. R. Heafford, *Pestalozzi, His Thought and Its Relevance Today* (London: Methuen, 1967), p. 88. The Heafford work provides a good introduction to Pestalozzi, as does Käte Silber, *Pestalozzi, The Man and His Work* (London: Routledge and Kegan Paul. Older references include the Barnard source cited above, Roger De Guimps, *Pestalozzi: His Life and Work.* (New York: Appleton-Century-Crofts, 1894); and H. Holman, *Pestalozzi: An Account of His Life and Work* (London: Methuen, 1908).

school experiences were painful. From earliest childhood he was "everybody's plaything" and bore the derisive title "Harry Oddity of Foolborough." He attended the local elementary school, went on through the Latin school, and then entered the Zurich Carolinium, or university. Pestalozzi's only close friend was his grandfather, a rural pastor, who he accompanied on his visits to the poor of the parish. Perhaps those pastoral calls provided the inspiration for Pestalozzi's life work. As he later wrote, "Ever since my youth has my heart moved on like a mighty stream, alone and lonely, towards my only goal—to stop the sources of the misery in which I saw the people around me sunk."

The young man's university career was relatively undistinguished. He failed his trial sermon and abandoned hope of becoming a clergyman like his grandfather. Next, he turned to politics in hopes of finding a career through which he could aid the oppressed and downtrodden. When Pestalozzi was a student he was much influenced by Enlightenment ideas then under discussion among his teachers. He eagerly responded to humanitarian calls for the improvement of society, and because of this, his reading of Rousseau's *Émile* and the *Social Contract* excited him greatly. When both were banned in Zurich, he and his friends founded a Helvetian Society to combat the social ills that were later to bring on the French Revolution. Publication of a radical tract entitled *Farmer's Conversation,* authored by the Society's members to protest the banning of Rousseau's writings, led to Pestalozzi's arrest. He was finally released but the episode confirmed his intention to devote his life to a reform movement.

At the age of twenty-three he married Anna Schulthess, his childhood sweetheart, and tried his hand at farming in the canton of Aargau. Called Neuhof, the farm was intended to be an exemplary showplace by means of which he could teach impoverished farmers how to prosper through using efficient agricultural techniques. At this time the Pestalozzis were blessed with a son, with whom the father tried out some of Rousseau's child-rearing ideas from the *Émile.* The experiment convinced Pestalozzi that Rousseau had been wrong in several respects. Events were to provide him with a further opportunity to work out his own ideas when the farm failed around 1774. Defeated and almost penniless, he turned Neuhof into an orphanage for twenty abandoned children. In five short years both the number of children and his problems had greatly increased. An uneducated servant girl by the name of Elizabeth Naef moved in to the Pestalozzi household to help save the situation. Before long a measure of order was restored, although the orphanage itself had to be discontinued. This latest failure destroyed his self-confidence almost completely. Of the experiment he wrote, "For years I have lived in the midst of fifty little beggars, sharing in my poverty my bread with them, living like a beggar myself in order to teach beggars to live like men." But perhaps there was another way to help the poor regain their dignity, through writing.

Pestalozzi's first major work was a didactic novel called *Leonard and Gertrude* (1781). Using Elizabeth as his model, he fashioned a hauntingly beautiful tale about a woman named Gertrude who triumphs over all obstacles to educate her children, reforms her drunken husband (Leonard), and through the power of example transforms the entire Swiss peasant village of Bennal. As a novel it was a great success from the start; as an educational work it was a total failure. The public loved the story, ignored the points it illustrated. There followed three less successful works, a number of journal articles, and a collection of essays, including *Evening Hours of a Hermit, Figures from My ABC Book, Legislation and Infant Murder,* and, at the urging of his friend Fichte, a scholarly *My Investigations Into the Course, Nature, and Development of the Human Race* which was promptly (and deservedly) forgotten by the European academic community.

In 1798 Switzerland was torn by the same contending forces that were tearing the French Revolution apart. An invasion into the cantons which stubbornly refused to join a French-controlled Swiss Union left widespread carnage and devastation in its wake. The new Swiss government sent Pestalozzi to the town of Stanz, at his own request, to supervise an orphanage for over eighty miserable, vermin-infested children, all victims of the war. He labored without respite for six months despite criticism of his unorthodox methods and the hostility of Catholic Stanz, which considered him a heretical Protestant interloper. A resumption of hostilities required the use of his orphanage as a military hospital. Pestalozzi was asked to leave. He departed for a three-week respite at a mountain health resort. When peace was restored, the orphanage was reopened, but its founder was not asked to return. Again, failure stared him in the face.

By this time his reputation for failure made it almost impossible for him to find employment. In 1799 he was put in charge (without pay) as an assistant schoolmaster to the poorest children of noncitizens in the village of Burgdorf, near Berne. Once more he proceeded in spite of loud criticism to implement his educational theories. Soon thereafter he was transferred to another school. Wherever he taught, his pupils did so well that at long last he was given a chance to found his own institute. His supporters organized a Society of the Friends of Education to popularize his ideas; and in 1801 he wrote *How Gertrude Teaches Her Children* to report on his work at Burgdorf. Within a short while he recruited several assistants, including Herman Krüsi, Georg Tobler, and J. Christoff Buss; together they opened a school in an old castle. The curriculum included geography, drawing, singing, history, language, arithmetic, and gymnastics. The school was enlarged in 1801 to include a teachers' training school, built on a promise from Swiss authorities to help support this venture. (The funds never materialized, however.) In the midst of his teaching, Pestalozzi somehow found time to write a *Guide for Teaching Spelling and Reading* to serve as a text for his teachers and a *Book for Mothers*. Two years later, in 1803, the school was moved to Munchenbuchsee, near Hofwyl, and relocated within an old abandoned convent. The next year war broke out again, forcing Pestalozzi and his staff to move to yet another castle, this time at Yverdon.

Yverdon quickly became a celebrated institution attracting educators from the entire Western world. One observer marveled, "I cannot think without emotion of this little company of brave men, struggling with the present that the future may be better, and finding alike their joy and their reward in the hope they have of raising children to the true dignity of humanity." Pestalozzi had finally realized his lifelong ambition to make some contribution to human welfare.

The last twenty years of his life at Yverdon were not especially happy. No longer a solitary teacher, he had gathered a large staff of assistants as the school's enrollment increased. Internecine strife among members of the faculty eventually resulted in the closing of the school and its founder retired to Neuhof, his reputation as a world-famous educator secure and still growing. He died two years later at the age of eighty-one. The most adequate summation of his career was provided by his epitaph: "Savior of the poor at Neuhof and Stanz, father of orphans at Burgdorf and Munchenbuchsee, founder of the popular school at Yverdon. The educator of humanity; man, Christian, and citizen. All for others, nothing for himself."

Pestalozzian Pedagogy

In *How Gertrude Teaches Her Children* Pestalozzi relates how he was discussing his educational ideas with a friend without being able to sum up his main aim in any simple catchphrase when the friend exclaimed, "You want to mechanize education!" Pestalozzi thought the description apt, but thought his questioner would have been equally valid if he had said, "You want to humanize education."[20] Pestalozzi's own summation was somewhat different: "When I now look back and ask myself: What have I specially done for the very being of education, I find I have fixed the highest supreme principle of instruction in the recognition of sense impression as the absolute foundation of all knowledge. Apart from all special teaching I have sought to discover the nature of teaching itself, and the prototypes by which nature herself has determined the instruction of our race." As he phrased it in his *Account of the Method* (1800), "I am trying to psychologize the instruction of mankind . . . to bring it into harmony with the nature of the mind. . . . I start from no positive form of teaching but simply ask what I must do to give a single child all the knowledge and practical skill he needs. . . ." His answer to his own question was that educational method must conform to the basic laws of human development and consciously augment them in the "natural, symmetrical, and harmonious" formation of the individual. This meant, Pestalozzi averred, the teacher's work is dictated by the unfolding of successive stages of human

20 Quoted in Heafford, op. cit., p. 43.

growth. In order for the child to develop as a whole—physically, morally, mentally—learning must take account of the individual's readiness at each stage, must begin at the level of direct experience, and must be organized around the fundamental elements of sense perception.

So far there is nothing original in Pestalozzi's thought. But though accepting sensory experience as the starting point for all knowledge, he went further than his predecessors in working out a theory of teaching and learning based on the principle that the most important sense impressions are those that put the mind in contact with objects. His concept of mind is dynamic, active; the mind is not a passive receptacle for impressions but a force engaged in analyzing, discriminating, organizing, and relating them into ideas or concepts, the building blocks of knowledge. It follows that in teaching, the pupil must be exposed to real things, not words or symbols, that he can see, hear, and manipulate. The child has to be trained to observe, analyze, compare, and count objects; this was the basic precept behind Pestalozzi's famous idea of the *object lesson*. Education is essentially a process through which sense impressions acquire meaning, very much in the sense of Kant's dictum that perception without concepts is blind and concepts without perception are empty. If learning is to be more than "empty chattering of mere words" and "outward show" it must be based on a well-organized theory of how sense impressions are converted into knowledge.

The mind begins with inchoate sensory impressions. "The world lies before our eyes like a sea of confused sense impressions, flowing into one another." Then it focuses on certain objects and makes them more *distinct* by abstracting them from the mass of sensations making up the impressions. (The "figure" has taken on individual form from out of the "ground," to use modern terminology.) At the next stage of cognition, distinct impressions become *clear*. Clearness implies that the mind is actively working on things, bestowing upon them the form and other sensory qualities by which they are represented. When clear images become *definite* ideas, they can be said to have become parts of knowledge. The business of education is to facilitate this transition from vague sense impressions to definite ideas through guided, direct observation and experience—what Pestalozzi called *Anschauung*. A lesson in which the child has an experience of something rather than being told about it, for example, is shown a tree instead of given a description of it, is an *Anschauung* lesson. It can be accomplished by helping the child separate objects in experience and make them more distinct, to help him relate objects to one another in terms of their resemblances and so help to make them clearer. When the mature adult requires definite ideas about something concerning which he has only confused and blurred impressions, Pestalozzi believed, he has to discover the *number, form,* and *names* of the items in question. Learning in the mind of a child is no different: his knowledge of things includes the same three elements.

Pedagogy, accordingly, must be based on instruction in the elements of number (arithmetic), instruction in the elements of form (drawing and then writing), and instruction in correlating object experiences with names (language) to give them meaning.

The ideas of number, form, and name are too difficult for the child to comprehend in the abstract, Pestalozzi maintained. The teacher must reduce them to their elements in sense experience. For example, the idea of *number* is learned by counting things, putting them together, and separating them. The elements of *form* are certain lines and angles out of which all complex figures proceed. In the study of *names* (language) the basic units are sounds. The child passes successively from vowels and consonants to syllables, links syllables to form words, and combines words into sentences. Pestalozzi's idea here is that instruction should follow the steps in the original development of the subject matter and each individual's learning should parallel the historical evolution of mankind as a whole.

An Assessment

His belief, probably taken from Rousseau, that ontogeny recapitulates phylogeny is almost certainly false. The theory of the history of language upon which he based the practice of beginning with speech components and working toward sentence wholes is highly improbable. Pestalozzi's view of the basic elements of experience is certainly mistaken even if he was on solid ground in insisting instruction should begin with the elements of experience. In language learning, for instance, the child begins with wholes —words and sentences—not with their basic elements. There is a certain confusion of psychological and logical orders involved also in basing instruction on the process of converting sense impressions into concepts. Even if knowledge is a progressive accumulation based on sorting, identifying, discriminating, and clarifying sensory data, it does not follow, as Pestalozzi thought, that the child learns best only through endless repetitions and exercises organized according to a logical progression. Insight, discovery, and accident have a place in the learning process as well.

In spite of these criticisms, it is the main idea about what Pestalozzi was trying to do that is important, rather than the defects in the procedures he laid down for accomplishing his end. He hoped to find the unalterable points of departure and links of all instruction in the laws of human unfolding. His aim was very similar to that of a later Swiss psychologist, Jean Piaget, who tried to specify the characteristics of child growth and development. If education is to be maximally effective, it has to accord with the child's nature. The surest indicator of the success of any method, that is, whether it does actually follow nature, is the interest exhibited by the student. "His desire to develop his mental powers . . . will necessarily diminish if the means whereby it is hoped to teach him to think do not appeal in an attractive way to his mental faculties," Pestalozzi wrote. The teacher can gauge the suitability of a lesson by its power to awaken self-activity in the learner. The child is interested only by what he can understand and that when presented in an exciting form. Speaking of his experience at Stanz, he noted that his method "quickly developed in the children a sense of capacities hitherto unknown. They realized their own power and the tediousness of the ordinary school tone vanished like a ghost. They wanted to learn, they found they could do it, they persevered, they succeeded, and they laughed. Their tone was not that of learners. It was the tone of unknown capacities roused from sleep." Intense interest manifest in student involvement arose when instruction followed the order of their minds' growth.

Pestalozzi never dealt extensively with educational problems connected with advanced stages of learning. He made no attempt to specify which subjects should be taught or the correct order of their presentation. About the only point he had to make was the vital importance of students having a personal acquaintance with the facts being taught. Whether this is possible was a question he was content to leave for others. His genius was more apparent when considering elementary education. Good instruction, he was fond of emphasizing, ought to be organic, complete. What is taught should be united in all its parts, should begin in a free and natural way with the first elements of the child's experience, and gradually progress from simpler to more complex things. The only way to ensure the penetration of learning to the whole being is to graduate it by easy stages. A subject must be learned thoroughly before proceeding on to something else, so that each step in the process grows out of the preceding step and grows into the next learning phase. Sometimes the teacher has to step back to allow the learner every chance to learn things himself; too much interference can stifle the desire to learn. Because every child is a totality, a unitary whole, education worthy of the name will seek to develop the whole child's potential as a unity. Moral, physical, and intellectual training are inseparable. A corollary is that instruction must aim to produce a person before it can develop his capacity to do some specific task. General education is at once logically and psychologically prior to vocational training.

Pestalozzi's concern for method proceeded from a somewhat different social philosophy than Rousseau's. Both agreed on the importance of education as a regenerative force, but whereas Rousseau abandoned hope that a corrupt society could produce good schools, Pestalozzi was willing to believe that a systematic pedagogy based on natural laws of human development would make it possible to extend the domestic virtues of an ideal home into the school. His own success in this was attested to by an observer's remark, exclaiming over what he had seen in one of Pestalozzi's projects: "Why, this is not a school but a family!" Reform need not wait for a utopian world where ideal parents and perfect homes have somehow sprung into existence, Pestalozzi said in effect; it can begin with a science of education to mediate between the child and his social environment, ever mindful of the truth that the individual is dependent on society for the stimulation of his natural powers. Skilled teachers using natural methods are the key to a better society. A good social order is founded on good individuals; nothing is gained either by thinking natural goodness will develop of itself if the child is isolated from society or by waiting until society has been magically transformed for the better before turning to questions of education. On this view, Pestalozzi's position is the more fruitful because by modifying Rousseau's beliefs he made their adoption possible.

His Influence

The school at Yverdon won worldwide attention. Napoleon and Talleyrand were among its countless famous visitors. King Frederick Wilhelm III visited Pestalozzi to learn more about his theories. International honors were heaped upon the humble schoolmaster: in 1792 he was made a citizen of the French Republic and the Czar of Russia knighted him in 1814. Fichte borrowed Pestalozzian ideas for his work in Berlin. Several teachers' institutes patterned on Pestalozzi's recommendations were opened, beginning with a seminary at Zurich in 1806. Graduates from Yverdon formed the core of a reform movement for Prussian schools, a movement that had counterparts in every major country of Europe. At the urging of J. P. Greaves, a member of England's Home and Colonial School Society, the Society's infant school program was revamped to bring it in line with Pestalozzi's main ideas. *Charles Mayo* (1792–1846) and his sister, Elizabeth Mayo, opened a Pestalozzian school for young boys, as well as a Home and Colonial College for teachers in England. Largely through their work, the Pestalozzian movement spread across the Atlantic to the United States. Before many decades had elapsed, the whole Western world had heard of Pestalozzi's work.

Of course not everyone (then or now) welcomed all of Pestalozzi's doctrines. Those who hoped to keep elementary education securely in sectarian hands and use it mainly for religious purposes fought a rear-guard action against spokesmen for Pestalozzian reforms. They were joined by groups who wanted to keep education confined to vocational training at a very rudimentary level. Nineteenth-century educational history is partly the story of resistance to the ideas that the study of objects should replace the study of words, that discussion is more important than parrotlike recitation, that observation and investigation should supersede mindless memorization, and that independent thought is more significant than institutional routine. In actual practice, if not in theory, the basic tenets of Pestalozzi have still not gained universal acceptance.

THE ORIGINS OF NATIONAL EDUCATIONAL SYSTEMS

Does the state have a right (or obligation) to compel parents to send their children to school? That was a major educational question debated everywhere in Europe during the latter part of the eighteenth century. For centuries education had been a family concern and was conducted according to custom, not law, under private arrangements. In the classical period, as has been seen, sporadic attempts were made to provide state aid for schools, institutions of higher learning were opened on a public basis, and teachers' salaries paid with tax revenues, but generally the state never intervened to regulate formal education for its citizens. With the dominance of the Christian Church in the Middle Ages, except for isolated instances where benevolent rulers appreciated the civil importance of education, schooling was an activity reserved for religious organizations. After the twelfth century there arose a rivalry between ecclesiastic and secular forces for the support of schools, illustrated in the history of the universities, municipal, and guild institutions. And succeeding centuries brought a period of "competitive cooperation" between church and state for promoting educational agencies. The confessional era of parochial schools, semipublic grammar schools, and territorial-sectarian universities witnessed increasing state involvement. The next phase no longer involved collaboration between church and state but led instead to the displacement of the former as a primary educational agency.[21] Church-controlled schools were destined to play less of a role in the growing national systems.

Of course for there to be any such national systems there had to be sovereign political states with established territorial boundaries and more or less centralized governmental power. In addition, the idea of state involvement in education depended upon nationalist sentiment—a shared feeling of identity among a people bound by ties of belief, custom, language and common origins. Thirdly, people had to perceive the connection between educational effort and national life. If man is largely a product of the education he receives and the state (as Plato believed) is the individual writ large, then the quality of the state depends in generous measure on the quality of education provided to citizens of the state. It is incumbent upon the state to support educational efforts that they might be directed to worthy ends. Turgot, who served briefly as Minister of Finance under France's Louis XVI, saw this plainly when he drew up his plan for a system of public education. Montesquieu's comment that education "ought to be relative to the principles of good government" served the same point.

Fourthly, the continued growth of national educational systems required the spur of a need for trained manpower. In England from about the 1770's there were stirrings of the great industrial expansion to come,

---

21 Good and Teller, op. cit., p. 296.

though industrial machines were slow to cross the channel. Industrial production was certainly rising in much of Europe, but it was a development in scale rather than a changing in kind until well into the nineteenth century. Nonetheless, to the extent that nobles were creating industries on their estates and middle-class entrepreneurs were opening small factories in the cities, there was created a need for people equipped with the skills necessary for an industrialized economy. These four factors all began to work together in the late eighteenth century and their cumulative effect was to hasten the expansion of institutionalized schooling at the national level.

French Education

In France the idea of state-controlled education did not arouse much sympathy until it became part of the program of social reform promulgated by critics like Rolland, Helvétius, Condorcet, and other intellectuals. The first major proposal for a national educational system was drafted by the Attorney General for the Parliament of Brittany, *Louis-René de Caradeuc de la Chalotais* (1701–1785). In two *Reports* drawn up in 1761–1762 Chalotais vigorously attacked the Jesuits for their domination over French schools, alleging that they were inefficient, that their decadent classicism was unsuited to modern needs, and that their "monasticity" discouraged lay participation in the conduct of education. He went on to demand a national, secular system of schools. His arguments were chiefly responsible for the expulsion of the Jesuits two years later. To fill the vacuum they left, Chalotais presented a scheme for a new organizational system and plan of studies, as outlined in his *Essay on National Education* (1763).

"I claim the right to demand for the nation an education that will depend upon the State alone," he began, "because it belongs essentially to it, because every nation has an inalienable and imprescriptible right to instruct its members, and finally because the children of the State should be educated by members of the State." He envisaged a three-tiered school structure: students between the ages of five and ten would be taught reading, writing, drawing, history, geography, and elementary mathematics through practices stressing rote memorization; abler students would continue their schooling until age sixteen with the simultaneous study of French and Latin, a year of rhetoric, two years of philosophy, and the earlier studies carried forward to higher levels; and, finally, an intellectual elite might specialize in particular subjects like jurisprudence, theology, and military science. Chalotais' proposals included the creation of a royally appointed commission to determine national educational goals, and the creation of new textbooks for students at all three levels. Against the objection that no well-trained corps of lay teachers existed to implement his plan, he confidently asserted the matter would take care of itself if the textbooks used were good enough. "These books," he wrote, "would be the best instruction the teachers could give, and would take the place of every other method. Once written they would make up for the lack of trained teachers. . . ."

Chalotais was an educational traditionalist in two respects. He had no objections to raise against a basically academic, classical curriculum, at least for the upper levels of his proposed school system. Also, he favored the restriction of formal schooling to the upper classes. It would not be wise or practical to educate the common people beyond their ordinary vocational needs, he argued. Too much learning can be dangerous and it does not necessarily contribute to the general welfare. It is interesting to note that his *Essay* was issued shortly after the publication of Rousseau's *Émile* and Chalotais pointedly omitted any reference to it. He was willing to entertain practical, workable suggestions for educational reform, changes involving administrative control and so forth, but nothing so drastic nor so sweeping as set down in the *Émile*.

The years immediately preceding the outbreak of revolution in 1789 saw a succession of proposals for state education. Rolland's *Report* to the Parliament of Paris in 1768, Rousseau's *Considerations on the Government of Poland* (1772), Helvétius' posthumously issued treatise *On Man* (1772), Turgot's *Memoirs* to the king in 1775, and Diderot's *Plan for a University*, written for the Russian Empress in 1776, all advocated some kind of nationalized system. The most radical offering came from Rolland: he urged education for everyone, with a complete nationwide pattern of colleges and lower schools under the direction of a central "correlating committee" headed by a director of education responsible to the king. Very little of a practical nature was accomplished, however, even though reactionary opposition to the national idea was swept away by revolution. A fantastic array of schemes advanced by Leppetier, Mirabeau, Lakanal, Robespierre, and other nationalists was considered. The most important and careful plan was advocated by *Marquis de Condorcet* (1743–1794) in his *Memoirs* of 1789 and in a *Report* for the Revolutionary Assembly in 1792. Most of its features were severely compromised and the final scheme, adopted in 1795, was highly disappointing. At best the latter provided for a village school system with private teachers paid through tuition fees.

Condorcet's plan was based on three main arguments. First, he tried to show that the right of the state to control education is not incompatible with personal liberty. On the contrary, the *failure* of government to establish schools for all people means individuals are deprived of their basic right to develop their natural ability through education. Good citizens need a certain minimal amount of knowledge if they are to perform their appropriate functions within the social order. Secondly, when universal education allows everyone the opportunity to perfect their various talents to the fullest extent, they become more qualified in discharging their political responsibilities. Political equality cannot become a reality until such a responsible citizenry has come into being. Thirdly, the perfectibility of mankind depends on education. All social institutions, including government, have a responsibility to advance the improvement of the race, he argued. By extending to people the means of securing their welfare, namely education, the state makes a major contribution to progress.

The specifics of Condorcet's scheme included primary schools for children aged six to ten, in every village; secondary schools, one in every large town, in which grammar, speech, writing, history, geography, agriculture, commerce, mathematics, and other natural sciences would be taught; "institutes" scattered across the country for the teaching of mathematics, physics, literature, art, and applied mechanical sciences; and lyceums (corresponding to universities) offering advanced studies in all fields. At Paris he would have founded a National Society of the Sciences and Arts which would function both as a scholarly research center and as a supervisory body over the lower levels of the school system. Primary- and secondary-level education was to be free and compulsory. At the upper levels, national scholarships were supposed to be created to enable poorer students to obtain a complete education. This grand scheme would confine itself to "positive" education in matters of "fact and numbers" but not intrude into matters of political, moral, or religious belief. No government, Condorcet stressed, has the right to impose particular values within the complement of national schools it supports.

Neither this nor other programs of the Revolution were carried through, because of lack of resources, scanty tax revenues, a shortage of trained teachers, and the universal social turmoil of the times. The actual establishment of universal free education was delayed for almost a century. Meanwhile, more modest advances were made with the founding of technical schools, conservatories, military academies, teacher-training institutes, and semiprivate secondary-level trade schools. For the most part, they were too poorly organized and too few in number to have any major social impact. Under Napoleon, approximately four hundred boarding schools or colleges were begun with limited financial assistance from the state, special schools of mining, engineering, law, and medicine were opened, and some work was done at Paris in establishing institutions for the physically handicapped. The greatest single accomplishment in the field of education during Napoleon's reign was the creation of the *Imperial University,* later called the University of France. This was not a school but an administrative system, begun in 1808, to oversee the appointment of teachers, to set school examinations, and to regulate finances. It lasted under one form or another until 1940. At the primary school level, almost all instruction continued to be conducted either by privately paid local schoolmasters or by members of some religious order. It would be some time yet before state appropriations would be made available for a comprehensive institutional educational structure under central direction.

English Education

The tradition reserving freedom of choice to parents in choosing schools and teachers for their offspring died hard in England. The affluent upper classes saw no need for the expansion of education to the lower classes; to attempt to educate the poor beyond their position in life would create widespread discontent and rebellion. A good number of people were convinced God loved the poor because he had made so many of them; attempting to change the status quo could easily contravene divine will. The prevailing social philosophy opposed any conception of the school as a national institution under state control, more or less open to all. The fear that the state's entrance into the field of education would lead to secularization was very prevalent. Perhaps more strongly than anywhere else, it was felt in England that education must be geared to class. Each should be educated to discharge his duties within his own social stratum, and this meant those at lower levels did not require formal schooling at all.

The fact that churches had exclusive responsibility for schools was another feature of English life that retarded the growth of a national state system. Around the time of La Salle's work in France, the dissenting churches founded a number of charity schools for children of the poor. In London a movement to establish poor schools was inspired by the labors of a Puritan clergyman, *Thomas Gouge* (1609–1681). Much more extensive were the efforts of the Anglican Church, beginning in 1698, with the founding of the *Society for the Promotion of Christian Knowledge* "to further and promote that good design of erecting catechetical schools in each parish in and about London." By 1750 some two thousand charity schools had been opened by the society. Each school was "a fortress and frontier garrison against popery" and a training center through which children of both sexes could learn a trade. Public reaction to these schools was mixed. Some, like Joseph Addison, lauded them as "the glory of the age we live in" while others, like Francis Place, condemned them because they "taught poor children next to nothing, and nothing likely to be useful to them." The fairest judgment seems to be that charity schools were a stopgap measure for an age not yet willing to sponsor a national state system. A sister philanthropic organization, the *Society for the Propagation of the Gospel in Foreign Parts,* aimed to carry on the same work beyond England's shores.

The cause of popular education received some support with the publication of *The Wealth of Nations* (1776) by economist and political theorist *Adam Smith* (1723–1790). He had spent a year in Paris at the time when the ideas of Chalotais and others were under intensive discussion. Smith agreed with the French reformers, at least to the extent that he urged more education for the common people. "For a very small expense," he noted, "the public can facilitate, can encourage, and can even impose [the] essential parts of education." Everyone should be taught reading, writing, accounting, some geometry, and elementary mechanics. "The public can facilitate their acquisition by establishing in every parish or district a little school, where children may be taught for a reward so moderate that even a common labourer can afford it." From this it is clear Smith intended a village school system partially supported by tuition fees, but whether the government was to help support the system also is uncertain. There was no suggestion that attendance at a village school should be compulsory.

Another movement to further popular elementary education was begun by *Robert Raikes* (1735–1811), a newspaper editor and businessman of Gloucester, who organized a Sunday school for paupers in 1780. Earlier, John Wesley and Joseph Alleine had tried to establish similar schools but with less success. At this time England was well advanced over nations on the continent in terms of industrialization. The invention of the mechanical shuttle, the steam engine, the cotton gin, and the spinning machine earlier in the century had moved industry from the home into the urban mill. Urbanization brought the growth of terrible slums. Living conditions were unbelievably depressed. Children of the millworkers were pressed into service alongside their parents six days a week, twelve hours a day. Sunday was their one free holiday, a day during which they roamed the streets aimlessly. Industrial congestion bred delinquency, debauchery, and crime among the masses, and the children were no exception. Raikes determined to remedy the situation by organizing a free secular school in which working children could be taught the rudiments of learning (without of course interfering with their work schedule the rest of the week). Raikes' venture was so successful that a *Society for the Support and Encouragement of Sunday Schools in the Different Counties of England* was founded five years later to enlist financial support for more schools. Methodists, Baptists, and the Friends were in the forefront of this movement. Sunday schools constantly suffered for lack of money and insufficient teachers, but many, who otherwise would not have had any education, learned to read in a school organized by a private religious group.

The next step toward an English state educational system was made possible through the rediscovery of a more efficient method of instruction. Around 1789 a British army chaplain by the name of *Andrew Bell* (1753–1832) had been serving as superintendent of an orphan asylum in Madras, India. Confronted with the problem of a teacher shortage, he hit upon the idea of "mutual tuition by the pupils," an arrangement whereby older pupils would be set to teaching younger students what they had learned. Dr. Bell recorded his experiences in a small pamphlet entitled *An Experiment in Education* (1797). In the meantime a Quaker educator, *Joseph Lancaster* (1778–1838), had opened a school for some one hundred poor children in London based on the same method of teaching. Lancaster enthusiastically endorsed the scheme of mutual instruction, now called the *monitorial method*, after the teacher-pupils who were known as monitors. The schoolmaster would meet with his monitors each day and teach them the daily lesson. Each of them in turn relayed the lesson to a small group of ten children to which he had been assigned. Before long Lancaster's roster of students had exceeded one thousand, without a proportionate increase in costs. The monitorial method seemed to offer at last a quick, cheap, and easy solution to educational problems of the day. So long as the system did not cost much, people favored its adoption. Lancaster became a public hero throughout England and almost every city sought to establish a Lancastrian school. The *Royal Lancastrian Institution,* afterward named the *British and Foreign School Society,* was organized in 1808 to gather funds for the movement. A second group, the *National Society for Promoting the Education of the Poor in the Principles of the Established Church,* under the superintendence of Bell set out to popularize the "Madras method" and to train teachers for managing schools.[22] Some estimates claim that by the 1830's over 50 per cent of the children of the working classes were enrolled in a school run by the two monitorial societies, the Sunday School society, or the Anglican *Society for the Promotion of Christian Knowledge.* All in all, the belief that there should be education for the underprivileged had won widespread acceptance, even though public opinion remained adverse to state intervention of any kind. Lancaster's call for a secular, universal system of state schools in his *Improvements in Education As It Respects the Industrious Classes* (1803) went unheeded.

Yet another impetus toward more education was the work of a philanthropic entrepreneur by the name of *Robert Owen* (1771–1858). To modern eyes Owen's concern smacks of *noblesse oblige,* paternalistic tokenism, but in his day the effort to improve living conditions among the workers of his cotton mill at Lanark, in Manchester, was highly unusual. He began a building program to provide decent homes for his employees, started a company store selling goods at prices the people could afford, and supported a monitorial school, free to all children from five to ten years of age. James Buchanan, a famous teacher, was brought to run the elementary school, called the *New Institution.* Owen also began the first British infant school at Lanark, which took in children "at one year or as soon as they could walk" and kept them until eligible to enter the primary school. Buchanan, Henry Brougham, Samuel Wilderspin, and others were instrumental in opening a number of nursery or infant schools in various parts of England. The London *Infant School Society* was founded in 1824 and through its efforts these schools became a permanent part of the English system. They were very much like kindergartens, except the British school was always more formal and academic in character. Other philanthropic societies begun to spread lower-level schools included the *British and Foreign School Society,* the *Glasgow Infant School Society,* and *The Irish Commissioners.*

---

[22] Lancaster's original school fell on hard times when Anglicans objected to the lack of sectarian dogma in the religious instruction offered. Dr. Bell came out of retirement to save the movement he believed he had begun from dissenters' heresies.

It can be argued that the very success of Owen's schools, as well as those founded by philanthropic or church-related organizations, in showing that the job of educating the lower classes was not impossible on a private, voluntary basis, helped to stifle more ambitious reform programs. If church and family could handle matters, there was no urgent need for the state to intervene. As late as the mid-1800's it was still considered improper to advocate governmental action in the sphere of education. A national school system in England was not achieved until late in the nineteenth century.

German Pietism and the Work of Francke

In German lands throughout the late seventeenth and early eighteenth centuries, the strength of a movement known as *Pietism* probably helped hasten the state's intervention in matters of formal schooling. Pietism had originated as a native protest or reaction against the French domination of German culture generally and the skeptical French influence upon German religious thought in particular. Such Pietist spokesmen as *Philip Jacob Spener* (1635–1705) argued strenuously that growing rationalist impiety was threatening wholesale spiritual degeneracy. Pietists were equally distrustful of the native churches that had seemingly lost Luther's original emotional, sacrificial faith. Just as the churches had succumbed to secular influences, it was claimed, their schools were endangered by the same fate. Germany's education was allegedly as immoral, ritualistic, and overintellectualized as its official religion.

Elector Frederick of Brandenburg evidently agreed with Spener. In 1694 he founded the new university at *Halle* to combat the institutional stagnation that had overtaken German higher learning. The reforms instituted resulted in drastic changes involving both the program of studies and the methods used in teaching. A brilliant faculty was assembled, composed of men who differed drastically in their scholarly views but who were united in their determination to break with the past. Rationalists and Pietists learned to coexist amicably under the principle of academic freedom in teaching and research, a principle formally recognized by the government. Scholastic studies were thrown out and replaced by modern subjects reflective of new philosophical and scientific themes. The old medieval lecture and the traditional disputation were given up, classes were conducted in the vernacular, and progressive teaching methods were introduced. Göttingen was the next university to implement changes along the same lines, thus establishing a pattern followed in succeeding years by almost all the universities in German lands.

The great evangelical missionary for the Pietist movement who labored to effect educational reforms below the university level was a professor of Oriental languages at Halle, *August Hermann Francke* (1663–1727). In 1695 he began a small free school for children of the poor which later became a burgh school supported by public contributions. He added an ordinary elementary school for children whose parents could afford tuition fees; this subsequently evolved into a Latin school or *gymnasium*. A third school reserved for sons of the nobility grew into a boarding school known as the *Paedagogium*. Two orphanages were added to Francke's growing complex of institutes, now commonly called the Halle Foundation. Still later, in 1697, he built a *Seminarium Praeceptorium,* or teacher-training center, the first institute of its kind in Prussia. By 1727 some two thousand pupils and over three hundred staff members were engaged in educational activity on the site of the first charity school.

In the burgh school, history, geography, counting, reading, writing, and music were taught. A full complement of courses in history, geography, music, mathematics, science, Latin, Greek, and Hebrew was offered in the *Gymnasium*. The *Paedagogium,* which was later placed under royal patronage, was an elaborate affair equipped with workshops, laboratories, and botanical gardens. *Frederick Wilhelm I,* King of Prussia, was most impressed with Francke's advances and came to share the latter's desire for making schools available to the common people. In 1716 Frederick decreed that attendance at elementary schools would be compulsory. The scheme floundered for the very simple reason that few hamlets or towns had bothered to open any formal schools at all. His son, *Frederick the Great,* was in agreement with the move for more education and arranged for the support of village schools under local clerical control. His *General School Regulations* of 1763 stipulated compulsory school attendance for all children between the ages of five and fourteen under penalty of heavy fines. Not much was done, however, to train teachers or to expand the system of village schools financed through tenants and landowners.

Johann Julius Hecker (1707–1768), a pupil of Francke and teacher in the Halle *Paedagogium* for six years, extended the master's work further. In 1747 he opened a school in Berlin to prepare boys for vocational careers patterned after the *Gymnasium,* the significant difference being that practical subjects were central to the curriculum. It was Hecker who drew up the Prussian school code later promulgated by Frederick the Great in the 1763 Regulations. A teachers' seminary also won enthusiastic support from the Prussian king. A second disciple of Francke, *Christopher Semler* (1669–1740), published a paper in 1739 describing the Halle innovations, in which the term *Realschule* ("real school") was first used. The subjects taught, Semler reported, were "the useful and in daily life indispensable sciences," such as mathematics, agriculture, and economics. The *Realschule* idea, appealing to the practical interests of German burghers, caught on quickly. Vocationally oriented institutions soon appeared in Dresden, Göttingen, and Prenzlau. They were to be the progenitors of an entire national system of such schools in the nineteenth century.

Benevolent Despotism

The interest shown by the two Prussian Fredericks in educational renewal was part of a widespread pattern among benevolent despots in the
eighteenth century. At their height of autocratic power, many rulers accepted certain humanitarian ideals of the Enlightenment (excepting those
potentially subversive of their rule) and made sincere efforts to advance the
welfare of the people through better schools. In all probability, the influence of the Enlightenment was inevitable, given France's long-standing pre-
eminence as cultural exemplar for the rest of continental Europe. Court
society everywhere had looked to France as a model of taste in literature,
the theater, art, music, and the refinement of social behavior and polite
etiquette characteristic of the *salon*. A French architect could justly boast
to a friend in 1765 as follows: "Travel through Russia, Prussia, Denmark,
Würtenburg, the Palatinate, Bavaria, Spain, Portugal, and Italy, everywhere you will find French architects in the highest places. . . . Paris is to
Europe what Athens was to Greece." When it appeared that France was
engaged in a massive program of social welfare, not to mention the rebuilding of schools, those in other lands who secretly harbored feelings of cultural inferiority hastened to follow suit. Especially in German lands, the
tradition of looking to Paris for cultural leadership was deeply engrained.
Thus, to a greater extent than is ordinarily recognized, the comprehensive
humanitarian problems of European despots (of which educational reform was
a visible manifestation) was a direct outgrowth of France's era of enlightenment. Frederick IV of Denmark, for example, made school attendance in his
realm compulsory as early as 1712. Classes in a wide variety of subjects were
opened to people of all ranks. Charles Frederick of Baden laid the foundations for a state-supported, state-controlled educational system, as did
Charles III of Spain. Between the accession of Philip V to the Spanish
throne in 1700 and the death of Charles III in 1788 there appeared a succession of able monarchs vitally interested in pedagogical problems. Modern
schools were founded, state financing was enlarged, qualifying examinations
for teachers were introduced, and numerous changes effected within the
universities. In Russia the reigns of Peter the Great (1689–1725) and
Catherine II (1762–1796) were marked by efforts at social reform, including
changes in education. When Maria Theresa of Austria came to power in
1740 she appointed a School Commission to oversee developments in lower
Austria. The next year the first Austrian teachers' institution was opened in
Vienna. A General School Code drawn up in 1774 by her Minister of Education, Abbot Felbiger, advocated supervisory commissions over schools in
each province, elementary schools in all villages, and an expansion of
teachers' normal schools. Maria Theresa's son, Josef II, continued her educational interests in a series of decrees between 1780 and 1790, the most important of which made all teachers civil servants.

This activity notwithstanding, it must be said that all of the despots mentioned harbored doubts on the wisdom of expanding educational opportunities too far. As Frederick the Great put it, "In country places a little reading and writing will be enough, for if the peasants learn too much, they will want to move into town and become clerks." Rulers were willing to educate leaders, but to give too much learning to commoners was possibly dangerous. Despots trembled on their thrones as the reverberations of the French Revolution spread across Europe. An 1805 decree under Franz I was typical: it ordered instruction in elementary schools to be curtailed to "absolutely necessary limits," so that "the common people shall get . . . only such ideas as will not trouble them in their work, and which will not make them discontented with their condition; their intelligence shall be directed toward the fulfillment of their moral duties, and prudent and diligent fulfillment of their domestic and communal obligations."

Toward a German National Educational System

Würtenburg was the first German state on record to organize a state-church school system in 1559 and to make attendance at classes in religion compulsory. This example was followed in the next hundred years by Brunswick (1569), Saxony (1580), Weimar (1619), and Gotha (1642). By the mid-1600's almost every German state had enacted a compulsory school law. Lack of funds and an absence of legislation for enforcement of decrees urging school attendance kept advances in these areas to a minimum. Moreover, what schools there were remained under church control or were private commercial ventures. Not until the latter half of the eighteenth century was there any significant move toward governmental involvement, though once it got underway it proceeded rather quickly. For the most part educational improvements depended on the initiative of people like Reyher, Francke, Semler, and Hecker, or independent philanthropists like *Eberhard von Rochow* 1734–1805). In the preface to his *Schoolbook for Country Children,* he wrote, "I live among country people and I pity them for the wretchedness of their condition and their ignorance and prejudices. They neither know how to make good use of what they possess nor how to give up cheerfully what they lack. They are not at peace with either God or king." Rochow's attempts to better the people's condition within his estate included the construction of school buildings, endowments for teacher's salaries, and the implementation of a curriculum composed of arithmetic, letter writing, religion, and nature studies. Clergy and nobility banded together to oppose Rochow when he tried to spread his ideas beyond his own land holdings. The idea of universal schooling, not to mention governmental supervision, had a long way to go before it would be popular.

The beginning of a transfer of power over schools from the hands of the churches to those of the state took place during the reign (1713–1740) of Frederick Wilhelm I. His *Regulatory Code* for Reformed Evangelical and Latin schools of Prussia was issued in the first year of his rule. Only four years later he posted an "Advisory Order" demanding parents under penalty of "vigorous punishment" to send their children to school to learn "all that could serve to promote their happiness and welfare." Succeeding years brought a series of decrees relating to upgraded teacher preparation, the building of schoolhouses, land grants for educational institutions, and state contributions for paying schoolmasters. Frederick the Great was equally sensitive to the educational needs of his people. His reign between 1740 and 1786 was distinguished for reforms in the old knightly academies and classical gymnasiums. One order established a standardized gymnasial "leaving certificate" (which was secured by passing an examination) as prerequisite to university admission. A 1750 law centralizing church consistories indirectly centralized the administration of schools as well, because ecclesiastical bodies governed the schools in their respective districts. Two major codes promulgated by Frederick the Great were the 1763 *General Land-Schule Reglement* (General School Regulations) mentioned previously, and a similar but broader set of regulations covering urban Catholic schools in Silesia, enacted in 1765. The two pieces of legislation were issued "to the end that ignorance, so injurious and unbecoming to Christianity, may be prevented and lessened, and the coming time may train and educate in the schools more enlightened and virtuous subjects." Their provisions fixed the dates of the school year, the hours of the school day, the major elements of the curriculum, and even prescribed how instruction was to be conducted. Tuition fees were set up on a uniform basis but supervision was left with local landowners or clergymen. These innovations met with widespread resistance from those fearful of political control.

Despite hostility, Frederick Wilhelm II (who otherwise was a relatively ineffectual leader) continued his uncle's enlightened policies in matters of social reform and simultaneously hastened the process of centralization of authority over the schools. One year after ascending to the throne, the king sponsored the creation of a National Board of Education, or *Oberschulkollegium*, to supervise secondary schools and institutions of higher learning in the state of Prussia. The climax to all preceding developments came in 1794 with passage of a General Civil Code (*Allegemeine Landrecht*) whose educational provisions forbade the founding of schools without the knowledge and consent of the state. They further announced that "schools and universities are state institutions . . . under the supervision of the state, and are at all times subject to its examination and inspection." Similar codes for schools in other German states besides Prussia appeared around the same time. Würtenberg issued a new School Code in 1792; the Saxon king, Augustus the Just, promulgated mandates in 1766 and 1773 to achieve greater state control; Weimar, Brunswick, and Gotha followed suit soon thereafter.

None of this might have happened had there not arisen in the meantime a movement whose practical consequences showed unmistakably what could be accomplished when enlightened teaching methods were employed in the sphere of popular education. If private volunteers could attain success without official state support, people began to ask, how much more might be done if the full resources of government were applied to coordinate disparate educational reforms? As usual, the movement began with the work of a single gifted individual.

The Philanthropinist Movement

Johann Bernard Basedow (1723–1790) was born in Hamburg, son of a wigmaker. Following a brilliant but erratic career in the Hamburg *Gymnasium* and the University of Leipzig, the young man spent three years as tutor to the young son of the Von Quaalen family at Holstein. The conclusions he reached through his early exposure to educational problems were given public expression in his master's thesis, *De Methodo Inusitato*, written in 1752 at the University of Kiel. The next fifteen years were frustrating ones for Basedow. Although he secured several important posts for short periods of time, his heterodox religious opinions prevented him from finding any permanent position. He returned his attention to matters of education around the time that Rousseau's *Émile* was stirring controversy. Basedow resolved to develop his own views, based on his personal experiences as a tutor, the broad themes presented in Rousseau's work, and the ideas presented by Chalotais in his *Essay on National Education*.

In 1768 he offered a program in *Appeal to Philanthropists and Men of Wealth Regarding Schools and Studies and Their Influence on Public Welfare*. It was basically a request for financial backing to establish schools based on "new" methods and to publish textbooks appropriate for his scheme. He proposed to organize two nonsectarian schools under state control: one for upper-class children aged ten to fifteen pursuing a preparatory course prior to entering secondary school, the other a common school for poorer children with a less academic course of studies. Like Chalotais, Basedow promised no special teachers would be needed, so long as good textbooks were made available. He concluded his appeal with a promise to write an *Elementary Book*, "the ABC of human knowledge, both real and verbal," written in the style of Comenius' *Orbis Pictus*—an illustrated, encyclopedic organization of all learning. This would become the basis of instruction for pupils up to age fifteen.

The response from wealthy humanitarians, trade associations, religious groups, and fraternal organizations was most gratifying. Subscriptions poured in from all parts of Europe. With the funds provided, Basedow wrote a *Book of Methods for Fathers and Mothers of Families and of Nations*. The underlying philosophy was an eclectic combination of the ideas of Comenius, Locke, and Rousseau. This was followed in 1774 by an incomplete Elementary Book which was published in a revised edition together with the first work under the title *Elementarwerk*. This massive treatise in four volumes with a hundred engraved illustrations was a curious, chaotic collection of theoretical discussions on educational method and articles on all branches of knowledge. The new education recommended was to stress learning by "natural means" through sensory experience. Children were to be taught to read and write through play activities and conversations instead of formal lessons. The *Elementarwerk* enjoyed immediate approval, and its author was hailed as the greatest educator since Comenius.

A second appeal for funds to begin a school met with less success. Basedow's plan was saved through the benevolence of Prince Leopold of Anhalt Dessau who promised to provide facilities and money for an institution run on Basedow's principles. The school was opened in 1774 under the name of the *Philanthropinum,* to call attention to its philanthropic aims. It aroused considerable interest. Basedow's approach to language teaching by conversational methods, the inclusion of handicrafts and manual training in the program, and a "realistic" curriculum of natural history, geography, geometry, physics, anatomy, arithmetic, religion, and etiquette brought pupils from as far away as Spain. Public exhibitions were held during which scholars could observe at first hand how the experiment worked. Field trips, physical sports and exercises, and other novelties were added. The famed philosophy professor at Königsberg, Immanuel Kant, wrote an article for the local newspaper in 1777 explaining why Basedow's work was important, expanding his comments later in his university lectures *On Pedagogy.*

As events progressed it became clear that instruction in real things—the world of science and nature—in place of words, and the practices of teaching through pictures, games, and exercises worked better with the younger pupils in attendance at Dessau than with older students. The school's plan or organization underwent modifications several times. Basedow himself left (or was forced to leave) the *Philanthropinum* in 1784; nine years later the school folded. In spite of this Basedow's work was a focal point for reform among philanthropists interested in educational improvements. A movement to found schools similar to the original Dessau model spread through Germany and Switzerland. Middle-class manual training schools and trade schools for commoners were opened everywhere in the German states by Basedow's followers. *Joachim Heinrich Campe* (1746–1818), who succeeded Basedow at the *Philanthropinum,* later opened another school at Hamburg before becoming the Director of Education for the state of Brunswick. Along with Christian Gotthilf Salzmann and other philanthropinists, he devoted the best part of his later career to expounding Basedow's ideas, most of which were published in a sixteen-volume work entitled *General Revision of the Whole System of Schools and of Education* (1785–1791). Owing to the fact that Basedow and his supporters had seemingly combined the best of Rousseau's natural pedagogy with the practical suggestions of Chalotais, they won support from people in high places. Baron von Zedlitz, Frederick the Great's minister of public education between 1771 and 1789, especially favored the idea of national education advanced earlier by Basedow. As part of the latter's program, there was a proposal for creating a Supreme Supervisory Council of Public Instruction governing a state school system. The founding of the *Oberschulkollegium* in 1787 was probably an outgrowth of that proposal.

The Achievement of Central Control

The 1794 Prussian Code stopped short of creating total and direct governmental jurisdiction over all schools. This step was taken fourteen years later, as an indirect result of an extraordinary turn of affairs. In 1806 the once proud Prussian armies were ignominiously routed by Napoleon's forces at the Battle of Jena. The Treaty of Tilset imposed the next year levied heavy indemnities on Prussia and half her territories were turned over to the French. The occupation which followed gave rise to a burst of Prussian nationalism. The philosopher Fichte in a series of addresses to the nation between 1807 and 1808 (which somehow passed through French censors) appealed to the defeated nation's leaders to rebuild their educational system as a means of rescuing the country. King Frederick Wilhelm III echoed Fichte's pleas. "The state," he announced, "must regain in mental force what it has lost in physical force." To accomplish this the now moribund *Oberschulkollegium* was dismantled and a new department of public instruction was set up in 1808 as a division of the Ministry of the Interior, with *Wilhelm von Humboldt* (1767–1835) serving as its first director. The true beginning of the modern German educational system dates from this time.

THE RATIONALIST TRADITION TODAY

Two major articles of faith characteristic of the eighteenth century were the belief that reason is a lever for human betterment and, because man is amenable to rational self-fulfillment, that education can contribute to social progress. Among a self-professed avant garde and some youthful revolutionaries at least, the first idea is almost moribund two centuries later, and with its decline the force of the second has diminished considerably. Paradoxically, however, much of the protest directed against contemporary institutions of education—even by those who profess to repudiate the rationalist faith—reveals a strong commitment to that credo. It is instructive to examine each theme in turn.

Faith in reason is probably more unfashionable than at any time since the Enlightenment. Many people no longer share the philosophes' belief that there are simple answers for all great social and political problems. Their affirmation that improvements would follow as a matter of course when reason held sway sounds naive. Nowadays reason appears to be a double-edged weapon, its offspring, technology, a monster out of control.

Bacon was right when he asserted that rational knowledge is power. Man powered with knowledge was, and is, like a god, but his power is proving independent of its generator: the theme of the Sorcerer's Apprentice has become chillingly familiar. Eighteenth-century rationalists had none of the fear and distrust of human power typical in the modern era, but of course they did not live in a world where man had the capacity to wreak ecological disaster, automate violence, and create ever more powerful engines of destruction. Armageddon seemingly looms just ahead. Again, contrary to rationalist expectations, the secularization of men's beliefs has done little to moderate fanaticism, hatreds, and bigotry. They remain as strong as ever.

All signs today point to a new "failure of nerve,"[23] a waning confidence in man's capacity to use his rationality for good. Against the visions of a golden age attained through the advance of human reason posited by Condorcet and his fellow rationalists, modern man counterposes the nightmarish antiutopia of a Brave New World or an Orwellian *1984*. Progress is no longer a foregone conclusion and it is not axiomatic that humanity is going to be an unqualified success. Among some intellectual seers, it has become fashionable to suggest that the world is absolutely out of control now, that it will not be saved through reason. As one critic put it: "Reason, although dead, holds us with an embrace that looks like a lover's embrace but turns out to be *rigor mortis*. Unless we are necrophiles, we had better let go."[24] Lest this be dismissed as theatrical rhetoric, it is important to note the recrudescence of antirational currents of thought in *all* sectors of contemporary culture.

Abraham Kaplan drew attention a few years ago to the ossification of philosophical thought which, he believes, has contributed to the contemporary crisis. "The new treason of the intellectuals," he wrote, "is that we have shared and even contributed to the current loss of faith in the power of the human mind to cope with human problems, faith in the worth of reasoned discussion, faith even in the possibility of objective truth." Philosophy, he claimed, has remained remote from any genuine inquiry into live issues. At a time when people hunger for principles to guide their lives, philosophers have been preoccupied with forms of analysis in which, they correctly assure the world, there are no guiding precepts to be found. "That philosophy has been set apart from our most basic concerns is a mark of this new failure of philosophic nerve," Kaplan continued. "If we ourselves cannot in good faith profess the love of wisdom, we might at least reaffirm the significance of its continued pursuit."[25]

23 See Sidney Hook, "The New Failure of Nerve," in *The Quest for Being* (New York: Delta, 1961), pp. 71–94.
24 Quoted in Joseph Wood Krutch, "If You Don't Mind My Saying So . . ." *American Scholar* (Autumn, 1969), p. 530.
25 Abraham Kaplan, "The Travesty of the Philosophers," *Change* (January–February, 1970), p. 13.

The denigration of reason is manifest in innuumerable ways: in the refurbishing of doctrines of the depravity of human nature, in the appearance of transcendental consolidations ranging from neo-fundamentalist theologies to astrological determinisms, in attacks on the whole liberal tradition of faith in intelligence. Prophecies of doom for Western culture are rampant. Artists (presuming they are sensitive barometers of the cultural climate) speak of decadence, isolation, alienation, and spiritual decay. Obscurantism in the arts is no longer apologetic; it has now become willful, most notably in the theater of the absurd and the novel of the antihero. Confidence in scientific method has been replaced by respect for one's viscera as an organ of knowledge—the truth of an assertion is proportional to how deeply it is felt.[26] It has become easy to herald the ideologies of panic as portents of spiritual revival. In the frenzied search for new centers of value, voices are raised inviting men to turn out the lights of intelligence and wallow in darkness.

Not everyone has abandoned the Enlightenment faith. Today's liberal–democratic reformers are optimistic, latter-day rationalists. They retain their faith in continuous, incremental reform and work for a victory of scientific acumen over irrationality. Unlike the visionaries of the past (they allege), for the first time in history man is in possession of a technology to create utopia and make it work. Technocrats among them are sublimely confident that science can be applied to the seemingly insurmountable social problems of the day. Human engineering will likewise solve the human problems—estrangement, individualism, stifled creativity—though these problems may take a little longer. In either case, man's problems *can be solved through intelligent action,* this is fundamental to the rational–liberal credo.

An increasing number of the young have rejected this creed, claiming anarchy is a necessary prelude to a glorious future. They are not at all sure meanwhile whether reason can or should prevail in the conduct of human affairs. Revolution is essential before the entrenched systems of "The Establishment" will give way to something better. Their call to unreason echoes the Persian poet's suggestion to "grasp this sorry scheme of things entire . . . shatter it to bits . . . remold it to our hearts' desire." The truth of Shaw's dictum, "Nothing important is ever done in this world until men are ready to kill each other if it is not done," is illustrated by the lengths of irrationality to which radical dissenters have felt they must go in order to effect reforms. Militants are likely to view calls to reasonableness as a subterfuge for avoiding action. They see no other course but to mutilate and destroy the present order and at most are willing to concede to society's leaders what Theodore Roosevelt reportedly admitted for William H. Taft: "He means well feebly." It has become horrifyingly apparent that at least some radical apocalyptics today, like the firebrands of the French Revolution, continue to welcome social chaos for its own sake and worship violence

26 Hook, op. cit., pp. 71–72.

as a purgative of the soul. Many will assent to the proposition that violent confrontation is cathartic for society's ills.

Mindful of the formidable obstacles to meaningful reform, another segment of the young has abandoned interest in programs of melioration altogether. It may still reject the rationalist tradition but the rejection assumes the form of a nihilistic subjectivism rather than activist anarchism. It implicitly repudiataes the idea that knowledge is a product of intelligence disciplined by logic and reason, the weighing of evidence, and the strictures of dispassionate investigation. What is sought is an unmediated personal vision, a series of intuitions undistorted by ideology, tradition, theory, or methodology. That sensibility, as Daniel Bell astutely observed, tries "to abolish constraint by substituting experience for art, sensation for judgment."[27] One end result (to borrow a term from Theodore Roszak) is a "counterculture" utterly opposed to the dominant strain of mainstream Western culture:

> What the counter-culture offers us, then, is a remarkable defection from the long-standing tradition of skeptical, secular intellectuality which has served as the prime vehicle for three hundred years of scientific and technical work in the West. Almost overnight (and astonishingly with no great debate on the point) a significant portion of the younger generation has opted out of that tradition, rather as if to provide an emergency balance to the gross distortions of our technological society, often by occult aberrations just as gross.[28]

The consequences for a system of education founded on a belief in the importance of rational intelligence are not difficult to imagine.

Indicative of the tempo of change in the national temper, it was this second current of thought that gained steadily in the early 1970's. The revolutionary rhetoric and confrontation that had seemingly become a way of life in the last years of the previous decade appeared to give way to a chastened air of reflection and retrenchment. Though punctuated with occasional mindless violence, a period of relative calm succeeded an era marked by calls to the barricades. Militant activists paused in their headlong pursuit of the apocalypse, gradually recognizing that if there was to be a revolution in society, it would not be a quick classic palace revolt but a long-term evolutionary development—in other words, not a revolution at all. "Cooptation" in the form of a "preventive counterrevolution" and an

---

[27] Daniel Bell, *The Reforming of General Education* (New York: Columbia University Press, 1966), pp. 308–309. Charles A. Reich in his *The Greening of America* (New York: Random House, 1970), similarly characterizes an attitude of mind he calls "Consciousness III" as deeply suspicious of logic, rationality, analysis, and principles.

[28] Theodore Roszak, *The Making of a Counter-Culture* (Garden City, N.Y.: Anchor, 1969), pp. 141–142. Quoted with permission. Consult also Charles E. Silberman, *Crisis in the Classroom: The Remaking of American Education* (New York: Random House, 1970), pp. 19–31.

attitude of "repressive tolerance" allegedly had contributed to the renunciation of violence as an acceptable instrument for social change. With the awareness that revolutionary violence could easily become an end unto itself, malcontents tended to retreat into privatism and abandoned hopes for any quick victories. Simultaneously, however, at least some protesters once again began to raise the question whether nonthinking and anti-intellectualism were viable alternatives or simply allies of the totalitarian-like repressions they had so arduously struggled against.

The second great theme of the rationalist tradition—that education could only bring increased happiness—has also come into hard times. In varying ways men like Rousseau, Condillac, Chalotais, Helvétius, Locke, Basedow, Pestalozzi, and other eighteenth-century reformers fervently shared the assumption that improved education would call a better world into being. Contrary to their more optimistic expectations, the vast expansion of formal education has not proved to be the panacea it was once hoped to be. Virtually every major nation in the West took giant strides in extending the opportunity to its citizens to attend school, even passed legislation requiring them to do so, during the late nineteenth and early twentieth centuries. Illiteracy rates in the developed nations plummeted. More people spent a larger portion of their lives in classrooms than ever before in history. Teaching techniques and tools were vastly upgraded and curricula proliferated at an astonishing rate to fulfill the needs of a varied clientele. But more and better education has not shown the way to a utopian society of peace and plenty for everyone. Crime rates have soared; wars have increased in frequency, scope, and destructive impact; economic dislocations have continued; the incidence of mental illness has gone up; and superstitions (albeit more sophisticated in character) persist among the masses. Inequities in the distribution of resources, opportunities, and responsibilities, often sanctioned by the predominating hierarchical structures of social organization, have not only continued but assumed more virulent forms. Racial prejudices, ethnic antagonisms, and nationalistic hatreds have endured among the educated as well as among the uneducated. Political leaders have not displayed any noticeable increased intelligence in their manipulation of public affairs, captains of business and industry are no wiser than before, and to an alarming extent modern society seems no closer to solving its major problems than it ever was; in fact, if anything, society's dilemmas have grown in magnitude. There is little or no evidence to suggest that an educated populace shows more magnanimity, more enlightened judgment, or greater perceptiveness of vision than men have shown in former times when only a tiny minority of people received a formal education. Particularly today when the prospect of planetary annihilation through nuclear conflict or ecological rape is imminent, historically speaking, there is growing doubt about the ability of presently constituted institutions to effect reforms. Because education is necessarily a long-range process, schools may not play any significant role in averting impending disaster. The crisis mentality of the times does not encourage critics of the existing order to sit back and wait for a new generation to be educated to their responsibilities for solving problems or even to hope that such an education will occur.

Aside from those who have passively withdrawn from the world through the use of drugs or under the auspices of some transcendental mysticism, malcontents among the present generation within the schools have evidenced a strong faith in the rationalist credo, even while the more radical members of activist groups proclaimed the death of reason and substituted confrontation for communication, destruction for dialogue. Basic to the stance of student rebellion is a moral disgust prompted by the belief that the existing order of things *need not be as it is and can be changed*. If the status quo is neither inevitable nor unalterable, it could be replaced by something better. Moral revulsion is meaningless unless human effort can make a difference. Protest began within the schools but only because that is where most of the young found themselves; their dissatisfaction has been directed not so much at the schools themselves as at the larger society with which educational institutions are allied. Yet to the extent that schools are assailed for bureaucratizing and dehumanizing those who have to learn within them, and, moreover, because schools serve the values obtaining in the social order, they have come in for a share of abuse.

The predominant characteristic of contemporary protest has been the inability of the young to identify with the goals of so much social engineering that schools presumably facilitate. The so-called generation gap talked about in recent years has become a *moral* chasm, across which the young stare at their elders with distrust, convinced that the values that make for success in the adult world are unacceptable.[29] Nor is the unrest a monolithic movement with a common ideology; the worldwide protest of the young against their elders transcends particular ideologies. This is to say that moral disapprobation today does not require any special theoretical justification, it is simply experienced at a different level altogether.

One of the great hazards of education, as eighteenth-century despots knew full well, is that increased learning often breeds discontent. It enables people to envisage alternatives to the status quo, whether personal or social. Although dissent is not confined to the young by any means, the phenomenon of student unrest is historically unique in the degree to which the young have developed a greater sense of consciousness of the problems of present-day society, a greater sensitivity to the alleged hypocrisy of an older generation, a deeper sense of loss over the apparent failure of conventional liberalism to extricate itself from status-quo politics, and the seeming inability of moderate reformist action to attack social ills head on. The habit

---

[29] For a good discussion of this interpretation, see J. Bronowski, "Protest—Past and Present," *American Scholar* (Autumn, 1969), pp. 535–546.

of mind informed by such concerns fastens readily upon schools because those most likely to feel dissatisfaction are directly involved in formal educational processes.

The specific complaints are too well known by now to require lengthy discussion. In part, faith in education has been severely compromised by the intractability of the institutions in which it is conducted. Schools tend to be blindly narcissistic about their own self-preservation, even at the expense of their inmates. For example, high school and college students sense something hypocritical about the demand levied by school officials that they, the students, "go through channels" in working for internal reforms, only to find that channels lead nowhere, or, alternatively, to be told that they must abide by established rules while their betters are free to depart from them whenever and however they see fit. The chorus of criticism by education's detractors (some of them not so young) has swelled in recent years, claiming that universities are hamstrung with inertia, that secondary schools are prison houses of the mind, and that elementary schools are repositories of trivia. Current teaching practices, some critics aver, unnecessarily neglect the affective domain for cognitive skills, that they place a premium on students' getting the "Right Answer" (unmindful of Margaret Mead's dictum that the "right" answer is often the trite answer), and that they utterly fail to honor the diversity of skills, interests, and abilities of those at whom teaching is directed. Given the evidence that no high correlation exists between school performance and life achievement and the school's unwillingness, so it is argued, to equip people to engage in socially useful labor which contributes to human betterment, hard questions are raised about the content, process, and direction of institutionalized schooling.

Beyond the schools, student protest has aimed at three interrelated sets of problems.[30] The first have to do with the question of man's continuing survival as a species. The very concept of Ultimate War, whether it employs thermonuclear weapons or biological and chemical agents of destruction, is repudiated in the belief that human conflicts should—must—be solved by means other than armed violence. Unlike earlier pacifist movements, the current campaign for a reordering of priorities (in a world where nations expend the greater share of their gross national product on armaments) and the demand for disarmament is predicated upon the assumption that *no* viable alternative exists if man is to survive. Student revolution has also been directed against the destruction of the natural environment which, it is claimed, will lead inevitably to mankind's extinction. Short of that, continued pollution will seriously damage the quality of life possible in a world choking on its own refuse. If this aspect of the struggle for reform seems to take on an apocalyptic character it is because protesters are convinced that

30 The interpretation follows Stuart Langton, "Demythologizing the Student Revolt," *Phi Delta Kappan* (June, 1970), pp. 540–544.

the annihilation of mankind or its preservation are the issues at stake.

The prevalence of human misery has offered youthful protest its second set of targets. Human misery and suffering as a result of poverty, hunger, disease, racism, and ignorance are viewed as absolutely intolerable now that man has the technology adequately to feed, clothe, shelter, educate, and preserve the health of all members of the human race. Presuming that man does not breed himself into cataclysmic disaster, it has become possible to eliminate or reduce drastically the major common ills of humanity. By reorganizing institutions so that exploitation and injustice are impossible or unproductive, by making the rational–liberal credo work, the glaring discrepancy between what men say and what they do can be ended. At the heart of the students' populist revolt is an acute sense of social responsibility and a profound determination to rid society of its terrible ills before it is too late.

The third aspect of dissent represents a response to a life style characterized by consensus and compromise, easy accommodation to social injustice, and collective myopia in the face of wrongdoing, buttressed by an elaborate apparatus of evasion and equivocation. Moreover, it is a repudiation of a way of life founded on superabundant materialism. The young reject the hallowed article of faith that More is Better, or that the good life can be defined in terms of economic success. They have sought new alteratives for organizing human behavior, ways which expand the range and quality of experience. The emergent posture of a new generation rejects a system whose environmental opportunities seem stale, narrow, demeaning, or lacking in imagination. A culture that distrusts genuine diversity, that punishes nonconformity, that prizes homogeneity of taste, attitude, and behavior and either restricts or assimilates (and then exploits) the deviant holds little appeal for an important segment of those under thirty. The new life style in process of birth seeks qualitatively different kinds of experiences, while rejecting the massive, interlocking and impersonal social system of contemporary society.[31] In asserting the value of emotionalism, protesters continue to look for an escape from all the forces of modern life that encourage alienation, depersonalization, isolation and that thwart the genuine possibilities of self-fulfillment.

If the preceding analysis is substantially correct, it shows that enough of the Enlightenment faith in progress remains to animate hopes that human effort will count for something in rebuilding society. The vision of a better world has not disappeared completely, though fewer panaceas for its realization seem at hand. Rightly or wrongly, the young blame their elders for a society in which the various social subsystems together have produced a world hovering on the brink of madness. Apologetics for those political, economic, and social subsystems of society begin to look patently absurd. Only fools, hypocrites, and incompetents, runs the argument, will defend

31 Ibid., p. 542.

that kind of society. Now the task is to create something better. In an age of rising expectations, an age of instant communication which demands instant answers, the rationalist belief in the efficacy of human action retains its sway over the young. Meanwhile, however, too many students feel caught in what Tolstoy called "the snare of preparation," which he insisted modern society has spread before the feet of students, hopelessly entangling them in a curious inactivity at the very period of life when they are longing to construct the world anew and to make it conform to their own ideals.

SUMMARY

The eighteenth century opened upon a scene of relative inactivity in the rebuilding of educational institutions at all levels. Far more progress was made, following Locke, in the realm of pedagogical theory than in actual practice. This was particularly true during the Enlightenment. Although the philosophes like Voltaire, Diderot, Montesquieu, and Turgot believed that education in the simple laws of nature was possible and desirable, they wrote very little on specific educational problems. Their energies were taken up in attacking the entrenched political, social, economic, moral, and religious structures of a corrupt society. A few rare individuals explored the pedagogical implications of Locke's view that environment is the determining factor in human development but none went so far as to lay down a comprehensive theory of education based on those views. That work was reserved for Jean-Jacques Rousseau. He tied his belief in the perfectibility of natural man through proper education (in the *Émile*) to a theory of societal growth that challenged the basic assumptions of Enlightenment rationalists. If society is a corrupting force, a good education is possible only by separating the student from it; education is the antidote to society. Whether Rousseau was able to resolve the contradiction inherent in this position is a question requiring further analysis. Two other solutions to the basic problem of education as he conceived it—state education and education in the home—were also considered in his other writings.

One of the eighteenth century's outstanding educators was Johann Heinrich Pestalozzi. He borrowed heavily from Rousseau's ideas but modified them in such a way that they could be adapted to practice within schools. More than anyone else, Pestalozzi built a systematic theory of instruction upon the prevailing sensationalist psychology of his day and showed how it could be applied successfully. Virtually all the fundamental precepts governing elementary education today were anticipated in his work. The Pestalozzian movement that grew up in the early 1800's undoubtedly hastened the day when the importance of early schooling received the recognition it deserves.

The late 1700's were an age in which beginnings were made in the building of Europe's national educational systems. Chalotais, Turgot, and Condorcet were among the most important participants in numerous discussions of a French state-supported system of schools. Their hopes, however, were not realized until well into the nineteenth century. In England activity centered around the private philanthropic labors of Thomas Gouge, Robert Raikes, and Robert Owen. The cause of popular state-supported education got some support from economist Adam Smith, not to mention many others, yet the English people by and large were content to leave schooling in the hands of private charitable societies. For a time the same situation obtained in the German states. The most significant practitioners of the day were Francke, Hecker, Semler, Rochow, Basedow, and Campe. Benevolent despots in German lands, especially the three Wilhelm Fredericks of Prussia, were the first to lend official support to a centralized school system. Their example was followed by enlightened rulers in Austria, Spain, and a number of other countries.

A retrospective look at the main intellectual themes of the Enlightenment suggests that the rational faith in the power of human reason has come in for serious questioning in recent decades. The related faith in education as a tool for rebuilding society still remains but it needs the inspiration of a new Rousseau or Pestalozzi to give it clearer definition.

QUESTIONS FOR DISCUSSION

1. What, if anything, is wrong with the theory of formal discipline? Does it not make sense to argue that if you can train the body, you can train the abilities of the mind? Are contemporary psychologists agreed that this theory is wrong? What about the related idea of transfer of training? Evaluate the idea that behind modern curriculum proposals, with their stress on the "structure" of a discipline and the learning of cognitive skills having broad applications, there is a covert theory of mental discipline and transfer of training.

2. To what extent are the sensationalist ideas of Locke, Condillac, and Helvétius— i.e., that environment is a powerful determinant of behavior—still operative today in modern programs of social reform, criminology, and the movements to provide "compensatory" education for the culturally deprived?

3. Compare the major educational ideas of Rousseau with those of A. S. Neill in *Summerhill*. How similar are their ideas on child rearing? What parallels can be found between Rousseau's theory of history and the Marxist view? Contrast Rousseau's thought with that of Jules Henry in *Culture Against Man,* Herbert Marcuse's in *Reason and Revolution,* or William Golding's in his novel *Lord of the Flies.*

4. Criticize, pro or con, Locke's claim that collective schooling is antieducational. What price has to be paid for modern public schooling, as opposed to private, tutorial arrangements? Are the disadvantages of mass education inherent?

5. How adequate is Condorcet's distinction between "positive" education in matters of "fact and number" and education concerning beliefs or values? Are *any*

subjects taught in schools value-free? Is it possible or desirable for a teacher to be totally objective and neutral?

6. Review the historic objections levied against national state-controlled educational systems. How valid were they? Might the same arguments be used today to criticize either European or American education? How similar were the objections to developing state education in France, Germany, or England to those raised in protest against increasing federal involvement in education within the United States?

7. Does anyone today echo the sentiments of the eighteenth-century benevolent despots in their misgivings about too much popular, universal education? Consider a possible similarity between the idea of educating people to keep them in their place within society and the frequent observation heard today that the real function of modern schooling is baby-sitting, keeping people off the streets, delaying their entrance into the job market.

8. What kinds of learning could *not* be achieved through use of a monitorial method of instruction? Assess the strengths and weaknesses of this approach if it were used in schools today.

9. How realistic was the idea of Chalotais and Basedow that if one has excellent textbooks, there is little need for good teachers? What theory of teaching undergirds their opinion? How important is the teacher today in implementing new curricular programs? If the programs are good enough, can they compensate for poor teachers?

10. A careful reading of Pestalozzi's work at Stanz, Neuhof, Burgdorf, and Yverdon suggests the possibility his success was owed to the power of personal character more than to any special methods in use. How important is the personality of an individual teacher in teaching effectiveness?

7 Education for a Progressive Society

The politicians tell us "You must educate the masses because they are going to be masters." The clergy join in the cry for education, for they affirm that the people are drifting away from the church and chapel into the broadest infidelity. The manufacturers and the capitalists swell the chorus lustily. They declare that ignorance makes bad workmen; that . . . the glory will be departed from us. And a few voices are lifted up in favour of the doctrine that the masses should be educated because they are men and women with unlimited capacity of being, doing, and suffering, and that it is as true now, as ever it was, that the public perish for lack of knowledge.

THOMAS H. HUXLEY
Address to the South London Working Men's College

Our schools are, in a sense, factories in which the raw product (children) are to be shaped and fashioned into products to meet the various demands of life. . . . It is the business of the school to build its pupils to the specifications laid down.

ELLWOOD P. CUBBERLEY
Public School Administration

SOCIAL AND INTELLECTUAL THEMES IN THE MODERN ERA

An Age of Progress

The closer one approaches the present, the more implausible it becomes to outline historical movements under a simple formula or a single theme. This is especially so in attempting to sketch out the broad intellectual and social contours of the nineteenth century. "No age," observed the historian J. T. Merz, "has been so rich in rival theories, so subversive of old ideas, so destructive of principles which stood firm for many ages." Its contrasts are striking: undreamt of wealth alongside unbelievable poverty, buoyant optimism coexisting with abject pessimism, religious piety with militant atheism, socialism with fascism, democracy with tyranny, stability with chaos. It was this incredible variety that must have prompted Matthew Arnold to lament the "multitudinousness" of his times and to observe that no one person could even begin to comprehend it all.

If there is any unifying thread binding the nineteenth century to the one preceding, it is to be found in the *doctrine of progress*. This Enlightenment legacy continued to command the assent of most thinkers, retaining its force as the basis of common belief in Europe throughout most of the 1800's. The Frenchman Javary, writing in the year of the Great Exhibition in London's Hyde Park (1851), observed, "If there is any idea that properly belongs to our century, it is, as it seems to me, the idea of progress, conceived as a general law of history and the future of humanity." Although tragic wars and revolutions throughout a quarter century extending from the French Revolution to Napoleon's downfall, must have suggested that progress was neither uninterrupted nor uniform, there was considerable evidence to confirm hopes in human advancement, uneven and irregular perhaps, but discernible nonetheless. At every turn it was plain that men were triumphing over the world around them, and at a rate never before thought possible.

When the century opened, men could look back in time to a world in which the better part of Europe's population had lived on isolated little farms, accessible only by dirt roads and barge canals, a world whose wealth derived almost completely from agriculture. Tools and textiles were wrought by small, independent craft guilds, and power was generated solely by human or animal muscle. Horse and sail were the chief means of transportation, and communications, always slow, were uncertain and sporadic. Now, less than a century later, the growing replacement of machinery for human toil, of inanimate for animate power, had brought about an industrial revolution. The processes of economic production had produced an entirely new world—an age of iron and coal and steam, of engines and machinery, of steamships and railroads, of telegraphs, and uncounted other marvels. Quicker travel and improved communication were making the earth a smaller place, and ingenious new devices were making life upon it more comfortable.

With industrialization came a rapid growth in population, a fantastic increase in agricultural productivity, and an expanded technology. The generation after 1830 witnessed an apparently uninterrupted advance in virtually all the sciences, accompanied by a growth of inventions the likes of which no man had seen before. It was no wonder that people welcomed and expected material improvements, not just for a privileged minority, but for everybody. Even the humblest man, it seemed, could hope to share in the benefits of a progressive society. In the midst of unparelleled change, proponents of the doctrine of progress could point with pride at the rise of business enterprise and all the successful new social adjustments to technological advancement, including mechanisms for the accumulation of capital, labor unions, an expansion of governmental functions and services, and consequently an over-all increase in the standard of living. Not only were science and technology reshaping man's physical and social environment, they were affecting his economics, conditioning his philosophy and religion, often influencing his art and literature as well.

It was even possible to argue that some progress had been made in the realm of politics. In the post-Napoleonic period, the regents of the various European states were plainly anxious to safeguard the status quo and to prevent a recurrence of revolutionary turmoil. Hopes for an enduring peace were bolstered when the Congress of Vienna reconvened to redraw the political map of the Continent along more secure lines, safeguarding its dictates by establishing a five-power "Concert of Europe" including Austria, Russia, Prussia, Great Britain, and France. Even when revolution did break out once again in the France of 1848, echoed by revolutionary movements in Germany, Italy, and Austria, prompt action on the part of those monarchs who survived ensured a swift return to normalcy. Surely it was significant, optimists claimed, that Europe experienced no major wars between 1818 and 1853. That fact by itself seemed to suggest that man as a political animal had finally reached his maturity.

The idea of the inevitability of progress received its greatest support, of course, from Darwin's theory of evolution. Much has been made of the intellectual impact this new view of man and his world made on nineteenth-century life. Actually, Darwin simply provided a scientific warrant for a concept already commonplace among scientists, historians, sociologists, and philosophers. As George Bernard Shaw sardonically observed, Darwin "had the luck to please everybody who had an axe to grind"—humanitarians who welcomed evolution as a confirmation of the Enlightenment faith in progress, moral philosophers who argued that material and social evolution was now shown to be a law of the universe, capitalists who translated the term "survival of the fittest" into the sphere of business competition, militarists who needed a rationale for conflict among sovereign nation states, unbelievers who wanted to overthrow the Book of Genesis, democrats and socialists with eyes fixed upon the vision of society evolving higher modes of social organization—just about everyone. Much as Newton's ideas had sanctioned so many political and philosophical ideas a century and a half earlier, Darwinism lent the authority of physical science to a variety of cherished doctrines in economics, philosophy, and all the nascent social sciences. Thus Lewis Morgan, the American anthropologist, could confidently assert in 1877: "Democracy in government, brotherhood in society, equality in rights and priviliges, and universal education, foreshadow the next higher plane of society to which experience, intelligence and knowledge are steadily tending." It sounded like Condorcet a century before.

An Age of Nationalism

It is often remarked that *nationalism,* a most potent force in nineteenth-century European politics, was reborn just at a time when the Enlightenment faith in a larger unified community of man had almost spelled its demise. For reasons too complex to treat succinctly, nationalism as a political phenomenon became the working form of such eighteenth-century beliefs as freedom, progress, and the perfectibility of mankind. *Liberty* became liberalism, *equality* became socialism and *fraternity*—last of the three great rallying calls of the French Revolution—tended to be confined within national boundaries. Instead of a vague, amorphous "humanity" to be bettered, individual men could fasten their hopes for improvement upon, and align their loyalties with, a definite territorial unit organized under a central political power. Because nationalism was congruous with the rise to power of a middle class, and with the facts of economic readjustment brought on by the early industrial revolution, it was not difficult to argue that the individual *within* the state stood the best chance of self-betterment.

Initially, all this notwithstanding, economic factors might have seemed to legislate *against* the possibility of strong nation states. There was a strong strain of individualism prevalent in the early 1800's, a doctrine which preached the virtues of "economic man" pursuing his own self-interest with a minimum of government interference. It was generally assumed, with Adam Smith, that private interests would tend to promote the public welfare, that the accumulative efforts of each individual on his own behalf would conduce to greater social harmony. Such slogans as "freedom of contract" and "free trade" figured prominently in the rhetoric of those, like Bentham and Mill, who sought to overthrow the old mercantilist system in favor of *laissez-faire.* "It is every day becoming more clearly understood," avowed Samuel Smiles in his tract *Self-help,* "that the function of government is negative and restrictive, rather than positive and active; being resolvable principally into protection of life, liberty, and property." Liberals never tired of inveighing against "too much government" and asserting the rights of the individual against the state. Apparently government had few economic functions to perform.

Then, before very many decades had passed, it was perceived that when capitalists were free to operate without hindrance in the marketplace, they promptly combined together to form monopolies in restraint of trade. Now the newly strengthened economic groups born of the industrial revolution began to exert pressure on government to take a strong hand in economic affairs. Not only should restraining monopolies be forbidden by law, reformers argued, the state should take positive steps to *enforce* competition. Thus there occurred that strange inversion whereby the old liberal belief in *laissez-faire,* threatened by steadily mounting socialist pressures for expanded state welfare programs, was transformed into a conservative doctrine of the capitalist middle class. Furthermore, as matters developed, even conservatives became allied with liberals in agitating for more governmental activism, particularly with respect to the erection of protective tariffs between nations. Yet if governments were to heed the cries from all sides for social or economic intervention, their powers necessarily had to be increased. Times change, as the English philosopher T. H. Green argued, and liberalism, formerly negative in its demands, should commit itself to a positive program of state action in such matters as freedom of contract for the sale of labor, public health, and public education; and the state should be armed with power to discharge these vital functions. When economic dislocations plunged the countries of Europe into depressions like those of the late 1800's, corporate business was quick to call upon the states to bolster the sagging economy. Only national governments, it was felt, could command the necessary resources to effect needed reforms. For several reasons, therefore, the concept of the strong, active nation state was winning widespread approval.

An Age of Bourgeois Domination

It was almost inevitable that economic changes would enhance the growth in power of the state, if only because those who made the loudest demands on government (whether for protectionism or free trade) had become a potent social force with which monarchs had to reckon. What industrialism had done was to raise to pre-eminence a new, prosperous, and influential middle class, a bourgeoisie whose position owed nothing to lineage and ancestry and whose wealth derived from investments in labor, and from surplus earnings acquired through trade, civil service, or shopkeeping. Karl Marx scarcely exaggerated when he claimed that this new bourgeois class, "during its rule of scarce one hundred years, has created more massive and more colossal productive forces than have all preceding generations together." Productivity had led to wealth, and wealth to power—not just economic influence, but political, social and cultural force as well. The middle class, in other words, was engaged in the process of reworking the world in its own image.

Basically, the bourgeois man elected for moderation and compromise in his world. He was congenial to the humanitarian aspirations of the Enlightenment, but he feared change unless it was modest and gradual. He welcomed the Darwinian struggle of economic life, but only if it could be counterbalanced by order, decorum, and restraint in private conduct. He favored political democracy so long as it did not include everyone or lead either to socialism or anarchism; he wanted peace if it did not threaten national dignity and honor; and he prized personal liberty so long as it was good for business, but he was keenly aware of the distinction between freedom and license. There was no question in his mind that limits upon social and individual freedom were both essential and inevitable. The middle-class man was inclined to let the pendulum swing back from the extreme unbelief of the eighteenth century and was inclined to profess a conventional brand of orthodox Christian piety. For him Comte's positivism, Marx's dialectical materialism, or Feuerbach's atheistic humanism obviously held scant appeal.

There was an element of tragedy in this bourgeois dominance, however, and it lay in the fact that middle-class affluence had been achieved at the expense of untold human misery. Beneath the bourgeoisie on the social ladder clung all those great suffering masses of men upon whose labors business prosperity had been built and whose lives were neither comfortable nor civilized. Indeed, for the underprivileged, life was decidedly "nasty and brutish." Therein lay the great failing of the nineteenth-century age of industrialism and progress: the horrendous living standards of the lower class. They mocked the optimism of the period and made fatuous talk about human betterment seem a pathetic joke. The industrial revolution had indisputably brought prosperity for some, but it had also brought in its aftermath terrible urban slums, child labor, and systematic exploitation. Families were crowded together in poorly built factory tenements, condemned to live out their lives in dark, foul-smelling warrens swept periodically with epidemics of typhoid, tuberculosis, and cholera. "The imagination can hardly apprehend the horror," notes English scholar G. M. Young, "in which thousands of families . . . were born, dragged out their ghastly lives, and died; the drinking water brown with faecal particles; the corpses kept unburied for a fortnight in a festering London August; mortified limbs quivering with maggots; courts where not a weed would grow, and sleeping-dens afloat with sewage."[1]

Those who serviced the burgeoning needs of industry, it became painfully evident, had simply exchanged the bondage of serfdom for the bondage of the factory. A report in 1860 of a county magistrate in Britain on conditions in the Nottingham lace trade was typical: Children, he exclaimed, were "dragged from their squalid beds at two, three or four o'clock in the morning and compelled to work for bare subsistence until ten, eleven or twelve at night, their limbs wearing away, their frames dwindling, their faces whitening, and their humanity absolutely sinking into a stone-like torpor, utterly horrible to contemplate."[2] Sensitive observers in all countries recoiled in horror at the grim picture of misery and depravation. "Oh God!" wrote Thomas Hood, "that bread should be so dear, and flesh and blood so cheap!"

An Age of Criticism

Criticism of the existing social order in the nineteenth century proceeded on several fronts. The most conspicuous target of course was industrialized

1 Quoted in Samuel C. Burchell, *Age of Progress* (New York: Time-Life Books, 1968), p. 75.
2 Ibid., p. 74.

injustice. The yawning chasm of capital and labor led Marx to draft his *Communist Manifesto* and stimulated Disraeli to note that Europe had "two nations," the Poor and the Rich. Revolution would surely follow, he warned, unless corrective measures were taken promptly. It is not to be wondered at that Marx thought the revolt of the proletariat would come first in the heavily industrialized nations and that in this so many people agreed with him. Anarchists, socialists, communists, all advanced social welfare schemes, ranging from proposals for piecemeal reform to demands for the total overhaul of society.

Another target for attack was the democratic–social ethos of middle-class culture itself. John Stuart Mill warned of the potential tyranny of bourgeois society which, he felt, might impose "an oppressive yoke of uniformity in opinion and practice." Alexis de Tocqueville shared the same misgivings. Balzac lamented the "materialism" of middle-class civilization and Zola skillfully dissected all its vices. Tories joined in the chorus of criticism, expressing disgust at the vulgar disorder of the times and wondered if the world was not entering upon an age of mass-produced mediocrity. John Ruskin objected to the ugliness and standardization of life he perceived, as did the Swiss writer Henri Amiel when he predicted dolefully that "the useful will take the place of the beautiful, industry of art, political economy of religion, and arithmetic of poetry." Dickens in London, Dostoevsky in St. Petersburg, and Victor Hugo, exiled from France, spoke with a single voice when they detected grave threats to human dignity in a world daily growing more inhumane.

If anything, this spirit of pessimism deepened in the closing decades of the century. Economic recessions, the "revolt of the masses" under revolutionary banners, and the steady emergence of imperialist powers founded on "blood and iron" help account for the change in spirit. At any rate, a more combative view of life made itself felt, evidenced by the frequency with which intellectuals resorted to such expressions as "struggle for existence," the "will to power," a "conflict of classes," and "warfare" between science and religion. Individualism receded before the principle of collectivism. Friedrich Nietzsche called for a transvaluation of morality, and urged the destruction of an ignoble bourgeois mentality, the ethic of the herd. "Democracy," he fumed, "has in all ages been the form under which organizing strength has perished . . . [it is] the historic form of the decay of the state." The historian Jacob Burckhardt wrote prophetically to a friend in 1871, "I have a premonition. Long voluntary subjection under individual *Führers* and usurpers is in prospect. People no longer believe in principles, but will, periodically, probably believe in saviors." In support for his thesis, he might have noted that protofascists like Thomas Carlyle were getting a wider hearing than ever before, and doctrines emphasizing the authority of a leader were steadily winning adherents. For the same reason, a character in one of Zola's novels saw "the red vision of revolution that . . . at the end of the century would carry everything away."

In the years after the Franco-Prussian War, international tensions tended to strengthen prophecies of impending doom. George Romanes must have spoken for many when he beheld the advance of a cataclysmic deluge, "black with destruction, resistless in might, uprooting our most cherished hopes, engulfing our most precious creed, and burying our highest life in mindless desolation." Imperialist ambitions fed upon a virulent resurgent nationalism (as expounded, for example, by Maurice Barrès in France and by Treitschke in Germany) which glorified the power of the state and insisted that, in the international arena, Might made Right. It was not without cause that Matthew Arnold feared mankind was poised "as on a darkling plain, swept with confused alarms of struggle and flight, where ignorant armies clash by night."

With the opening decade of the twentieth century, however, dire predictions of calamity seemed unwarranted. On the contrary, with such few exceptions as the abortive Russian Revolution of 1905, peace and tranquility reigned unchallenged. All visible signs pointed to a new dawning era of prosperity and harmony. It was, as historians are fond of pointing out, an "age of innocence." The march of progress seemed as relentless as ever and mankind could still hope that the specter of war had been laid aside, that poverty and disease could be conquered permanently, and that the nations of Europe were evolving effortlessly toward a higher civilization. These hopes were dashed abruptly in 1914 when the Archduke Franz Ferdinand, nephew of Franz Josef and heir to the Hapsburg crown, was assassinated by Serbian nationalists in the obscure little Bosnian town of Sarajevo. Four weeks later Europe plunged into a four-year holocaust that was to claim the lives of millions. It was mankind's first introduction within modern times to a world in which war or the threat of war had become a permanent condition. Pitirim Sorokin, in his *Social and Cultural Dynamics,* expressed the general disillusionment and anguish of the postwar period. "I am not ashamed to confess," he wrote, "that the World War and most of what took place after it were bewildering. . . . I expected the progress of peace but not of war; the bloodless reconstruction of society but not bloody revolutions; humanitarianism in nobler guise but not mass murders; an even finer form of democracy but not autocratic dictatorships; the advance of science but not of propaganda and authoritarian *dicta* in lieu of truth; the man-sided improvement of man but not his relapse into barbarism."

Subsequently Europe staggered into the greatest economic collapse she had known in over three centuries, followed by a still more destructive worldwide conflict. The horrors of mechanized murder and mass exterminations only served to underscore Ortega y Gassets's earlier warning about the consequences of allowing the powers unleashed by science to fall into the hands of irrational men. "The type of man dominant today," he observed, "is a primitive one, a *Naturmensch* [an irrational man] rising up in the midst of a civilized world"—one who controls civilization's instrumentalities but does not know how to employ them to moral ends. Ordinary men did not require an Ortega or a Freud to remind them of irrationality; they saw the results around them all too clearly—universal devastation, hunger, poverty, and death, all part of the grim chronicle of man's inhumanity to man.

The single greatest change wrought in the early twentieth century was the gradual loss of European autonomy. Two long and destructive wars, fought largely on European soil, contributed powerfully to that loss. For over a millennium, from the very inception of Western Judeo-Christian civilization, European developments had depended primarily upon the complex interplay of techniques, ideas, institutions, events, and personalities indigenous to that continent. But since 1914 European history increasingly reflected the impact of outside forces, especially from America and the underdeveloped countries of the world. Moreover, despite popular optimism and a remarkable economic recovery, Europe's intellectual life continues to reflect an age of social disintegration and spiritual anxiety. Alienation is still as prevalent as ever.

Basic to much of current thought is a mood of restlessness and uncertainty. Science has been shown to have its limits, especially when men turn to the most fundamental questions of life; conventional religion continues to offer solace, though an equally strong spirit of secularism permeates Western society; Marxist socialism has rigidified into a complacent orthodoxy; contemporary literature and art bear witness to the fragmentation of personality; philosophy has seemingly retreated within itself or fallen prey to the forces of obscurantism; and the forces of political irrationalism and primitivism may yet plunge the world into new barbarisms from which recovery will be impossible. Many still concur with T. S. Eliot's judgment that contemporary "hollow man" lives in a "wasteland," or spiritual vacuum, from which (as Sartre implied) there is no way out. Perhaps, without the *de facto* wisdom of some far-removed historian, no further judgment can be rendered, except to note with Ortega once again, "No one knows toward what centre human beings are going to gravitate in the near future, and hence the life of the world has become scandalously provisional. . . . Life to-day is the fruit of an interregnum, of an empty space between . . . that which was, that which is to be."

On the other side, there is still evidence to show that the general optimism of the Enlightenment has managed to survive two world wars, a cold war, the welfare state, and the warfare state, all the cruelest miseries of the past two centuries. Over and against a tragic view of life, there remains a certain perennial confidence that mankind will endure, a belief that though no final victories are easily won it is still worth struggling, and that mankind still has within his grasp an unrealized potential for improvement. From an educational standpoint alone, the record of recent times reveals how for the first time in Western history the nations of Europe began to make educational provision for whole populations, not just for the well-born and the wealthy, but for everybody. That development by itself may yet be accounted as one of the most significant advances of the modern era.

The Educational Ramifications

It remains to treat briefly a few of the major *educational* implications of the social and intellectual movements of the last two hundred years. Because formal education is inherently a refractive phenomenon, it was almost inevitable that a complex interplay of *nationalist sentiment* and educational endeavor would take place. Just as it proved difficult, if not impossible, to meet the needs of nineteenth-century society in the areas of public health, social welfare, and economic stability without expanding the role of central government, so too there was a growing recognition from 1800 on that society's educational requirements could not be fulfilled adequately without assistance on a nationwide basis, usually originating at the national governmental level (England was a partial exception). Furthermore, as education became a state function, instruction was bent increasingly to serve the ends of the state. Nationalism was both a result and a determining influence on the development of state educational systems. In Prussia, for example, the first major educational efforts of the early nineteenth century, it will be shown, were initiated with the avowed aim of fostering state patriotism. France followed much the same course of action, largely in direct imitation of the Prussian model. This is to say that nationalist feelings played an important role in the establishment of schools, and once begun, educational agencies were expected to inculcate nationalist sentiment in the children who attended them.

The slow evolution from private, voluntary schools to state-controlled institutions roughly paralleled the decline of the *economic doctrine of laissez-faire* in business. So long as people accepted the idea that prosperity depended upon governments adhering to a "hands-off" policy, it was unlikely that popular opinion would accept active state support, supervision, and control of educational agencies. This was especially true in Great Britain, where the tradition of private philanthropic control of the schools died hard. Naturally many factors were responsible for expanded state intervention when it did occur, but it is not difficult to see a rough correspondence between economic and educational thought in late-nineteenth-century Europe.

The *industrial revolution's influence* on education was twofold. First, to the extent that industrialization depended upon advances in science and technology, it became apparent that school curricula had to be revised to include the new learning and thus to prepare people to live successfully in a technological society. The real beginnings of industrial trade schools and technical training institutes date from the period when this need was first realized. Secondly, as the factory system enhanced rigid class differences, the awareness grew that some educational provision had to be made for the offspring of the toiling masses as well as for the sons of the middle class. Opinion divided on what kind of elementary popular education should be provided, some arguing that schoolroom instruction should be employed to *enhance* social class distinctions, others arguing that it should obliterate or at least mitigate them, but almost no one defended the proposition that workers' children should be allowed to grow up without benefit of schooling at all. Parenthetically, it is worth noting that the *cultural domination of the bourgeoisie* practically guaranteed that formal education at the post-elementary level would be controlled largely by middle-class values.

No less important was the indirect influence science and technology had in stimulating efforts to build a definite science of education. This development gained little headway until the late 1800's, although its beginnings can be seen in the work of the educational theorist Herbart. When scientists demonstrated for all to see how man's control over his natural environment was vastly enhanced by the application of scientific method, it was but a short step to conclude that with the development of the infant social science disciplines, educators might finally be able to introduce a greater measure of rigor and control to the conduct of teaching–learning processes.

Finally, modern *social criticism,* strengthened by the belief in the possibility of human progress, has had a powerful influence on educational developments. So long as men have harbored aspirations for a better society and have believed it within their power to effect reforms, schools have been enlisted in the fight against ignorance, poverty, prejudice, and social immorality. Education, reformers extending back over the centuries have hoped, can provide a fulcrum and lever for moving the social order toward its own transformation. This was very much in the thinking of liberal–democratic reformers when they agitated for the expansion and equalization of educational opportunity for everyone, as a logical imperative following from the broadening of social and political democracy. Today, particularly among educational practitioners, it would seem that the business of keeping school is incompatible with a tragic or pessimistic view of common man, or at least not in keeping with an attitude of passive resignation in the face of ignorance.

In order to illustrate these broad themes more clearly, it becomes necessary to retrace back to the beginnings of the last century and show how educational theory and practice have evolved in the modern era. Much of the history of educational developments since 1800 structures itself along the lines each separate nation pursued more or less on its own. A full discussion of the various national educational systems is better reserved for a comparative study of modern education; economy of space here dictates that only a few representative patterns be considered. Germany was the earliest of the major European nations to build a comprehensive educational structure, followed next by France and then by England. The first development will be viewed against the contributions of two important German educational theorists, Johann Herbart and Friedrich Froebel.

TOWARD A SCIENCE OF EDUCATION: JOHANN FRIEDRICH HERBART

The Continuing Influence of Pestalozzian Pedagogy

Nearly all of the early nineteenth century's major educational theorists were indebted in varying degree to the work and teachings of Pestalozzi. *Johann Gottlieb Fichte* (1762–1814), whose *Addresses to the German Nation* (1807–1808) were partly an appeal for educational effort to rejuvenate the nation after its defeat at the Battle of Jena in 1806 acknowledged his debt to the great Swiss reformer. In his ninth address Fichte wrote,

> It was the reading of his works, and constant meditation on his ideas, that suggested my own system to me. In spite of obstacles of every kind, Pestalozzi, inspired by a mighty and invincible sentiment, the love of the poor and the outcast, has succeeded in making an intellectual discovery that is destined to revolutionize the world. He has sought an education for the common people, and by the force of his genius and his love he has created a true national education that is capable of rescuing the nations and humanity as a whole from the deplorable situation into which they have now fallen.

Others were not so sure. Was it true, educational writers began to ask, that Pestalozzi had succeeded where so many others had failed in discovering techniques for deploying a "natural" method in the day-to-day teaching of children? Ever since the time of Comenius, educators had groped for ways of adapting instruction to the psychological nature of the child. Possibly their efforts had failed for want of a more adequate psychology of learning.[3] Locke had drafted one approach; Rousseau adapted it and gave it expression in his own pedagogical theories. But neither Rousseau nor Pestalozzi, in the eyes of later educators, had gone far enough in identifying the psychological foundations upon which their labors rested. The German philosopher Herbart made the point in his *Science of Education* when he observed that the motive for his "not exactly toilless investigations" had been the conviction that "a large part of the enormous gaps in our pedagogical knowledge results from lack of psychology." As early as the time of his first speech to some young mothers and their friends in Bremen, entitled "On Pestalozzi's Newest Work, 'How Gertrude Teaches Her Children,'" Herbart professed dissatisfaction with the disorganization evident in Pestalozzian pedagogical theory and the lack of scientific preci-

---

3 See Edward J. Power, *Evolution of Educational Doctrine: Major Educational Theorists of the Western World* (New York: Appleton-Century-Crofts, 1969), pp. 308–309.

sion to his instruction that only a more adequate psychology could remedy. Friedrich Froebel, a second important theorist, also tried to bring a firmer psychological basis to educational theory, but his approach was certainly less mathematical, less mechanical, less analytic than Herbart's.

Herbart's Life and Works

Johann Friedrich Herbart (1776–1841) was born at Oldenburg in north-western Germany, son of a prominent attorney. He was tutored at home under the close supervision of his mother until the age of twelve and then sent to the Oldenburg *Gymnasium* for a six-year program of studies. At a very early age the young Herbart showed scholarly promise and a strong bent toward philosophy. He studied under Fichte at the University of Jena for three years before taking employment as a private traveling tutor to three sons of the Swiss governor at Interlaken. This opportunity to engage in the practical business of teaching, coupled with a visit to Burgdorf in 1799 to observe the work of Pestalozzi, accentuated his interest in educational problems. He became convinced that educational methodology could be made a systematic science if it were given a proper philosophical basis. A beginning in this work was made in his first appreciative analysis of the methods and aims of Pestalozzi, entitled *Pestalozzi's Idea of an ABC of Sense-Impression,* published in 1802. Meanwhile Herbart had returned briefly to Oldenburg, left for Bremen to complete his doctoral studies, and, at the age of twenty-six, accepted a post at the University of Göttingen to teach philosophy and pedagogy. His *The Aesthetic Presentation of the World as the Chief Business of Education,* appended in 1804 to the second edition of his first work, was another attempt to improve upon "the grand idea of the noble Pestalozzi, and to expand it into a comprehensive theory of education. Among the major works authored during this period, his *General Principles of Pedagogy* (1806) ranks as the most important. At Göttingen Herbart opened a "seminary of pedagogy" to implement and develop his theories on education.

In 1809 at the tender age of thirty-three he was called to succeed Kant as professor of philosophy at Königsberg, in eastern Prussia. He remained there until 1833, lecturing on pedadogy and philosophy, and writing his major works, the *Introduction to Philosophy* (1813), *Psychology as a Science* (1824–1825), and *General Metaphysics* (1828–1829), as well as many less significant treaties. In addition to his pedagogical seminars and philosophy lectures, Herbart opened a demonstration school (later expanded into a teachers' training college) in which he reportedly supervised some of the instruction personally. From the age of fifty-seven until his death in August of 1841, he taught at Göttingen once again while writing his *Outlines of Pedagogical Lectures* and other restatements of earlier works.

Philosophical Foundations

Herbart's educational theory is closely integrated with his theories of ethics and psychology, both of which were built up from a more general metaphysical theory. Only those portions of his philosophical viewpoint directly relevant to Herbartian pedagogy need be explored. He began by describing philosophy as the elaboration (*Bearbeitung*) of concepts, an activity of applying logical principles to the clarification of concepts furnished by experience. When one undertakes to analyze experiential concepts, a host of difficulties arise, he noted. In the ordinary way of describing things, contradictions quickly become apparent, as, for example, when one tries to describe an object in terms of its qualities. A ball is a single unitary thing, yet in order to describe *what kind* of ball it is one has to mention its size, color, hardness, composition, and so on. The object in question seems to be a plurality of qualities or attributes. Is the ball merely a collection of sensations or is there some underlying something that "holds together" the hardness, size, color, weight, and other qualities of it? If the former, then the ball is no longer a single object; if the latter, then one cannot say the ball *is* hard or soft, heavy or light, large or small; it is whatever holds together its perceivable characteristics.

Herbart's solution to this problem was to postulate a plurality of independent substances or entities called "reals" (*Realen*) which enter into differing relations with one another, and to assert that phenomenal qualities and changes correspond to those relations. The experiences one has of the qualities which define or identify an object like the ball are the results of relations between noumenal "reals," perceived indirectly through phenomena. The ball appears as a unit; actually it is made of a plurality of simple, unchangeable, unextended entities. One perceives the ball's various attributes according to their correspondence with the relations in which reals or underlying entities stand to one another.

This position can be more easily understood by referring to Kant's belief that reality lies hidden behind the appearance of things, that things-in-themselves can never be known or perceived directly but only through what Locke called ideas, or with Kant, presentations (*Vorstellungen*) in the mind. The sensations of experience furnish the raw stuff of thought upon which the mind imposes forms or categories of organization so as to render them intelligible. The categories are, as it were, the *necessary conditions* for having any experiences at all. For reasons too involved to bear extended explanation, both Kant and Herbart believed that an account of reality in the form of a comprehensive system of mutually consistent noncontradictory propositions requires the postulate of the existence of "reals" or noumenal substances, unknowable apart from their manifestations through the phenomena of experience.

There are many reals, each trying to preserve its self-identity in the face of "disturbances" from other such entities. Every disturbance arising from the reciprocal interactions of entities stimulates self-preservative reactions on the part of other entities. Phenomenal occurrences—changes in things experienced—are grounded on and are explicable by the behavior of their underlying "reals." With Herbart, this is the metaphysical basis upon which an intelligible psychological theory is to be constructed.

The soul or mind is a simple and unextended substance, or real, and its basic nature "is totally unknown and will forever remain so." One's consciousness or ego is not mind itself, "only the sum of the actual presentations" or mental states which are generated through experience. The soul, considered simply as such, is not conscious at all; like any other phenomenon it is the product of an unknowable "real" soul. It follows, according to Herbart, that the soul has no forms or categories and its activities are derived entirely from outside itself. "The soul is originally a *tabula rasa* in the most absolute sense, without any form of life or presentation: consequently, there are in it neither primitive ideas, nor any predisposition to form them. All ideas, without exception, are a product of time and experience." Consciousness (one's awareness of self as a subject) is merely the result of the conflict of reals, it is an aggregate of ideas or presentations having an existence and nature all their own. Herbart's point here is that the soul struggles to preserve itself against the disturbances of other reals, and the self-preserving reactions are expressed in sensations and ideas. Mental activity is constituted by the relations and interactions between ideas or sensations. It might be said for Herbart the mind is only a point where presentations come together and struggle for dominance. Knowing, feeling, willing result from the relations between presentations of other reals. If there were no conflict of reals there would be no mind, no consciousness.

Because ideas are the products of interacting reals, it is important to understand the nature of this conflict. Each presentation is a form of activity which "strives to present itself" to consciousness (itself, naturally, the presentation of a real). Ideas vary in their force. If they are associated with one another, are *similar* or *complementary*, there is no conflict. Like presentations attract one another to form *"apperceptive masses"* which occupy the focus of consciousness and expel antagonistic presentations into the unconscious. When two presentations are *contrary,* and therefore mutually exclusive, one comes to the fore and the other disappears from consciousness. It becomes a mere tendency to reappear as an idea at another time. When an idea similar to others already in consciousness appears, it fuses into the apperceptive mass and strengthens it. Again, others are neither like nor contrary, but merely *disparate.* They do not form masses, but what Herbart called a complex. In these three major relations of presentations —fusions into masses, complexes, and expulsion into unconscious tendencies —are to be found the genesis of all ideas held by an individual. The mind, then, is mainly an aggregate of ideational complexes and apperceptive masses. The science of the "statics and mechanics" of ideas (namely, psychology), Herbart believed, could be mathematicized by quantifying the relations among ideas of varying intensity. Further, he thought that in principle it would be possible to determine mathematically the sequence and rate at which inhibited ideas forced below the level of consciousness would return to consciousness, the cause of their return, and the kinds of associated ideas any given repressed presentation would bring with it. Herbart even went so far as to speculate on what kind of mathematical formulas would be required to express these mental activities.

Herbartian Ethics and Curriculum

The second basis for Herbart's thinking on education was an ethical theory. The more basic question of the moral end of education supersedes psychological questions about its means or processes. "The one task, and the whole task, of education," Herbart affirmed, "may be summed up in the concept of morality." By goodness or morality he meant an all-round development of character and mind which, in terms of the proximate goals of the teacher, implies the proper growth of mind and body through "educative instruction," that is, teaching which brings that growth into existence. Mere knowledge is not enough. Nor can morality be taught in the ordinary sense of the word. Morality is based on knowledge because one cannot realize the first without the second, of course, but the knowledge required is of a very special sort. In order for knowledge to inform character there must be what he called many-sided *interest,* absorption in the facts to be taken in. Interest is not some temporary extraneous attitude of mind, but, rather, an involvement of self-activity of the learner. This attention to what is being learned depends on the apperception, or taking in, of a new experience and relating it to previous experiences. The ideas involved organize themselves into an apperceptive mass and grow steadily in their power over consciousness. Ordinarily an individual acquires interest from two sources: first, those associated with contacts with the physical environment, and, secondly, those based on acquaintance with social relations among men in society. In the first group of potential interests, Herbart distinguished empirical interests of facts, speculative interests aroused by connecting facts through general laws (say, the theorems of logic or mathematics), and esthetic interests aroused by the contemplation of beauty in art, music, poetry, and literature. Ethical interests from the second source include "sympathetic" concerns for one's fellow men, social interests in organized societal life, and religious concerns. Any of these classes of interests arising from either source can be character-forming influences, properly handled. Morality as the concomitant of good character, as Herbart defined it, is never fully realized solely through eliciting interests but its realization is achieved through instruction based on any of the interests classified. The ultimate end product is a man who knows what he ought to

do and has the will to affect his conduct, whose moral knowledge is rooted
in a harmonious balance among the various strivings of his will, whose acts
are in accord with the ideals of perfect benevolence and justice which are
manifested in the attitude he assumes toward others, and, finally, whose
moral stance accepts the idea of retribution and compensation, respectively,
for evil and good actions, be they executed by him or by others.

Herbart professed to see an exact correspondence between his classifica-
tion of objects of interest and the organization of an ideal curriculum. He
divided his projected course of studies into two parts: the *scientific,* including geography, mathematics, and nature study as well as manual training,
and the *historical,* including languages and history. Instruction revolving
around human institutions and social relations was crucial, he believed,
because it teaches the learner his duties, obligations, and responsibilities, as
determined by the society of which he is a part. Education's intent to
develop personal character does not preclude its complementary goal of
training the individual to be socially useful, however. Both "scientific" and
"historical" subjects studied together will elicit a broad range of interests
which will eventually contribute to the production of a moral individual.
The curriculum outlined by Herbart was to guarantee the "many-sided
interest" he believed was a precondition for virtue. The other side of this
many-sidedness is the need for a *unification* of interests. "The many sides,"
Herbart asserted, "should represent sides of the same person, like different
surfaces of one body." Good methodology satisfies this requirement of
unifying interests.

There are two phases, two mental aspects, involved: *absorption* and
reflection. Absorption means any single idea is acquired by concentrating
upon it to the exclusion of all others. In psychological terms, a strong
apperceptive mass is built up the more often attention is focused upon it;
this is the so-called law of frequency of return to consciousness. The student
must shut out all contradictory ideas and fasten completely upon a single
idea in order for it to become fixed in the mind. Reflection is a coordinating act of comparison by which the single idea apprehended through
absorption is associated with like ideas from previous experiences and
contrasted with unlike ideas; this is the law of association of similar ideas
in learning. "Absorption and reflection, as forming the act of mental respiration," Herbart claimed in a vivid metaphor, "should always alternate
with one another." Parenthetically, it should be noted that later Herbartians turned their master's dictum on this point into a rigid dogma known
as the *theory of concentration and correlation.* It required the organization
of all aspects of a course of studies around a single subject, upon which the
student was supposed to "concentrate," in Herbart's sense of absorption.
"Correlation" meant reflection, relating the subject to other studies previously learned. The presumption was the learner would build up an apperceptive mass of like ideas instead of being left with a confused welter of
unsystematized impressions.

The Five Steps

The elaboration of a twofold mental "respiration" led Herbart to delineate four successive stages for instruction which, he said, "are universal and must be followed in all instruction without exception." His disciples expanded this into five steps and heeded the advice not to deviate from them with a vengeance. (It can almost be laid down as a general rule that the original, creative ideas of an innovator invariably will be warped beyond recognition by his less inspired followers.) Teachers were taught to divide a lesson plan according to the "formal steps of the recitation" and not to depart from them under any circumstances. The first step, the stage of *preparation,* required the teacher to bring to attention whatever ideas had already been learned consistent with the new learning to be imparted and to aid the student's concentration on it. The second stage, called *presentation,* as the label suggests, meant explaining the material as vividly and clearly as possible, beginning with its simplest component elements and only then moving on to more challenging parts. Herbart recommended using concrete objects whenever possible to make the lesson understandable. Although his followers separated these first two steps, Herbart himself collapsed them into one he called the stage of *clearness* (or absorption).

The third step was termed *association.* Once absorption has brought an object of thought into clear consciousness, the idea must be associated with older ideas learned before. By pointing out similarities and differences between the new material and the old, the teacher assists the child in assimilating new learning into the apperceptive mass. This stage of mental activity obviously corresponds to what Herbart originally called reflection.

The fourth step was system or *generalization.* This was intended as the natural extension of the preceding stage of association. At this point the new learning is organized into a unity, its features made more explicit, and concepts are formed from the relations between older and newer learning. The pupil's understanding is more complete when the work of this step is completed.

Last of all came what Herbart called *method.* (His supporters called it *application.*) This involves the trying out or use of learning in particular situations, putting it to the test to see its relationships with all other learning. Learning is not meaningful, Herbart seemed to imply, unless its relations with new problems are perceived by the learner.

Later Herbartianism

This entire program of correlating the content of instruction with moral training according to clearly defined principles of methodology seemed ideally suited to the needs of the German people at a time when education was regarded as a powerful tool for social regeneration. Herbart's main accomplishment appeared to reside in the fact that he had taken Pestalozzi's doctrines and made them more workable by furnishing them with the systematic philosophical and psychological basis they required. By rejecting the doctrine of Rousseau that education must be antisocial while developing naturally innate abilities, repudiating Locke's formulation of the mind as a *tabula rasa*, and also throwing out Pestalozzi's theory of the harmonious training of mental faculties, he was in effect breaking new ground. He was positing a broad social as well as a personal–moral aim for education in a way that had not been attempted before. With Herbart, greater recognition was given to the importance of preparing men to live effectively within organized society, as well as the need for a science of pedagogy deduced from the nature of men's responsibilities, activities, and interests in the social order. The unusual feature of Herbart's thought was its capacity to tie social and moral ends in education together neatly within the setting of a broader metaphysical and psychological theory.[2]

His own assessment of his labors was pessimistic. "My poor pedagogy has not been able to lift up its voice." This judgment proved premature. Among those who helped make Herbartianism an important force in nineteenth-century educational thought were *Karl Volkmar Stoy,* a lecturer at the University of Jena, and *Tuiskon Ziller* and *Moritz Drobisch,* teachers at Leipzig. Those two universities became centers for Herbartian ideas, particularly with Ziller's publication of *An Introduction to General Pedagogy* (1856), his *Foundations of Educative Instruction* (1864), and the founding in 1869 of an *Association for Scientific Pedagogy* to advance Herbart's theories. Only fifteen years after Herbart died, his ideas had caught the imagination of large numbers of people in both Europe and America. An Austrian scholar, *W. F. Volkman,* published a massive review of the growing Herbartian literature. In 1858 Gustav Adolf Lindner wrote his famous textbook *Empirical Psychology,* which made Herbart's pedagogy a dominant influence in German teachers' seminaries for over two decades. Herbartianism also gave impetus to questions of methodology and learning theory within American educational circles, most markedly after *Charles DeGarmo* translated Lindner's work into English. Charles McMurray's *General Method* (1892) and Frank McMurray's *The Method of the Recitation* were only two of the most influential books written to acquaint Americans with Herbart's ideas. Until it became the *National Society for the Scientific Study of Education* early in the twentieth century, the *National*

2 Fuller treatments of Herbartian thought are to be found in Charles DeGarmo, *Herbart and the Herbartians* (New York: Charles Scribner's Sons, 1896); C. C. Van Liew, *Life of Herbart and Development of His Pedagogical Doctrines* (London: Swan Sonnenschein, 1893); Gabriel Compayré, *Herbart and Education by Instruction* (New York: T. Y. Crowell, 1907); Percival R. Cole, *Herbart and Froebel, An Attempt at Synthesis* (New York: Teachers College, Columbia University, 1907); and in Charles J. Brauner, *American Educational Theory* (Englewood Cliffs, N.J.: Prentice-Hall, 1964), Chapter 4. Alexis Lange's *Herbart's Outlines of Educational Doctrine* (New York: Macmillan, 1901) and William J. Eckoff's *Herbart's ABC of Sense-Perception and Minor Pedagogical Works* (New York: Appleton-Century-Crofts, 1896), although old, are among the better compilations of Herbart's works in English. A more recent treatment is to be found in Harold B. Dunkel, *Herbart and Herbartianism: An Educational Ghost Story* (Chicago: University of Chicago Press, 1970).

Herbartian Society, founded in 1892, was a determining force shaping American pedagogy for many years. There is no question that this ferment strengthened research in the areas of teacher preparation, educational psychology, and instruction—all of which tended to support Herbart's original contention that education is too important an undertaking to be conducted without benefit of sound underlying principles.

FROEBEL AND THE KINDERGARTEN MOVEMENT

Froebel's Career

Born the son of a rural German pastor, *Friedrich Wilhelm August Froebel* (1782–1852) grew up under the harsh care of a stepmother after the death of his mother. His early childhood was an exceptionally unhappy one, filled with loneliness and frustrations. The young Froebel's feelings of neglect were so much reflected in his poor school performance that he was considered feeble-minded by his teachers. Between the ages of ten and fifteen he discovered a more normal existence under the care of a great-uncle in Switzerland. The respite ended after his return home and in desperation the father apprenticed his son to a forester for two years. Friedrich hated the work and slunk home once more, considered an utter failure by himself and his family.

At the age of eighteen Froebel was enrolled briefly at the University of Jena, where the leading lights of the day—Schelling, Hegel, Fichte, Herder, Goethe, and Schlegel—provided a heady intellectual atmosphere. He was unable to complete a course of studies and had to be bailed out of prison for indebtedness by his father. By this time a third return home had taken its toll: the boy was humiliated, totally lacking in self-confidence, deeply despondent. The next few years found him working at a variety of jobs, none of which attracted his interest. Around 1805 he happened to visit a Pestalozzian Institute in Frankfurt and became intensely interested in what he observed there. He returned repeatedly until the school's head, Gottlieb Anton Gruner, offered him a job teaching a class of young boys. Immediately Froebel felt he had at last found his life career. "It seemed as if I had found something I had never known, but always longed for," he reported later. "From the first hour my occupation did not seem in the least alien to me. . . . I felt I had already been a teacher for a long while. I found myself in my native element."

Froebel continued to teach at the Institute for two years, all the while becoming convinced he lacked a proper foundation for his teaching. He returned to his studies, accepted a post as tutor of three boys, and took them out into the country in hopes of educating them very much after the fashion of Rousseau's *Émile* (although he probably was unacquainted with the work). This endeavor was a complete failure. Next he traveled to

Yverdon with his charges in tow to study under Pestalozzi and to teach in the school. When it seemed the institution was on the verge of collapse, Froebel withdrew his three students, returned to Germany, and continued to tutor them privately for another year. The following years were occupied with further academic pursuits, first at the University of Göttingen, where he studied languages, and then at the University of Berlin, where he undertook the study of mineralogy.

During his thirty-first year he served as a volunteer soldier in the German army against Napoleon. During this period of military service he met two younger men who later became his ardent disciples, *Heinrich Langenthal* and *Wilhelm Middendorf*. In 1816 he founded a school at Keilhau in his native state of Thuringia, giving it the pretentious title "The Universal German Educational Institute." This venture was made possible through the service and financial support of his widowed sister-in-law, who hoped to marry the young schoolmaster. Their alliance was to prove disastrous for Froebel even though at first the new school was a success. Frau Froebel enrolled her three sons and the two sons of another brother under their uncle's tutelage. The curriculum offered by Froebel as student enrollments grew included "religion, reading, writing, arithmetic, drawing, the German language, singing, mathematics, nature study, geography, Greek, piano, and physical exercises." The next year Middendorf, and later Langenthal, joined the faculty. For a time the Institute prospered and was operated along lines similar to Pestalozzi's schools at Burgdorf and Yverdon. Then in Berlin Froebel met an attractive, wealthy young widow, married her, and brought her back to Keilhau. Understandably, his sister-in-law bitterly resented the intruder. In a fit of pique she withdrew her support from the school. Her children only dimly understood what was happening but their reaction to the new school mistress plunged all concerned into constant turmoil. Froebel turned into a tyrant under the pressure of his troubles. Charges brought by his sister-in-law led to a government investigation of the Institute. Although they were never substantiated, the damage had been done. The school gradually sank into debt, enrollments shrank, and its founder was finally expelled from his position.

Froebel's next venture was short-lived. He interested a Swiss noble, the Duke of Meningen, in sponsoring a Pestalozzian school with himself as its director. When it collapsed he founded another educational institution but charges brought against him by his embittered nephews (still angry over what had happened to their mother at Keilhau) necessitated his resignation. The school was turned over to Middendorf, who had followed Froebel to Switzerland. A third school was opened at Burgdorf, again on the Pestalozzian pattern. There Froebel remained for some time writing, teaching, and working part time in a nearby orphanage.

Sometime during this stage of his career, Froebel began to question seriously the basic tenets of Pestalozzian doctrines. "Our greatest teachers," he wrote, "Pestalozzi himself not excepted, seemed to me too bare, too empirical and arbitrary, and therefore not sufficiently scientific in their principles, that is, not sufficiently led by the laws of our being." Specifically, he sensed the need for a more organized sequence of experiences for young children to stimulate their innate capacities, order their internal mental life, and advance the process of educational growth. Froebel also came to appreciate the tremendous importance of the home environment for infancy and the need to train mothers for their task of guiding the correct development of their children. This latter idea was given concrete exposition in his publication *Mother and Nursery Songs* (1843). Prior to this time he was engaged in writing his major pedagogical treatise, *The Education of Man,* issued in 1826.

In order to develop his thinking more clearly, Froebel departed Burgdorf for Berlin to inspect the urban nursery schools then beginning to appear throughout the city. Seized by a burst of inspiration, he rented an abandoned mill at Blankenburg and opened his own school in 1837 for children age one to seven. It was to realize his earlier ambition to experiment with a freer, less academic environment for small children, as indicated in previous correspondence: "I shall not call this . . . an infant school because I do not intend the children to be schooled, but to be allowed under gentlest treatment to develop freely." This Blankenburg institution lasted until 1844. On May 1, 1840, Froebel reported, he suddenly hit upon an appropriate name for the kind of place he wanted to develop: it was to be a *kindergarten,* a "children's garden," where infants were free to blossom and unfold according to their own natural development. The next four years were taken up by the work of producing games and other instructional materials that could be literally "packaged" and sent to other educators for use in their own kindergartens.

Froebel could not rest content with these labors alone. He began traveling all over Europe to spread the kindergarten idea through lectures and demonstrations. During the winters he ran an institution at Keilhau designed to train teachers for this new kind of education. One of the pupils at this training institute was a young lady by the name of *Louise Levine.* Although thirty years younger than Froebel, she became his constant companion, accompanying him in his travels as he demonstrated kindergarten exercises and materials to educators. Some years before his wife had died but the fact that he did not immediately marry Louise scandalized nearly everyone, especially his relatives and associates at Keilhau.

Among the many kindergartens founded by Froebel was one at Bad Liebenstein, along with a demonstration school for teachers. The work aroused the interest of a wealthy Baroness, *Bertha von Marenholtz-Bülow* (1810–1893), who from 1849 when she first made Froebel's acquaintance until her death devoted her time working in Switzerland, Italy, France, Germany, and England to popularize his ideas. Her *Reminiscences of Fried-*

rich Froebel and other numerous writings directly accounted for the favorable reception the kindergarten movement received in many countries. In the meantime Froebel had had a run-in with his nephew, Carl Froebel, during a sojourn in Berlin. The younger Froebel had authored on his own a number of works supportive of kindergarten education. Unfortunately he was confusedly identified by Prussian authorities with his uncle and because Carl was a leading socialist revolutionary, the entire educational movement became politically suspect. In 1851 the Prussian minister of education issued an edict proscribing the kindergarten idea as "a socialistic system designed to foster atheism among the country's youth." Baroness von Marenholtz-Bülow managed to get the order annulled but the affair probably hastened Froebel's death. He died at Bad Liebenstein in the company of his beloved Louise (whom he had finally married), his teaching associates, and students. The monument over his grave bore a fitting quotation from the poet Schiller: "Come, let us live for our children."

His Philosophy

The opening passage of *The Education of Man* begins, "All things live and have their being in and through God, the divine unity. All things exist only through the divine effluence that lives in them." The universe is a totality, a whole, an "all-pervading, energetic, living, self-conscious, and hence eternal Unity" which is God. The divine oneness is manifest in all created existing things, but is not to be identified with the totality of existents.[5] God is an active, continuous principle of self-creativity whose conscious, and hence fullest, expression is man. The development of man's internal potential, the unfolding of his inner nature, is only one phase of the universal, unfolding activity of creation that comprehends all things. Each individual is a part of a self-realizing whole that comes into being through its own activity. "In all things there lives and reigns an eternal law" of growth manifest, respectively, in the "outer" world of nature, and the "inner" reality of the human spirit: a principle of unity and connection revealed, depending on which aspect is considered, in the multiplicity of natural phenomena and the individuality of man's consciousness. Phrased differently, God achieves universality in the diversity of existing things and within the human soul, both of which are products of an ongoing process of generation.

Froebel drew two main conclusions from this conception of the universe. First, all things have a threefold nature: anything is *unique* as an object or individual in its own right; it is *diverse,* because it is made up of many constituent elements or entities, and it is *universal,* insofar as it is part of the universal divine whole. Secondly, the triune nature of all things leads directly to his idea of education as a process by which the divine unity,

---

[5] This would be the philosophical position known as *pantheism:* everything is God and God is everything. Froebel's position is technically termed *panentheism.*

God, achieves greater self-consciousness. "Education," he said, "consists in leading man, as a thinking, intelligent being, growing into self-consciousness, to a pure and unblemished, conscious and free representation of the inner law of divine unity, and in teaching him ways and means thereto." Human development is a striving for actualization, a conscious evolution toward completeness which can be given a measure of direction and control. Some of the direction comes from within; part of it comes through the good offices of the teacher in providing the child with opportunities to define or exercise his internal formative impulses. As a *unique* entity, the child must be allowed to unfold at his own rate, in his own way. As a *diverse* phenomenon, the individual's personality has many aspects to it that need to be educated so that they grow together in a harmonious whole. And as a *universal,* the child must be brought to an awareness of his identity with everything else in the universe. Froebel phrased it as follows: "By education, then, the divine essence of man should be unfolded, brought out, lifted into consciousness, and man himself raised into free, conscious obedience to the divine principle that lives in him, and to a free representation of this principle in his life." He continued, "Education as a whole, by means of instruction and training, should bring to man's consciousness, and render efficient in his life, the fact that man and nature proceed from God and are conditioned by him—that both have their being in God."

His Pedagogy

Froebel set forth three postulates following from the idea of education as an evolutionary process determined mainly from within, and through which the divine spirit reveals itself. (1) Educational growth proceeds of its own accord. The teacher's intervention should "necessarily be passive, following, not prescriptive, categorical, interfering." At most, an educator can direct growth, not force it. (2) The unfolding process follows a genetic order of development or "inner" law (which Froebel believed, along with Pestalozzi and others, recapitulated the evolution of the human race) that must be taken into account when planning the curriculum. He argued that it is vital "to note the moment, the proper place, for the introduction of a new branch of instruction. . . . The whole attention of the teacher must be directed to these budding-points of new branches of instruction." (3) This implies that education must be ordered around the interests and spontaneous activities of the child. Nothing is served by extraneously imposing learning materials upon a child at points where the natural self-activities of the child do not warrant their introduction.

In considering the nature of child development further, Froebel was led to the conclusion that human growth is governed by two complementary laws, the law of *opposition* or *polarity* and the law of *connection*. All things in the universe have their contrasting opposites: up and down, inner and outer, spirit and matter, male and female, animate and inanimate. So far as human growth is concerned, the basic opposition is between the inner nature of the child and the outer character of the environment. Learning means coming to terms with the environment and being influenced by it through various activities. Self-initiated action, exploration, and discovery are the ways through which the external world shapes the child's internal nature. The law of connection comes into play when the developing child begins to apprehend relationships among things that at first seemed to be opposed. He intuitively grasps the idea of the indwelling unity of all creation. Froebel was most insistent on this point: "The essential business of the school is not so much to communicate a variety and multiplicity of facts as to give prominence to the ever-living unity that is in all things." As will be shown, this conviction that an ontological unity can be represented to the child was a major principle underlying much of Froebel's pedagogy. By assuming that the deepest spiritual laws of the universe were objectively symbolized by the phenomena of nature, he was convinced that even small children could understand the fundamental unity of cosmic evolution and their own participation in it. The entire theory of "gifts" so prominent in Froebelian educational thought was based on this idea.

Central to his view was an identification of three distinct stages in the blossoming of the child's inner nature, each requiring its own techniques. (Froebel was careful to point out that because individuals develop at different rates they enter the stages of growth at differing ages.) The first, the period of *infancy,* begins at birth and usually lasts until age three. The main concern of parents should be to foster a loving, happy environment in order for the child to feel secure and protected. Bodily exercises and training of the senses are the only educative activities appropriate during the first years of life.

Childhood, from three to seven ordinarily, is the kindergarten period during which the most fundamental instincts are aroused through musical rhythms, drawing activities, and spontaneous play activities. Froebel defined play as the "independent, outward expression of inner impulse and life." Education is mainly a matter of letting the child's "first voluntary employments"—observing his surroundings, grasping objects, playing with them—stimulate his natural evolution through action on his external environment. Play is important for its own sake. "Is not the most beautiful expression of child life at this time," Froebel asked, "a playing child?—a child wholly absorbed in his play?—a child that has fallen asleep while so absorbed?"

Boyhood, the period extending from around age seven to ten, is the "period of learning" when "instruction predominates." The child's formative instincts appear, making action more purposive or goal-centered. Activities are no longer engaged in for their own sake, but as means for accomplishing some end. Feeling gives way to thought; the place of play is taken over by organized learning. Basically four subjects or groups of studies make up the proper curriculum: religion, natural sciences, languages, and art. Speaking of these, Froebel remarked, "In religion the aspiration of the soul, which is directed toward unity in man, prevails and seeks the fruition of its hopes. In the contemplation of nature and mathematics, the aspiration of intellect, which refers to individuality in man, prevails and seeks certainty. In language, the demand of reason, which refers to diversity and unites all diversity, prevails and seeks satisfaction." An elaborate rationale was offered for these claims. Finally, "A universal and comprehensive plan of human education must . . . necessarily consider at an early period singing, drawing, painting, and modeling; it will not leave them to an arbitrary, frivolous whimsicalness, but treat them as serious objects of the schools." Never before, and possibly never after Froebel, were such activities considered so educationally important.

Historically, except for the discussion of the stage of childhood, his outline of successive steps of development never gained much influence. Froebel himself thought they were critical: "How different could [human growth] be in all respects if parents were to view and treat the child with reference to all stages of development and age, without breaks and omissions; if, particularly, they were to consider the fact that the vigorous, complete development and cultivation of each successive stage depends on the vigorous, complete and appropriate development of all preceding stages of life!" In this vein, Froebel set himself squarely in the tradition of Comenius, Locke, Rousseau, Pestalozzi, and Herbart.

Gifts and Occupations

The most controversial feature of Froebelian pedagogy was his theory of "gifts." During the kindergarten period he recommended three main kinds of activities: (1) games and songs (well illustrated in his *Mother and Nursery Songs*) so that the child would come to know the inner life of other people and animals; (2) gardening and the care of pets, so that the child would develop "sympathy" or empathy with plants and animals; and (3) "occupations" designed to serve the child's inner nature through familiarity with inanimate objects. These activities might include picture coloring, weaving, sewing, modeling, drawing, paper cutting, and so forth. A fourth kind of play activity involved certain concrete objects, presented to the child in a definite sequence, for use in teaching basic cosmic truths about man in his universe. Froebel observed that the young child fills his world with an elaborate symbolism. He projects his imagination outward onto objects so they become whatever he wishes them to be. The stick becomes a sword, the tree a mighty castle or fort, a pile of lumber a sturdy pirate ship. Instead of taking certain objects and endowing them with symbolic meaning, Froebel reflected, perhaps certain objects could be found inherently possessed of symbolic significance and which, once presented to the child, could help him in apprehending the ultimate truths they represent. Three such shapes—the ball, the cube, and the cylinder—are innately possessed of the capacity to teach symbolically realities otherwise understood only through laborious philosophical reflection, he decided.

Consider the ball. It is a perfect symbol whose symmetrical shape and continuous surface are ideally suited to communicate the basic unity underlying the universe. Even its name incorporates universality: b—all.[6] Hence the ball is an extremely valuable plaything; with it the child grasps not only a physical object but a faint perception of oneness, of his own nature and its relationship with everything else in the world. Aside from its symbolic value, the ball ministers to the child's development through motor activities when he plays with it. The universe also manifests diversity or multiplicity. The cube, with its many edges and sides, helps the child comprehend this complementary truth. Finally, the law of connection suggests a synthesis between the divine oneness and the phenomenal many, the basic unity of God and the separateness of all distinct things in existence. The cylinder, because it combines the roundness of the ball and the flat sides of the cube, is a perfect symbol of the synthesis of unity and diversity.[7] Froebel advocated a whole system of classroom games and exercises structured around geometrical forms, sometimes providing wooden cubes, balls, and cylinders to be placed in the hands of the children.

It hardly seems necessary to point out the grotesque errors in Froebel's entire theory of symbolism. As a matter of historical record, his followers were quick to discard his rather obtuse philosophy and with it the theory of gifts, while retaining what was genuinely helpful for a theory of instruction for young children, including his belief that education must serve the natural unfolding of the child's nature, the idea that the teacher must grade instruction according to the level of the learner's understanding, his awareness of the virtues of self-activity, educational play, the theme of social participation, and the emphasis upon school as a place where growth occurs under the benevolent guidance of sympathetic teachers. Somewhat defensively Froebel tried to defend his beliefs about gifts against criticism. "God clothed his own image in a mass of clay," he wrote, "and was not ashamed of his creation; neither will I be ashamed to set forth in little blocks of wood my ideas upon the nature of man." Typical was the acidic comment of Susan E. Blow, otherwise a loyal devotee of Froebelian pedagogy: "What must any sane person think of an effort to render perceptible not only the unity of the world, but absolute existence? And is not any educator clearly daft who attempts to set forth in little blocks of wood his ideas upon the nature of man?"[8] Froebel's stubborn refusal to modify his

6 "*Der Ball ist ein B(ild des)All.*" ("The ball is a picture of everything.")

7 Other "gifts" for postkindergarten children were to include more complex cubes, square and triangular tablets, sticks, and rings. Froebel built an elaborate symbolism around all of these.

8 Susan E. Blow, *Educational Issues in the Kindergarten* (New York: Appleton-Century-Crofts, 1908), pp. 52–53 ff.

thinking on this point marred what was otherwise a remarkably perceptive theory of teaching.[9]

The Influence of Froebelism

The kindergarten movement spread widely in the years after Froebel's death. Little was accomplished in Germany, Austro-Hungary, or Prussia, but in Lausanne and Geneva, Switzerland, Henriette Breyman preached the new gospel to receptive audiences. Schools were established throughout Dutch and Italian cities. In England and France the infant school development prevented any marked expansion of kindergartens despite the popularization of Froebel's ideas through the *International Kindergarten Union* founded by Elenore Heerwart. Adele von Portugall was the exception to this rule, enjoying an unusual success in starting kindergartens in Manchester. French educators borrowed many of Froebel's precepts for their own maternal schools. The greatest enthusiasm for the movement was in the United States, where it had been exported by Germans after the revolutions of 1848. The first German kindergarten in America was established in 1855 in Watertown, Wisconsin, by Mrs. Carl Schurz, one of Froebel's students. By 1870 at least ten more were organized in German communities. Mrs. Elizabeth Peabody, who served as editor of the *Kindergarten Messenger* between 1873 and 1877, founded the first English-language kindergarten at Boston in 1860. Eight years later a training school for kindergarten teachers was opened in Boston by Matilde Kriege; a similar institution began operations under the direction of Marie Boelte in New York City around the same time.[10] In 1873 the first public-school kindergarten opened its doors in St. Louis, thanks to the patronage of that city's famous school superintendent, William T. Harris. The growth of other kindergartens proceeded rapidly thereafter.

Indirectly, Froebel lent strength to another important educational movement—the drive to include manual training in schools—through his idea that kindergarten "occupations" could be adapted as a form of creative expression for upper-level schools. A beginning was made in Finland by *Uno Cygnaeus* (1810–1888), a Froebelian disciple who drafted a course of manual studies for his country's schools. In 1866 compulsory training in manual arts was instituted in Finnish rural schools. Within a few short

---

[9] For further reading, consult H. C. Bowen, *Froebel and Education by Self-activity* (New York: Charles Scribner's Sons, 1901); Robert Ulich, *History of Educational Thought* (New York: American Book Company, 1950), pp. 284–291; E. M. and H. K. Moore's translation of Froebel's *Autobiography* (London: Allen & Unwin, 1886); the W. N. Hailmann translation of Froebel's *Education of Man* (New York: Appleton-Century-Crofts, 1892; Evelyn Lawrence, ed., *Friedrich Froebel and English Education* (New York: Philosophical Library, 1953); and Fanny Franks, *The Kindergarten System* (London: Swan Sonnenschein, 1897).

[10] It is curious that in its early years, as now, the kindergarten has been almost exclusively a woman's domain. There were no prominent male leaders in the kindergarten movement either in Europe or the United States.

years the Swedes incorporated the idea in their folk schools, following the lead of *Otto Solomon* (1849–1907). Before long there were manual activities including domestic arts, carpentering, and industrial vocations as regular parts of the primary curriculum in the urban schools of France and England. Germany's efforts in the same direction were delayed until after the close of the nineteenth century. Secondary school manual and practical arts education in the United States got its start from a Russian demonstration at the Centennial Exhibition of 1876. The Russians' display of student work from the Imperial Technical Institute in Moscow prompted demands for a similar kind of organized technical education at the high school level in all parts, a demand satisfied in succeeding years with new courses and specialized institutions. Of course by the late 1800's vocational education had been shorn of its original Froebelian underpinnings but there is no denying its first modern inspiration belonged to that German theorist whose concern for humane education among very young children was a lifelong passion. In varied forms the ideas of Froebel were destined to remain a permanent part of the contemporary educational legacy.

GERMAN STATE EDUCATION SINCE THE NAPOLEONIC WARS

Education for Patriotism

Prussia's defeat at the hand of Napoleon roused *Frederick Wilhelm III*, the reigning monarch, to issue a call for political renewal, partly through education. Fichte phrased it more strongly still: "It is education alone which can save us from all the evils by which we are oppressed." Fichte spoke at a time when his fellow countrymen were bent under the occupation forces of French conquerors. The sphere of educational activity, he noted, was the only domain in which a subject people could begin the work of social reconstruction. "National education" in citizenship and loyalty to the fatherland could be the means for re-creating a nation fit to regain its place as a leader in the civilized world. The easy cosmopolitanism so prevalent among German intellectuals was a luxury that could no longer be afforded, Fichte told his audience. A universal system of compulsory education for all classes and both sexes was sorely needed now, a kind of schooling designed to foster patriotic virtues, practical experience in some kind of manual trade, and the formation of good moral character. The new system Fichte advocated in actuality bore little resemblance to that laid down by Pestalozzi, despite his enthusiastic praise for the man, though his fervent nationalism probably blinded him to the differences. In order to preserve German culture and language, national boarding schools should be created in which children would be given vigorous physical exercises, taught practical work skills, the elements of religion, and strong nationalist sentiment.

Georg Wilhelm Friedrich Hegel (1770–1831) caught the nationalist temper of the times in his exposition of pedagogical principles. Above all, he avowed, the ultimate responsibility for education rests with the state as "the higher authority in respect to which the laws and interests of the family and the civic community are subject and dependent." This became the dominant theme of almost all Germans writing on educational matters in the early 1800's. Friedrich Froebel's aggressive nationalism was evident in the name he gave to his first school at Keilhau—"The Universal German Educational Institute"—and in his comment that anyone worthy of becoming an educator would not hesitate to lay down his life or shed his blood in defense of his country.

Fueled with this general spirit of aggressive nationalism, an ambitious program of educational renewal was undertaken. Compulsory school laws were enforced, reforms begun in the secondary humanistic schools, and a new university at Berlin opened with Fichte as its head. The nascent liberalism evident in changes at the elementary school level gave hope to reformers everywhere that a pedagogical reformation was in process of birth. In 1808, seventeen Prussian teachers were sent to Yverdon to study Pestalozzi's methods, armed with instructions to "warm yourselves at the sacred fire which burns in the heart of this man." *William Harnisch* (1787–1864), in his *Schools for the People, on Pestalozzian Principles* (1812), laid down a comprehensive reform program. "I have been inspired," he exclaimed, "by the ideal of a popular education for the development of a community which shall include the whole nation and all the people." *F. A. W. Diesterweg* (1790–1866) began to extend Pestalozzian ideas throughout the whole Prussian school system. In 1810 a state qualifying examination for all secondary school teachers was ordered and in the next decade several teachers' seminaries were opened. Under Humboldt's able direction the newly formed Department of Education in the Ministry of the Interior became an active force in Prussian schooling. The right of university students to study abroad was secured. Humboldt's 1810 Memorial for the University of Berlin sketched the proper relationship of the state to institutions of higher learning. "The state should not treat the universities as if they were higher classical schools or schools of special sciences," he announced. "On the whole, the state should not look to them at all for anything that directly concerns its own interests." Unhappily, this declaration of university autonomy and academic freedom did not last long after Humboldt's brief tenure was over.

Other advances of the early 1800's included the requirement of a *Probejahr*, or probationary year of teaching before any teacher was given a permanent position, the establishment of "leaving" examinations for students desiring to enter a university or the civil service, the extension of state provincial school boards in Prussia to replace local church school boards, property taxes for state aid to education, and the laying out of a uniform course of instruction, including Latin, Greek, German, mathematics, history, geography, religion, and the sciences for two kinds of secondary schools. But after 1817, when a liberal official by the name of Stein was replaced by *Karl von Altenstein* as Minister of Education, Frederick Wilhelm's reign was marked by increasingly illiberal measures. The tendency to centralize the administration of the schools entailed a constriction of earlier progressive programs and it became common, after the Congress of Vienna, to view education less as a means for social reform and more as a tool of the aristocracy to keep commoners in line and to foster loyalty to the government. Outlining a government program for the lower schools, Altenstein remarked, "I do not think that the principles enunciated will raise the common people out of the sphere designated for them by God and human society."[11] Once the Napoleonic menace to Prussia had passed, Frederick Wilhelm repudiated his liberal beliefs, allowed the church and aristocracy to return to their influential positions, and restored a measure of control over the schools to ecclesiastical authorities. Extended schooling was considered a vice, not a virtue. The king's changed attitude was revealed in his comment, "We do not confer upon the individual or upon society any benefit when we educate him beyond the bounds of his social class and vocation." And in the 1830's a Prussian Cabinet Minister declared, "It is not becoming for subjects to judge the actions of the head of state by the measure of their limited understanding." This viewpoint was to prevail for the rest of the nineteenth century and well into the twentieth.

The divided institutional structure of Prussian education, so long a tradition in German lands, became even more pronounced under Altenstein and his successors. Folk schools (*Volksschulen*) for the commoners, who made up over 90 per cent of the population, gradually replaced the old private religious vernacular centers. These schools of the laboring classes were explicitly designed as instruments of "social predestination," that is, their function was to provide just enough of the rudiments of learning to keep the common man happy in his appointed position, to indoctrinate him in his social obligations. The typical curriculum for children aged six to fourteen was taught by a folk teacher, who was considered a state employee, although his support came mainly from tuition payments. Not until 1888 was folk school instruction completely paid through state funds.

Prussian secondary schools were reserved for the middle and upper classes and supported by tuition fees. They included lower preparatory departments, beginning with the primary grades, so as to allow the children of wealthier citizens the luxury of not having to attend a folk school. Very early in the century the *Paedagogium,* the *Collegium,* the *Akademie,* and the *Latin school* types had been consolidated into two basic kinds of schools: (1) the nine-year *Gymnasium,* whose first six years were sometimes distinguished as the *Progymnasium,* and (2) the *Realschule* or *Burgerschule.* Both were intended to prepare their students for leadership positions in society,

[11] E. Reisner, *Nationalism in Education Since 1789* (New York: Macmillan, 1927), p. 145.

the former emphasizing classical studies, the latter stressing modern subjects. As a rule, modern languages and sciences were also taught on a limited basis in the *Progymnasium*. Because Wilhelm Humboldt was an ardent classicist, he continued the tendency to favor the humanistic school over its competitor, an inclination which received official sanction in 1834 when the state's *Gymnasium* leaving examination was made the only entry to the universities. The *Realschule* survived as a middle-class institution under private or municipal control until 1859, when it too was incorporated into the state's provincial school board system. Thereafter, three main types of schools had approval: (1) a *Realgymnasium,* begun in 1870, with a nine-year course combining Latin and classical studies; (2) the *Gymnasium* (of the kind dating back to Sturm's school in 1538), which was the most revered institutional type, offering courses in Greek, Latin, and other classical subjects; and (3) the *Realschule,* which gave an abbreviated six-year academic course and no Latin instruction, the main emphasis being on mathematics, modern languages, and the sciences. After 1870 an *Oberrealschule,* with a sequence of scientific studies lasting nine years, was created. Its curriculum was basically an extension of that offered in the *Realschule.* As a distinct type, the *Realschule* and its enlarged *Oberrealschule* dated back to 1747, when the first *Realschule* was opened in Berlin. The General School Regulations of 1872 tended to break up the sharp distinction between schools for the classes and those of the masses in the creation of a middle school, or *Mittelschule,* as an intermediary institution for the lower classes between the folk school and the *Realschule* or *Realgymnasium.* The course of instruction varied from three to nine years and serviced the need of minor officials and the burgher class. The *Mittelschule* was supported by private tuition and found only in the larger German cities. Despite the diversity of schools, attendance was compulsory only up to the age of fourteen and the sexes were rarely educated together.

Frederick Wilhelm IV ascended the Prussian throne in 1840. Like his predecessor, he viewed the schools as instruments for combatting rising social, religious, and political heterodoxy. From the very beginning, tyrannical restrictions were imposed on teachers' training institutes to curb any hints of liberal sentiment. The new minister of education, *Karl von Raumer,* outlawed the kindergarten and proscribed the reading of works by Diesterweg and Froebel. Frederick's worst fears were realized with the outbreak of revolution in 1848 in Italy, Switzerland, France, and the Austrian and German states. But instead of acceding to the popular demand for constitutional government and an end to reactionary rule, this not-so-benevolent monarch boasted he could handle the situation through force. "As long as I hold the sword-hilt in my hand," he proclaimed, "I shall know how to deal with such a nuisance." The "nuisance" referred to was the abortive revolution in his own domain, a movement crushed in short order. Frederick laid the blame for unrest squarely upon the schools. At a conference of representatives of teachers' seminaries in 1849 he raged, "You and you alone are to blame for all the misery which the last year has brought upon Prussia! The irreligious pseudo-education of the masses is to be blamed for it, which you have been spreading under the name of true wisdom, and by which you have eradicated religious belief and loyalty from the hearts of my subjects and alienated their affections from my person. This sham education, strutting about like a peacock, has always been odious to me."[12]

Any hopes that Frederick's replacement would take a kindlier approach to educational problems were dashed when illness forced his retirement and his brother was appointed regent to reign in his stead. After Frederick's death in 1861, *Wilhelm I* lent full support to all the forces of extreme nationalism and conservatism that had dominated German education during previous reigns. Education legislation remained paternal, restrictive, and cautious. *Prince Otto von Bismarck* was called into service as the Prime Minister and an aggressive "cultural struggle" (*Kulturkampf*) launched to unite all peoples behind the throne as custodian of Germanic ideals. Bismarck rammed through legislation expelling the Jesuits from Prussia in 1872 and broke up the Catholic bureau in the Ministry of Education. All remaining schools were withdrawn from Church control. The May Laws of 1873 provided for total state inspection of all schools by nonclerical officers of the state. Education was to be primarily concerned with the unification of social classes, the promotion of an aggressive patriotism, and the training of people for specific vocations.

The final consolidation of the German states was a direct result of the Franco-Prussian War of 1871. On January 18 of that year, the king was proclaimed emperor over twenty-six formerly separate states, with only Austria excepted. The outcome was an illiberal, undemocratic, highly centralized political bureaucracy over which Bismarck wielded actual control. When *Wilhelm II* came to power in 1888, almost all effective power was retained by Bismarck, the real force behind the throne. The chief thrust of the schools remained what it had always been: to keep people submissive, obedient, orderly, and economically productive.

Emperor Wilhelm II was especially concerned to see that educational institutions were enlisted in the fight against communist and socialist influences. In 1889 he laid upon the school an obligation to "make a special effort to furnish even the youth with the conviction that not only are the teachings of social democracy contrary to the commandments of God and to Christian morals, but also impracticable of realization and dangerous to the individual and to society at large." Special attention was paid to the curricula of teachers' seminaries so that their products would emerge free of any taint of leftist leanings. Logic, psychology, grammar, composition,

[12] Frederick Paulsen, *German Education Past and Present* (London: Allen & Unwin, 1908), pp. 245 ff.

mathematics, some science, economics, and generous amounts of chauvinistic history made up the usual study program. Every teacher was expected to go forth preaching the superiority of German language, literature, and customs. Absolute fidelity to the Hohenzollern regime on the part of student and teacher alike was expected as a matter of course.

The forward-looking changes of Bismarck's rule must not be overlooked. Germany assumed a lead in the field of vocational education (for reasons already mentioned) and kept it well into the twentieth century. The *Mittelschule,* as well as a number of trade schools for industrial workers, enjoyed unparalleled support in virtually every German city. Most were run on a private basis. Thanks to the organizing work of *Georg Kerschensteiner* (to cite but one of many commercial educators), some instruction in the various trades became a part of the curriculum (though separated from the academic regimen) in public city schools throughout the empire. Advanced technical institutes guaranteed German pre-eminence in scientific endeavor, unquestionably helping to make Germany a major industrial power prior to World War I. At the university level, beginning with the University of Leipzig in 1826, extraordinary attention was given to scientific, agricultural, engineering, and technical studies—so much so in fact that scholars the world over flocked to Germany for instruction. Johns Hopkins University in the United States was founded in 1876 in direct imitation of the German model. Research became at least as important as teaching in most German universities, particularly at Halle, Göttingen, Jena, Heidelberg, and Berlin.[13] At the turn of the century Germany's universities were the finest in the world.

The real determining force that set the direction for German secondary education, and indirectly higher education as well in the waning years of the 1800's, was Wilhelm II's pressure on behalf of modern studies. At an 1890 educational convocation he attacked gymnasial education for trying to produce "young Greeks and Romans" instead of "national young Germans." Henceforth, he continued, German "general culture" should be the official focus of all the schools.[14] The Kaiser's official regulations of 1892 threw state support to three six-year institutions: the *Realschule,* the *Progymnasium,* and the *Realprogymnasium* (the lower department of the *Realgymnasium*). The effect of Wilhelm's edicts was a de-emphasis on classical training in German schools for the remainder of his reign.

Toward a More Democratic Education

Following the devastation of World War I the German *Weimar Republic* in 1919 began with high hopes for a resuscitated national educational

[13] This development has had decidedly mixed results in the American university of today, when questions are being raised about the propriety of certain kinds of research and about the balance that should obtain among service, research, and teaching functions of institutions of higher learning.

[14] Isaac L. Kandel, *History of Secondary Education* (Boston: Houghton Mifflin, 1930), p. 257.

system. The new Constitution proclaimed, "In all schools effort shall be made to develop moral education, a sense of responsibility for the public welfare, personal and vocational competence in the spirit of German nationality and reconciliation with the nations. . . ." Reserved for the central government was the right to "define the guiding principles of the educational system, including higher education; that the public school system be developed as an organic whole, and the middle and higher, that is, secondary schools, become extensions of a common school." To effect these changes at least three new kinds of schools were opened, differing only in minor details from state to state within the Republic: (1) a common four-year "foundation" elementary school or *Grundschule,* compulsory for all German children, whose instruction was preparatory to the upper primary grades; (2) a rural six-year *Aufbauschule* for children over twelve; and (3) the German High School or *Deutsche Oberschule,* a secondary-level institution stressing national culture, which was given a place alongside the *Gymnasium, Oberrealschule,* and *Realgymnasium.* Both of the last two newly created schools prepared students to enter the university, as did the *Gymnasium.* Attempts to provide free secondary education floundered in the face of opposition from the upper classes, with their traditional aristocratic bias. The status of teachers' seminaries was upgraded, however, and new standards of accreditation introduced. Many other reforms were begun under the Weimar regime, but most passed into oblivion when the National Socialists came to power after 1933.

Under the Third Reich

The Nazi period in German educational history is both fascinating and terrifying.[15] Immediately after coming to power, Adolf Hitler tightened central administrative control over all schools and turned the system into a gigantic militaristic propaganda machine under the Reich's Ministry of Science and Education. The *Grundschule* and upper levels of the *Volksschule* were retained, from which graduates might enter the *Gymnasium,* the *Deutsche Oberschule,* or the *Aufbauschule.* The role of the first was severely restricted and the course of instruction in the other two shortened to allow more time for political indoctrination, military training, and a *Landjahr,* introduced in 1934, which was a year of compulsory work and physical training city children spent among peasant farmers in rural areas. In order to be admitted to a university all males had to complete six months of compulsory labor service (the *Arbeitsdienst*) and two years of military duty. The few remaining private or sectarian schools which had been allowed under a Concordat of 1933 were systematically undermined or forced out of existence. All people were to be educated in the image of

[15] See G. Ziemer, *Education for Death* (New York: Oxford University Press, 1941). An excellent summary treatment is given in James Mulhern, *A History of Education,* 2nd ed. (New York: Ronald Press, 1959), pp. 670–680.

the National Socialist Man. As one state official described it, "We begin with the child when he is three years old. As soon as he begins to think, he gets a little flag put in his hand; then follows the school, the Hitler Youth . . . and military training. We don't let him go; and when adolescence is past, then comes the working period, which takes him again and does not let him go till he dies, whether he likes it or not."

Many kinds of institutions were created or expanded to help the totalitarian Nazi state mold its citizens. For graduates of the primary and middle schools desiring to prepare for a trade there were commercial schools (Fachschulen) and higher technical high schools (Hochschulen). For political leaders, local leadership schools, National Political Educational Institutions, the Adolf Hitler Schools, and institutions to train the party elite, called Ordensburgen, were begun. For adults a Volksbildungstätte, or Popular Education Center, was provided in every community for the ideological re-education of the masses. The Ministry of Education, in cooperation with a branch of the Labor Front known as the "Strength Through Joy Association," coordinated a vast array of adult education programs. Special Nazi teacher training schools were established to ensure the production of loyal, reliable instructors. All boys had to join the youth organizations, in order of age, beginning with the Pimpf, the Jungvolk, and the Hitler Youth, or Hitlerjugend. (This last was a consolidation of many German student organizations, some of them dating back to 1896.) Girls, on the other hand, joined the Jungmädel and then the Bund Deutscher Mädel, and participated in activities having to do with home economics, eugenics, physical improvement, and political instruction. Nazi theory firmly endorsed the ancient German social ideal for women of "Kinder, Küche, Kirche" (children, kitchen, church) and forbade coeducation except where local conditions made separation of the sexes impossible.[16]

Hitler's Reich Minister, Bernard Rust, was charged with responsibility for purging Jews and other "non-Aryans" from the faculties of the universities. Both in Italy and in Germany the universities were among the first institutions to capitulate formally to fascist doctrine. Rust explained the basis of his program: "The National Socialist system of education is not the outcome of pedagogical planning but of political struggle and of the laws which govern such a struggle. . . . The National Socialist historical epoch will build a school which will be its true image." At the same time, the political office of the Nazi party launched a press campaign for the total exclusion of all Jewish children from the schools. "The second demand for racial thought for a new straightening out of the school sphere," it announced, "concerns the racial harmony between teacher, pupil, and cur-

16 "The goal of feminine education," Hitler declared, "must be fixed as the education of the future mother." Alfred Rosenberg echoed the prevailing theory when he suggested that "the absence of all-round abilities in women is directly to be attributed to the fact that woman is vegetative."

riculum. . . . Fruitful education is only possible if the teacher and his pupils
show the same racial attitude. The teacher of an alien race [i.e., a Jew] has
become for us unthinkable; but the demand that the community of the
school class itself, with which the instructor has to work, shall present a
racial unity is just as essential. From this demand follows that those groups
of the population of an alien race still living among us shall be fundamentally separated in the schools from children of our own kind." Accordingly, Rust ordered all Jewish children to leave ordinary elementary
schools, promising that special Jewish schools would be "everywhere established." Meanwhile, pure "German" schools would be free to foster discipline and devotion in the sons and daughters of the superior Ayran race.
As the Teachers' Journal (*Allgemeine Deutsch Lehrerzeitung*) in August
of 1933 declared, "We care nothing about an insipid enumeration of 'objective' facts; we want a historical science for Germans." Later in the same
year, the Journal said, "The taste for militarism must be inculcated in
children. . . . Germans will be victorious in the next war; it is the will and
the way of God. . . . No one can resist our health within and our young
strength."[17] It took six years, millions of lives, and measureless human
misery to prove that prediction wrong.

Recent German Education

"De-Nazification" and "democratization" were the most urgent priorities
for German education in the immediate postwar period. In the Potsdam
Agreement of August, 1945, it was agreed that "German education shall be
controlled so as completely to eliminate Nazi and militaristic doctrines and
to make possible the successful development of democratic ideas." The
Allied Control Council of 1947 enacted a series of reforms, including
decentralization of school administration, new curricula, provision for
greater equality of education opportunity, the stipulation that all children
had to attend school from the age of six to fifteen, state aid to nonpublic
schools, and free public education through the secondary level. The
Americans and British attempted in their sectors to build a six-year *Grundschule* program, followed by a six-year secondary instructional sequence.
The rebuilding work proceeded against overwhelming odds: in some of
the areas within the American sector, for example, as much as 90 per
cent of the schools were buried under rubble. The French imposed a
four-year foundation school similar to those of the Weimar Republic
and a nine-year secondary school program. In the Russian zone, an
eight-year elementary school type was created, along with a four-year
vocational school. All private and religious schools were abolished and
education was returned to its role of political indoctrination, this time in

---

[17] *Educational Yearbook, 1934* (New York: Teachers College, Columbia University,
1934), pp. 487–488, 489. Contemporary urgings that education be "politicized"—to the
left or right—bear an uncomfortable resemblance to such teachings of the Nazi era.

the tenets of Communism.[18] In East Germany it was decreed that at least 60 per cent of all university students must come from the "working classes" and that teachers were to be hired mainly on the basis of their political reliability. Higher education was geared to specialized technical training and political re-education, a characteristic feature of eastern German universities today. In the western sector, the Free University of Berlin was created in 1948, a precursor for other democratically oriented institutions of higher learning organized since.

Education in the present Federal Republic of West Germany is supervised by the various independent states and only loosely coordinated by the central government. The usual state institutional pattern includes a four- to six-year "foundation" school leading to a four-year "middle" school, and' three types of secondary schools: the academic *Gymnasium,* a scientific *Realgymnasium,* and a multicurricular high school. Part-time or continuing vocational schools, advanced technical institutions, and adult education programs meet the diverse needs of those not electing to pursue a university preparation regimen of studies.

Over a quarter of a century has elapsed since the fall of Nazi Germany. A new generation has come to power anxious to dispel the shadow of the past, a generation which feels little or no responsibility for the mistakes of previous generations. Whether the long Prussian tradition of militarism, authoritarianism, imperialism, and extreme nationalism that culminated in Nazism has finally been eradicated completely, only the future will tell. It is a question which historians, political scientists, novelists, poets—and educators—have been left to ponder.

FRENCH STATE EDUCATION SINCE THE REVOLUTION

After the Deluge

It might have seemed at first that the French Revolution would put an end to the conservatism and traditionalism that typified education on all levels and among all classes, the Church's domination of the schools, and the belief that schools should be bastions of orthodoxy protecting a social order founded on privilege and class. Mention has already been made of the welter of educational reform bills introduced before the revolutionary National Assembly (1789–1791). Talleyrand promoted the idea of a state system of free primary schools, secondary schools open to all, and higher institutions of religion, law, military science, and medicine, with state Commissioners of Education administering the structure. Condorcet's bill would have founded a similar system so that there might be "among the citizens

---

[18] It is debatable how much "freer" English, French, and American schools were in this respect, insofar as they were specifically designed to foster democratic attitudes and values among the defeated Germans.

an equality in fact, making real the political equality recognized by law."
Neither bill was acted upon. A radical proposal to re-create the ancient
Spartan system for French education, proposed by Lepelletier de Saint
Fargeau, also failed. Measures were taken, in the midst of the Assembly's
deliberations, to undermine the position of the Church in education
through passage of the Civil Constitution of the Clergy in 1790, causing
many members of religious orders to abandon their teaching positions. Two
years later the *Comité de l'Instruction Publique* outlawed all ecclesiastical
corporations, including religious schools, and in 1793 total state control
of all education was proclaimed. But the problem remained of how to
create a new school system in accordance with the Constitutional provision
of 1791 for "a public system of education, common to all citizens, free for
those parts of education indispensable to all men." The revolutionary
Lakanal prophesied that out of the old royalist order there would emerge
"the great edifice promised so long to French patience," the question was
how and when. A scarcity of resources, the lack of an efficient tax system,
the general turmoil of the times, and an absence of professional teachers
meant the grandiose programs of the Revolution had to be deferred. And so
the Assembly argued at length, labored mightily, and brought forth a
meager compromise measure in 1795. The *Danou Law* provided for the
establishment of a primary school in each canton, to be supported almost
entirely by tuition fees, and a limited number of secondary "central schools"
free to talented poor students. A few higher "special" schools for the bourgeoisie to pursue scientific studies were also authorized. The law of Lakanal
establishing a more extensive system of elementary and higher schools was
largely ineffective. Both pieces of legislation fell far short of the noble
aspirations held by leading educators of the day, for want of means of enforcement and lack of funds.

One of Lakanal's proposals led to the opening in 1795 of an *École
Normale Supérieure* for training teachers, an institution later revived and
strengthened by Napoleon. This action marked the first step of a rapid
transition to a uniform centralized school system administered and inspected by government officials. Although the changeover was effected much
more quickly than in German lands, for example, it meant a consolidation
of authority and subordination to the central government differing little in
character from prerevolutionary times. The resulting school system was too
weak and ineffectual to bring the French people together, as had been
hoped, and it certainly failed to realize the earlier aims of synthesizing the
ideas of Rousseau, the philosophes, and the practical suggestions of a
Talleyrand or Condorcet.

The Napoleonic Era

In 1799 *Napoleon* overthrew the Directory, seized power, and proclaimed
himself First Consul. Five years later France became an empire, with

Napoleon as its emperor.[19] Until defeated in battle and banished to Saint Helena in 1815, Napoleon ruled the country with as firm a hand as any of the Bourbon kings. His reign was both despotic and reactionary. One of his first acts was to disband the humanistic *Collège de Louis le Grand* (founded in 1567) and use its endowments to create four military schools. In 1801 he signed a Concordat with the Catholic Church restoring state stipends to priests and returning primary education to the control of the religious orders. The Brothers of the Christian Schools were recalled the next year and accorded special recognition as a teaching congregation. There followed a series of edicts reflecting his belief that "of all political questions, that [of education] is perhaps the most important." There cannot be a firmly established political state, he affirmed, without an educational system founded on sound principles, the most important being political indoctrination of all subjects. To realize this end Napoleon appointed *Count de Fourcroy* (1755–1809) as his first Director General of Public Instruction and commanded him to draw up an educational plan for the country. It was enacted into law in 1802. This law required each *commune* (the smallest local governmental unit) to establish a school and sponsor a schoolmaster. Elementary teachers were directly responsible to the local authorities while their schools were placed under the supervision of the prefect of instruction in each *département* (the next state administrative unit). State financial aid was restricted to scholarships for poorer students; all others had to pay tuition to attend school. Departmental authorities were enjoined to see that teachers confined instruction to the three R's and "to watch that the teachers do not carry their instructions beyond these limits."

Napoleon was much more concerned with secondary education. The same law of Floréal 2 of the year 10, according to the old revolutionary calendar (May 2, 1802), instituted two types of secondary-level residential boarding schools: *communal collèges* (private or municipal), offering instruction in mathematics, history, geography, Latin and French; and *lycées,* the standard secondary school for the study of rhetoric, logic, physical education, drawing, and ancient and modern languages. Each *lycée* had to have at least eight "professors," an administrative superintendent, a supervisor of studies, and a business steward. Cities in which *lycées* were located provided the facilities, the state furnished the building, and the schools were maintained through a combination of state stipends, tuition fees, and rooming and boarding fees. *Collèges* were intended as an inferior type of institution offering an abbreviated *lycée* course for the lower middle classes, whereas the regular secondary schools sponsored a more complete program for the intellectual elite. The former usually operated on a private basis under state license; the latter were overseen directly by superintendents of secondary studies appointed by the Director General. These two types of

---

[19] He reportedly remarked later, "I found the crown of France lying on the ground and I picked it up with a sword."

institutions largely fixed the two-track line of development French education followed throughout the next hundred and fifty years.

The 1802 law did more than expand secondary education. It also ordered
the creation of special "faculties" or higher schools of law, medicine, mathematics, natural history, science, and later, theology. By special decree
Napoleon created two schools of mining and engineering as well as a school
of arts and trades. Thus, very early in the Napoleonic era the state had
moved in as the dominant agency in control of all education above the
primary level and had confirmed the direction of all instruction to serve
state ends. This work was completed in May of 1806 with another law
tightening state control of schools within an organized administrative structure. "There shall be created," the law began, "under the name of the
Imperial University, a body exclusively commissioned with teaching and
public education throughout the Empire." All schools were to be placed
under the control of a quasimonopolistic administrative structure and required to "make as a basis of their instruction (1) the precepts of the
Catholic religion, and (2) fidelity to the Emperor, to the imperial monarchy,
the depository of the happiness of the people, and to the Napoleonic
dynasty, the conservator of the unity of France, and of all the ideas proclaimed by the Constitution." Two years later Emperor Napoleon decreed
the creation of a *University of France* within which all public instruction
was to be confined. "No school, nor establishment for instruction," he
ordered, "can be formed independent of the Imperial University, and without the authority of its head." The university was set up with a grand
master and a twenty-six member council appointed by Napoleon. France
was divided up, for administrative purposes, into twenty-seven *académies,*
each with its *recteur* and educational council. Central and local inspec-
torates were created with state inspectors appointed by the university's head
to supervise local school operations. A central normal school for preparing
lycée graduates to teach was set up in 1810 and expanded five years later.

Many of the Napoleonic educational changes failed to win approval from
the people, and private and Church-related secondary schools continued to
be patronized. A further effect was the end put to the French tradition of
theorizing about education. Most discussion now moved outside regular
educational circles as all public schools came under direct state control. The
resurgence of religious teaching congregations under Napoleon and the
succeeding monarchy gave increased impetus to those who opposed clerical
influences in the schools. On the one hand, there was a group of revolutionary thinkers, such as *Jean Joseph Jacotot* (1770–1840) and *Edouard
Seguin* (1812–1880), who set themselves in firm opposition to the direction
public education was taking; on the other, there appeared a succession of
women writers concerned mainly with domestic education within the home.
Among the latter group, the most important were *Madame de Staël* (*On
Germany,* 1810), *Madame Campan* (*On Education,* 1824), *Madame de*

Remusat (*The Education of Women*, 1824), and *Madame Necker de Saussure* (*Progressive Education*, 1836–1838).

During the Restored Monarchy

Once Napoleon was removed from power France became a monarchy again. Under the *Restoration* (1815–1830) very little in the way of educational reform was accomplished. Louis XVIII was made king, ruled until his death in 1824, and was succeeded by his brother, Charles X. State appropriations for schools were slowly increased and efforts renewed to improve teachers' qualifications by requiring them to obtain state certification, but all the religious orders were excused from the requirement. The Napoleonic university system continued unchanged in most respects. Between 1816 and 1824 clerical control over the primary schools steadily increased, thanks to a series of favorable governmental rulings. In the latter year this process was hastened by the appointment of Frayssinous, Bishop of Hermapolis, as first Minister of Public Instruction and Ecclesiastical Affairs. State subsidies to the *lycées* were tried on an experimental basis, as was the introduction of the monitorial system of instruction to the lower schools. If anything, Charles' reign was marked by a regression in the quality of instruction for prospective teachers after the suppression of the old *École Normale Supérieure* and its temporary replacement with twelve elementary normal schools.

The July Monarchy

In July of 1830 King Charles discovered his subjects would not tolerate any attempt to further repress civil liberties guaranteed under the Constitution; the people arose in revolt, threw him out, and installed a new king, Louis-Phillippe, of the House of Orléans, in his place. Under an able Minister of Education by the name of *François Pierre Guillaume Guizot* (1787–1874), several notable educational changes were put into effect. New normal schools were opened, state grants to elementary schools greatly increased, and the clerical exemption from examinations for teaching certificates abolished. *Victor Cousin* (1792–1867), the Director of the revived *École Normale Supérieure* of France, in 1831 was dispatched to investigate educational experiments underway in Prussia. His *Report on the Condition of Public Instruction in Germany, and Particularly in Prussia* (1831) included, among other things, a declaration that "in the present state of affairs, a law concerning primary education is indispensable in France." The main question, Cousin added, was "how to produce a good one in a country where there are no precedents or experience in so essential a matter." His widely read *Report* led the next year to a comprehensive law establishing the basis for a national primary school system, just as Napoleon's law of 1802 and his decree of 1808 laid the foundation for the French national administration of secondary schools. The Law of 1833 obliged every commune to open an elementary school, towns and cities were to open higher primary schools, and each commune had to provide a school building, maintain it, and pay a minimum salary to the teacher. Tuition rates for those able to afford it as well as teachers' salary schedules were fixed by the state. The government also reserved for itself authority in making teacher appointments. Lower schools would be free to the poor. Each *département* (the next administrative subdivision above the *commune*) was supposed to open a teacher training institute. State certificates of competence for teachers were required and all schools, private ones included, had to submit to inspection by a corps of state inspectors.

Guizot issued a *Manual of Primary Instruction* to ensure a uniform plan of lower school education. The primary schools were to teach the three basic skills of reading, writing, and arithmetic; morals and religion; and French grammar. In the upper primary grades, mathematics, geometry, geography, music, political history, elementary science, drawing, and religion were required subjects. The duties of primary school teachers were clearly defined: they were to foster "the faith in Providence, the sanctity of duty, submission to paternal authority, the respect due to the laws and rights of all. . . ." As the system evolved, the lower levels of the primary school (for students up to age eleven) became separated from the upper levels. The latter became a continuation of the former (but *not* on the secondary level) attended by commoners, whereas the *collèges* and *lycées* became secondary schools reserved for the wealthier upper classes. This meant in effect an extension downward of the two-track system. Working people moved from lower primary to upper primary schools; "professional" people moved directly into a *lycée* or, less often, into a communal *collège*. The upper levels of the commoners' primary schools later were consolidated into a separate institution called the *école primaire supérieure*. On the whole, education under the July Monarchy moved farther away from the secularizing tendencies of pre-Napoleonic times. Guizot firmly endorsed the principle of *la liberté d'enseignement*, the right of religious institutions to open their own primary schools. Indirectly, religious institutions had the unfortunate effect of enhancing the rigidly authoritarian, autocratic character of French education as a whole during this period.

The reign of Louis-Philippe witnessed a number of other pedagogical developments. In 1837 infant schools that had been introduced during the Restoration were formally made a part of the public school system. Around the same time Guizot enlarged the state's contingent of primary school inspectors and inspectors general, approvingly calling them the "sinews of public instruction." By 1840 state aid to all levels of education had been vastly increased. Yet despite all efforts to achieve an equitable educational system for all people, a great deal remained to be done. As one dissatisfied critic put it in 1846, "The only government which has occupied itself wholeheartedly with the education of the people is that of the Revolution." The complaint was not without justification.

Further Developments During the Second Republic and Empire

The revolutions of 1848 that broke out all over Europe began in France. Louis-Philippe was compelled to abdicate and a Second Republic was proclaimed, with *Louis Napoleon* (a nephew of Napoleon I) elected as President. The new regime was extremely short-lived. In December of 1853 the Republic was dissolved and Napoleon became the dictatorial head of a new empire. Any doubts about the character of the new government were laid to rest when he officially assumed the title Emperor Napoleon III. The years between 1848 and 1870 represented a particularly reactionary period in educational legislation. Determined never again to allow the forces of liberalism to gain the upper hand as they had briefly in 1848, state officials did everything possible to make the schools serve monarchical interests. As in Prussia, popular public education was suspected of having been a major source of political discontent. The famous *Falloux Law* of 1850 was an explicit response to the Catholic Church's bid to re-establish its place in the educational system. A whole series of privileges was extended to private secondary schools, including a curtailment of the state's right to inspect confessional educational institutions, the granting of permission to employ teachers without a degree, and a reduction in salary for public primary school teachers so that religious schools could better compete with public institutions. Under Napoleon III the University of France's power became almost absolute. Both primary and secondary school administrations were combined under a new Minister of Public Instruction, the force of inspectors was enlarged, and a revamped system of *académies, départements,* and *communes* brought into existence to keep schools in line. Teachers' seminaries were either forced to curtail their curricula or close down altogether. An official government edict ordering teachers to shave off their moustaches was issued, so as to remove from "their faces, as well as their minds" every symbol of rebellion, every trace of the Revolution of 1848.[20] Teachers were not permitted to read any newspaper except the official state publication. A decree of 1852 took matters another step when it was declared legal for the emperor through his Minister of Education to dismiss any educational official or professor if he chose, "in the interest of the public peace."

The foregoing makes it obvious how frightened the bourgeoisie were by the events of 1848. It is often observed that the mid-nineteenth century was the highwater mark of clerical influence in French schools. Unquestionably the primary reason that the Catholic Church's position was strengthened was because it was looked upon as a stabilizing influence. Possibly the only liberal measure enacted during the Second Empire was a law of 1867 drafted by *Victor Duray* (1811–1894) improving normal schools, drawing attention to the need for better education for women, and creating a curriculum for the *lycée* which emphasized modern scientific and technical subjects over the traditional classical studies.

[20] The expression (and interpretation) of social or political attitudes through facial hair is obviously not unique to the present era.

After the Franco-Prussian War

The advent of the Third Republic came about as a result of France's disastrous defeat at the hands of the Prussians in 1870. Louis Napoleon was taken captive, occupation armies entered Paris, and a new government was established. There followed a "bloody week" of rioting among Jacobins, socialists, communists, Republicans, and Bourbon royalists, succeeded by years of political indecision. Finally, the Republicans won out in the elections of 1877. One of the outstanding leaders of the new era was *Jules François Camille Ferry* (1832–1893), twice Prime Minister, and Minister of Public Instruction from 1879 to 1880, and again in 1882. "Let it be understood," he announced in an address of 1876, "that the first obligation of a democratic government is to exercise control over public instruction." Accordingly, the so-called Ferry Laws of 1881–1886 were aimed at the re-creation of a system of free, public, compulsory, and secular schools. Their major provisions included:

1. Free primary and nursery education in public schools.
2. Compulsory education for all children between the ages of six and thirteen.
3. The secularization of state education and abolition of religious instruction in state-controlled institutions.
4. The requirement of state certification for all teachers, without exceptions.
5. The elimination of members of religious orders from teaching positions in public schools.
6. More secondary education for girls.
7. An enlarged state aid-to-education program.
8. The elimination of boarding fees for public teachers' seminaries.

Subsequent legislation granted more autonomy to the universities, provided for the maintenance through tax funds of primary schools in every administrative district, and provided for the expansion of normal schools.

In the late 1800's there arose a groundswell of popular dissatisfaction with lingering clerical influences in French education. Such private sectarian schools as had survived were subject to more stringent inspection and regulation. Opposition to the practices authorized originally under Napoleon's Concordat with the pope grew steadily, along with the belief that the Church was plotting with monarchists to overthrow the government. "Clericalism, that is our enemy!" stormed the republican orator Gambetta. His anticlerical party was swept into power on the rising tide of opinion hostile to ecclesiastical authority, and this was interpreted as a mandate for laws passed in 1901 and 1904 suppressing religious orders and restricting their teaching activities. Prime Minister Waldeck-Rousseau went so far as to declare the Church a hostile, rival power to the state. In 1905 the total and complete separation of Church and government was authorized by Parliament. For a time it looked as though France's long "love–hate" relationship with the Church would end with private schools being disbanded entirely; had it not been for World War I this probably would have come to pass. Instead, sectarian schools have continued to exist up to the present time. But the public system of education at any rate has been almost always secular since 1905.

French Education in the Twentieth Century

Under the Third Republic, the French national system gradually assumed the basic form it bore until very recently. The Minister of Public Instruction gained a seat both in the Presidential Cabinet and in Parliament. Under him a permanent civil service staff was created, along with the system of checks and balances involving a Higher Council of Public Instruction and a Consultative Committee. The first body advised on matters of curricula, teaching methodology, examinations, and supervision. Its members were elected from the teaching profession at large. The latter body dealt with questions of teacher appointments and promotions. The school system was organized around seventeen *circonscriptions académiques* (academies) headed by *recteurs,* advised by a staff of inspectors and academic councils. Beneath these *recteurs* were prefects governing local *départements* with the aid of elective departmental councils. School administration at the *commune* or township level was left to local municipal officials.

In the late nineteenth century, controversy over the classical curriculum in French secondary education reached a high pitch. The *Ribot Commission of 1898,* appointed to examine the controversy, recommended four seven-year study sequences for children aged eleven to eighteen in all secondary institutions: one stressing Latin and Greek, a second emphasizing Latin and modern languages, a third offering Latin and modern languages as well as some scientific subjects, and a fourth exclusively concerned with scientific studies, all leading to university studies. Although modern subjects at last gained a more equal recognition along with classical subjects, they failed to win equal prestige from the people. It was hard to break down the classical tradition in secondary education. The four-track arrangement persisted until 1925, when a common secondary curriculum for all was devised.

The period between the wars did not bring many changes. The Astier Law of 1919 supported a growth in technical and vocational education and placed this kind of training under the control of the Minister of Public Instruction, thereby making technical institutions regular parts of the state system. The year 1933 witnessed the first time that the principles of free schooling in both technical and general secondary education was recognized by law. One major advance was the establishment of a common elementary school, the *école unique,* to consolidate preparatory classes for the *lycée* with the upper levels of the ordinary primary school. In effect this meant a breakdown in the traditional pattern of two separate school systems carried within one centralized administrative organization—a lower school system for the many and a secondary–higher system for the few. Further efforts to democratize the French system were brought to an abrupt halt by World War II.

On July 16, 1940 the Reynaud government resigned, Marshal Pétain assumed the reins of power, and promptly replaced the old Revolutionary slogan—"liberty, equality, fraternity"—with a new ideal: "family, work, country." All traces of democracy vanished overnight. Under the fascist Vichy regime, any discussions critical of the government were forbidden in the schools. Subsidies were given to private schools, clerics were allowed to teach in public schools once more, and Jews were debarred from holding any teaching posts whatsoever. Fresh emphasis was given to Latin and the humanities in the *lycée*. Teachers' colleges were abolished in favor of a brief postsecondary course of instruction to prepare primary school teachers. Everywhere the tendency was to make educators the scapegoats for France's defeat.

While the country was still occupied by the Germans, a committee appointed by the Free French government in exile met in Algiers to devise a new educational program. "Those who could claim to have come from the summit of our educational system," the commission noted bitterly, "are those whose cowardice has been the most scandalous." After the Liberation a new commission headed by *Paul Langevin* and *Henri Wallon* submitted a report on educational reform. A revamped system, the Langevin Plan's authors declared, should "bring about in a measure compatible with the diversity of individual aptitudes, the equality of all education in respect of education, to allow each, in the interest of all, to fully develop his personality." The dual aim of the schools was defined as "an initiation into culture" and "vocational preparation, to allow for each and every one the training as a man and as the workman he is most likely to become." The Delbos Act of 1949 and André Marie Act of 1953 were legislative attempts to put the plan into practice, but only limited success was achieved because of heavy opposition from conservatives.

The French system today is still undergoing change. Its essential features include public and private nursery and primary schools; *lycées* and *collèges classiques,* providing a classical and modern education: the parallel *collèges modernes,* whose curricula stress technical instruction; and new specialized trade schools, called *collèges techniques.* Limited experimentation with *classes nouvelles* ("new classes") in some secondary schools is conducted in which self-initiated learning, independent study, and "activity" methods of instruction play an important part. Under the Fourth Republic there were state subsidies to assist Catholic schools (which still attack the secular public schools for being "godless"), but these have been controlled through the state examination system through which most students must pass enroute to higher educational levels. At fourteen, students receive the *certificat* or *brevet* diplomas, and the *baccalauréat* diploma at age eighteen or nineteen.

The granting of diplomas depends upon successful completion of state-administered examinations. The Fifth Republic, begun in 1958 under Charles de Gaulle, brought tighter regimentation of the schools under the Ministry of Education, a continuing policy of using education to foster nationalism in the minds of the country's students, and a greater recognition of the importance of modern subjects in an industrial, technological age.[21]

ENGLISH NATIONAL EDUCATION SINCE THE INDUSTRIAL REVOLUTION

The Early Nineteenth Century

There were several reasons why the English did not achieve a national state system of education until at least a generation after France or Prussia. In the first place, the structure of English government was less centralized. Secondly, several decades were required to create a consensus of favorable public opinion among a people whose deeply ingrained traditions resisted control and regimentation. Thirdly, the very success of private agencies raised hopes that redoubled effort might continue to prove adequate for meeting the nation's educational needs without government intervention.[22] Fourthly, church–state relations in England developed quite differently than they did on the Continent. From its inception the Church of England was tied to what became parliamentary government and, consequently, the growing power of the state was rarely perceived as a threat to the church as it was in other lands. As G. Baron notes, "At all times the Church possessed the confidence that came from its close links with all levels of the governmental structure, as exemplified by the intermingling of spiritual and temporal members in the House of Lords." It was always an integral part of the government structure and the only source of institutional authority in the field of education.[23] The result was England never had a totally secular system; her leading schools at all levels have been either Anglican or interdenominational in character, and those favoring a separate system remained an ineffectual minority until very recent times. The accepted aim of the schools was to prepare the upper middle class and aristocracy for upper civil service positions; any suggestion that schools should be expanded for the benefit of the masses was stoutly resisted.[24] As for the bour-

21 A good historical summary of the French educational development is provided in W. D. Halls, *Society, Schools and Progress in France* (Oxford: Pergamon Press, 1965), pp. 14–30.

22 Harry G. Good and James D. Teller, *A History of Western Education*, 3rd ed. (New York: Macmillan, 1969), p. 410.

23 G. Baron, *Society, Schools, and Progress in England* (Oxford: Pergamon Press, 1965), p. 4.

24 Historically, the degree of independence from state supervision enjoyed by an English school has been taken as a measure of its status. Even today, the term *state school* evokes distaste and condescension. Ibid., pp. 10–11.

geois man himself, he rested content, assured that a strict Victorian up-bringing in the home would set his offspring on the path of righteousness and that when the time came to send them on to boarding school, teachers could be depended upon to carry through. The little English boy would become a virtuous adult who knew his duty, who did not need a policeman because he had his conscience, and who could do what he liked because he could not possibly like to do anything improper or very dangerous to society. The story of England's education since the eighteenth century is a wonderful example of her people's penchant for "muddling through," for effecting change through long, slow, and peaceful evolution.

As England moved into the nineteenth century she relied on a combina-tion of private, religious, and philanthropic agencies to advance education. The *Society for the Support and Encouragement of Sunday Schools in the Different Counties of England* (founded in 1785 to establish schools in every parish), the *Ragged School Union* (an outgrowth of John Pounds' work in London to provide waifs and street urchins some elementary instruction), and the *Society for Bettering the Condition and Increasing the Comforts of the Poor* (founded in 1796 to encourage the growth of charity, monitorial, and Sunday schools) were the three most conspicuous agencies for educating the lower classes in "an honest, upright, grateful, and industrious poverty." Other religious groups and private entrepreneurs joined in opening educa-tional institutions to a varied clientele. For the rich, classical "grammar" or "public" schools existed in abundance to prepare students for the uni-versities. And the French Revolution only confirmed the upper-class sus-picion that general popular education above the most rudimentary level might inflame the masses and lead to domestic revolt. Hence, the diverse philanthropic organizations actually had to stress how *little* was taught in their schools in order to garner public support.

Interestingly enough, a small but influential group of reformers some-times turned the argument around: if commoners were *not* educated, they claimed, ignorance would only breed discontent and revolution. As Adam Smith phrased it, "The inferior ranks of the people" ought to be educated to some socially useful task and thus render them "less apt to be misled into any wanton or unnecessary opposition to measures of government." Thomas Malthus (1766–1834) spoke frequently of the "great national dis-grace that the education of the lowest classes in England should be left to a few Sunday Schools, supported by a subscription from individuals who can give to the course of instruction in them any kind of bias which they may please." He was joined by Robert Owen, unhappy with the meager results of his own schools at New Lanark. "According to the present system," Owen lamented, "children may learn to read, write, account, and sew, and yet acquire the worst habits and have their minds irrational for life." In his *New Moral World* Owen laid out a revolutionary scheme for educating people "of a new race, physically, intellectually, and morally." The only outcome of his work was a greater acceptance of the idea of infant schools, following the efforts of David Stow in Scotland and Samuel Wilderspin in England, and the later founding of the *Home and Colonial Infant School Society* to establish and train teachers for work in infant schools. Owen's school and others like it were eventually taken over by Pestalozzian disciples, the Lancastrians' Society, or Bell's National Society.

Against those few individuals who urged maintenance of a general, compulsory, state education separated from the church stood a solid block of *laissez-faire* factory owners and middle-class managers. State interference, they argued, would paralyze all private enterprise and destroy people's character by withdrawing incentives for helping themselves. Private charitable efforts to alleviate the misery of the poor and to provide instruction in the three R's was necessary and desirable, they said, but education was no business of the state. Edward Baines (1774–1848), editor of *Leeds Mercury*, spoke for the majority when he wrote, "Civil government is no fit agency for the training of families or of souls. . . . Throw the people on their own resources in education, as you did in industry; and be assured, that in a nation so full of intelligence and spirit, freedom and competition will give the same stimulus to improvement in our schools, as they have done in our manufactures, our husbandry, our shipping, and our commerce."[25] The trouble was, Baines was just plain mistaken: with each passing year of the industrial revolution more and more poor people massed together in factory towns, swarms of workers turned the manufacturing centers into cesspools of social misery and ignorance, and the efforts of philanthropists to improve the welfare of the poor made little impact. But the managerial class, joined by the landed aristocracy and the church, successfully resisted all attempts to introduce any national system of popular education. For the time being the government rested content to let private groups take care of whatever needed to be done.

The first step along the route traversed by countries on the Continent toward increased government action in the sphere of education dates to 1802 with the passage of the *Health and Morals of Apprentices Act*. This limited the daily hours of labor apprentices in textile mills to twelve, proscribed night employment, and ordered that "every such apprentice shall be instructed in some part of each working day, for the first four years at least of his or her apprenticeship, in the usual hours of work, in reading, writing, and arithmetic . . . according to the age and ability of such apprentice, by some discreet and proper person, to be provided and paid by the master or mistress of such apprentice, in some room or place in such mill or factory to be set aside for that purpose." The law was widely evaded and few benefited from it, but a beginning had been made, an important precedent set for state intervention in matters of schooling.

A series of reform acts beginning in 1830, when the Whigs came to power,

[25] Quoted in Cubberley, op. cit., p. 641.

represented the next breach in a solid wall of class privilege and social in-equity. The year following the Political Reform Act of 1832 brought a new *Factory Act* prohibiting the employment of children under nine, ordered two hours' school attendance daily for children between the ages of nine and thirteen, and voted a small amount of money to the Anglican National Society and the Nonconformist Foreign Society "in aid of public sub-scriptions for the erection of school-houses for the education of children of the poorer classes." Partly in response to agitation from *Lord Henry Brougham* (1778–1868), whose *Observations on the Education of the People* (1825) went through countless editions and through whose efforts bills were introduced, addresses were made, and committees of inquiry launched, the Parliamentary grant was increased in 1839, more funds were allocated for the building of a state training college for teachers, and a special Committee of the Privy Council was appointed "for the consideration of all matters af-fecting the education of the people." These measures were followed by many others extending funds to other sectarian and nonsectarian educational or-ganizations, instituting state-paid inspectors to oversee expenditures, and the expansion of teachers' seminaries. *James Kay-Shuttleworth,* called by Matthew Arnold the founder of the public instruction system in England, presided as first secretary over the Privy Council (which became the De-partment of Education in 1856). Relentless pressure for more state par-ticipation in educational reform was kept up by such illustrious leaders as Jeremy Bentham, William Blackstone, John Stuart Mill, and Thomas Carlyle.

Such activity remained highly controversial. Some regarded government action on behalf of education as unwarranted interference with a sacred right reserved by God for parents or the church. The Anglican claim to be the sole educator of the country in turn was opposed by Catholics, Wesleyans, and other nonconformists fearing ecclesiastical domination. *Herbert Spencer* (1820–1903), among the most uncompromising opponents of national educa-tion, viewed it as a move toward political tyranny over the human mind. Education, he argued in his *Social Statics* (1851) and the famous four essays on *Education* (1861), is basically an individual concern; state action beyond the narrowest limits would do irreparable harm. The bitter controversy raged on throughout the nineteenth century. Whenever public school laws were proposed, a storm of protest would arise from private agencies, ec-clesiastical bodies, and political factions.

The first significant national commission appointed to undertake a com-prehensive study of the "state of 'popular' education in England, and to consider what measures, if any, are required for the extension of sound and cheap elementary instruction to all classes of the people" was appointed in 1858. The *Newcastle Commission* issued its report in 1861. It concluded that any major increase in government control over "public" schools (meaning those institutions not managed for private gain) would lead inevitably to infringements on individual prerogatives, and voted firmly against all proposals to make primary education universal, free, or compulsory. The commission's report did recommend improvements in teacher preparation, the extension of public day schools, and a vicious practice known as "payment by results," by which state grants to schools were based on the number of students passing annual examinations administered by state officials. Obviously this scheme led teachers to emphasize drill and memorization for examination questions. The whole idea was not shelved until after 1890. A second body, the *Taunton Schools Inquiry Commission* (1864–1867), was appointed to investigate curricula, state supervision of academic standards, teacher certification, and matters of endowed school organization. This body proved more progressive in its recommendations for an extension and democratization of the entire English system of secondary education. Yet another agency, the *Clarendon Commission,* was formed to make specific suggestions for revising the classical curriculum of the public grammar schools. Its report urged the inclusion of more social studies, science, and modern languages in upper-class schools, but generally endorsed the prevailing system. No important results were secured. Instead Parliament chose to ignore the commission's findings and passed an *Endowed School Act* (1869) limiting the state to an advisory role in the financial management of schools. Nothing had been done to correct deplorable conditions in lower schools for commoners and the public schools continued pretty much as before, preserving rigid class separations, devoted to classical ideals, concerned mainly with producing English "gentlemen" schooled in the mores of an aristocratic tradition.

Curricular Debates

Another phase of educational ferment during the nineteenth century, tied to the question of a national school system, had to do with the relative merits of a humanistic versus a scientific curriculum. Spencer's question, "What knowledge is of most worth?" helped set the terms of a debate that continued on into the twentieth century. The aim of education, Spencer maintained, is to help individuals prepare for living as whole and complete a life as possible. The sciences that teach people to use knowledge to solve their own problems, based on personal experience and judgment, are those that belong at the top of a scale of worthwhile knowledge, whereas the literary arts, resting on tradition and an outmoded culture, should be placed at the bottom. Beginning with an exposition of Pestalozzi's educational principles (especially those relating to learning by discovery and the concept of learning as an individual process), he concluded that the literary traditions prevalent in established schools were incompetent to educate people for a changing society. Although Spencer believed educational reforms should be directed on a voluntary, private basis, *George Combe* (1788–1858) took up the same argument and ran it in the opposite direction. Vested interests and natural inertia, he argued in his *Lectures on Popular Education* (1833), can be overcome and more scientific studies introduced only when the power of the state is brought in to compel reform. *John Tyndall* (1820–1893) added his voice to those pleading for modifications in the schools' literary–classical regimen. "While thankfully accepting what antiquity has to offer," he wrote in *On the Importance of the Study of Physics*, "let us never forget that the present century has just as good a right to its forms of thought and methods of culture as any former centuries had to theirs." A representative spokesman for the opposing side was *Thomas Arnold* (1795–1842), headmaster of Rugby for fourteen years. "Expel Greek and Latin from your schools," he wrote in 1834, "and you confine the views of the existing generation to themselves and their immediate predecessors, you will cut off so many centuries of the world's experience, and place us in the same state as if the human race had come into existence in the year 1500. . . .[The ancients'] observation has been exercised in a field out of reach of common men, and that having thus seen in a manner with their eyes what we cannot see for ourselves, their conclusions are such as bear on our own circumstances." Parliament was inclined to favor Arnold's view whenever legislation was introduced to modify school curricula at the secondary level.

A more balanced view, though inclined to favor scientific over classical studies, was advanced by one of the century's most distinguished intellectual leaders, *Thomas H. Huxley* (1825–1895).[26] For the purpose of attaining real culture," he noted in his *Science and Education*, "an exclusively scientific education is at least as effectual as an exclusively literary education." For the most part Huxley's time was taken up advancing the cause of science, although he personally favored a sane balance of liberal and scientific subjects for the school curriculum. (He was perfectly accurate in predicting to a friend that when the balance had swung in the opposite direction at some future date, equally bad arguments would be advanced on behalf of an exclusively scientific course of study as those put forth in his own time championing a totally literary curriculum.) To a group of school teachers at South Kensington in 1861, he warned, "The modern world is full of artillery; and we turn out our children to do battle in it, equipped with the shield and sword of an ancient gladiator." Huxley never tired of urging that scientific interests be made the focus of attention in education. He told the 1884 Select Committee on Education in Science and Art that "the whole theory on which our present educational system is based, is wrong from top to bottom; that the subjects which are now put down as essential . . . are luxuries, so to speak; and that those which are regarded as comparatively unessential and as luxuries are essential." Needless to add, very few people

---

[26] Huxley is one of the most underrated educational theorists of the 1800's, The brief treatment he is accorded in most histories of education (including this one) is very undeserved. See Cyril Bibby, *T. H. Huxley: Scientist, Humanist and Educator* (London: Macmillan, 1959).

were willing to entertain the notion of a complete curricular overhaul emphasizing science.[27]

Founding of a State Education System

To *Karl Marx* (1818–1883), who spent the last thirty-four years of his life in England, the main question was not merely what subjects should be studied but whether education of any kind could be an instrument of liberation for the masses. His taunting criticisms of social conditions in an industrial economy and vivid portrayal of the dehumanizing character of society exposed the fundamental weakness of nineteenth-century liberalism. For Marx the ordinary man had become a means to further someone else's ends; he was an object to be manipulated, an economic commodity. Laborers were forced to sell themselves piecemeal, he raged, "like every other article of commerce." *Laissez-faire* capitalism perpetuated an ideology camouflaging the exploitation of man, he argued, and what the ruling class called freedom was merely a deception to conceal the reality of slavery. Until the revolution of the proletariat comes to pass, so his argument ran, workers would remain alienated, estranged, spiritually deformed. The classless society would offer "free education for all children in public schools" and thereby help bring about a transformation of man. Marx summarized his educational position with an explanation: "The communists have not invented the intervention of society [or the state] in education; they do but seek to alter the character of that intervention, and to rescue education from the influence of the ruling class." The Marxist version of a social order in which dignified education for the free individual would be possible won scanty support. But Marx lived to see the day when his belief that the "voluntary system" of independent private schools was failing to educate the English people became commonplace among a growing majority of the nation's leadership.

The *Forster Act* of 1870, sometimes called the *Elementary School Act,* was a compromise measure to improve and expand lower schools. The country was divided into school districts administered by local elective school boards. Private groups were given one year in which to found schools in every district (with financial aid from the state). If, when the time period had expired, voluntary agencies had not made adequate provision for elementary schooling in a district, the board was authorized to levy taxes, set tuition fees, and open a compulsory *board school* for children aged six to thirteen. Poorer children could attend without charge. In voluntary schools religious instruction might be given only if the students' parents lodged no objections; in state schools the law provided that "no religious

[27] Huxley did not rest content with assembly hall rhetoric in his desire to bring about educational reform; his entire career was marked by active involvement in the field of education. Looking back on his pioneering efforts with the London School Board in trying to establish schools for orphans, he reflected that "that period of my life was perhaps the part of it least wasted."

catechism or religious formulary which is distinctive of any particular denomination" could be taught. Continuing government aid to private, sectarian schools was specifically authorized. Succeeding legislation in 1876, 1880, and 1891 made elementary education fully compulsory and almost entirely free. At the close of the nineteenth century a *National Board of Education* under a parliamentary secretary and president was created to centralize administrative supervision over a wide range of state and public institutions. Its function was to "suggest and assist" in matters of instruction and curriculum, setting standards for teacher certification, and the enforcement of compulsory attendance laws. Thus, as England entered the present century, there were two elementary school systems: one "voluntary" and run by philanthropic or denominational sponsors, the other created by the state to meet needs unsatisfied through private action. At the secondary level, the traditional private "grammar" schools, such as Eton, Rugby, St. Paul's, Westminster, Merchant Taylor's, and Harrow, predominated. Though under attack by democratic and liberal forces for their elitist character, rigid classical curriculum, and policies of exclusion, these prestigious institutions remained the only avenues open to positions in the church, government civil service, and industry.

Modern English Education

In 1902 the English government abandoned its long-standing policy of merely supervising and assisting private groups in the maintenance of educational institutions. The *Balfour Act* abolished elective school boards and placed control with local governments over both *council schools* (so-called because they were administered by local councils) and voluntary schools. Tax funds for facilities and special services for both school systems were authorized as well as a reorganizational plan to connect state secondary schools more closely with lower-grade schools. Considerable opposition was aroused by these provisions from a public not yet willing to accept the principle of state control over private educational agencies.

During World War I the *Fisher Act* of 1918 was passed and a giant attempt made to bring together all public educational agencies under unified control, including elementary, secondary, technical, and higher institutions. The age of compulsory attendance was raised to fourteen, primary schools fees were eliminated, and local authorities were given permission to found nursery schools for children under the age of five. Scholarship funds for needy secondary school students were also provided for through tax revenues. Conservative elements in Parliament, fearing the immediate advent of socialism if the latter provisions of the Fisher Act were carried through, moved rapidly to shut off appropriations. As a result, the reform legislation remained inoperative. The same fate befell later attempts through the 1920's and 1930's to raise the age for compulsory continuation schooling beyond the age of fourteen and to open postprimary education for those interested in a technical career or unable to enroll in a private secondary-level grammar school. Some progress, however, was made with the opening of *central* institutions serving surrounding elementary schools. These institutions specialized in industrial, technical, commercial, and domestic subjects and generally offered a course of studies lasting four or five years. Instruction was pitched at a considerably lower level than in public or private secondary schools. The nearest American equivalent would be a junior high school, except that the former were terminal institutions.

On the eve of World War II the English school structure had evolved into a fixed pattern. Supervision and administration of all education was in the hands of the National Board. The actual power of this agency was severely compromised, either by law or for lack of resources. Infant and nursery schools, although under official state control, were conducted mainly by private groups. Elementary education was handled by a combination of denominational, philanthropic, or private schools and state schools overseen by local councils. The elementary schools taught reading, writing, arithmetic, history, geography, nature study, drawing, hygiene, physical education, and manual or domestic training. Considerable latitude was given in matters of instruction and course arrangement. Elementary or primary schools were followed, roughly speaking, by five institutional types: (1) the *central schools,* cited previously; (2) *local day schools* managed privately as classically oriented academies supported by tuition charges; (3) *public secondary schools* maintained by county boroughs or counties, teaching English language and at least one foreign language (usually Latin or French), history, science, music, manual arts, drawing, mathematics, geography, and physical education; (4) the *great public schools,* privately conducted for the rich upper classes; and (5) a diverse array of *private secondary schools,* offering broad, flexible curricula. The total picture is obscured by the fact that historically no hard-and-fast distinction between "elementary" and "secondary" education has been preserved in the English tradition. Despite attempts to introduce fixed limits through the *Hadow Reports* (1926–1939), some schools took young children through to the doorstep of the university; others admitted pupils at the age of nine or twelve and retained them until age eighteen.

Wartime conditions impelled Richard A. Butler, President of the Board of Education, to call for a more effective system of education for national renewal in the postwar period. The *Butler Education Act* of 1944 was a kind of turning point in English educational developments. The National Board was disbanded, to be replaced by a Ministry of Education possessed of broad powers to concentrate school administration under a central authority, while preserving local and private initiative in some areas. The law extended the compulsory attendance period to age fifteen and for the first time provided machinery for enforcing it. Voluntary schools were retained under a system of partial state support, but made subject to inspection by Ministry officials. The Minister of Education was empowered to "control and direct" institutions for "further education," including adult evening programs, county colleges offering part-time continuing education for drop-outs from regular schools, and county secondary schools responsible to local authorities. The Butler Act included measures treating all secondary-level education as a continuation of primary instruction and supplying some type of free postelementary schooling for all people. One result was that state primary schools became vestibules for a broader range of secondary schools, which helped to break down class barriers within the system.[28]

Today both separation and interpenetration characterize the British educational system, with one pattern obtaining for England and Wales, another similar pattern for Scotland, and yet another for Northern Ireland. All share common features. The broad outlines of the educational ladder include *nursery schools* for children up to the age of five, *infant schools* for those under seven, and *junior schools* for students aged seven to eleven. Elementary science, arithmetic, geography, national and local history, language, and mathematics are subjects forming the common curriculum. Basically four types of secondary institutions exist. There are traditional *grammar* or *academic* schools offering courses in geography, history, science, mathematics, plus a heavy emphasis on the traditional liberal arts and classics; so-called *modern schools,* teaching general liberal arts in the lower grades and practical business subjects in the upper levels; *technical schools,* with a curriculum weighted toward specialized studies in the sciences, business and industrial subjects, and technical training; and a few *"comprehensive" high schools* sustaining academic, vocational, and technical courses of study. At the postsecondary stage there are specialized technical institutes, teacher-training schools, and of course the prestigious colleges of the major universities like Cambridge and Oxford. More numerous but somewhat lacking in the same social esteem are municipal or *provincial universities,* such as those at Reading, Liverpool, Bristol, Durham, Leeds, Aberdeen, Birmingham, Glasgow, Manchester, and Edinburgh. Kings College and University College of the University of London also attract large numbers of students.

Something of the selection process still operating can be seen in the state's examination system. Elementary school students in some schools around the age of eleven still take an examination that largely determines their subsequent education. Two thirds go on to technical or modern schools; the remaining third with highest grades go on to a grammar school. Two more comprehensive examinations are required before the more brilliant students are admitted to a university. Only within the past two decades has it become possible for individuals to rise to positions of influence

---

[28] This infuriated many people who clung to traditional class divisions. Groups of mothers actually picketed Parliament to protest the elimination of educational class segregation.

and power without graduating from the "proper" grammar school and university college. Among the upper classes, it is still fashionable to praise a classical education and to judge public school curricula on the basis of how well they prepare graduates resembling those from Eton, Westminster, and other "status" institutions.

One curious feature of the English development is the absence of any direct attempt to use education for propagating nationalist doctrines, at least in the overt sense in which Prussian or French schools indoctrinated their students. Love of country has undoubtedly been fostered through study of the nation's past and its literature, and there is no denying that much attention is paid to the rights, duties, and social mores appropriate for an Englishman, yet explicit citizenship training has always been condemned. The English ethos has produced a profound respect for aristocratic and class virtues, but always combined with tolerance for diversity, individuality, and independence. Public ceremony, ritual, and a feeling for tradition have seemed to foster national loyalty at least as well as schoolbook instruction; whether this is a function of England's unique history is an open question.

RUSSIAN AND SOVIET EDUCATION

Before the Nineteenth Century

The growth of Russian state-supported schools followed a pattern unique to itself in many respects, primarily because those great cultural forces that convulsed the West, including the twelfth-century humanistic revival, the Renaissance, and the religious upheavals of the sixteenth and seventeenth centuries, had little impact on Russia. Until relatively recent times, historically speaking, the country remained isolated from most of the major intellectual and social movements of Western Europe. As a partial result, widespread schooling did not appear until late in the 1700's. Documentary evidence for schools prior to unification under Archduke Ivan IV (the Terrible), early in the seventeenth century, is fragmentary at best.[29] Evidently institutionalized schools on a significant scale first arose in the late 1500's in the southwestern portion of the empire. It can be shown that in addition to private tutorial instruction, there were several monastic schools in existence by then, supported by the Orthodox Church, as well as a limited number of church-sponsored vernacular elementary schools located in the larger villages and towns. For the most part, educational agencies were unorganized, isolated from one another, and subject to no unified direction or supervision. This situation continued to prevail throughout most of the seventeenth century.

[29] A helpful treatment of Russian education prior to 1917 is to be found in William H. E. Johnson, *Russia's Educational Heritage* (Pittsburgh: Carnegie Press, 1950).

In the last half of the 1600's there occurred a gradual metamorphosis of schools from a Greek–Slavonic to a Latin basis, hastened in all probability by the teaching efforts of the Jesuits. The founding of schools for advanced instruction at Lavr, Lutsk, Kiev, and Moscow was prompted by opposition to Roman Catholic influences, as illustrated for instance in a statement of purpose for the Lavr institution, whose avowed aim was "to teach free knowledge in Greek, Slavonic and Latin, at the same time preserving the Christian truth of Eastern Orthodoxy." At a lower level, several sectarian secondary schools were begun in an effort to resist the Latinization of Russian culture. Most had a very short-lived career.

The first Romanov monarch to make any substantial contribution to the spread of institutionalized schooling was Czar *Peter I* (the Great), who ascended to the throne in 1701. Peter's driving ambition was to open "a window on the West" and to encourage the importation of ideas from Russia's European neighbors. As part of his westernization program, he sponsored the establishment of several "cypher" schools in order to better provide the government with a cadre of semiskilled and technical workers, a secular school for military and civil service training at St. Petersburg, and a School of Mathematical and Navigation Sciences at Moscow (the first nonclassical higher school in the world). Among his many other contributions, he founded the Ecclesiastical College, or Holy Synod, an agency designed to help regulate the church's work in organizing seminaries for its clergy.

Peter's successor, Elizabeth, continued with her father's program of state encouragement of formal education, helping to found a number of private boarding schools and presiding at the opening of Moscow University in January of 1755. The next major advances were made during the reign of Empress *Catherine II* (the Great), who ruled from 1762 until her death in 1796. Under the stimulus of counsel from the French Encyclopedist Diderot and the German educator Friedrich von Grimm, Catherine initiated ambitious plans for a network of women's institutes and classical *gymnasia* for sons of the nobility. Her decree of 1775 increased the number of *guberniyas,* provinces, to fifty, and set up in each a Board of Public Assistance charged with founding schools in every provincial city. For lack of funds the scheme never fully materialized, although the empress continued to evidence a strong interest in school reform. In 1782 she created a Commission for the Establishment of Schools and directed that it devise a comprehensive plan for a national school system. The commission issued its proposals four years later under the title "Statutes for Public Schools in the Russian Empire." Again, because insufficient funds were available, and for lack of administrative supervision, the plan was never carried through. A severe shortage of trained teachers, disinterest on the part of local communities, and active opposition from the nobility also account for the Commission's failure. Meanwhile, a private reformer by the name of

Nikolai Ivanovich Novikov was active in the work of raising money at the local level for a system of progressive community schools. Besides founding a major pedagogical seminary, Novikov founded the "Friendly Learning Society" in 1782, an organization dedicated to expanding local elementary schools and preparing teachers to work in them. Despite its heroic labors, it is estimated that only one in eight hundred Russians at the end of the eighteenth century received any formal instruction in a school setting.

Under the Reign of Alexander I

There followed a brief reactionary period (1796–1801) under Catherine's son and successor, Paul I, during which no significant legislation relative to education was enacted. Paul was succeeded by Czar *Alexander I* in 1802. One of his first actions was to establish a Ministry of Public Education to supplant the Commission for the Establishment of Schools, created by Catherine I. Count *Peter Vasilevich Zavadovskii* was appointed first head of the newly created ministry and proceeded to reorganize the stagnating Russian school system into six "educational circuits" (*uchebnye okrugi*) with a university in each circuit, at St. Petersburg, Moscow, Vilna, Dorpat, Kazan, and Kharkov. At that time only three full-fledged universities were in existence—at Moscow, Vilna, and Dorpat. The new concept behind the circuit system was expressed by journalist Ivan Petrovich Pnin (1773–1806) as follows:

Education, as accepted in the present sense, consists in that each member of society, no matter what profession he finds himself in, knows and fulfills thoroughly his responsibilities; that is to say, when the superiors on their part sacredly carry out the obligations of the power entrusted to them and when the lower class people inviolately live up to the responsibilities of their obedience. If these two classes do not transgress their bounds but preserve the proper equilibrium in their relations, then education has attained the desired aims.[30]

It would be difficult to find a more unequivocal statement than this on behalf of class-bound education for the preservation of the societal status quo.

For many reasons Zavadovskii experienced little success in building a true national system of state-controlled schools. Progress was hampered by the fact that Czar Alexander was either unwilling or unable to release public funds for the planned construction of universities. In addition, the few secondary-level *gymnasia* the ministry did manage to open attracted few students. Class antagonisms favored private preparatory schools for the sons of the nobility, and poorer people were unable to raise the tuition fees charged by schools under the supervision of the government. State control of education was abandoned altogether in 1817 when the Czar issued a manifesto

[30] Quoted in ibid., p. 74.

handing schools over to the care of the Orthodox church. Henceforth, announced Leonti Magnitskii, new ecclesiastical superintendent of education, "the aim of government in the education of students is the bringing up of true sons of the Orthodox Church, loyal subjects of the State, good and useful citizens of the Fatherland." A period of extreme repression ensued, during which time instruction at all school levels was confined to the teaching of religion and morals. Secular subjects, as such, assumed a markedly subordinate place in the curricula.

By 1824 when Admiral *Alexander Semenovich Shishkov* became Minister of Public Education, the ministry had regained most of its administrative integrity. Indicative of the direction state education would take under the new regime, the minister observed: "To instruct all the people, or even a disproportionate number of them, in literacy would do more harm than good. To teach rhetoric to the son of a farmer would make him a bad and useless citizen, if not a really dangerous one. But instruction in the rules and principles of Christian conduct and good morals is needed by everybody." (Similar statements of this same distrust of popular education in Prussia and France have already been cited.) Although Alexander I died the year following Shishkov's appointment, his successor, Nicholas I, saw no reason to alter his brother's choice of a Minister of Public Education. In fact, in 1826 he appointed Shishkov as head of a commission to revise the school system which, it was claimed, had "no steadfast plan by which it might always be guided." Predictably, the result was a thoroughgoing repudiation of the "ladder" concept of schools in favor of independent, disconnected school units adapted to the social position of the social class from which pupils came—village schools for peasant children, country (district) schools for merchants' children, *gymnasia* and universities for the noble-born. Most of the few private schools then operating were brought under state inspection and supervision, to ensure complete subservience of all formal education to the authority of the central government. This remained the general pattern for the next three decades: official primary schools for the lower class, an indeterminate number of unregistered private schools, a few *gymnasia,* universities under tight state control, and a growing number of public and private technical institutes.

An Era of Reform and Expansion

Czar *Alexander II* (1818–1881), eldest son of Nicholas I, came to the throne in 1855. His reign, lasting throughout the late 1800's, was distinguished by several important educational reforms. Not only did he increase greatly the material prosperity of the serfs, he responded generously to their demand for an improved system of primary schools. His law of January, 1864, created elective county councils, called *Zemstvos,* with responsibility for levying taxes to "provide and maintain" schools within their area of jurisdiction. The *Elementary School Code* of June, 1864, declared that "the elementary schools have the aim of strengthening the religious and moral understanding of the people, and of disseminating the essentials of useful knowledge." All such schools were ordered placed under the direct authority of one of three administrative bureaus: the Ministry of Public Education, the Ministry of Public Domains and Internal Affairs, or the Holy Synod of the Church. The *Zemstvos* were further provided with special school boards in each district to supervise all educational agencies maintained by rural and town councils.

Alexander made a similar attempt to upgrade and expand secondary schools. His *Secondary School Code* of December, 1864, gave recognition to two types of postelementary institutions: a *Realgymnasium* (or *Progymnasium*), modeled after the German *Realschule,* and the "classical" *Gymnasium.* The aim of the latter, the code proclaimed, was "to convey general education to the youth being trained in them, and at the same time to serve as preparatory institutions for entrance into universities and other specialized schools." Ordinarily, the graduate of a *Realgymnasium* was not expected to pursue an advanced instruction, although entrance to some technical or business school was not closed to him altogether. The czar also was instrumental in the re-establishment or founding of several universities and half a dozen higher professional institutes. The Empress Maria, wife of Alexander II, shared her husband's early enthusiasm for education and opened several schools for women under her special protection.

It was at this time that a brief but remarkable school experiment was undertaken by Count Lyóf Nikoláyevitch, better known as *Leo Tolstoy* (1828–1910), representing his attempt to explore alternative methods of instruction in the school. "All are agreed," he wrote, "that schools are imperfect; I, personally, am convinced that they are noxious." Tolstoy was very much disturbed by the discrepancy he found between the schoolchild as "a vivacious, inquisitive being, with a smile in his eye and on his mouth, seeking information as a pleasure . . ." *outside of the classroom* and that same child *in school,* when he became "a weary shrinking creature repeating, merely with his lips, someone else's thoughts in someone else's words, with an air of fatigue, fear and restlessness: a creature whose soul has retreated like a snail into its shell." He called this strange unhappy condition the "school state of mind," which consists "in all the higher capacities, imagination, creative power and reflection, yielding to a semi-animal capacity to produce words without imagination or reflection."

Around the midpoint of the century, Tolstoy opened his own village school at Yasnáya Polyána, hoping that if he as teacher followed a principle of noninterference and maximum freedom for the students, learning could be greatly facilitated. "The only criterion of pedagogy is freedom . . .," he maintained, "the less the children are compelled to learn, the better is the method; the more—the worse. . . . In instruction [there can be] no necessity of compelling children to learn anything that is tiresome and repulsive to them, and, if necessity demands that children be compelled, it only proves the imperfection of the method." For two years Tolstoy conducted his school, basing his instruction on the maxim that "the method which does not demand an increase of discipline is good; the one which demands greater severity is bad."

Was the experiment successful? Tolstoy unashamedly admitted that his classroom could become noisy, explaining, "this disorder, or free order, is terrible to us only because we are accustomed to something quite different in which we have been educated . . . force is used only through haste and insufficient respect for human nature . . . we need only to wait a little and the disorder (or animation) calms down naturally by itself, growing into a much better and more permanent order than what we have created." Furthermore, he recounted later, it was not uncommon for a noisy class to transform itself without compulsion into a group of quiet children, utterly absorbed in their lessons: "To tear [a student] from his reading would now need as much effort as formerly to tear him from his wrestling." This was not the report of some idealistic dreamer but of an experienced educational practitioner. Needless to add, it would be many years before Tolstoy's views on education would win a sympathetic hearing. With the exceptions of A. S. Neill, Bertrand Russell, Homer Lane, and to a lesser extent Maria Montessori, few prominent writers on education even in the present century have shown themselves willing to countenance such a radical humanism in pedagogical practice.

Reaction and Repression

It is interesting to speculate how the Russian educational system might have developed had it not been for the strenuous opposition of the czar's advisory officials and a dramatic incident which led to an abrupt reversal of Alexander's policies. For years certain government officials had greatly feared the expansion of educational opportunity represented by *Zemstvos* schools. Allowing the lower classes to attend school, they argued, was an open invitation for disaster. Schools would become nests for atheism, free-thinking, anarchism, socialism, and all sorts of subversive doctrines. After an assassination attempt was made on the czar's life in 1866, Alexander allowed himself to be persuaded, thinking that perhaps after all his advisors had been right in their assertion that political disunity would follow upon the heels of expanded schooling for the masses. There followed a long period of repression and reaction under the direction of Count Dmitri A. Tolstoi, Chief Procurator of the Holy Synod and then Minister. Schools were closed on a wholesale basis or forbidden to teach anything not expressly approved by the government. The coronation of the czar's son, Alexander III, in the closing years of the nineteenth century, brought a continuation of the same reactionary policies. Count T. D. Delianov, Minister of Education, and then K. P. Dobedonostsev, worked assiduously to complete the work of their predecessors. Among the changes wrought, there occurred a complete downfall of autonomy within the universities, the elimination of any school officials suspected of liberalism, a restoration of strong class distinctions at the secondary school level, and a concerted effort to restore all primary schools to a sectarian basis.

As Russia entered the twentieth century she was burdened with a population still largely illiterate, a school system in disarray, a woefully under-developed technology, an unresponsive bureaucracy at all levels of government, and an autocratic monarch tragically insensitive to the needs of his people. Sporadic attempts at reform never succeeded and when violent uprisings did take place, they were ruthlessly crushed. This was the situation of instability as Nicholas II led his empire into the throes of World War I.

Experimentation Under Lenin's Regime

In March of 1917 an army of peasants led by dissident army officers, with strong support from the middle class, overthrew Russia's imperial government and thereby ended centuries of czarist rule. Waiting on the sidelines was a revolutionary faction (the Bolsheviks) of the Russian Social Democratic Labor Party. In November of that same year, after a period of unrelieved confusion under the provisional government of Alexander Kerensky, the Bolsheviks (headed by Lenin and Trotsky) seized power. The beginnings of modern Soviet education date to the start of Lenin's regime, when the Ministry of Education was replaced by the People's Commissariat for Education and a State Commission for Education.[31]

The early years of the Revolution brought a period of experimentation and radical innovation in education. Reflective of Lenin's strong belief in early indoctrinative training, "preschool education" (*doshkolnoe obrazovanie*) was vastly expanded. Infant nurseries, the *Yasli,* were begun for children as young as six weeks, as well as connecting schools to care for children aged two to three. A kindergarten (*Detski sad*) school system was begun for three- to seven-year-olds, in order to emancipate women from the home and enable them to join the growing labor force required in a crash program of national industrialization. Until the early 1930's there was no unified federal agency for education as such, although control of schools was implied by the omniscient presence of the Communist Party. Considerable self-determinative power was allowed the separate constituent republics, and naturally wide variations in local school practice resulted. Generally the emphasis was upon "life adjustment" curricula, with few

[31] For informative sources on Soviet education see George S. Counts, *The Challenge of Soviet Education* (New York: McGraw-Hill, 1957); George Z. F. Bereday et al., eds., *The Changing Soviet School* (Boston: Houghton Mifflin, 1960); Edmund J. King, ed., *Communist Education* (London: Methuen, 1963); Nigel Grant, *Soviet Education* (Baltimore: Penguin, 1964); Edmund J. King, *Other Schools and Ours*, rev. ed. (New York: Holt, Rinehart and Winston, 1963), Chapter 6; and A. G. Korol, *Soviet Education for Science and Technology* (Boston: Massachusetts Institute of Technology, 1957).

grading standards, examinations, or formalized study sequences. Until 1930 no compulsory school attendance laws existed.

As determined by a Communist Party Congress in 1919, proletarian education aimed basically at three interrelated goals: the total extermination of czarist nationalist sentiment, inculcation of loyalty to the official Communist ideology and its party apparatus, and involvement in real-life work experience. Originally envisioned by Marx and championed by Lenin's wife, N. K. Krupskaya, "polytechnical" or "work" schools were designed to involve children in industrial work processes, to acquaint them with the use of tools, building materials, and methods and to foster positive attitudes toward manual labor.

A new phase in Soviet education began after enactment of the first Five-Year Plan of 1928, a period in which educational processes came under increasing centralized control and were conducted with greater thoroughness. The so-called activity or project method was still employed, whereby a brigade (Druzhina) of children was set to helping with the harvest, assisting workers in cultivation, and working on urban renewal projects. The next twelve years, from about 1929 until 1942, also saw a concerted effort to consolidate elementary education and to coordinate it with intermediate and higher education. A three- or four-year elementary school (Nachalnoya shkola) for children aged seven to eleven was begun or strengthened, and then another three-year study sequence was added to it, conducted either in the village school or, more often, in a larger building in a nearby town. Thus, a four-year school became a seven-year school (Srednaya shkola), providing instruction for children up to age fourteen. The term ten-year school later was used when still another three years of instruction was added on, meaning provision for the entire period between the ages of seven and seventeen or later. Complete "secondary" education, or the stage of schooling from age fifteen to eighteen (Polnoe srednee obrazonvanie), has had no precise institutionalized equivalent in the European or American educational structures.[32]

After 1930 school attendance was made mandatory for children in rural areas between the ages of eight to twelve, and in urban areas it was extended to age fifteen. Six years later the Central Committee decreed that all the old "self-determining" teaching methods whereby children were sometimes allowed to control their advancement through the various forms (grades) were to be abolished. Extensive authority was returned to classroom teachers, and at the same time, a halt was ordered to an extensive program of intelligence testing and student performance evaluation by the use of standardized instruments. Leaders of an incipient "child study" movement were discredited or forced into retirement. The "work" school concept was

---

[32] Since 1959 the term eight-year school has been used to refer to the schooling years until age fifteen, and an eleven-year school is one extending to the age of entrance to a university, usually at eighteen.

also abolished in most areas, although it survived in some regions of the country under different forms.

Recent Developments

The trend toward greater formalization of education has continued steadily in the last half century. Since 1933 a federal "Committee for Higher Technological Education" (now the Federal Ministry of Higher Education) has maintained strict control over higher education, and to a lesser extent, over lower school curricula as well. In the early 1940's the period of compulsory attendance was ordered begun at age seven and extended to age fourteen for those in the country and to age seventeen for those in urbanized areas. Today, officially at least, school attendance is mandatory throughout a ten- or eleven-year training period. In rural areas it has proved impossible to offer more than four to seven years of schooling, but efforts are underway to extend this uniformly to ten or eleven years through the Union.

The contemporary school structure admits of many local variations, but basically it consists of the following elements: nursery schools and kindergartens directed by the Federal Department of Health, coeducational schools of the types previously described for students aged seven to fifteen, and residential trade schools or vocational–technical schools (*remeslennoye uchilishche*) offering utilitarian subjects for students who have completed the eight-year general studies course.[33] Many who attend these institutions are selected on the basis of results from a stringent examination administered to all pupils around the age of fourteen or fifteen. Others, placed in a "college preparatory" track, complete the regular academic curriculum in "polytechnical" and "general" secondary schools and, following a two-year work experience, go on to the universities, the many military academies, teacher-training institutes, technical and industrial schools, or, in some cases, special colleges designed to educate Party functionaries and leaders. At all levels there are evening and correspondence schools, institutions for educating the physically or mentally handicapped, and community centers offering remedial instruction in a variety of subjects.

Of special interest is the technical college or school (*tekhnicheskoye uchilishche*, or *Tekhnikum*), with a four-year course for fifteen-year-old entrants, or a shorter course for eighteen-year-olds with a middle-school certificate. Its course of study is designed to prepare medium-skill specialists and technicians for intermediate management positions. Upon completion

---

33 These one- to three-year institutions, numbering over 4,000, cater especially to "nonacademic" students who do not expect to pursue advanced training. They are designed to introduce "practical work experience" to pupils around the age of fifteen and may be residential boarding schools with tuition, board, and clothing provided by the state. They were begun during the Stalinist period and were then called Labor Reserve schools. Traditionally they have been located adjacent to farm collectives or even within factories.

of the course of study, some of its graduates go on to universities, but for the most part this "intermediate" kind of education overlaps so-called higher training and is deemed sufficient for an increasing percentage of the population. Its nearest American equivalent, roughly speaking, is a junior or community college.

Since World War II education has been free to everyone, although there are fees at the middle-school level for uniforms, books, and other supplies. "Progressive" teaching methods are not employed and the curriculum is weighted heavily in favor of mathematics and science, history and political science, and languages. Despite an abortive effort by Nikita Khrushchev to popularize boarding schools in which children would be confined to a socialist environment twenty-four hours a day, most modern Russian schools are attended by students who live at home with their parents. There are no private schools in the Soviet Union, but Moslems, Jews, and the Orthodox church are allowed to maintain seminaries for the training of the clergy. Because the Union of Soviet Socialist Republics covers an area of nearly nine million square miles and includes in its population over a hundred distinct nationalities, each with its own language, customs, and cultures, it has proved difficult to maintain a centralized state bureaucracy governing all educational institutions. Nonetheless, in a sense outsiders find difficult to understand, all schools are rigidly fixed to serve the interests of a monolithic state, as interpreted by the Communist Party.

The official school ideology, as V. P. Yelyutin, Minister of Higher Education, expressed it in 1959, has remained constant: "The role of Soviet education is to assist in the building of a communist society, in shaping the materialist world outlook of the students, equipping them with a good grounding in the different fields of knowledge and preparing them for socially useful work." As the Central Committee of the Party expressed it in a 1958 policy statement: "Upbringing must inculcate in the school children a love of knowledge and of work, and respect for people who work; it must shape the communist world outlook of the pupils and rear them in the spirit of communist morality and of boundless loyalty to the country and the people, and in the spirit of proletarian internationalism."[34]

The Soviet educational pattern has been adopted in more or less unmodified form in almost all of the eastern satellite countries of Europe. East Germany, Poland, Hungary, Rumania, Bulgaria, and Czechoslovakia all display the same characteristics: a communist monopoly on schools, a uniform curriculum, heavy emphasis upon "polytechnic" and working experience, illiberal instructional methodologies, and so on.[35] The only discernible difference is that some kind of private religious instruction under state patronage has been allowed, particularly in Hungary and Poland.

[34] Both statements quoted in Grant, op. cit., p. 23.
[35] English-language sources on East European education are few in number. See Nigel Grant, *Society, Schools and Progress in Eastern Europe* (London: Pergamon Press, 1969).

OTHER NATIONAL STATE SYSTEMS OF EDUCATION

Almost all nations of the Western hemisphere developed state systems of education along the lines traced by England, France, Germany, or the United States, although naturally the specific characteristics of institutions were adapted to particular national needs and circumstances. Some proceeded in direct imitation of the patterns already discussed, others evolved more or less independently. Most of the European systems had their actual beginnings in the aftermath of the Napoleonic Wars and the rewriting of Europe's political geography. Italy, for example, borrowed heavily from the educational traditions of her French conquerors during the late eighteenth century, because with the exception of some brief reform activity in Savoy earlier in the 1700's and the laws enacted by Maria Theresa when the Italian states were part of the Austrian empire, little had been done by the various independent principalities in the sphere of education. The strongly centralized structure of French control that left little room for local administrative autonomy became the pattern in Italy after the establishment of a constitutional monarchy in 1870. Prime Minister Cavour (1810–1861) began the work of founding state schools as early as the 1840's, and such bodies as a Minister of Public Instruction and Council of Public Education were created well before the midpoint of the nineteenth century. But the real basis for Italian state education (until the last few decades) goes back to a General School Law enacted in 1859 providing for a two-class system, consisting of a six-year primary school, a five-year *ginnasio,* and a two-year *liceo,* paralleled by a seven-year secondary-level technical and vocational course of studies. Spain likewise opted for the French pattern of school control.

In the Netherlands public education dates back to a school law of 1806, modified by the educational provisions of the constitutions of 1815 and 1848. State control of education was gradually increased thereafter and the administrative structure evolved very much as it did in England, with supervision of schools divided between the national government and local units. Norway, Sweden, and Denmark have retained modified versions of the English system, except that, in Denmark especially, schools have taken on a unique character of their own. The Danish educational ladder today is comprised by the nursery school, kindergarten, and a primary *Folkeskole* for children up to the age of fourteen, which is followed either by a two-year vocational school (*Havedskole*) or a three-year *Realskole. Havedskole* graduates typically continue their education in residential folk high schools, evening schools, or agricultural institutes. *Realskole* graduates may go on to a variety of specialized schools or to a three-year *Gymnasie,* preparatory to a technical college or university. In West Germany, as has been seen, the control of education is lodged in the individual states of the Republic, with the central government acting mainly as a coordinating agency to ensure some broad measure of uniformity in standards and tax support. The United States has carried the principle of decentralized control much farther than either France or Germany, with responsibility for the administration and supervision of public schools spreading down from the federal government to state and local levels.

Possibly the only generalization that applies universally across the spectrum of national school systems is that it was not until the nineteenth century that governments began to appreciate the pivotal role that schools could play in advancing national objectives. Increasing state involvement in education has brought such positive benefits as greater uniformity in standards of instruction, compulsory attendance laws, the raising of the leaving age, an increase in the percentage of the nation's gross national product allocated to schools, the partial replacement of private tuition fees by tax funds for institutional support, and the expansion of educational opportunity to more people. On the negative side, government intervention has normally confirmed dual school systems with separate tracks for an aristocratic elite and the common masses. Popular education has been encouraged by government in its tendency to address narrowly conceived vocational concerns and schools have been used to solidify rigid class divisions. Until fairly recently, state paternalism inclined to discourage formal instruction above a very rudimentary level, for the very simple and straightforward reason that heads of state knew full well ideas are dangerous; they always threaten the established order of things. Moreover, tightly regimented structures of control have tended to choke off local initiative. Economy and efficiency have been purchased at the cost of diversity to some extent, depending on which national context is considered.

Lastly, schools have been used extensively to promote obedience and loyalty to the state. The chauvinistic brand of nationalism so characteristic of nineteenth-century thought could hardly have persisted without reinforcement by educational agencies, although it is certainly true that among the more developed countries in the West, nationalism is less parochial in tone than it has been for over a hundred and fifty years. The quality of nationalist sentiment embodied in the schools has been modified accordingly: evidence suggests that the more blatant forms of chauvinism are not nearly so prevalent in the curricula of the various national educational systems as they once were. One of the greatest challenges confronting educators today involves the meaning of nationalism based on geographical identity in a world drawn ever closer together by modern means of mass transportation and communication. For the first time in human history the question must be seriously entertained whether the ideals of internationalism and a worldwide cooperative community of interdependent states are luxuries or absolute necessities. The imperatives for educational theory and practice following from those ideals have not been articulated clearly, neither have they won universal acceptance among those charged with the conduct of schools. If and when the concept of absolute national sovereignty is recognized as an atavistic legacy of the past and there emerges a convergent awareness of the unity of mankind as one species, education will have an important role to play in a new cosmopolitan social order.

POSITIVISM AND THE NEW EDUCATIONAL TECHNOCRATS

The Scientific–Technological Movement in Modern Education

Throughout the two and a half millennia that reflective men have been pondering the basic issues of education, concern has focused primarily upon two elements of the teaching–learning process: the teacher or instructional agent and the materials of instruction. When the learner has been considered at all, the problem posed has been getting him to conform to the strictures of time, texts, and teachers. More frequently, controversy has revolved around the appropriateness of the *content* of the curricula (and more broadly the social ends it serves) as well as the instructional *procedures* employed. With respect to the first, criticism traditionally has been directed against outmoded or irrelevant learning; with regard to the second, against cruelty and inefficiency on the part of teachers. Sensitive souls across the centuries have been troubled by the chasm between educational aspirations and achievements on these two counts and have sought some rational reconciliation of pedagogical reality with exhortation.

This reconciliatory effort goes back at least as far as the rise of realism. Central to its reform program of the early seventeenth century was a demand that the practice of education be based upon the application of scientific understanding to problems of learning and teaching. Bacon had first shown the way; educators were required now to adapt the new scientific learning for the improvement of instruction. Something of this spirit can be discerned in the thought of Comenius—in his passion for systematizing, in his attempt to build a philosophical substructure for a psychology of learning, and in his careful attention to the pedagogical imperatives he felt followed from that psychology. Ratke's "new method" was likewise a brave, if premature, attempt to introduce greater control and precision based on scientific insights into teaching methodology. Those who followed Locke believed that at long last a coherent theoretical base had been uncovered upon which a systematic discipline of education might be raised.

Conspicuous by its absence up until then was any systematic concern for the nature of the learner as a critical factor in the educational equation. Though countless theorists had given perfunctory attention to the psychological characteristics of the child, including Quintilian, Erasmus, and Montaigne, it was not until Rousseau that proper regard was given to the idea that the learner—his growth and development—furnishes the logical point of departure for any educational endeavor. Pestalozzi saw this clearly and tried to "psychologize" education, employing Rousseau's conceptual frame of reference. In Herbart and Froebel these tendencies were taken much further, so that by the late nineteenth century enough momentum had been gained that forward-looking educators anticipated the achievement of a definite science of education in the very near future—a science taking into account *all* the important variables of teacher, learner, curriculum, and instruction.

Of particular concern in the late 1800's was the need to adapt educational effort to the psychology of the child. Based upon her pioneering work at the *Casa dei Bambini* in Rome, the great Italian educator Maria Montessori (1870–1952) insisted that the teacher had to be prepared to learn: "From the child itself he will learn how to perfect himself as an educator." Deploring the methods then in use, she scorned conventional classrooms where "the children, like butterflies mounted on pins, are fastened each to his place, the desk, spreading the useless wings of barren and meaningless knowledge which they have acquired." Shortly thereafter, John Dewey was to make much the same point: "The primary root of all educative activity," he wrote in one of his early essays, "lies in the instinctive impulsive attitudes and activities of the child, and not in the presentation and application of external material . . . accordingly, numberless spontaneous activities of children . . . are capable of educational use; nay, are the foundation-stones of education method."

Psychologists joined with philosophers and educators in urging a more careful analysis of child development. "Teachers as a rule do not study the nature of the children they instruct," complained the American psychologist G. Stanley Hall, guiding light of the child-study movement. Nothing less than a total revolution in teaching methods was needed, he argued, based upon expanded psychological insight. The early twentieth century witnessed a thoroughly international effort to follow Hall's counsel. Building upon the work of the English biologist Francis Galton and his investigation of inherited differences in human beings, the Frenchman Alfred Binet and the American J. McKeen Cattell devised new scientific instruments for the measurement of intelligence. Jean Piaget at Geneva embarked upon detailed, systematic research into the development of reasoning and thought in young children, a labor complemented by Charlotte Bühler and her colleagues in Vienna who undertook longitudinal studies of maturation in young children and its effect on learning. Susan Isaacs at the Malting House School at Cambridge and Anna Freud and Dorothy Burlingham in Britain's Residential Wartime Nurseries similarly labored to show how the organic structure of human personality provides a foundation for behavior in infants. Arnold and Beatrice Gesell, writing in *The Normal Child and Primary Education* (1912), expressed the growing concern for an educational psychology as follows: "Education cannot, by formulating courses of study, force intellectual functions. The laws which govern the growth of mind are as immediate and irresistible in their operation as those which govern the growth of the body. If we force either the one or the other, personality is foiled."

In America Alexander Bain's *Education as a Science* (1879) and an 1882 essay bearing the same title authored by F. A. P. Barnard were typical of the literature on scientific pedagogy of the day, as were numerous articles addressed to the same subject in the journals of the various child-study organizations, the National Education Association, and the house organ of the Herbartian Society. The Herbartians, however, instead of pinning hopes for a nascent science of education on a body of psychological knowledge, tacitly assumed that scientific information could be systematically organized within a rationalistic philosophical framework and interpreted to provide a convincing demonstration of how to conduct educational practice. Wilhelm Dilthey, a professor at the University of Berlin, made the same basic assumption.[36] The Herbartians were opposed by men like Paul Monroe and E. L. Thorndike in the early part of the twentieth century, who insisted that Herbartian philosophy was no substitute for a laborious, piecemeal, and thoroughly empirical inspection of teaching and learning processes if a scientific theory of instruction was ever to be achieved. Both Dewey and William James further perceived that scientific knowledge of the nature of human development and learning, although essential, would not *automatically* provide a theory of teaching. As James pointed out in his *Talks to Teachers on Psychology* (1901), psychology is (or aspires to be) a definite science, but teaching is basically an art, and "the sciences never generate arts directly out of themselves." The teaching act does not consist simply of the mechanical application of certain rules or principles; the repertoire of instructional responses is almost infinite. Furthermore, many different theories of teaching can be based on the same careful observation and analysis of the teaching act; that is, a variety of teacher behaviors is compatible with the same basic empirical conclusions about how people learn.

It is equally true, however, that although the practice of education is basically an art, just as is the practice of engineering or law or medicine, it is also generally recognized that if today's doctors are better physicians than those of the past, it is not because they are more artful but because they are more scientific.[37] It is this undeniable truth that has lent authority to continuing calls for more information about teaching and learning applicable to school practice. "One of the transcendent needs of educational research today," two commentators note, "is the systematic and scientific evaluation of changes and innovations. . . . We need to be able to test and measure education outcomes, to check on assertions about the beneficial

---

[36] An historical account of the "science of education" concept is to be found in Brauner, op. cit., pp. 88–110, 124–125 ff.

[37] For an illuminating discussion of these points, see Philip G. Smith, *Philosophy of Education* (New York: Harper & Row, 1965), pp. 38–42.

or detrimental effects of educational procedures."[38] Scientific prediction and control offer the best promise for workable, practical instructional strategies, for principles of efficient curriculum organization, and for adequate evaluation instruments to measure learning. For many reasons, the argument runs, this bright promise of scientific improvement in education has gone unrealized.

It is remarked frequently, for example, that the schools were bypassed by the scientific and industrial revolutions, in the sense that genuinely new patterns of educational activity were not achieved as a result of their influence. Past reforms led to changes in the objectives and content of the curricula, but virtually all of these innovations left traditional modes of teaching and learning intact. Now the demand is heard not simply that the content of curricula be made to reflect man's expanding scientific–technological knowledge (a process largely completed), but that *the terms under which teaching and learning take place* be based more closely on scientific understanding. On the other hand, just as reformers from Comenius to Pestalozzi, Herbart, and Froebel were opposed on various grounds in their efforts to build a systematic pedagogy, today's reformers meet with strong resistance from those grown fearful of the impact of science and its offspring, technology, upon education. Opposition sometimes shows itself as simple, visceral antiscientific sentiment; other kinds of protest deserve far more serious consideration. Especially troubling is the argument that the original humane goal of a "science of education" has been perverted and distorted in such a way as to make it unrecognizable to earlier scientific reformers.

Science and technology have invaded the schoolhouse in three basic ways: (1) in terms of an (allegedly) enlarged understanding of the processes by which students acquire information and come to understand it; (2) by transforming inherited teaching methodologies; and (3) by revising the patterns under which schools are organized and administered. Any sane assessment of the scientific–technological movement in contemporary education must consider carefully each of these three developments. Though interrelated by intent and basic method, such fundamental transformations pose separable concerns and issues.

Psychology and the Improvement of Learning

The argument that educators can profit from a better understanding of the psychology of the learner seems unassailable considered by itself. Effective teaching methods must accord with the maturational development of the child, must "interface" with the evolving structure of personality, and must take into account such important variables as interest, motivation, learning style, idiosyncratic behavior patterns, special disabilities, affective needs, and psychophysiological limitations imposed by genetic endowment

[38] Raymond S. Adams and Bruce J. Biddle, *Realities of Teaching* (New York: Holt, Rinehart and Winston, 1970), p. 98.

or by interaction with the environment. Systematic understanding of all these factors is indispensable if the teacher is to facilitate learning. Rather obviously, nothing is to be gained by trying to defend human dignity or integrity by shielding teaching–learning processes from the probings of scientific psychologists—a point often missed by critics of, for example, B. F. Skinner's theory of "operant conditioning." On the other hand, most psychological learning theory has been preoccupied with the study of variables in extremely simple, stimulus–response situations and shows its inadequacies when applied in any reasonable fashion to real-life classroom learning situations. Even when due allowance has been made for the pretentious verbiage currently in vogue among educational psychologists, the better part of which is drawn from the rat laboratory, the fact remains that investigations of meaningful learning phenomena have dealt with human subjects as though they were all alike. Moreover, the "average" learner whose responses form the basis for erudite psychological conclusions turns out all too often to be a creation of statistical manipulation rather than a reflection of any flesh-and-blood subject. Still more fundamental is the question of whether better than a half century of hard empirical study *has* won any confirmed, testable results in the behavioral sciences. (It is not totally inapropos to wonder whether anything substantive has been added to man's traditional, informal understanding of himself with the exception of new conceptual frameworks for organizing his insights.)

These caveats aside, the gap between rhetoric and reality in education can never be closed without better understanding of the nature of learning and human development. Except when the psychologist lays down unwarranted, procrustean conclusions based upon a particular view of psychological functioning, he is a valuable ally of the educator and should be recognized as such. The educator will welcome any advances in psychological knowledge, while keeping in mind that the art of teaching is separable from, though dependent on, a scientific pedagogical psychology.

Technology and the Industrial Revolution

The transformation of instructional techniques through technology raises a different set of issues. "Conventional wisdom" of educational folklore has tended to recoil from the prospect of a school technology based upon computer-assisted instruction, teaching machines, and other automated devices, fearing that cold, impersonal machines will not only mechanize but dehumanize teaching.[39] The new educational technocrats who serve as proponents of a mechanized instructional technology have the stronger argument here on several points. First, they correctly point out that the hardware and processes used in schools today constitute a "technology" of sorts, though

39 See Ronald Gross and Judith Murphy, eds., *The Revolution in the Schools* (New York: Harcourt, Brace, 1964), pp. 10–11.

rarely considered as such.[40] "Gutenberg" technology relies on time-honored media, such as pencil and paper, chalkboards, textbooks, and teachers. It is instructor-centered and textbook-based. It is characterized by a high degree of active involvement on the teacher's part and a relatively high degree of passivity on the part of the learner. Whether its component elements be textbooks and chalk or sophisticated computerized information storage and retrieval systems, an instructional technology is relatively neutral. It is virtually value-free. It can be used to promote any objectives whatsoever. Students who protest against an impersonal, sterile educational environment do not object to computer hardware itself so much as they resist how it is used and the goals toward which mediated instruction is directed. The point deserves amplification because it has become a bone of contention between educational humanists and technocrats in recent years.

Possibly an educational system that accommodates human individuality is possible *only* through more efficient technologically based teaching approaches. A convincing case can be made for the thesis that automated media may offer the best chance yet to break out of the rigid instructional pattern decried through the centuries by reformers like Rousseau, Pestalozzi, Froebel, and Montessori. As both Locke and Montaigne pointed out, the ideal educational situation is one in which the learner is paired with a wise tutor who not only knows his subject matter, but is skilled in the diagnosis of learning problems and fluent in his knowledge of the psychological make-up of his charge.[41] He can tailor instruction to fit the special capabilities and requirements of the individual learner. Yet in order to reproduce such a system today, given the modern commitment to mass education, it would require unimaginable expenditures of money and an army of millions of teachers to provide even a ratio of two or three pupils to an instructor, an approach patently impractical of realization. Because the nature and extent of human variability are so overwhelming, technocrats argue, the only hope of truly individualizing instruction, of duplicating the tutorial mode within the foreseeable future, is to employ computers, involving real-time interaction between the student at a terminal and a stored learning program within the machine itself. Arguments on behalf of computers used this way reduce to three allegations: (1) that machines can better adapt to individual learning differences and thereby free the human teacher from the drudgery of rote teaching; (2) that computer-programmed instruction creates a more responsive learning environment; and (3) that computers facilitate more sensible modes of instructional evaluation.

[40] David Engler, "Instructional Technology and the Curriculum," *Phi Delta Kappan* (March, 1970), pp. 379–381.

[41] An eloquent defense of computer-based instruction along these lines appears in Harold E. Mitzel, "Computers and Adaptive Education," *American Education* (December, 1970), pp. 23–26. An excellent critique of the uses and abuses of educational technology, particularly with reference to computer-assisted instruction, appears in Charles E. Silberman, *Crisis in the Classroom: The Remaking of American Education* (New York: Random House, 1970), pp. 186–203.

On the first point, properly planned programs in all probability can be shown to be superior in that the learning format allows students to progress at individual rates with differing materials. If learning rates are a function of personality organization, sensory receptivity, and the like, the optimal instructional aid will adapt the presentation of material to the requirements of an individual learner. Instead of having to teach a body of subject matter by exposition to whole classes and thereby carry out a very low-order skill, the teacher is free to spend time on higher-order activities: reinforcing curiosity, inspiring creativity, developing interpersonal attitudes, diagnosing learning handicaps, prescribing remedial or supplementary instruction, and so forth. Simple exposition is the only role relegated to the computer program.

Secondly, for simple learning tasks there is impressive evidence that constant reinforcement, evaluation, performance recording, curricular continuity—in short, "feedback"—can be handled more efficiently by a teaching machine. In this (limited) sense, the computer does create a more responsive learning environment.

Finally, the intriguing suggestion is made that computers can help educators overcome the dogma of a half century of standardized testing and classical psychometrics. Traditionally, an "adversary" system has obtained in the classroom in which a pupil's performance is measured solely in relation to the achievements of his classmates. More relevant possibly would be an evaluation indicating what *proportion of instructional objectives* a learner has met. Mastery-oriented or "criterion-referenced" evaluation, which depends upon the assumption that there are operational correlatives to the achievement of learning goals—an assumption intrinsic to computer-programmed instruction—allegedly represents an alternative to the old system of deliberately designing evaluation instruments so that a certain proportion of students will err on a given percentage of test items. The usual examination, in effect, is constructed to maximize the differences among pupils' respective scores.[42] With computer-assisted instruction, in contrast, the tendency would be to remove harmful classroom competition and to substitute for it an opportunity for each student to progress at his own rate toward mastery of the learning program's objectives. Though the use of computers in the classroom would not be essential for the adoption of such a method, it would certainly encourage a basic shift in practice toward criterion-referenced instruction and evaluation.

Opponents of computer-assisted instruction evidence no reluctance to question these arguments and to raise separate objections of their own. First, it is claimed that although such subjects as mathematics, physics, and a wide class of performance–task skills lend themselves to a programmed format, other subjects, such as literature, civics, sociology, and the fine arts, do not. Hence the utility of computers, it is said, is somewhat limited.

42 A more complete discussion is given in Mitzel, op. cit., p. 26.

Secondly, besides the inordinate cost of computer hardware and software, it has proved far more difficult than anticipated to prepare good programs. Critics wonder whether a new mandarinlike class of programmers equipped with specialized, esoteric skills will not be required to devise new curricula. It is unlikely in any event that classroom teachers can be trained to perform such tasks. But this phenomenon, in turn, suggests the possibility of an undesirable concentration of power over the content of instruction in the hands of a very few, if and when computers are employed in the schools on a large-scale basis.

Thirdly, opponents allege, computers will inevitably accentuate the tendency to define learning primarily in terms of acquiring data, and knowledge in terms of replication rather than interpretation. The propensity to ignore the affective domain and concentrate on cognitive learning of a very low level will be perpetuated. The question is asked whether proper attention *will* be given to interpretation, synthesis, and application of materials learned. Can an automated technology in the classroom take account of the feelings, inclinations, attitudes, and values of students, or at least permit human teachers to do so? Mindful of Lewis Mumford's dictum that "every technical process tends, in its perfection, to eliminate the active worker from participation and to produce an effective substitute: the automaton," critics remain unconvinced that teachers may not be automated out of existence, or at least not have their functions so reduced that their contribution is negligible. So far there has been much brave talk about what the machines will do and precious little about the tasks reserved for human beings.

The standard rejoinder is to point out that a final decision on the matter rests with human beings: it is they who will finally decide whether they will become more fully "human" or mere appendages to a mechanical contrivance. The time when it becomes necessary to stop mechanizing learning, so the argument runs, is when it begins to robotize the young, and that possibility is not considered likely. Critics harbor doubts all the same and wonder if that time has not already been reached. Less persuasive is the argument advanced by proponents of computer-assisted instruction who stress the *inevitability* of a mechanized educational technology. Although it may be true that scientific technology will increase its influence over methods of instruction and that to resist the trend will probably prove as ineffectual as efforts by the eighteenth-century Luddites to destroy factory machines and turn back the industrial revolution, an altogether different issue is involved when the *desirability* of such changes is thrown into question.[43]

The incipient transformation of education by science is not confined to the utilization of an automated technology. More pervasive in its influence

[43] See Donald N. Michael, *Cybernation: The Silent Conquest* (Santa Barbara, Calif.: Center for the Study of Democratic Institutions, 1962).

is a habit of mind, a global attitude toward a broad range of teaching and learning processes, ostensibly derived from the scientific point of view. It represents in effect a new catechism for schoolmen, lauding the virtues of precision and control. The new technocratic priesthood coming to power worships at the shrine of scientific objectivity, and its rituals evidence an overwhelming passion for certainty and objectivity. Because they deliberately view human beings from a purely "nonsubjective" standpoint, contemporary educational technocrats find it unprofitable to deal with phenomena which cannot be isolated in a laboratory or described in quantitative terms. Their desire is to move toward those aspects of educational processes easiest to control.

Presumably this ambition lies beneath much of the current rhetoric about defining educational objectives in operational or behavioral terms.[44] Unless the teacher can specify the behavioral correlates of learning, it is said, there is no way to ascertain whether in fact the desired learning has taken place, no procedure for measuring the outcomes of instruction. Instead of formulating goals in terms of "appreciation" or "insight" or "understandings," teachers should stipulate what the child should be able to *do* that he could not do prior to learning. Typically this means establishing minimal performance criteria on some body of information such that the student should be able to supply a certain percentage of right answers on a quiz testing the material. This becomes the instructional objective. The point frequently glossed over is that behavioral criteria are likely to be arbitrary for certain kinds of learning. Getting the correct answer may possibly indicate learning has taken place; it certainly reveals little about the student's feelings, attitudes, or understandings evoked about the learning. It does not tell the instructor whether the material has been perceived in any *meaningful* way. Or there may be reliable behavioral manifestations, but they are of a long-range nature and the teacher is not in a position to observe them. The social studies teacher trying to impart the concept of "democracy" might discover the student knows how to define and apply the idea. In principle at least, the teacher could even measure the student's attitudes toward democracy, given a sufficiently sophisticated instrument. Nonetheless the real measure of learning will not be revealed until some time after the student has left the classroom: in his participation in community affairs, in his voting pattern, and so on. Furthermore, it is not unreasonable to claim that some kinds of learning do not lend themselves to operational definition in *any* terms.

The technocratic mania for seeking security and safety through behavioral objectives for instruction produces some gross oversimplifications. The usual focus is on those behaviors that are easiest to define, such as the acquisition of concepts and facts, to the neglect of higher-level conceptual proc-

44 See Robert F. Mager, *Preparing Instructional Objectives* (Palo Alto, Calif.: Fearon Publishers, 1962).

esses and affective learning. Interpreted as a call for clarity in defining educational goals, the operationalist argument is laudable. As a generalization intended to reshape all instruction, however, it is simply grotesque. The requirements of *evaluation* can too easily overpower proper regard for the content and aim of teaching. Much the same criticism needs to be raised against those technocrats who tout classroom "interaction analysis" as a panacea for all educational ills or who reduce the concept of "teaching" to simple "behavior modification."

The New Cult of Efficiency

The third way in which scientific thought has affected education has to do with patterns of school organization and supervision. Accustomed to the use of mechanistic modes of thought for describing phenomena in the physical world, and guided by the criterion of efficient control, today's technocrats now find it congenial to describe such social institutions as schools in mechanical terms. Their analyses go well beyond the "cult of efficiency" earlier in the twentieth century when business–industrial values and managerial concepts were applied to educational administration.[45] The current technocratic obsession involves the application to education of "systems" models adapted from among those long used to describe mathematical and mechanical relationships and, more recently, used in developing modern industrial and military complexes.[46]

In the *investment* model, educational expenditures are analyzed as investments that result in predictable economic returns. Man is the machine, schooling is the input, and the output is the product of trained manpower or "human resources" that can be aggregated into the gross national product. Another variation is the *production* model in which the school is viewed essentially as a machine, educational expenditures are the input, and the output is analyzed in terms of manpower needs and supply. The *managerial–accounting* approach provides yet another model in which the operation of schools is analyzed in terms of functional efficiency, through cost–benefit ratio studies and integrated program planning and budgeting. Theoretically such a model answers the need for specific and quantitative information about all aspects of the educational process. It is presumed, among other things, that schools can be thought of as systems existing for the purpose of achieving limited but easily defined objectives. The goals are set by those that operate the system and remain reasonably static. Once assigned, material and human "resources" can be "plugged in" and manipulated in ways calculated to achieve those goals with maximal efficiency.

---

[45] Raymond E. Callahan, *Education and the Cult of Efficiency* (Chicago: University of Chicago Press, 1962). See also H. Thomas James, *The New Cult of Efficiency and Education* (Pittsburgh: University of Pittsburgh Press, 1969).

[46] A good introduction to the topic and a bibliography is provided by Bela H. Banathy, *Instructional Systems* (Palo Alto, Calif.: Fearon Publishers, 1968).

Among the objections made against such an approach is that it encourages the dependence of teachers on those who design and run the system. Classroom control is turned over to personnel not directly involved in the teaching process. Instead of aiming to produce free individuals with greater self-insight and understanding of their moral and civil responsibilities in the world, the educational process tends to be directed to the pursuit of external governmental or corporate-defined objectives.[47] It is further alleged that treating the people who live in and use the system as passive objects to be manipulated involves an equation of men with machines. A controlled system encourages the precision with which students can be shaped into identical sets of replaceable units to fit similar sets of institutional roles, the possibility of which creates nagging doubts about how the process affects basic human dignity. A systems approach either produces alienated teachers and students who will eventually rebel, or, worse yet, people who assume the characteristics of automatons. Opponents of the systems technique have a double fear in this respect: because no model is adequate to perform in a predictive sense when applied to human behavior comparable to its capabilities in the physical world, it will be applied to inconsequential ends, leaving broader educational issues to go by default; or models will prove sufficiently potent to make men reason only within their limitations. Either alternative is unpalatable; both serve as symptom of the larger crisis confronting education today: the need to discover ways of obtaining a high measure of control over educational processes without sacrificing certain people-centered values.

Unquestionably the greatest threat posed to humanistic values is the propensity to elevate to the status of unquestionable dogma the concepts of "accountability" and "assessment" in education. In an age of scarce tax dollars, proponents claim, educators must begin defining the benefits to be derived from schooling and developing ways of measuring results quantitatively, because education represents an investment from which society has a right to demand tangible returns. Alex M. Mood was more candid than some have been in recent years when he admitted that this can eventually mean assigning "cost–benefit" values even to such educational outcomes as "the culturally enriched life, the soaring abstractions of the philosophers, the magnificent cosmological concepts of God's great universe . . . or cavorting on the moon."[48] This extreme example of technocratic philistinism in its worst form is admittedly uncommon, and fortunately so, but it serves as a warning of the dangers implicit in the allegedly "scientific" approach to education.

---

[47] Consult John F. Cogswell, "Humanistic Approaches to the Design of Schools," in Arthur M. Kroll, ed., *Issues in American Education* (New York: Oxford University Press, 1970), pp. 98–117.

[48] Alex M. Mood, "The Operations Analysis Program of the U.S. Office of Education," in Werner Z. Hirsch et al., eds., *Inventing Education for the Future* (San Francisco: Chandler, 1967), p. 185.

The Resurgence of Positivism

It is when proponents of the "science of education" movement begin to harbor unwarranted ambitions that they become a threat to the creation of an educational system fit for human beings. The most basic hazard lies deeper than its surface manifestations in the implementation of an electronic instructional technology, the development of a scientific pedagogy for teaching and learning, or the questionable adoption of "systems" models for schools. The new technocrats constitute a menace insofar as they express, reinforce, and lend aid and comfort to a more general attitude (perhaps "ideology" is a better word) known as *positivism*. Fathered by Auguste Comte early in the nineteenth century, positivism emphasized the need for verifiable knowledge, for total objectivity, for the elimination of nonquantifiable speculation. It evidenced complete impatience with subjectivity, with the intrusion of questions of ends rather than techniques; it eschewed values for facts, intuition for science.

As Professor Michael B. McMahon has perceptively noted, positivism has become a rather common attitude today and has made its influence felt in certain pedagogical assumptions, among them the belief that the most significant aspects of learning can be accurately measured, that the administration of an examination is the best way of gauging the effect of learning on the student, and that objective measurement is necessarily beneficial to the learning process.[49] Some symptoms of the positivist mentality on the part of educators are the concentration on teaching objective external data and insisting that empirical performance is the only way of evaluating whether the data has been learned; an excessive concern for quantification, to the point where human behavior is distilled into standardized norms and statistical formulas; the pervasive use of objective rather than subjective tests or themes as a source of grades; the propensity to value individual students in terms of their performance, as measured against some scale; and an abiding distrust and suspicion of student subjectivity. McMahon concludes that while the appurtenances of an educational technology are essential, "in attempting to streamline education . . . we cannot afford to assume that a student's most significant insights can be objectively measured, that the ritual of scientism can explain the meaning of existence, that the totality of the human being lends itself to definitive quantification."[50] Protestations to the contrary, it is precisely those assumptions that today's educational technocrats are willing, even anxious to embrace.

Taken together—a scientific technology of instruction, reductionist views of teaching and learning, positivistic objectivity, organizational structures favoring efficiency over humanness—the elements of a science of education may yet prove beneficial, certain warning flags notwithstanding. Or they

[49] Michael B. McMahon, "Positivism and the Public Schools," *Phi Delta Kappan* (June, 1970), p. 516.
[50] Ibid., p. 517.

may produce an unmitigated disaster never foreseen by those historic pioneers who helped to bring it all about. "We have not yet learned to enjoy the blessings of automation without sacrificing human values in any area of activities," Harry Broudy once observed. "Is there reason to believe that we can do otherwise in automated instruction?" He concluded sagely that despite the hazards, "we have no real choice but to try to outwit the machine age, to seek therein the potentialities for human values that it undeniably has."[51] He might with equal justice have been speaking of all the changes wrought in education by the scientific–technological revolution.

SUMMARY

The organizing theme of this chapter might easily have been education for a stratified class society, education for an industrial society, or even education for a technological society. Many forces and values operated to determine the directions education has taken during the past two hundred years, among them, an unflagging hope for social and personal progress. Schools were utilized to strengthen existing class divisions, to make useful economic producers out of the great unwashed masses, to engender state patriotism and submission to despots, and occasionally to develop the innate capabilities of people as individuals in their own right. At the opening of the nineteenth century, the educational principles of Pestalozzi dominated most of European pedagogical thought, influencing such leading theorists as Fichte, Herbart, and Froebel. But the individualistic ideals of a Pestalozzi soon gave way before a still stronger social force—the spirit of nationalism. And it was nationalist sentiment that provided the backdrop against which educational theory and practice evolved during the next hundred years and more.

In Prussia the growth of an organized school system was closely tied to political events during the reigns of Frederick Wilhelm III and Frederick Wilhelm IV, followed by the two Kaisers. A tightly knit, regimented structure arose, with authority vested in the central government. Formal schooling was a handy device for promoting nationalist ideals and strengthening authoritarian traditions within the German states. Moves to democratize the system during the Weimar Republic were completely obliterated when the National Socialists came to power. The postwar reconstruction of German education required a virtual overhaul of long-standing ideals and cherished values. The story of French education since the Revolution contains many of the same elements: the struggle to establish schools, the enactment of legislation for educational improvements, and the development of distinct institutional types. Today schools in France remain under a strongly centralized structure of control, a pattern widely imitated in

51 Quoted in Gross and Murphy, op. cit., p. 11.

such countries as Spain and Italy. In England the achievement of a national state-supported system of schools was delayed until late in the 1800's. Private philanthropic agencies and church-related organizations continued to assume most of the responsibility for meeting educational requirements until early in the twentieth century. In its present form English education retains the principle of diversified control to a greater extent than any other major European country. As in other countries, however, the concept of private "class" education has died hard. Developments in such countries as Finland, Denmark, and Sweden have been influenced by the patterns established by Germany, France, England, and the United States. The pattern of educational growth in the Soviet Union, at least since 1917, has been unique to itself.

The hope of building a systematic discipline or science of education can be traced historically to the reformers of the early seventeenth century. In diverse ways educators like Comenius, Locke, Pestalozzi, Herbart, and Froebel were progenitors of the scientific movement in education. The full impact of this movement has not been felt until comparatively recent times, mainly for want of an adequate technology to service its requirements. Today's educational technocrats bear scant resemblance to their more humanistically oriented precursors in earlier centuries. The major challenge for contemporary education is to utilize scientific knowledge and technological know-how to achieve greater control over educational processes without forsaking some of those basic human values that education is designed to serve in the first place.

QUESTIONS FOR DISCUSSION

1. It was fashionable in the late eighteenth and early nineteenth century to assert the transcendent common bonds of humanity over national barriers. The concept of internationalism is once again in the ascendancy, at least among the intellectual leaders of many developed nations. What circumstances in the modern world reinforce this venerable ideal of an international community of man? What changes in education would be required to foster a cosmopolitan spirit among the peoples of the various nation states? Alternatively, what arguments can be mustered on behalf of *national sovereignty* as the supreme principle governing international relations?

2. Why were the Herbartian steps of instruction fixed in a rigid pattern to be slavishly followed without deviation? What other curricular or instructional innovations have been turned into absolute dogmas by educators?

3. What specifically was wrong with Froebel's theory of symbolism and gifts? Do kindergarten activities today take advantage of the young child's symbol-building capacity?

4. How important was the Prussian tradition of authoritarianism in paving the way for German acceptance of National Socialism? What other social forces account for that extraordinary period in German history?

5. Why did state control of education in nineteenth-century France tend to discourage the activity of educational theorizing?

6. Why did religious groups in France and England oppose the growth of a national system of state-supported schools throughout the 1800's? Was their hostility necessary or inevitable?

7. Compare Edward Baines' argument that private enterprise is the best mechanism for stimulating educational improvement with those advanced today in the United States against further federal involvement in education. In what ways are the arguments similar and how do they differ?

8. Review the opposing positions presented by John Tyndall and Thomas Arnold on the question of a classical versus a scientific curriculum. Are the arguments still alive today? If not, why are they a dead issue? If the debate is still active in contemporary educational thought, what new forms has it assumed?

9. It has been argued that teaching is basically an art. Is there any reason for supposing that it could not become an exact science? Assess the claim that many theories of teaching are compatible with a single analysis of learning processes. If the claim is valid does it not imply that the analysis is either arbitrary or incomplete?

10. Consider the following assertion of Raymond Houghton [quoted from "The Focus of Humanism and the Teacher," in Robert R. Leeper, ed., *Humanizing Education: The Person in the Process* (Washington: A.S.C.D., National Education Association, 1967), p. 59]: "The screaming cry of the approaching 21st century is that education is that which transpires after the last fitful burp of the computer." What does Houghton mean? What claim is being made about the nature of education?

8 Education for a Free Society

*To be an American is, primarily, to acknowledge a political commit-
ment, not a national or cultural identification. This country was—the
national myth has it—an empty place, where people came to make a
novel political covenant among one another.*

WILLIAM PFAFF
The Decline of Liberal Politics

*If a nation expects to be ignorant and free, in a state of civilization,
it expects what never was and never will be.*

THOMAS JEFFERSON
Letters

THE AMERICAN FAITH IN EDUCATION

An archetypal element in the social–political thought of America since
its inception has been an enduring faith in the power of popular education
and a belief that schools are powerful instrumentalities for the achievement
of a wide range of social goals. This is to say that the controlling power
and effectiveness of education has been considered almost infinite, in the
dual sense as cure for social, moral, economic, and political maladies and
as the means for enforcement of overarching social values and responsibilities.[1] Americans at various times have expected the schools to inculcate

[1] The point is elaborated in Rush Welter, *Popular Education and Democratic Thought
in America* (New York: Columbia University Press, 1969), pp. 3ff. An opposing interpretation is supplied by Arthur N. Chamberlin, *Mann, Dewey and Disaster,* an article reprint
by the Center for Independent Education, Wichita, Kansas (February, 1971).

468

religious orthodoxy, to instill moral virtue, to develop rationality or "critical thinking," to educate for the productive use of leisure time, and to enrich the affective life. They have been called upon to teach order, discipline, and democracy, the virtues of thrift, cleanliness, and honest labor, the evils of alcohol, tobacco, atheism, drugs, war, peace, sex, and communism; and they have been asked to help acculturate immigrants, to foster patriotism, tolerance, and, above all, to produce a universally high standard of literacy.[2] All this the schools sometimes did and still do.

To stress the impossibility of fully meeting these demands or to note the ignoble ends and narrow interests that schools have serviced all too frequently is to miss the point. The American faith in education, whether justified or not, was part and parcel of the original American Dream itself. The early colonists, for example, hastened to establish schools in order to conserve cherished traditions amid the threat of changing conditions in the New World. The founding fathers expressed strong concern for a system of education to buttress the infant republic. Jacksonian democrats quickly perceived the potential of schooling to help dislodge an allegedly "aristocratic" residue in early republican institutions, and post-Civil War progressivists worked hard to enlist the schools in the struggle for social reform. In the same way earlier, Whigs and Democrats both viewed universal education as an important element in social melioration—and that common faith has persisted on down through most of the twentieth century. The evidence is impressive on behalf of this basic commitment to popular education as a shared element throughout almost the whole range of American political thought.

In colonial days *religious* motives were largely responsible for the founding of schools, because even the humblest man had to be able to read the word of God if he were to attain eternal salvation. "It's with an ignorant sinner in the midst of all means," avowed Thomas Hooker, "as with a sick man in an Apothecaries shop, full of the choicest medicines in the darkest night: though there be the choicest of all receipts at hand, and he may take what he needs, yet because he cannot see what he takes, and how to use them, he may kill himself, or increase his distempers, but never cure any disease." Ben Franklin heartily agreed with Milton's declaration that " the end of learning is to repair the ruins of our first parents by regaining to know God aright."

Americans have been confident that schools could make men *virtuous.* Thus Noah Webster, writing in 1796, asserted, "Education forms the moral character of men, and morals are the basis of government." Almost a hundred years later the late-nineteenth-century Protestant clergyman A. D. Mayo echoed Webster's judgment, "How to make our children unselfish, just, kind, pure, honest, truthful, lovers of all men, able to live in our

2 Peter Schrag, "End of the Impossible Dream," *Saturday Review* (September 19, 1970), p. 68.

order of American society resisting its awful temptations and seizing its grand opportunities . . . —this is the task for the teachers in the American school-room." Mayo was convinced that Americanism and Christian morality were inseparable, "The problem before the common-school teacher in America is to hold before the child, by precept and example, in the most practical way, that Christian morality which is essential to high character in a true American." Thousands have adhered to that belief ever since.

Secular concerns played an important role in the American educational faith. The popular mythology had it that the schools offered the ultimate promise of equality and opportunity; that they enabled American society to remain somehow immune from the *economic* injustices and social ills that plague the rest of humanity; that they, in short, provided a guarantee of an open society. As Horace Mann summarized it in 1848 in one of his annual reports as secretary of the Massachusetts Board of Education, the school for all classes could be "a great equalizer of the conditions of men, the balance wheel of the social machinery. . . . It does better than disarm the poor of their hostility toward the rich: It prevents being poor." Marx was proven wrong, Americans asserted, because schools could provide a ladder to economic success and well-being. Senator F. A. Sawyer of South Carolina expressed that credo in 1870 as follows, "A laudable ambition to better their condition takes early possession of the educated sons of the American farmer, mechanic, or laborer. . . . Free schools have made [of them] an aristocracy of labor, and their places as mere manual laborers are supplied from other lands or by those who have failed to take the full benefit of the education all can now secure. . . ."

Another cornerstone of popular support for education was the belief that schools were the single most important agency for *cultural assimilation,* for introducing refugees from foreign shores to the great American "Melting Pot." Declared President J. H. Smart of the National Education Association in 1881, "I believe that the American school-room is the place in which that wonderful change takes place, by which the children of every land and every tongue, of every religious creed and of every political faith, are transformed by subtle assimilating processes, from aliens and strangers, into a sympathetic membership in the greatest and best political organization the world has ever seen."

Despite their faith in the power of the schools, Americans frequently evidenced strong distrust in *too much* education—"fancy book larnin'." Schools were deemed important agents of recruitment for the labor force, but the object of education was not to fill up a man's mind with "useless facts" so that he became a "learned ignoramus," rather it was to teach him how to use his mind to some practical endeavor. Education best served society, it was widely argued, when it developed each individual's highest abilities and intellectual powers. Henry Ford's advocacy of this position was typical: "The best that education can do for a man is to put him in possession of his powers, give him control of the tools with which destiny has endowed him, and teach him how to think."[3]

On one point Americans of all persuasions agreed: the indispensability of education for *good citizenship*. "A good system of education should be the first article in the code of political regulations," Webster insisted, "for it is much easier to introduce an affectual system for preserving morals than to correct by penal statutes the ill effects of a bad system." With Webster, as with so many other writers, the *political* function of the schools was expressed primarily in negative terms of what education would protect *against*—civil or ecclesiastical tyranny, anarchy, factionalism, disruption of law and order. In striking contrast to the argument advanced by some eighteenth- and nineteenth-century European writers, fearful of the consequences of an educated populace, Webster noted, "Were the poor laboring people . . . as well informed as those who have leisure and opportunity to read all that is said on popular affairs, faction would be deprived of nine tenths of its force. Opposition to our government would hardly exist in any shape. . . ." He concluded confidently, "Knowledge must be diffused among all classes of citizens; and when they understand public affairs, they will not do wrong." J. L. M. Curry, writing in 1884, agreed: "Education should be so conducted as to make good, law-abiding, self-supporting, productive people. . . . Without it, the functions of citizenship cannot . . . be safely discharged, or the just expectations of American citizens be realized. . . . The educated citizen becomes a bulwark of society as he has a stake in public order and welfare."

This theme went unchallenged as the decades passed, and the rationale for schools remained unchanged. Echoing Horace Mann's contention that there is no other human instrumentality so indispensable to the continuance of republican government, J. R. Preston, Mississippi's State Superintendent of Public Instruction in the early 1890's, spoke for many when he told his listeners, "To make a citizenship whose intelligence, moral rectitude, and steadfast virtues will counteract . . . disintegrating forces and social disorders is the function and the mission of our public schools." More positively, of course, schools were aimed at promoting a harmonious social order, a new society in which the "wretched masses yearning to breathe free" could do so without political or religious hindrance. Democratic

---

[3] H. L. Mencken saw the darker side of the picture, noting that in the American experience "teaching people to think" often meant precisely the opposite. The school's aim, he alleged, is "to make the pupil a good citizen, which is to say, a citizen differing as little as possible, in positive knowledge and habit of mind, from all other citizens. In other words, it is the mission of the pedagogue, not to make his pupils think, but to make them think right. . . . His fundamental function in America is to manufacture an endless corps of sound Americans. A sound American is simply one who has put out of his mind all doubts and questionings, and who accepts instantly, and as incontrovertible gospel, the whole body of official doctrine of his day, whatever it may be and no matter how often it may change." Henry Louis Mencken, *A Mencken Chrestomathy* (New York: Alfred A. Knopf, 1953), pp. 315–316.

government—the bulwark of civil liberty—made qualitatively new demands on the citizenry, American political theorists maintained, for unless each and every individual was educated to the highest level possible, he could not exercise his franchise intelligently at the polling booth. It is in this sense that American education can be said to represent a long and persistent attempt to realize a more "open," free society. There is no difficulty in showing the extent to which the schools failed in realizing this ancient aspiration. More significant and challenging, however, is a demonstration of how well schools *did* succeed in helping to give substance to the American Dream. As one historian has phrased it, Americans "substituted theories of education for theories of society based upon class order and theories of politics based upon class struggle, and developed the characteristic patterns of American political belief in virtual indifference to the social and political assumptions that shaped most of European political thinking."[4] It should be added, however, that this was only a gradual evolutionary development, not an instantaneous decision on the part of the body politic. It was well over a century after the first American settlements were made before the substitution really began.

THE COLONIAL PERIOD

The American educational experience began with colonists in an alien, forbidding wilderness attempting to re-create, preserve, and transmit their European cultural inheritance. Theirs was a deliberate effort to sustain the values, institutions, modes of behavior, and beliefs of the Old World. The primitive environment in which the earliest settlers found themselves was fraught with unknown hazards and unexpected difficulties: If America was a land of opportunity, it was equally a land of hardships. Perpetuating a civilized existence under frontier conditions was always an audacious undertaking if only because there was neither a dependable set of precedents nor a fund of experience to draw on; and novel conditions, it was soon discovered, dictated changes in the colonists' cultural patterns, social relationships, attitudes, and aspirations.[5] Many of their imported traditions, including educational ones, were found wanting in the struggle to master a new way of life. A fresh beginning had to be made.

This need for innovation assumes significance when it is recalled that the colonists of New England at least did not actively welcome change as such; they saw themselves primarily as Englishmen, working in an unfamiliar environment to reproduce an improved version of the theocentric civilization

---

[4] Welter, op. cit., p. 4.

[5] Bernard Bailyn, *Education in the Forming of American Society* (New York: Vintage, 1960), p. 22. See S. Alexander Rippa, *Education in a Free Society, An American History* (New York: David McKay, 1967), p. 4.

from which they had been expelled. They had little inclination to experiment, no desire to abandon familiar educational traditions except as circumstances required new social modes of organization.[6] Basically, they tried to reconstruct the Reformational society they had known on the other side of the Atlantic Ocean. In terms of educational activity America's first European settlers opted for schools to serve the needs of a hierarchically ordered community, a society explicitly authoritarian, having no precedent for anything but a very limited kind of formal training and schools left largely to private initiative. In light of the subsequent directions American schools took in later centuries, the colonial period in education marked a false beginning, a start from which it was necessary to turn away before education could become a cardinal principle of the American democratic faith.[7]

Regional differences among the colonies were pronounced. In the South, as nowhere else, the tendency was to try to reproduce as closely as possible a life style characteristic of old England. In the Middle Colonies a pluralist society developed, made up of diverse groups from varied cultural backgrounds. The northeast colonies of New England were more homogeneous in character—puritanical, authoritarian, and communal. In their educational effort, despite regional differences, all reflected a common propensity to rely on the family and the church as the main educative agencies. Few formal institutions of instruction were in existence, at least until the late seventeenth century. The burden of transmitting culture devolved on the family because it was the primary social unit as well as the most important agency for economic production. For all but the very affluent it was universally accepted that one would win entrance into the world of trade, merchandising, agriculture, and commerce through apprenticeship training. Whatever else was required in the way of instruction could be handled ordinarily on a private, voluntary basis by religious or philanthropic agencies. The kind of education demanded for all but the very few was necessarily basic and utilitarian. Although the idea was accepted that a commonwealth depended on an educated citizenry, most people assumed this meant no more than minimal literacy. For these reasons, schooling was not well articulated and remained very informal.

During all the seventeenth and most of the eighteenth century, the American colonies were governed by local legislative assemblies, by individual proprietors, or by royal governors, ultimately responsible to the English crown. From the outset, though schooling was more or less under the jurisdiction of governmental authority, considerable latitude was permitted in the local conduct of schools. As Bailyn aptly notes, the role of the state in formal education, though forceful, was indirect: "It was exhortatory, empowering, supervisory, regulatory; it was, with rare exceptions, neither

[6] David B. Tyack, *Turning Points in American Educational History* (Waltham, Mass.: Blaisdell, 1967), p. 4.

[7] Welter, op. cit., p. 22.

initiating nor sustaining."[8] Because church and state were bound together, wherever schools were to be found the religious influence on the content of instruction was pervasive. This remained the usual pattern until well into the nineteenth century.[9] Vernacular schools existed mainly to ensure doctrinal conformity to the precepts of their sponsors. Secondary-level Latin grammar schools, as in Europe, taught the religion of the local dominant sect, usually the Anglican or Puritan church. As a kind of subordinate aim, higher schools were designed to perpetuate class distinctions imported from the Old World. In this they exceeded very well, despite a growing demand in the 1700's from the commercial classes for a more utilitarian schooling, open to a wider segment of the population.

Meanwhile, what had once been a predominantly rural and agrarian society was evolving into a more cosmopolitan urban social order. Changing ways of life called forth new ideas and values, among them the Enlightenment concept of religious freedom. As yet little headway had been made in establishing common schools where people of different racial, ethnic, or religious origins could be educated together. But gradually the right was won for minority religious groups to found their own schools during a period when more powerful religious bodies insisted on sectarian instruction in the schools. Thus a positive gain had been made for the cause of freedom in the colonial period, and this institutional pluralism in religion and education was an important development in the American experience.[10]

The Battle Against "Old Deluder Satan" in New England

"We shall be as a city upon a hill," Governor John Winthrop announced, "the eyes of all people are upon us; so that if we shall deal falsely with our god in this work we have undertaken and so cause him to withdraw his present help from us, we shall be made a story and a by-word through the world." Almost twenty thousand refugees from Europe's religious, political, and economic turmoil had immigrated to the New World to carve out a home for themselves by the time Winthrop and his band won a charter (1629) as "The Governor and Company of the Massachusetts Bay of New England." Beginning with the Separatist Pilgrims' settlement at Plymouth in 1620, the New England colonies grew steadily. Their economy was based on shipbuilding, the Indian fur trade, fishing, textile manufacturing, industry, and commerce. A township system of local government sprang up as economic conditions encouraged the growth of small settlements and compact little cities. The rigid class structure of the Old World was success-

---

[8] Bailyn, op. cit., p. 20.

[9] Gerald Gutek, *An Historical Introduction to American Education* (New York: T. Y. Crowell, 1970), p. 21. Consult Lloyd P. Jorgenson, "The Birth of a Tradition," *Phi Delta Kappan* (June, 1963), pp. 407–414.

[10] R. Freeman Butts has advanced the thesis that a search for freedom—personal and social—is the persistent thread that runs through the story of American education. See his "Search for Freedom," *NEA Journal* (March, 1960), pp. 33–48.

fully preserved. At the top were the aristocratic landed gentry, the civil magistrates and, of course, the clergy. Beneath them were the free trades-men, farmers, and skilled artisans. On the bottom, as always, were unskilled laborers, indentured servants, and occasionally a few slaves. Within two generations Boston traders and other merchant-capitalists had founded dynasties and accumulated untold riches. By the mid-seventeenth century, Winthrop's "city upon a hill" was a prosperous, thriving venture.

The Massachusetts Bay Colony, under Winthrop's iron rule, became a veritable citadel of Puritan orthodoxy, a "Bible Commonwealth" modeled after Calvin's Geneva. Puritanism, the controlling ideology, was founded on absolute faith in God's majestic omnipotence and man's total impotence. Jonathan Edward's sermon addressed to children entitled "Sinners in the Hands of an Angry God" drove home the point that man is utterly power-less to save himself from the torments of eternal damnation. "You are all naturally in a miserable state and condition," he thundered. "In a little while you will be in eternity, some sooner and some later. . . . God is angry with you every day. How dreadful to have God angry with you. How dreadful it will be to be in Hell among the devils and to know that you must be there to all eternity. Consider how it will be when you come to die and are unconverted." Only God could save poor sinners suspended precariously over the devil's lair. According to the Calvinist doctrine of predestination, those headed for heavenly bliss had been saved by God to be examples of piety to their unenlightened brethren. They were a divine elect charged with safeguarding the purity of the faith. Those who opposed the Puritan oligarchy were not among the chosen few naturally and their dissent need not be tolerated; indeed, to do so might be an act of defiance against God's will. And so there emerged a dour, narrow theocratic state, committed to social unity through religious conformity. Puritan thought exalted the virtues of sobriety, asceticism, diligence, and thrift in personal conduct. Those whose souls were destined to be saved, it was thought, would manifest their spiritual purity in their work. God would reward the honest laborer who pursued his vocation faithfully. His successful struggle for economic survival would be an outward sign of an inner state of grace. In this way the Protestant ethic extolled a creed ideally suited to the mercantile class.

In Puritan eyes, the child was but a small-sized adult, conceived in sin and born with a corrupted nature. Constant discipline was needed to curb the child's evil impulses, suppress his carnal desires, and bring him to the ways of God. As Jonathan Edwards warned, "Let children obey their par-ents, and yield to their instructions, and submit to their orders, as they would inherit a blessing and not a curse. For we have reason to think, from many things in the word of God, that nothing has a greater tendency to bring a curse on persons in this world, and on all their temporal concerns, than undutiful, unsubmissive, disorderly behavior in children towards their parents." When gentle admonitions failed, parents resorted to blows and whippings. If those did not suffice, the community's preachers stoked the fires of hell to a pure white heat, inviting children to contemplate their fate below if they did not obey in this world above. And if even this did not achieve the desired effect, there was always the threat of physical death itself. No "rude, stubborn and unruly" child could be allowed to continue unpunished. Accordingly, the Commonwealth passed a law stating that "if a man have a stubborn or rebellious son of sufficient years of understanding, viz. 16, who will not obey the voice of his father or the voice of his mother, and when they have chastened him will not harken to them, then shall his father and mother being his natural parents, lay hold on him, and bring him to the magistrates assembled in court, and testify to them by sufficient evidence that this their son is stubborn and rebellious, and will not obey their voice and chastizement, but lives in sundry notorious crimes, *such a son will be put to death*" (emphasis added). This then was the harsh, unforgiving world of the New England Puritan.

The colonial determination to seek God's acceptance led early to some concern for education, both so that children might learn to read the Bible and to provide for a literate clergy. Despite the rigors of frontier life the first settlers found time to build schools and enact legislation relating to education. "After God had carried us safe to New England," reports the *New England's First Fruits* (1643), "and we had built our houses, provided necessities for our livelihood, reared convenient places for God's worship, and settled the civil government: one of the next things we longed for, and looked after was to advance learning and perpetuate it to posterity; dreading to leave an illiterate ministry to the churches, when our present ministers shall lie in the dust." The first major step was taken only two decades after the first settlement of the Bay Colony. In 1642 the General Court of Massachusetts passed a compulsory education law requiring selectmen to evaluate the literacy of their towns' children and to levy penalties against those apprentices' masters or parents whose charges could not "read and understand the principles of religion and the capital laws of the country." In some respects the 1642 law was like the English Poor Law of 1601 providing instruction for pauper apprentices. Nothing was said about making the establishment or maintenance of schools obligatory nor was it suggested that school attendance be made compulsory, only that all children be taught the rudiments of reading. It was further ordered that children be removed from their parents' custody if any educational neglect continued, with a fine imposed on offenders.

Five years later, in 1647, the government enacted the famous *"Old Deluder Satan" Act.* Its Preamble began, "It being one of the chief projects of that old deluder Satan to keep men from the knowledge of the Scriptures, as in former times by keeping them in an unknown tongue, so in these latter times by persuading from the use of tongues, that so at least the true sense and meaning of the original might be clouded by false glosses of saint-seeming deceivers, that learning may not be buried in the grave of our fathers in the church and commonwealth, the Lord assisting our endeavors"—a compulsory school maintenance law was absolutely necessary. Towns of fifty or more families were instructed to appoint someone to teach "all such children as shall resort to him to write and read," the schoolmaster to "be paid either by the parents or masters of such children, or by the inhabitants in general." Larger towns of a hundred or more householders were also ordered to establish a secondary-level grammar school and employ a teacher to prepare youths for advanced education. The "Deluder Satan" Act was the *first* legal claim in America of the government's right to require education, compel towns to organize schools, and permit civil authorities to levy taxes for school support. Connecticut followed with similar statutes between 1650 and 1700, as did New Hampshire between 1693 and 1719. Widespread noncompliance and lax enforcement were the general rule for many decades, although legislative attempts were made to correct the situation by increasing the fines for disobedience.[11]

Most colonial towns already were maintaining some kind of formal school long before the statutes of 1642 and 1647. One common type was the *dame school*. It was a direct import from England, where widows or spinsters opened a room (usually the kitchen) in their private homes to children of the community. There they taught girls sewing, knitting, religion, and the rudiments of reading. Young boys also attended, with all students' fees paid by their parents or the local town officials. Few pupils remained more than a few weeks and rarely beyond a single year. The quality of instruction was exceedingly poor. Most "dames" themselves had little or no schooling and could do nothing more than teach elementary counting and the letters of the alphabet. The public attitude toward dame schools is best revealed in one town's statement, "Twelve months of school taught by a female is to be counted as equivalent to four and four-fifths months of a master's school."

Town schools were the other elementary-level institutional type in New England. Better than half the towns of Massachusetts had founded such schools by the mid-1600's; the others remained content with privately managed ventures supported wholly through tuition charges. Occasionally a master's fees would be supplemented by small grants from public funds. Larger cities boasted many private schools competing with the tax-supported town schools. Reading and writing schools, as they were called, offered instruction in elementary arithmetic, writing, reading, and religion. The teaching master might be an itinerant "n'er-do-well" or a highly capable college graduate, an indentured servant, or a ministerial candidate awaiting

---

11 See M. W. Jernegan, *Laboring and Dependent Classes in Colonial America, 1607–1783* (Chicago: University of Chicago Press, 1931), p. 125. It distorts the facts to suppose the main motive for increased education in the colonies was the democratic spirit. Religious concern, not social or political ones, were namely responsible for interest in schools. John Winthrop, for one, was typical in his outspoken contempt for democracy. It was, he alleged, "the meanest and worst of all forms of government."

a parish assignment. Discipline in the town school was harsh, strict, and physical. Many a student learned his ABC's to the tune of a thrashing birch rod wielded by a quick-tempered, unforgiving teacher. Classes were entirely ungraded. Rote memorization and recitation were the instructional methods commonly employed in these simple primary schools.

The first "text" from which children learned was the *hornbook*, a sheet of parchment paper fastened on a board and fitted with a transparent cover of cow's horn to keep the paper clean. On it were written the letters of the alphabet, vowels, syllables, the text of the doctrine of the Trinity, and the Lord's Prayer. The next and most widely used colonial school book was the *New England Primer*, first appearing in 1660 and issued under numerous editions in following decades.[12] It contained the alphabet, syllabic combinations known as the "syllabarium," and a series of rhymed couplets illustrated with woodcuts for each letter of the alphabet. These began "In Adam's fall, We sinned all" and concluded with "Zaccheus he, Did climb the tree, his Lord to see." Also included were prayers, hymns, catechisms, the Lord's Prayer, church creeds, the Ten Commandments, and short sermons bearing such titles as "The Dutiful Child's Promises" and "The Duty of Children Towards Their Parents." Stern Calvinistic doctrine was taught on every page through poems describing the misery of human life, the horrors awaiting the ungodly beyond the grave, and promises of rich rewards, temporal and spiritual, for those who learned their lessons well. One edition of the *Primer* contained for the edification of its readers John Cotton's immortal "Spiritual Milk for American Babes, Drawn Out of the Breasts of Both Testaments for Their Souls Nourishment" as well as John Roger's poem, "Exortation to His Children." This latter work was enlivened by a woodcut showing Rogers (a Protestant martyr during the reign of Queen Mary) being burned at the stake, with his wife and children looking on. The final feature was an allegorical tale warning youth that the devil lurked at every turn, ready to seize upon the souls of the unwary. Only the most obstinate pupil could miss the point that his sole hope for a successful departure from this earthly vale of tears lay in strict application to school lessons.

Other popular texts of the colonial period included Isaiah Thomas' *Tommy Book for All Little Masters and Misses* (1638), Thomas Dilworth's speller, *A New Guide to the English Tongue* (1740), his *The Schoolmasters Assistant*, an arithmetic text (1734), and above all, a lengthy best-selling poem by Michael Wigglesworth entitled *The Day of Doom* (1662).

The earliest provision for secondary education made in colonial New England dates to the spring of 1635 when the citizens of Boston held a mass meeting, resolved to establish a grammar school (later called the *Boston Public Latin School*) partly supported by public tax revenues, and elected *Philemon Pormort* as its first schoolmaster. Although the Boston school

---

[12] It was so popular that it has justly been called the "Little Bible of New England" and the catechistic reflection par excellence of Puritan ideology. See Paul Leicester Ford, ed., *The New England Primer* (New York: Dodd, Mead, 1899).

and others like it in Roxbury and elsewhere were intended to be nearly free, tuition charges had to be introduced to supplement town salaries paid to masters. Plymouth opened a similar "free schoole" in 1670 and fifteen years later ordered every county town to build a Latin school to prepare the sons of the social, religious, and political aristocracy for a college career. Portsmouth was the first community in New Hampshire to hire a grammar school teacher, trailed by the Connecticut towns of Hartford, Fairfield, New London, and New Haven. By the early 1700's Latin schools were in existence throughout the New England area. Later in the century as the tight little town system began to dissolve, local schools at both elementary and secondary levels were replaced by centrally located district schools. Connecticut began the practice officially in 1715, New Hampshire joined in the next year, and Massachusetts finally sanctioned the district school concept in 1789.

The Latin grammar school was a decidedly mixed success. It filled a genuine need in preparing students for the clergy or high government positions, but its aristocratic bias was poorly adapted to the changed circumstances of the New World. The Latin school catered to the needs of what was, after all, a very small percentage of the population; only a select few were able to pursue learning beyond the elementary level. Enrollment in a Latin school took place around the age seven or eight. The seven-year course of studies included geometry, arithmetic, algebra, trigonometry, geography, and religion, plus liberal doses of Latin, with readings from classical authors such as Terence, Caesar, Livy, Virgil, Cicero, Horace. This was followed by materials drawn from Homer, Hesiod, and Isocrates.[13] Teachers in secondary institutions were invariably licensed by the church, though no moves were made to set standards of certification. Perhaps the exceptionally meager salaries (sometimes paid in corn, barley, wheat, or other foodstuffs) account for the generally low caliber of Latin schoolmasters. Great teachers like Elijah Corlett or Ezekiel Cheever (master of the famous Ipswich Grammar School between 1650 and 1670 and later headmaster at Boston for almost forty years) were rarities. Most colonial pedagogues were badly prepared, indifferent teachers with little concern for the intellectual welfare of their students. It must be remembered, though, that Latin grammar schools offered the only type of secondary education available in colonial America until the late eighteenth century. At that time private academies began to appear in large numbers. One of the most outstanding of these was the Philadelphia Academy founded by Benjamin Franklin in 1751. Others included the Washington Academy in New Jersey, the Newark Academy in Delaware, and Phillips Academy in Massachusetts. All catered to children of middle-class merchants able to pay stiff tuition fees.

13 Samuel Eliot Morison, *The Intellectual Life of Colonial New England* (New York: New York University Press, 1956), pp. 105–106.

Harvard College opened its doors in 1638 to train Latin school graduates for the ministry or other professional positions. The new college was supported by both public and private resources, with tuition fees accounting for only a small proportion of its revenues. A bad beginning was made in the appointment of Nathaniel Eaton as its first head and professor. He reportedly beat his students unmercifully and kept them virtual house prisoners, while his wife fed them vermin-infested food. Both were finally dismissed for embezzlement and Henry Dunster was appointed president in Eaton's stead. It was Dunster who upgraded instruction, won college status for the infant institution, and greatly expanded the curriculum. In 1650 Harvard was awarded its official charter and dedicated to "the advancement of all good literature, arts, and sciences" so that its students might be brought to "knowledge and godlynes." Emmanuel College in England was the blueprint for Harvard in its formative years. The curriculum was distinctly medieval in organization and spirit, consisting of the subjects of the Trivium and Quadrivium, with Hebrew, Greek, and ancient history added on. With the exception of William and Mary (founded in 1693), no other college existed in the English colonies before 1700.

Later institutions of higher learning continued the tradition begun at Harvard of sectarian classical instruction for an aristocratic upper class. Rutgers, Brown, Princeton, and Dartmouth were all denominational schools originally. Partial exceptions were represented by Yale, King's College, and the College of Philadelphia, in that secular interests were represented on their respective boards of governors. Gradually, throughout the prerevolutionary period, new scientific studies infiltrated into college curricula to alter the classical orientation of liberal education. By and large, enrollments remained small and the tradition of keeping higher studies in the hands of the socially privileged lost little of its strength.

In New England as elsewhere, apprenticeship training was ideally suited to meeting the needs of a colonial economy and hence became the pervasive educational pattern for most people. The 1642 and 1648 Massachusetts laws ordered masters of apprentices to give instruction in reading, religion, and capital laws, but at best trainees or indentured servants received the bare bones of a formal education. Those in the "servant class"—orphans, illegitimate children, the offspring of the destitute, and those apprenticed to a trade—could expect to remain functionally illiterate, save in unusual cases. Education was not an effective means of upward social mobility among the lower classes during this period.

Educational Beginnings in the Middle Colonies

New York, New Jersey, Pennsylvania, and Delaware enjoyed none of the cultural, religious, and ethnic homogeneity of the New England colonies. As a result, formal education remained under the control of insular little groups pursuing their separate ends. Each religious group, whether

German Pietists, Mennonites, Lutherans, Dutch Calvinists, Jews, Roman Catholics, Scotch-Irish Presbyterians, or English Quakers, tried to educate its own parish children in the precepts of a particular tradition. Geographical barriers combined with ethnic and religious differences to retard the growth of a common educational pattern similar to that founded by the Puritans.

In the English proprietary colony of Pennsylvania, *William Penn* tried without success to get a public school system started. His two Frames of Government, passed by the colonial legislature in 1682–1683, vested power with the governor to "erect and order all public schools" for teaching reading, writing, arithmetic, and religion. Sectional differences frustrated this ambitious plan and nothing much came of it. A later compromise measure abandoned the idea of state control over schools, providing only "that it shall and may be lawful to and for all religious societies or assemblies, and congregations of Protestants . . . [to] erect schools." With this encouragement, private groups assumed the responsibility of founding schools for their own constituencies. The Quakers in particular were active in this work, following a colonial legislative council act of 1698 giving them the right to establish schools "where poor children may be freely maintained, taught, and educated in good literature, until they be fit to be put out as apprentices, or capable to be masters or ushers in said schools." The Friends were also authorized to begin a public school "where all children and servants, male and female, whose guardians and masters be willing" could attend. Two factors prompted this activity. The first was a 1682 statute making some schooling for apprentices obligatory. The second was fear of competition from Anglican charity schools to which some Quaker parents were sending their children. The William Penn Charter School, founded at Philadelphia in 1689, was probably designed to counter subversive influences, and eventually expanded into a cluster of free elementary schools. At least one major Latin grammar school was also opened under Quaker auspices.

Although the colonial government reserved the formal right to license schoolmasters, actual control was usually vested with local communities. In Quaker and Mennonite institutions, students were taught to read from either the Bible or a scriptural text, *New Primer,* by Pastorius. Evidently many excellent teachers served in these parochial schools, among them the Mennonite preacher Christopher Dock. His *Schul-Ordnung* (1770) was the earliest text on pedagogy printed in the New World. As the German immigrants expanded their schools, parallel efforts were made by the Anglican *Society for the Propagation of the Gospel in Foreign Parts.* Between 1710 and 1776 at least a dozen charity schools were opened to combat the effects of education conducted by German-speaking sects. Benjamin Franklin was one of many leaders lending support to the drive for English schools in the colony.

A roster of Protestant Latin schools built in the colonial period would include the Presbyterians' New London Academy, William Tennent's "Log College" (Princeton's predecessor), the Moravians' Nazareth Hall for boys, the Moravian Female Seminary, and Linden Hall Female Seminary. In the Philadelphia area several private schoolmasters opened elementary and upper-level tuition schools for the richer classes. Most of them were free of sectarian allegiances.

Quakers led the way in providing primary schools for New Jersey, and Presbyterians did the same in the field of secondary education. From its beginning as a colony in 1665, New Jersey was always a haven for religious freedom (Catholics excepted). The Dutch Reformed Church, the Presbyterians, and the Friends as the dominant sects undertook to provide schools, reserve land for educational purposes, and support legislation for tax-supported town schools. When initial efforts to build a colony-wide school system floundered, a law was passed in 1695 requiring each settlement to appoint a committee "yearly and every year" to secure the services of a schoolmaster. The details of organization, curriculum, and type of sectarian instruction imparted in local schools were left to the discretion of the townspeople. In 1702, when the English gained control, public support for schools was seriously eroded, and popular education again became the exclusive concern of private bodies or philanthropic societies.

The history of education in the Dutch colony of New Netherland is the story of a determined effort to preserve a particular culture against the enculturative onslaughts of English colonists. The single most powerful educative agencies of the region were the Dutch Reformed Church and the Dutch West India Company. The church founded great numbers of elementary reading and writing schools, with financial assistance from the company. The latter paid teachers' salaries in the schools of New Amsterdam, contributed to the salaries paid in smaller town schools, and otherwise helped keep Dutch educational agencies in operation. The church, on the other hand, licensed schoolmasters, and directed local parishes in setting supplementary tuition fee rates. The specifics of church school administration always remained at the local consistory level. The first known school of the Dutch was founded around 1633 at New Amsterdam with Adam Roelantsen its first licensed headmaster. This and other church schools lasted for over a century, even after the English gained control. At Brooklyn, the first charter granted for a school was issued jointly by the local government and the church in 1661. New Amstel, in Delaware, had a similar school by 1656. Outside of urban areas, feudal patroons given land by the West India Company were chiefly responsible for building schools on their estates, although of course the church retained ultimate control over the kind of education offered.

Dutch schools usually stayed open throughout the year and had long morning and afternoon sessions. Girls were permitted to attend but the subjects they could study were limited by statute law. Tuition fees were charged in order to supplement funds from the church, not counting the poor who were given instruction without charge. The subjects studied, according to one contemporary report, included "reading, writing, ciphering, and arithmetic . . . the fundamental principles of the true Christian religion and salvation . . . the customary forms of prayers" and "manners." As the years rolled by, the doughty Dutch burghers began to fear such instruction would be insufficient to prevent their cultural assimilation. In this they were absolutely correct. English influence rose steadily in spite of tenacious attempts to stem the tide. In 1755, for example, long after New Netherlands had become a possession of the English Crown, the townspeople of New York sent all the way to Holland for a schoolmaster ignorant of English language to supervise instruction in the local consistory. "A man who knew no English would not surreptitiously spread that commercial language, and certainly he would not favor loosening church ties with Holland."[14]

The *laissez-faire* attitude of English colonial rule after 1664, more than anything else, accounts for the universal decline in tax-supported schools during the next century. A very few Latin grammar schools in New York and philanthropic charity schools for the poor were exceptions to the pattern of private or church control of all educational institutions. The only other schools not conducted by sectarian interests were commercial ventures stressing utilitarian instruction in accounting, modern languages, navigation, and the like. They were to be found exclusively in large cities such as New York and Philadelphia.

In the Southern Colonies

The first permanent English settlement in the trackless expanse of the New World was made at Jamestown in 1607. The next century witnessed a startling transformation of the entire Atlantic coastal region, stretching from the Chesapeake Bay area in the north to the southernmost portion of the Florida peninsula. What was once a densely forested wilderness gave way to an orderly civilized expanse of cultivated fields, bustling port towns like Savannah and Charleston, and stately river plantations. After the Treaty of Utrecht in 1713 the African slave trade plus a superabundance of fertile land made possible an elegant if still rural agrarian society. The basic economy of the southern colonies was founded on tobacco and trade with Mother England. A planter aristocracy arose, consisting of wealthy landed proprietors housed on vast estates. Freed by cheap slave labor for other

14 William H. Kilpatrick, *The Dutch Schools of New Netherland and Colonial New York* (Washington, D.C.: Government Printing Office, 1912), U.S. Bureau of Education Bulletin No. 12, pp. 154–155. Dutch schoolmasters were busy people. One statement of a master's responsibilities indicates he was to act "as process-server . . . also to serve the church, leading the singing and in reading, to arrange the seats, to ring the bell, and furthermore to hold school, to dig graves, and to look after everything else that is needful thereto."

tasks, the colonial gentry soon gained control over all positions in the social–political order, from places on the local courts to seats on governors' councils. Affluence bred privilege, prestige, and a sense of social duty. Throughout the prerevolutionary era the upper-class elites carried on the traditions of their well-bred English forefathers, convinced that economic power entailed a responsibility to conduct affairs of state in a manner befitting their station in life. Such illustrious leaders as John Marshall, Thomas Jefferson, and George Washington were all imbued with this consciousness of civic obligation. The vast majority of the population, on the other hand, were either slaves, indentured servants, or poor yeoman farmers. Those belonging to the lower free class, unless they found employment in the growing towns, were consigned to eking out a living on less fertile lands or beyond the edges of established civilization.

Because almost all the early settlers were of English stock, there was no tradition of public support for schools. As in England, education in the colonial South was primarily a private affair. The rich could afford to hire tutors for their children. Poorer families received little or no formal education, partly because distances between plantations were too great to permit the establishment of community schools, partly because the upper classes perceived no need for popular education apart from apprenticeship training. Sir William Berkeley's *Report on Virginia* (1671) was not atypical in its expression. "I thank God," the Governor exclaimed, "there are no free schools nor printing, and I hope we shall not have these [for a] hundred years, for learning has brought disobedience, and heresy, and sects into the world, and printing has divulged them, and libels against the best government. God keep us from both!" With apprehensions like these, it is small wonder that the cause of formal education made little headway in the colonies.[15]

On the rural plantations, private teachers instructed their charges from Lilly's *Latin Grammar,* Euclid, and possibly expurgated editions of the classics. Young ladies were taught French occasionally, the basics of reading, writing, and arithmetic, and, of course, the social graces. Sometimes itinerant tutors traveled from estate to estate if they could not find full employment with a single manor. In one or two coastal cities, private schools flourished for those who could afford the tuition costs. Otherwise, provisions for formal schooling were limited to the work of private charities and the *Society for the Propagation of the Gospel.* Their basic purpose was purely missionary: to instruct the poor in religion for the salvation of their souls. Even this encountered stiff opposition. A 1740 law in South Carolina prohibiting the teaching of slaves and Indians was copied widely throughout the South. In Virginia the sole legislative action relating to education

[15] For another interpretation, however, see William W. Brickman, *Guide to Research in Educational History* (New York: New York University Bookstore, 1949), p. 113.

was a series of decrees between 1624 and 1660 establishing standards for teachers in Anglican catechetical centers. A few *"Old Field" Schools* (so-called because classes were conducted privately in buildings on lands abandoned for agricultural purposes) were permitted in rural areas but given no public support. In the towns, for example at James City in 1646, there were *workhouse schools* for pauper apprentices jointly sponsored by the colonial administration and the various counties; still, they were so few in number that little was accomplished to correct the working classes' illiteracy.

In the Carolinas the Anglican *Society* was the only active educational agency. Limited help came from the South Carolina legislature in 1710 with aid to a "Charleston Free School" and in the form of grants two years later to parish schools, though church-sponsored schools were few and far between. The same held true for North Carolina: some money was given to a coeducational school at Newbern; in all other instances the Anglicans had to go it alone. The only school of any reputation in Georgia during the early 1700's was the Bethesda Orphan House, founded by evangelist George Whitefield in 1737. More successful was the work in Maryland when Anglicans began a system of county secondary "free" schools between 1696 and 1723. Little is known about the fate of that system, other than the fact that by 1728 poor children were taught without charge in county institutions. In addition, Maryland Catholics were successful as early as 1671 in getting legal sanction for "a school or college." How enduring this particular venture might have been remains unclear.

Sometimes philanthropic aristocrats in the southern colonies were moved to make funds available in their wills for a "free school" for orphans and other indigents. The first charity school started in this way goes back to 1635 when a Benjamin Symmes left an endowment of two acres of land and the milk from eight cows. In 1659 Thomas Eaton made a similar bequest of five hundred acres, a herd of cattle, and two black slaves for the purpose of beginning a charity school. Both the Eaton Free School and Symmes' Free School continued in existence for over a century and a half until 1805, when they were merged to form the now-famous Hampton Academy. Evidence suggests that many schools of the same type offered a rudimentary education to sons and daughters of impoverished parents throughout the prerevolutionary period. In spite of this, illiteracy must have been fairly widespread in the South until the 1800's.

William and Mary College, surely the most distinguished institution in the southern colonies, got its start from a 1661 act of Virginia's General Assembly sanctioning "a college of students of the liberal arts and sciences." No action was taken until 1693, when an official charter was granted for "a certain place of universal study, or perpetual College of Divinity, Philosophy, Language, and other good arts and sciences." James Blair, an ambitious commissioner to the Bishop of London, had arrived eight years earlier to get the project underway. Despite legislative opposition at the time the new college finally opened.[16] During its early years enrollments stayed small and its academic reputation left something to be desired (for example, frequent complaints were voiced against its professors for public drunkenness and night-long card-playing in the public taverns), yet it went on to become an outstanding institution. Among the college's later graduates were Thomas Jefferson, James Monroe, and John Marshall. Something of the institution's stature is revealed in the fact that the first Phi Beta Kappa Society was begun there in 1776. For those of the upper class unwilling to send their sons abroad for advanced training at an English college, William and Mary served admirably as a domestic substitute.

REVOLUTION AND REPUBLICANISM

Portents of the direction American education would take in the future were not lacking during the prerevolutionary period. Long before war clouds began to gather on the political horizon, there was growing dissatisfaction with imported European educational traditions. Eighteenth-century secularism was rapidly eradicating the last theocratic strongholds in America. Doctrinal intransigence gave way to uneasy accommodation as ecclesiastical monopolies lost power and it became impossible for a particular sect to retain exclusive control over education.[17] Minority religious groups won the right—slowly and painfully—to establish their own schools throughout the colonies and to conduct them as they saw fit. This was but one departure from the ordinary situation in much of Europe.

Secular modes of thought impressed themselves upon the content of formal instruction in other ways as well. The demand was heard for more practical, utilitarian kinds of learning, once again a departure from the prevailing Old World pattern. An emerging democratic society needed more schools, better teachers, and, above all, a type of education adopted to the commercial needs of a rising middle class. *Benjamin Franklin* (1706–1790) both epitomized and personified the values of that growing colonial bourgeoisie. In his *Poor Richard's Almanack,* published between 1732 and 1757, he gave eloquent if homely expression to the ideas of a people distrustful of purely ornamental learning, class privilege, and classicist intellectualism. Something of Franklin's attitude toward education is revealed in a brochure he published in 1749 under the title *Proposal Relating to the Educa-*

[16] Religious motives played a large role in its founding. When Virginia's attorney-general opposed the allocation of funds which he felt were needed elsewhere, Blair remarked that the people of Colonial Virginia were no different from Englishmen; they too had "souls to be saved." The attorney-general is said to have responded, "Damn your souls; make tobacco!" Fortunately for the cause of colonial higher education, religious needs won out over economic interests.

[17] An outstanding account of this development is given in Franklin Hamlin Littell, *From State Church to Pluralism* (Garden City, N.Y.: Anchor Books, 1962).

tion of Youth in Pennsylvania. He urged there the creation of three schools, a classically oriented institution, an English grammar school, and a mathematics trade center, for teaching "those things that are likely to be most useful" in the various professions. The advocacy of an educational system to serve practical ends was typical of his day. The original plan itself was severely compromised and only one academy was actually begun. It was officially chartered in 1753, elevated two years later to the status of a college, and subsequently became the University of the State of Pennsylvania—the first instance of a legally established state university. Throughout a long and colorful career, Franklin never wearied of preaching the worldly, down-to-earth virtues of middle-class education.

It is undeniable that colonial educational forms persisted well into the republican era. Yet it was clear on the eve of the American Revolution that the future nation would be compelled to devise its own unique institutional types. In order to service the requirements of a dynamic, expanding society, a new educational system would have to be created from top to bottom. The search for alternatives to existing trade schools, private or religious elementary schools, and classically oriented grammar schools of the eighteenth century is a major theme in the story of American education during the next half century.

Education and the Founding of "A More Perfect Union"

Well after the cannons fell silent at Yorktown and a new nation had made good its declaration of independence, there remained widespread fears of a strong centralized government. One symptom of distrust was the inability of the founding fathers to agree on the government's role in the field of education. Neither the Articles of Confederation nor the Constitution specifically authorized federal activity on behalf of schooling. Few disputed James Madison's assertion that "a popular government, without popular information, or the means of acquiring it, is but a prologue to a farce or tragedy; or perhaps both." The constitutional delegates were in agreement with him that "a people who mean to be their own governors must arm themselves with the power which knowledge gives." The question was whether a public, tax-supported system of education was desirable or necessary, or whether schooling should remain in the hands of private interests. For the time being, it was decided (at least officially) to remain silent on the matter.

Under the "reserved powers clause" of the Tenth Amendment to the Constitution's Bill of Rights, authority "not delegated to the United States by the Constitution, or prohibited by it to the States [was] reserved to the States respectively, or to the people." As a result, educational authority was conceded to the various states, thus laying the basis for the state systems that later developed. And if those who had written the national Constitution made no mention of schools, drafters of state constitutions were not

nearly so reticent. John Adams, who helped prepare Massachusetts' constitution, declared that a people's liberties and rights depend on "spreading
the opportunities and advantages of education in the various parts of the
country and among the different orders of the people." His state document
called for a "school in every town" and urged legislators "to cherish the
interests of literature and the sciences, and all the seminaries of them."
Massachusetts was the first state to pass compulsory school-support legislation. Every community of fifty or more families was obliged to open at least
one elementary school; larger towns had to add and support a grammar
school, under penalty of fines. Very much in the New England colonial
tradition, the state delegated most powers to local school districts. This
became the usual practice in the remaining states, thereby beginning the
vast local variations in public schools that exist today.

For a time the Middle Atlantic states tried to fulfill their educational
needs through a combination of private institutions, including Sunday
schools, privately endowed academies, and philanthropically sponsored
monitorial schools. It should have been apparent at the outset that greater
state support would be required, but only New York State enacted meaningful legislation to bring "all the colleges, academies, and schools" under a
state board of regents. In 1790 the practice was begun in New York of
providing state funds for education through the sale of public lands. Even
this modest gesture exceeded steps taken in other states. As the nineteenth
century began, seven state constitutions made mention of governmental
responsibility in the sphere of education. Few had done anything concrete
to match the noble pronouncements about the importance of free, universal
schooling included in their respective constitutions. That lack of effective
action was to continue for several years.

The situation in the new state of Indiana in 1816 was typical. Its constitution included the following statement: "Knowledge and learning generally
diffused through a community being essential to the preservation of a free
government, . . . it shall be the duty of the general assembly . . . to provide
by law for a system of education, ascending in regular graduation from township schools to a state university, wherein tuition shall be gratis, and
equally open to all."[18] However, education "free and open to all," it was
added, was to be delayed "until circumstances will permit." As one might
expect, the popular interpretation of "circumstances" practically guaranteed
that little would be done for some time.

In the meantime the federal government had taken one important step
on behalf of expanded education. Under authority of the Articles of Confederation, the Congress enacted a *Land Ordinance of 1785* providing for
a survey of the Northwest Territory—a parcel of land bounded by the
Ohio River to the south and the Appalachians to the east. Because the

18 Quoted in Carl L. Becker, *Freedom and Responsibility in the American Way of
Life* (New York: Vintage, 1955), p. 50.

separate states had ceded their titles to the central government, it was federally authorized that these western lands be divided into townships and further subdivided into sections. In the same year (1787) that a portion of the territory was sold for development, an official ordinance was passed ordering the proceeds from the rental or sale of every sixteenth section of land in a township to be reserved for educational purposes. "Religion, morality, and knowledge being necessary to good government, and the happiness of mankind," the law read, "schools and the means of education shall be forever encouraged." Nothing was said about the specific ways in which money was to be used to support schools, but at least a valuable precedent had been laid down for helping new states develop revenues for education. Ohio, in 1802, and almost every other state admitted to the union thereafter adhered to the provisions set forth in the federal government's ordinance.

The Question of a National Educational System

What is required in the way of formal instruction to safeguard the liberties of a democracy? How could the new United States ensure its domestic development, strengthen the acumen of its citizens, and foster a common national identity? These were some of the questions pondered by America's leaders when they looked at education during the fledgling nation's first critical years. One of the foremost advocates of reform was *Thomas Jefferson* (1743–1826)—statesman, Secretary of State, diplomat, governor, Vice-President, and President. "It is an axiom in my mind," he declared in 1786, "that our liberty can never be safe but in the hands of the people themselves, and that too of the people with a certain degree of instruction. This it is the business of the state to effect," he concluded, "and on a general plan." In 1779 Jefferson introduced to the Virginia legislature a Bill for the More General Diffusion of Knowledge calling for a state-supervised system of free elementary schools for white children in all counties. Teachers in the schools would be paid through taxes. A basic three-year curriculum was envisioned, to be followed by up to six more years of instruction in English grammar, Latin, Greek, geography, mathematics, and related subjects. Some twenty grammar boarding schools in each district of the state were proposed in the bill. Most students would be charged tuition. A select minority of charity pupils would be allowed to attend boarding schools; the most talented among them might even complete the course of studies and go on to William and Mary for a university degree at public expense.

Here was a remarkable proposal for broadening the state's educational framework. If passed, the bill would have opened the schoolhouse door to anyone desiring instruction (except blacks). Because the proposed system would have been publicly supported and controlled, in effect it would have enhanced the government's role in spreading learning among commoners.

Unsurprisingly, that measure and a similar Bill for Establishing a System of Public Education, introduced by Jefferson in 1817, failed to win approval from the state legislature. In retrospect, neither measure was very comprehensive: they both failed to make attendance compulsory, they denied equal opportunities to girls and to nonwhites, and the chance to advance beyond a rudimentary education was still tied to one's ability to pay for it. On the other hand, these proposals went far beyond any existing provisions and they did reflect in a very practical way Jefferson's belief in public education as the basis for a free society and his appreciation of the need for a literate citizenry in a democratic social order. Historically, his bills were important insofar as they helped to articulate a conviction shared by others that secular education should be a political rather than a religious responsibility. The only major achievement secured by Jefferson in his fight to improve schooling was the founding of the University of Virginia in 1825. Looking back on a distinguished career of public service, he counted that one educational success among the greatest triumphs of his life.

Some of the schemes for educational advancement offered during the first two decades after the Revolution were much broader in scope than anything proposed by Jefferson. In 1795 the American Philosophical Society offered a reward for the best essay on a "system of liberal education and literary instruction, adapted to the genius of the Government of the United States; comprehending also a plan for instituting and conducting public schools in this country, on principles of the most extensive utility."[19] The prize was shared by Samuel Knox's *An Essay on the Best System of Liberal Education* (1799) and Samuel Harrison Smith's *Remarks on Education* (1798). Knox's proposal fastened primarily on the question of curricular content instead of the issue of school control. He urged a classical course of studies in the humanities plus instruction to encourage American nationalist sympathies. Smith echoed the plea for patriotism through education, adding that the United States as a democratic model was on trial in the rest of the world. The Old World watched with interest to see if this new nation could harness the human resources essential for its sovereignty and continued prosperity. Benjamin Rush's *Thoughts upon the Mode of Education Proper in a Republic* (1786), Joseph Priestly's *The Proper Object of Education in the Present State of the World* (1791), Noah Webster's *Essays* (1790), and William Godwin's *The Enquirer, Reflections on Education, Manners, and Literature* (1797) all sounded the same theme. Residual Old World loyalties and sectarian or regional affiliations could not be allowed to impede allegiance to national unity. Only the federal government and its state divisions, one Robert Coram told his audience in 1791, could support a uniform educational system capable of creating the shared national loyalty so sorely needed.

[19] See Allen Oscar Hansen, *Liberalism and American Education in the Eighteenth Century* (New York: Macmillan, 1926), pp. 110 ff.

Virtually every major spokesman on the issue saw the shortcomings of existing educational provisions. Washington, in his *Farewell Address* of 1796, cited the tremendous importance of schools for the national welfare. Thus it was ironic that in an era when sentiment for universal free schooling ran high, so little agreement was found on how best to use education to buttress republican principles. The problem grew more severe with each passing year. Between 1800 and 1820 it has been estimated the country's population increased by nearly two million people. As the frontier moved westward, illiteracy probably increased rather than diminished. Before the Civil War the original union of thirteen states had grown to thirty-one states, half a dozen of them west of the Mississippi. Revived sectionalism and an ethic of rugged individualism together blocked any move for a nationally coordinated program of educational growth. Public education remained the responsibility of state legislatures, with responsibility for the administration and enforcement of school laws left to local officials.

In the end a delicate balance was achieved between state and local control. At first, state legislatures enacted *permissive* laws allowing school districts to levy taxes for the support of education, providing a majority approved within the district. Next, states *encouraged* districts to enact local tax ordinances by granting state aid to districts agreeing to support public education. State funds were raised from lotteries, taxes, or occasionally from the sale of public lands. Then the states *ordered* the establishment of school districts with taxing powers. Schools were compulsory but not yet free. They were supported through tuition fees and a "rate bill," a tax imposed on parents based on the number of children they had in the district's school. Lastly, the rate bill was abolished entirely and schools ordered to be self-supporting on the basis of taxes alone. Only then was free elementary-level education open to all.

Local boards of education, it was felt, ought to retain direct control in order to keep the schools close to the people. The local boards were to operate under the general authority of a state board of education, the latter either elected by the people or directly appointed by the governor. In this way the potential danger of a local school board neglecting its district's needs was averted. State agencies could impose minimum standards for all the schools of the state. Contrariwise, the fact that direct management of schools was left with locally elected (or appointed) officials, according to the prevailing theory, would ensure freedom, diversity, and administrative flexibility.[20] At the national level it would be many years before the federal government would play an appreciable role in education.

The Republican Educational Dilemma

Like all successful revolutionaires, America's founding fathers were mainly interested in consolidating and conserving their gains so as to ensure

[20] Butts, op. cit., p. 39. See also Gutek, op. cit., p. 53.

the continued survival of the new republic. On the one hand, they greatly feared European cultural contamination, with its age-old feudal traditions, its encrustation of illiberal institutions, and its perennial antagonism toward social egalitarianism. The strength of the newly founded United States, after all, lay in its repudiation of the Old World legacy. On the other, they were apprehensive lest the revolutionary movement begun in 1776 prove uncontrollable, leading straight to anarchy and factionalism and thus destroying the very civil liberties it had been intended to protect. This abiding problem of finding the balance between freedom and order surfaced once again in republican attitudes toward education. It was acknowledged that democracy needed a wider dissemination of learning, but it was felt that the schools should also serve to overcome any threatening excess of popular social ferment. As a result, republican educational theory fell far short of the radical democratic faith that succeeded it in the early nineteenth century, even though it marked a distinct advance beyond attitudes toward popular education prevalent in the colonial period.

Leading public figures like John Adams and Francis Marion harbored few doubts about the advisability of extending educational opportunity. Only when the new nation and the various states developed legislation to sustain more schools, they proclaimed, would the continued success of the republican experiment be assured. It was James Madison, for example, who argued that a national university along the lines encouraged by Washington and Jefferson would broaden the opinions, reinforce the patriotism, and harmonize the beliefs of those who attended it, and thus "contribute not less to strengthen the foundations than to adorn the structure of our free and happy system of government." Rhetoric aside, and for reasons previously touched on, such early republican enthusiasm for education was to prove insufficient for creating a national university or for building state systems of public schools. The heavy influence of colonial precedent was one factor involved. Most of the states concentrated their efforts on strengthening existing educational institutions rather than trying to begin new ones. Secondly, the mechanism chosen for funding education—revenues accumulated from the sale of lands or from other nontax sources—led inevitably to a postponement of school development until the chronic shortage of funds had been overcome.

Beside this restricted approach to educational expansion, republican thinking was also limited in its tendency to stress the conservative function of schools, at least as much as it was inclined to emphasize their positive contributions. Education, Jefferson once wrote, is "the most certain and the most legitimate engine of government. Educate and inform the whole mass of the people, enable them to see that it is their interest to preserve peace and order, and they will preserve it, and it requires no very high degree of education to convince them of it." The same theme, this time outlining the role of schools in the state of North Carolina, was sounded by James Turner in 1803, when he emphasized learning as "the mortal enemy to arbitrary governments, and the surest basis of liberty and equal rights." Law and order, freedom with social stability—these were the paramount concern of republicans when they talked about the function of the schools. Implicit in those concerns was a deeply rooted ambivalence toward the common man.

Frequently, a distinctly antiegalitarian note crept into republican thinking throughout the last years of the eighteenth century. In his fight for a state university, for instance, Jefferson perhaps inadvertently betrayed his bias when he commented that a national school would "promote in every order of men the degree of instruction proportioned to their condition, and to their views in life." The presumption was clear: the type of education needed by republican leaders and that required for the masses of men should not be the same. This *noblesse oblige* attitude, combined with the tendency to treat education primarily as the safeguard for civil liberties, revealed a critical inadequacy in terms of meeting the requirements of a new generation. Not only did republican thought neglect questions of personal or social utility in learning, it remained authority-oriented and geared to the existing arrangement of society. Although a second generation of republican advocates of public education proposed a more generous scheme for opening schools than their predecessors had achieved, the underlying social and political assumptions governing popular education had not really changed; they represented more nearly a liberalization of colonial attitudes than an adumbration of democratic beliefs.[21] The next development toward more democratic schooling had to await the first few decades of the nineteenth century.

LIBERALISM AND THE RISE OF THE COMMON MAN

Forces for Change

In the opening years of the nineteenth century the United States still depended mainly on charity schools, church-related institutions, dame schools, privately managed ventures, and tutorial instruction for the rudimentary schooling of its populace. Although secular influences were beginning to have some impact, particularly through the labors of William Maclure, Joseph Neef, and others busy importing the tenets of Pestalozzianism, an unregenerate Puritanism continued to dominate pedagogical theory and practice in the better part of the country.[22] The teacher was still the unquestioned authority in the classroom, standing *in loco Dei* to the child. Absolute obedience in childhood, it was held, would help prepare

21 Welter, op. cit., p. 37.
22 See W. S. Monroe, *History of the Pestalozzian Movement in the United States* (Syracuse, N.Y.: C. W. Bardeen, 1907).

the pupil for obedience to higher authorities in later life. Calvin E. Stowe, in his report on education in Europe in 1837 could just as easily have been describing the typical American classroom: "A stiff Orbilius of a master, with wooden brains and iron hands, orders [the boy] to sit perfectly still, with nothing to employ his mind or his body, till it is his turn to read. Thus confined for hours, what can the poor little fellow do but begin to wiggle like a fish out of water, or an eel in a frying pan? For this irrepressible effort at relief he receives a box on the ear . . . and next comes the merciless ferula." Attempts by enlightened reformers to break old molds, to introduce a more humane conception of the educational process, met with limited success, at least until the century was half over.

One notable change was the adoption of new textbooks stressing secular democratic principles, in preference to the old *New England Primer*. Noah Webster's famous "blue-backed speller," the *Elementary Spelling Book,* first issued in 1783, was a special favorite among schoolmasters. Liberally laced with aphorisms on the importance of respect for one's elders, thrift, obedience, dependability, industry, and moral virtue, it attracted the favor of middle-class educators wherever it was introduced. Exceeding even the Webster speller in sales were the *Readers* of William Holmes McGuffey.[23] They too placed great importance on the character traits of obedience, temperance, honesty, and patriotic fervor. Literally millions of copies poured off the press after 1836 to meet the insatiable demand for better teaching tools.

Ideologically, these early textbooks reflected the changing mores of nineteenth-century American culture. Publishers assured the public that their wares were "decidedly moral and religious," but an advertisement for *McGuffey's Eclectic Fourth Reader* in 1844, for example, announced, "No *sectarian* matter has been admitted into this work." Reflective of the growing need to accommodate to some religious consensus, the publisher went on to explain, "It has been submitted to the inspection of highly intelligent clergymen and teachers of the various Protestant and Catholic denominations, and nothing has been inserted, except with their united approbation. . . ." Furthermore, in the attempt to avoid any political offense, prospective buyers were told that "no *sectional* matter, reflecting upon the local institutions, customs, or habits of any portion of the United States, is to be found among their contents, and hence they [the *Readers*] are extensively used at the South and at the North, in the East as well as the West."

Textbook publishers readily reflected the political conservatism prevalent among educators in the early part of the century. "What better proof can we give of our wisdom," asked one schoolbook rhetorically in 1815, "than to be content in the situation in which Providence has placed us?" Another

23 Ruth Miller Elson, *Guardians of Tradition: American Schoolbooks of the Nineteenth Century* (Lincoln: University of Nebraska Press, 1964), pp. 160ff.

reminded its young readers that "the poor, disciplined into order, respect the rich." Equally important was the need to inculcate the virtues of hard work and diligence, nicely illustrated in Webster's turn-of-the-century "moral catechism," in which children were reminded, "Labor keeps the body in health, and makes men relish all their enjoyments. 'The sleep of the laboring man is sweet,' so is his food. . . . The rich and indolent first lose their health for want of action—They turn pale, their bodies are enfeebled, they lose their appetite for food and sleep, they yawn out a tasteless stupid life without pleasure, and often useless to the world. . . ." And, of course, school texts aimed to foster patriotic sentiment and love of country. "Our literature cannot fail to be patriotic," one author proclaimed, "and its patriotism will be American—composed of a love of country, mingled with an admiration for our political institutions."

Reminiscent of the saccharine tales of Dick and Jane, Jerry and Alice, that filled elementary reading books until recently, nineteenth-century spellers treated their readers to the exploits of "merry little George," who found a bright silver dollar and then wondered how to spend it, or of the happy little chimney sweep who successfully resisted the temptation to steal a lady's watch. About the only color and drama to be found appeared in tales of disobedient little children who invariably came to a bad end—the suspense provided by uncertainty as to whether the miscreant eventually would be drowned, burned, bitten by dogs, or simply crushed under the wheels of a passing carriage. At least these *dénouements* were an improvement over colonial versions where assorted devils or an avenging angel of the Lord carried off the offender to eternal perdition.

Common Schools for a Democracy

The basic educational problem facing Americans in the early 1800's was whether there should not be a major expansion of schooling to all classes of people—a universal system of publicly financed and publicly controlled "common schools." The crusade began in the East where industrialism, urbanization, and a growing democratization of politics were awakening people to the need for reform. As early as 1816 Governor Caleb Strong of Massachusetts was recommending legislation to provide for the education of children working in the mills of the textile industry. The cry was taken up by various workingmen's movements as they assailed undemocratic republican theories of education. They argued that the "axe of knowledge" was needed to chop down the last "root of aristocracy" and thereby destroy the last vestiges of antidemocratic privilege. Spokesmen for the working class decried the "monopoly of talent" represented by subsidies to a few select private schools which, they alleged, "consigns the multitude to comparative ignorance, and secures the balance of knowledge on the side of the rich and the rulers." Only when "the means of equal knowledge" was rendered "by legal provision, the common property of all classes," announced one workingmen's committee, could the abrogation of class-oriented education be assured.[24]

Despite the apparent logical inconsistency involved in championing *laissez-faire* economic doctrine and active state support for education, the Democratic Party was the first major political body to equate democracy with public education. Those who put Andrew Jackson and then Martin Van Buren into the White House accepted most of the arguments on behalf of common schools offered earlier by the workingmen's associations, and went on to advance arguments of their own. Such ideologues as George Bancroft, William Cullen Bryant, William Legget, and John L. O'Sullivan were acutely aware that the uncertain mixture of formal and informal educational institutions, private and public responsibilities, "aristocratic" and "pauper" schools could not long endure in the face of mounting popular pressures. Interestingly enough, it was not long before they were joined by National Republicans and Whigs who found it necessary to respond to the same pressures. At first an attempt was made to employ the concept of popular schooling restrictively, but gradually, in a progression extending from positions developed by Edward Everett, Samuel Sewall, Edward T. Channing, Jared Sparks, and Orville Dewey, a much more egalitarian perspective emerged.

By the 1830's it was perfectly possible for even a staunch political conservative to champion the cause of democratic schooling. Thus, for example, in an 1833 essay in the *North American Review,* Orville Dewey offered the following justification: "There are tendencies to a radical reform, so radical indeed, that if not restrained it will tear up every social institution by the roots, and leave nothing behind it but disorder, waste, and ruin. But," he continued, "we confess, without intending to say anything paradoxical, that we look to the very power which has given the impulse to control it. That power, undoubtedly, is education. . . ." Within a very few years, consequently, radical reformers and die-hard conservatives had found common ground in their dedication to the idea of public education.

It should not be supposed that the concept of a common school went unopposed. Tax-leery property owners joined with some wealthy industrialists in asserting that education should remain a private affair and not a public concern, that taxes on the affluent to support schooling for the poor would be a gross encroachment on sacrosanct property rights. Factory owners quickly projected their losses if children were sent to schools instead of laboring in the mills, and concluded the whole idea was bad for business. Some political figures viewed popular education as either a clever socialist plot to eliminate natural class distinctions or a subtle maneuver aimed at placing one political party over another. It was foolish, they claimed, to

[24] See Walter Hugins, *Jacksonian Democracy and the Working Class: A Study of the New York Workingmen's Movement, 1829–1837* (Stanford, Calif.: Stanford University Press, 1960), pp. 132–134.

think that schools could obliterate the inevitable differences among men by gathering them together for a common instructional program. The *Philadelphia National Gazette* in 1830 assailed the common school movement as futile: "Universal opulence, or even competency, is a chimera, as man and society are constituted. There will ever be distinctions of conditions of capacity, of knowledge and ignorance, in spite of all the fond conceits which may be indulged, or the wild projects which may be tried, to the contrary. The 'peasant,'" the editorial concluded confidently, "must labor during those hours of the day, which his wealthy neighbor can give to the abstract culture of his mind."[25] Not a few recent immigrants voiced their apprehension that a common, public school system would strip their offspring of the last vestiges of their ancestral ethnic identity—a legacy they wanted to preserve in the American cultural environment. At the same time, rural dirt farmers saw no real need for more elaborate educational institutions than their forefathers had attended. On different grounds, common cause was made by well-to-do taxpayers whose children attended private schools. Needless to add, proprietors of private agencies hardly waxed enthusiastic over the possibility of publicly supported competition. Further support was provided by unregenerate political reactionaries like James Kent, John Randolph, and Orestes A. Brownson. Their educational position was nicely circumscribed by Federalist Judge Joseph Story, who counseled teachers in 1834 to "repress the inordinate love of innovation of the young, the ignorant, and the restless."

Rural complacency and urban parsimony gained strength from religious intransigence. More than a few religious leaders refused to surrender moral and spiritual education to teachers whose religious beliefs might be noncommittal or unorthodox. Important religious values would be irretrievably lost, they argued, if the people abandoned church-controlled education. Still others, like Frederick Packard, secretary to the American Sunday School Union, attacked public schools on the grounds that they would lead inevitably to the total secularization of American society. Such fears were aptly expressed by the Presbyterian Synod of New Jersey in 1845, when it predicted that "the race of irreligious and infidel youth, such as may be expected to issue from public schools, deteriorating more and more, with the revolving years will not be fit to sustain our free institutions."

The campaign for common educational agencies proceeded despite this strong opposition. Widespread support continued to come from the ranks of the laboring classes, thoroughly disgusted with the "pauper" stigma attached to existing public facilities. Such spokesmen as *Frances Wright,* a Scottish advocate of working men's rights who had emigrated in 1819, and *Robert Dale Owen,* a prominent leader in the New York Workingmen's Party, proclaimed the need for schools maintained at public expense. A

25 Quoted in Alexander Rippa, *Education in a Free Society, An American History* (New York: David McKay, 1967), p. 106.

Philadelphia Working Men's Committee in 1830 drew attention to the fact that in some state districts no schools at all existed. Countless embattled humanitarians added to the clamor by arguing that unless better education was provided, growing social-class stratification would become irreversible. The enfeebled school apparatus available during the Jacksonian period of social reform positively outraged sensitive observers. They saw that only vastly strengthened schools could become a powerful force to help correct the execrable ills of industrial urbanization. Failing this, there would be no way out for the victimized thousands caught in mills and factories.

Among those publicizing the need for common schools was a zealous pedagogue by the name of *James G. Carter* (1795–1849). His polemical articles, published in the *Boston Transcript* between 1824 and 1826, drew attention to Massachusetts' decrepit schools, untrained teachers, and ineffectual administrative practices. Following a long and bitter struggle, it was Carter who was chiefly responsible for legislation passed in 1837 establishing the first state board of education. Trenchant criticism of poor schools was forthcoming from reformers like Caleb Mills in Indiana, Michigan's Isaac Crary, Robert Breckenridge in Kentucky, Ninian Edwards in Illinois, Calvin Wiley and Archibald D. Murphey of North Carolina, and Charles F. Mercer in Virginia. Calvin Stowe's report to the Ohio legislature on the strengths of Prussian schools impressed on the popular consciousness the shortcomings of American schools.[26] The American Lyceum movement, organized by Josiah Holbrook in 1826, lent its prestigious support to the common school movement. In this it was joined by groups such as the American Institute of Instruction, the Pennsylvania Society for the Promotion of Public Schools, and the Western Literary Institute and College of Professional Teachers.

In essence, proponents wanted an entirely new kind of elementary vernacular school for the country. The common school, they alleged, was absolutely essential for bringing together people of diverse backgrounds and creating a united citizenry dedicated to American democracy. A better mechanism was needed not only to Americanize the hordes of European immigrants pouring in yearly, but to provide that minimal literacy essential for informed voters. Editorials in William Russell's *American Journal of Education,* the *Connecticut Common School Journal* of Henry Barnard, and Horace Mann's *Common School Journal* constantly made the point that socioeconomic improvement for the working middle class demanded community schools free to everyone, supported through taxes, sustaining a useful, practical course of studies. Gradually people began to heed their message.

[26] Stowe was particularly enthusiastic about the Prussians' adoption of general taxation for the support of education, uniform requirements for teacher certification, and a standardized curriculum. Victor Cousin's report on Prussian innovations to the French people was widely reprinted in the United States and also helped awaken public opinion in favor of an expanded school system.

There can be little doubt that *Horace Mann* (1796–1859) was the single most influential apologist for common schools. Giving up a bright future in law and politics, he was persuaded to accept the newly created post as Secretary of the Massachusetts State Board of Education in 1837. He labored unceasingly in that position for almost twelve years. Overwork and ill health necessitated his resignation in 1848, whereupon he took John Quincy Adams' vacated seat in the House of Representatives. Five years later he assumed the presidency of Antioch College. Shortly before his death at the age of sixty-three, he delivered the famed commencement address containing the admonition, "Be ashamed to die until you have won some victory for humanity." All the evidence of Mann's life shows how assiduously he labored in the field of education for his victories.

His first task as Board of Education Secretary set him to stumping the lecture circuit to inform an indifferent public about their educational disabilities. Wherever he journeyed, Mann tirelessly espoused the cause of free common schools. Against criticism from skeptical mercantile entrepreneurs, he argued that taxation for popular education was "the cheapest means of self-protection and insurance." When appeals to civil responsibility failed, Mann shrewdly suggested that enlightened self-interest of itself should show how important were schools where people would learn to respect property rights and social liberties. When critics alleged that common schools would threaten class privilege, he neatly reversed their argument, claiming that only common schooling would suffice for preventing the growth of socialistic tendencies or anarchism among the lower working people. Furthermore, he was fond of saying, high-quality schools attracting the children of all classes would act as a deterrent to social-class conflict if and when people of differing origins mingled freely together. An added benefit would be the assimilative effect of bringing newly arrived "foreigners" into the mainstream of American life. Arguments like these made a powerful impression on his listeners. For those who prided themselves on their Americanism, Mann's thesis that democratic equalitarianism was incompatible with a dual system of schools for commoners and aristocrats appeared eminently reasonable.

Mention has already been made of religious opposition to common schools. Mann had an argument ready for his critics here too. Secularism need not invade the schoolroom, he was convinced; there was a central core of Christian beliefs that could be taught without becoming entangled in sectarian bias. Just as a pupil is taught about politics, without the presumption that he will be indoctrinated into any particular party, but to prepare him to share in the political decision-making process, so religious education in a public school "is not imparted to him for the purpose of making him join this or that denomination when he arrives at years of discretion, but for the purpose of enabling him to judge for himself, according to the dictates of his own reason and conscience, what his religious obligations are

and whither they lead." Mann's solution never proved satisfactory, owing
to disagreements on *which* religious truths should be taught, but the argument undoubtedly allayed enough religiously motivated distrust to allow
common schools to get a firm footing. In passing it is worth mentioning
that a vocal segment of public opinion today apparently supports Mann's
original thesis about religion in the schools.

In his *Common School Journal* and some dozen *Annual Reports* Horace
Mann pricked the public's conscience on the much-neglected issue of teacher
education. There is "no other worldly interest," he exclaimed in a burst of
hyperbole, of comparable importance than the improvement of professional
teacher preparation. At his urging, the state legislature funded three teachers' normal schools and enacted other measures to improve the situation.
Topics discussed in his *Reports* included the need for more financial support for schools, the advantages of consolidating districts, teachers' salaries,
and the training of educational administrators.

Mann's seventh *Report* was the result of five months spent in Europe in
1843 observing Pestalozzian reforms in Prussian schools. What prevented
American educators from adopting such marvelously effective practices in
domestic classrooms, he asked. A bitter reply came from thirty-one tradi-
tional-minded Boston schoolmasters identifying themselves as "prostrated
and pulverized by the hand of Horace Mann." Their plea for "stern virtue,
and inflexible justice, and scorn-despising firmness of the Puritan founders"
in school pedagogy infuriated their critic. His able rejoinder brought a
galaxy of distinguished supporters into the fray. When the controversy
subsided, Mann had won the attention of people the country over. He
lived to see his views vindicated in innumerable ways: flourishing teachers'
seminaries, a lengthened school year, a doubling of state appropriations to
education, millions of dollars funneled into plant construction, enlarged
libraries, compulsory school legislation, and a renewed interest in educational questions as far away as South America. Most importantly, by the
century's midpoint it was clear that universal, free, compulsory common
schools were destined to become a fixed element in the American educational structure.

Also significant in spearheading the common school movement were the
contributions of *Henry Barnard* (1811–1900). In 1838 he took the post of
Secretary to the Connecticut State Board of Education. For the next four
years until the agency was temporarily abolished, he traversed the state
preaching the need for public schools. Then Barnard filled a similar post as
state educational commissioner for Rhode Island. Like Mann, he induced
the legislature to increase school appropriations, organized demonstration
schools and teachers' normal institutions, and mobilized support for libraries in every community. At the age of forty-one he returned to Connecticut
to serve as a normal school president and resumed his post with the revived
State Board. He helped begin the *American Association for the Advancement of Education* and, as its president, edited thirty volumes of the

American School Journal. Barnard was called to the chancellorship of the University of Wisconsin in 1859 and to the presidency of St. John's College in Maryland in 1866. Two years later Congress responded to his pleas for a federal office of education and appointed him the first United States Commissioner of Education. He resigned in 1870, devoting the remaining three decades of his life to editing the *Journal.*

Barnard was a voice to be reckoned with in American educational circles during the nineteenth century. Possibly no one did more than he to acquaint teachers with the advances of European pedagogy, in particular, the teachings of Pestalozzi, Herbart, and Froebel. Politically conservative, his educational views displayed a liberal, progressive outlook. He was at his most eloquent when persuading the upper classes to lend their support to the common school cause or when advocating a utilitarian curriculum for America's expanding industrial requirements. The success enjoyed by the drive for public schools owed a great deal to his unrelenting propaganda on its behalf.

Massachusetts was the first state to take positive steps toward free compulsory schooling. Between 1789 and 1827 local district committees were charged with founding schools and given taxing authority. Compulsory taxation was followed by the abolition of the rate bill in 1827. Free education had become a settled legal issue in a majority of the states before the century's close, including Pennsylvania (1834), Rhode Island (1848), Indiana (1852), Ohio (1853), Illinois (1855), Vermont (1864), Connecticut (1868), and New Jersey (1871). Only in the South did reform legislation lag until some time after the Civil War. In the interval between 1852 and 1900, thirty-four states enacted compulsory school attendance laws. (Some states failed to follow suit until as late as 1918.) Two additional elements that went into the building of a modern elementary school system were the adoption of discrete grade levels and the implementation of a sequential or correlated curriculum, consisting of seven or eight levels (for children aged five or six to fourteen).[27] Yet another important advance was the gradual consolidation of separate reading and writing schools into a single institution. All three practices were begun first at the Quincy Grammar School in Massachusetts in 1850 under the direction of John Philbrick. Thus, from its precarious inception in the early 1800's and a century-long battle, the indigenous common school evolved into the familiar little red schoolhouse of yesteryear, ultimately the elaborate elementary school known today.

Pre-Civil War Origins of the Modern High School

Criticism of Latin grammar schools reached a new pitch in the post-Revolution period. Changing social conditions lent authority to the call for

[27] There may be historical irony in the fact that one thrust of contemporary educational reform aims at the elimination of primary school grade levels in favor of an ungraded classroom.

a more useful kind of secondary education than was generally available. It was felt an industrial society deserved something more appropriate than aristocratic institutions preoccupied with training the select few for college careers. In the new republic that was the United States, popular opinion looked with disfavor upon schools tied to an allegedly "dead" classical tradition. Vocational training of immediate utility now became the keynote of educational reform.

For a time the demand for vernacular, secular instruction was filled by privately managed ventures. Pedagogical entrepreneurs were more than willing to open schools for teaching any subjects whatsoever, so long as pupils were willing to pay the fees. Private schools were patronized mainly by the sons and daughters of middle-class merchants. Some founders of private ventures possessed impeccable academic credentials. Others were more dubious. As a rule, admissions standards were conspicuous by their absence, the quality of teaching was uncertain, and the instructional content unpredictable. Insolvency, new demands by a changing clientele, and the growth of another kind of postelementary school gradually relegated private-venture schools to a relatively insignificant position in the educational picture.

More enduring were the hundreds of *academies* which sprang up in the late 1700's. They remained in vogue for half a dozen decades or more.[28] In some cases they tried to supplant Latin schools while also taking on the major functions of private institutions. Those that did so offered both college preparatory work in classical subjects and vocational studies. The combination of a utilitarian regimen with traditional instruction in Greek, Latin, rhetoric, and logic was a large undertaking, all things considered; few really succeeded. Some academies opted instead for teaching "natural philosophy," that is, physical sciences like biology, chemistry, and physics. Others specialized in instruction for terminal students, usually involving algebra, mathematics, bookkeeping, surveying, navigation, accounting, or public speaking. "Finishing schools" for well-bred young ladies fastened on the fine arts, social amenities, and domestic science. Especially favored were "normal" academies for prospective teachers. Because they catered to the diverse needs of middle-class America, academies deservedly got an enthusiastic reception wherever they appeared. Townsfolk living in widely dispersed communities knew that without a nearby academy, their offspring would be deprived of any opportunity for post-elementary instruction. Public financing on a formal basis was out of the question in most communities; the tax base of the typical rural town in nineteenth-century America was usually insufficient to do more than provide rudimentary support for a one-room elementary schoolhouse. Therefore, the academy

[28] An authoritative reference for the period is Theodore R. Sizer, *The Age of the Academies* (New York: Bureau of Publications, Teachers College, Columbia University, 1964).

has to depend on local civic pride to supply endowments for its maintenance. The gift to one academy in Indiana for one year was typical: "one day's work, one horse collar, one steel trap, five pounds of coffee, six pounds of sugar, fifty pounds of flour and four bushels of wheat." Despite this irregular mode of financing, it has been estimated that more than a quarter-million students were in attendance in over six thousand academies at the nineteenth century's midpoint.

Academies were ordinarily semiprivate, rather than exclusively private affairs like their predecessors. They might be tied to a religious denomination or be under the control of a secular governing board of trustees. Supported by sectarian endowments, philanthropic stipends, or tuition fees (or a combination of all three revenue sources), academies soon found it necessary to seek financial aid from the state. The overwhelming majority were chartered by state legislatures in any case, and it was not long before ways were found to lend support. In New York, for example, two pieces of legislation passed in 1784 and 1787 bestowed regulatory powers over academies through the Board of Regents. Those schools conforming to specified academic standards as determined by periodic inspections were rewarded with grants-in-aid. In Massachusetts, land was allocated to proprietary corporations organized to found academies, providing they abided by certain state-determined criteria.

The earliest academies of note included Dummers, at Bayfield, Massachusetts, founded in 1778; Phillips, located in Andover and established in 1778; and Phillips, opened in 1783 at Exeter, New Hampshire. Less than a quarter century after the Revolution, the total number of academies in all parts of the country exceeded one hundred. A few are still in existence today. Wherever possible, these new schools adopted the boarding-school arrangement. A few boasted completely coeducational facilities; more commonly they restricted enrollment to one sex only. With the passage of time, some boys' institutions set an example by opening a part-time girls' division, but it was not until after the Civil War that secondary schooling for the combined sexes became commonplace.

The late 1700's witnessed a steady stream of textbooks geared to new instructional needs, corresponding to the unimpeded proliferation of academy curricula. Nicholas Pike's arithmetic texts, reprints of Thomas Dilworth's grammars, Webster's advanced readers, the well-known *English Grammar* of Lindley Murray, and Jedidiah Morse's history and geography represented only a fraction of the resources in widespread use. All had this much in common: they tried to remedy a lack of adequate tools for teaching modern subjects to the populace at large. Judged by the standards of an earlier era, they were a vast improvement over what had been available on a limited basis to private tutors. Without them, the academy movement would scarcely have been as successful as it proved to be.

Commentators disagree on the caliber of teaching in the early academies.

Perhaps the fact that no single pattern held sway renders broad generalizations untrustworthy. There were undoubtedly shoddy schools in the hands of charlatans, just as there were many outstanding institutions. The important point to be kept in mind, whatever their over-all character, is that academies marked a genuine advance for the indigenous American educational structure. Diversified curricula, the lack of stringent entrance requirements, and tuition fees set well within the reach of the bourgeoisie account for part of this. Democratized secondary schooling was opened to more people than would have been dreamt possible only a half-century before. As the nineteenth century wore on, more and more people were discovering the advantages of institutionalized education above a rudimentary level.

The expansion of secondary schools by itself was not nearly enough, according to some far-sighted innovators. Early in the 1800's, as a kind of counterpoint to the free common school rhetoric, voices were heard pressing for *free* secondary schools as well. Most of the arguments on behalf of tuition-free elementary education could be extended upward to academies. Was it desirable or necessary, reformers questioned, to have private groups retain control of postelementary teaching? Did tuition charges prevent able, poor students from continuing their studies? At issue was the idea of a system of state-controlled and state-supported public secondary schools. The first public institution of the type sought opened in Boston in 1821. It was originally known as the *English Classical School;* later the name was changed to the Boston High School. In its curricular orientation this historic institution was weighted toward vocational studies for "merchants and mechanics." A second public high school was begun at Portland, Maine, in the same year and New York City established another four years later. Five years following the founding of their first venture, the Boston School Committee started a Girls' High School. The response of the public was astounding. Enrollments exceeded all expectations, so much so in fact that the school was temporarily closed until 1852 for fear that the demand for female education would bankrupt the state's school fund.

It will be recalled that Massachusetts' 1827 school law had ordered all large towns to give tax support to secondary schools. Around 1850 the state could pride itself on having over one hundred intermediate schools within its own boundaries. On the eve of the Civil War the public high school was to be found in leading cities everywhere in the country. George S. Boutwell, Secretary of the Massachusetts Board of Education declared, "The high school must be a public school, accessible to the public upon terms of equality, without special charge for tuition." As yet this was not fully the case. Many, perhaps most, high schools were still charging students fees. It would require several more years before Boutwell's declaration was translated into national reality. Meanwhile the public high school was becoming a fixed part of America's emerging institutional ladder. During the 1850's several secondary schools began the practice of admitting students on the basis of examinations covering subjects taught in the common schools. All that remained was to devise a curricular sequence correlated with those lower schools in order to make the public high school an integral extension of elementary institutions.

The Changing Scene in Higher Education

Practically all the American colonial colleges were self-conscious replicas of English collegiate institutions at Oxford and Cambridge. Such leading higher schools as Harvard, William and Mary, Brown, King's College, and Rutgers were originally small in size. They drew their students from a socially privileged class and schooled them thoroughly in the humanistic classical tradition. Their basic intent, proclaimed in their founding charters, was to train a literate clergy and, more broadly, to educate society's civil leaders. Most were bound firmly to a particular denominational body, dedicated to teaching its special precepts.

A certain loosening of this pattern gained momentum during the early republican era. Deistic currents of thought and Unitarian liberalism were two forces softening the strict sectarian allegiance of many leading denominational schools, especially in the East. Some acquired completely interdenominational governing boards; a few went so far as to cut their church ties entirely. The Enlightenment interest in Newtonian science was bound to have an impact on the content of instruction. Alongside the usual offerings in philosophy, logic, rhetoric, and mathematics, several schools introduced courses in modern languages, natural science, and even vocational subjects like animal husbandry, business law, economics, and commercial management. As early as 1754, for example, King's College prided itself on a broad comprehensive program embracing "everything useful" in the disciplines.

Over fifty new colleges were founded in the period 1800–1825 in the Middle Atlantic states, in the South, and along the expanding western frontier. Some were Protestant denominational schools clinging to sectarian educational goals. A few others, in contrast, devoted themselves to agricultural and technical–vocational pursuits. An ever-increasing number of colleges were state-supported ventures—secular in tone, decidedly nonclassical in orientation, and less restrictive in their admission policies than ever before. *State universities* were another innovation transforming American higher education. When nothing came of attempts by Washington, Jefferson, and others to found a national university under federal auspices, state legislatures created publicly controlled institutions on their own.

The university-building process moved along three routes. Some schools, as in Vermont (1777), North Carolina (1776), and later in Kentucky, were begun from the ground up. Some were outgrowths of an expanded collegiate program. The University of Pennsylvania evolving out of Franklin's

Academy at Philadelphia is a case in point. Elsewhere, universities were part of an interrelated system of higher institutions correlated through the legislature. Georgia and New Hampshire tried to create governing bodies to consolidate educational centers into universities, somewhat reminiscent of the Napoleonic University of France. A New York State act of 1784 created a University of the State with authority to "found schools and colleges in any part of the state . . . every such school or college being at all times to be deemed a part of the University and, as such, subject to the control and direction of the said Regents." Less successful was an attempt in Louisiana in 1805 to create a University of New Orleans with power to establish a complex of county schools. The University of Michigan, created in 1817, was originally intended as a central agency for founding other state schools at all levels. Regardless of how they were begun, state-founded, state-controlled universities shared financial assistance, their curricula invariably were broader than the old classical programs, and they were thoroughly nonsectarian. Indiana began its first state university in 1820, Wisconsin in 1848, and a few other states did the same prior to the Civil War.

Support and encouragement for state universities were reflected in the national government's policy of handing over public lands to the various states for the express purpose of beginning institutions of higher learning, beginning with the Ordinances of 1785 and 1787. Later on, it became a fixed procedure for federal authorities to turn over two townships of land to each state joining the Union. Ohio's Enabling Act ordering land grants for universities created a model for other states as they were admitted. In the 1850's and 1860's a united front of businessmen, labor leaders, and farmers began demanding an expansion of land-grant schools to better serve their needs. Liberal arts colleges and denominational schools, they alleged, were not responsive to the demands of a technological age. Reformers harkened back to the early precedent of giving land to the states for schools and seized upon it to support their argument for a greatly enlarged educational program. Jonathan Baldwin Turner of Illinois was one of the first to lay out a plan for a state university financed partly through a federal land grant. In 1853 the legislature appealed to Congress for an endowment to realize the plan. The result was a bill advanced by Justin S. Morrill, a Congressman from Vermont, calling for land-grant assistance for mechanical and agricultural institutions. After much debate Congress passed the first *Morrill Act* in 1862. It allowed each state thirty thousand acres of land from the public domain for each senator and representative in Congress. Income from the land was to be used to support colleges whose main objective would be agricultural–mechanical training. Sometimes the resulting institutions were autonomous units; more frequently they were assimilated to state universities. The latter was the case in Maine (1865), Illinois and West Virginia (1867), California (1868), Nebraska (1869), Ohio (1870), and

Arkansas (1871). A second Morrill Act in 1890 authorized the creation of Negro schools in areas where restrictive admissions policies governed state universities and provided direct financial help to state-sponsored higher institutions.

The first Morrill Act was a significant milestone in the university movement. Not only did it greatly increase the number of state-controlled schools, it altered the direction taken by university-level instruction. For all intents and purposes the dominance of postsecondary schooling by classical–professional interests was over. However, private colleges continued to play an important role of their own in higher education. Events were to demonstrate that the rise of public universities was *not* incompatible with the existence of smaller, private institutions.

This issue was decided early in the nineteenth century. In 1816 the New Hampshire legislature determined to found a state university by revoking a 1769 charter granted to Dartmouth College by King George III. The private college's board of trustees opposed the move and took its case to court. Daniel Webster, arguing on behalf of Dartmouth, maintained that the state legislature could not retroactively annul the original charter because the Constitution forbade the impairment of all contracts. Any private institution of higher education holding a contractual charter should be guaranteed freedom from state control. Chief Justice John Marshall, speaking for the Court, agreed. Dartmouth was allowed to retain its status as a private corporation. This famous decision of 1819 assured the legal existence of all independently maintained educational institutions. From that time on no state body attempted by fiat or decree to absorb private colleges and turn them into public agencies.

Religious considerations aside, one reason the smaller collegiate institution was guaranteed a future in American higher education was the refusal of universities to consider women's educational needs. There was a deeply rooted prejudice against women pursuing formal training above the elementary level, unless the schooling was of the genteel "finishing school" variety. For this reason sporadic attempts were made to extend educational opportunities to women, either on a coeducational basis or in separate academies whose instruction went beyond the ordinary secondary level. One of the earliest women's schools was opened at Middlebury, Vermont, by Emma Hart Willard in 1807. Again in 1821 she created the Troy Female Academy, for girls seeking advanced instruction in subjects other than the domestic arts. When Catherine Beech tried to found a female seminary in Hartford, Connecticut, around 1828, public opposition grew so strong the school had to close. More enduring was the Mount Holyoke Female Seminary in Massachusetts, established by Mary Lyons in 1837. It was an exception to the usual short-lived women's colleges that sprang up in all parts of the country around the same time.

Resistance to the education of women continued unabated for many decades. Even when permission was given for coeducation at established schools, it was extended grudgingly and on a limited basis. Exceptions were Oberlin College in Ohio and Antioch College under Horace Mann. One compromise measure sometimes adopted was to found subordinate adjuncts to regular universities. Radcliffe College at Harvard and Barnard College at Columbia were begun in this way.

The one place where women could receive postsecondary instruction was in a normal school. Coincident with the growth of common schools, an awareness developed of the need for better teacher-training facilities. Samuel Hall's *Lectures to School-Masters on Teaching* (1833), written during his tenure as head of the normal department at Phillips Andover Academy, drew attention to the need for more centers where teachers could be prepared to work in lower schools. Under the pressure generated by people like Walter Johnson, Thomas Gallaudet, James G. Carter, and Horace Mann, teacher education programs were expanded drastically.[29] Massachusetts in the late 1830's and New York in the early 1840's assumed the lead, followed later by the Midwestern and Western states. Normal schools, properly speaking, did not offer a collegiate or university education. The typical curriculum lasted two years and only later was expanded to four. The level of instruction in most teachers' seminaries (including the better normal schools) was definitely inferior to that given in either private colleges or state universities. Eventually pedagogy became an established area of scholarly study and teacher training assumed its rightful place within universities' professional divisions, but those developments were a post-Civil War phenomenon.

Just at the time that denominational colleges were enjoying a resurgence of popularity, when public colleges were beginning to get increased state support, and legislatures were founding state universities, there began an important controversy in American higher education that was to continue for almost a century. It began around 1836, roughly at the time that Victor Cousin's report on Prussian education became available in an English translation. Leading educators in the United States, impressed with developments in the German universities, journeyed abroad to inspect the innovations then in progress. The universities at Leipzig, Berlin, Halle, Königsberg, and Göttingen were especially favored for the purpose. Scholars returned resolving to adapt American institutions of higher learning to German models studied. Henry P. Tappan, later president of the University of Michigan, offered a thoughtful analysis of the direction to be taken in his much-read *University Education* (1851). Others joining in the debates on university reform came to include Daniel C. Gilman at Johns Hopkins,

[29] A detailed examination of the movement appeared in Charles Harper, *A Century of Public Teacher Education* (Washington, D.C.: National Education Association, 1939). A highly informative analysis of the historical development of teacher education in the United States and a controversial assessment of its present status may be found in Silberman, op. cit., Chapters 9–11.

F. A. P. Barnard of Columbia, and David Starr Jordan of Leland Stanford. Their most frequently urged proposal was the redirection of the university away from its teaching function at the undergraduate level in favor of research activities and graduate training. Although some efforts had been made as early as 1814 at Yale in the field of graduate education, few major institutions before 1860 granted postbaccalaureate degrees or mounted advanced instructional programs. Few could have anticipated the momentous changes that were destined to rework the entire character of higher education within less than a century.[30]

CHANGES AND CHALLENGES IN MODERN AMERICAN EDUCATION

Aftermath of the Civil War

The firing on Fort Sumter in April of 1860 was followed by five years of devastating internecine warfare. When the holocaust was over and the South had been brought to its knees, a wounded nation struggled painfully back toward normalcy. In the former Confederate states, according to one observer's report, there remained only a "wilderness of ruins." The legacy of civil conflict was a maelstrom of sectional hatreds and bitter animosity. Resentment in the South at "scalawags" and carpetbaggers was matched by a vindictive lust for revenge among Congressional Radicals from the North. Schools lay in ruins. Economic dislocations coupled with political upheaval made the road back to educational reconstruction long and difficult. The problem was particularly acute in the southernmost portions of the country, although pressing educational needs cried for attention everywhere in the United States.

Efforts to rebuild the shattered system of schools were prompted in large measure by a postwar tendency to view education as the social cement for bringing the nation together once again. Northern spokesman frequently maintained that the South could be "redeemed" and its freedmen elevated only through a national program of public education. A government based on universal suffrage needed a far more generous conception of education for all the people, it was maintained, especially through a radical expansion of federal aid to common schools and colleges. Less enlightened was the tendency on the part of some political figures to oversimplify grossly all the complex issues that had led to the Civil War in the first place. Senator Henry W. Blair of New Hampshire, for example, went so far as to reduce the issues to those of simple ignorance on the part of Southerners. "Had

---

[30] Useful treatments of the history of American higher education are to be found in Frederick Rudolph, *The American College and University: A History* (New York: Alfred A. Knopf, 1962); and William Brickman and Stanley Lehrer, eds., *A Century of Higher Education: Classical Citadel to Collegiate Colossus.* (New York: Society for the Advancement of Education, 1962).

common schools been universal throughout the country there would have been no civil war," he told the Senate in 1884, "for intelligence among the masses of the people would have abolished the causes which led to it, and the chains of the bondmen would have dissolved like the mists of the morning in their warmth and light, instead of awaiting to be broken by the terrible hammer of Thor."

Postbellum Expressions of the American Faith in Education

That unflagging faith in the power of education evidenced by Americans in the early republican and Jacksonian periods and now in the immediate postbellum era continued with undiminished influence in the latter half of the nineteenth century. Before turning to a consideration of specific educational developments of the past hundred years, it is instructive to note briefly how this faith was given new expressions throughout the later 1800's.

American *farmers* constituted one power bloc anxious to extend both formal and informal educational opportunities to a broader segment of the rural population of the United States. Following the successful conclusion of the war, they set out to organize themselves into associations designed to enhance their political influence and increase their economic power. One of the tactics they proposed to utilize on their behalf was formal schooling. In the forefront of the effort to encourage national aid to education, to reinforce compulsory school laws, and to upgrade common schools was the *National Grange* of the Patrons of Husbandry. Grange associations sought two fundamental kinds of improvement: (1) better elementary school curricula, because lower-level education comprised the total formal schooling most rural inhabitants were able to obtain, and (2) the inclusion of practical subjects as well as the traditional academic disciplines. Basing their demands on simple social justice, farmers advocated, in the words of one spokesman, "a class of schools and system of instruction, which shall bring the means of a practical education suited to the wants of every condition of life, within the reach of every child in the community." The speaker at a national convention of Grangers in 1875 similarly urged delegates to help "establish a system of education, so much needed by the agriculturists of our land . . . by which equal justice can be given to all industries, and which will cause moneyed monopolists hereafter to cease oppressing the laboring classes among us." Like the Jacksonian democrats and workingmen's associations earlier in the century, organized farmers shared the belief that education was the great social equalizer par excellence.

Agitation on the part of *labor reformers* throughout the 1870's and 1880's also was directed at educational expansion as an integral part of a program of broad social improvement. Spokesmen for union associations like Wendell Phillips, Ira Steward, and Charles Litchman consistently detected possibilities for labor reform through the schools. As William H. Sylvis, a leading figure in the National Labor Union, put it in the *Workingmen's*

Advocate, "Give [workers] but time and opportunity to think, with even limited education, and neither the heat of furnaces, the clang of machinery, the stifled air of manufactories, nor the heat of midsummer's sun, would be sufficient to chain them to the contracted sphere assigned them by the aristocracy of intellect." By the 1890's, when the American Federation of Labor had come to dominate the labor movement, it had become a fixed article of faith that industrial workers' associations had a continuing moral obligation to lend support to education. Added strength to the idea that formal schooling would eventually compensate for pressing social and economic problems was forthcoming from the hordes of newly arrived immigrants who increasingly made up the rank and file of the trade unions. Despite the harsh fact that initial exposure to American culture via the schools did not always prove an unmixed blessing, for ethnic prejudices ran strong and cultural assimilation even under the best of circumstances could be a wrenching trauma, immigrants fastened high hopes on the schools for the betterment of their sometimes wretched condition.

Still another force working on behalf of the schools was the *Populist movement.* The People's party drew its main strength from a broad gamut of Farmers' Alliances in the 1880's, agricultural organizations patterned after the Grange but more strongly committed to some form of political activism. Like the Grange in their demand for more technical education in the elementary schools, the alliances took a strong interest in formal education at all levels. Gradually the various groups gravitated together and formed an organized Populist movement harboring aspirations to mount a new, third political party. Thomas J. Davis, writing in the *National Economist* in 1891, underscored the concern for better agricultural education in land-grant colleges and a strengthened system of high schools, "The first purpose, principles and aims of the Alliance and all other industrial organizations are education. The second purpose is the action, the good, the benefit we may obtain as a result of such education." The only significant difference between the views expressed by Alliance spokesmen and Populist leaders, as opposed to those of the earlier farmers' associations, was a denial of the old Jacksonian belief that minimal government would secure the general welfare if people were adequately educated. Now the argument had shifted: education can be an effective tool of politics, it was said, but not until state and federal government moved actively to ensure equal educational opportunity for everyone.

It would require a separate volume to treat at length some of the other social and intellectual movements engaged in educational work during the late nineteenth and early twentieth centuries. Postbellum evolutionary social theory, as expounded by Lester Frank Ward and Andrew Carnegie, among others, must be counted as one intellectual force underscoring the popular faith in education as an instrument for social progress. As Carnegie expressed it in his *Triumphant Democracy* (1886), the public school represented a "true panacea for all the ills of the body politic." The optimistic, expansive, reformist progressive ideology also joined in the chorus of praise for the schools. The Protestant "social gospel" movement of the late 1800's, in alliance with the ideologues of middle-class economic liberalism, undoubtedly reinforced the popular faith as well. Perhaps the only useful generalization that can be made in this connection is that it was not until well into the twentieth century before liberal democratic theories first came under sustained attack, in particular, the progressivist faith in universal suffrage made competent through education. For most of the nineteenth century at least, the growth of the American school system must be interpreted against a prevailing confidence in the power of educational agencies to effect broad social reforms.

The Unfulfilled Promise of Equal Educational Opportunity

Shortly after Civil War hostilities had ceased, General O. O. Howard visited a school for freedmen in South Carolina and asked the pupils what message he should take to their compatriots in the North. "Massa," said one little Negro youngster, "tell 'em we is rising." The first generation of emancipated blacks believed fervently that education would lead them to a promised land of opportunity—a hope quickly shattered for a people destined to remain economically suppressed, legally disenfranchised, socially barred by rigid caste rules, and frequently subjected to terror and outright humiliation.[31] The story of Negro education in the United States is part and parcel of a larger failure on the part of American society to give reality to the noble goal of emancipation.

Certainly one of the most urgent priorities requiring a sustained national effort within the field of education in postwar years, and as part of a comprehensive mandate for social reform, was schooling for newly freed Afro-Americans. Working against fearful economic odds and Southern white antagonism, Northern organizations such as the American Missionary Association and the Boston Educational Commission labored hard to provide school facilities for former slaves. "What a magnificent revenge Massachusetts has now . . . upon South Carolina," observed one of the hundreds of Yankee schoolteachers who migrated south to teach blacks. "Oh for an hour of the wizard's cunning, to evolve the spirit of Calhoun from the trance of death, and show him the thronging thousands of the people he despised as brutes, crowding around the school-house doors." The Civil Rights Act of 1866, passage of the Fourteenth Amendment in 1868, and the Reconstruction Act of 1867 were complementary attempts to enfranchise blacks and hasten their entrance into the mainstream of American life. Years would pass, all these acts notwithstanding, before legislative fiat became social reality. The *Freedmen's Bureau* of the War Department, created by Congress in 1865 to protect Negroes' civil rights, faced awesome obstacles

31 The story is recounted in Tyack, op. cit., p. 264.

in its drive for greater co-racial equality. Its emissaries were indisputably well intentioned, but inept. In the midst of a tumultous era characterized by intransigence and repressive legislation, however, one ray of hope was to be found in the benevolence of philanthropic foundations. In 1867 George Peabody, a wealthy financier, established grants amounting to two million dollars for the rebuilding of schools in the South. Skillful administrators of the *Peabody Education Fund* like Barnas Sears and Jabez Curry did much to stimulate southern support for public schools, including institutions for Negroes.

The *Slater Fund,* begun by the well-to-do industrialist John F. Slater, also rendered support to education in Southern states. Development of normal schools for blacks to enable them to educate themselves was an important objective of the foundation. Such philanthropy stimulated other bequests for the expansion of Negro education in the next four decades. Another encouraging development was the rise of dynamic leaders like *Booker T. Washington* and *W. E. Burghardt Du Bois* who helped articulate blacks' demands for social justice, symbolized their aspirations toward economic fulfillment, and pricked the conscience of the racial majority. White leadership in the postwar drive for improved education was represented by Edward Abbott, Walter Hines Page, and a host of other reformers.

It was an uphill battle on at least two counts. First, white supremacists were determined to keep their former slaves "in their place" by the enactment of disenfranchisement legislation. After the Compromise of 1877 which returned control of state governments to Southerners, blacks were legally barred from any significant participation in political processes. Second, such schools as were in existence were kept racially segregated. Public education in the South had always lagged behind the rest of the country, and in the antebellum period very few "common" schools for either race were available. Even when the Southern states began to include statutes for expanded schooling in their respective constitutions throughout the period 1867–1877, a careful separation of school systems was maintained. Not surprisingly, Negroes' schools were inadequately funded, poorly staffed by underpaid and inexperienced teachers, and allocated decrepit facilities.

Moreover, popular theories of racial inferiority greatly reinforced stereotypes of the Negro as a fawning "Uncle Tom" or a servile "Stepin Fetchit." When blacks dared to step out of their assigned roles, in demanding better education, for example, there were always the pogroms of the Ku Klux Klan and legalized "Jim Crowism" to drive them back. Nor did persecution stop at the Mason-Dixon line. As Negroes migrated northward to the urban cities in search of economic opportunity, the arrivals soon found themselves imprisoned in slum ghettos by residential segregation. Racial fears mounted as the influx of blacks continued and white attitudes hardened. Violence erupted frequently, as it did in the Chicago riot of July, 1919, in which thirty-eight people were killed, five hundred and thirty-seven wounded, and over a thousand left homeless. Meanwhile, school segregation in both the North and the South—a blatant repudiation of the true common school ideal—practically guaranteed that mutual distrust and intolerance would feed on economic and social inequalities. Not only did education fail to bridge the yawning chasm of racism, it aggravated it.

Separate schools for the races hardened into a universal pattern for almost a century after the Civil War. As late as 1951 twenty states either compelled or permitted by law the separate education of the races. Even in states where integrated education was decreed by law, segregated housing patterns effectively blocked moves toward institutional integration. Legal sanction for the principle of "separate but equal" educational facilities came with the United States Supreme Court's 1896 decision in *Plessy* v. *Ferguson,* and had the unintended effect of helping those more interested in the separation of schools than in their equality. In the latter half of the nineteenth century, separatist black institutions such as General Samuel Chapman Armstrong's Hampton Institute, Washington's Tuskegee Institute, Fisk University and Atlanta University endeavored to meet the educational needs of an oppressed people. As was to be expected, considering the temper of the times, they met with limited success.

It was not until the present century that Afro-Americans began to storm the citadel of white racial supremacy on an organized basis. An important phase of the struggle took place in the nation's courts and one by one the barriers came crashing down. Judicial decisions struck hard at denials of due process of law and legislative violations of the Fourteenth Amendment. In 1938 the outcome of the *Gaines Case* compelled the University of Missouri to provide an equal education for a black applicant to its law school. The *Sweatt* and *McLaurin* decisions of 1950 required Texas and Oklahoma to allow Negroes to pursue a higher education on an equal basis with whites. Finally, on May 17, 1954, in *Brown* v. *Board of Education of Topeka,* the Supreme Court repudiated its earlier "separate but equal" doctrine and ruled that segregated public schools deprived individuals of their constitutionally guaranteed equality of protection under the law. Speaking for a unanimous Court, Chief Justice Warren concluded, "In the field of public education the doctrine of 'separate but equal' has no place. . . . Separate educational facilities are inherently unequal." This was followed a year later by a ruling ordering total school desegregation with "all deliberate speed."

Two decades of unrelenting turmoil ensued in the wake of the Court's historic rulings. De facto segregation made it virtually impossible to comply with judicial orders without destroying what some considered a vital institution—the neighborhood school. Various schemes for busing students from one area to another in order to redress racial imbalances within schools were tried and sometimes abandoned. Resistance, even outright defiance of the Court, was widespread in some states. An increasingly militant civil rights movement in the 1960's eradicated some barriers, but others still remained. Passage of the 1964 Civil Rights Act, the Voting Rights Act of 1965, and later legislation only aggravated racial controversy. A decade after the Court's 1954 decision less than 3 per cent of the classrooms in eleven Southern states were racially integrated. Nor was the situation much improved in the North. As the United States moved through the 1970's, it was clear that schools had become arenas in which the continuing battle for equality among the races would be conducted.

With the passage of time, furthermore, the issues of education for blacks shifted in new directions. A split developed between black "moderates" seeking to achieve the traditional goals of racial equality and total integration, on the one hand, and militant "radicals" who, ironically, sought to reverse the slow trend of previous decades and in the name of racial pride and dignity championed the cause of separatism. One frequently heard call was for closer "community control" of predominantly black schools by and for blacks. From an educational point of view there was a certain element of tragedy involved in such demands, because it developed that racially organized school control could lead to a repudiation of progressive pedagogical practices in favor of a more authoritarian approach. Observers tended to account for the threatened reversion in terms of the socioeconomic biases sometimes evidenced by the lower classes on behalf of traditional pedagogy. And despite some gains, most blacks still belonged to an underprivileged socioeconomic class. In the 1970's it remained uncertain whether the forces for racial integration or for separatism would prevail.

Compounding the tragedy of an unfulfilled educational promise was the situation confronting other minority groups in the population, including Indians and Americans of Puerto Rican, Mexican, and Chinese extraction. They too could look back upon a history of separatism, prejudice, discrimination, inequality, and inadequate schooling. Education for a truly free society, so far as these minority groups were concerned, was still an unrealized aspiration for the future.

Consolidation of an Educational Ladder

Ensuring the education of all children at public expense was a momentous task faced by the nation in the post-Civil War period. A long line of hard-working educational reformers such as *William T. Harris,* superintendent of schools in St. Louis, and *Francis Wayland Parker,* superintendent at Quincy, Massachusetts (later director of the Cook County Normal School in Chicago), explored various ways of meeting unprecedented educational challenges. The thrust of experimentation in pedagogy was toward adoption of progressive European advances, the creation of new administrative modes of organization, the development of a body of empirical knowledge to guide instructional practice, and the nurture of public support for tax-supported schools.

In order for the schools to function effectively, the realization developed that compulsory attendance was essential. Massachusetts had a law on its books by 1852 requiring children aged eight to fourteen to attend schools for a minimum of twelve consecutive weeks during the year. Within a quarter century at least five states had enacted laws with equally stringent provisions, and by the twentieth century almost all had passed compulsory school attendance legislation. Slowly, laws were strengthened by lowering the required entrance age, raising the minimum leaving age, extending the number of weeks a child had to go to school, and making provision for stricter enforcement of these standards. Indirectly, the proliferation of attendance laws aided the expansion of elementary schools during the 1870's and 1880's as more and more students crowded into classrooms.

At the state level it became a settled conviction that the various legislatures should act to create educational agencies and superintendencies, without of course eroding the tradition of local support and control. Gideon Hawley served as the first superintendent of public instruction for the State of New York, beginning in 1812. By the close of the 1800's a majority of states had created such positions and appointed someone to oversee the activities of their respective state educational boards. Locally elected school boards and their administrative heads continued to supervise schools at the district level. A good deal of human ingenuity went into preserving that balance of divided responsibility between centralized state boards and their district counterparts. The effort was justified, in the minds of many, as the best way to ensure quality education without the potential hazards of totally centralized control. No major criticism of this administrative structure was launched until after the midpoint of the twentieth century, when acrimony over the federal government's educational role introduced a new element into the situation.

It is safe to say that the common elementary school of seven or eight graded levels was an established institution by 1860. It was open to almost everyone on a tuition-free basis and supported through public taxation. The fight for enactment (if not enforcement) of compulsory school maintenance laws was over. The next struggle of the post-Civil War period was waged to secure a solid legal basis for public secondary education.[32] The culmination of extended litigation over the issue came in a judicial decision handed down by the Michigan Supreme Court in 1874. The famed *Kalamazoo Case* arose when a group of Michigan taxpayers filed suit to prevent their local school board from allocating public funds to support secondary schools. Justice Thomas M. Cooley, on behalf of a unanimous bench, handed down a judgment affirming the school board's use of tax monies. When the state levied taxes, said Cooley, its intention was to sustain free schooling for all age groups. This decision prompted state legislatures across the country to pass laws *allowing*, then *requiring*, school boards to main-

---

[32] Details are recounted in Edward Krug, *The Shaping of the American High School* (New York: Harper & Row, 1964).

tain high schools. Ultimately it became possible for children to pass from kindergarten through elementary school and on through high school entirely within the system of publicly supported institutions.[33] A true educational "ladder" of graduated classes was brought into existence, with instruction at the lower level leading naturally to secondary studies. Remaining were questions of the high school's central purpose and its appropriate relation to higher education.

It was only natural, all things considered, that the nature of the high school as a new institutional type should be somewhat ambiguous. Its predecessor, the academy, had been a thoroughly multipurpose agency itself. But as academies began to die out in the 1880's, it became increasingly important to define the functions that high schools would assume. The problem was not crucial in urban areas where high schools were common, but in rural areas the decline of the old academies sometimes meant that rural youth had less of a chance to obtain a secondary-level education than they had earlier in the century. It was true, as one observer noted in 1890, that "the mass of the rural population—that is to say, three-quarters of the American people—is unprovided with secondary schools." Academies were evolving into colleges, some had regressed to the status of primary schools, a few had been transformed into sectarian agencies or elite college preparatory institutions, some were in the process of becoming public high schools, and many had simply withered away for lack of financial support.

The basic issue was whether the high school should view itself as a terminal institution for those directly entering trades or whether its college-preparatory function should be made central. If the latter, the linkage between high school and college for many years was precarious at best. Collegiate officials complained loudly about the poor preparation entrants had received in the lower schools. High school officials for their part were upset over the lack of any pattern governing admission standards of colleges. One principal reported in 1891 that entrance requirements "are found to range from the merest rudiments of arithmetic, reading, and writing, up to the highest mathematics, Greek, moral philosophy, and the history of art. It is hardly an exaggeration to say," he remarked, "that the histories of all states and all times are included, from Babylonian and Assyrian history . . . down to the history of Texas and North Carolina. . . ." Matters were temporarily resolved, first, by having colleges accredit high schools and, later, by abandoning the practice of requiring college applicants to pass entrance examinations in favor of a policy of admitting high school graduates directly. This practice inevitably tended to orient secondary schools toward preparation for advanced studies. Yet as enrollments grew, a decreasing proportion of high school students hoped to go on to college and consequently needed a very different kind of instructional pro-

[33] Gutek, op. cit., p. 78.

gram. Toward the close of the last century the question of fundamental purpose had assumed major proportions.

Charles W. Eliot (1834–1926), President of Harvard, was selected by the National Educational Association in 1892 to head a *Committee of Ten* to investigate matters. The selection of Eliot was a natural one, owing to his long-standing interest in improved institutional efficiency. The Committee's final report the next year was most peculiar. It acknowledged the high school's main function in providing terminal education, then went on to urge reforms geared toward college-preparatory programs. Earlier introduction of basic subjects, less differentiation of instruction for terminal and college-bound students, and a unit or credit system of classes were some of its basic proposals. More commissions were convened to examine the high school in succeeding years, including the NEA's *Committee on College Entrance Requirements* and its *Commission on the Re-organization of Secondary Education*. A *Committee of Fifteen,* organized in 1893, was charged with the parallel task of examining elementary schools.

Controversy continued over the high school's role. The *Commission on Re-organization* made the first of several attempts to articulate the "cardinal principles" of secondary education. Later statements appeared in 1933, 1938, and 1944 under the auspices of other bodies such as the Educational Policies Commission. G. Stanley Hall, a respected voice in educational circles, decried the domination of high schools by colleges and demanded far-reaching curricular revisions. A "social efficiency" movement in the early twentieth century, begun by leaders such as David Snedden, wanted to apply the criterion of social utilitarianism to assess the worth of all subjects taught at the secondary level. Effective participation in a democratic society for everyone, not merely preparation for college for a minority, was lauded as the high school's chief aim. George S. Counts claimed in 1922 that the typical American high school was hopelessly out of tune with the aspirations of a majority of people.[34] Equally articulate spokesmen for the opposing view that too many vocational–commercial courses had found their way into the curriculum prompted an *Eight-Year Study* by the Progressive Education Association in 1933. Sad to say, the results of that ambitious analysis contributed little to subsequent discussions, because of the outbreak of World War II in 1939.

The comprehensive high school, with multiple curricular "tracks" for all pupils, was one response to conflicting demands. It attempted to meet the varying needs of a heterogeneous clientele by making available both an academic, intellectualist regiment of studies and a technical–vocational sequence. What it failed to do was quell debate; in the years after World War II, criticism intensified more than ever. Critics indicted the school for shirking the needs of terminal students, for slighting the interests of scholar-

[34] George S. Counts, *The Selective Character of American Secondary Education* (Chicago: University of Chicago Press, 1922).

ship, for "watering down" the curriculum, for being too academic, and for being pedagogically reactionary. No one, it seems, was ever fully satisfied. The Russian launching of Sputnik I in 1957 unleashed a new deluge of criticism. Alarms were sounded that American education had let its people down; and crash programs were begun in mathematics, science, and foreign languages. It was clear the stimulus of international competitiveness had lent new urgency to school reform measures.

The early 1960's witnessed continuing nationwide attention to secondary school problems. James B. Conant's *The American High School Today* (1959) was an influential appraisal of comprehensive schools, comparing them with smaller, specialized high schools. Contained in Conant's first report were strongly worded recommendations for the consolidation of school districts and the elimination of institutions too small to maintain viable programs, and practical suggestions for improvng instructional practice. The basis for high school organization, urged Conant, should be a core of "general education" courses for everyone, including science, mathematics, social studies, and English. Under an elective system, students could decide whether to pursue vocational subjects or a college-preparatory program. Counseling programs, ability grouping by subject matter, and expanded individualized instruction were cited as mandates for school reconstruction.[35] A second report in 1961, *Slums and Suburbs,* pointed out the threat of shifting living patterns for secondary education. Slum schools in the urban ghetto could scarcely equal the high-quality programs of upper-middle-class suburban institutions. Conant argued persuasively that the very existence of the comprehensive high school was threatened—poorer schools favored vocational education for producing marketable skills, whereas affluent ones concentrated wholly on getting students ready for college. According to Conant, exclusive attention to either objective was disastrous, the developing bifurcation of schools "social dynamite."

In 1961 the Educational Policies Commission argued that the "central purpose of American education" should be to develop in students the power to think effectively. The commission urged in secondary schools a retreat from performance subjects and increasing emphasis on intellectual skills. Helping the individual expand his rational capabilities, it was concluded, is an objective which increases in importance with the passage of time.[36] A decade later no consensus of opinion had been reached. The American people were as divided as ever on the basic issues of educational purpose. The decade of the 1970's promised not less but more sharply edged commentary on the nation's schools. An incipient revolt led by radical students, as much as by academicians, seemed to point the way toward a

---

[35] Conant's general stance is bluntly assessed in James E. McClellan, *Toward an Effective Critique of American Education* (Philadelphia: J. B. Lippincott, 1968), pp. 61–127.

[36] A cogent discussion of the Commission's thesis is to be found in James E. Russell, *Change and Challenge in American Education* (Boston: Houghton Mifflin, 1965).

populist revolution in all aspects of social life. The unanswered question was whether the schools would be swept along or engulfed in the transformation of American society.

Church, State, and the Question of Religion in Schools

The struggle over religion in the schools was almost inevitable when the state began to increase its control in the area of education at the expense of religious groups. As the public school system expanded in the nineteenth century and as increasing amounts of public money were used for its support, advocates of sectarian schools demanded a share of the taxpayers' largesse. Despite the principle of church-state separation formalized in the Constitution's First Amendment, early state constitutions expressly endorsed public support for denominational institutions. Where church and state were united, no hard and fast distinctions obtained between "public" and "sectarian" schools. Religious teaching within a publicly supported school was common practice. New Hampshire was the first state in 1792 to go on record against sectarian instruction in public education. Contention arose when people began to oppose state aid to private schools and question the propriety of teaching religious doctrines in state-controlled institutions. The controversy has not yet subsided.

Nineteenth-century America had a flourishing parochial school system. Lutherans maintained over two hundred private schools by 1820; Episcopalians sponsored their own facilities in a dozen states by 1865; and following the admonitions of their First Provincial Council of Baltimore in 1829, and two later Plenary Councils of 1852 and 1884, Catholics made a vigorous effort to build a separate school system. Presbyterians were warning against the "vain and pernicious" philosophy in secular schools as early as 1799. A dozen years later they were still affirming that education was "the legitimate business of the church, rather than of the state."[37] And although enthusiasm among Protestants for a parochial school movement waned in the 1850's, in view of the fact that the common school drive was a Protestant phenomenon from its inception, the growth of public schools only acerbated the problems of Catholics. In fact, the whole theory of religious but nonsectarian schools (accepted by Mann, for example) was a thoroughly Protestant thesis, one never congenial to Catholics. Their fears were solidly grounded, as events were to show, when popular opinion began to regard common schools as bastions against papist heresy.

It is not widely known that the common school movement took place at a time when the country was in the throes of a virulent wave of anti-Catholicism.[38] For example, in 1834 inflammatory sermons preached by a

[37] Lewis J. Sherrill, *Presbyterian Parochial Schools, 1841–1870* (New Haven: Yale University Press, 1932), p. 2. See Francis X. Curran, *The Churches and the Schools: American Protestantism and Popular Elementary Education* (Chicago: Loyola University Press, 1954).
[38] Jorgenson, op. cit., pp. 409 ff.

group of Boston clergymen incited a mob to burn down an Ursuline convent school just outside the city. Six years later in New York City, Catholic Bishop John Hughes petitioned the state's legislature for tax funds to support a church-controlled school system. His appeal aroused furious protests. The legislature's response in 1842 was to announce that "no school . . . in which any religious sectarian doctrine or tenet shall be taught . . . shall receive any portion of the school moneys to be distributed." Religious issues involving schools were not laid to rest there, however. Dissent over a Philadelphia school board's ruling in 1844 that Catholic school children could receive Bible reading from the Douay edition erupted into physical violence. Before it was over, buildings had been burned to the ground, blocks of homes were in ruins, and almost a hundred people had been killed or wounded.

Succeeding years brought legislative action but no resolution of the fundamental issues. Massachusetts, in 1855, following a prolonged dispute decided "money shall never be appropriated to any religious sect for the maintenance . . . of its own schools." Illinois took the same stand in 1870 when it forbade the spending of tax funds "in aid of any church or sectarian purpose." Catholics continued to charge that the allegedly "nonsectarian" schools were actually Protestant and therefore sectarian. Their demands for a share in public tax revenues to support their own schools went on. Nearly every state enacted laws similar to those of Illinois and Massachusetts, but not without extremely bitter opposition.

For a short time it looked as though the very existence of a private school system in twentieth-century America was in jeopardy. On November 7, 1922, Oregon voters approved a petition requiring all children between the ages of eight and sixteen to attend a *public* school. Proponents of the law frankly admitted that it was a move designed to close down parochial institutions in the state. Litigation followed when the proposed law was challenged on various grounds, chief among them the claim that it would destroy the property value of private schools without due process. The case finally reached the Supreme Court.[39] Its decision in *Pierce* v. *Society of Sisters* (1925) struck down the statute for interfering "with the liberty of parents and guardians to direct the education and upbringing of children under their control." The state could require children to attend school but parents were free to choose whether their offspring received an education under private or public auspices.

One argument advanced on behalf of public support for religious schools was that such agencies were educating children who otherwise would burden the public school system, necessitating a greater expenditure of public funds for their schooling. Because Catholics had to pay for parochial education while being taxed in addition for public schools, they were

[39] Lloyd P. Jorgenson, "The Oregon School Law of 1922: Passage And Sequel," *Catholic Historical Review* (October, 1968), pp. 463–464.

carrying a double financial burden. Therefore the state should allocate its resources more equitably. Some non-Catholics agreed in part, suggesting that the principle of church–state separation did not prohibit the state from giving *indirect* aid to sectarian schools in the form of "student services"—bus transportation, free lunches, medical services, and police and fire protection. Over the protests of others arguing against any aid whatsoever, that view gained in favor with the passage of time. In 1946 the Supreme Court held in *Everson* v. *Board of Education* that bus transportation to parochial schools paid for by taxpayers was not in violation of the First Amendment. It was the first of a series of rulings upholding various forms of indirect aid.

The related issue of religious instruction in public schools also came before the courts. In 1948 the Supreme Court in *McCollum* v. *Board of Education* ruled against a Champaign, Illinois, school board that had supported a program of voluntary religious instruction using public school facilities. Because the board had employed a tax-supported institution "to aid religious groups to spread their faith," the Court maintained, it fell squarely under the ban of the First Amendment. Four years later, in the case of *Zorach* v. *Clauson,* a New York State plan for "released time" from school activities for religious instruction was declared legal. "We cannot read into the Bill of Rights . . . a philosophy of hostility to religion," the majority brief explained. The vexing problem of Bible-reading in public schools was finally taken up by the court in the historic case of *School District of Abington Township* v. *Schempp* (1963). The Court declared that state laws making it mandatory were in violation of Constitutional prohibitions. Neither the recitation of the Lord's Prayer nor selections from the Bible were permissible. In a separate decision the Court forbade as a First Amendment violation the reading of a "nonsectarian" prayer prepared by state education officials. Teaching *about* religion could be included "as part of a secular program of education" but any direct religious observances were proscribed.

In the late 1960's and early 1970's Americans remained deeply divided on the questions of parochial school support and religious activities within public schools. Some, like James Conant, said advocacy of the use of taxpayers' money to assist private schools was akin to asking American society to use its own hands to destroy itself. Parochial schools, he claimed, posed a major threat to democratic unity. Others argued that tax support was the only practical way to protect a people's right to sustain private schools. There was widespread conviction that public schools were "godless" cesspools of secularism, just as there was concern that education had not yet completely divorced itself from religious commitments. A society aspiring to be free had not yet resolved the dilemma of religious freedom and the schools.[40]

40 Consult Henry Ehlers, ed., *Crucial Issues in Education,* fourth ed. (New York: Holt, Rinehart and Winston, 1969), pp. 150–179.

Shifting Currents in Higher Education

The age of the small college was over in the United States by 1900. Land-grant institutions, brought into being by the Morrill Acts of 1862 and 1890, were commencing to offer programs in agriculture, applied sciences, and vocational preparation that bore little resemblance to the college curricula of an earlier day. Though smaller general-purpose schools continued to thrive, the opening of Johns Hopkins University in 1876 had ushered in an era of the university as a dominant institutional type. Thanks to Daniel Coit Gilman's pioneering endeavor, a new kind of educational center had been brought into being. Essentially it was a grafting of the German graduate school onto the liberal arts college, yet the end product resembled neither institution completely. Its primary purpose, as Abraham Flexner was later to remark, was scholarship and the production of new knowledge through research.[41] Harvard, Columbia, Yale, Princeton, Chicago, and other major institutions soon adopted its organizational structure and accepted the university's interests as their own. Before long, land-grant colleges were scrambling to emulate the university model.

Paralleling the explosive expansion of secondary schooling, student enrollments in universities' undergraduate schools, not to mention their graduate divisions, mounted steadily. Around the focal liberal arts program with its traditional concern for general education, each university developed a cluster of graduate professional schools specializing in business, dentistry, nursing, education, engineering, social work, law, and agriculture. From the very beginning this combination created a certain tension or confusion of purpose. Was it true, as university founders boldly proclaimed in the 1880's, that their institutions existed primarily to advance the bounds of human understanding, to produce scholars, to sustain the life of the mind? Or was it to train tomorrow's "nonacademic" leaders to discharge their respective functions in the practical world of business and industry? Were these missions complementary or did they conflict? Throughout the twentieth century, questions such as these kept higher education in a constant state of turmoil.

Robert Maynard Hutchins' *Higher Learning in America* (1936) was a scathing condemnation of the modern university and a typical document in the literature of the period. The American university, Hutchins asserted, was a hybrid creation, a monstrosity of muddled purpose and uncertain construction. Considered in light of its European ancestors, it was a horrendous failure. The "true" university had for its sole aim the disinterested pursuit of truth for its own sake. It aspired to produce men of wisdom and goodness through rational knowledge. Instead, Hutchins held, the typical

[41] Abraham Flexner, *Universities: American, English, German* (New York: Oxford University Press, 1930). Consult Richard Hofstadter and C. De Witt Hardy, *The Development and Scope of Higher Education in the United States* (New York: Columbia University Press, 1952).

American institution of higher learning had fallen prey to a misguided sense of service. Its utilitarian spirit betrayed an anti-intellectual bias. It sought to be all things for all people and consequently by default neglected its fundamental purpose. The university was too overspecialized in trying to offer every conceivable kind of vocational program. In short, by pandering to society's short-range immediate needs it had abrogated its responsibility for addressing the ultimate concerns of human life.

Few were swayed by such criticism. Most Americans put a premium on socially useful knowledge, and the demands they made upon their institutions of higher education reflected that bias. The corollary to social and political democracy, it was popularly believed, was a democratized educational system catering to the needs of the masses, not the scholarship-oriented minority. This was so much the case that it became appropriate in the 1960's to speak of the *multiversity:* no longer an ivy-covered, cohesive community where scholars and students gathered in quiet repose, but a complex of disparate academic communities pursuing their separate goals, only loosely coordinated under a common administrative unit.[42] If it still made sense to speak of any *single* purpose for the multiversity, it was to offer instruction in *all* the arts, sciences, and applied technologies needed by a complex society. The sheer size of universities alone had made for qualitative changes in higher education.

At least two other developments were unique to the American experience. One was the transformation of professional training programs from non-institutionalized apprenticeship experiences to highly systematized academic courses of study incorporated into the university structure. Instruction in law, medicine, teacher preparation, and business became highly formalized. The other was the rise of two-year "junior" or community colleges.[43] The first institution of this type was opened as early as 1901 in Joliet, Illinois; hundreds more were founded in succeeding years at an accelerating rate. It has been estimated that by 1970 they were being created at the rate of one per week. In the first few decades of their existence, junior colleges' goals remained poorly defined. Some aimed to prepare students for the upper levels of the university; others concentrated on terminal semi-professional programs of study. Recent patterns of growth have tended to confirm the latter function of the community college. Two-year schools at the postsecondary level appear to have met a long-standing need for a kind of training experience that neither a college nor a university is equipped to provide and seem destined to become an increasingly important component in the over-all structure of institutionalized education.

Possibly the increase of federal participation in education in the twenti-

[42] Clark Kerr, *The Uses of the University* (Cambridge, Mass.: Harvard University Press, 1963), pp. 18–19.
[43] A general overview is given in Samuel Baskin, ed., *Higher Education: Some Newer Developments* (New York: McGraw-Hill, 1965). See also Leland L. Medsker, *The Junior College: Progress and Prospect* (New York: McGraw-Hill, 1960) and James W. Thornton, *The Community Junior College* (New York: John Wiley & Sons, 1966).

eth century should rank among the most momentous forces affecting schools at all levels. In the 1800's the separate states stoutly resisted direct expenditures of funds by the national government, ever fearful of encroachments on their own authority. The Morrill Acts, an 1887 Hatch Act for establishing agricultural experiment stations, and similar legislation in the form of land or tax incentives were welcomed. Proposals to increase the government's role via direct cash grants (with suitable controls) were not. When the Congress suggested it might extend direct financial assistance to schools, the thorny issue of support to parochial institutions intervened. Some Congressmen denounced federal aid as an interference with states' rights when proponents insisted that grants-in-aid be distributed equally between white and black schools. Critics argued that the federal government might inadvertently destroy state and local initiative if it stepped in to correct educational deficiencies. Few issues aroused so much ire as the question of federal–state relations in education.

The twentieth century brought a partial reversal of public opinion. The *Smith-Hughes Act* of 1917 financing vocational programs in high schools won acceptance, as did its expansions in the *George-Reed Act* of 1929 and the *George-Deen Act* of 1936. The *Smith-Lever Act* of 1914 creating the Agricultural Extension Service met no effective resistance, even though it placed the national government in the role of sponsor for educational programs in home economics, farming, and related fields. The same effect was brought about by passage of the *Vocational Rehabilitation Act* of 1920 and the *Social Security Act* of 1935—the government was allocating funds for vocational programs to rehabilitate the physically handicapped. During the New Deal, countless institutions of higher education became involved in instructional ventures associated with the federally created Civilian Conservation Corps, the Works Progress Administration, and the National Youth Administration.

In the post-World War II era, the *Servicemen's Readjustment Act* of 1944 (popularly known as the G.I. Bill) was the first of several legislative acts funneling government monies into education—billions of dollars in all. The *National Science Foundation,* founded in 1950, was a tax-sustained federal agency for the promotion of education and basic scientific research. Under the *National Defense Education Act* of 1958, millions of dollars went for programs in mathematics, foreign language, science, and personnel services. The NDEA Act was expanded by Congress in 1964 to extend state-coordinated programs in a variety of other disciplines. The *Elementary and Secondary Education Act* of 1965 and a *Higher Education Facilities Act,* under several "Titles," authorized assistance for extension services, plant construction, student loans, community service activities, capital improvement expansions, and instruction for the economically "disadvantaged." By the early 1970's the balance of power in education had shifted discernibly in the federal direction.

Some groups, including the American Association of School Administrators, characterized federal-state-local relations in educational policy formulation as a "partnership." Critics were apprehensive that it would produce a situation where federal control made all public educational institutions direct arms of the centralized government. They pointed to the unarguable fact that government intervention has redirected research in higher education, created new curricular programs at lower levels, and transformed the organizational structure of American schooling. Federal supporters have responded by pointing out that only the national government has the power to equalize educational opportunity for all. The question is often asked what should be the response of an equalitarian society when differential tax bases in the various states (and possibly public apathy) produce discrepancies amounting to eight hundred dollars in per capita expenditure for education from one state to another. Few would care to claim this produces genuinely equal educational opportunity. Others worry whether federal efforts to redress sectional inequities may not give rise to all the hazards of centralized control. Clearly the question of whether the federal colossus will be a benign partner in, or a fearful master of, the educational process remains an unsettled issue in the minds of many.

THE EVOLUTION OF AMERICAN EDUCATIONAL THEORY: AN OVERVIEW

The Original Dream

America's Declaration of Independence was a symbolic rejection of the past, of hereditary authority and historically enshrined privilege. It continued to express the hope of successive generations of immigrants and their children aiming to escape the past and to break with old ways. Their conviction was that nothing in their inheritance could serve as a model for what America was, or for what she was capable of becoming. Above all, they embraced the tenets of modern liberalism, including its belief that any social proposal or political order was to be judged in terms of effects on human interests; the "engineering" approach to social action; its economic doctrine of *laissez-faire;* the precept that man's institutions should fragment power rather than consolidate it; and the liberal concern for social reform. With fewer fixed traditions to worry about, there was more room to make decisions on the basis of efficiency and individual happiness. Nowhere else did belief in free-ranging intelligence, good will, and the idea of progress flourish as it did in America.[44] It was only to be expected that themes such as these would show up in the schools. If virtue is the child of knowledge, and vice of ignorance, education would serve to make the people moral and happy. Thus liberalism's articles of faith were always manifest in American educational theory.

[44] Charles Frankel, *The Case for Modern Man* (Boston: Beacon Press, 1965), pp. 10–11, 28–38.

in 1859, graduated from the University of Vermont at the age of twenty, and taught briefly in a lower school before returning for graduate studies in philosophy. Dewey received his doctorate at Johns Hopkins and in 1884 accepted a teaching post at the University of Michigan. Following a decade at Michigan and Minnesota, he moved to the University of Chicago where he spent ten years writing, teaching, and supervising an experimental laboratory school. In 1904 he was persuaded to move to Columbia University. He retired in 1930, though remaining active in his work until his death in 1952.

Like Hall, Dewey perceived serious inadequacies in progressivism's philosophical undergirding. Speaking of progressive educators, he observed, "If they do not intellectually organize their own work, while they may do much in making the lives of children . . . more joyous and more vital, they contribute only incidental scraps to the science of education." Something very different, a radically new kind of philosophic stance, was required, Dewey affirmed. "Unless a philosophy is to remain symbolic—or verbal—or a sentimental indulgence for a few, or else mere arbitrary dogma," he announced in his *Democracy and Education* (1916), "its auditing of past experience and its program of values must take effect in conduct." Specifically, *education* ought to be the laboratory in which philosophic distinctions become concrete and are tested. "If a theory makes no difference in educational endeavor," he asserted, "it must be artificial. The educational point of view enables one to envisage the philosophic problems where they arise and thrive, where they are at home, and where acceptance or rejection makes a difference in practice. . . ." It was this that led Dewey to advance his controversial dictum that philosophy and education are inseparable, "If we are willing to conceive education as the process of forming fundamental dispositions, intellectual and emotional, toward nature and fellow men, philosophy may even be defined as the general theory of education."

For Dewey philosophy was not a repository of static wisdom, still less a compendious world view in the grand tradition of his predecessors. In *Creative Intelligence* (1917) he wrote, "The chief characteristic of the pragmatic notion of reality is precisely that no theory of Reality in general is possible or needed." Philosophy was to be considered more as a *process of inquiry*, the act of applying critical intelligence to human experience and extracting meaning from it. One of his persistent themes was that all thought must refer to experience, that all valid judgment and knowledge—including philosophical knowledge—proceeds from an analysis of experience. It followed for Dewey there can be no such thing as a truth antecedent to, independent of, and separate from the knowing process. "Absolute" certain knowledge is impossible; one must speak of knowledge claims only in terms of "warranted assertability," i.e., their verifiable consequences in action. Ideas are but instruments or tools for making sense of one's environment, not disembodied entities reflecting some external state of affairs.

Americans were willing to borrow freely from European pedagogy—particularly from Froebel and Herbart—but insofar as European thought concerned questions of specific purposes, curricular content, or instructional methodology, it was not immediately applicable to the American milieu. The *first* major challenge for educators in the United States was to create schools in which citizens could be educated to their responsibilities as members of a democratic community. A school system had to be devised to counteract the centrifugal tendencies of a polyglot population and weld it together into a self-governing unity. Thomas Jefferson anticipated to some degree Horace Mann's vision of "the great circle of beneficence of which universal education is center and circumference." More broadly, America's acknowledged crusaders for better education, in a line tracing from Jefferson down through Horace Mann, James Carter, and Henry Barnard, sought three things: (1) *universal* education (common, public, available equally to all), (2) *compulsory* education (obligatory upon everyone), and (3) *free* education (for all classes of people).[45] Only when these achievements were assured could educational discussion focus on other issues.

Progressivism

The second phase in educational development took place between the Civil War and the early decades of the twentieth century. Now attention turned to needed improvements in pedagogy, the opening of the newly created institutional school structure to more people, and the business of forging close relations between the school and a changing society. The initial stages of this practical work were undertaken in rural areas by people such as Walter Hines Page, Robert Ogden, and Seaman A. Knapp, and in urban areas by William T. Harris, Bishop Spalding, and Francis Wayland Parker.[46] The *theoretical* base for this endeavor was less a philosophy and more a generalized faith. Its essence was caught by Ralph Waldo Emerson early in the nineteenth century when he wrote, "Efficient universal education, that makes men producers as well as consumers, is the surest guarantee of progress in the arts of peace—is the mother of national prosperity. . . . Let us make our education brave and preventive. Politics is an afterwork, a poor patching. . . . We shall one day learn to supersede politics by education. What we call our root-and-branch reforms . . . is only medicating the system. We must begin higher up, namely in Education."[47]

Inspired by words like Emerson's, reformers worked assiduously for the

45 For a discussion of these points, see Max Lerner, *Education and a Radical Humanism* (Columbus: Ohio State University Press, 1962), p. 27.

46 See Lawrence A. Cremin, *The American Common School* (New York: Teachers College, Columbia University, 1951) and Merle Curti, *The Social Ideas of American Educators* (Patterson, N.J.: Littlefield, Adams, 1965). Both contain good bibliographical references.

47 Quoted in Merle Curti, *The Social Ideas of American Educators* (Patterson, N.J.: Littlefield, Adams, 1965), p. 50.

transformation of the schools.[48] Account should be taken of the fact that educational progressivism was but one aspect of a much broader, diffuse reform movement of the nineteenth century. *Progressivism* was the ideology of a crusade for social, political, and economic amelioration, founded on a belief in the power of human intelligence to affect human progress. Philosophically, it presumed a world order amenable to direction and control, provided man used the critical methods of science to harness his energy. It endorsed the democratic process both as the means for overcoming traditional modes of action and as end, ultimately to be realized in the establishment of a rational society in which individuals could realize their fullest potential. Progressivism was basically an optimistic viewpoint, drawing its strength from many sources, mainly social Darwinism. As interpreted in diverse ways by such writers as Herbert Spencer, Lester Frank Ward, and William Graham Sumner, it made human progress seem almost as inexorable as the laws governing the physical universe.

The *educational* manifestation of progressivism arose from the desire to enlist the schools for building a better society. *Jacob A. Riis,* a muckraking journalist of the late 1890's who saw the importance of public education in fighting "the battle with the slum," was a representative spokesman for progressivism. So was *Jane Addams,* founder of the well-known Hull House in Chicago (1889). Her demand for an educational system lending "human significance" to the lives of poverty-stricken immigrants was a characteristic progressivist rallying call.[49] *Felix Adler,* originator of the Ethical Culture Society and an active agent for school reform in New York in the late 1800's, was another eloquent partisan of progressivist educational ideals.

What the movement in education lacked was a solid theoretical base. Perhaps the infant science of psychology could provide the foundation, saving it from the "armchair" theorizing of the past. At the turn of the century G. Stanley Hall complained, "We still have no philosophy of education, save only the rags and tatters of systems, and . . . the whole field has so long been a cave of the winds." Educators watched with interest as a generation of social scientists, including Hall, William James, and Edward L. Thorndike, labored to put psychology on a firm footing. In so doing, they generated a body of knowledge of tremendous potential significance for education. As time passed, psychologists such as Alfred Binet, John B. Watson, Arnold L. Gesell, and Jean Piaget were attacking a broad spectrum of problems, ranging from questions of testing and evaluation to the measurement of human development. Their insights represented a rich fund of resources which progressivist educators were quick to exploit.

By the twentieth century the main outline of progressivist pedagogy could be discerned, as pious aspiration if not always as accomplished prac-

[48] From which comes the title for Lawrence A. Cremin's excellent history of progressivism, *The Transformation of the School* (New York: Alfred A. Knopf, 1962). See also Patricia Albjerg Graham, *Progressive Education: From Arcady to Academe* (New York: Teachers College Press, Columbia University, 1967).

[49] Jane Addams, *Democracy and Social Ethics* (New York: Macmillan, 1902).

tice. Briefly, it embraced the following: (1) concern for the child in all his complexity—his interests, needs, desires, feelings, and attitudes; (2) recommendation of an advisory rather than authoritarian or directive role for the teacher; (3) advocacy of problem-solving techniques of instruction in preference to those stressing student passivity, rote memorization, and deductive learning; (4) rejection of the doctrine that education is more a preparation for living than a part of the process of living; (5) emphasis on a supportive, humane classroom environment where cruel punishments have no place; (6) support for patterns of educational organization encouraging cooperative, communal experiences through which pupils would actually practice democratic modes of behavior; and (7) curricula geared to the maturational level of each student, with learning proceeding out of pupils' spontaneous interests.

It is often alleged that *John Dewey* was the founder of the progressive education movement. The foregoing should make it plain that it antedated him by several decades. Although it is true that Dewey's pragmatist philosophy (sometimes termed *instrumentalism* or *experimentalism*) was appealed to for support by progressive educators and, admittedly, his position sanctioned some of their proposals, Dewey himself was as much critic as advocate of progressive education. But however the matter is considered, it was John Dewey who became symbol and prophet for an incipient educational revolution, a comprehensive program for reform whose roots went deep into the liberal–democratic tradition of nineteenth-century progressivism. It remains to sketch briefly Dewey's expression of that program.

John Dewey

No textbook gloss is a satisfactory substitute for reading Dewey's works directly and it would be pointless to try to do more than convey the broad contours of his educational thought.[50] He was born in Burlington, Vermont,

[50] "Everybody talks about Dewey, no one reads him." Two convenient sources to consult for samples of his earlier writings are Martin S. Dworkin, ed., *Dewey on Education: Selections* (New York: Bureau of Publications, Teachers College, Columbia University, 1959) and Reginald D. Archambault, ed., *John Dewey on Education: Selected Writings* (New York: Random House, 1964). Dewey's *Experience and Education* (New York: Macmillan, 1938) and *Democracy and Education* (New York: Macmillan, 1916) are his two major works on education. For a near-complete listing of his writings and the vast literature that has grown up around them, consult Milton Halsey Thomas, ed., *John Dewey: A Centennial Bibliography* (Chicago: University of Chicago Press, 1962). Among the more useful references: Paul Arthur Schilpp, ed., *The Philosophy of John Dewey* (Evanston, Ill.: Northwestern University Press, 1939); Kathern C. Mayhew and Anna Camp Edwards, *The Dewey School* (New York: Appleton-Century-Crofts, 1936); Melvin C. Baker, *Foundations of John Dewey's Educational Theory* (New York: King's Crown Press, 1955); C. W. Hendel, *John Dewey and the Experimental Spirit in Philosophy* (New York: Liberal Arts Press, 1959); Oscar Handlin, *John Dewey's Challenge to Education* (New York: Harper & Row, 1959); John Blewett, ed., *John Dewey: His Thought and Influence* (New York: Fordham University Press, 1960); and Arthur G. Wirth, *John Dewey as Educator* (New York: John Wiley & Sons, 1966). Especially useful for the beginning student is Reginald D. Archambault, ed., *Dewey on Education: Appraisal* (New York: Random House, 1966).

Dewey was most insistent on this point and it is crucial to his educational perspective. The individual is an organism constantly seeking to effect adaptive adjustments with his surroundings. All the events and processes which affect the human being and the responses they elicit constitute the domain of experience. Experience is the total complex of activities and undergoings perceived, appropriated, and reacted to by the individual. Phrased another way, experience is the product of an *interaction* between the organic energies of a subject and the conditions impinging upon him. Hence it scarcely makes sense to speak of knowledge and knowing apart from experiencing. The act of knowing something occurs only insofar as the knower makes a response to an experience in an effort to understand, control, and make use of it. Mind, accordingly, "as a concrete thing is precisely the power to understand things in terms of the use made of them." Furthermore, if knowledge arises from experience, and the latter is a process of adjustment to an ever-changing environment, according to Dewey, one can articulate the *pattern* or structure of the knowing process. This he termed variously the method of "critical intelligence," the method of reflective thinking, or, more simply, the scientific method.[51]

Thinking is an active process of experimentation and problem-solving, one that begins with a problematic situation involving doubt and uncertainty and concludes with a resolution or readjustment between the thinker and his environment. As Dewey put it in *How We Think* (1910), the "demand for the solution of a perplexity is the steadying and guiding factor in the entire process of reflection." Thought is initiated with the need to adjust to a condition of indecision, with the "occurrence of a felt difficulty." Some obstacle presents itself. The subject seeks to locate and identify the source of perplexity. The situation is analyzed and tentative hypotheses are formulated about it. Next an imaginative rehearsal of the various possible solutions to the problem is undertaken. Finally, there occurs experimentation or testing of the most likely hypothesis (conceptually or through overt action) to see if it resolves the felt difficulty. Solution of the problem re-establishes equilibrium. Further experience has corroborated the hypothesis and consequently allows the unimpeded resumption of experience. Consequently all valid knowledge has its source in the outcome of ideas verified experimentally through interaction with the environment. More precisely, knowledge is made up of hypotheses which serve as guides for such activities as observation, analysis, manipulation, inference, and so on. The components of knowledge are controlled by the consequences of such activities; that is, they are warranted or proved unwarranted. Thinking therefore proceeds in two phases: *engaging in activity* to try out ideas and *undergoing the consequences* of that activity. The end product, knowledge, allows for a re-

---

[51] Dewey has been misunderstood on this point. By "scientific method" he meant the generic logical pattern of thinking, not the application of specialized techniques for solving particular scientific problems.

construction of past experience so that future experiences can be handled more efficiently, more productively, more intelligently.

Cast in educational terms, Dewey's view of the thinking process implies that all genuine reflection is a process of action upon and reaction to a problematic situation. The tedious memorization of unconnected and meaningless data is no substitute for real learning. The scientific method as a mode of inquiry, Dewey held, warrants the assumption that learning is more efficient as it is directed within problematic situations from the pupil's standpoint. Always the educational emphasis should be on the purposes, needs, and abilities of the child because these set the problems which will motivate reflection.

Education, as Dewey defined it, is "that reconstruction or reorganization of experience which adds to the meaning of experience, and which increases ability to direct the course of subsequent experience." Almost obscured by his ponderous phrasing is a major generative idea: the refusal to isolate education from other aspects of life, in fact, the identification of education with the process of experiencing itself. In *Democracy and Education* he made the point as follows, "Since education is not a means to living, but is identical with the operation of living a life which if fruitful and inherently significant, the only ultimate value which can be set up is just the process of living itself. And this is not an end to which studies and activities are subordinate means; it is the whole of which they are ingredients. . . ." Dewey was careful to point out that education as a process of reconstructing experience is not devoid of purpose or aim. "It has all the time an immediate end, and so far as activity is educative, it reaches that end—the direct transformation of the quality of experience. . . ." Further, "what is really *learned* at every stage of experience constitutes the value of that experience."

"*Growth*" is a pivotal concept for Dewey; it explains *why* learning is important at any "stage of experience" and suggests *how* the "quality of experience" is transformed. In his view education is a "continuous process of growth, having as its aim at every stage an added capacity of growth." His reason is basic: "Since life means growth, a living creature lives as truly and positively at one stage as at another, with the same intrinsic fullness and the same absolute claims. Hence education *means* the enterprise of supplying the conditions which insure growth, or adequacy of life, irrespective of age. . . . Living has its own intrinsic quality and . . . the business of education is with that quality." It could be said, with Dewey, that education is simply growth leading to further growth. Education is an "open-ended" process—it aims to produce experiences for the sake of experience.

Dewey was more careful than his critics in pointing out that not all experience or growth is necessarily educative. An experience is miseducative when it arrests or distorts the growth of further experience, when it restricts the possibility of having richer continuing experiences. Traditional education fails, he noted, not because it does not provide experiences but because *it provides the wrong kinds.* Everything hinges upon the *quality* of the experience had. Only those to which the individual responses with an informed awareness of the problems and challenges of his environment are truly educative. The critical problem for education is presenting the kind of present experiences that "live fruitfully and creatively" in subsequent experiences. The teacher's task is to engage the student in activities which are both immediately enjoyable and conducive to further (socially) desirable experiences. Educative activities are to be judged, as Dewey made clear in *Experience and Education* (1938), on the basis of whether or not they enable the student to handle future experiences in a productive way.

As early as 1902 when he wrote his essay "The Child and the Curriculum," Dewey was emphasizing the continuity of experience or the "experiential continuum" as a standard for separating growth-producing experiences from miseducative ones. If learning is not something passive, but an active participation of the learner in experiencing (perceiving meaning in problematic situations), education proceeds when the child is led on to discover, "work over," assimilate, and thoughtfully reflect upon further experiences as these are provided by the sequence and structure of the curriculum.

There are two sides to the educational process, as Dewey defined them in "My Pedagogic Creed" (1897). One side is *psychological.* This implies that what is learned and how it is taught must be geared to the maturational level, learning readiness, needs, and interests of the child. No education is adequate if it fails to take into account the psychological characteristics of the child. The other is *social.* In anthropological terms, *education* is another term for socialization—the process of converting the child's basic capacities, instincts, and dispositions into their social equivalents. The difficulty is that an individual's cultural or social environment is vastly complex. Hence the need for the *school* as a specialized, simplified environment. Defined in *School and Society* (1899), the school should be "an embryonic community life, active with types of occupations that reflect the life of the larger society, and permeated throughout with the spirit of art, history, and science." Its agencies "are concentrated [so that they] will be most effective in bringing the child to share in the inherited resources of the race [and enable him] to use his own powers for social ends." By condensing, consolidating, reducing social life to its basic elements and grading their presentation in terms of the maturational level of children, the school facilitates socialization. What is more, the pupils *understand* their social environment more thoroughly.

In transmitting culture, the school as an agent for "social progress and reform" is necessarily selective. It seeks to eliminate pernicious elements, habits detrimental to growth, and stresses only those aspects of social life thought to be valuable for the individual in society. When Dewey spoke of

the close connections that should obtain between the school and its cultural
context, he qualified this with the assertion that a "purification" of the environment should take place. Teachers are not slavishly bound to the status
quo; their mission is to pass on attitudes and values likely to benefit both
individuals and the larger society of which they are members.

Evidently Dewey envisioned a classroom environment very different from
that found in the schools of his day. He repeatedly criticized the traditional
schoolroom for "its passivity of attitude, its mechanical massing of children,
its uniformity of curriculum and method." He had nothing but scorn for
its substitution of "the forms and tools of learning" for the "substance of
experience" itself. Successful methods of instruction, he insisted, "depend
for their efficiency upon the fact that they go back to the type of situation
which causes reflection out of school in ordinary life. They give the pupil
something to do, not something to learn; and the doing is of such a nature
as to demand thinking, or the intentional noting of connections. . . ." When
students are truly engaged in learning, classroom discipline is internal to
the situation rather than a matter of coercion from without, according to
Dewey. There is no need for the teacher to substitute discipline for motivation, because the latter is generated out of the requirements of the task at
hand.

To the question of what pupils should study, Dewey responded that subject matter should consist of "whatever is recognized as having a bearing
upon the anticipated course of events, whether assisting or retarding it."
In his view the content and method of instruction are one: Method means
whatever arrangement of subject matter makes it most effective in use. It
is never something external to the material. Subjects should be learned "not
as gymnastic appliances but as conditions for the attainment of ends." They
will grow out of the interests and powers of each child and progress as the
pupil seeks solutions to the particular problems posed by them. One byproduct of cooperative endeavor in problem-solving, as Dewey saw it, is
that pupils would learn how to relate to others in socially important ways.
The process of discussing, deliberating, and experimenting by the group
would greatly enrich the experience of each member of the group.[52]

The last architectonic theme in Dewey's thought to be touched on is the
relation between "education" and *"democracy."* This was an idea he
returned to again and again, that "a democracy is more than a form of government; it is primarily a mode of associated living, of conjoint com-

[52] Dewey's laboratory school at Chicago, according to contemporary observers, was
designed to "exhibit, test, and verify, and criticize" his educational principles. Their
account describes the spirit of "freedom and mutual respect" that characterized the
institution. A child-centered curriculum produced pupils with an "alert curiosity about
and keen interest in all life." Shared discussions, the pooling of experiences, a stress on
activity methods resulted in "the growth of self-directive power and judgment" on the
part of all concerned. Though extant reports are not unbiased, they do suggest that
Dewey's practical effort to implement his ideas was not unsuccessful. See Mayhew and
Edwards, op. cit., *passim.*

municated experience." It refers to far more than an operational way of social or political organization based on free choice, responsible action by a majority, and preservation of the rights of a minority. The essence of Dewey's view is that education's ultimate end is "the development of a democratic community" in which "consciously socialized interest" and freedom predominate. Democracy means a form of association of socially interdependent individuals, a spiritual community united by virtue of a common faith and a shared commitment to certain social values. Relations among members of a "true" democratic community, Dewey seemed to suggest, would be free of irrational conflicts because all constituents of a democracy would employ rational methods of reflection to select ideals directive of conduct. Common ends, agreed-upon means, and responsible ways of cooperation would produce a society capable of preserving social order, all the while protecting the autonomy of each individual. It is frequently remarked by commentators that Dewey's version of democracy was almost an ecstatic vision; better yet, a secular eschatology.

Education was to be the means for bringing a genuine democracy into being. Among the many corollaries for pedagogical thought developed by Dewey was an abiding commitment to equality of concern for each person in the community. Each individual should be allowed to actualize his own unique potential and the school should be the chief agent for identifying, then liberating personal capacities. In sharp contrast with ordinary school procedure, this seemingly implies that *equality of opportunity* is absolutely incommensurate with *equal treatment* of all. In order to nourish the abilities of each child, no common standards can apply. Because people differ, there must be as many standards of progress and achievement as there are individuals involved. Just as the judicious parent refuses to treat his children identically precisely because no two people are the same, so the school must take seriously the notion of "individualized education" in its most radical sense. "What the best and wisest parent wants for his own child," Dewey remarked, "that must the community want for all its children. Any other ideal for our schools is narrow and unlovely; acted upon, it destroys our democracy." It could be argued that educators since Dewey have been unwilling—or unable—to realize in practice this mandate for institutionalized education.

The Post-Dewey Era

Lawrence Cremin has argued (in his *Transformation of the School* and elsewhere) that Dewey's most seminal contribution was the development of a body of pedagogical theory which could encompass the tremendous diversity of the progressive education movement. At the very least, Dewey launched an effective protest against a rigid etiquette of behavior in the classroom and the separation of classroom learning from the process of living without. A reasoned assessment of his work will conclude that it was neither as infallible as Dewey's more enthusiastic disciples claimed nor as mistaken as his bitterest critics alleged. Many of his ideas have proven singularly resistant to obsolescence, as witnessed by current controversy over their contemporary significance and relevance.

In the years following publication of his major works, Dewey's thought became identified in the minds of many as the official ideology for educational progressivism, so much so in fact that when the latter fell into disfavor and lost its popular influence as a reform movement, Dewey's educational theory also became moribund. During the heyday of progressivism, however, the tenets of Dewey were extended in several directions. *William Heard Kilpatrick* (1871–1965), an influential exponent and interpreter of Dewey, formalized the master's theory of experience in education in his "project method" doctrine and in so doing, some theorists alleged, popularized educational instrumentalism only by introducing numerous distortions. A split developed between child-centered progressivists, some of whom fell prey to a certain sentimentality about children that Dewey had explicitly warned against, and those like George S. Counts (*Dare the School Build a New Social Order?*) who sought to enlist education as an agent for social reform. More recently, *Theodore Brameld*, a one-time progressivist, has promulgated a point of view termed *Reconstructionism* calling upon schools to lead in the creation of a worldwide democratic community.[53]

The first significant wave of reaction against progressivism generally, and Dewey's philosophy of education in particular, was initiated in the late 1930's by *Essentialists* such as *Isaac Kandel* and *William Chandler Bagley* who argued strenuously in support of school systems stressing "basic disciplines" and for systematic instruction in the skills indispensable to a stable society. Bagley's presentation of a paper on behalf of the newly formed Essentialist Committee for the Advancement of American Education at a 1938 educational conference in Atlantic City, New Jersey, marked a major turning point in contemporary educational criticism. Meanwhile, Neo-Thomists, Realists, Idealists, and assorted partisans of other philosophical persuasions kept up the attack on philosophical pragmatism, although discussion was confined largely to the pages of learned journals.

Almost a decade later, despite calls for a searching reappraisal of school purposes, progressivism remained the official dogma dominating popular educational theory. The famed "life-adjustment" movement, originating with the Vocational Education Division of the U.S. Office of Education, and the various documents produced by the Educational Policies Commission between 1944 and 1948 bore testimony to the continuing impact of the progressivist movement. Not until the postwar years was there any sub-

---

53 Brameld's many writings include *Philosophies of Education in Cultural Perspective* (New York: Dryden Press, 1955); *Education as Power* (New York: Holt, Rinehart and Winston, 1965); *Education for the Emerging Age* (New York: Harper & Row, 1965); *The Use of Explosive Ideas in Education* (Pittsburgh: University of Pittsburgh Press, 1965); and *The Climactic Decades: Mandate to Education* (New York: Praeger, 1970).

stantial body of literature attacking the ills of schools, blaming their deficiencies on the influence of established pedagogical folklore.

The offensive began with publication of Bernard Iddings Bell's *Crisis in Education* and Mortimer Smith's *And Madly Teach,* both appearing in 1949. Spurred by fear of subversive infiltration into the classroom and an unprecedented demand for technically trained manpower by an expanding industrial economy, critics assailed the schools for weakened standards of achievement, for diluted curricula, and ineffective discipline. Allen Zoll's National Council for American Education and Milo McDonald's American Education Association were begun to challenge the influence of the Progressive Education Association, originally founded in 1919 under the guidance of Stanwood Cobb. By 1955 the progressivist association had fallen into disfavor and suffered a quiet death.

The decade of the 1950's brought new diatribes against official school ideology. Some of the more influential works of the period included Arthur Bestor's *Educational Wastelands,* Albert Lynd's *Quackery in the Public Schools,* Paul Woodring's *Let's Talk Sense About Our Schools,* Robert Hutchins' *The Conflict in Education,* Mortimer Smith's *The Diminished Mind,* and Rudolph Flesch's *Why Johnny Can't Read.*[54] With scant philosophical rigor but no lack of fervor, critics demanded more basic training in academic disciplines, all the while attacking the vested interests of "educationist hacks." The Soviet Union's launching of Sputnik in October of 1957 lent more fuel to the fire. Alarmed at the apparent failure of the United States to compete technologically in the international arena, there arose a strident call for total reorientation of American schools.[55] Admiral Hyman Rickover (*Education and Freedom*) and Max Rafferty, California's one-time State Superintendent of Public Instruction (*Suffer Little Children, What They Are Doing to Your Children*), were in the forefront of the battle to discredit the few remaining defenders of the progressivist tradition. By 1960 their number had dwindled considerably.

Analogously, the pre-eminent position pragmatism had long enjoyed in philosophical theory about education was challenged successfully after the mid-twentieth century by existentialism, logical positivism, and linguistic analysis. Although existentialist theorists continued to address human issues on a grand scale, adherents of the analytical revolution in contemporary critical philosophy tended on the whole to view their philosophic role more narrowly than heretofore. Piecemeal investigations of the logic governing educational discourse and the activity of conceptual analysis replaced discussion of the broad objectives of the schools. With the constriction of topics investigated by philosophers came an evident loss of public

[54] See C. Winfield Scott et al., eds., *The Great Debate, Our Schools in Crisis* (Englewood Cliffs, N.J.: Prentice-Hall, 1959).

[55] Interestingly enough, twelve years later when America placed a man on the moon, the schools received no credit whatsoever for the achievement.

interest. Educational philosophy became a more technical, arcane enterprise with little direct bearing on the issues of controversy among educational practitioners. Intellectual excitement was generated elsewhere. The cutting edge of inquiry had seemingly passed on to other disciplines, particularly to the social-behavioral sciences.

It was Jerome Bruner (not to mention many others), writing in the early 1960's, who saw clearly that progressivism was no longer a major motive force in American educational theory.[56] The rise of a new technology, the cataclysms of two global wars, and the reign of skepticism were only some of the forces making a new direction imperative. Dewey's apparent rejection of the tragic view of life, the pragmatist conception of truth as the product of inquiry into the consequences of action, and the progressivist faith in the growth capacity of the individual had lost intellectual support. The doctrine that society could use its schools to help shape its members in its own best image was now under serious questioning. On the other hand, certain tag ends of the progressivist credo lost little of their original vitality throughout the remainder of the decade. They included a concern for tailoring instruction to meet vocational needs, adapting curricula to the differing abilities of children, and a demand for applying scientific research in the social sciences to pedagogical practice.

The Neo-romantic Revolt

As is so often the case in the history of ideas, precisely at the time when the precepts of Bestor, Conant, Rickover, and Smith seemed assured of a secure place in the newly established educational orthodoxy, a host of new critics appeared on the scene proclaiming the total moral bankruptcy of institutionalized public instruction. Unlike their predecessors they did not call for more and better education of the traditional variety; they wanted nothing less than a comprehensive revolution in the structure and content of formal schooling. Some observers wondered if the ghost of John Dewey had not been resurrected in a new guise.[57]

The new critics never spoke with a single voice. They constituted a diverse group without a consistent program for reform. But all seemed to share an intemperate anger, even contempt, directed at conventional educational folk wisdom. Their members included Paul Goodman (*Growing Up Absurd, Utopian Essays, The New Reformation, Compulsory Mis-education, The Community of Scholars*), John Holt (*How Children Fail, How Children Learn, The Under-Achieving School*), Edgar Friedenberg (*Coming of Age in America*), Jonathan Kozol (*Death at an Early Age*), George Dennison (*The*

---

[56] See his "After Progressive Education, What?" *Saturday Review* (June 17, 1961), 58–59, 76–78. For a cogent analysis at the failures of educational reforms in the 1950's and '60's, consult Silberman, op. cit., Chapter 5.

[57] Peter Schrag, "Education's 'Romantic' Critics," *Saturday Review* (February 18, 1967), reprinted in Stan Dropkin et al., eds., *Contemporary American Education* (New York: Macmillan, 1970), pp. 265–274.

Lives of Children), A. S. Neill (*Summerhill*), Herbert Kohl (*The Open Classroom, 36 Children*), James Herndon (*The Way It Spozed to Be*), John Keats (*The Sheepskin Psychosis*), and many others.[58] With Rousseau and Dewey, they shared a faith in the native capabilities of the young and a belief that "everything is good as it comes from the hands of the creator; everything degenerates in the hands of man." As Holt wrote, "nobody is born stupid"; educators simply "encourage children to act stupidly."[59] Neo-romantic radicalism as an educational movement was clearly set to challenge virtually all the fundamental premises of educational theory and practice.

The new critics inverted most of the accepted truths cherished by conventional educators. Against the belief that schools are helping to build a better social order, they alleged that schools perpetuate a sick and inhuman social order. They argued that so-called educational institutions are actually symbols of society's deep-rooted fear, hatred, and distrust of the young. Schools do not teach essential skills; primarily they emphasize the learning of skills needed to beat the System. Discipline has replaced worthwhile learning, they complained, and teaching too often interferes with meaningful human growth. Society at large needs not individuals "adjusted" to the inhumane pattern of social organization, but individuals adjusted to themselves. Above all, they attacked educators for being *too* successful in achieving the purposes of an allegedly sick society. Neo-romantics deplored the dehumanization, apathy, and boredom prevalent in classrooms; they rejected as a fetish the concern for educational "accountability" because of the emphasis it gives to the objective, quantitative, measurable side of learning to the apparent exclusion of the subjective and the personal; and, finally, they assailed public schools for bureaucratic inertia and an obsessive preoccupation with trivia.

As the country moved into the decade of the 1970's, it was unclear whether the schools would once again be successful in disarming their critics through the tactic of compromise or outright assimilation. No common themes, no single unifying set of ideas—philosophical or otherwise—had gained widespread acceptance. It was apparently a time of transition, characterized by groping efforts to articulate the direction American education would take in future years.

SUMMARY

All nation states require a charter "myth," including a founding ideology. In the United States the myth of eighteenth- and nineteenth-century liberal-

[58] A helpful anthology of writings is provided in Beatrice and Ronald Gross, eds., *Radical School Reform* (New York: Simon & Schuster, 1970).
[59] Quoted by Schrag, op. cit., p. 265.

ism proclaimed the death of traditional conservatism, the birth of a great egalitarian society where everyone is created equal, where advancement is attained through ability alone, and where those who do not succeed are necessarily incompetent. America celebrated social pluralism, rugged individualism, free enterprise, and open economic competition. The new republic was the great melting pot, the refuge for "oppressed masses yearning to breathe free," the textbook case for proving Marx wrong. Hawthorne spoke of "a country where there is no shadow, no antiquity, no mystery, no picturesque and gloomy wrong, nor anything but a commonplace prosperity, in broad and simple daylight. . . ."[60] The Great Society of the United States was a totally new experiment in the conduct of human affairs.

De Tocqueville, always an astute observer, early perceived the darker side of the picture, as did Charles Dickens. Writing to a friend back home in 1842, the latter deplored "the desperate contests between the North and the South; the iron curb and brazen muzzle fastened upon every man who speaks his mind . . . the stabbings and shootings, the coarse and brutal threatenings exchanged . . . the intrusion of the most pitiful, mean, malicious, creeping, crawling, sneaking party spirit into all transactions of life." With undisguised revulsion Dickens concluded on a pessimistic note, "I believe the heaviest blow ever dealt at Liberty's head will be dealt by this nation in the ultimate failure of its example to the earth." For him at least, America was not the litmus paper of earthly possibility. Today, domestic observers can point to vast inequalities of wealth, to thousands living in a state of poverty, deprivation, and near-starvation amidst affluence, to the rebellion of blacks and other minorities demanding their share in the American Dream, and to the "hollow homogenizing tendencies" of a mass society, in support of the argument that building a free society has always been an unfinished business.[61] For a growing number of Americans, reiteration of pious pronouncements about America's founding myth no longer suffices. The national self-image has begun to tarnish.

Still in all, an analysis of America's educational development lends qualified support to the myth of a free society, *if* interpreted as a goal toward which men struggled rather than as something wrought at a single stroke by the founding fathers. Americans *have* always cherished the belief that a free, democratic society rests upon the knowledge, wisdom, and intelligence of its citizenry, however much they have disagreed on what this entailed. Lacking proper education, society would surely perish. As a result, the growth of schools in the United States involved a persistent search for compromise between individual liberty and social necessity. It is a story of delicately balanced personal and collective rights.

In the colonial period, against totally unabridged individual freedom was posed the government's right to require parents to have their children

60 Quoted in Frankel, op. cit., p. 38.
61 The quoted phrase appears in Lerner, op. cit., p. 29.

educated, to force local communities to establish schools and hire teachers, and to use public tax funds for educational support. It was decided then that private entrepreneurs as well as religious groups should be free to found their own schools.

During the republican era there arose the idea that everyone should be educated together in a common school, although those few who chose to do so could attend a private institution. Acceptance was won for the right of states to compel districts to levy school taxes, abolish tuition charges, and open elementary education to the masses. It was further conceded that the right of society to protect itself through education took precedence over the freedom of local authorities to ignore educational deficiencies. A pattern of divided authority evolved in which responsibility for schools was shared between local boards and state agencies. Ultimately, "public" schools were to remain under local control, so as to avoid making them arms of the government. "State" schools, in the European sense, were anathema.

American opinion held that public monies should not be used to assist private schools nor should common schools be allowed to come under sectarian interests. The freedom of all was best safeguarded if religion and education were separated. The second half of the nineteenth century saw the extension of the common school idea to secondary education. It was felt that the opportunity to attend free public high schools was essential to a free society. In higher education the right of private institutions to retain their independent status was secured through court action. Gains for freedom were won in the founding of land-grant schools to meet the needs of a middle-class population, in the broadening of curricula beyond their traditional classical base, and through the opening of academies and colleges to women. Often overlooked for its historic significance was growing public acceptance for the concept of academic freedom.

Since the start of the present century, certain long-sought educational goals have been achieved. Universal elementary education was a *fait accompli* by 1960. Ten years later the same held true for secondary schooling. It was firmly established that the state could supervise, inspect, and establish minimal standards for *all* schools and require children to attend some school, but could not stipulate which school.[62] The freedom to maintain private schools and indirectly receive state support received judicial sanction. The last few years have brought a renewal of controversy over what freedom of choice in education actually means, however. Some hold that true freedom is possible only with a system of free, publicly supported private schools; others hold that a free society cannot endure without public schools for everyone.

The major issues of educational freedom in America today are exceedingly complex. Does federal government intervention abridge or enhance freedom? For whom? Does the expense of postsecondary education prevent

62 Butts, op. cit., p. 43.

the exercise of a right to a college education? Should the cost of higher education be borne entirely by the state? What does academic freedom mean in a society torn by dissent? What are the permissible limits of student protest and how much "freedom to learn" should students enjoy? How free are schools if teachers and students do not help determine their operation? Does poor-quality education set limits on freedom? These are but a few of the urgent questions still unanswered.

Within the realm of educational theory the first great task for educators was to construct a rationale for a universal, public, free system of schools. The second task was to delineate a theoretical base for the humanization of education. The third major problem is to formulate a coherent order of priorities for organized schooling. The uniqueness of the historical situation today resides in the fact that the actual existence of human society is seriously threatened. Some sober-minded prognosticators are convinced that the alternatives for the future are either radioactive annihilation or a dehumanized ant-hill society. No less reassuring are those who point to the mind-boggling devastations attendent upon man's continued pollution of the environment in ecological upheaval. In an age when mankind is taking its first faltering steps toward the stars, little evidence indicates contemporary educators are prepared to plot a trajectory into an uncertain tomorrow.

QUESTIONS FOR DISCUSSION

1. Advocates of an "open-admissions" policy for institutions of higher learning argue that the contrary policy of "selective admissions" is incompatible with the democratic precept of equality of opportunity. In light of America's educational development, attack or defend this thesis.

2. Still unresolved today is the question of public and private education. Some groups hold that there should be an *unlimited* role for private enterprise in educational matters instead of a *limited* role for public enterprise. For example, perhaps we should divide up public funds among religious and racial groups so they can set up their own private schools, thereby creating many free private educational systems instead of one free public system. Which alternative allows for greater freedom? Which best serves the interests of a free society?

3. Why have so many colleges in the United States sought frantically to attain the status of a full-fledged university? Is there a separate, unique role for the small liberal arts school in the age of the multiversity? If so, how does its role differ from that of a two-year junior or community college?

4. What specific events or social and intellectual phenomena have contributed to the alleged decline of the liberal–democratic tradition in American life? Why is progressivism no longer a dominant movement within educational circles?

5. Evaluate Dewey's claim that all genuine reflection is a process of action on and reaction to a problematic situation. Are we *always* trying to "solve a problem" when we think?

6. Think back upon your own school experiences—what you were taught and how the schools you attended were organized. Do your personal reflections

support or cast doubt on the idea that American schools aim to foster knowledge about, and allegiance to, the cardinal principles of social–political democracy?

7. On historical grounds should contemporary teacher-preparation programs be housed in separate "normal" institutions or be incorporated as a professional division within universities? What advantages or disadvantages accrue either way?

8. Examine a representative sample of elementary readers and other textbooks in use today. Do the values presumably fostered by these instructional aids differ from those stressed in their nineteenth-century equivalents?

9. An historical interpretation that explains too much is always suspect. In the discussion of the growth of Europe's national educational systems, it was argued there was a correspondence between *laissez-faire* economic theory in the early 1800's and a popular unwillingness to support state intervention on behalf of education. Yet in the treatment of early nineteenth-century American education, the argument was made that Jacksonian democrats, though advocates of *laissez-faire,* actively supported governmental efforts to build a common school system. How can this apparent contradiction be resolved?

10. An organizing theme for this chapter is the idea of education for a "free" society. How misleading is this historical generalization, given the fact that other societies have obviously employed educational means on behalf of greater political and social freedom? What evidence can be adduced to show the extent to which contemporary America represents a "closed" society?

11. The critic H. L. Mencken is quoted to the effect that although American educators profess to teach critical thinking, they sometimes do just the opposite. In balance, which course of action has American education tended to favor?

12. What evidence can you find from your own reading and experience to support (or refute) the claim that professional educators today are still responding to their critics of the 1950's and early 1960's, but largely ignoring the complaints of neo-romantic "radical" critics a decade later? If there is a lag in the educational response to criticism, what factors are responsible?

13. What analogies might be drawn between the historic mission of the school in assimilating immigrants into the mainstream of American life and today's "compensatory" education for disadvantaged minority groups?

14. The American public school system of today is an historical product of many centuries. Is it *essential* that those who work within that system be aware of its historical development? Or are contemporary issues so different from those of the past that an educator gains little by studying America's educational inheritance?

Appendix

Research Tools in General and Educational History

There are countless general guides to books and journals providing historical background for the student. Among the most helpful: *Guide to Historical Literature* (1961) supported by the American Historical Association; its predecessor, *A Guide to Historical Literature* (1930); Hannah Lofas, *Historical Non-Fiction* (7th revision, enlarged, 1960); the *International Bibliography of Historical Science,* published in Washington by the International Committee of Historical Sciences; Louis B. Frewer, *Bibliography of Historical Writings Published in Great Britain and the Empire* (1947); American Universities Field Staff, *A Select Bibliography* (1960); and the *Jahresberichte der Geschichtswissenschaft,* published in thirty-six volumes in Berlin, covering the period from 1878 to 1916.

It would be impossible to list even the most important original writings, interpretive works, and specialized histories dealing with particular historical periods. The serious student will find that original research in the history of education is inseparable from general historical research. Some of this is inaccessible without at least a reading knowledge of other languages besides English. The following is a partial list of guides to the historical literature.

ANCIENT HISTORY

The Cambridge Ancient History (twelve volumes, 1923–1939); *History of the Greek and Roman World* (seven volumes, 1934—); Louis Laurand, *Manuel des Études Grecques et Latines* (two volumes, 1957); Jules Marouzeau, *Dix Années de Bibliographie Classique* (two volumes, 1927) and its annual continuation; Charles Daremberg and Edmond Saglia, *Dictionnaire des Antiquités Grecques et Romaines* (five volumes, 1813–1919); and August F. Pauly and George Wissowa, *Pauly's Realencyclopadie der Elassischen Alterumswissen-Schaft* (1893—).

MEDIEVAL HISTORY

A. Molinier, *Les Sources de l'Histoire de France Depuis ses Origines Jusqu'à 1815* (1901–1935); *Cambridge Medieval History* (eight volumes, 1911–1936); Louis J. Paetow, *Guide to the Study of Medieval History* (revised edition, 1931); Cyr Ulysse Chevalier, *Répertoire des Sources Historiques du Moyen Âge* (two volumes, 1894–1904); and Francesco Cognasso, *Avviamento Agli Studi di Storia Medieval* (1951).

MODERN HISTORY

Cambridge Modern History (thirteen volumes, 1902–1926); Frederich C. Dahlmann-Waitz, *Quellenkunde der Deutschen Geschichte* (9th ed., two volumes, 1931–1932); *Historical Abstracts* (1955—); Stanley Pargellis and D. J. Medley, *The Eighteenth Century, 1714–1789* (1951); Charles Cross, *The Sources and Literature of English History from the Earliest Times to About 1485* (2nd ed., 1915 and reprinted in 1951); and *The Cambridge History of the British Empire* (1929–1959). Guides to American history are numerous; perhaps the most exhaustive is that made available through the General Reference and Bibliography Division of the U.S. Library of Congress, *A Guide to the Study of the United States of America* (1960). See also Oscar Handlin et al., *Harvard Guide to American History* (1963). An annotated bibliography of guides can be found in Allan Nevins, *The Gateway to History* (1962). John Herman Randall's *The Making of the Modern Mind* (revised edition) Cambridge: Riverside Press, 1954, is indispensable in its own right as a reference work in intellectual history; it is also notable for its selected reading lists at the end of each chapter. Butt's *A Cultural History of Western Education,* 2nd ed. (New York: McGraw-Hill, 1955) offers an outstanding bibliography of sources to be consulted for background reading, particularly materials most relevant for research in educational history.

Among the better general guides of basic source tools in education, the student will find the following helpful: Carter Alexander and Arvid J. Burke, *How to Locate Educational Information and Data* (4th edition, 1958); William W. Brickman, *A Guide to Research in Educational History* (1959); Deobold B. Van Dalen and William J. Meyer, *Understanding Educational Research: An Introduction* (1962) Chapters 5 and 9; the *Dictionary of American Biography* (1928–1936); *Microfilm Abstracts* (1938–1952); *Dissertation Abstracts* (1953–date); Henry Barnard's *American Journal of Education* (thirty-two volumes, 1855–1882); Carter V. Good's *Dictionary of Education* (2nd ed., 1959); Paul Monroe, ed., *Cyclopedia of Education* (five volumes, 1911–1919); Harry N. Rivlin and Herbert Schueler, eds., *Encyclopedia of Modern Education* (1943); and Theodore Manheim et al., *Sources in Education Research* (1969). William C. Budd and Sam P. Kelley, *Educational Research by Practitioners: An Elementary Casebook* (1970) contains two historical cases in educational research with critical commentary; and Edward Blishen, ed., *Encyclopedia of Education* (1970) contains an informative article by W. H. G. Armytage entitled "Historiography of Education."

The American Educational Research Association of the National Education Association publishes the *Review of Educational Research* (1931–date), not to be confused with Phi Delta Kappa's *Research Studies in Education* (1941–date). Useful bibliographies or bibliographical essays can often be found in one-volume monographic studies of special topics or general textbooks in educational history (listed in this volume). See *Butts* (2nd ed., 1955), *Butts and Cremin* (1953), *Cremin* (1951) and (1961), *Cubberley* (almost all of his histories), *Curti* (1935), *Drake* (1955), *Knight* (1951), *Noble* (1954), *Frost* (1966), *Mayer* (1966), and *Brubacher* (2nd ed., 1966). The latter's list of references, arranged by topics, and Butts' bibliography, arranged by historical periods, are quite good. An especially complete bibliographical essay for American educational history is provided in *Bailyn* (1960). A still more comprehensive list of primary and secondary sources in American history of education is to be found in *Welter* (1969).

Listings such as Pedagogy, Education, Teaching, Teacher, Schools and so forth appear in many guides to periodical literature. These include: *Education Index; Catholic Periodical Index; Poole's Index to Periodical Literature* (1802–1881) and its *Supplements* (five volumes, 1892–1906); the *Nineteenth Century Readers' Guide to Periodical Literature* (1890–1899); *Cumulative Index* (1899–1903); *Readers' Guide to Periodical Literature* (1900–date); the *Supplement to Readers' Guide,* changed in 1920 to *International Index;* the *Social Science Abstracts* (1929–1933); *Annual Magazine Subject Index* (1907–date); *Educational Review, Analytical Index to Vols. 1–25* (1891–1903), edited by C. Nelson, and *Vols. 25–50* (1904–1915), edited by N. M. Butler; and the United States Bureau of Education's *Analytical Index to Barnard's American Journal of Education* (1892), listed above.

One research tool often overlooked is the newspaper index. The *New York Times*, for example, keeps an excellent one. Addresses and proceedings, annual reports, and the yearbooks of professional and learned societies contain valuable data. The *Addresses and Proceedings* of the National Education Association; the *Yearbook* of the John Dewey Society; the *Educational Yearbook* (1924–1944); the *Yearbook* of the National Society for the Study of Education (NSSE); and the *Year Book of Education* are particularly helpful for pursuing topics in recent American educational history. Yearbooks are most easily located by the names of the organizations publishing them. Other publications of educational associations are listed in *The Education Index*. Also appearing are listings of publications of the United States Office of Education. In the *Annual Reports of the Commissioner of Education* (1867–date) and its *Index,* and in the former U.S. Bureau of Education's *Special Reports* and *Circulars of Information* (1887–1903), the student will find a wealth of information. The Department of Education was created in 1867; two years later it was renamed the Office of Education. In 1870 its name was changed to the Bureau of Education. It retained this title until 1929, when the earlier designation of Office of Education was again assigned to it. These name changes should be noted when searching for publications issued at different times.

Chapter 16 in Alexander and Burke suggests ways of locating educational information and data in government data. Reports of state governments, the archives of state historical societies and reports of boards of education in the various states sometimes prove useful on highly specialized subjects. Philip M. Hamer's *Guide to Archives and Manuscripts in the United States* (1961) should be examined before attempting to consult such regional sources.

Many educational journals carry articles relating to both American and European educational history. Particular subjects can be traced through *The Education Index.* Among the better periodicals and journals which include historical materials, one might mention *Educational Record, Educational Forum, Phi Delta Kappan, Harvard Educational Review, Journal of Negro Education, Social Education, Catholic Educational Review,* and *School and Society.* The *History of Education Quarterly* (formerly *The History of Education Journal*) devotes itself primarily to American developments, but not exclusively (see below). *Educational Theory* occasionally contains an article of historical significance from a philosophical perspective. General historical journals such as the *American Historical Review* should not be overlooked; they sometimes include studies in the history of education.

The *Review of Educational Research* (Volume 22, February, 1952) carries some good materials entitled "Historical and Philosophical Foundations of Education," Chapter 1 in "The Social Framework of Education." Volumes 6 (October, 1936) and 9 (October, 1939) have listings entitled "History of Education and Comparative Education." Also worth consulting is William W. Brickman's "Educational Literature Reviews" in *School and Society:* October 26, 1946; December 28, 1946; April 26, 1947; November 29, 1947; March 27, 1948; March 5, 1949; May 28, 1949; March 4, 1950; May 6, 1950; October 28, 1950; and December 20, 1950. Stuart G. Noble's "An Evaluation of State Histories of Education" in *The High School Journal* (Volume 12, October, 1929 and November, 1929) and his "State Histories of Education" in *Review of Educational Research* (Volume 6, October, 1936) retain some value. As part of a series of research studies edited by Franklin Parker, Lloyd P. Jorgenson's "Materials on the History of Education in State Historical Journals" has appeared in four parts in the *History of Education Quarterly:* Summer, 1967; Fall, 1967; Winter, 1968; and Spring, 1969. Book reviews, bibliographical notations, and monographs in the same journal relating to specialized aspects of European educational history frequently appear. The *International Review of Education,* published abroad, sometimes carries monographs of international import involving continental developments in the history of education, as does *Paedagogica Historica,* edited at Gent, Blandijnberg (Belgium) by the Center for the Study of the History of Education.

Some Primary Writings in Educational History

The following is a fairly representative bibliography of sources arranged by historical periods and authors. Not included are documents of uncertain authorship, writings of indirect significance for education, reports, government documents, and so forth. The works cited below include instructional books of historical importance, philosophical treatises, sociological analyses, interpretive surveys, biographies, and other writings with direct relevance to understanding Western educational developments. The student will note a lack of consistency in titles; some have been translated (or transliterated), others appear in their original format. Wherever possible, the most common usage has been followed.

In some instances, important educators wrote nothing. In other cases, a major theorist is known primarily by his noneducational writings, but these works have been omitted. For the modern period, judgments about which authors and works will enjoy enduring historical significance are necessarily tentative.

Many editions, compilations, and translations of these original sources are available.

ANCIENT EDUCATION

Aristophanes—*The Clouds;* Aristotle—*The Ethics, The Politics;* Augustine—*Confessions;* Capella—*Marriage of Philology and Mercury;* Cato—*De Agricultura;* Cicero—*De Oratore;* Clement—*The Educator, Stromata;* Donatus—*Grammer;* Gregory of Nazianzus—*Panegyric;* Homer—*The Illiad, The Odyssey;* Isocrates—*Exchange of Estates, Against the Sophists;* Jerome—*Letters, to Laeta, to Gaudentius;* Juvenal—*Satires;* Lucian— *Teacher of Orators, Anacharses;* Martial—*Epigrams;* Plato—*Republic, Laws, Meno, Apology, Euthyphro, Lysis, Protagoras;* Pliny—*Epistles;* Plutarch—*Training of Children;* Priscian—*Grammar, Institutiones Grammaticae;* Quintilian—*Institutio Oratoria;* Suetonius—*Lives of Rhetoricians;* Tacitus—*De Oratoribus;* Thucydides—*Pericles' Oration;* Varro—*Disciplinarum Libri Novem;* Xenophon—*Memorabilia, Cyropedia.*

MEDIEVAL EDUCATION

Abelard—*Sic et Non;* Alcuin—*On the Seven Liberal Arts;* Aquinas, Thomas—*Summa Theologica;* Averroës—*Commentaries;* Avicenna—*al Shifa, Canon of Medicine;* Bede—*Chronicles;* Benedict—*Rules;* Boethius— *Consolations, Translations of Aristotle;* Cassiodorus—*Institutes of Sacred Literature;* Isodore—*Etymologies, Origines;* John of Salisbury—*Metalogicus;* Lombard, Peter—*Sentences;* Map, Walter—*Latin Students' Songs;* Maurus, Rabanus—*Education of the Clergy;* St. Victor, Richard—*On Instruction;* Strabo, Walafred—*Biography;* de Villedieu, Alexander—*Grammar.*

RENAISSANCE AND REFORMATION EDUCATION

Agricola, Rudolph—*On the Regulation of Study;* Alberti, Leone Batista —*On the Care of The Family;* Ascham, Roger—*The Schoolmaster;* Boccaccio—*Decameron;* Bude, Guillaume—*On the Education of a Prince;* D'Arrezo, Leonardo Bruni—*On Studies and Letters;* Elyot, Thomas—*The Boke Named the Governour;* Erasmus, Desiderius—*System of Studies, Liberal Education of Boys, Education of a Prince, Colloquies;* Guarino, Battista—*Concerning the Order and the Method to Be Observed in Teaching and in Reading the Classical Authors;* Knox, John—*First Book of Discipline;* Luther, Martin—*Letters to Mayors and Aldermen, Sermon to Parents;* Melanchthon, Phillip—*Visitation Articles;* Montaigne, Michel de—*Of Pedantry, Of the Education of Children, Of the Affection of Fathers to Their Children;* Mulcaster, Richard—*Positions, Elementarie;* Petrarch— *My Secret, Lives of Ancient Men;* Piccolomini, Aneas Sylvius—*On the Education of Boys;* Rabelais, François—*Pantagruel, Gargantua;* Vegius, Mapheus—*On the Education of Boys and Their Moral Culture;* Vives, Juan Luis—*On a Plan of Studies for Youth, On the Instruction of a Christian Woman, Concerning the Teaching of the Arts;* Wimpheling, Jacob—*Adolescentia, The Guide to German Youth;* Zwingli, Ulrich—*The Manner of Instructing and Bringing Up Boys.*

EDUCATION DURING THE SIXTEENTH AND SEVENTEENTH CENTURIES

Bacon, Francis—*Novum Organum, The Advancement of Learning, Essays, New Atlantis, Utopia;* Brinsley, John—*Ludus Literarius;* Comenius, John Amos—*Gates of Languages Unlocked, Vestibulum, The Atrium, Palatium, Thesaurus, Orbis Pictus, The Great Didactic;* Dury, John—*Reformed Schools;* Hartlib, Samuel—*A Description of the Famous Kingdom of Macaria;* Hoole, Charles—*A New Discovery of the Old Art of Teaching School;* Locke, John—*Some Thoughts Concerning Education, An Essay Concerning Human Understanding;* Milton, John—*Tractate on Education;* Petty, William—*Advice of W. P. to Mr. Samuel Hartlib;* Ratke, Wolfgang —*Methodus Nova;* de la Salle, John Baptist—(Institute of the Brothers of the Christian Schools) *Conduct of the Schools;* Woodward, Hezekiah—*A Gate to Science.*

EIGHTEENTH-CENTURY EDUCATION

Basedow, Johann Bernard—*Book of Methods for Fathers and Mothers of Families and for Nations, Elementary Book, Elementarwerk;* de Condillac, Etienne Bonnot—*Course of Studies;* Diderot, Denis—*Systematic Refutation of the Book of Helvetius on Man, Plan of a University;* Dock, Christopher —*Schulordnung;* D'Erceville, Barthelemy Rolland—*Compterendu, Plan of Education;* Franklin, Benjamin—*Proposals Relating to the Education of Youth in Pennsylvania;* Helvetius, Claud Adrien—*Treatise on Man;* Murray, Lindley—*English Grammar;* Pestalozzi, Johann Heinrich—*Leonard and Gertrude, How Gertrude Teaches Her Children, Mother's Guide, My Investigations into the Course of Nature in the Development of the Human Race;* Rousseau, Jean-Jacques—*Émile, Nouvelle Héloïse, On the Origin of Inequality Among Men;* Smith, William—*General Idea of the College of Mirania;* Turgot, Aune Robert Jacques—*Memoirs.*

MODERN, RECENT, AND CONTEMPORARY EDUCATION

Adler, Mortimer—*Liberal Education in an Industrial Democracy;* Bagley, W. C.—*Determinism in Education, Education and Emergent Man;* Barzun, Jacques—*Teacher in America, House of Intellect;* Bode, Boyd—*Progressive Education at the Crossroads;* Brameld, Theodore—*Education as Power;* Bruner, Jerome—*The Process of Education;* Buber, Martin—*Between Man and Man;* Childs, John L.—*Education and Morals, Education and the Philosophy of Experimentalism;* Conant, James B.—*Education and Liberty;* Counts, George S.—*The Social Foundations of Education, Education and the Promise of America, Education and American Civilization, Dare the Schools Build a New Social Order?;* Dewey, John—*School and Society, How We Think, Experience and Education, Democracy and Education, Human Nature and Conduct, My Pedagogic Creed;* Eliot, T. S.—*Selected Essays;* Emerson, Ralph Waldo—*Education, The American Scholar;* Froebel, Friedrich—*Education of Man;* Goodman, Paul—*Growing Up Absurd, Compulsory Mis-education, The Community of Scholars;* Herbart, Johann Friedrich—*Science of Education, Outlines of Educational Doctrine;* Hook, Sidney—*Education for Modern Man;* Horne, Herman H.—*Idealism in Education;* Hutchins, Robert M.—*The Higher Learning in America, The Conflict in Education;* Huxley, Thomas H.—*Science and Education;* James, William—*Talks to Teachers;* Kilpatrick, William H.—*Foundations of Method, Philosophy of Education, The Educational Frontier, Education for a Changing Civilization;* Mann, Horace—*Annual Reports;* Maritain, Jacques—*True Humanism, Education at the Crossroads;* Meiklejohn, Alexander—*Education Between Two Worlds;* Neill, A. S.—*Summerhill;* Rugg, Harold—*American Life and the School Curriculum;* Russell, Bertrand—*On Education, Education and the Social Order;* Skinner, B. F.—*Science and Human Behavior, Walden Two;* Spencer, Herbert—*Essays on Education;* Thorndike, Edward L.—*Educational Psychology;* Van Doren, Mark—*Liberal Education;* Whitehead, Alfred North—*The Aims of Education and Other Essays.*

Textbooks and General References in the History of Ancient, European, and American Education*

Adamson, J. W. *A Short History Of Education.* New York: Macmillan, 1920.
Beck, Robert Holmes. *A Social History of Education.* Englewood Cliffs, N. J.: Prentice-Hall, 1965.*

* References marked with an asterisk are especially useful.

Boone, R. G. *Education in the United States: Its History from the Earliest Settlements.* New York: Appleton-Century-Crofts, 1890.

Boyd, William. *The History of Western Education,* 8th ed. New York: Barnes & Noble, 1966.*

Browning, Oscar. *A History of Educational Theory.* New York: Harper & Row, 1905.

Brubacher, John S. *A History of the Problems of Education,* 2nd ed. New York: McGraw-Hill, 1966.*

Burridge, Trevor D. *What Happened in Education: An Introduction to Western Educational History.* Boston: Allyn & Bacon, 1970.

Butts, R. Freeman. *A Cultural History of Education.* New York: McGraw-Hill, 1947.

———. *A Cultural History of Western Education,* 2nd ed. New York: McGraw-Hill, 1959.

Butts, R. Freeman, and Lawrence A. Cremin. *History of Education in American Culture.* New York: Holt, Rinehart and Winston, 1953.*

Cole, L. *Education from Socrates to Montessori.* New York: Holt, Rinehart and Company, 1950.

Cole, P. R. *History of Educational Thought.* London: Humphrey Milford, 1931.

Compayré, G. *History of Pedagogy.* Boston: D. C. Heath, 1891.

Cordasco, Francesco. *A Brief History of Education.* Patterson, N.J.: Littlefield, Adams, 1965.

Cubberley, Ellwood P. *The History of Education.* Boston: Houghton Mifflin, 1920.*

———. *Public Education in the United States.* Boston: Houghton Mifflin, 1934.

Curtis, S. J., M. E. A. and Boultwood. *A Short History of Educational Ideas.* London: University Tutorial Press, 1953.

Davidson, T. *History of Education.* New York: Charles Scribner's Sons, 1900.

Dexter, E. G. *A History of Education in the United States.* New York: Macmillan, 1904.

Drake, William E. *The American School in Transition.* Englewood Cliffs, N.J.: Prentice-Hall, 1955.

Duggan, Stephen. *Students' Textbook in the History of Education.* New York: Appleton-Century-Crofts, 1936.

Dupuis, A. M. *Philosophy of Education in Historical Perspective.* New York: Rand McNally, 1966.

Eby, Frederick. *The Development of Modern Education,* 2nd ed. Englewood Cliffs, N.J: Prentice-Hall, 1952.

Eby, F., and Arrowood, C. F. *The Development of Modern Education.* Englewood Cliffs, N.J: Prentice-Hall, 1934.

———. *The History and Philosophy of Education.* Englewood Cliffs, N.J.: Prentice-Hall, 1940.

Edwards, N., and H. G. Richey. *The School in the American Social Order.* Boston: Houghton Mifflin, 1963.

Finney, R. *The American Public School.* New York: Macmillan, 1921.

French, William M. *America's Educational Tradition.* Boston: D. C. Heath, 1964.*

Frost, S. E. *Historical and Philosophical Foundations of Western Education.* Columbus, Ohio: Charles E. Merrill, 1966.*

Good, Harry G. *History of American Education.* New York: Macmillan, 1962.

———. *A History of Western Education,* 2nd ed. New York: Macmillan, 1960.

Good, Harry G., and James D. Teller. *A History of Western Education,* 3rd ed. New York: Macmillan, 1969.*

Graves, Frank P. *A History of Education before the Middle Ages.* New York: Macmillan, 1925.

———. *A History of Education During the Middle Ages.* New York: Macmillan, 1910.

————. *A History of Education in Modern Times.* New York: Macmillan, 1913.

————. *A Student's History of Education.* New York: Macmillan, 1936.

Hart, J. K. *Democracy and Education.* New York: Century Company, 1918.

Kandel, I. L., ed. *Twenty-five Years of American Education.* New York: Macmillan, 1929.

Kane, W. T. *An Essay Toward a History of Education,* rev. ed. Chicago: Loyola University Press, 1954.

Knight, E. K. *Fifty Years of American Education.* New York: Ronald Press, 1952.

Knight, Edgar W. *Education in the United States,* 3rd ed. Boston: Ginn, 1951.

————. *Twenty Centuries of Education.* Boston: Ginn, 1940.

Lawrence, Elizabeth. *The Origins and Growth of Modern Education.* Baltimore: Penguin, 1970.

Marique, P. *History of Christian Education,* 3 vols. New York: Fordham University Press, 1924–1932.

Mayer, Frederick. *American Ideas and Education.* Columbus, Ohio: Charles E. Merrill, 1964.

————. *Foundations of Education.* Columbus: Charles E. Merrill, 1965.

————. *A History of Educational Thought,* 2nd ed. Columbus: Charles E. Merrill, 1966.

McCallister, W. J. *The Growth of Freedom in Education.* London: Constable & Company, 1931.*

McCormick, Patrick J. *History of Education.* Washington, D.C.: Catholic University of America Press, 1915.

McCormick, Patrick J., and Francis P. Carridy. *History of Education.* Washington, D.C.: Catholic University of America Press, 1953.

Melvin, A. G. *Education, A History.* New York: John Day, 1946.

Messenger, J. F. *Interpretive History of Education.* New York: T. Y. Crowell, 1931.

Meyer, Adolphe E. *Educational History of the American People.* New York: McGraw-Hill, 1957.

Monroe, Paul. *A Brief Course in the History of Education.* New York: Macmillan, 1909.

————. *Founding of the American Public School System.* New York, Macmillan, 1940.

————. *Textbook in the History of Education.* New York: Macmillan, 1907.

Moore, E. C. *The Story of Instruction,* two vols. New York: Macmillan, 1936–1938.

Mulhern, James. *A History of Education,* 2nd ed. New York: Ronald Press, 1959.*

Myers, E. D. *Education in the Perspective of History.* New York: Harper & Row, 1960.

Nakosteen, Mehdi. *History and Philosophy of Education.* New York: T. Y. Crowell, 1931.

————. *History of Islamic Origins of Western Education, 800–1350.* Boulder: University of Colorado Press, 1964.

Noble, S. G. *A History of American Education.* New York: Holt, Rinehart and Winston, 1938.

Painter, F. V. N. *History of Education.* New York: Appleton-Century-Crofts, 1904.

Pounds, Ralph L. *The Development of Education in Western Culture.* New York: Appleton-Century-Crofts, 1968.*

Power, Edward J. *Evolution of Educational Doctrine: Major Educational Theorists of the Western World.* New York: Appleton-Century-Crofts, 1969.*

————. *Main Currents in the History of Education.* New York: McGraw-Hill, 1962. Revised 1969.*

Pulliam, John D. *History of Education in America.* Columbus, Ohio: Charles E. Merrill, 1968.

Reisner, Edward H. *Historical Foundations of Modern Education.* New York: Macmillan, 1928.

Rudy, W. *Schools in an Age of Mass Culture.* Englewood Cliffs, N.J.: Prentice-Hall, 1965.*

Ryan, Patrick J. *Historical Foundations of Public Education.* Dubuque, Ia.: William C. Brown, 1968.*

Smith, W. A. *Ancient Education.* New York: Philosophical Library, 1955.

Thayer, V. T. *Formative Ideas in American Education.* New York: Dodd, Mead, 1965.

Thut, I. N. *The Story of Education.* New York: McGraw-Hill, 1957.

Thwing, C. F. *A History of Education in the United States Since the Civil War.* Boston: Houghton Mifflin, 1910.

Ulich, Robert. *Education in Western Culture.* New York: Harcourt, Brace, 1965.*

———. History of Educational Thought. New York: American Book Company, 1950.

Weimer, Hermann. *Concise History of Education from Solon to Pestalozzi.* New York: Philosophical Library, 1962.

Welter, Rush. *Popular Education and Democratic Thought in America.* New York: Columbia University Press, 1969.*

Wilds, Elmer H. *The Foundations of Modern Education.* New York: Farrar and Rinehart, 1942.

Wilds, Elmer H., and Kenneth V. Lottich. *The Foundations of Modern Education,* 3rd ed. New York: Holt, Rinehart and Winston, 1964.* Revised 1970.

Wise, John E. *The History of Education.* New York: Sheed & Ward, 1964.

Books of Readings and Collections of Sources

Adamson, J. W., ed. *The Educational Writings of John Locke.* New York: Macmillan, 1913.

———. Pioneers of Modern Education. New York: Cambridge University Press, 1905.

Archambault, R. D., ed. *Dewey on Education: Appraisals.* New York: Random House, 1966.

Arnold, Matthew. *Reports on Elementary Schools, 1852–1882.* London: Macmillan, 1889.

Baker, M. C., ed. *Foundations of John Dewey's Educational Theory.* New York: King's Crown Press, 1955.

Baskin, W., ed. *Classics in Education.* New York: Philosophical Library, 1966.

Blewett, John, ed. *John Dewey: His Thought and Influence.* New York: Fordham University Press, 1960.

Born, Lester K., ed. *The Education of a Christian Prince by Desiderius Erasmus.* New York: Columbia University Press, 1936.

Boyd, William, ed. *The Minor Educational Writings of Jean Jacques Rousseau.* Glasgow: Blackie, 1910.

Brubacher, John S., ed. *Eclectic Philosophy of Education.* Englewood Cliffs, N.J.: Prentice-Hall, 1951.

Butler, Vera M., ed. *Education as Revealed by New England Newspapers Prior to 1850.* Philadelphia: Majestic Press, 1935.

Champagnac, E. T., ed. *Ludus Literarius, or the Grammar Schools, by John Brinsley.* London: Constable, 1917.

———, ed. *Mulcaster's Elementarie.* New York: Oxford University Press, 1925.

————, ed. *A New Discovery of the Old Art of Teaching Schoole, by Charles Hoole.* Liverpool: Liverpool University Press, 1913.

Connell, W. F., et al., eds. *Readings in the Foundations of Education.* New York: Rand McNally and Company, 1967.

Cooke, E., ed. *Letters on Early Education, Addressed to J. P. Greaves.* Syracuse, N.Y.: C. W. Bardeen, 1898.

Cubberley, Ellwood P., ed. *Readings in the History of Education.* Boston: Houghton Mifflin, 1920.*

————. ed. *Readings in Public Education in the United States.* Boston: Houghton Mifflin, 1934.

Drake, William E., ed. *Intellectual Foundations of Modern Education.* Columbus, Ohio: Charles E. Merrill, 1967.

Eckoff, W. J., trans. *J. F. Herbart, ABC of Sense Perception and Minor Pedagogical Works.* New York: Appleton-Century-Crofts, 1903.

Elliott, E. C., and M. M. Chambers, eds. *Charters and Basic Laws of Selected American Universities and Colleges.* New York: Carnegie Foundation, 1934.

Evans, Henry R., and Edith A. Wright, eds. *Expressions on Education by Builders of American Democracy.* Washington, D.C.: U.S. Office of Education, Bulletin 1940, No. 10, 1941.

Felkin, H. E., and E. Felkin, eds. *Herbart's Lectures and Letters in Education.* Syracuse, N.Y.: C. W. Bardeen, 1898.

Fitzpatrick, E. A., ed. *St. Ignatius and the Ratio Studiorum.* New York: McGraw-Hill, 1933.

Fletcher, S. S., and J. Welton, eds. *Froebel's Chief Writings on Education.* New York: Longmans, Green, 1912.

Green, J. A., ed. *Pestalozzi's Educational Writings.* London: Edward Arnold, 1916.

Hall, Clifton, et al., eds. *Readings in American History of Education.* Glenview, Ill.: Scott, Foresman, 1963.

Hart, J. K., ed. *Creative Moments in Education.* New York: Holt, Rinehart and Winston, 1931.*

Heartman, Charles F., ed. *The New England Primer, Issued Prior to 1835.* New York: Bowker, 1934.

Heinemann, A. H., ed. *Froebel's Letters.* Boston: D. C. Heath, 1900.

Hillard, George S., ed. *Life, Letters, and Journals of George Ticknor,* two vols. Boston: James R. Osgood, 1875.

Hinsdale, B. A., ed. *Documents Illustrative of American Educational History.* U.S. Commissioner of Education Report, 1892–1893, Vol. 11, 1895.

Hofstadter, R., and W. Smith, eds. *American Higher Education.* Chicago: University of Chicago Press, 1961.

Johnson, Clifton, ed. *Old-time Schools and Schoolbooks.* New York: Macmillan, 1904.

Johnson, J. A., et al., eds. *Foundations of American Education: Readings.* Boston: Allyn and Bacon, 1969.

Jones, L. W., trans. *Cassiodorus & Aurelius: An Introduction to Divine and Human Readings.* New York: Columbia University Press, 1946.

Keatinge, M. W., ed. *Comenius.* New York: McGraw-Hill, 1931.

Kenyon, F. G., ed. *Books and Readers in Ancient Greece and Rome.* New York: Oxford University Press, 1932.

Klain, Zora, ed. *Educational Activities of New England Quakers: A Source Book.* Philadelphia: Westbrook, 1928.

Knight, Edgar W., ed. *Reports on European Education by John Grissom, Victor Cousin, Calvin E. Stowe.* New York: McGraw-Hill, 1930.

Knight, Edgar W., and C. L. Hall, eds. *Readings in American Educational History*. New York: Appleton-Century-Crofts, 1951.

Leach, A. F., ed. *Educational Charters and Documents, 598 to 1909*. London: Cambridge University Press, 1911.

———. *English Schools at the Reformation*. Westminster: Archibald Constable, 1896.

Littlefield, George E., ed. *Early Schools and School-books of New England*. Boston: Club of Odd Volumes, 1904.

Michaelis, E., and H. K. Moore, eds. *Froebel's Letters on the Kindergarten*. Syracuse, N.Y.: C. W. Bardeen, 1897.

Monroe, Paul, ed. *Readings in the Founding of the American Public School System*. University of Michigan. University Microfilms, 1940.*

———, ed. *Source Book of the History of Education*. New York: Macmillan, 1921.*

———. *Sourcebook of the History of Education for the Greek and Roman Period*. New York: Macmillan, 1913.

Nash, Paul et al., eds. *The Educated Man: Studies in the History of Educational Thought*. New York: John Wiley & Sons, 1965.*

Nash, Paul, ed. *History and Education*. New York: Random House, 1970.

———. *Models of Man, Explorations in the Western Educational Tradition*. New York: John Wiley & Sons, 1968.

Nettleship, H. *The Study of Latin Among the Romans in the First Century A.D.*, 2nd series. London: Oxford University Press, 1895.

Norton, A. O., ed. *Readings in the History of Education*. Cambridge, Mass.: Harvard University Press, 1909.

Painter, F. V. N., ed. *Great Pedagogical Essays: Plato to Spencer*. New York: American Book Company, 1905.

———. *Luther on Education*. St. Louis, Mo.: Concordia Publishing House, 1928.

Perry, Leslie R., ed. *Bertrand Russell, A. S. Neill, Homer Lane, W. H. Kilpatrick; Four Progressive Educators*. New York: Macmillan, 1967.

Price, Kingsley, ed. *Education and Philosophical Thought*, 2nd ed. Boston: Allyn and Bacon, 1962.

Rippa, S. Alexander, ed. *Educational Ideas in America: A Documentary History*. New York: David McKay, 1969.

Turnbull, G. H., ed. *Hartlib, Drury and Comenius*. Liverpool: Liverpool University Press, 1947.

Tyack, David B., ed. *Turning Points in American Educational History*. Waltham, Mass.: Blaisdell, 1967.*

Ulich, Robert, ed. *Three Thousand Years of Educational Wisdom: Selections from Great Documents*, 2nd ed. Cambridge, Mass.: Harvard University Press, 1965.*

Vassar, Rena L., ed. *Social History of American Education*, two vols. Chicago: Rand McNally, 1965.*

Woodward, W. H., ed. *Desiderius Erasmus Concerning the Aim and Method of Education*. New York: Cambridge University Press, 1904.

Wright, Arthur D., and G. E. Gardner, eds. *Hall's Lectures on School-keeping*. Hanover, N.H.: The Dartmouth Press, 1929.

Young, Robert F., ed. *Comenius in England*. New York: Oxford University Press, 1932.

Specialized Histories of Education and Works of Historical Interest in Education

Abelson, P. *The Seven Liberal Arts.* New York: Bureau of Publications, Teachers College, Columbia University, 1906.

Adams, C. F. *The New Departure in the Common Schools of Quincy.* Boston: Estes & Lauriat, 1879.

Adams, F. *The Free School System of the United States.* London: Chapman & Hall, 1875.

Adams, J. *Herbartian Psychology Applied to Education.* Boston: D. C. Heath, 1897.

Adams, J. T. *Frontiers of American Culture.* New York: Charles Scribner's Sons, 1944.

Adams, John. *The Evolution of Educational Theory.* London: Macmillan, 1915.*

Adamson, J. E. *The Theory of Education in Plato's Republic.* New York: Macmillan, 1903.

Adamson, John W. *The Educational Writings of John Locke.* New York: Longmans, Green, 1912.

———. *English Education (1789–1902).* Cambridge: Cambridge University Press, 1930.

———. *Pioneers of Modern Education.* London: Cambridge University Press, 1905.

Ainsworth, Oliver M., ed. *Milton on Education.* Ithaca, N.Y.: Cornell University Press, 1928.

Alexander, Thomas. *The Prussian Elementary Schools.* New York: Macmillan, 1919.

Alexander, Thomas, and Beryl Parker. *The New Education in the German Republic.* New York: John Day, 1929.

Allen, Hollis P. *The Federal Government and Education.* New York: McGraw-Hill, 1950.

Allen, Jack. *The American Public School.* New York: McGraw-Hill, 1969.

Allen, P. S. *The Age of Erasmus.* Oxford, England: Clarendon Press, 1934.

Allen, W. O. B., and E. McClure. *Two Hundred Years; History of the S. P. C. K., 1698–1898.* London: Christian Knowledge Society, 1898.

Alston, Patrick L. *Education and the State in Tsarist Russia.* Stanford, Calif.: Stanford University Press, 1969.

Anderson, Archibald, Virgil A. Clift, and H. Gordon Hullfish, eds. *Negro Education in America.* New York: Harper & Row, 1962.

Anderson, J. *Socrates as an Educator.* Sydney: Angus and Robertson, 1962.

Anderson, L. F. *History of Common School Education.* New York: Holt, Rinehart and Winston, 1909.

———. *History of Manual and Industrial School Education.* New York: Appleton-Century-Crofts, 1926.

———. *Pestalozzi.* New York: McGraw-Hill, 1931.

Andrews, Benjamin F. *The Land Grant of 1862 and the Land-Grant College, Bulletin No. 13.* Washington, D.C.: Government Printing Office, 1918.

Archer, R. L. *Rousseau on Education.* London: Edward Arnold Publishers, Ltd., 1912.

———. *Secondary Education in the 19th Century.* Cambridge, England: Cambridge University Press, 1921.

Ariès, Philippe. *Centuries of Childhood, A Social History of Family Life.* New York: Vintage, 1965.*

Armytage, W. H. G. *The American Influence on English Education.* New York: Humanities Press, 1967.

———. *Four Hundred Years of English Education*. New York: Cambridge University Press, 1969.

———. *The French Influence on English Education*. New York: Humanities Press, 1968.

Arrowood, Charles F. *Thomas Jefferson and Education in a Republic*. New York: McGraw-Hill, 1930.

Ascham, R. *The Schoolmaster*, D. C. Whimster, ed. London: Methuen, 1934.

Ashmore, Harry. *The Negro and the Schools*. Chapel Hill: University of North Carolina Press, 1954.

Atkins, J. W. H. *Literary Criticism in Antiquity*. New York: Peter Smith Publisher, 1952.

Auchmuty, J. J. *Irish Education*. Dublin: Hodges, Figgs, 1937.

Babbitt, Irving. *Rousseau and Romanticism*. Boston: Houghton Mifflin, 1930.

Bagley, William C. *A Century of the Universal School*. New York: Macmillan, 1937.

Baierl, J. J., et al. *Religious Instruction and Education*. New York: Joseph F. Wagner, 1938.*

Bailyn, Bernard. *Education in the Forming of American Society*. New York: Vintage, n.d.*

Baldwin, Charles S. *Ancient Rhetoric and Poetic*. New York: Macmillan, 1924.

———. *Medieval Rhetoric and Poetic*. New York: Macmillan, 1928.

Baldwin, T. W. *William Shakespeare's Small Latin and Lesse Greeke*. 2 vols. Urbana: University of Illinois Press, 1944.

Barclay, W. *Educational Ideals in the Ancient World*. London: Collins, William & Sons, 1959.

Bardeen, C. W. *The Orbis Pictus of John Amos Comenius*. Syracuse, N.Y.: C. W. Bardeen, 1887.

Barker, Ernest. *British Universities*. New York: Longmans, Green, 1946.

Barlow, Melvin L. *History of Industrial Education in the United States*. Peoria, Ill.: Charles A. Bennett, 1967.

Barnard, Henry C. *The French Tradition in Education*. London: Cambridge University Press, 1922.

———. *German Educational Reformers*. Hartford, Conn.: Brown, Russell, & Gross, 1878.

———. *German Teachers and Educators*. Hartford: Brown & Gross, 1878.

———. *A History of English Education from 1760*, 2nd ed. Mystic, Conn.: Verry, Lawrence, Inc., 1963.

———. *The Little Schools of Port Royal*. London: Cambridge University Press, 1913.*

———. *Normal Schools, and Other Institutions, Agencies, and Means Designed for the Professional Education of Teachers*. Hartford, Conn.: Case, Tiffany, and Company, 1851.

———. *Pestalozzi and His Educational System*. Syracuse, N.Y.: C. W. Bardeen, 1906.

———. *The Port Royalists on Education*. London: Cambridge University Press, 1918.

Bates, S. P. *Method of Teachers' Institutes and the Theory of Education*. New York: A. S. Barnes & Burr, 1864.

Battersby, W. J. *De La Salle: A Pioneer of Modern Education*. New York: Longmans, Green, 1949.

Beale, H. K. *A History of Freedom of Teaching in American Schools*. New York: Charles Scribner's Sons, 1927.*

———. *Are American Teachers Free?* New York: Charles Scribner's Sons, 1936.*

Beck, Calton E., et al. *Education for Relevance: The Schools and Social Change*. Boston: Houghton Mifflin, 1968.

Beck, Frederick A. G. *Greek Education: 450–350 B.C.* New York: Barnes and Noble, 1964.

Becker, Carl H. *Secondary Education and Teacher Training in Germany.* New York: Teachers College, Columbia University, 1931.

Beesley, P. *The Revival of the Humanities in American Education.* New York: Columbia University Press, 1940.

Bell, S. *The Church, the State, and Education in Virginia.* Lancaster, Pa.: Science Press, 1930.

Benedict, Agnes E. *Progress to Freedom: The Story of American Education.* New York: G. P. Putnam's Sons, 1942.

Bennett, C. A. *A History of Manual and Industrial Education up to 1870.* Peoria, Ill.: Manual Arts Press, 1926.

———. *A History of Manual and Industrial Education, 1870–1917.* Peoria, Ill.: Manual Arts Press, 1937.

Benson, C. H. *Popular History of Christian Education.* Chicago: Moody Press, 1943.

Berelson, B. *Graduate Education in the United States.* New York: McGraw-Hill, 1960.

Bernbaum, Gerald. *Social Change and the Schools, 1918–1944.* New York: Humanities Press, 1967.

Best, John Harding, ed. *Benjamin Franklin on Education.* New York: Bureau of Publications, Teachers College, Columbia University, 1962.

Bibby, Cyril. *T. H. Huxley: Scientist, Humanist, and Educator.* London: Macmillan, 1959.

Biber, E. *Henry Pestalozzi.* London: John Souter, 1831.

Binns, Henry B. *A Century of Education, 1808–1908: History of the British and Foreign School Society.* London: J. M. Dent, 1908.

Birchenough, Charles. *History of Elementary Education in England and Wales.* London: W. B. Clives, 1925.

———. *History of Elementary Education in England and Wales.* London: University Tutorial Press, 1938.

Birge, E. B. *History of Public School Music in the United States.* Philadelphia: Oliver Ditson, 1937.

Bittner, W. S. *The University Extension Movement.* Washington, D.C.: U.S. Bureau of Education, Bulletin 84, 1919.

Blow, Susan E. *Letters to a Mother on the Philosophy of Froebel.* New York: Appleton-Century-Crofts, 1899.

Boas, L. S. *Woman's Education Begins: The Rise of Women's Colleges.* Norton, Mass.: Wheaton College Press, 1935.

Bode, Boyd H. *Modern Educational Theories.* New York: Macmillan, 1927.

Bolgar, R. R. *The Classical Heritage and Its Beneficiaries.* London: Cambridge University Press, 1954.

Bolton, F. E. *The Secondary School System of Germany.* New York: Appleton-Century-Crofts, 1905.

Bond, Horace Mann. *The Education of the Negro in the American Social Order.* Englewood Cliffs, N.J.: Prentice-Hall, 1934.

Bonner, S. F. *Roman Declamation.* Berkeley: University of California Press, 1950.

Borrowman, M. *The Liberal and Technical in Teacher Education.* New York: Bureau of Publications, Teachers College, Columbia University, 1956.

Bosanquet, Bernard. *The Education of the Young in the Republic of Plato.* Cambridge, Mass.: Harvard University Press, 1917.

Bourne, H. R. Fox. *The Life of John Locke.* London: Henry S. King, 1876.

Bowen, H. C. *Froebel and Education Through Self-activity.* New York: Charles Scribner's Sons, 1906.

Connell, W. F. *The Educational Thought and Influences of Matthew Arnold.* London: Routledge & Kegan Paul, 1950.

Cooke, E. *Pestalozzi's How Gertrude Teaches Her Children.* Syracuse, N.Y.: C. W. Bardeen, 1898.

Coon, C. L. *North Carolina Schools and Academies 1790–1840.* Raleigh, N.C.: Edwards and Broughton, 1915.

Cope, H. F. *The Evolution of the Sunday School.* Boston: Pilgrim Press, 1911.

Corcoran, T. *Studies in the History of Classical Teaching.* London: Longmans, Green, 1911.

Counts, George S. *The Challenge of Soviet Education.* New York: McGraw-Hill, 1957.

———. *Education and American Civilization.* New York: Bureau of Publications, Teachers College, Columbia University, 1952.

———. *Secondary Education and Industrialism.* Cambridge, Mass.: Harvard University Press, 1929.

———. *The Selective Character of American Secondary Education.* Chicago: University of Chicago Press, 1922.

———. *The Social Foundations of Education.* New York: Charles Scribner's Sons, 1934.

Cowley, E. B. *Free Learning.* Boston: Bruce Humphries, 1941.

Cox, F. A. *The Life of Philip Melanchthon.* London: Gale, 1817.

Crane, T. R., ed. *The Colleges and the Public, 1787–1862.* New York: Bureau of Publications, Teachers College, Columbia University, 1963.

Cranston, M. *John Locke.* London: Longmans, Green, 1957.

Cremin, Lawrence A. *The American Common School.* New York: Bureau of Publications, Teachers College, Columbia University, 1951.

———. *A History of Teachers College, Columbia University.* New York: Columbia University Press, 1954.

———. *The Transformation of the School.* New York: Alfred A. Knopf, 1961.*

Cruickshank, M. *Church and State in English Education 1870 to the Present Day.* New York. St. Martin's Press, 1963.

Cubberley, Ellwood P. *Public Education in the United States: A Study and Interpretation of American Educational History.* Boston: Houghton Mifflin, 1934.

———. *State School Administration.* Boston: Houghton Mifflin, 1927.

Culver, R. B. *Horace Mann and Religion in the Massachusetts Public Schools.* New Haven, Conn.: Yale University Press, 1929.

Curoe, Philip R. *Educational Attitudes and Policies of Organized Labor in the United States.* New York: Bureau of Publications, Teachers College, Columbia University, 1926.

Curti, Merle. *The Social Ideas of American Educators,* rev. ed. Patterson, N.J.: Littlefield, Adams, 1965.*

Curtis, S. J. *History of Education in Great Britain.* London: University Tutorial Press, 1950.

Curtius, E. R. *European Literature and the Latin Middle Ages.* New York: Harper & Row, 1963.

Dabney, Charles W. *Universal Education in the South,* two vols. Chapel Hill: University of North Carolina Press, 1936.

Daly, L. J. *The Medieval University.* New York: Sheed & Ward, 1961.

Danforth, Eddy, Jr. *College for Our Land and Time: The Land Grant Idea in American Education.* New York: Harper & Row, 1956.

Darroch, Alexander. *Herbart and the Herbartian Theory of Education.* New York: Longmans, Green, 1903.

Davidson, Thomas. *Aristotle and Ancient Educational Ideals.* New York: Charles Scribner's Sons, 1901.

———, *Aristotle and the Ancient Educational Ideal.* New York: Charles Scribner's Sons, 1904.

———. *Education of the Greek People.* New York: Appleton-Century-Crofts, 1904.

———. *Rousseau and Education According to Nature.* New York: Charles Scribner's Sons, 1909.

Davis, Calvin O. *A History of the North Central Association of Colleges and Secondary Schools.* Ann Arbor, Mich.: The North Central Association of Colleges and Secondary Schools, 1945.

Dawson, Christopher. *The Crisis of Western Education.* Garden City, N.Y.: Image Books, 1961.

Dearborn, N. H. *The Oswego Movement in American Education.* New York: Bureau of Publications, Teachers College, Columbia University, 1925.

De Garmo, Charles. *Herbart and the Herbartians.* New York: Charles Scribner's Sons, 1896.

De Guimps, Roger. *Pestalozzi: His Life and Work,* J. Russell, trans. New York: Appleton-Century-Crofts, 1895.

De La Fontainerie, F. *The Conduct of the Schools of Jean Baptiste de la Salle.* New York: McGraw-Hill, 1935.

———. *French Liberalism and Education in the Eighteenth Century.* New York: McGraw-Hill, 1932.

De Montmorency, J. E. G. *National Education and National Life.* London: Swan Sonnenschein, 1906.

———. *The Progress of Education in England.* London: Knight, 1904.

———. *State Intervention in English Education.* London: Cambridge University Press, 1902.

De Wulf, Maurice. *Scholasticism Old and New,* P. Coffey, trans. New York: Benziger Brothers, 1907.

Dexter, Edwin G. *A History of Education in the United States.* New York: Macmillan, 1904.

Dircks, Henry. *A Biographical Memoir of Samuel Hartlib.* London: J. R. Smith, 1865.

Dobbs, A. E. *Education and Social Movements, 1700–1850.* London: Longmans, Green, 1919.

Dobson, J. F. *Ancient Education and Its Meaning to Us.* New York: Longmans, Green, 1932.

Donohue, John W. *St. Thomas Aquinas and Education.* New York: Random House, 1968.

Doughton, I. *Modern Public Education, Its Philosophy and Background.* New York: Appleton-Century-Crofts, 1935.

Douglas, P. H. *American Apprenticeship and Industrial Education.* New York: Columbia University Press, 1921.

Drane, A. T. *Christian Schools and Scholars.* New York: Benziger Brothers, 1924.

Draper, W. H. *University Extension 1873–1923.* London: Cambridge University Press, 1923.

Drever, J. *Greek Education: Its Practices and Principles.* London: Cambridge University Press, 1912.

Du Bois, W. C. Burghardt. *Black Reconstruction.* New York: Harcourt, Brace, 1935.

Duckett, Eleanor S. *Alcuin, Friend of Charlemagne.* New York: Macmillan, 1951.

Dunkel, Harold B. *Herbart and Education.* New York: Random House, 1969.

———. *Herbart and Herbartianism: An Educational Ghost Story.* Chicago: University of Chicago Press, 1970.

Dunn, W. K. *What Happened to Religious Education?* Baltimore: Johns Hopkins Press, 1958.

Dunshee, Henry W. *History of the School of the Collegiate Reformed Dutch Church of the City of New York.* New York. Aldine Publishing, 1883.

Earle, Alice M. *Child Life in Colonial Days.* New York: Macmillan, 1899.

Ebner, Eliezer. *Elementary Education in Ancient Israel.* New York: Bloch Publishing Company, 1956.

Eby, Frederick. *The Development of Modern Education.* Englewood Cliffs, N.J.: Prentice-Hall, 1952.

———. *Early Protestant Educators.* New York: Columbia University Press, 1936.

Eckelberry, R. H. *The History of the Municipal University in the United States.* Washington, D.C.: U.S. Government Printing Office, 1932.

Edgar, John. *History of Early Scottish Education.* Ebinburgh: James Thin, 1893.

Eells, W. C. *The Junior College.* Boston: Houghton Mifflin, 1931.

Ellspermann, G. L. *The Attitude of the Early Christian Latin Writers Toward Pagan Learning and Literature.* Washington, D.C.: Catholic University of America Press, 1949.

Elsbree, W. S. *The American Teacher.* New York: American Book Company, 1939.

Emerson, M. I. *Evolution of the Educational Ideal.* Boston: Houghton Mifflin, 1914.

English, H. B. *Historical Roots of Learning Theory.* Garden City, N.Y.: Doubleday, 1954.

Ennis, Mary Gratin. *The Vocabulary of the Institutiones of Cassiodorus, With Special Advertence to the Technical Terminology and Its Sources.* Washington, D.C.: Catholic University of America Press, 1939.

Ensign, F. C. *Compulsory School Attendance and Child Labor.* Iowa City: Athens Press, 1921.

Farrell, A. P. *The Jesuit Code of Liberal Education.* Milwaukee: Bruce Publishing, 1938.

Farrington, Frederic E. *French Secondary Schools.* New York: Longmans, Green, 1910.

———. *The Public Primary School System of France.* New York: Teachers College, Columbia University, 1906.

Felkin, H. M., and E. Felkin, trans. *J. F. Herbart, on the Aesthetic Revelation of the World As the Chief Work of Education.* London: Swan Sonnenschein, 1892.

———. *Herbart's Science of Education.* Boston: D. C. Heath, 1908.

Field, Louis F. *The Child and His Book. Some Account of the History and Progress of Children's Literature in England.* London: W. Gardner, Darton & Company, 1895.

Fitzpatrick, E. A. *The Educational Views and Influence of De Witt Clinton.* New York: Bureau of Publications, Teachers College, Columbia University, 1911.

———. *La Salle, Patron of All Teachers.* Milwaukee: Bruce Publishing, 1951.

———. *St. Ignatius and the Ratio Studiorum.* New York: McGraw-Hill, 1933.

Fleming, Sandford. *Children and Puritanism.* New Haven, Conn.: Yale University Press, 1933.

Fletcher, Arthur W. *Education in Germany.* Cambridge, England: W. Haffer & Sons, 1934.

Flexner, Abraham. *Daniel Coit Gilman: Creator of the American Type University.* New York: Harcourt, Brace, 1946.

———. *Universities: American, English, German*. New York: Oxford University Press, 1930.

Forbes, C. A. *Greek Physical Education*. New York: Appleton-Century-Crofts, 1929.

Ford, Paul L. *The New England Primer*. New York: Dodd, Mead, 1899.

Forest, I. *Pre-school Education*. New York: Macmillan, 1927.

Foudy, John. *The Education Principles of American Humanism*. Washington, D.C.: The Catholic University of America Press, 1945.

Frankena, William K. *Three Historical Philosophies of Education*. Chicago: Scott, Foresman, 1965.*

Franks, Fanny. *The Kindergarten System*. London: Swan Sonnenschein, 1897.

Freeman, K. *Schools of Hellas*. London: Macmillan, 1922.

Fulop, Miller R. *The Power and Secret of the Jesuits*. New York: Viking Press, 1930.

Gabel, R. J. *Public Funds for Church and Private Schools*. Washington, D.C.: Murray & Heister, 1937.

Gambrell, Mary L. *Ministerial Training in 18th Century New England*. New York: Columbia University Press, 1937.

Gascoin, C. J. B. *Alcuin, His Life and Work*. New York: Russell and Russell, 1904.

Gay, Peter, ed. *John Locke on Education*. New York: Bureau of Publications, Teachers College, Columbia University, 1964.

Gibson, James. *Locke's Theory of Knowledge and Its Historical Relations*. Cambridge, England: Cambridge University Press, 1960.

Gifford, Walter J. *Historical Development of the New York High School System*. Albany, N.Y.: J. B. Lyons, 1922.

Gilland, T. M. *Origin and Development of the Powers and Duties of the City School Superintendent*. Chicago: University of Chicago Press, 1935.

Ginzberg, Louis. *Students, Scholars, and Saints*. Philadelphia: Jewish Publication Society, 1928.

Glover, Terrot R. *Life and Letters in the Fourth Century*. New York: G. E. Stecher, 1924.

Godbold, A. *The Church College of the Old South*. Durham, N.C.: Duke University Press, 1944.

Goebel, Edmund J. *A Study of Catholic Secondary Education During the Colonial Period up to the First Plenary Council of Baltimore, 1852*. New York: Benziger Brothers, 1937.

Goodsell, Willystine. *A History of the Family as a Social and Educational Institution*. New York: Macmillan, 1915.

———. *Pioneers of Women's Education*. New York: McGraw-Hill, 1931.

Gould, Elizabeth. *Izekiel Cheever, Schoolmaster*. Boston: Palmer, 1904.

Graham, Hugh. *Early Irish Monastic Schools*. Dublin: Talbot, 1923.

Grant, Nigel. *Soviet Education*. Baltimore: Penguin Books, 1964.

Grattan, C. Hartley, ed. *American Ideas About Adult Education, 1710–1915*. New York: Bureau of Publications, Teachers College, Columbia University, 1959.

Graves, Frank P. *Great Educators of Three Centuries*. New York: Macmillan, 1912.

———. *Peter Ramus*. New York: Macmillan, 1912.

———. *What Did Jesus Teach? An Examination of the Educational Material and Method of the Master*. New York: Macmillan, 1925.

Greeley, Andrew M., and Peter H. Rossi. *The Education of Catholic Americans*. Garden City, N.Y.: Anchor, 1966

Green, F. C. *Jean-Jacques Rousseau: A Critical Study of His Life and Writings*. New York: Barnes & Noble, 1969.

Green, J. A. *The Educational Ideas of Pestalozzi*. London: University Tutorial Press, 1911.

————. *Life and Work of Pestalozzi*. London: W. B. Clive, 1913.

Greenough, J. C. *The Evolution of the Elementary Schools of Great Britain*. New York: Appleton-Century-Crofts, 1903.

Grizzel, E. D. *Origin and Development of the High School in New England before 1865*. New York: Macmillan, 1923.

Gruber, F. C. *Foundations for a Philosophy of Education*. New York: T. Y. Crowell, 1961

Gutek, Gerald Lee. *Pestalozzi and Education*. New York: Random House, 1968.

Gwynn, Aubrey Osborn. *Roman Education from Cicero to Quintilian*. London: Oxford University Press, 1926.

Haarhoff, T. *Schools of Ancient Gaul*. New York: Oxford University Press, 1920.

Hadas, Moses. *History of Latin Literature*. New York: Columbia University Press, 1952.

————. *Humanism: The Greek Ideal and Its Survival*. New York: Harper & Row, 1960.

Hall, A. J. *Religious Education in the Public Schools of the State and City of New York*. Chicago: University of Chicago Press, 1914.

Halls, W. D. *Society, Schools and Progress in France*. New York: Pergamon Press, 1965.

Hambly, W. D. *Origins of Education Among Primitive Peoples*. London: Macmillan, 1926.

Hamlyn, V. W. C. *The Universities of Europe at the Period of the Reformation*. Oxford: G. Shrimpton, 1876.

Handlin, Oscar. *John Dewey's Challenge to Education*. New York: Harper & Row, 1959.

Hans, Nicholaus A. *History of Russian Educational Policy, 1701–1917*. New York: Russell and Russell, 1964.

————. *New Trends in Education in the 18th Century*. New York: Grove Press, 1951.

Hansen, A. O. *Liberalism and American Education in the Eighteenth Century*. New York: Macmillan, 1926.

Hanus, Paul H. *Adventuring in Education*. Cambridge Mass.: Harvard University Press, 1937.

Harper, C. A. *A Century of Public Teacher Education*. Washington, D.C.: National Education Association, American Association of Teachers College, 1939.

————. *Development of the Teachers College in the United States*. Bloomington, Ind.: McKnight & McKnight, 1935.

Harris, J. Henry. *Robert Raikes; The Man and His Work*. New York: E. P. Dutton, 1899.

Harrison, J. F. C. *Learning and Living, 1790–1960; A Study in the History of the English Adult Education Movement*. Toronto: University of Toronto Press, 1961.

Haskins, C. H. *The Rise of Universities*. New York: Holt, Rinehart and Winston, 1923.

Haynes, B. R. *History of Business Education in the United States*. Cincinnati: South-Western Publishing, 1935.

Heafford, M. R. *Pestalozzi*. London: Methuen, 1967.*

Healy, John. *Ireland's Ancient Schools and Scholars*. Dublin: Sealy, Bryers and Walker, 1893.

Heatwole, C. J. *A History of Education in Viriginia*. New York: Macmillan, 1916.

Heffron, Ida Carson. *Francis Wayland Parker, a Biography*. Los Angeles: Ivan Deach, Jr., 1934.

Herford, W. H. *The Student's Froebel*. Boston: D. C. Heath, 1900.

Hinsdale, B. A. *Horace Mann and the Common School Revival.* New York: Charles Scribner's Sons, 1900.

Hobhouse, W. *The Theory and Practice of Ancient Education.* New York: Stechert-Hafner, 1910.

Hodgson, G. *Primitive Christian Education.* Edinburgh: T. T. Clark, 1906.

———. *Studies in French Education from Rabelais to Rousseau.* New York: Franklin, Burt, 1908.

Höffding, Harold. *Jean Jacques Rousseau and His Philosophy.* London. Oxford University Press, 1930.

Hofstadter, Richard, and C. Dewitt Hardy. *The Development and Scope of Higher Education in the United States.* New York: Columbia University Press, 1952.

Hofstadter, Richard, and Walter P. Metzger, *The Development of Academic Freedom in the United States.* New York: Columbia University Press, 1955*

Hollis, Andrew P. *The Contribution of the Oswego Normal School.* Boston: D. C. Heath, 1898.

Holman, Henry. *English National Education: A Sketch of the Rise of Public Elementary Schools in England.* Glasgow: Blackie, 1898.

———. *Pestalozzi: An Account of His Life and Work.* London: Longmans, Green, 1908.

Holmes, D. O. W. *The Evolution of the Negro College.* New York: Bureau of Publications, Teachers College, Columbia University, 1934.

Holmes, P. *A Tercentenary History of the Boston Public Latin School 1635–1935.* Cambridge, Mass.: Harvard University Press, 1935.

Holtz, A. A. *A Study of the Moral and Religious Elements in American Education up to 1800.* Menasha, Wis.: George Banta, 1917.

Honeywell, R. J. *The Educational Work of Thomas Jefferson.* Cambridge, Mass.: Harvard University Press, 1937.

Hook, Sidney. *John Dewey: An Intellectual Portrait.* New York: John Day, 1939.

Horne, H. H. *The Democratic Philosophy of Education.* New York: Macmillan, 1932.

Howell, W. S. *The Rhetoric of Alcuin and Charlemagne.* Princeton, N.J.: Princeton University Press, 1941.

Hubbell, L. G. *The Development of University Departments of Education.* Washington, D.C.: Catholic University of America Press, 1924.

Hudson, William H. *Rousseau and Naturalism in Life and Thought.* New York: Charles Scribner's Sons, 1903.

Huebener, Theodore. *The Schools of West Germany.* New York: New York University Press, 1962.

Hughes, J. L. *Froebel's Educational Laws for All Teachers.* New York: Appleton-Century-Crofts, 1897.

Hughes, Thomas A. *Loyola.* New York: Charles Scribner's Sons, 1904.

———. *Loyola and the Educational System of the Jesuits.* New York: Charles Scribner's Sons, 1897.

Hutchins, Robert M. *The Higher Learning in America.* New Haven: Yale University Press, 1936.

Hyma, Albert. *Erasmus and the Humanists.* New York: Croft Educational Services, 1930.

Hyman, H. M. *To Try Men's Souls.* Berkeley: University of California Press, 1959.

Inglis, A. J. *The Rise of the High School in Massachusetts.* New York: Bureau of Publications, Teachers College, Columbia University, 1911.

International Kindergarten Union. *Pioneers of the Kindergarten.* New York: Century Company, 1924.

Jackson, George L. *The Development of School Support in Colonial Massachusetts.* Bureau of Publications, Teachers College, Columbia University, 1909.

Jackson, S. L. *America's Struggle for Free Schools.* Washington, D.C.: Public Affairs Press, 1941.

Jackson, Samuel M. *Huldreich Zwingli.* New York: G. P. Putnam's Sons, 1903.

Jacobsen, J. V. *Educational Foundations of the Jesuits in Sixteenth Century New Spain.* Berkeley: University of California Press, 1938.

Jaeger, Werner. *Early Christianity and Greek Paideia.* Cambridge, Mass.: The Belknap Press of Harvard University, 1961.

———. *Paideia.* New York: Oxford University Press, 1945.*

Jarvis, Josephine. *Froebel: Pedagogics of the Kindergarden.* New York: Appleton-Century-Crofts, 1905.

Jebb, R. C. *Attic Orators.* New York: Macmillan, 1893.

Jenkins, Ralph C., and Gertrude C. Warner. *Henry Barnard, An Introduction.* Hartford: The Connecticut State Teachers Association, 1937.

Johnson, Clifton. *The Country School in New England.* New York: Appleton-Century-Crofts, 1893.

———. *The District School As It Was.* Boston: Lee & Shepard, 1897.

———. *Old Time Schools and School Books.* New York: Macmillan, 1925.*

Johnson, George M. *Education Law.* East Lansing: Michigan State University Press, 1969.

Johnson, H. *An Introduction to the History of the Social Sciences in School.* New York: Charles Scribner's Sons, 1932.

Johnson, W. H. E. *Russia's Educational Heritage.* Pittsburgh: Carnegie Press, Carnegie Institute of Technology, 1950.

Jones, Lloyd. *The Life, Times, and Labours of Robert Owen.* London: Swan Sonnenschein, 1905.

Jones, M. G. *Charity School Movement: A Study of 18th Century Puritanism.* Hamden, Conn.: Shoe String Press, n. d.

Judd, C. H. *Evolution of a Democratic School System.* Boston: Houghton Mifflin, 1918.

Kandel, Isaac L. *American Education in the Twentieth Century.* Cambridge, Mass.: Harvard University Press, 1957.

———. *Comparative Education.* Boston: Houghton Mifflin, 1933.

———. *History of Secondary Education.* Boston: Houghton Mifflin, 1930.

———. *The Impact of War upon American Education.* Chapel Hill: University of North Carolina Press, 1948.

———. *The Making of Nazis.* New York: Teachers College, Columbia University, 1934.

———. *The Reform of Secondary Education in France.* New York: Teachers College, Columbia University, 1924.

Keatinge, M. W. *Comenius.* New York: McGraw-Hill, 1932.

———. *The Great Didactic of John Amos Comenius.* New York: Russell & Russell, 1907.

Kelly, R. L. *The American Colleges and the Social Order.* New York: Macmillan, 1940.

Kelly, Thomas. *George Birkbeck, Pioneer of Adult Education.* Liverpool: University of Liverpool Press, 1957.

Kemp, W. W. *The Support of Schools in Colonial New York by the Society for the Propagation of the Gospel in Foreign Parts.* New York: Teachers College, Columbia University, 1913.

Kennedy, George. *The Art of Persuasion in Greece.* Princeton, N.J.: Princeton University Press, 1963.

Kibre, P. *The Nations in the Medieval Universities*. Cambridge, Mass.: Medieval Academy of America, 1948.

———. *Scholarly Privileges in the Middle Ages*. Cambridge, Mass.: Medieval Academy of America, 1962.

Kilpatrick, William H. *The Dutch Schools of New Netherland and Colonial New York*. Washington, D.C.: Government Printing Office, 1912.

———. *Froebel's Kindergarten Principles Critically Examined*. New York: Macmillan, 1916.

———. *Heinrich Pestalozzi: The Education of Man*. New York: Philosophical Library, 1951.

Kingsley, Charles. *Alexandria and Her Schools*. London: Macmillan, 1854.

Kinloch, T. F. *Pioneers of Religious Education*. New York: Oxford University Press, 1939.

Klain, Z. *Educational Activities of New England Quakers*. Philadelphia: Westbrook, 1928.

Kleinz, John P. *The Theory of Knowledge of Hugh of St. Victor*. Washington, D.C.: The Catholic University of America Press, 1944.

Kliebard, Herbert M., ed. *Religion and Education in America, A Documentary History*. Scranton, Pa.: International Textbook Company, 1969.

Kline, George L., ed. *Soviet Education*. London: Routledge & Kegan Paul, 1957.

Kneller, George F. *The Educational Philosophy of National Socialism*. New Haven: Yale University Press, 1941.

Knight, E. W. *The Academy Movement in the South*. Chapel Hill: University of North Carolina Press, 1919.

———. *History and Management of Land-grants for Education in the Northwest Territory*. New York: G. P. Putnam's Sons, 1885.

———. *The Influence of Reconstruction in Education in the South*. New York: Teachers College, Columbia University, 1913.

———. *Public Education in the South*. Boston: Ginn, 1922.

Knowles, M. S. *The Adult Education Movement in the United States*. New York: Holt, Rinehart and Winston, 1962, part I.

Koos, Leonard V. *The Junior College Movement*. Boston: Ginn, 1925.

Korol, Alexander. *Soviet Education for Science and Technology*. New York: John Wiley & Sons, Inc., 1957.

Krug, E. A. *The Shaping of the American High School*. New York: Harper & Row, 1964.*

Krüsi, Hermann, Jr. *Pestalozzi, His Life, Work, and Influence*. New York: American Book Company, 1875.

Kuhn, A. L. *The Mother's Role in Childhood Education: New England Concepts, 1830–1860*. New Haven: Yale University Press, 1947.

La Fontainerie, F. *The Conduct of the Schools of Jean Baptiste de la Salle*. New York: McGraw-Hill, 1935.

———. *French Liberalism and Education in the Eighteenth Century*. New York: McGraw-Hill, 1932.

Laistner, M. L. W. *Thought and Letters in Western Europe, A.D. 500–900*. New York: The Dial Press, 1957.

Lancaster, Joseph. *Improvements in Education*. London: Darton and Harvey, 1805.

Lane, F. H. *Elementary Greek Education*. Syracuse, N.Y.: C. W. Bardeen, 1895.

Lang, O. H. *Comenius: His Life and Principles of Education*. New York: E. L. Kellog, 1891.

Lange, A. F., and C. De Garmo. *Outlines of Educational Doctrine*. New York: Macmillan, 1901.

Laurie, Simon S. *Development of Educational Opinion*. New York: Macmillan, 1903.

——. *Historical Survey of Pre-Christian Education*. New York: Longmans, Green, 1915.

——. *John Amos Comenius*. Syracuse, N.Y.: C. V. Bardeen, 1892.

——. *John Amos Comenius, Bishop of the Moravians: His Life and Educational Works*. Boston: Willard Small, 1885.

——. *The Rise and Early Constitution of Universities*. New York: Appleton-Century-Crofts, 1903.

——. *Studies in the History of Educational Opinion Since the Renaissance*. New York: Longmans, Green, 1903.

Lawrence, Evelyn, ed. *Friedrich Froebel and English Education*. New York: Philosophical Library, 1953.

Lawson, John. *Medieval Education and the Reformation*. New York: Humanities Press, 1967.

Leach, A. F. *Schools of Medieval England*. New York: Macmillan, 1915.

Learned, W. S. *The Oberlehrer; A Study of the Social and Professional Evolution of the German Schoolmaster*. Cambridge, Mass.: Harvard University Press, 1914.

Lee, E. A. *The Development of Professional Programs of Education*. New York: Columbia University Press, 1925.

Lee, Gordon C., ed. *Crusade Against Ignorance: Thomas Jefferson on Education*. New York: Teachers College, Columbia University, 1962.

Leonard, F. E. *A Guide to the History of Physical Education*. Philadelphia: Lea & Febiger, 1923.

Lexis, W. H. *A General View of the History and Organization of Public Education in the German Empire*, G. J. Tawson, trans. Berlin: A. Ascher & Company, 1904.

Liebeschütz, Hans. *Medieval Humanism in the Life and Writings of John of Salisbury*. London: The Warburg Institute, 1950.

Lilge, Frederic. *The Abuse of Learning: The Failure of the German University*. New York: Macmillan, 1948.

Lindsay, T. M. *Luther and the German Reformation*. New York: Charles Scribner's Sons, 1900.

Livingood, F. G. *Eighteenth Century Reformed Church Schools*. Norristown, Pa.: Norristown Press, 1930.

Livingstone, Richard W. *Greek Ideals and Modern Life*. New York: Biblo & Tannen, 1935.

——. *Plato and Modern Education of Young Children in England*. New York: Teachers College, Columbia University, 1932.

Lodge, Rupert C. *Plato's Theory of Education*. New York: Harcourt, Brace, 1948.*

Loomis, B. W. *The Educational Influence of Richard Edwards*. Nashville, Tenn.: George Peabody College for Teachers, 1932.

Lull, H. G. *Inherited Tendencies of Secondary Instruction in the United States*. Berkeley: University of California Press, 1913.

Luqueer, F. L. *Hegel as Educator*. New York: Macmillan, 1896.

Mackenzie, M. *Hegel's Educational Theory and Practice*. London: Swan, Sonnenschein, 1909.

MacVannel, J. A. *The Educational Theories of Herbart and Froebel*. New York: Teachers College, Columbia University, 1905.

Mageuney, E. *Christian Education in the Dark Ages*. New York: Catholic Library Association, 1900.

——. *Christian Education in the First Centuries*. New York: The Cathedral Library Association, 1907.

Mahaffy, J. P. *Old Greek Education*. London: Routledge & Kegan Paul, 1881.

Mallet, Charles E. *A History of the University of Oxford*, three vols. London: Methuen, 1924–1927.

Mangun, V. L. *The American Normal School: Its Rise and Development in Massachusetts.* Baltimore: Warwick and York, 1928.

Mann, Horace. *Lectures and Annual Reports on Education.* Cambridge, Mass.: Cornhill Press of Boston, 1867.

Mann, Mary. *Life and Works of Horace Mann.* Boston: Walker Fuller, 1867.

Marenholz-Buelow, Baroness Bertha von. *Reminiscences of Friedrich Froebel,* Mrs. Horace Mann, trans. Boston: Lee and Shepard, 1892.

Maritain, Jacques. *Three Reformers: Luther, Descartes, Rousseau.* New York: Charles Scribner's Sons, 1929.

Marrou, H. I. *History of Education in Antiquity.* New York: Mentor, 1964.*

Martin, G. H. *Evolution of the Massachusetts Public School System.* New York: Appleton-Century-Crofts, 1894.

Mason, J. D. *Gentlefolk in the Making.* Philadelphia: University of Pennsylvania Press, 1935.

Masso, G. *Education in Utopias.* New York: Teachers College, Columbia University, 1927.

Matthews, J. C. *The Contributions of Joseph Baldwin to Public Education.* Nashville, Tenn.: George Peabody College for Teachers, 1932.

Mayer, Frederick A. *Education and the Good Life.* Washington, D.C.: Public Affairs Press, 1957.

Mayer, M. H. *The Philosophy of Teaching of St. Thomas Aquinas.* Milwaukee: Bruce Publishing Company, 1929.

Mayhew, K. C., and A. C. Edwards. *The Dewey School.* New York: Appleton-Century-Crofts, 1936.*

McCabe, Joseph A. *A Candid History of the Jesuits.* London: E. Nash, 1913.

————. *Peter Abelard.* New York: G. P. Putnam's Sons, 1901.

McCallister, W. A. *Growth of Freedom in Education.* New York: Richard R. Smith, 1931.

McCluskey, N. G. *Public Schools and Moral Education.* New York: Columbia University Press, 1958.

McCormick, John E. *St. Thomas and the Life of Learning.* Milwaukee: Marquette University Press, 1937.

McCrie, Thomas. *The Life of John Knox.* Edinburgh: J. Ogle, 1813.

McGarry, Daniel D. *The Metalogicon of John of Salisbury.* Berkeley, Calif.: University of California Press, 1955.

McGrath, Fergal. *Newman's University: Idea and Reality.* New York: Longmans, Green, 1951.

McMahon, Clara P. *Education in Fifteenth-Century England.* Baltimore: Johns Hopkins Press, 1947.

Medsker, Leland L. *The Junior College: Progress, Prospect.* New York: McGraw-Hill, 1960.

Meiklejohn, A. *Education Between Two Worlds.* New York: Harper & Row, 1942.

Meriwether, C. *Our Colonial Curriculum 1607–1776.* Washington, D.C.: Capitol Publishing, 1907.

Meyer, A. E. *The Development of Education in the Twentieth Century.* Englewood Cliffs, N.J.: Prentice-Hall, 1949.

Miller, G. F. *The Development of the Academy System in New York.* Albany, N.Y.: J. B. Lyon Company, 1922.

Miller, Nathan. *The Child in Primitive Society.* New York: Brentano's, 1928.

Milne, J. M. *History of Educational Journalism.* Syracuse, N.Y.: C. W. Bardeen, 1893.

Minnich, H. C. *William Holmes McGuffey.* New York: Macmillan, 1936.

Misawa, Tadasu. *Modern Educators and Their Ideals.* New York: Appleton-Century-Crofts, 1909.

Moberly, Walter. *Plato's Conception of Education and Its Meaning Today.* New York: Oxford University Press, 1944.

Moehlman, C. H. *School and Church.* New York: Harper & Row, 1944.

Monroe, J. Paul. *The Educational Ideal.* Boston: D. C. Heath, 1906.

———. *Thomas Platter and the Educational Renaissance of the Sixteenth Century.* New York: Appleton-Century-Crofts, 1904.

Monroe, Will S. *Comenius and the Beginnings of Educational Reform.* New York: Charles Scribner's Sons, 1900.

———. *Comenius' School of Infancy.* Boston: D. C. Heath, 1896.

———. *History of the Pestalozzian Movement in the United States.* Syracuse, N.Y.: C. W. Bardeen, 1907.

Montessori, Maria. *The Advanced Montessori Method.* Cambridge, Mass.: Bentley, Robert, Inc., 1964.

Moore, E. C. *The Story of Instruction: The Beginnings.* New York: Macmillan, 1936.

Morison, Samuel E. *The Founding of Harvard College.* Cambridge, Mass.: Harvard University Press, 1935.

———. *The Development of Howard University Since the Inauguration of President Eliot (1869–1929).* Cambridge: Harvard University Press, 1930.

Morley, John. *Rousseau and His Era.* London: Macmillan, 1910.

Mulhern, James. *A History of Secondary Education in Pennsylvania.* Lancaster: Pa. Science Press, 1933.

Mullinger, J. Bass. *The Schools of Charles the Great.* New York: Stechart, 1911.

Myers, A. J. W. *Horace Bushnell and Religious Education.* Boston: Menthorne & Burack, 1937.

Needham, J. *The Teacher of Nations.* London: Cambridge University Press, 1942.

Nettleship, R. L. *The Theory of Education in the Republic of Plato.* London: Oxford University Press, 1935.

Nevins, Alan. *The State Universities and Democracy.* Urbana: University of Illinois Press, 1962.

Newman, John Henry. *The Idea of a University.* New York: Longmans, Green, 1927.

Newton, Alfred W. *The English Elementary School.* London: Longmans, Green, 1919.

Nietz, J. A. *Old Textbooks.* Pittsburgh: University of Pittsburgh Press, 1961.*

Noffsinger, J. S. *Correspondence Schools, Lyceums, Chautauquas.* New York: Macmillan, 1926.

Norton, A. O. *The First Normal School in America.* Cambridge, Mass.: Harvard University Press, 1926.

Ogilvie, Vivian. *The English Public School.* London: B. T. Batsford, Ltd., 1957.

Oliphant, James. *The Educational Writings of Richard Mulcaster.* Glasgow: J. MacLehose & Sons, 1903.

Osman, Howard. *Utopias and Education.* Minneapolis: Burgess, 1969.

Paetow, L. J. *The Arts Course at Medieval Universities.* Urbana: University of Illinois Press, 1910.

———. *The Battle of the Seven Liberal Arts.* Berkeley, Calif.: University of California Press, 1914.

Page, David P. *Theory and Practice of Teaching or the Motives and Methods of Good School-Keeping.* New York: A. S. Barnes and Company, 1885.

Painter, F. V. N. *Luther on Education.* Philadelphia: Lutheran Publication Society, 1889.

Pangburn, J. M. *The Evolution of the American Teachers College.* New York: Teachers College, Columbia University, 1932.*

Parker, I. *Dissenting Academies in England.* London: Cambridge University Press, 1914.

Parker, S. C. *The History of Modern Elementary Education.* Boston: Ginn, 1912.

Parker, William B. *The Life and Public Services of Justin Smith Morrill.* Boston: Houghton Mifflin, 1924

Parks, E. P. *The Roman Rhetorical Schools as a Preparation for the Courts Under the Early Empire.* Baltimore: The Johns Hopkins Press, 1945.

Parry, A. W. *Education in England in the Middle Ages.* London: University of London Press, 1920.

Paulsen, Friedrich. *The German Universities: Their Character and Historical Development.* New York: Macmillan, 1895.*

————. *German Education, Past and Present,* T. Lorenz, trans. New York: Charles Scribner's Sons, 1912.

————. *German Universities and University Study.* New York: Charles Scribner's Sons, 1906.

Payne, William H. *Rousseau's Émile.* New York: Appleton-Century-Crofts, 1914.

Peterson, A. D. *A Hundred Years of Education.* London: Gerard Duckworth, 1952.

Peterson, H. *Great Teachers.* New Brunswick: Rutgers University Press, 1946.

Pierce, P. R. *The Origin and Development of the Public School Principalship.* Chicago: University of Chicago Press, 1935.

Pinloche, A. *Pestalozzi and the Foundation of the Modern Elementary School.* New York: Charles Scribner's Sons, 1901.

Pitkin, R. S. *Public School Support in the United States During Periods of Economic Depression.* New York: Stephen Daye Press, 1933.

Pollard, Hugh M. *Pioneers of Popular Education.* Cambridge, Mass.: Harvard University Press, 1957.

Poole, R. S. *Illustrations of the History of Medieval Thought and Learning.* New York: Macmillan, 1920.

Potter, Alonzo, and George B. Emerson. *The School and the Schoolmaster.* New York: Harper & Row, 1842.

Potter, D. *Debating in the Colonial Chartered Colleges.* New York: Teachers College, Columbia University, 1944.

Power, Edward J. *A History of Catholic Higher Education in the United States.* Milwaukee: Bruce Publishing, 1958.

————. *Medieval English Nunneries.* New York: Biblo & Tannen, 1922.

Price, Kingsley. *Education and Philosophical Thought.* Boston: Allyn and Bacon, 1962.

Prince, J. W. *Wesley on Religious Education.* New York: Methodist Book Concern, 1926.

Pruette, Loraine. *G. Stanley Hall; A Biography of a Mind.* New York: Appleton-Century-Crofts, 1926.

Quick, R. H. *Essays on Educational Reformers.* New York: Appleton-Century-Crofts,

Rait, R. S. *Life in the Medieval University.* London: Cambridge University Press, 1912.

Rand, Edward K. *Founders of the Middle Ages.* Cambridge, Mass.: Harvard University Press, 1929.

Randels, G. B. *Doctrines of Herbart in the United States.* Philadelphia: University of Pennsylvania Press, 1909.

Rashdall, H. *Universities of Europe in the Middle Ages,* three vols. New York: Oxford University Press, 1936.*

Ratner, Joseph. *Philosophy of Dewey.* New York: Holt, Rinehart and Winston, 1928.

Raymont, T. *History of the Education of Young Children.* London: Longmans, Green, 1937.

Reeder, R. R. *Historical Development of School Readers and Methods of Teaching Reading.* New York: Macmillan, 1900.

Reigart, J. F. *The Lancasterian System of Instruction in the Schools of New York City.* New York: Teachers College, Columbia University, 1916.

Reisner, E. H. *Evolution of the Common School.* New York: Macmillan, 1930.

———. *Nationalism and Education Since 1789.* New York: Macmillan, 1925.

Reller, T. L. *The Development of the City Superintendency of Schools.* Philadelphia: T. L. Reller, 1935.

Rice, E. A. *A Brief History of Physical Education.* New York: A. S. Barnes, 1926.

Rice. E. W. *The Sunday School Movement and the Sunday School Union 1817–1917.* Philadelphia: American Sunday School Union, 1917.

Richard, James W. *Philip Melanchthon, the Protestant Preceptor of Germany.* New York: G. P. Putnam's Sons, 1898.

Rickover, H. G. *Education and Freedom.* New York: E. P. Dutton, 1959.

Robinson, J. H., and H. W. Rolfe. *Petrarch: The First Modern Scholar and Man of Letters.* New York: G. P. Putnam's Sons, 1914.

Robson, J. A. *Wyclif and the Oxford Schools.* London: Cambridge University Press, 1961.

Rolfe, H. W. *Petrarch: The First Modern Scholar and Man of Letters.* New York: G. P. Putnam's Sons, 1909.

Ross, E. D. *Democracy's College.* Ames: Iowa State University Press, 1942.

Rousseau, Jean Jacques. *Émile,* Barbara Foxley, trans. New York: E. P. Dutton, 1938.

Ruccius, Walter M. *John Bugenhagen Pomeranus.* Philadelphia: The United Lutheran Publishing House, 1916.

Rudolph, F. A. *The American College and University.* New York: Alfred A. Knopf, 1962.*

Rugg, Harold. *American Life and the School Curriculum.* Boston: Ginn, 1936.

———. *The Teacher of Teachers.* New York: Harper & Row, 1952.

Rusk, R. R. *Doctrines of the Great Educators.* London: Macmillan, 1918.

Russell, F. W. *The School of Plato.* London: Methuen, 1896.

Russell, James Earl. *German Higher Schools; The History, Organization and Methods of Secondary Education in Germany.* New York: Longmans, Green, 1899.

Ryan, M. B. *John of Salisbury on the Arts of Language in the Trivium.* Washington, D.C.: Catholic University of America Press, 1958.

Sadler, J. E. *J. A. Comenius and the Concept of Universal Education.* New York: Barnes & Noble, 1966.

Saettler, Paul. *A History of Instructional Technology.* New York: McGraw-Hill, 1968.

Salmon, D. *Joseph Lancaster.* London: Longmans, Green, 1904.

———. *The Practical Parts of Lancaster's Improvements and Bell's Experiments.* London: Cambridge University Press, 1932.

Salmon, D., and W. Hindshaw. *Infant Schools, Their History and Theory.* London: Longmans, Green, 1904.

Samuel, R. H. and Thomas, R. Hinton. *Educationand Society in Modern Germany.* London: Routledge & Kegan Paul, 1949.

Sandys, John Edwin. *Harvard Lectures on the Revival of Learning.* London: Cambridge University Press, 1905.

————. *A History of Classical Scholarship.* New York: Hafner Publishing Company, 1958.

————. *A History of Classical Scholarship from the 6th Century B.C. to the End of the Middle Ages.* London: Cambridge University Press, 1920.

Scanlon, D. G. *International Education: A Documentary History.* New York: Teachers College, Columbia University, 1960.

————. ed. *Traditions of African Education.* New York: Teachers College, Columbia University, 1964.

Schachner, Nathan. *The Medieval Universities.* Philadelphia: J. B. Lippincott, 1938.*

Schmidt, G. P. *The Liberal Arts College.* New Brunswick, N.J.: Rutgers University Press, 1957.

————. *The Old Time College President.* New York: Columbia University Press, 1930.

Schwendener, N. *A History of Physical Education in the United States.* New York: A. S. Barnes, 1942.

Schwickerath, R. *Jesuit Education: Its History and Principles.* St. Louis: B. Herder, 1904.

Scott, Emmett J., and Lyman B. Stowe. *Booker T. Washington, Builder of a Civilization.* Garden City, N.Y.: Doubleday, 1916.

Scott, J. F. *Historical Essays on Apprenticeship and Vocational Education.* Ann Arbor, Mich.: Ann Arbor Press, 1914.

Seybolt, R. F. *Apprenticeship and Apprenticeship Education in Colonial New England and New York.* New York: Teachers College, Columbia University, 1917.

————. *The Evening School of Colonial New York City.* Albany, N.Y: University of the State of New York, 1921.

Sheldon, Edward A. *Lessons in Objects.* New York: Charles Scribner's Sons, 1863.

Sherill, L. J. *Presbyterian Parochial Schools 1846–1870.* New Haven, Conn.: Yale University Press, 1932.

————. *The Rise of Christian Education.* New York: Macmillan, 1944.*

Shirreff, Emily. *A Short Sketch of the Life of Froebel.* London: Chapman & Hall, 1887.

Shoemaker, Ervin C. *Noah Webster: Pioneer of Learning.* New York: Columbia University Press, 1936.

Sikes, J. G. *Peter Abelard.* Cambridge, England: The University Press, 1932.

Silber, K. *Pestalozzi: The Man and His Work,* 2nd ed. New York: Humanities Press, 1965

Sizer, T. R. *The Age of the Academies.* New York: Teachers College, Columbia University, 1964.*

Smail, W. M. *Quintilian on Education.* New York: Oxford University Press, 1938.

Small, W. H. *Early New England Schools.* Boston: Ginn, 1914.

Smalley, B. *The Study of the Bible in the Middle Ages.* Oxford: Blackwell, 1941.

Smith, F. W. *The High School.* New York: Sturgis & Walton, 1916.

————. *History of English Elementary Education Since 1760.* London: University of London Press, 1931.

Smith, J. W. A. *The Birth of Modern Education: Contribution of the Dissenting Academies.* London: Independent Press, 1954.

Smith, Margaret K. *Herbart's Text-Book in Psychology.* New York: Appleton-Century-Crofts, 1891.

Smith, Preserved. *Erasmus.* New York: Harper & Row, 1923.

Smith, S. M. *The Relation of the State to Religious Education in Massachusetts.* Syracuse, N.Y.: Syracuse University Book Store, 1926.

Smith, W. A. *Ancient Education*. New York: Philosophical Library, 1955.

———. *The Junior High School*. New York: Macmillan, 1925.

Snell, Reginald. *Progressive Schools, Their Principles and Practice*. London: Hogarth Press, 1934.

Snider, Denton J. *The Life of Friedrich Froebel, Founder of the Kindergarten*. Chicago: Sigma Publishing Company, 1900.

Snow, L. F. *The College Curriculum in the United States*. New York: Teachers College, Columbia University, 1907.

Spinka, Matthew. *John Amos Comenius: That Incomparable Moravian*. Chicago: University of Chicago Press, 1943.

Steiner, Bernard C. *Life of Henry Barnard, The First United States Commissioner of Education, 1867–1870*. Washington, D.C.: U.S. Government Printing Office, 1919.

Stettbacher, Hans, ed. *Pestalozzi, a Pictorial Record for the Centenary of His Death*. Zurich: Zentralbibliothek, 1928.

Stewart, G. *A History of Religious Education in Connecticut*. New Haven, Conn.: Yale University Press, 1924.

Stout, J. E. *The Development of High School Curricula in the North Central States 1860–1918*. Chicago: University of Chicago Press, 1921.

Stowe, A. M. *The English Grammar Schools in the Reign of Queen Elizabeth*. New York: Teachers College, Columbia University, 1908.

Surtz, Edward. *The Praise of Pleasure; Philosophy, Education and Communism in More's Utopia*. Cambridge, Mass.: Harvard University Press, 1957.

Suzzalo, Henry. *The Rise of Local School Supervision in Massachusetts*. New York: Teachers College, Columbia University, 1906.

Swift, F. H. *Education in Ancient Israel*. Chicago: Open Court, 1919.

———. *Public Permanent Common School Funds in the United States 1795–1905*. New York: Holt, Rinehart and Winston, 1911.

Swint, Henry W. *The Northern Teacher in the South, 1862–1870*. Nashville, Tenn.: Vanderbilt University Press, 1941.

Taylor, A. E. *Plato: The Man and His Work*. New York: Dial Press, 1927.

Taylor, Howard Cromwell. *The Educational Significance of the Early Federal Land Ordinances*. New York: Teachers College, Columbia University, 1922.

Taylor, Jerome. *The Didascalion of Hugh of St. Victor*. New York: Columbia University Press, 1961.

Tewkesbury, D. G. *The Founding of American Colleges and Universities Before the Civil War*. New York: Teachers College, Columbia University, 1932.

Tharp, Louise Hall. *Until Victory; Horace Mann and Mary Peabody*. Boston: Little, Brown, 1953.

Thayer, Vivian T. *The Misinterpretation of Locke as a Formalist in Educational Philosophy*. Madison: University of Wisconsin Press, 1921.

———. *The Passing of the Recitation*. Boston: D. C. Heath, 1928.

Thomas, Russell. *The Search for a Common Learning*. New York: McGraw-Hill, 1962.

Thompson, James Westfall. *Ancient Libraries*. Berkeley, Calif.: University of California Press, 1940.

———. *The Literacy of the Laity in the Middle Ages*. New York: Burt Franklin, 1960.

———. *The Medieval Library*. Chicago: University of Chicago Press, 1939.

Thorndike, L. *University Records and Life in the Middle Ages*. New York: Columbia University Press, 1944.

Thorpe, Francis N. *Franklin's Influence in American Education*. Washington: U.S. Bureau of Education, 1903.

Thuring, Charles F. *A History of Higher Education in America.* New York: Appleton-Century-Crofts, 1906.

Thursfield, R. E. *Henry Barnard's American Journal of Education.* Baltimore: Johns Hopkins Press, 1945.

———. *Henry Barnard's Journal of Education.* Baltimore: Johns Hopkins Press, 1946.

Thut, I. N., and Don Adams. *Educational Patterns in Contemporary Societies.* New York: McGraw-Hill, 1964.

Thwing, Charles F. *The American and the German University. One Hundred Years of History.* New York: Macmillan, 1928.

———. *A History of Higher Education in America.* New York: Appleton-Century-Crofts, 1906.

Tiedt, Signey W. *The Role of the Federal Government in Education.* New York: Oxford University Press, 1966.

Todd, A. J. *The Primitive Family as an Educational Agency.* New York: G. P. Putnam's Sons, 1913.

Todd, Lewis Paul. *Wartime Relations of the Federal Government and the Public Schools, 1917–1918.* New York: Teachers College, Columbia University, 1945.

Totah, K. A. *Contribution of the Arabs to Education.* New York: Teachers College, Columbia University, 1926.

Townsend, W. J. *The Great Schoolmen of the Middle Ages.* London: Hodder and Stoughton, 1881.

Truscott, Bruce. *Red Brick University.* London: Pelican Book, 1951.

Tuer, Andrew. *History of the Horn-book.* New York: Charles Scribner's Sons, 1897.

Turnbull, G. *The Educational Theory of J. G. Fichte.* Liverpool: Liverpool University Press, 1926.

———. *Samuel Hartlib: A Sketch of His Life and His Publications on John Amos Comenius.* London: Oxford University Press, 1920.

Ufer, Christian. *Introduction to the Pedagogy of Herbart.* Boston: D. C. Heath, 1901.

Ulich, Robert. *The Education of Nations.* Cambridge, Mass.: Harvard University Press, 1961.

———. *History of Educational Thought.* New York: American Book Company, 1945.

———. *A History of Religious Education: Documents and Interpretations from the Judeo-Christian Tradition.* New York: New York University Press, 1968.

———. *Sequence of Educational Influences Traced Through Unpublished Writings of Pestalozzi, Froebel, Diesterweg, Horace Mann, and Henry Barnard.* Cambridge, Mass.: Harvard University Press, 1935.

Updegraff, Harlan. *The Origin of the Moving School in Massachusetts.* New York: Teachers College, Columbia University, 1908.

Untersteiner, M. *The Sophists,* K. Freeman, trans. Oxford: Blackwell, 1954.

Van Dalen, D. B., et al. *World History of Physical Education.* Englewood Cliffs, N.J.: Prentice-Hall, 1953.

Vandewalker, N. C. *The Kindergarten in American Education.* New York: Macmillan, 1908.

Van Liew, C. C. *Life of Herbart and Development of His Pedagogical Doctrines.* London: Swan, Sonnenschein, 1893.

Waddell, H. *The Wandering Scholars.* Garden City, N.Y.: Anchor, 1955.

Walch, M. R. *Pestalozzi and the Pestalozzian Theory of Education.* Washington, D.C.: Catholic University of American Press, 1952.

Walden, J. W. H. *The Universities of Ancient Greece.* New York: Charles Scribner's Sons, 1909.

Walker, O. *Of Education, Especially of Young Gentlemen.* London: Oxford, 1673.

Walker, Williston. *John Calvin.* New York: G. P. Putnam's Sons, 1906.

Walsh, J. J. *Education of the Founding Fathers of the Republic.* New York: Fordham University Press, 1935.

Walz, John A. *German Influence in American Education and Culture.* Philadelphia: The Carl Schurz Memorial Foundation, 1936.

Ward, A. W. *The Counter Reformation.* London: Longmans, Green, 1889.

Ward, Herbert. *The Educational System of England and Wales and Its Recent History.* London: Cambridge University Press, 1935.

Warfel, Harry Redcay. *Noah Webster, Schoolmaster to America.* New York: Macmillan, 1936.

Washington, Booker T. *Twenty-Five Years of Tuskegee.* Garden City, N.Y.: Doubleday, 1906.

————. *Up from Slavery; An Autobiography.* Garden City, N.Y.: Doubleday, 1913.

Watson, Foster. *The Beginning of the Teaching of Modern Subjects in England.* London: Isaac Pitman & Sons, 1909.

————. *English Grammar Schools to 1660.* London: Cambridge University Press, 1908.

————, ed. *Vives and the Renascence Education of Women.* New York: Longmans, Green, 1912.

————. *Vives on Education.* Cambridge, England: The University Press, 1913.

Webb, C. C. J., ed. *John of Salisbury, Policraticus.* Oxford, England: Clarendon Press, 1909.

Webb, Sidney. *London Education.* New York: Longmans, Green, 1904.

Webster, Hutton. *Primitive Secret Societies.* New York: Macmillan, 1932.

Wells, Guy F. *Parish Education in Colonial Virginia.* New York: Teachers College, Columbia University, 1923.

Wesley, E. B. *The National Education Association: The First Hundred Years.* Washington, D.C.: National Education Association, 1957.

West, A. F. *Alcuin and the Rise of Christian Schools.* New York: Charles Scribner's Sons, 1909.

Westaway, K. M. *The Educational Theory of Plutarch.* London: University of London Press, Ltd., 1922.

Wiggin, G. A. *Education and Nationalism.* New York: McGraw-Hill, 1963.

Wiggin, Kate D., and Nora A. Smith. *Froebel's Gifts.* Boston: Houghton Mifflin, 1896.

Wilderspin, Samuel. *Infant Education; or Practical Remarks on the Importance of Educating the Infant Poor.* London: Simpkin and Marshall, 1929.

Wilkins, A. S. *National Education in Greece in the Fourth Century Before Christ.* New York: G. E. Stechert and Company, 1911.

————. *Roman Education.* Cambridge, England: The University Press, 1931.

Williams, E. I. F. *Horace Mann, Educational Statesman.* New York: Macmillan, 1937.

Wilmot-Buston, E. M. *Alcuin.* New York: P. J. Kenedy & Sons, 1922.

Wilson, J. Dover. *The Schools of England; A Study in Renaissance.* Chapel Hill: University of North Carolina Press, 1929.

Wilson, Louis N. *Granville Stanley Hall.* New York: G. E. Stechert, 1914.

Wirth, Arthur G. *John Dewey as Educator.* New York: John Wiley & Sons, 1966.*

Wish, Harvey. *Society and Thought in Early America.* New York: Longmans, Green, 1950.

Woeful, Norman. *Molders of the American Mind.* New York: Columbia University Press, 1933.

Wood, Norman. *The Reformation and English Education*. London: Routledge & Kegan Paul, 1931.

Woodring, Paul. *New Directions in Teacher Education*. New York: The Fund for the Advancement of Education, 1957.

Woodson, Carton G. *The Mis-Education of the Negro*. Washington, D.C.: The Associated Publishers, 1933.

Woodward, W. H. *Desiderius Erasmus Concerning the Aim and Method of Education*. New York: Teachers College, Columbia University, 1964.

———. *Education During the Renaissance, 1400–1600*. New York: Cambridge University Press, 1924.

———. *Erasmus Concerning Education*. London: Cambridge University Press, 1904.

———. *Vittorino da Feltre and Other Humanist Educators*. New York: Teachers College, Columbia University, 1963.

Woody, Thomas. *Early Quaker Education in Pennsylvania*. New York: Teachers College, Columbia University, 1920.

———. *Educational Views of Benjamin Franklin*. New York: McGraw-Hill, 1931.

———. *A History of the Education of Women in the United States*. Lancaster, Pa.: Science Press, 1929.

———. *Life and Education in Early Societies*. New York: Macmillan, 1949.

Wymer, Norman. *Dr. Arnold of Rugby*. London: Robert Hale, 1953.

Zeller, Eduard. *Plato and the Other Academy*. New York: Longmans, Green, 1876.

Ziemer, Gregor A. *Education for Death; The Making of the Nazi*. New York: Oxford University Press, 1941.

Zweig, Stefan. *Erasmus of Rotterdam*. New York: The Viking Press, 1934.

Index

581